MW00617732

DICTIONARY
OF
OBJECT
TECHNOLOGY

SIGS Reference Library Series

Donald G. Firesmith
Editor-in-Chief
Knowledge Systems Corporation

Additional Volumes in Preparation

DICTIONARY
OF
OBJECT
TECHNOLOGY

The Definitive Desk Reference

Donald G. Firesmith
and
Edward M. Eykholt

SIGS
BOOKS

New York • London • Paris • Munich • Cologne

Library of Congress Cataloging-in-Publication Data

Firesmith, Donald G., 1952-

Dictionary of object technology : the definitive desk reference/ Donald G. Firesmith and Edward M. Eykholt.

p. cm.

Includes bibliographical references.

ISBN 1-884842-09-7 (alk. paper)

1. Object-oriented programming (Computer science) — Dictionaries. 2. Computer science — Dictionaries. I. Eykholt, Edward M., 1962-. II. Title.

QA78.64.F56 1995		95-6869
005.1'1—dc20		CIP

PUBLISHED BY

SIGS Books, Inc.

71 West 23rd Street

New York, New York 10010

Voice: +1 (212) 242-7447

SIGS Books ISBN 1-884842-09-7

Prentice Hall ISBN 0-13-373887-6

To my wife, Becky, who once again was forced to play the role of book widow. Thank you for your understanding and keeping the world at bay while I wrote.

—Don

To my wife, Lori, and our daughter, Lauren. Thank you for your patient and supporting love.

—Ed

About the Authors

Donald G. Firesmith has recently joined Knowledge Systems Corporation as a Senior Member of the Technical Staff. For the previous five years, he was the president of Advanced Software Technology Specialists (ASTS), a small consulting and training company specializing in the practical application of object technology. For ASTS and organizations such as Semaphore, he has provided training in object-oriented management, analysis, design, and testing to over 2,500 software managers and engineers in North America, Europe, and the Pacific Rim. As the developer of the Firesmith method, a fourth-generation object-oriented systems development method, and OOSDL, a second-generation object-oriented specification and design language, he has long been an innovator and leader in object-oriented methodology. He is a columnist for the *Report on Object Analysis and Design (ROAD)* and a frequent contributor for the *Journal of Object-Oriented Programming (JOOP)*, as well as a regular speaker at international conferences on object technology. His first book was *Object-Oriented Requirements Analysis and Logical Design: A Software Engineering Approach,* published by John Wiley & Sons in February 1993, and he is currently working on a book on object-oriented testing and the second edition of his first book.

Prior to founding ASTS, Firesmith was a software methodologist for Magnavox Electronic Systems Company, where he developed object-oriented standards and procedures and ran an Object-Oriented Design help desk for a 1.3 million line object-based command and control project for the U.S. Army. Before that, he did proposal work, project evaluations, configuration management, data management, and product assurance for Computer Sciences Corporation in Germany, Switzerland, and the United States. He was also director of data processing on an American Indian reservation after starting out as a traditional hacker doing analysis, design, coding, testing, and maintenance for an actuarial consulting company.

Firesmith holds a BA degree in math and German from Linfield College and an MA degree in mathematics from Arizona State University. He also spent a year at Ludwig Maximillian Universität in Munich and one post-master's year at Arizona State.

He can be contacted at the following address:

Donald G. Firesmith
Knowledge Systems Corporation
4001 Weston Parkway
Cary, North Carolina 27513, USA
Phone: +1 (919) 481-4000
Fax: +1 (919) 677-0063
E-mail: dfiresmith@ksccary.com

Edward M. Eykholt (pronounced "eye-colt") is a sales engineer with Rational Software Corporation in McLean, Virginia, where he provides presales technical support for the Rational Rose® product line of object-oriented software eingineering tools. Prior to mid-1995, he was a business systems consultant with AT&T Global Information Solutions in Dayton, Ohio. At AT&T, Eykholt facilitated dialog between business and information-technology professionals in order to achieve consistent understanding and expectations between them, assuring that IT supported business strategies and requirements. He has utilized object-oriented analysis & design, business process reengineering and information engineering techniques. He has previous experience in Accounting Systems and Product Management. Eykholt received his Bachelor of Science degree in Electrical Engineering (1985) and Master of Science in Management (MBA, 1987) from Purdue University, West Lafayette, Indiana.

He can be contacted at the following address:

Edward M. Eykholt
Rational Software Corporation
8000 Westpark Drive, 5th Floor
McLean, Virginia 22102, USA
Fax: +1 (703) 761-4407
E-mail: eykholt@rational.com

Foreword

The Object Management Group (OMG) defined OMG Interface Definition Language to be the standard language for interfaces between objects. But what about a standard language for the people who work with these objects? OMG recognizes the need for this, and we include a glossary section in most of our specifications; but these glossaries are available primarily to people who read highly technical standards documents. We are pleased that our definitions, along with others, have been incorporated into this comprehensive *Dictionary of Object Technology,* where they will get increased exposure, distribution, and recognition.

With this dictionary, Don Firesmith and Ed Eykholt provide a tool that makes possible a common "people interface," which can accompany the common object interfaces in our future. Let's examine some people interfaces and the benefits that will follow from a common terminology:

Within an Enterprise: It is common, especially within large enterprises, for one or a few "evangelists" to advocate object technology (OT) to the rest of the staff. Frequently (although not always) new to objects themselves, these forward-looking people have to digest input from a variety of sources and translate it into a business case for objects along with a technical justification and road map. These people are key to the future of object technology, because their position gives them credibility while their actions translate simultaneously to advantages for their company (i.e., increased computing capability combined with long-term savings) and increased sales for the vendors who provide the technology. This dictionary will be an important resource for people in this position—especially those accorded "guru" status within their company for being, and staying, just one jump ahead of everyone else.

For Training: There's a lot of education going on in OT. Some is formal—classroom training provided not only by companies set up for this purpose, but also by system and software vendors who find it necessary in this new and emerging market. Some isn't called training, but really is—every time an evangelist talks to someone new to object technology, that's training, too. Vocabulary is such an important part of training that at least one company has published a "glossary of object-oriented terms" sized to fit the student's coat pocket; this item is a popular giveaway at trade shows and has benefitted many as they became familiar with the basic terms of OT.

The Sales Relationship: This relationship is key to the growth of OT. Customers must receive value for their dollar, especially for end-users who must look on information technology as a cost center rather than a as profit center. Vendors, who may have substantial up-front investments in development, need income to repay these development costs and fund future work. Both sides agree that a solid long-term relationship must be based on common understanding. The availability of a comprehensive, neutral reference work like the *Dictionary of Object Technology* makes this kind of relationship easier to form and maintain.

Technical "People Interfaces": Large development projects will have separate teams for Analysis/Design and Development. The interface between these teams is crucial, but distinct concerns and separate terminology may hinder technology transfer. And, although object technology makes it easier to split a development effort into teams working in parallel, it imposes a responsibility for coordination and understanding, which requires a common vocabulary.

Documentation: A final area wherein meaning must be conveyed precisely, and words must be used carefully. Documentation writers' work will be easier if they can find the term they want and not have to create one (with a usage conflicting with someone else's), and readers will benefit as commonality of usage increases among the available works.

Of course we recognize that dictionary writers do not impose or pass judgment; they only note the usages of a term and record them in their work. But authors should not underestimate the power of a dictionary to bring down the wrath of readers on those who perpetuate ambiguous or uncommon usage! Pay attention to the power of the pen at work here—by noting usages and recording them in an authoritative way for all to read, the dictionary authors hasten the maturation of the terminology they at first set out only to record. Thus terminology and technology mature hand-in-hand, each assisting the other along the way.

We will know that object orientation has fully matured when programmers are no longer asked if they know OT; it's just the way everyone programs (remember when "structured programming" was all the rage?). We're not there yet, but the publication of this comprehensive dictionary by Firesmith and Eykholt marks a key milestone along the road. Watch for OO terminology to mature more quickly for a while thanks to this effort, and for this newly matured terminology, which we hope will be clearer and more compact, to be recorded in future editions.

Jon Siegel, Ph.D.
Director of Program Management
Object Management Group
492 Old Connecticut Path
Framingham, Massachusetts 01701, USA

Preface

If language be not in accordance with the truth of things, affairs cannot be carried on to success.
—Confucius

Like most specialized fields, object technology has its own vocabulary, which is *large* and *complex*. In its present state, it is unfortunately also *inconsistent*. Parts of it might even be called *ugly*. The degree to which this is true is astounding and is clearly an indication of the present lack of standardization within our industry. Our industry is very active and is rapidly evolving, with simultaneous and often independent progress on standards, methods, and programming languages. Comparatively few people have focused on making sure everyone's evolving terminology is consistent.

Consider the following parable: Five blind men from India were once on a journey together and came across their first elephant. Upon encountering the side of the elephant, the first man declared, "Careful, my friends, there is a wall here." The second man then reached out, touched the rough leg of the elephant, and said, "No, brother, it is only a tree." The third was brushed by the elephant's ear and stated, "Someone must have left a fan tied to the tree." The fourth then bumped into one of the elephant's tusks and said, "Someone must have also left a spear here." Finally, the elephant brushed its trunk up against the last blind man, who stepped back in fear and warned, "Careful, there is also a big snake in the tree!"

Just like the blind men, different methodologists and language designers have approached the same concept and articulated their understanding of it based on their perspective. Often, a single object-oriented term has been given multiple, even conflicting, definitions. Conversely, the same or similar concept definitions have been given to many different terms; synonyms for the same concept abound. Preferring a high level of abstraction, some methodologists have defined object-oriented concepts in terms of what they truly "are" or should be. For example, they have defined an object as *a model of a single thing within the application*. Others feel that they have taken a more pragmatic approach by defining the very same concepts in terms of how these concepts are currently implemented in their favorite object-oriented programming language. For example, an object has been defined as *an encapsulation of data and associated operations* or even as *a region of storage*.

It is not unusual for the vocabulary of a relatively young paradigm like object technology to evolve and include bridges and baggage from older paradigms; this is arguably healthy. People are influenced by their perspective of, history with, and interface to the "elephant" they are trying to understand and describe. Each of these perspectives is valuable but must be assimilated to achieve a true, complete picture. The perspectives on object technology are subject to these same truths, and the definitions of terms vary for these same reasons. Listen to this dictionary and you will hear them: "It is an abstraction!" "An encapsulation!" "An instance!"

> *When I use a word, it means just what I choose it to mean, neither more nor less.*
> —Humpty Dumpty in *Through the Looking Glass* by Lewis Carroll

An early step in every object-oriented development method encourages establishing a common understanding of, and vocabulary and semantics for, the most essential domain concepts. The object-technology industry is also working toward this kind of common language, although it still has a long way to go. Imagine the capabilities of the industry when it does reach a critical mass of semantic consistency. To achieve this vision of effectiveness, the standards organizations, methodologists, and programming languages will all need to converge toward, or at least map to, one shared metamodel. Our hope is that this dictionary will speed this progress by providing a mechanism for clear and conscious choices about our language.

> *The ill and unfit choice of words wonderfully obstructs the understanding.*
> —Francis Bacon (1561–1626)

In our research for the dictionary, we became extremely sensitive to the use of terms and the casualness with which they sometimes appear to have been introduced and used. The mixing of the terms *object* and *class* is a classic example. No doubt, individual writers have always fully intended to convey complete, precise meaning. In an industry that presently has an inconsistent vocabulary, clarity of meaning is essential for its continued progress. Although many have argued that the industry needs to standardize the *icons* it uses to draw object-oriented diagrams, we would contend that it is far more important to standardize the terminology. Icons are merely syntax, whereas terminology, when used consistently, provides the true semantics of the field.

A major problem for us was to determine whether this dictionary should specify only "correct" or "appropriate" usage and ignore "incorrect" usage or whether it should document the way the terms and definitions are currently used in practice. The difference between these two approaches can be seen in the differences between typical French and English dictionaries. The correct use of the French language is specified by a governmental body, and French dictionaries therefore specify the correct use of the language. On the other hand, English dictionaries tend to assume that languages evolve through widespread usage, which determines current correctness. There are pros and cons with both approaches, and we were certain that our choice could be attacked, no matter which choice we made.

If we only documented "correct" usage, then how could we determine correctness when there is so much disagreement among the experts? When methodologists cannot even agree on notation that is mere syntax, what chance would we have of obtaining a consensus on terminology and semantics within a reasonable time frame given the great investment in documentation, training, and egos involved? We could not even rely on popularity, because several misuses of terminology are quite popular (e.g., the confusion between the terms *is a* and *a kind of*). We would, at the very least, open ourselves up to potentially legitimate charges of favoritism by only including terms and definitions that we professionally agree with. Such a dictionary would have less universal appeal, and the neophyte to object technology would be less likely to find in the dictionary terms and definitions that are used in practice.

The other choice was to attempt to document all terms and definitions as they are used. This would unfortunately run the risk of further popularizing and justifying poor or incorrect usage. Some have therefore advised us to only include "correct" usage, and others have even voiced concern that a dictionary including all viewpoints could do more harm than good.

Ultimately, we have decided in favor of impartiality, fairness, and completeness. This dictionary includes all of the terms and definitions that we could include given the time and resources that we had available. As such, it includes some terms and definitions that we personally disagree with—in some cases, even emphatically. Just because a term or definition is in this dictionary does not mean that we endorse its use. We have attempted to address the issue of appropriateness or correctness in terms of rationale and commentary, listing the relative merits and disadvantages of the various terms and definitions. We also recognize that this dictionary must be a living document, and, as with all software projects, subject to significant iteration.

> *Don't sir, accustom yourself to use big words for little matters.... The practice of using words of disproportionate magnitude is, no doubt, too frequent.*
> —Samuel Johnson (1709–1784)

One common accusation of the industry is its introduction of complicated jargon, making object technology unnecessarily difficult for someone new to it. Skeptics would say this jargon is even intentionally introduced by the "elite priests" for the purpose of cultivating the mystery that keeps them elite and their consulting rates high. This notion is, of course, ludicrous! Practitioners want to increase understanding. *Every* field has its own specialized jargon that concisely conveys a precise meaning. Although the term *polymorphic substitution* is foreign to a novice, it does convey the exact meaning intended between those familiar with the technology (or having access to an appropriate dictionary). Although experts need to be cautious not to unintentionally snow those who don't share their understanding, everyone should be realistic and expect the use of jargon to continue and even increase as the industry matures. One of the primary intentions we had in introducing this dictionary was to make the industry more approachable and understandable.

The Making of the Dictionary

The concept for the dictionary originated with Firesmith's extensive company glossary and his long standing interest in the appropriate use of object terminology. He recognized the industry's need for better understanding of its terminology and the catalytic value a widely accessible dictionary would have to the development of the industry. He collaborated with Eykholt, whom he was mentoring at the time, to write this dictionary.

The main body of the dictionary originally started out containing only the entries in the 40+ page *ASTS Abbreviations and Glossary* produced by Donald Firesmith's former company Advanced Software Technology Specialists. We then developed draft appendices consisting of quoted definitions from industry associations (i.e., the OMG and ODMG), 13 major methodologists, and four of the most popular object-oriented programming languages. The resulting draft appendices were then sent to the authors of the books containing their original quotes for review, and the resulting comments where incorporated into the draft appendices. The entries in the updated draft appendices where then merged into the main dictionary. During the merging process, we clarified, synthesized, delineated, organized, and cross-referenced the terms, which resulted in one consistent style. Terms and definitions from other sources such as journal articles and conference papers were also included in the main dictionary. Finally, comments resulting from a technical review of the resulting manuscript were also incorporated.

The manuscript rapidly grew to slightly over 1,000 pages, and in spite of being some four times larger than originally estimated, the dictionary was nearly on schedule when disaster struck. Unfortunately, the publisher of the majority of the methodology books withdrew their verbal permission allowing the dictionary to freely quote definitions from their books and instead demanded royalties far beyond what the project could afford. We were therefore reluctantly forced to delete approximately 400 pages of method-specific appendices from the final manuscript. We were, however, able to obtain reproduction rights to the quotations in the industry group and language-specific appendices.

In researching sources to include, we needed to narrow our selection from the large and rapidly growing number of published books in the field; we could not have included every good source. In fact, several additional significant books were published during the seven months it took to complete the manuscript. Our choice of which books to include was based on when a book was published, its popularity, and its influence on the industry. We also wanted to cover a complete set of perspectives on the object paradigm. We unfortunately needed to exclude many significant works, most of which are in alignment with the terminologies and concepts of one or more of the works we did choose. Although we were tempted to include several vendor-specific influences on the industry, we felt it was best to avoid the pitfalls of the favoritism we would have needed to show during our selections. Our sincere respect goes to those we excluded.

In the appendices, as well as the main dictionary, we included only terms closely related to object technology. Therefore, the appendices are not complete glossaries of terms from their sources. For example, we excluded many features of programming languages unrelated to object technology. In citing sources for the dictionary appendices, we made every attempt to convey the meaning intended by the authors. For this reason, the appendices are almost entirely quoted definitions and commentary. In some cases, the sources already had precise glossaries that we readily incorporated, but other sources had no glossaries or precise definitions of terms. In several cases, we created the first glossaries for these sources. For these reasons, the quality and consistency of the appendices vary greatly. We invited the authors of the sources to review our representation of their work, and most of them responded with recommended changes. The review time was brief, unfortunately, due to our desire to introduce the benefits of the dictionary into the market and make these definitions readily available. The *Acknowledgments* section lists the actual reviewers, who are all very well respected in the industry.

Future Directions

Although the evolution of terminology used in the industry is not predictable, we are confident that convergence will ultimately occur. Like all object-oriented models, this dictionary and the terminology it documents will evolve. In future editions of the dictionary, we will incorporate these changes, and we hope to make redundant terms and definitions obsolete as they are superceded by better and more popular terms. We welcome your feedback and will sincerely consider incorporating all suggested changes. We ask that you submit suggested changes via electronic mail to Firesmith's address listed in the *About the Authors* section. The description of the changes should be complete and match the format of the main dictionary, including examples, rationale, commentary, kinds, citation, and bibliography. The *Guide to the Dictionary* describes these headings.

It is our sincere hope that this work will advance the reader's personal growth, as well as that of the industry. It is promising that the industry is achieving pockets of significant commercial success, in spite of the complexity and inconsistencies of its language. As an industry, let's hope and work for the exact opposite of what happened at the Tower of Babel:

> And the Lord said, "They are one people and they all have one language. And this is only the beginning of what they will do, and nothing that they propose to do will be impossible for them. Come let us go down and there confuse their language that they may not understand one another's speech."
> —Genesis 11, *The Bible*

Donald G. Firesmith and Edward M. Eykholt
Cary, North Carolina
March 25, 1995

Acknowledgments

The authors and publisher sincerely thank the copyright holders and publishers who have allowed us to cite the significant number of quotes contained in the appendices: Christine Anderson of the Ada9X Project Office; Paul Becker of Prentice Hall; Paul Dzeus of the Addison-Wesley Publishing Company; Esther Hanlon of Butterworth-Heinemann; Jon Seigel of Object Management Group, Inc.; Douglas Sery of Morgan Kaufmann Publishers; and author Bertrand Meyer.

We also sincerely thank the copyright holders and publishers who worked with us but whose material we did not cite in the appendices: Bill Kelly of John Wiley & Sons; R. Jill Phillips of Benjamin/Cummings Publishing Company; Yvonne Zasloawska of Addison-Wesley Publishers, Ltd.; as well as authors Peter Coad, Brian Henderson-Sellers, and James J. Odell.

The introduction to each appendix contains copyright and permission notices for the quoted material.

We very sincerely thank the reviewers of this dictionary:

Douglas K. Barry . . . . Object Database Management Group
Grady Booch . . . . The Booch Method
Peter Coad . . . . The Coad Method
Adele Goldberg . . . . Smalltalk
Rick Grehan. . . . . Main dictionary
Brian Henderson-Sellers. . . . . MOSES and the main dictionary
Agneta Jacobson . . . . Objectory
Mark Mayfield. . . . . The Coad Method
Gunnar Övergaard . . . . Objectory
James Rumbaugh. . . . . OMT
Jon Siegel . . . . OMG
Tucker Taft. Ada95
Richard S. Wiener . . . . Main dictionary

Guide to the Dictionary

Order of the Listings

All main entries in the dictionary are listed in strict alphabetical order and set in boldface type. When multiple derived versions of a word occur, these are also listed immediately following their base word, indented, and preceded by bullets. For example, the definitions of various kinds of classes can be found listed alphabetically after the main entry for class:

class *n.* ...
- **abstract class** *n.* ...
- **active class** *n.* ...
- **aggregate class** *n.* ...
- **ancestor [class of a given class]** *n.* ...
  - **parent class [of a given class]** *n.* ...
  - **proper ancestor [of a given class]** *n.* ...
  - **repeated ancestor [of a given class]** *n.* ...

To make the dictionary user-friendly and to make it easy to find not just definitions of terms but also their relationships, many terms are found listed in the above manner as well as under their own alphabetical position. For example, the term *abstract class*, above, also has its own separate entry.

Definitions and Their Main Proponents

The entries and definitions in the main part of the dictionary have been almost entirely collected from the draft appendices of this dictionary. Whereas the definitions in the appendices consist of direct quotations from their sources, the definitions in the main dictionary have been merged from their original sources and paraphrased, with the goals of increased understandability and uniformity. Significant effort has been made to ensure that the original intent of each definition has been preserved. For each entry, a form of etymology has been indicated following the definition. Because the *original* sources of these terms have not always been known to us and because of the limited time and resources we had with which to research and create the dictionary, we have primarily restricted ourselves to documenting as sources the sources of the draft appendices in which the terms and definitions are used. Because it has not always been clear which of these sources used the term or definition first, we have chosen to list the sources after the definitions in alphabetical order. If we knew the primary or original source, we have tried to note this in the commentary or rationale sections. In alphabetical order, these sources are as follows:

[Ada95]. . . . . Ada95 programming language
[Atkinson] . . . . Colin Atkinson

[Berard] .... Edward Berard
[Booch]. .... Grady Booch
[CLOS] .... CLOS programming language
[Coad] .... Peter Coad et al.
[Coleman] .... Derek Coleman et al. (Fusion)
[C++] .... C++ programming language
[Eiffel] .... Eiffel programming language
[Embley] .... David W. Embley et al.
[Firesmith] .... Donald G. Firesmith
[Graham] .... Ian Graham
[Henderson-Sellers] Brian Henderson-Sellers
[Jacobson] .... Ivar Jacobson et al.
[Kim] .... Won Kim
[Lorenz] .... Mark Lorenz
[Martin/Odell]. .... James Martin and James Odell
[Meyer]. .... Bertrand Meyer[1]
[OADSIG]. .... Object Analysis and Design Special Interest
                Group of the OMG
[ODMG] .... Object Database Management Group
[OMG]. .... Object Management Group
[Rumbaugh]. ...... James Rumbaugh et al.
[Shlaer/Mellor] .... Sally Shlaer and Stephen Mellor
[Smalltalk] .... Smalltalk programming language
[Wirfs-Brock] ..... Rebecca Wirfs-Brock et al.

Terms with Multiple Definitions

Many terms have been given multiple definitions, typically by different methodologists. Definitions of the same term that are significantly different from each other are grouped with each group of definitions numbered consecutively. Minor variants of meaning within each group are labeled with letters. The ordering of multiple definitions is based on an informal combination of actual and recommended usage, with the more popular or recommended usages listed first. For example:

    abstract class *n.* **1.** (a) any incomplete class that therefore cannot be used to instantiate semantically meaningful objects. [Firesmith, Henderson-Sellers, Smalltalk, Wirfs-Brock] (b) any class that cannot have direct instances but whose descendants can have instances. [Rumbaugh] (c) any class that should not have instances. [Wirfs-Brock] **2.** any class with no instances. [Booch, Coad, Lorenz] **3.** (a) any class that can be

---

[1]Bertrand Meyer is a methodologist (Design by Contract method), as well as the language developer of Eiffel. For this reason, Eiffel and Meyer are both included in the etymology of the main dictionary entries.

used only as a parent class from which to derive child classes. [Coleman, C++, Firesmith, Henderson-Sellers, Jacobson] (b) any base class that declares the existence of one or more features (e.g., attributes, operations) that must be implemented by its derived classes prior to instantiation. [C++]

Parts of Speech

Each entry is labeled with its corresponding part of speech. These labels appear in italics following the entry and include:

abbr.	abbreviation
adj.	adjective
n.	noun
pl.	plural
v.	verb

The suffixes following verbs denote the past tense and the present participle. For example:

abstract *v. -ed, -ing*

Usage Information

Each major entry in the dictionary may be followed by usage information. This information, which is listed in the following order after the definitions, may also be subdivided and numbered only if it applies to one of the multiple numbered meanings of the major entry.

Synonyms:	A list of entries with the same meaning as the current entry.
Antonyms:	A list of entries with meanings opposite to that of the current entry.
Contrast with:	A list of entries with meanings contrasting that of the current entry. This list will typically include other related specializations of a more general concept. The reader can reference the more general concept for a complete list of its indented specializations.
See also:	A list of related entries.
Examples:	One or more examples of the entry.
Rationale:	A list of rationales for the choice of the term or its definition.
Commentary:	Comments such as consequences of the definition, or potential problems with the definitions.
Kinds:	A specialization hierarchy of the different kinds of the original term. The listed kinds are not necessarily (1) an exhaustive set, (2) mutually exclusive of each other, or (3) within the same dimensional context of each other. For example, associations come in the following kinds:

- ATTRIBUTE ASSOCIATION
- BASE ASSOCIATION

- BINARY ASSOCIATION
- CLASS ASSOCIATION
  - INHERITANCE ASSOCIATION
- DEPENDSON ASSOCIATION
- DERIVED ASSOCIATION
- DYNAMIC ASSOCIATION
  - COMMUNICATION ASSOCIATION
- EXTEND ASSOCIATION
- FUNCTION
- INSTANCE ASSOCIATION
- META ASSOCIATION
- QUALIFIED ASSOCIATION
- RELATION
- STATIC ASSOCIATION
  - ACQUAINTANCE ASSOCIATION
    + CONSISTS-OF ASSOCIATION
    + PART-OF ASSOCIATION
  - INHERITANCE ASSOCIATION
- TERNARY ASSOCIATION
- UNQUALIFIED ASSOCIATION
- USES ASSOCIATION

Use of Synonyms in the Main Dictionary

Many object-oriented terms have numerous synonyms. When multiple synonyms exist, the authors selected a single primary synonym for use in all definitions in order to avoid confusion, promote understandability, and standardize the definitions. The most prominent terms are listed below:

Primary synonym	Other synonyms
ANCESTOR	BASE CLASS, SUPERCLASS
CHILD	DERIVED CLASS, HEIR, DIRECT OR IMMEDIATE SUBCLASS
DESCENDANT	DERIVED CLASS, SUBCLASS
FEATURE	MEMBER, RESOURCE
MESSAGE	CALL, OPERATION INVOCATION, REQUEST, STIMULUS
PARENT	BASE CLASS, DIRECT OR IMMEDIATE SUPERCLASS

Use of Synonyms in the Appendices

The use of synonyms in appendices varies depending on the context of the citation. Sometimes, for example, a methodologist prefers one term for domain analysis and another for implementation. These terms may still be listed as synonyms unless they are clearly articulated as separate. Commentary is included when the intended preferences are known.

The synonyms are not always defined symmetrically, unless we found support from the source for the symmetry. This situation may actually represent a casual usage of subtyping; for example, in a citation such as "a *parent* is also called an *ancestor*; the terms are synonymous." Even though multiple terms are listed as synonyms, it might be wise for the reader to look up the entries for all of the synonyms. In the appendices, terms include citations of how they are used, and citations of synonymous terms are not usually included in the same entry. The authors refrained from making too many interpretations of the intentions of a given standards organization, methodologist, or programming-language designer. The same is not true for the main dictionary, however, where the authors did feel it was appropriate to interpret the industry's terminology as a whole; as a result, synonyms are more precisely synchronized in the main dictionary.

Table of Contents

Abbreviations

Ace	assembly of classes in Eiffel
AD	assembly diagram [Firesmith]
ADT	abstract data type
AGD	aggregation diagram [Firesmith]
AKO	A-Kind-Of [Graham]
ADFD	action–data-flow diagram [Shlaer/Mellor]
ADL	ASTS Diagramming Language
ADM	ASTS Development Method
AO	application object
API	application programming interface
ASF	atomic system function
BAA	Business Area Analysis [Martin/Odell]
BID	blackbox-interaction diagram [Firesmith]
BLOB	binary large object
BOA	Basic Object Adapter [OMG]
BOMSIG	Business Object Model Special Interest Group [OMG]
BON	Business Object Notation
BTD	blackbox-timing diagram [Firesmith]
CASE	computer-aided software engineering
CBO	coupling between objects
CCM	Class-Centered Modeling
CD	context diagram [Firesmith]
CDT	class description table
Cecil	C-Eiffel Call-In Library
CF	Common Facilities, CORBA Facilities [OMG]
CHD	Class Hierarchy Diagram [Siemens/Nixdorf]
CLOS	Common LISP Object System
CND	configuration diagram [Firesmith]
COM	Common Object Model [Microsoft]
COMMA	Common Object Methodology Metamodel Architecture [Henderson-Sellers]
COOMM	Common Object-Oriented Meta-Model [Graham]
CORBA™	Common Object Request Broker Architecture [OMG]
COSS	Common Object Services Specification [OMG]
CRC	class responsibility collaborator [Wirfs-Brock]
CSD	Class Structure Design [Martin/Odell]
DBMS	database management system
DD	distribution diagram [Firesmith]
DFD	data-flow diagram
DIT	depth of the inheritance tree
DM	data management [Coad]
DNU	doesNotUnderstand [Smalltalk]
DSOM	Distributed System Object Model [IBM]
DST	Distributed Smalltalk
ECOOP	European Conference on Object-Oriented Programming
EM	event model [Henderson-Sellers]
ERD	entity relationship diagram
FM	Firesmith Method [Firesmith]
GOF	Gang of Four
gen-spec	generalization-specialization
GOOD	Generalized Object-Oriented Design
GOPRR	graph-object-property-role-relationship
GSN	general semantic net [Firesmith]
GUI	graphical user interface
HI	human interaction [Coad]
HOOD	Hierarchical Object-Oriented Design
HOOT	Hotline on Object-Oriented Technology

ID	interaction diagram [Firesmith]
IDL™	Interface Definition Language [OMG]
IDP	Iterative Development Process [Henderson-Sellers, Lorenz]
IE\O	Information Engineering \with Objects
IIP	incremental, iterative, parallel
IM	inheritance model [Henderson-Sellers]
ins	inherits [Jacobson]
INHD	inheritance diagram [Firesmith]
JAD	1 joint application design [Martin/Odell] 2 joint application development [Firesmith]
JEM	joint enterprise modeling [Martin/Odell]
JOOP	Journal of Object-Oriented Programming
KISS	Kristen Iteration Selection and Sequence Method
Lace	Language for Assembling Classes in Eiffel
LCOM	lack of cohesion in methods
LID	local [object] identifier
LOOK	Lectures and Object-Oriented Konference
MD	module diagram [Firesmith]
MERODE	Model-Driven Entity-Relationship Object-Oriented Development
MM-Path	method/message path
MNU	messageNotUnderstood [Smalltalk]
MOO	multiuser dungeon (MUD) object-oriented
MOSES	Methodology for Object-oriented Software Engineering of Systems [Henderson-Sellers]
MooD	Methodology for Object-Oriented Development [Siemens/Nixdorf]
MTD	Marketing to Design

MUD	multi-user diagram
MVC	Model–View–Controller [Smalltalk]
MVCD	model-view-controller diagram
NICE	The Nonprofit International Consortium for Eiffel
NIH	not invented here
NIHCL	National Institute of Health Class Library
NOC	number of children
NT	not this time [Coad]
OA&D	object analysis & design
OAD	Object Association Diagram [Siemens/Nixdorf]
OAM	object-access model [Shlaer/Mellor]
OBA	Object Behavior Analysis [Goldberg/Rubin, Martin/Odell]
OBD	Object Behavior Design [Martin/Odell]
objref	object reference
O/C	object/class
OCD	object context diagram [Siemens/Nixdorf]
OCM	object-communication model
OCS	object class sticker [Siemens/Nixdorf]
OCT	object class template [Siemens/Nixdorf]
ODBMS	object database management system
ODL	Object Definition Language [OMG]
ODT	object-description table
ODMG	Object Database Management Group
OFD	object-flow diagram
ODT	object-description table
OID	1 object identifier 2 object identity
OIG	object interaction graph
OIM	object information model
OLE	Object Linking & Embedding [Microsoft]

OMA	Object Management Architecture [OMG]
OMG™	Object Management Group
OML	Object Manipulation Language [ODMG]
OMFT	OMG Object Model Task Force
OMT	Object Modeling Technique [Rumbaugh]
OO	object-oriented
OOA	object-oriented analysis
OOAD	1 object-oriented analysis and design
	2 object-oriented application development
OOCM	Object-Oriented CASE Methodology [Martin/Odell]
OOD	1 object-oriented design
	2 object-oriented development
OODA	object-oriented domain analysis
OODB	object-oriented database
OODD	object-oriented domain design
OODL	object-oriented dynamic language
OODLE	Object-Oriented Design LanguagE [Shlaer/Mellor]
OODN	Object-Oriented Design Notation [Page-Jones]
OODP	object-oriented domain programming
OOIE	Object-Oriented Information Engineering
OOID	object-oriented implementation design
OOIT	object-oriented integration and testing
OOLD	object-oriented logical design
OOP	object-oriented programming
OOPL	object-oriented programming language
OOPSLA	Object-Oriented Programming Systems, Languages, and Applications
OORA	object-oriented requirements analysis

OOSA	object-oriented systems analysis
OOS	Object-Oriented Systems
OOSC	Object-Oriented Software Construction
OOSD	Object-Oriented Software Development
OOSDL	Object-Oriented Specification and Design Language [Firesmith]
OOSE	object-oriented software engineering
OOSIG	Object-Oriented Special Interest Group
OOT	object-oriented technology
OOUI	object-oriented user interface
OPRR	object-property-role-relationship
OQL	Object Query Language
OORAM	Object-Oriented Role Analysis and Modeling
OORASS	Object-Oriented Role Analysis, Synthesis, and Structuring
ORB™	Object Request Broker [OMG]
ORCA	Object-Oriented Requirements Capture and Analysis
ORDBMS	Object Relational Data Base Management System
ORM	object-relationship model [Embley]
OS	Object Services [OMG]
OSA	1 Object-oriented Systems Analysis [Embley]
	2 Object-Structure Analysis [Martin/Odell]
OSD	1 Object-oriented Systems Design [Embley]
	2 object-state diagram [Siemens/Nixdorf]
	3 object-structure design [Martin/Odell]
OSI	object-oriented systems implementation [Embley]
OSQL	object structured query language

OSS	object-oriented systems specification [Embley]		[Firesmith]
OSTF	OMG Object Services Task Force	**SN**	semantic net [Firesmith]
		SOM	System Object Model [IBM]
OT	object technology	**SOMA**	Semantic Object Modeling Approach [Graham]
OWL	Object Windows Library [Borland]	**SOT**	state operation table
PD	1. problem domain [Coad]	**SRM**	subsystem relationship model [Shlaer-Mellor]
	2. presentation diagram	**SRS**	subsystem responsibility specification [Henderson-Sellers]
PDD	presentation dependency diagram [Firesmith]		
PIPO	platform-independent portable objects	**SSM**	service structure model [Henderson-Sellers]
PLoP	Pattern Languages of Programming	**ST**	Smalltalk
		STIC	Smalltalk Industry Council
POS	Persistent Object Services [OMG]	**STD**	state transition diagram
		TD	timing diagram [Firesmith]
PRD	presentation diagram [Firesmith]	**TM**	task management
		TOOLS	Technology of Object-Oriented Languages and Systems
RD	Recursive Design	**TS**	Typed Smalltalk
RDD	Responsibility-Driven Design	**UDC**	user-defined class [Firesmith]
RFC	response for a class	**UDT**	user-defined type [Firesmith, Martin/Odell]
ROAD	Report on Object Analysis and Design		
		UI	user interface
RTOOSA	Real-Time Object-Oriented Structured Analysis	**UID**	universal [object] identifier
		UON	Uniform Object Notation
SAM	subsystem access model [Shlaer/Mellor]	**VCPU**	virtual CPU [machine]
		VPE	visual programming environment
SASY	Software Architects' SYnthesis model		
		vtbl	virtual-function table
SBM	Solution Based Modeling	**WID**	whitebox-interaction diagram [Firesmith]
SCM	subsystem communication model [Shlaer/Mellor]		
		WMC	weighted methods per class
SCOOP	Seminars and Conference in Object-Oriented Programming	**WTD**	whitebox-timing diagram [Firesmith]
SD	system diagram [Firesmith]	**WOOD**	Workshop on Object-Oriented Development
SEI	Software Engineering Institute		
SE/OT	Systems Engineering for Object Technology	**X3J13**	ANSI Common Lisp Object System [CLOS] Committee
SI	system interaction [Coad]	**X3J16**	ANSI C++ Committee
SIGDB	OMG's Special Interest Group on Object Databases	**X3J20**	ANSI Smalltalk Committee
		X3J4	ANSI Object COBOL Committee
SLD	scenario lifecycle diagram		

A

abstract *v. -ed, -ing* to concentrate on the most important or essential aspects of anything while suppressing or ignoring less important, immaterial, or diversionary details. [Booch, Firesmith]
See also: ABSTRACTION.
Commentary: Developers abstract to view problems with varying degrees of detail depending on current context and needs. Developers abstract to manage complexity and promote correctness, extensibility, maintainability, reusability, and understandability. [Firesmith]

abstract actor *n.* any actor that is not instantiated directly but rather is used as a source of common *roles* that other actors can inherit. [Jacobson]
Contrast with: ABSTRACT USE CASE.

abstract class *n.* **1.** (a) any incomplete class that therefore cannot be used to instantiate semantically meaningful objects. [Firesmith, Henderson-Sellers, Smalltalk, Wirfs-Brock] (b) any class that cannot have direct instances but whose descendants can have instances. [Rumbaugh] (c) any class that should not have instances. [Wirfs-Brock] **2.** any class with no instances. [Booch, Coad, Lorenz] **3.** (a) any class that can only be used as a parent class from which to derive child classes. [Coleman, C++, Firesmith, Henderson-Sellers, Jacobson] (b) any base class that declares the existence of one or more features (e.g., attributes, operations) that must be implemented by its derived classes prior to instantiation. [C++]
Synonym: **3** DEFERRED CLASS.
Antonym: CONCRETE CLASS.
Contrast with: **1** DEFERRED CLASS.
Example: In a graphics application, a concrete circle class can inherit from an abstract shape class. [Firesmith]
Commentary: An abstract class is used as a parent that can provide common features, provide a minimal protocol for polymorphic substitution, or declare missing (i.e., deferred) common features that its children must supply prior to instantiation. [Firesmith, Lorenz] Definition **2** is questionable because even concrete classes have no instances before they are instantiated or after all instances have been destroyed. Definition **3**(b) ignores the distinction between abstract and deferred classes. An abstract class is referred to as a "semifinished product" in Oberon-2.

Kinds:
- DEFERRED CLASS
  - FULLY DEFERRED CLASS
  - PARTIALLY DEFERRED CLASS
- **deferred class** *n.* **1.** any abstract class that declares the existence of one or more features (e.g., attributes, operations) that must be implemented by its descendants prior to instantiation. [Firesmith] **2.** any base class that declares the existence of one or more features (e.g., attributes, operations) that must be implemented by its derived classes prior to instantiation. [C++, Henderson-Sellers]
Contrast with: ABSTRACT CLASS, CONCRETE CLASS, EFFECTIVE CLASS.
Commentary: A deferred class should be used if one or more polymorphic features are required to implement a complete abstraction. [Firesmith] A deferred class describes a group of possible implementations of an abstract data type. A deferred class describes an incompletely implemented abstraction, which its proper descendants will use as a basis for further refinement. Any class that is declared as deferred is invalid unless it has deferred features. [Eiffel, Meyer]
Kinds:
  - FULLY DEFERRED CLASS
  - PARTIALLY DEFERRED CLASS
- **fully deferred class** *n.* any deferred class whose features are all deferred. [Eiffel, Firesmith, Meyer]
Antonym: PARTIALLY DEFERRED CLASS.
- **partially deferred class** *n.* any deferred class, some of whose features are not deferred. [Firesmith]
Antonym: FULLY DEFERRED CLASS.
abstract coupling *n.* any coupling dependency of a class on another abstract class.

abstract data type (ADT) *n.* **1.** (a) any localization of a single *data* type and its associated operations that is encapsulated so that the implementations of the data and operations are hidden. [Firesmith, Jacobson] (b) any encapsulated user-defined type that hides the implementations of its data and operations. [Martin/Odell] **2.** any data structure known from an official interface rather than through its representation. [Eiffel, Meyer] **3.** any user-defined type used as a description or specification of a class without implementation details. [Henderson-Sellers]
Contrast with: CLASS.

abstract factory [pattern] *n.* the creational object design pattern that provides an interface for creating families of related or dependent objects without specifying their concrete classes. [Gamma, Helm, Johnson, and Vlissides]
Synonym: KIT.

abstract form *n.* the text of any class without its nonpublic elements. [Eiffel, Meyer]
Synonym: SHORT FORM.
See also: DECLARATION, INTERFACE.
Commentary: The abstract form captures the type of the class and should be used to document its interface. [Eiffel, Meyer]

abstract method *n.* **1.** any method that is declared by, but not implemented in, an abstract class. **2.** any method that is implemented in a base class and that provides a default behavior that is intended to be overridden in its concrete derived classes. [Wirfs-Brock]
Synonyms: 1 ABSTRACT OPERATION, ABSTRACT SUBPROGRAM, DEFERRED METHOD, DEFERRED OPERATION, DEFERRED ROUTINE.

Commentary: **1** The term *abstract method* may be something of an oxymoron if method is considered to mean the implementation of an operation. [Firesmith]

abstract object type *n.* any abstraction used to group common characteristics of real-world object types. [OADSIG]
Contrast with: ABSTRACT TYPE.

abstract operation *n.* **1.** any incomplete operation that does not have a method. [Firesmith] **2.** any operation that is declared by, but not implemented in, an abstract class. [Booch, Rumbaugh]
Synonyms: ABSTRACT METHOD, ABSTRACT SUBPROGRAM, DEFERRED OPERATION.
Contrast with: BASE OPERATION, DEFERRED OPERATION.
Example: any pure virtual member function in C++ is an abstract operation. [Booch]
Commentary: The term deferred operation is more commonly used. [Firesmith]

abstract property *n.* any incomplete property that does not have a type. [Firesmith]

abstract state machine *n.* any encapsulation of a hidden set of states and operations that either change or return the states. [Firesmith]
Commentary: The instances of many objects and classes are abstract state machines. [Firesmith]

abstract subprogram *n.* any subprogram that has no body but is intended to be overridden at some point when inherited. [Ada95]
Synonyms: ABSTRACT METHOD, ABSTRACT OPERATION, DEFERRED OPERATION.

abstract type *n.* **1.** any type without an implementation that cannot therefore be instantiated. **2.** any tagged type intended for use as a parent type for type extensions, not allowed to have objects of its own. [Ada95]

Contrast with: ABSTRACT CLASS.

abstract use case *n.* any use case that will not be instantiated on its own, but is meaningful only to describe parts shared among other use cases. [Jacobson]
Antonym: CONCRETE USE CASE.
Contrast with: ABSTRACT ACTOR.

abstraction *n.* **1.** (a) any model that includes the most important, essential, or distinguishing aspects of something while suppressing or ignoring less important, immaterial, or diversionary details. [Booch, Firesmith, Henderson-Sellers] (b) the result of removing distinctions so as to emphasize commonalties. [Martin/Odell] **2.** the cognitive tool for rationalizing the world by considering only those details necessary for the current purpose. [Coad, Firesmith, Henderson-Sellers, Rumbaugh] **3.** any relationship between a group of object types such that one object type represents a set of characteristics that are shared by other object types. [Lorenz, OADSIG]
Contrast with: ABSTRACT.
Kinds:
- CLASS ABSTRACTION
- CLUSTER ABSTRACTION
- DATA ABSTRACTION
- EXCEPTION ABSTRACTION
- FUNCTIONAL ABSTRACTION
- KEY ABSTRACTION
- OBJECT ABSTRACTION
- PROCESS ABSTRACTION

- **class abstraction** *n.* any model of a set of related object abstractions. [Firesmith]
- **cluster abstraction** *n.* any model of a set of related class abstractions. [Firesmith]
Commentary: A cluster abstraction is captured by a cluster rather than an aggregate class or parent class.

- **data abstraction** *n.* any abstraction (i.e., model) of a characteristic, property, trait, quantity, or quality of some object or class. [Firesmith]
Contrast with: ABSTRACT DATA TYPE.
- **exception abstraction** *n.* any model of an error condition and its handling. [Firesmith]
- **functional abstraction** *n.* any model of a sequential operation. [Firesmith]
Contrast with: PROCESS ABSTRACTION.
- **key abstraction** *n.* **1.** any essential abstraction that is a part of the vocabulary of the application domain. [Firesmith] **2.** any essential object or class that forms a part of the vocabulary of the application domain. [Booch]
Synonyms: BUSINESS OBJECT, DOMAIN OBJECT, MODEL OBJECT.
Contrast with: KEY CLASS.
Commentary: Not every essential abstraction is an object or class. [Firesmith]
- **object abstraction** *n.* any model of a single thing from the problem space (i.e., real world) or the solution space. [Firesmith]
- **process abstraction** *n.* any model of a concurrent operation. [Firesmith]
Contrast with: FUNCTIONAL ABSTRACTION.

abstraction hierarchy *n.* any hierarchy of superclass/subclass relationships. [Henderson-Sellers]
Synonym: CLASS HIERARCHY, INHERITANCE HIERARCHY.
Commentary: The term is also used to refer to a network in which multiple generalization occurs. [Henderson-Sellers]

abstraction level *n.* any collection of logically related abstractions at the same level in some ordered structure. [Firesmith]
Synonym: LEVEL OF ABSTRACTION.
Examples: Classes at the same level in an inheritance structure, objects at the same level in a collaboration structure. [Firesmith]
Kinds:
- HIGH LEVEL OF ABSTRACTION
- LOW LEVEL OF ABSTRACTION

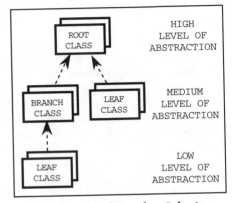

Abstraction Level Based on Inheritance

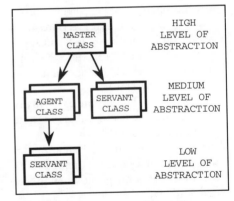

Abstraction Level Based on Message Passing

- **high level of abstraction** *n.* any abstraction level near the root of a hierarchy of abstractions. [Firesmith]
Antonym: LOW LEVEL OF ABSTRACTION.
Examples: An ancestor is at a higher

level of abstraction than its descendants in an inheritance structure. A client is at a higher level of abstraction than its servers in a message-passing structure. An aggregate is at a higher level of abstraction than its parts in an aggregation hierarchy. [Firesmith]

Commentary: A high level of abstraction typically implies either more complete (aggregation), more abstract (inheritance), or closer to the masters (message passing). [Firesmith]

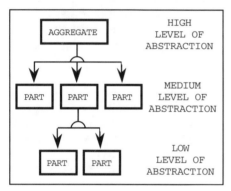

Abstraction Level Based on Aggregation

- **low level of abstraction** *n.* any abstraction level far from the root of a hierarchy of abstractions. [Firesmith]

Antonym: HIGH LEVEL OF ABSTRACTION.

Examples: A part is at a lower level of abstraction than its aggregate in an aggregation hierarchy. A descendant is at a lower level of abstraction than its ancestors in an inheritance structure. [Firesmith]

Commentary: A low level of abstraction typically implies either less complete (aggregation), less abstract (inheritance), or closer to the servants (message passing). [Firesmith]

access control *n.* the language mechanism that controls access to the features of some thing. [Booch, C++]

Synonym: VISIBILITY CONTROL.

Contrast with: INFORMATION HIDING, PRIVATE, PROTECTED, PUBLIC.

See also: BODY, IMPLEMENTATION, INTERFACE, PROTOCOL.

Commentary: The term *access control* was chosen over the term *visibility control* to emphasize that changes in access status would not quietly change the meaning of a program. The C++ access control mechanisms protect against accident, but not against fraud. Any programming language, such as C++, that provides access to raw memory will leave data open to deliberate tampering in ways that violate explicit type rules. [C++]

access declaration *n.* any declaration of a qualified name in the public or protected part of a derived class declaration that adjusts access to a member of a direct or indirect base class. [C++]

Commentary: An access declaration may not be used to restrict access to a member that is accessible in the base class, nor may it be used to enable access to a member that is not accessible in the base class. [C++]

access interaction *n.* any interaction that obtains information about objects. [Embley]

accessible slot *n.* a slot is *accessible* in an instance of a class if the slot is defined by the class of the instance or is inherited from a superclass of that class. [CLOS]

Commentary: At most one slot of a given name can be accessible in an instance. [CLOS]

accessing message *n.* any message used

to get or set the value of an instance attribute.
Synonyms: ACCESSOR MESSAGE.
Contrast with: ACCESSING METHOD, ACCESSING OPERATION, ACCESSOR METHOD, ACCESSOR OPERATION, PRESERVER OPERATION.

accessing method *n.* any relatively standard small and simple method that is used to either get or set the value of an instance attribute. [Lorenz]
Synonyms: ACCESSING OPERATION, ACCESSOR METHOD, ACCESSOR OPERATION.
Contrast with: ACCESSING MESSAGE, ACCESSOR MESSAGE, PRESERVER OPERATION.
Example: The *balance* and *balance:* methods get and set the value of an account's balance. [Lorenz]
Commentary: Accessing methods are generally named after the attribute that they access and allow one to perform laissez-faire initialization. [Lorenz]

accessing operation *n.* any relatively standard small and simple operation that is used to either get or set the value of an instance attribute.
Synonyms: ACCESSING METHOD, ACCESSOR METHOD, ACCESSOR OPERATION, PRESERVER OPERATION.
Contrast with: ACCESSOR MESSAGE, PRESERVER MESSAGE.

accessor message *n.* any message used to *get* or *set* the value of an instance attribute.
Synonyms: ACCESSING MESSAGE.
Contrast with: ACCESSING METHOD, ACCESSING OPERATION, ACCESSOR OPERATION, PRESERVER OPERATION.

accessor method *n.* any relatively standard small and simple method that is used to either get or set the value of an instance attribute.
Synonyms: ACCESSING METHOD, AC-

CESSING OPERATION, ACCESSOR OPERATION, PRESERVER OPERATION.
Contrast with: ACCESSING MESSAGE, ACCESSOR MESSAGE.

accessor [operation] *n.* **1.** any relatively standard small and simple method that is used to either get or set the value of an instance attribute. [Firesmith, Shlaer/Mellor] **2.** any fundamental field operation required to query values. [Martin/Odell]
Synonyms: ACCESSING METHOD, ACCESSING OPERATION, ACCESSOR METHOD.
Contrast with: ACCESSING MESSAGE, ACCESSOR MESSAGE, PRESERVER MESSAGE.
Kinds:
- CREATE ACCESSOR
- DELETE ACCESSOR
- READ ACCESSOR
- WRITE ACCESSOR

● **create accessor** *n.* any accessor operation that creates a new instance of an object. [Shlaer/Mellor]
Synonym: CONSTRUCTOR, CREATE OPERATION.
Antonym: DELETE ACCESSOR.

● **delete accessor** *n.* any accessor operation that deletes an instance of an object. [Shlaer/Mellor]
Synonym: DELETE OPERATION, DELETE OPERATOR, DESTRUCTOR.
Antonym: CREATE ACCESSOR.

● **read accessor** *n.* any accessor operation that returns the value of a property. [Firesmith, Shlaer/Mellor]
Antonym: WRITE ACCESSOR.

● **write accessor** *n.* any accessor operation that updates the value of a property. [Firesmith, Shlaer/Mellor]
Antonym: READ ACCESSOR.

acquaintance association *n.* any static association between objects in which one object knows of the existence of another. [Jacobson]

Contrast with: STATIC ASSOCIATION.

See also: ATTRIBUTE, ENTITY OBJECT.

Commentary: An acquaintance association does not give the object the right to exchange information with the other object (for which a dynamic association is needed). Like attributes, acquaintance associations are typically implemented as ordinary references or pointers to instances. [Jacobson]

Kinds:
- CONSISTSOF ASSOCIATION
- PARTOF ASSOCIATION

- **consistsOf association** *n.* any acquaintance association from an aggregate object to an object of which it consists. [Jacobson]

  Antonym: PARTOF ASSOCIATION.

  See also: AGGREGATE.

  Example: A food order consists of a dish and a beverage. [Jacobson]

- **partOf association** *n.* any acquaintance association from an object to the aggregate object of which it is a part. [Jacobson]

  Antonym: CONSISTSOF ASSOCIATION.

  See also: AGGREGATE.

  Example: A dish and a beverage are parts of a food order. [Jacobson]

action *n.* **1.** the term used during state modeling for any operation that, for all practical purposes, takes zero time to execute. [Booch, Firesmith, Rumbaugh] **2.** any operation that must be executed upon arrival in a state. [Shlaer/ Mellor] **3.** any operation performed by an object. [Embley]

Contrast with: ACTIVITY.

Examples: The updating of an attribute usually takes such a short time to accomplish that is may be considered an action for state modeling purposes.

[Firesmith] The passing of a message, the invocation of an operation, the starting and stopping of an activity, the updating of an attribute. [Booch, Firesmith] An *action* may cause events, create or destroy objects and relationships, observe objects and relationships, and send or receive messages. [Embley]

Rationale: Standard term used by Booch, Embley, Firesmith, Rumbaugh, and Shlaer/ Mellor.

Commentary: Definition 1 is the most popular definition.

Kinds:
- INTERRUPTIBLE ACTION
- NONINTERRUPTIBLE ACTION

- **interruptible action** *n.* any action associated with a state that may be suspended before it finishes executing and may resume execution at a later time. [Embley]

  Synonym: INTERRUPTIBLE OPERATION.

  Antonym: NONINTERRUPTIBLE ACTION.

- **noninterruptible action** *n.* any action associated with a state transition that the analyst expects to run to completion unless exceptions or system failures occur. [Embley]

  Synonym: INTERRUPTIBLE OPERATION.

  Antonym: INTERRUPTIBLE ACTION.

action data flow diagram (ADFD) *n.* any data flow diagram that provides a graphic representation of the units of processing (a.k.a. processes) within an action and the intercommunication between them. [Shlaer/Mellor]

action data flow diagram document *n.* any document that contains the action data flow diagrams for all the actions, ordered first by state model (using the state model's key letter) and then by state number. [Shlaer/Mellor]

action diagram *n.* any diagram that organizes procedural code into components surrounded by brackets. [Martin/Odell]

action time *n.* the time required to execute the corresponding action. [Shlaer/Mellor]

activate *v. –ed, –ing* to prepare a persistent object to execute an operation. [OMG]

activation *n.* the preparation of a persistent object to execute an operation. [OMG]

Example: Copying the persistent form of the operations and stored attributes into an executable address space to allow execution of the operations on the attributes.

active *adj.* 1. describing a concurrent object or class that executes without the need for incoming messages. [Firesmith] 2. describing a concurrent object or class encapsulating at least one thread of control (e.g., operation). [Booch]

Synonym: 2 CONCURRENT.

Antonym: 1 PASSIVE.

Rationale: Definition 1 is consistent with the traditional use of the term to describe Ada tasks without entries. [Firesmith]

active class *n.* 1. (a) any class of concurrent objects. (b) any concurrent class that may execute without the need for incoming messages. [Firesmith] 2. any class that is concurrent. [Booch] 3. any class that is generated by an object that has a separate state machine for each instance. [Shlaer/Mellor]

Synonym: 2 CONCURRENT CLASS.

Antonym: PASSIVE CLASS.

active iterator *n.* any iterator that consists of multiple low-level methods whereby the user has the ability to decide which methods(s) are to be performed at each node. [Berard]

Antonym: PASSIVE ITERATOR.

See also: HOMOGENEOUS COMPOSITE OBJECT.

Commentary: Although users of active iterators have a great deal of control, they must be careful to ensure that all nodes have been accessed and to avoid unintentional changes in the object during iteration. [Berard]

active object *n.* 1. any concurrent object that may execute without the need for incoming messages. [Firesmith] 2. any object that sends messages to other objects but does not receive messages. [Booch] 3. any object with one or more threads of control. [Booch]

Synonyms: 2 MASTER OBJECT 3 ACTOR, CONCURRENT OBJECT.

Antonym: PASSIVE OBJECT.

Commentary: 1 Every active object is concurrent, but not all concurrent objects are active. Sequential objects are reactive, whereas active objects may be proactive. [Firesmith]

active process *n.* the process whose actions are currently being carried out. [Smalltalk]

active view *n.* the view that is currently being used by the operator. [Firesmith, Smalltalk]

Contrast with: BROWSER, COLLAPSED VIEW, STANDARD SYSTEM VIEW, SUBVIEW.

activity *n.* the term used during state modeling for any operation that takes significant time to execute. [Booch, Firesmith, Rumbaugh]

Antonym: ACTION.

Rationale: Standard term used by Booch, Firesmith, and Rumbaugh.

activity schema *n.* any diagram showing a sequence of operations. [Martin/Odell]

actor *n.* **1.** (a) any external class that models one of a set of roles played by a perspective user of a business system or information system. [Jacobson, Rumbaugh] (b) any class, type, or category of external user. [Jacobson] (c) any person, any organization, or any other thing that participates in one or more ways over time. [Coad] **2.** any object in the Actor language. **3.** (a) any object with one or more threads of control. [Booch] (b) any object that can spontaneously change its internal state. **4.** any object that sends messages to other objects but does not receive messages. [Booch]

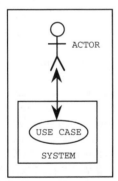

Actor (Definition 1)

Synonyms: **1** AGENT, TERMINATOR; **3** ACTIVE OBJECT, CONCURRENT OBJECT; **4** ACTIVE OBJECT, MASTER OBJECT.
Contrast with: AUDIENCE, USER.
Example: A role played by a user of the information system is an actor. [Jacobson]
Commentary: A *user* is the actual person or thing that uses the system, whereas an *actor* represents a specific role that a user can play. Actors capture the roles that users can play, and a single user can play the roles of multiple ac-

tors. Unlike other objects, the actions of actors are nondeterministic. [Jacobson] Definitions **1** and **2** are the most popular. Using the term *master* instead of *actor* for definition **4** avoids ambiguity. *Kinds:*
- ABSTRACT ACTOR
- PRIMARY ACTOR
- SECONDARY ACTOR

- **abstract actor** *n.* any actor that is not instantiated directly but rather is used as a source of common roles that other actors can inherit. [Jacobson]
Contrast with: ABSTRACT USE CASE.
Commentary: A technique to extract abstract use cases is to identify abstract actors, which typically describe *roles* that should be played against the system. [Jacobson]

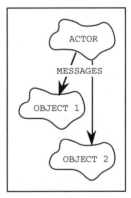

Actor (Definition 4)

- **primary actor** *n.* any actor that is going to use the system directly and that will perform one or any of the main tasks of the system. [Jacobson]
Antonym: SECONDARY ACTOR.
- **secondary actor** *n.* any actor that exists only so that the primary actors can use the system. [Jacobson]
Antonym: PRIMARY ACTOR.

actual *n. short for generic actual parameter* **1.** either the explicit generic actual parameter given in a generic parameter association for each formal or the corresponding default expression or default name if no generic parameter association is given for the formal. [Ada95] **2.** the view denoted by a generic actual parameter. [Ada95] **3.** the value of a generic actual parameter. [Ada95]
Synonym: GENERIC ACTUAL ARGUMENT, GENERIC ACTUAL PARAMETER.
Contrast with: FORMAL ARGUMENT.

actual argument *n.* any argument that contains the actual value supplied by the client. [Firesmith]
Synonym: ACTUAL PARAMETER.
Antonym: FORMAL ARGUMENT.

actual parameter *n.* any parameter that contains the actual value supplied by the client. [Firesmith]
Synonym: ACTUAL ARGUMENT.
Antonym: FORMAL ARGUMENT, FORMAL PARAMETER.

actual subtype [of an object] *n.* the subtype of which the object is declared. [Ada95]
Contrast with: NOMINAL SUBTYPE.

actualization *n.* the process by which a generic class is instantiated to generate a normal (nongeneric) class. [Atkinson]
Commentary: When a generic class is actualized, the actual parameters satisfying the specified requirements must be supplied for all generic formal parameters. [Atkinson]

[object] adapter *n.* any object request broker (ORB) component that provides object reference, activation, and state-related services to an object implementation. There may be different adapters provided for different kinds of implementations. [OMG]

adapter [pattern] *n.* the structural class/object design pattern that converts the interface of a class into one that clients expect, thereby allowing classes to work together that otherwise could not because of incompatible interfaces. [Gamma, Helm, Johnson, and Vlissides]
Synonym: WRAPPER.

ad hoc polymorphic operation *n.* any polymorphic operation that has a single method containing multiple implementations of the same functional abstraction, one of which is selected at run-time using a case statement, switch statement, or similar language construct. [Firesmith]
See also: AD HOC POLYMORPHISM.

ad hoc polymorphism *n.* **1.** any polymorphism in which multiple implementations of a single operation are included within a single method and where one of these implementations is selected at run-time (e.g. using a case statement, switch statement, or similar language construct). [Firesmith] **2.** the type of polymorphism whereby different operations on different types have the same name. [OMG]
Contrast with: INCLUSION POLYMORPHISM, INHERENT POLYMORPHISM, OVERLOADING, PARAMETRIC POLYMORPHISM.
Rationale: **1** This kind of polymorphism is *ad hoc* in that it does not make use of any of the powerful tools of object orientation. [Firesmith]
Commentary: **1** The implementation selected is typically dependent on either an argument of the message or the state of the receiver. This form of polymorphism is neither maintainable, extensible, nor object-oriented. [Firesmith] Definition **2** confuses ad hoc polymorphism with a kind of overloading.

:after method *n.* any auxiliary method

that specifies code that is to be run after primary methods. [CLOS]

Antonym: :BEFORE METHOD.

Contrast with: :AROUND METHOD.

Commentary: An :after method has the keyword *:after* as its only qualifier. [CLOS]

agent *n.* **1.** anything (e.g., an object, class, cluster) that has one or more clients and one or more servers. [Booch, Firesmith] **2.** anything in the environment that sends asynchronous messages to an application and receives the results of the messages. [Coleman]

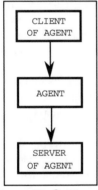

Agent (Definition 1)

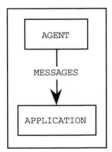

Agent (Definition 2)

Synonym: **2** ACTOR, TERMINATOR.

Contrast with: **1** MASTER, SERVANT.

Rationale: **1** This is the original meaning of the term *agent*.

Commentary: **2** The terms *terminator* and *actor* are far more popular and logical than this usage of the term *agent*.

aggregate *adj.* describing anything (e.g., scenarios, systems, clusters, classes, objects, or states) that contains at least one other such thing as a component part. [Firesmith]

n. **1.** (a) any composite (e.g., scenarios, systems, clusters, classes, objects, or states) that contains at least one other such thing as a component part. [Firesmith] (b) any object composed of other objects by means of the *consistsOf* association. [Jacobson] (c) any identifiable union of objects that has meaning and that is modeled by an aggregate object. [Jacobson] **2.** any array or an object of a class with no constructors, no private or protected members, no base classes, and no virtual functions. [C++]

v. **–ed, –ing** to encapsulate some things as component parts into an aggregate thing. [Firesmith]

Synonym: COMPOSITE.

Antonym: ATOMIC.

Kinds:
- AGGREGATE CLASS
  - COLLECTION CLASS
  - CONTAINER CLASS
  - STRUCTURE CLASS
- AGGREGATE CLUSTER
- AGGREGATE KEY
- AGGREGATE NAME
- AGGREGATE OBJECT
  - COLLECTION OBJECT
  - CONTAINER OBJECT
  - STRUCTURE OBJECT
- AGGREGATE OPERATION
- AGGREGATE PATTERN
- AGGREGATE SCENARIO

A

- AGGREGATE STATE
- CONSTANT AGGREGATE
- FIXED AGGREGATE
- RECURSIVE AGGREGATE
- VARIABLE AGGREGATE
- **aggregate class** *n.* **1.** any class, the instances of which are aggregate objects. [Coleman, Firesmith] **2.** any class that contains one or more classes as component parts. [Firesmith] **3.** any class that is constructed primarily via inheritance from other classes and rarely adds its own properties or behaviors. [Booch]
Synonym: COMPOSITE CLASS.
Antonym: ATOMIC CLASS.
Contrast with: CONTAINER CLASS, NESTED CLASS.
Example: A class of traffic signals, each of which contains traffic light objects. [Firesmith]
Rationale: **1** This definition is the most popular and is the recommended usage. **3** This definition is ambiguous.
Kinds:
  - COLLECTION CLASS
  - CONTAINER CLASS
  - STRUCTURE CLASS
- **collection [class]** *n.* any homogeneous aggregate class of collection objects (i.e., aggregate objects, the purpose of which are to hold component objects of a single type and its subtypes). [Firesmith]
Contrast with: CONTAINER CLASS, STRUCTURE CLASS.
Examples: A class of arrays, bags, dictionaries, lists, queues, sets, or stacks. [Firesmith]
Commentary: Collections enforce strong typing. Collection classes are often generic, with the parameter designating the (super)type of the component objects. [Firesmith]
- **container [class]** *n.* any heterogeneous aggregate class of container objects (i.e., aggregate objects, the purpose of which are to hold unrelated component objects of multiple unrelated types). [Booch, Firesmith, Rumbaugh]
Contrast with: COLLECTION CLASS, STRUCTURE CLASS.
Example: A class of car trunks. [Firesmith]
Commentary: Containers allow more freedom by violating strong typing. [Firesmith]
- **structure [class]** *n.* any aggregate class of structure objects (i.e., aggregate objects, the component parts of which are interrelated). [Firesmith]
Contrast with: COLLECTION CLASS, CONTAINER CLASS.
Example: A class of car engines. [Firesmith]
- **aggregate cluster** *n.* any cluster that contains one or more clusters (i.e., subclusters) as component parts. [Firesmith]
Antonym: ATOMIC CLUSTER.
- **aggregate key** *n.* any key that consists of multiple properties. [Firesmith]
Antonym: ATOMIC KEY.
- **aggregate name** *n.* any name with multiple components. [Firesmith]
Antonym: ATOMIC NAME.
- **aggregate object** *n.* **1.** any object that contains one or more objects as component parts. [Booch, Embley, Firesmith, Rumbaugh] **2.** any instance of an aggregate class. [Firesmith]
Synonym: SUPERPART.
Antonym: ATOMIC OBJECT, SUBPART.
Example: A paragraph object con-

tains one or more sentence objects. [Firesmith]

Kinds:
- - COLLECTION OBJECT
- - CONTAINER OBJECT
- - STRUCTURE OBJECT
- **collection [object]** *n.* **1.** any homogeneous aggregate object, the purpose of which is to hold component objects of a single type and its subtypes. [Firesmith] **2.** any instance of a collection class. [Firesmith]
Contrast with: COLLECTION OBJECT, STRUCTURE OBJECT.
Examples: Any individual array bag, dictionary, list, queue, set, or stack. [Firesmith]
Commentary: Collections enforce strong typing. Collections often provide appropriate operations to access and iterate over their contents. [Firesmith]
- **container [object]** *n.* **1.** (a) any heterogeneous aggregate object, the purpose of which is to hold unrelated component objects of multiple unrelated types. [Firesmith] (b) any instance of a container class. [Firesmith] **2.** any object that exists to contain other objects and that provides appropriate operations to access and iterate over its contents. [Rumbaugh]
Contrast with: COLLECTION OBJECT, STRUCTURE OBJECT.
Example: Any individual car trunk can be modeled as a container object. [Firesmith]
Commentary: Containers allow more freedom by violating strong typing. Definition **2** does not clearly distinguish between collection,

container, and structure objects. [Firesmith]
- **structure [object]** *n.* **1.** any aggregate object, the component parts of which are interrelated. [Firesmith] **2.** any instance of a structure class. [Firesmith]
Contrast with: COLLECTION OBJECT, CONTAINER OBJECT.
Example: Any car engine can be modeled as a structure.
- **aggregate operation** *n.* any operation that has been functionally decomposed into two or more suboperations. [Firesmith]
Antonym: ATOMIC OPERATION.
- **aggregate scenario** *n.* any scenario that contains one or more subscenarios as component parts. [Firesmith]
Antonym: ATOMIC SCENARIO.
- **aggregate state** *n.* any generalized superstate that is decomposed into one or more specialized substates. [Firesmith]
Synonym: SUPERSTATE.
Antonym: ATOMIC STATE.
Example: The aggregate state *functioning* may be decomposed into an *enabled* substate and a *disabled* substate. [Firesmith]
Commentary: The term *aggregate state* is preferred over the term *composite* state. [Firesmith]
- **constant aggregate** *n.* any aggregate, the aggregation structure of which and the component parts of which cannot change. [Firesmith]
Antonym: VARIABLE AGGREGATE.
Contrast with: FIXED AGGREGATE.
- **fixed aggregate** *n.* **1.** any aggregate, the aggregation structure of which cannot change, but the component parts of which can change. [Firesmith]

2. any aggregate with a predefined number and types of component parts. [Rumbaugh]
Contrast with: CONSTANT AGGREGATE, VARIABLE AGGREGATE.

- **recursive aggregate** *n.* any aggregate that contains, directly or indirectly, an instance of the same kind of aggregate. [Firesmith, Rumbaugh]
Example: A document may have other documents inside it.
- **variable aggregate** *n.* **1.** any aggregate, the aggregation structure and component parts of which can change. [Firesmith] **2.** any aggregate with a finite number of levels but a varying number of parts. [Rumbaugh]
Contrast with: CONSTANT AGGREGATE, FIXED AGGREGATE.

aggregation *n.* **1.** the whole-part relationship from an aggregate to its component parts. [Firesmith, Henderson-Sellers, Rumbaugh] **2.** any relationship, such as *consistsOf*, *contains*, or a similar relationship between object types that defines the composition of an object type from other object types. [OADSIG] **3.** (a) any mechanism for structuring the object model whereby a new class is constructed from several other classes and relationships. [Coleman] (b) the process of forming an aggregate object from other objects as its component parts. [Firesmith, Martin/Odell]
Synonym: COMPOSITION.

aggregation cardinality constraint *n.* any cardinality constraint that restricts the cardinality of an aggregate.

aggregation coupling *n.* **1.** the coupling dependency of an aggregate on its component parts. [Firesmith] **2.** the coupling dependency between component parts within an aggregate. [Firesmith]
Example: An internal combustion engine is built from its component parts (e.g., pistons, spark plugs, valves), which in turn depend on one another for proper functioning. [Firesmith]
Commentary: Whereas the aggregate depends on and is defined in terms of its component parts, the component parts should usually not depend on the aggregate. Definition 1 applies to all aggregates, whereas definition 2 applies to structures, but not to collections and containers. [Firesmith]

aggregation diagram (AGD) *n.* any specialized semantic net that documents all or part of an aggregation hierarchy. [Firesmith]
Contrast with: INHERITANCE DIAGRAM.

aggregation hierarchy *n.* any hierarchy consisting of an aggregate, its component parts, the component parts of these component parts, etc. and the aggregation relationships between them. [Firesmith]
Synonyms: ASSEMBLY STRUCTURE, CONTAINMENT HIERARCHY, PARTITION HIERARCHY, WHOLE-PART STRUCTURE.

aggregation [relationship set] *n.* any relationship that declares an object, called a *superpart* or *aggregate*, to be composed of other objects, called *subparts* or *components*. [Embley]
Synonym: AGGREGATION, COMPOSITION, IS-PART-OF RELATIONSHIP SET.
Contrast with: IS-MEMBER-OF RELATIONSHIP SET.
See also: RELATIONSHIP SET, SUBPART CLASS, SUPERPART CLASS.

a-kind-of relationship *n.* the relationship between a specialization and its generalization(s). [Firesmith]
Contrast with: IS-A RELATIONSHIP.

Examples: Examples include the subtyping relationship from a subtype to its supertype and the specialization inheritance relationship from a derived class to its base class whereby instances of the derived class are a kind of the base class. [Firesmith] A car is a kind of vehicle.

Commentary: Many developers confuse the *a-kind-of* relationship between types or classes with the *is-a* relationship between objects and their types or classes. [Firesmith]

aliased view [of an object] *n.* any view of an object that can be designated by an access value. [Ada95]

Example: Objects allocated by allocators are aliased. Objects can also be explicitly declared as aliased with the reserved word *aliased*. [Ada95]

Commentary: The *Access* attribute can be used to create an access value designating an aliased object. [Ada95]

alternative course [of a use case] *n.* any variant of a basic course, possibly including errors that can occur. [Jacobson]

Antonym: BASIC COURSE.

Commentary: Robustness is increased as more alternative courses are described (i.e., as the more sequences have been anticipated). [Jacobson]

ambiguous *adj.* describing any expression that can reference more than one feature due to polymorphism, inheritance, or dynamic binding. [C++, Firesmith]

Example: Different ancestor classes define different features with identical signatures whose overloading can not be resolved. [Firesmith]

Commentary: When virtual base classes are used, a single function, object,

type, or enumerator may be reached through more than one path through the directed acyclic graph of base classes. This is not an ambiguity. [C++]

analysis *n.* **1.** the development activity consisting of the discovery, modeling, specification, and evaluation of requirements. [Firesmith] **2.** the development activity during which is discovered the desired behavior of a system together with the roles and responsibilities of the central objects that carry out this behavior. [Booch]

Commentary: Analysis is largely a process of *discovery*, whereas design is largely a process of *invention*. [Booch, Firesmith]

Kinds:

- OBJECT-ORIENTED ANALYSIS
  - OBJECT-ORIENTED DOMAIN ANALYSIS
  - OBJECT-ORIENTED REQUIREMENTS ANALYSIS
  - OBJECT-ORIENTED SYSTEMS ANALYSIS

- **object-oriented analysis (OOA)** *n.* the discovery, analysis, and specification of requirements in terms of objects with identity that encapsulate properties and operations, message passing, classes, inheritance, polymorphism, and dynamic binding. [Firesmith]

Contrast with: OBJECT-ORIENTED DESIGN (OOD).

Commentary: The requirements are typically developed and organized in increments of clusters and subsystems. [Firesmith] Booch restricts OOA to a single project, whereas Martin makes OOA enterprise wide.

Kinds:

- OBJECT-ORIENTED DOMAIN

ANALYSIS
- OBJECT-ORIENTED REQUIREMENTS
  ANALYSIS
- OBJECT-ORIENTED SYSTEMS
  ANALYSIS
- **object-oriented domain analysis (OODA)** *n.* the object-oriented analysis of *application-domain-independent* requirements, typically for reuse on multiple projects within that application domain. [Firesmith] *Contrast with:* OBJECT-ORIENTED REQUIREMENTS ANALYSIS. *See also:* OBJECT-ORIENTED DOMAIN DESIGN.
- **object-oriented requirements analysis (OORA)** *n.* the object-oriented analysis of *application-domain-dependent* software requirements for use on a single project. [Firesmith] *Contrast with:* OBJECT-ORIENTED DOMAIN ANALYSIS. *See also:* OBJECT-ORIENTED DESIGN, OBJECT-ORIENTED SYSTEMS DESIGN.
- **object-oriented systems analysis (OSA)** *n.* **1.** the object-oriented analysis of *application-domain-dependent* software requirements for use on a single project. [Firesmith] **2.** the study of a specific domain of interacting objects for the purpose of understanding and documenting their essential characteristics. [Embley] *Antonym:* 1 OBJECT-ORIENTED DOMAIN ANALYSIS. *Contrast with:* OBJECT-ORIENTED REQUIREMENTS ANALYSIS.

analysis modeling *n.* **1.** any modeling during analysis, the purpose of which is to obtain a thorough understanding of the requirements of either an application domain or a specific application by modeling the real world as a collection of collaborating objects. [Firesmith] **2.** the analysis activity that seeks to obtain a thorough understanding of a problem domain by representing the real world as a collection of intercommunicating objects. The purpose of analysis modeling is to obtain a thorough description of a problem domain, so that:
- The requirements in the problem domain of some application can be formalized.
- The environment in which those applications are to be used is well understood. [OADSIG]

ancestor [class of a given class] *n.* **1.** any class from which the given class is directly or indirectly derived via inheritance. [Firesmith, Jacobson, Rumbaugh] **2.** either the given class or any class from which the given class is directly or indirectly derived via inheritance. [Meyer] *Synonyms:* 1 BASE CLASS, SUPERCLASS. *Antonyms:* DERIVED CLASS, DESCENDANT CLASS, SUBCLASS. *Contrast with:* PARENT CLASS. *Rationale:* The term *ancestor* is preferred over the older and more popular Smalltalk term *superclass* because of the potential for confusion between inheritance and aggregation when the corresponding term *subclass* is used. The term *ancestor* is preferred over the C++ term *base class* because base class often implies direct inheritance. The term *ancestor* is relatively common without being language-specific. [Firesmith] *Commentary:* 2 In keeping with common usage, a class should not be allowed to be its own ancestor. *Kinds:*

- DIRECT ANCESTOR
- IMMEDIATE ANCESTOR
- INDIRECT ANCESTOR
- PARENT CLASS
- PROPER ANCESTOR
- REPEATED ANCESTOR
- ULTIMATE ANCESTOR

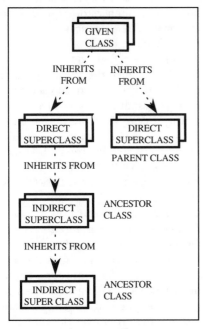

Ancestor Class

- **direct ancestor [class of a given class]** *n.* any ancestor class from which the given class is directly derived via inheritance. [Firesmith, Jacobson]
  Synonyms: DIRECT BASE CLASS, DIRECT SUPERCLASS, IMMEDIATE ANCESTOR, IMMEDIATE BASE CLASS, IMMEDIATE SUPERCLASS, PARENT CLASS.
  Antonyms: CHILD CLASS, IMMEDIATE DESCENDANT, IMMEDIATE DERIVED CLASS, IMMEDIATE SUBCLASS.
- **immediate ancestor [class of a given class]** *n.* any ancestor class from which the given class is directly derived via inheritance. [Jacobson]
  Synonyms: DIRECT ANCESTOR, DIRECT BASE CLASS, IMMEDIATE BASE CLASS, IMMEDIATE SUPERCLASS, PARENT CLASS.
  Antonyms: CHILD CLASS, DIRECT DERIVED CLASS, DIRECT DESCENDANT, IMMEDIATE DERIVED CLASS, IMMEDIATE DESCENDANT, IMMEDIATE SUBCLASS.
- **indirect ancestor [class of a given class]** *n.* any ancestor class from which the given class is indirectly derived via inheritance. [Firesmith]
  Synonyms: INDIRECT BASE CLASS, INDIRECT SUPERCLASS.
  Antonyms: CHILD CLASS, DIRECT DERIVED CLASS, DIRECT DESCENDANT, DIRECT SUBCLASS.
  Rationale: The term *indirect ancestor* is preferred over the terms *indirect base class* and *indirect superclass* because of the preference of the term *ancestor* over the terms *base class* and *superclass*. [Firesmith]
- **parent [class of a given class]** *n.* any ancestor class from which the given class is directly derived via inheritance. [Firesmith]
  Synonyms: DIRECT ANCESTOR, DIRECT BASE CLASS, DIRECT SUPERCLASS, IMMEDIATE ANCESTOR, IMMEDIATE BASE CLASS, IMMEDIATE SUPERCLASS, PARENT CLASS.
  Antonyms: CHILD CLASS, DIRECT DERIVED CLASS, DIRECT DESCENDANT, DIRECT SUBCLASS, IMMEDIATE DERIVED CLASS, IMMEDIATE DESCENDANT, IMMEDIATE SUBCLASS.
  Rationale: The term *parent* is preferred over the term *direct ancestor* because of its common usage in English and in biological inheritance. The term

direct ancestor is in turn preferred over the terms *direct base class* and *direct superclass* because of the preference of the term *ancestor* over the terms *base class* and *superclass*. [Firesmith]

- **proper ancestor [class of a given class]** *n.* any ancestor class of the given class other than itself. [Meyer]
Antonym: PROPER DESCENDANT.
Contrast with: PARENT CLASS.
Commentary: Meyer's proper ancestor is the same as Firesmith's ancestor.

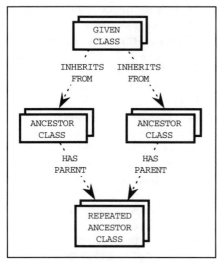

Repeated Ancestor Class

- **repeated ancestor [of a given class]** *n.* any ancestor class from which the given class is multiply derived via inheritance. [Eiffel, Firesmith, Meyer]
Antonym: REPEATED DESCENDANT.
- **ultimate ancestor [class of a given class]** *n.* any ancestor of the given class that is not a descendant of any other ancestor. [Firesmith]
Contrast with: ROOT CLASS.

ancestor object *n.* any object to which other objects can delegate responsibilities in languages that support delegation rather than inheritance. [Firesmith]
See also: DELEGATION, PROTOTYPE.
Commentary: The term *ancestor class* involves inheritance, whereas the term *ancestor object* involves delegation. In both cases, the ancestor is the *source* of information (e.g., concerning properties, behavior, rules).

ancestor [type of a given type] *n.* **1.** any type from which the given type is directly or indirectly derived via inheritance. [Firesmith] **2.** Type T1 is an ancestor of type T2 if and only if either T1 is the same as T2 or if T2 is directly or indirectly derived from T1. [Ada95]
Synonym: BASE TYPE, SUPERTYPE.
Antonym: DERIVED TYPE, DESCENDANT TYPE, SUBTYPE.
Contrast with: PARENT TYPE.
Rationale: The term *ancestor* is preferred over the older and more popular Smalltalk term *supertype* because of the potential for confusion between inheritance and aggregation when the term *supertype* is used. The term *ancestor* is preferred over the C++ term *base type* because base class often implies direct inheritance. The term *ancestor* is relatively common without being language-specific. [Firesmith]
Kinds:
- DIRECT ANCESTOR
- INDIRECT ANCESTOR
- PARENT TYPE
- REPEATED ANCESTOR
- ULTIMATE ANCESTOR

- **direct ancestor [type of a given type]** *n.* any ancestor type from which the given type is directly derived via inheritance. [Firesmith]

Synonyms: DIRECT BASE TYPE, DIRECT SUPERTYPE, PARENT TYPE.

Antonyms: CHILD TYPE, DIRECT DERIVED TYPE, DIRECT DESCENDANT, DIRECT SUBTYPE.

Rationale: The term *parent* is preferred over the term *direct ancestor* because of its common usage in English and in biological inheritance. The term *direct ancestor* is in turn preferred over the terms *direct base type* and *direct supertype* because of the preference of the term *ancestor* over the terms *base type* and *supertype*. [Firesmith]

- **indirect ancestor [type of a given type]** *n.* any ancestor type from which the given type is indirectly derived via inheritance. [Firesmith]

Synonyms: INDIRECT BASE CLASS, INDIRECT SUPERCLASS.

Antonyms: CHILD TYPE, DIRECT DESCENDANT, DIRECT DERIVED CLASS, DIRECT SUBCLASS.

Rationale: The term *indirect ancestor* is preferred over the terms *indirect base class* and *indirect superclass* because of the preference of the term *ancestor* over the terms *base class* and *superclass*. [Firesmith]

- **parent [type of a given type]** *n.* any ancestor type from which the given type is directly derived via inheritance. [Firesmith]

Synonyms: DIRECT ANCESTOR, DIRECT BASE TYPE, DIRECT SUPERTYPE.

Antonyms: CHILD TYPE, DIRECT DERIVED TYPE, DIRECT DESCENDANT, DIRECT SUBTYPE.

Rationale: The term *parent* is preferred over the term *direct ancestor* because of its common usage in English and in biological inheritance. The term *direct ancestor* is in turn

preferred over the terms *direct base type* and *direct supertype* because of the preference of the term *ancestor* over the terms *base type* and *supertype*. [Firesmith]

- **repeated ancestor [type of a given type]** *n.* any ancestor type from which the given type is multiply derived via multiple inheritance. [Firesmith]

Antonym: REPEATED DESCENDANT.

- **ultimate ancestor [type of a given type]** *n.* **1.** any ancestor type of the given type that is not a descendant of any other ancestor. [Firesmith] **2.** the ancestor of the type that is not a descendant of any other type. [Ada95]

Contrast with: ROOT TYPE.

anchored type *n.* any type that carries a provision for automatic redefinition in descendants of the class where they are used. [Eiffel, Meyer]

Commentary: An anchored type is of the form "like *anchor*" where *anchor,* called the anchor of the type, is an entity, or current. An anchored type avoids code duplication when you must deal with a set of entities (attributes, function results, routine arguments), which should all follow suit whenever a proper descendant redefines the type of one of them, to take advantage of the descendant's more specific context. [Meyer]

anonymous class [of a given object] *n.* the unspecified class of the given object, the class of which is not relevant to the current discussion. [Firesmith]

anonymous type [of a given object] *n.* the unspecified type of the given object, the type of which is not relevant to the current discussion. [Firesmith]

anonymous union *n.* any union that defines an unnamed object (and not a type). [C++]

Commentary: A union for which objects or pointers are declared is not an anonymous union. [C++]

anthropomorphize *v.* *-ed, -ing* to attribute human qualities to objects and classes. [Firesmith, Lorenz]

See also: PERSONIFICATION.

Examples: During analysis and design, developers often anthropomorphize their objects and classes. They may play the role of their objects and classes in order to validate their interactions and the scenarios that involve them. [Firesmith]

Commentary: Anthropomorphism helps developers make the paradigm shift and think like an object, instead of merely describing the data and functions that are to be localized into objects. [Firesmith]

ANY (Kernel Library Class) *n.* the general-purpose class that serves as parent to any class without an inheritance clause, and hence as universal ancestor. [Eiffel, Meyer]

Synonym: OBJECT. [Smalltalk]

application *n.* **1.** any part of a software system used to deliver end-user functionality. [OADSIG] **2.** any complete program. [Wirfs-Brock] **3.** any collection of classes that work together to provide related functionality to the end user. [Lorenz]

Synonyms: PROGRAM, PROCESS, RUNNING APPLICATION.

Kinds:
- DYNAMIC OBJECT-BASED APPLICATION
- STATIC OBJECT-BASED APPLICATION
- **dynamic object-based application** *n.*

1. one or more programs consisting of a collection of interacting objects. **2.** the end-user functionality provided by one or more programs consisting of a collection of interacting objects. [OMG]

Synonyms: PROGRAM, PROCESS, RUNNING APPLICATION.

- **static object-based application** *n.* any set of related types and classes used to provide end-user functionality. [OMG]

Synonym: PROGRAM.

application class *n.* **1.** (a) any class of objects that model and interface with an end-user application. [OMG] (b) any class of objects encapsulating entire applications. [ODMG] **2.** any essential class of model objects that captures a key abstraction of the application domain. [Lorenz]

Synonyms: **2** BUSINESS CLASS, CORE CLASS, DOMAIN CLASS, KEY CLASS, MODEL CLASS.

Contrast with: CONTROLLER CLASS, KEY ABSTRACTION, PRESENTATION CLASS, SUPPORT CLASS, VIEW CLASS.

See also: **1** WRAPPER.

Example: An *Account* class would be an application class for the banking industry. [Lorenz]

application dictionary *n.* any comprehensive dictionary defining all object-oriented abstractions (e.g., objects, classes, clusters, properties, operations, exceptions, relationships) in an application. [Firesmith]

Contrast with: DATA DICTIONARY.

Rationale: The term *application dictionary* is recommended as being less subject to misinterpretation than the traditional term *data dictionary.* [Firesmith]

application domain *n.* the subject matter of the system from the perspective

of the end user of the system. [Shlaer/
Mellor]
Contrast with: ARCHITECTURAL DO-
MAIN, IMPLEMENTATION DOMAIN, SER-
VICE DOMAIN.

application facilities *n.* an obsolete term
for any facility that supports a specific
vertical market segment. [OMG]
Synonym: VERTICAL COMMON FACILI-
TIES.
Antonym: HORIZONTAL COMMON FA-
CILITIES.

application object (AO) *n.* **1.** any object
that models and interfaces with an end-
user application. Example operations on
such objects are open, install, move, and
remove. [OMG] **2.** any object encapsulating an entire application. [ODMG]

architecture *n.* **1.** the logical or physical partitioning of some dynamic behavior or static structure. [Booch,
Firesmith] **2.** the partitioning of a system into subsystems and the allocation
of the subsystems to tasks and processors. [Rumbaugh]
Commentary: The architecture captures the strategic and tactical analysis
discoveries and design inventions, typically in terms of objects, classes, clusters, and the mechanisms that glue them
together. [Booch, Firesmith]
Kinds:
- DYNAMIC ARCHITECTURE
- MICROARCHITECTURE
- OBJECT-ORIENTED ARCHITECTURE
- STATIC ARCHITECTURE

- **dynamic architecture** *n.* the logical
or physical partitioning of some dynamic behavior. [Firesmith]
Antonym: STATIC ARCHITECTURE.
Examples: The partitioning of an application's dynamic behavior into multiple
mechanisms, scenarios, or concurrent

threads of control. [Firesmith]
- **microarchitecture** *n.* the patterns from
which a well-structured object-oriented system is composed. [Booch]
See also: PATTERN.

- **object-oriented architecture** *n.* any
architecture consisting of objects,
classes, and the collaboration and inheritance relationships among them.
[Firesmith]

- **static architecture** *n.* the logical or
physical partitioning of some static
structure. [Firesmith]
Examples: The partitioning of a system into subsystems, an assembly
into clusters, or a cluster into classes.
[Firesmith]
Antonym: DYNAMIC ARCHITECTURE.

architecture concept *n.* any concept that
is a framework of functional components, embracing a set of standards,
conventions, rules, and processes that
support the integration of a wide
range of information technology, enabling them to be used effectively within
an enterprise. [OADSIG]
Contrast with: GROUP AND VIEW CON-
CEPT, OBJECT BEHAVIOR CONCEPT, OB-
JECT STRUCTURE CONCEPT.

architectural domain *n.* the domain that
provides generic mechanisms and structures for managing data and control for
the system as a whole. [Shlaer/Mellor]
Contrast with: APPLICATION DOMAIN,
IMPLEMENTATION DOMAIN, SERVICE
DOMAIN.

argument *n.* any value that must be supplied by a client as part of a message,
operation invocation, or generic instantiation. [Firesmith, Martin/Odell]
Synonym: PARAMETER.
Kinds:
- ACTUAL ARGUMENT

- FORMAL ARGUMENT
  - GENERIC FORMAL ARGUMENT
- MESSAGE ARGUMENT
- **actual argument** *n.* any argument that contains the actual value supplied by the client. [Firesmith]
  Synonym: ACTUAL PARAMETER.
  Antonym: FORMAL ARGUMENT.
- **formal argument** *n.* any argument that specifies the type of the actual value to be supplied by the client. [Firesmith]
  Synonym: FORMAL PARAMETER.
  Antonym: ACTUAL ARGUMENT.
  Commentary: The specification of a formal argument may include its name, its mode (e.g., in, out, or in and out), its type, and any default value). [Firesmith]
  - **generic formal argument** *n.* any formal argument of a generic that must be supplied by the client as part of the instantiation process. [Firesmith]
    Synonym: GENERIC FORMAL PARAMETER.
    Commentary: Actual arguments must be supplied for each generic formal argument prior to instantiation.
- **message argument** *n.* an object that specifies additional information for an operation. [Smalltalk]
  Commentary: The value returned by the message is typically not considered an argument.

argument name *n.* **1.** the name of any pseudo-variable that holds an argument. [Firesmith] **2.** the name of a pseudo-variable available to a method only for the duration of that method's execution; the value of the argument names are the arguments of the message that invoked the method. [Smalltalk]

argument passing mode *n.* the direction (i.e., in, out, and inout) of information (i.e., data or object) flow for an argument. [Firesmith]

arity *n.* **1.** the number of separate classes that participate in a relationship. [Coleman] **2.** the number of connections to objects in a relationship. [Embley]
Synonym: CARDINALITY.
Contrast with: MULTIPLICITY.
Commentary: The term CARDINALITY is much more popular than the term ARITY.

:around method *n.* any auxiliary method that specifies code that is to be run instead of other applicable methods but that is able to cause some of them to be run. [CLOS]
Commentary: An *:around* method has the keyword *:around* as its only qualifier. [CLOS]

assembly *n.* **1.** any cluster that is not contained within any other cluster. An application typically consists of multiple component clusters. An assembly has an interface exporting its protocol of visible component clusters and an implementation containing its hidden component clusters. [Firesmith] **2.** formerly, any logical collection of objects, classes, and component subassemblies. [Firesmith]
Synonym: 2 CLUSTER.
Contrast with: 1 CLUSTER.
See also: 1 ASSEMBLY DIAGRAM.
Commentary: 1 An assembly usually is a major software configuration item and often corresponds to an entire program. A large application may have multiple assemblies. Assemblies are decomposed into clusters, which in turn are decomposed into classes. [Firesmith] 2 Firesmith has abandoned this usage of

the term *assembly* in favor of the more popular term *cluster* and restricted the term *assembly* to mean definition 1 above. [Firesmith]

assembly diagram (AD) *n.* any configuration diagram documenting the static architecture of an assembly in terms of its component clusters and the dependency relationships between them. [Firesmith]
Antonym: SYSTEM DIAGRAM.

assembly structure *n.* an obsolete term for *Whole-Part Structure*, any hierarchy consisting of a whole, its component parts, their component parts, etc., and the *has-a* relationships between them. [Coad]
Synonym: AGGREGATION HIERARCHY, WHOLE-PART STRUCTURE.

assertion *n.* **1.** any Boolean condition or relationship that must be true at certain points during execution. [Booch, Firesmith, Rumbaugh] **2.** any rule stated as a predicate that is part of the definition of an object type. **3.** any element of formal specification expressing a correctness condition. [Eiffel, Meyer]
Contrast with: CONSTRAINT.
Commentary: Assertions are typically written as expressions involving the properties of an object or class. Assertions involving multiple objects or classes are typically encapsulated in a single class, the instances of which have the visibility of all the objects and classes involved in the assertion. [Firesmith]
Kinds:
  • INVARIANT
    - CLASS INVARIANT
    - EXTENT INVARIANT
    - INSTANCE INVARIANT
    - MESSAGE INVARIANT
    - SCENARIO INVARIANT

    • POSTCONDITION
    • PRECONDITION
  • **invariant** *n.* any assertion, the scope of which is the entire lifecycle of the associated thing. [Firesmith, OADSIG]
  Contrast with: PRECONDITION, POSTCONDITION.
  Example: The length times the width of a rectangle must equal the rectangle's area.
  Commentary: Invariants are used to ensure that abstractions are never violated. Many equate the term *invariant* with the term *instance invariant*. [Firesmith]
  Kinds:
    - CLASS INVARIANT
    - EXTENT INVARIANT
    - INSTANCE INVARIANT
    - MESSAGE INVARIANT
    - SCENARIO INVARIANT

  - **class invariant** *n.* any invariant involving the properties of a class that must be true on elaboration, prior to the execution of each class operation, and after execution of each class operation. [Firesmith]
  Example: an invariant involving generic formal parameters. [Firesmith]

  - **extent invariant** *n.* any invariant involving the properties of an extent that must be true prior to the execution of each constructor and after execution of each destructor. [Firesmith]
  Example: the maximum number of instances.

  - **instance invariant** *n.* any invariant involving the properties of an instance that must be true on instantiation, prior to the execution of each instance operation, after execution of each instance operation, and prior to destruction. [Firesmith, Meyer, OADSIG, Rumbaugh]

Examples: The length times the width of a rectangle must equal the rectangle's area. [Firesmith] The age of a person cannot be less than zero. A book is overdue if today's date is after the due date. [OAD-SIG]

- **message invariant** *n.* any invariant that must evaluate to true after execution of the associated operation(s) if it holds prior to receipt of the message. [Firesmith]

- **scenario invariant** *n.* any invariant that must evaluate to true after execution of each associated operation and exception handler if it holds prior to the start of the scenario. [Firesmith]

• **postcondition** *n.* **1.** (a) any assertion on an operation or scenario that must be true immediately following the execution if all preconditions were true immediately prior to execution. [Coad, Eiffel, Firesmith, Meyer] (b) any condition that describes the correct effect of its associated operation or scenario. [Coleman, Firesmith] (c) any constraint that guarantees the results when the operation is executed. [Martin] (d) any condition that the operation itself agrees to achieve. [Rumbaugh] **2.** an invariant satisfied by an operation. [Booch]

Synonym: OPERATION POSTCONDITION RULE.

Contrast with: INVARIANT, PRECONDITION.

See also: ASSERTION.

Example: A postcondition of the push operation on a stack is that the stack not be empty.

Commentary: Postconditions are "guarantees" that are used to ensure that the associated operation or scenario was correctly executed. [Firesmith] Definition **2** uses the term *invariant* instead of the more appropriate term *assertion*.

• **precondition** *n.* **1.** (a) any assertion on an operation or scenario that must evaluate to true prior to execution. [Coad, Firesmith] (b) any predicate that characterizes the conditions under which an operation may be invoked. [Coleman] (c) any requirement that clients must satisfy whenever they call a routine. [Eiffel, Meyer, Rumbaugh] (d) any constraint that guarantees the results when the operation is executed. [Martin] **2.** any invariant assumed by an operation. [Booch]

Synonym: OPERATION PRECONDITION RULE.

Contrast with: INVARIANT, POSTCONDITION.

See also: ASSERTION.

Example: A precondition of the push operation on a stack is that the stack not be full.

Commentary: Preconditions are used to ensure that the associated operation may be correctly executed. Definition **1**(d) makes the client rather than the server responsible for satisfying the precondition. Definition **2** uses the term *invariant* instead of the more appropriate term *assertion*. [Firesmith]

assignment *n.* the operator that assigns the value of one object, pointer, or reference to another. [Firesmith]

association *n.* **1.** (a) any semantic relationship between two or more classes or types. [Booch, Firesmith, Henderson-Sellers, Martin/Odell, OADSIG] (b) any class of links between the instances of two or more classes or types. [Firesmith, Rumbaugh] **2.** any relationship between two objects or classes describing their interaction. [Henderson-Sellers] **3.** (a) any *is-member-of* relationship, containing a *set class* and one or more *member classes*. [Embley] (b) any object class whose instances are sets. [Embley] **4.** any directed binary relation between instances or classes. [Jacobson]

Synonym: **3** SET CLASS [Embley].
Contrast with: LINK.
Examples: The *employer* and *employee* relations between the object types *company* and *person* are associations.
Commentary: An association may be unidirectional [Firesmith, Jacobson], bidirectional [Firesmith, Rumbaugh], or have an explicit inverse relation [OADSIG]. It is always the associating object that acts on and knows of the associated object, never the other way around. [Jacobson]
Kinds:
- ATTRIBUTE ASSOCIATION
- BASE ASSOCIATION
- BINARY ASSOCIATION
- CLASS ASSOCIATION
  - INHERITANCE ASSOCIATION
- DEPENDSON ASSOCIATION
- DERIVED ASSOCIATION
- DYNAMIC ASSOCIATION
  - COMMUNICATION ASSOCIATION
- EXTEND ASSOCIATION
- FUNCTION
  - BASE FUNCTION
  - CHANGE-CLASS FUNCTION
  - COMPUTED FUNCTION
  - FRIEND FUNCTION
  - GENERIC FUNCTION
  - MEMBER FUNCTION
  - VIRTUAL FUNCTION
    + VIRTUAL MEMBER FUNCTION
    > PURE VIRTUAL FUNCTION
- INSTANCE ASSOCIATION
- META-ASSOCIATION
- QUALIFIED ASSOCIATION
- RELATION
- STATIC ASSOCIATION
  - ACQUAINTANCE ASSOCIATION
    + CONSISTSOF ASSOCIATION
    + PARTOF ASSOCIATION
  - INHERITANCE ASSOCIATION
- TERNARY ASSOCIATION
- UNQUALIFIED ASSOCIATION
- USES ASSOCIATION

- **attribute association** *n.* any association that captures the relationship from the object to that part of its attribute that holds the value of the attribute. [Jacobson]
Contrast with: ATTRIBUTE TYPE.
See also: ATTRIBUTE, HAS RELATIONSHIP.
Commentary: The attribute association represents the unit that holds the value of the attribute, whereas the attribute type shows the attribute's structure and type. The attribute association has a name that, like the name of acquaintance associations, describes the role that the attribute plays in relation to the object. The association can also have a cardinality. [Jacobson]

- **base association** *n.* **1.** any association that cannot be defined in terms of other associations. [Firesmith] **2.** any association of base links. [Firesmith]
Antonym: DERIVED ASSOCIATION.
Commentary: Base associations may be used to define derived associations. [Firesmith]

- **binary association** *n.* any association between two classes. [Firesmith, Rumbaugh]
  Contrast with: TERNARY ASSOCIATION.
- **class association** *n.* any association linking two classes. [Jacobson]
  Contrast with: INSTANCE ASSOCIATION, META ASSOCIATION.
  Example: The inherit association is a *class association*, that is, an association between classes. [Jacobson]
  Commentary: Class associations are drawn with dashed arrows. [Jacobson]
  - **inheritance association** *n.* any class association, meaning that the definition of the operations and attributes of one class is also used in the inheriting class, which might do additions and redefinitions. [Jacobson]
    See also: INHERITANCE.
- **dependsOn association** *n.* any association from one subsystem to another that means that objects in the first subsystem will use, in some way, objects in the second subsystem. [Jacobson]
- **derived association** *n.* **1.** any association that is defined in terms of other associations. [Firesmith, Rumbaugh] **2.** any association of derived links. [Firesmith]
  Antonym: BASE ASSOCIATION.
- **dynamic association** *n.* any association that captures a dynamic interaction. [Jacobson]
  Antonym: STATIC ASSOCIATION.
  - **communication association** *n.* any association that models the communication of one object with another. [Jacobson]
    Contrast with: STATIC ASSOCIATION.
    Commentary: The communication association does not show what

kind of stimuli is sent between the objects; this is a level of detail that is saved for interaction diagrams. Communication associations are not named because they are dynamic. [Jacobson]
- **extends association** *n.* any association from one use case to another, specifying how the first use case description extends (i.e., is inserted into) the second use case description. [Jacobson]
  Contrast with: USES ASSOCIATION.
  See also: PROBE.
  Commentary: When performing a use case, it might be performed either with or without the extended description according to some condition. The description of the second use case should be completely independent and unknowing of first use case. Ideally, the first use case should take the initiative and insert itself into the second use case. [Jacobson]
- **function** *n.* **1.** any operation that returns a value. [Ada95, C++, Eiffel, Firesmith] **2.** (a) any input/output mapping resulting from some object's behavior. [Booch] (b) any operation that maps an object of one set into a set of objects in the same or different set. [Martin/Odell]
  Synonym: **1** METHOD, OPERATION, SERVICE.
  Contrast with: **2** PROCESS.
  Commentary: The term *function* is included as a kind of association due to the definition of Martin and Odell.
  Kinds:
  - BASE FUNCTION
  - CHANGE-CLASS FUNCTION
  - COMPUTED FUNCTION
  - FRIEND FUNCTION

- GENERIC FUNCTION
- MEMBER FUNCTION
- VIRTUAL FUNCTION
    + VIRTUAL MEMBER FUNCTION
        > PURE VIRTUAL FUNCTION
- **base function** *n.* any function whose mapping is fixed by assertion. [Martin/Odell]
Antonym: COMPUTED FUNCTION.
- **change-class function** *n.* the function *change-class* changes the class of an instance from its current class, C_{from} to a different class, C_{to}. [CLOS]
- **computed function** *n.* any function whose mapping is derived or computed. [Martin/Odell]
Antonym: BASE FUNCTION.
- **friend function** *n.* the C++ term for any external function whose implementation may reference the hidden members of another class which permits the violation of information hiding. [C++, Firesmith]
Synonym: FRIEND OPERATION.
Contrast with: FRIEND CLASS.
- **generic function** *n.* **1.** (a) a parameterized function encapsulated within an object or class. [Ada, Firesmith] (b) any function whose behavior depends on the classes or identities of the arguments supplied to it. [CLOS] **2.** any function that may be redefined by derived classes. [Booch] **3.** a function object that contains a set of methods, a lambda-list, a method combination type, and other information. [CLOS]
Synonyms: **1** GENERIC OPERATION, PARAMETERIZED OPERATION. **2** VIRTUAL MEMBER FUNCTION.
See also: LAMBDA-LIST.

Commentary: Definition **1** is far more traditional and popular than definitions **2** and **3**.
- **member function** *n.* the C++ term for any function encapsulated within an object or class. [Booch, C++, Firesmith]
- **virtual function** *n.* any function that may be dynamically bound to an object at run-time. [Booch]
Synonyms: DYNAMIC OPERATION, VIRTUAL MEMBER FUNCTION, VIRTUAL OPERATION.
Contrast with: STATIC OPERATION.
    + **virtual member function** *n.* any C++ member function that may be dynamically bound to an object at run-time. [C++, Firesmith]
Synonyms: DYNAMIC OPERATION, VIRTUAL FUNCTION, VIRTUAL OPERATION.
Contrast with: STATIC OPERATION.
        > **pure virtual function** *n.* the C++ term for any virtual function whose implementation is deferred and must be supplied by a descendant base class before the descendant class can be instantiated. [Firesmith]
Contrast with: ABSTRACT.
Commentary: Pure virtual functions are used to create deferred classes. [Firesmith]
• **instance association** *n.* any association linking two instances. [Jacobson]
Antonym: CLASS ASSOCIATION.
Contrast with: META ASSOCIATION.
• **meta association** *n.* any association linking a class to an instance or vice versa. [Jacobson]
Contrast with: CLASS ASSOCIATION, INSTANCE ASSOCIATION.
• **qualified association** *n.* any binary

association, a multiplicity of which is constrained by a qualifier. [Firesmith, Rumbaugh]

Antonym: UNQUALIFIED ASSOCIATION.

See also: QUALIFIER.

- **relation** *n.* any object type modeling an association whose extension is a set of tuples. [Martin/Odell]

  Contrast with: RELATIONSHIP.

  See also: ASSOCIATION, OBJECT TYPE, PLACE, TUPLE.

  Example: The *employment* association is a relation between the *organization* and *person* object types.

- **static association** *n.* any association that captures a static relationship. [Jacobson]

  Antonym: DYNAMIC ASSOCIATION.

  Kinds:
  - ACQUAINTANCE ASSOCIATION
    + CONSISTSOF ASSOCIATION
    + PARTOF ASSOCIATION
  - INHERITANCE ASSOCIATION

  - **acquaintance association** *n.* any static association between objects, in which one object knows of the existence of another. [Jacobson]

    See also: ATTRIBUTE, ENTITY OBJECT.

    Contrast with: STATIC ASSOCIATION.

    Commentary: An acquaintance association does not give the object the right to exchange information with the other object; for that, a dynamic association is needed. Acquaintance associations are normally implemented in the same way as attributes, namely as ordinary instance references or pointer variables to instances. [Jacobson]

    Kinds:
    + CONSISTSOF ASSOCIATION
    + PARTOF ASSOCIATION

  + **consistsOf association** *n.* any ac-

quaintance association from an aggregate object to an object of which it consists. [Jacobson]

Antonym: PARTOF ASSOCIATION.

See also: AGGREGATE, ACQUAINTANCE ASSOCIATION.

Example: A food order consists of a dish and a beverage. [Jacobson]

Commentary: The association *consistsOf* is used to express that an aggregate object is a compound of other objects. [Jacobson]

+ **partOf association** *n.* any acquaintance association from an object to the aggregate object of which it is a part. [Jacobson]

Antonym: CONSISTOF ASSOCIATION.

See also: AGGREGATE, ACQUAINTANCE ASSOCIATION.

Example: A dish and a beverage are parts of a food order. [Jacobson]

Commentary: The association *partOf* is used to express that an aggregate object is a compound of other objects. [Jacobson]

- **inheritance association** *n.* any class association whereby the definition of the operations and attributes of one class is also used in the inheriting class, which might do additions and redefinitions. [Jacobson]

  See also: INHERITANCE.

- **ternary association** *n.* any association among three classes. [Firesmith, Rumbaugh]

  Contrast with: BINARY ASSOCIATION.

- **unqualified association** *n.* any association, no cardinality of which is constrained by a qualifier.

  Antonym: QUALIFIED ASSOCIATION.

  See also: QUALIFIER.

- **uses association** *n.* any association from an abstract use case to a concrete

use case in which the description of the abstract use case is used in the description of the concrete use case. [Jacobson]
Contrast with: EXTENDS ASSOCIATION.
See also: INHERITANCE.

association attribute *n.* any attribute of an association as a whole.
Contrast with: LINK ATTRIBUTE.

associative class *n.* **1.** any class that is a reification of an association. [Firesmith] **2.** any class of associative objects. [Firesmith]
Contrast with: ASSOCIATIVE OBJECT.

associative object *n.* **1.** any object that is a reification of a link (i.e., an instance of an association). [Firesmith, Shlaer/Mellor] **2.** any instance of an associative class. [Firesmith]
Contrast with: ASSOCIATIVE CLASS.

associative retrieval *n.* any retrieval of objects from an objectbase that is based on the values of the properties of objects rather than on their object identifiers or names.

associator operation *n.* any operation that creates, destroys, or maintains the referential integrity of a link. [Firesmith]
Example: When a bidirectional link is moved from one object to another, associator operations in the three objects involved must work together to break the original link and establish the new one. [Firesmith]

ASTS Development Method (ADM) *n.* the former name of the Firesmith method, an object-oriented system and software development method designed primarily for large, complex, distributed applications. [Firesmith]
Synonym: FIRESMITH METHOD.
Commentary: ASTS stood for Advanced Software Technology Specialists.

ASTS diagramming language (ADL) *n.* the former name for the language used to formally specify the icons, diagrams, and dialog boxes of Firesmith's ASTS development method (ADM). [Firesmith]
Synonym: FIRESMITH DIAGRAMMING LANGUAGE.
Commentary: ASTS stood for Advanced Software Technology Specialists.

asymmetric constraint *n.* the structural constraint on a given relationship R, which requires that if A is related by R to B, then B is not related by R to A. [Firesmith]
Antonym: SYMMETRIC CONSTRAINT.
Example: The *is parent of* link and association are asymmetric. If A *is a parent of* B, then B *is not a parent of* A. [Firesmith]

asynchronous message *n.* **1.** any message involving two threads of control that do not synchronize during message passing so that neither the sender nor the receiver of the message is blocked waiting for the other. [Firesmith] **2.** any message that can be sent at any time. [Booch]
Synonyms: ASYNCHRONOUS INTERACTION, ASYNCHRONOUS REQUEST, SIGNAL.
Antonyms: SYNCHRONOUS INTERACTION, SYNCHRONOUS MESSAGE, SYNCHRONOUS REQUEST.
Contrast with: SEQUENTIAL MESSAGE.
Commentary: An asynchronous messages does not return a value, because that would cause the sender to wait for the receiver. If information needs to be returned to the sender, the receiver will send a return message to the sender of the original message. Definition **2** can be derived from definition **1**.

asynchronous interaction *n.* any interaction via an intermediate. [Embley]

Synonyms: ASYNCHRONOUS MESSAGE, ASYNCHRONOUS REQUEST, SIGNAL.
Antonyms: SYNCHRONOUS INTERACTION, SYNCHRONOUS MESSAGE, SYNCHRONOUS REQUEST.
Examples: Communication via mail objects can be implemented as an asynchronous interaction. [Embley]

asynchronous request *n.* any request involving two threads of control that do not synchronize so that neither the sender nor the receiver of the request is blocked waiting for the other. [OMG]
Synonyms: ASYNCHRONOUS MESSAGE, ASYNCHRONOUS INTERACTION, SIGNAL.
Antonyms: SYNCHRONOUS INTERACTION, SYNCHRONOUS MESSAGE, SYNCHRONOUS REQUEST.

atom *n. short for* atomic object. [ODMG]

atomic *adj.* describing something that does not contain another such thing. [Firesmith]
Antonym: AGGREGATE.
Rationale: An atom cannot be split into component parts, at least not by chemical means.

atomic class *n.* **1.** any class that does not contain any classes as component parts. [Firesmith] **2.** any class, the instances of which are atomic objects. [Firesmith]
Antonym: AGGREGATE CLASS.

atomic cluster *n.* any cluster that does not contain any subclusters as component parts. [Firesmith]
Antonym: AGGREGATE CLUSTER.

atomic key *n.* any key that consists of a single property. [Firesmith]
Antonym: AGGREGATE KEY.
Rationale: An employee's social security number (i.e., a single attribute) can be used to uniquely identify specific employees in an object database. [Firesmith]

atomic literal *n.* any literal having no structure (i.e., containing no objects). [ODMG]
Contrast with: ATOMIC OBJECT, STRUCTURED LITERAL.
Example: An integer, a float, a Boolean, or a character are examples of atomic literals.

atomic name *n.* any name with only a single component. [Firesmith]
Antonym: AGGREGATE NAME.

atomic object *n.* any object that does not contain any objects as component parts. [Firesmith]
Synonym: ATOM.
Antonym: AGGREGATE OBJECT.
Contrast with: SUBPART, SUPERPART.
Commentary: An atomic object may, however, have one or more objects *as attributes* or *links* to one or more objects. Note that this definition assumes a clear distinction between attributes, links, and component parts. [Firesmith]

atomic operation *n.* **1.** any operation that either consistently updates the states of all participating objects, or does not update the state of any. [Firesmith, OMG] **2.** any operation that is guaranteed to execute to completion without interruption. [Firesmith] **3.** any operation that has not been functionally decomposed into component suboperations. [Firesmith]
Antonym: AGGREGATE OPERATION.
See also: TRANSACTION.

atomic scenario *n.* any scenario that does not contain any subscenarios as component parts. [Firesmith]
Antonym: AGGREGATE SCENARIO.

atomic state *n.* any state that does not contain any specialized substates. [Firesmith]
Antonym: AGGREGATE STATE.

35

atomic system function (ASF) *n.* any elemental function visible at the system boundary consisting of a message into the system, followed by all associated sequences of method executions linked by messages terminating in one or more output events.
Synonym: USAGE SCENARIO.
Contrast with: USE CASE.
Commentary: A typical ASF involves many objects and classes, and an object or class is typically involved in many ASFs.

atomicity *n.* the property which ensures that an operation either changes the state associated with all participating objects consistent with the request, or changes none at all. If a set of operations is atomic, then multiple requests for those operations are serializable. [OMG]
See also: TRANSACTION.

attached link *n.* any link to an existing object. [Firesmith]
Contrast with: DANGLING LINK, VOID LINK.
Commentary: Even though links are typically unidirectional, the link is said to be attached to the object, and the object is also said to be attached to the link. [Firesmith]
Kinds:
• ATTACHED POINTER
• ATTACHED REFERENCE

• **attached pointer** *n.* any pointer that currently points to an existing object. [Firesmith]
Antonym: VOID POINTER.
Commentary: The pointer is said to be attached to the object, and the object is also said to be attached to the pointer. [Firesmith]

• **attached reference** *n.* any reference that currently refers to an existing object. [Eiffel, Firesmith, Meyer]
Antonym: VOID REFERENCE.
Commentary: The reference is said to be attached to the object, and the object is also said to be attached to the reference. [Eiffel, Firesmith, Meyer]

attachment *n.* to attach a link (e.g., reference or pointer) to an object. [Eiffel, Firesmith, Meyer]
Contrast with: BINDING.
See also: LINK, POINTER, REFERENCE.
Commentary: One of the effects of a creation instruction is to attach the instruction's target to an object. The attachment status of an entity is not eternal. It may be changed one or more times during system execution by reattachment operations. [Eiffel, Meyer]

attribute *n.* **1.** (a) any named property used as a data abstraction to describe its enclosing object, class, or extent. [Firesmith, Rumbaugh] (b) any named property of an object that takes a literal as its value, does not have an OID, defines the abstract state of its object, and appears within the interface rather than the implementation. [ODMG] (c) a data item associated with class instances. [Coad, Eiffel, Meyer] **2.** any instance of an attribute class or attribute type. [Firesmith, Jacobson] **3.** any part of an aggregate object. [Booch] **4.** (a) an identifiable link or association between the object and some other entity (e.g., object, data value) or entities that describes the object. [Martin/Odell, OMG] (b) a set of named values associated with an object, class, or relationship. [Coleman] (c) a unit of information consisting of an attribute association and an attribute type that is stored in and describes an object. [Jacobson] **5.** an abstraction of a single characteristic possessed by all entities that were, themselves, abstracted as an object. [Shlaer/Mellor] **6.** the information that a class keeps on itself; the state data of a class. [Lorenz] **7.** something that an object *knows*. [Coad] **8.** a characteristic that can be queried. [Ada95]

Synonym: MEMBER DATA.

Commentary: Definitions **1** and **2** are often used together. Definition **1b** prohibits objects as attributes, is unnecessarily restrictive, and requires a hybrid approach. Definition **3** confuses attribute and part. Definition **4** has the referent of the attribute exist independently of the object that encapsulates the attribute.

Kinds:
- ASSOCIATION ATTRIBUTE
- BASE ATTRIBUTE
- CLASS ATTRIBUTE
- CLASS VARIABLE
- COMMON INSTANCE ATTRIBUTE
- CONSTANT ATTRIBUTE
- DERIVED ATTRIBUTE
- DESCRIPTIVE ATTRIBUTE
- DETERMINANT ATTRIBUTE
- DISCRIMINATOR
- EVENT ATTRIBUTE
- EXTENT ATTRIBUTE
- INSTANCE ATTRIBUTE
  - DEFAULT ATTRIBUTE
- LINK ATTRIBUTE
- NAMING ATTRIBUTE
- OPERATION ATTRIBUTE
- QUALIFIER
- REFERENTIAL ATTRIBUTE
- STATE ATTRIBUTE
- STATE-DEPENDENT ATTRIBUTE
- STATE-INDEPENDENT ATTRIBUTE
- TEMPORARY ATTRIBUTE
- VARIABLE ATTRIBUTE

● **association attribute** *n.* any attribute of an association as a whole.

Contrast with: LINK ATTRIBUTE, REFERENTIAL ATTRIBUTE.

● **base attribute** *n.* any attribute that cannot be derived from other attributes. A base attribute is stored rather than calculated by an operation. [Firesmith]

Antonym: DERIVED ATTRIBUTE.

● **class attribute** *n.* **1.** any attribute of a class as a whole. [Firesmith, Jacobson] **2.** any attribute whose value is common to a class of objects. [Rumbaugh]

Synonyms: **1** CLASS VARIABLE, **2** COMMON INSTANCE ATTRIBUTE.

Contrast with: COMMON INSTANCE ATTRIBUTE, INSTANCE ATTRIBUTE, EXTENT ATTRIBUTE.

Examples: **1** Generic parameters are class attributes, **2** C++ static data members are class attributes.

● **class variable** *n.* **1.** any variable shared by all the instances of a single class. [Smalltalk] **2.** any variable attribute of a class descriptor object. **3.** any variable describing the class as a whole.

Synonyms: **2** CLASS ATTRIBUTE, **3** COMMON INSTANCE ATTRIBUTE.

Example: In C++, a class variable is declared as a static member.

● **common instance attribute** *n.* any instance attribute that has the same value for all instances of the same class. [Firesmith].

Synonym: CLASS ATTRIBUTE.

Contrast with: CLASS ATTRIBUTE, EXTENT ATTRIBUTE, INSTANCE ATTRIBUTE, OPERATION ATTRIBUTE.

Example: The interest rate for a type of savings account is a common instance attribute. [Firesmith]

Commentary: Common instance attributes are usually stored once in the class rather than redundantly in each instance. [Firesmith]

- **constant attribute** *n.* **1.** any attribute whose value cannot change at runtime. [Firesmith] **2.** any attribute whose value is the same for every instance and cannot be changed at runtime. [Eiffel, Meyer]
  Antonym: VARIABLE ATTRIBUTE.

- **derived attribute** *n.* any attribute that is calculated in terms of other properties (i.e., attributes, links, or component parts). A derived attribute is calculated by an operation rather than stored. [Firesmith, Rumbaugh]
  Antonym: BASE ATTRIBUTE.
  Example: Age can be calculated from date of birth and current date.

- **descriptive attribute** *n.* any attribute that provides facts intrinsic to each instance of the object. [Shlaer/Mellor]
  Examples: The altitude, latitude, and longitude of an airplane; the current and desired state of a valve; and the address and salary of an employee are descriptive attributes.

- **determinant attribute** *n.* any attribute other than the current state attribute on which the events generated by the action depend. [Shlaer/Mellor]
  Rationale: Such attributes are known as determinant attributes, because they determine how a thread of control develops as it passes through the action.

- **discriminator** *n.* **1.** any attribute that indicates which property of the parent is used to differentiate between its children. A discriminator therefore differentiates the members of a partition. [Firesmith, Henderson-Sellers, Rumbaugh] **2.** any attribute that is an instance of a discriminator class. [Firesmith]
  See also: PARTITION.

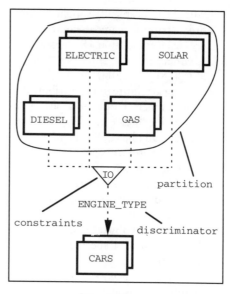

Discriminator

Example: The attribute ENGINE_TYPE of a car can be used as a discriminator to partition cars into disjoint derived classes or types; that is, cars can be subtyped as either diesel, electric, gas, or solar powered. [Firesmith]

- **event attribute** *n.* **1.** any attribute of an event object. **2.** any parameters of a message. [Rumbaugh]

- **extent attribute** *n.* any attribute that describes an extent. [Firesmith]
  Contrast with: INSTANCE ATTRIBUTE, CLASS ATTRIBUTE.
  Example: The current, maximum, and minimum number of instances are all extent attributes. [Firesmith]

- **instance attribute** *n.* any attribute that describes an individual instance. [Firesmith, Jacobson]

Contrast with: CLASS ATTRIBUTE, EX-TENT ATTRIBUTE.

- **default attribute** *n.* any instance attribute the default value of which is used if not explicitly supplied. [Kim]

• **link attribute** *n.* any attribute of each link in an association. [Rumbaugh]
Contrast with: ASSOCIATION ATTRIBUTE, REFERENCE ATTRIBUTE.

• **naming attribute** *n.* any attribute that provides facts about the arbitrary labels and names carried by each instance of an object. [Shlaer/Mellor]
Contrast with: IDENTIFIER.
Examples: The aircraft ID and name of an airplane, the code of a valve, and the name and ID of an employee are all naming attributes.

• **operation attribute** *n.* any attribute that is local to a specific operation. [Firesmith]
Synonym: TEMPORARY ATTRIBUTE.

• **qualifier** *n.* any attribute of an object that distinguishes it from other objects, thereby acting as a relationship cardinality constraint. [Firesmith, Rumbaugh]
See also: QUALIFIED ASSOCIATION.

• **referential attribute** *n.* any attribute that captures the facts that tie an instance of one object to an instance of another object. [Shlaer/Mellor]
Contrast with: LINK ATTRIBUTE.

• **state attribute** *n.* any attribute whose value helps determine the state of its encapsulating object or class. [Firesmith]
Contrast with: STATE COMPONENT, STATE LINK.

• **state-dependent attribute** *n.* any attribute that has meaning only during specific states. [Coad, Firesmith]
Antonym: STATE-INDEPENDENT AT-TRIBUTE.

Contrast with: STATE-DEPENDENT OP-ERATION.

• **state-independent attribute** *n.* any attribute that has meaning during all states. [Firesmith]
Antonym: STATE-DEPENDENT ATTRI-BUTE.
Contrast with: STATE-INDEPENDENT OPERATION.

• **temporary attribute** *n.* any attribute that is local to a specific operation. [Jacobson]
Synonym: OPERATION ATTRIBUTE.

• **variable [attribute]** *n.* **1.** any attribute the value of which can change at runtime. [Firesmith, Jacobson] **2.** any attribute associated with a particular instance, the value of which can be changed by a routine. [Eiffel, Meyer]
Antonym: CONSTANT ATTRIBUTE.

attribute association *n.* any association which captures the relationship from the object to that part of its attribute that holds the value of the attribute. [Jacobson]
Contrast with: ATTRIBUTE TYPE.
See also: ATTRIBUTE.
Commentary: The attribute association represents the unit that holds the value of the attribute, whereas the attribute type shows the attribute's structure and type. The attribute association has a name that, like the name of acquaintance associations, describes the role that the attribute plays in relation to the object. The association can also have a cardinality. [Jacobson]

attribute class *n.* any class of objects used as attributes. [Firesmith]
Contrast with: ATTRIBUTE TYPE.

attribute description *n.* **1.** any short, informative description that tells how the formal attribute reflects the real-world characteristic of interest. [Shlaer/Mellor] **2.** any filled-in template of information about an attribute, including: description, legal values, units of measure, required (yes/no), get/set constraints, rules for setting a default value, applicable states, and traceability codes. [Coad]

attribute domain *n.* the set of values an attribute can take on. [Shlaer/Mellor]

attribute signature *n.* the signature of any attribute, declaring its:
– name
– mutability (i.e., constant or variable)
– type
– initial value (if any) [Firesmith, ODMG]

attribute type *n.* **1.** any type of object used as an attribute. [Firesmith, Jacobson] **2.** any characteristic that specifies a mapping to a nonobject type. [OADSIG] **3.** any function that links a given set of objects to another set of objects. [Martin/Odell]
Synonym: **3** FUNCTION.
Contrast with: ATTRIBUTE CLASS, FIELD, INSTANCE VARIABLE.
See also: ASSOCIATION.
Examples: Customer Name and *Customer Address* would be attribute types of the *Customer* object type.

audience [of a given interface] *n.* the set of direct clients of the given interface. An interface may be intended for use by the ultimate user of the service (functional interface), by a system-management function within the system (system management interface), or by other participating services in order to construct the service from disparate objects (construction interface). [OMG]
Contrast with: ACTOR, CLIENT, TERMINATOR.

See also: CONSTRUCTION INTERFACES, FUNCTIONAL INTERFACES, SYSTEM MANAGEMENT INTERFACES.

authorization *n.* the access privileges a user has to a particular object in an object database. The specification of authorization consists of the user, the object, and the access type. [Kim]
Kinds:
• STRONG AUTHORIZATION
• WEAK AUTHORIZATION

• **strong authorization** *n.* any authorization on a class in an inheritance hierarchy that cannot be overridden by a descendant. [Kim]
Antonym: WEAK AUTHORIZATION.

• **weak authorization** *n.* any authorization on a class in an inheritance hierarchy that can be overridden by a descendant. [Kim]
Antonym: STRONG AUTHORIZATION.

automatic class *n.* any class of automatic objects (i.e., objects that are local to each invocation of a block). [C++]
Contrast with: STATIC CLASS.

automatic garbage collection *n.* the language mechanism for automatically performing heap compaction and deallocating the memory of objects (and data structures) that can no longer be accessed and that is therefore no longer needed. [Firesmith]
Commentary: Smalltalk and Eiffel provide automatic garbage collection.

automatic object *n.* any object that is local to each invocation of a block. [C++]
Contrast with: STATIC OBJECT.

automatic transition *n.* **1.** any state transition that fires without being triggered by an incoming message. **2.** any unlabeled transition that automatically fires when the activity associated with the source state is completed. [Rumbaugh]

Synonym: 1 SPONTANEOUS TRANSITION.
Examples: An automatic transition may result from the execution of a concurrent modifier operation, the completion of an operation associated with the source state, or result from an interrupt raised by a terminator.

auxiliary method *n.* any method that modifies the main, primary action of effective methods. [CLOS]
Kinds:
- :AFTER METHOD
- :AROUND METHOD
- :BEFORE METHOD

- **:after method** *n.* any auxiliary method that specifies code that is to be run after primary methods. [CLOS]
  Antonym: :BEFORE METHOD.
  Contrast with: :AROUND METHOD.
  Commentary: An *:after* method has the keyword *:after* as its only qualifier. [CLOS]

- **:before method** *n.* any auxiliary method that specifies code that is to be run before primary methods. [CLOS]
  Antonym: :AFTER METHOD.
  Contrast with: :AROUND METHOD.
  Commentary: A *:before* method has the keyword *:before* as its only qualifier. [CLOS]

- **:around method** *n.* any auxiliary method that specifies code that is to be run instead of other applicable methods, but that is able to cause some of them to be run. [CLOS]
  Contrast with: :AFTER METHOD, :BEFORE METHOD.
  Commentary: An *:around* method has the keyword *:around* as its only qualifier. [CLOS]

available feature *n.* any public feature that is either exported to all classes or selectively exported to specific classes and their descendants [Eiffel, Meyer]
Contrast with: SECRET FEATURE.
Kinds:
- GENERALLY AVAILABLE FEATURE
- SELECTIVELY AVAILABLE FEATURE

- **generally available feature** *n.* any public feature that is exported to all classes. [Eiffel, Meyer]
  Synonym: EXPORTED FEATURE.
  Contrast with: SELECTIVELY AVAILABLE FEATURE.

- **selectively available feature** *n.* any feature that is only available to specific classes and their descendants. [Eiffel, Meyer]
  Contrast with: GENERALLY AVAILABLE FEATURE.

B

balking message *n.* any synchronous message that can be successfully passed only if the receiver is immediately ready to accept the message. [Booch, Firesmith]

base *adj.* describing something that is not derivable from like things. [Firesmith]
Antonym: DERIVED.

base association *n.* **1.** any association that cannot be defined in terms of other associations. [Firesmith] **2.** any association of base links. [Firesmith]
Antonym: DERIVED ASSOCIATION.

base attribute *n.* any attribute that cannot be derived from other attributes. A base attribute is stored rather than calculated by an operation. [Firesmith]
Antonym: DERIVED ATTRIBUTE.

base class *n.* any class that is not application-specific, but instead is used to support those classes that are. [Lorenz]
Synonym: SUPPORT CLASS.
Antonym: DOMAIN CLASS.
Commentary: This definition is ambiguous and is not as intuitive as the term support class.

base class [of a given class] *n.* **1.** the C++ term for any ancestor class of the given class (i.e., a class from which the given class

has been derived). [C++, Firesmith] **2.** any class that is not derived via inheritance from any other class. [Booch] **3.** the class from which the type of a category is derived. [Eiffel, Meyer]

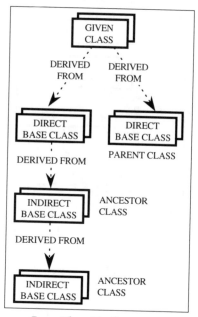

Base Class (Definition 1)

Synonyms: **2** ROOT CLASS [Booch], **3**

SUPPORT CLASS [Lorenz], 4 ANCESTOR CLASS.
Commentary: Definition **1** is by far the most popular. Definitions **2** and **3** are ambiguous (especially on C++ projects) and are not as intuitive as the terms *root class* and *support class.*
Kinds:
- DIRECT BASE CLASS
- INDIRECT BASE CLASS
- VIRTUAL BASE CLASS
- **direct base class [of a given class]** *n.*
1. the C++ term for any parent class of the given class. [C++]
Synonyms: DIRECT SUPERCLASS, PARENT CLASS.
Antonym: INDIRECT BASE CLASS.
Contrast with: ANCESTOR CLASS.
Commentary: A direct base class of the given class is also its parent ancestor class. [Firesmith]

Base Class (Definition 2)

- **indirect base class [of a given class]** *n.* **1.** the C++ term for any indirect ancestor class of the given class. [Firesmith] **2.** any base class from which a given class is indirectly derived via intermediate base classes. [C++]
Synonyms: ANCESTOR CLASS, INDIRECT SUPERCLASS.
Antonyms: DIRECT BASE CLASS, DIRECT SUPERCLASS, INDIRECT DERIVED CLASS.
Commentary: An indirect base class of the given class is any of its ancestors class that are not also its parent.
- **virtual base class** *n.* the C++ term for any base class whose members are *shared* by all of its child classes, which declare the base class as virtual. [C++]
Contrast with: ABSTRACT CLASS, BASE CLASS.
Example:
```
class VBC {};
class C1 : virtual public VBC
  {};
class C2 : virtual public VBC
  {};
class C12 : public C1, public C2
  {};
```
The child classes C1 and C2 share the information defined in the virtual base class VBC. Therefore, the ancestor derived class C12 does not inherit the members of VBC twice, which it would have if C1 and C2 had not declared VBC as virtual. [C++]
Commentary: A virtual base class provides a local point for sharing information, a statically typed interface to the information shared by its derived classes. One can cast from a derived class to a virtual base class. Casting from a virtual base class to a derived class is disallowed to avoid requiring an implementation to maintain pointers to enclosing objects. [C++]

base function *n.* any function whose mapping is fixed by assertion. [Martin/Odell] *Antonym:* COMPUTED FUNCTION.

base link *n.* any link that cannot be derived from other links. [Firesmith] *Antonym:* DERIVED LINK.

base method *n.* any method that provides behavior that is generally useful to subclasses. [Wirfs-Brock] *Synonyms:* BASE OPERATION. *Contrast with:* ABSTRACT OPERATION, DERIVED OPERATION.

base operation *n.* **1.** any operation that cannot be derived from other operations. **2.** any operation that is implemented by a class, and generally useful as is by subclasses. *Synonyms:* **1** BASE METHOD. *Antonyms:* ABSTRACT OPERATION, DERIVED OPERATION.

base relationship *n.* any relationship that cannot be derived from other relationships. [Firesmith] *Antonym:* DERIVED RELATIONSHIP. *Kinds:*
- BASE ASSOCIATION
- BASE LINK

- **base association** *n.* **1.** any association that cannot be defined in terms of other associations. [Firesmith] **2.** any association of base links. [Firesmith] *Antonym:* DERIVED ASSOCIATION.
- **base link** *n.* any link that cannot be derived from other links. [Firesmith] *Antonym:* DERIVED LINK.

base type *n.* **1.** the C++ term for any type from which another type is derived via subtyping. [C++, Firesmith] **2.** the Eiffel term for the type of the anchor of an anchored type. [Eiffel] *Synonym:* **1** ANCESTOR TYPE, PARENT TYPE, SUPERTYPE. *Antonym:* **1** DERIVED TYPE.

Contrast with: **1** BASE CLASS.
See also: **2** ANCHOR.

baseball model *n.* the Coad object-oriented development cycle implying both iteration and concurrent development. [Coad] *Contrast with:* FOUNTAIN MODEL. *Commentary:* This is represented by a graphic resembling a baseball showing bidirectional interactions between object-oriented analysis, object-oriented design, and object-oriented programming.

Basic Object Adapter (BOA) *n.* any interface intended to be widely available and to support a wide variety of common object implementations. It includes convenient interfaces for generating object references, registering implementations that consist of one or more programs, activating implementations, and authenticating requests. It also provides a limited amount of persistent storage for objects that can be used for connecting to a larger or more general storage facility, for storing access control information, or other purposes. [OMG]

basic course [of a use case] *n.* the most common or important sequence in the use case that gives the best understanding of the use case. [Jacobson] *Antonym:* ALTERNATIVE COURSE. *See also:* USE CASE. *Commentary:* Variants of the basic course and errors that can occur are described in *alternative courses*. The basic course is always designed before the alternative courses. [Jacobson]

basic service *n.* any service that each object in an object model provides. [Coad] *See also:* SERVICE. *Examples:* The basic services are: create an object, get and set attribute values, add and remove object connections, and delete.

B

Commentary: Basic services are not shown in an object model. However, they are included in a scenario view, as needed along the way.

basic type *n.* any class type, defined by a nongeneric basic class of the Kernel Library. [Eiffel]

bearer *n.* any object that presents an interface. [OMG]

Commentary: An object may be fundamentally characterized by the fact that it has a given interface (a specific object bears an interface) or an object may have an interface that is ancillary to its primary purpose in order to provide certain other capabilities (a generic object bears the interface). [OMG]

:before method *n.* any auxiliary method that specifies code that is to be run before primary methods. [CLOS]

Antonym: :AFTER METHOD.

Contrast with: :AROUND METHOD.

Commentary: A *:before* method has the keyword *:before* as its only qualifier. [CLOS]

behavior *n.* **1.** (a) the externally visible dynamics of an object or class in terms of its interactions with others (i.e., in terms of incoming and outgoing messages and exceptions). [Firesmith] (b) an object's externally visible and testable actions (ordinary English meaning) and reactions in terms of its message passing, exception raising, and state transitions. [Booch] **2.** (a) the set of services provided by an object or class via the messages in its protocol. [Firesmith] (b) the set of messages to which an object or class can respond. [Wirfs-Brock] (c) the operations exported by the protocol of an object or class. [ODMG] **3.** (a) the observable effects of performing the requested operation including its results. [Henderson-Sellers, OMG] (b) a service provided by a class upon request through a message. [Lorenz] **4.** a metaphor referring to the way objects change over time within a defined *structure*. [Martin/Odell] **5.** any set of synchronization constraints that defines how the methods of an object may execute in relation to one another (i.e., how their execution may be temporally interleaved). [Atkinson]

Synonym: **2** PROTOCOL. **3** RESPONSIBILITY.

Contrast with: ATTRIBUTE, PROPERTY.

See also: **5** BEHAVIORAL CLASS.

• **conferred behavior** *n.* the behavior that a class/object obtains through interaction with behaviored clients. [Atkinson]

behavior consistency *n.* any state consistency ensured by the behavior of an object. [OMG]

behavioral class *n.* any class that defines an abstract behavior in terms of Boolean expressions over "history" functions. [Atkinson]

See also: BEHAVIOR, BEHAVIORED CLASS, MIXIN.

Commentary: A behavioral class is not a class in the normal sense, because it cannot be directly instantiated, but is called a class to emphasize the fact that it may serve as a parent. [Atkinson]

behavioral constraint *n.* any constraint that limits the behavior of an object or class. [Firesmith]

Contrast with: STRUCTURAL CONSTRAINT.

• **real-time constraint** *n.* any behavioral constraint specifying temporal requirements. [Firesmith]

Commentary: Analysts should add real-time constraints whenever time is important.

behavioral model *n.* any model that describes the dynamics of the object types within the problem domain. [OADSIG] *Examples:* A behavioral model could include event lists, state transition diagrams, life cycle diagrams, event diagrams, event traces, scenarios, use cases, and object request diagrams.

behavioral pattern *n.* any design pattern that is primarily concerned with behavior, the assignment of responsibilities among objects, and the patterns of collaboration between objects. [Gamma, Helm, Johnson, and Vlissides] *Kinds:*
- BEHAVIORAL CLASS PATTERN
  - INTERPRETER
  - TEMPLATE METHOD
- BEHAVIORAL OBJECT PATTERN
  - CHAIN OF RESPONSIBILITY
  - COMMAND
  - ITERATOR
  - MEDIATOR
  - MOMENTO
  - OBSERVER
  - STATE
  - STRATEGY
  - VISITOR

- **behavioral class pattern** *n.* any behavioral design pattern that uses inheritance to distribute behavior among classes. [Gamma, Helm, Johnson, and Vlissides] *Kinds:*
  - INTERPRETER
  - TEMPLATE METHOD

- **interpreter [pattern]** *n.* the behavioral class design pattern that models a grammar as a class hierarchy and implements an interpreter as an operation on instances of grammar classes. [Gamma, Helm, Johnson, and Vlissides]

- **template method [pattern]** *n.* the behavioral class design pattern that models an abstract algorithm in which each step invokes either an abstract or primitive algorithm. [Gamma, Helm, Johnson, and Vlissides]

- **behavioral object pattern** *n.* any behavioral design pattern that uses aggregation to distribute behavior among objects. [Gamma, Helm, Johnson, and Vlissides] *Kinds:*
  - CHAIN OF RESPONSIBILITY
  - COMMAND
  - ITERATOR
  - MEDIATOR
  - MOMENTO
  - OBSERVER
  - STATE
  - STRATEGY
  - VISITOR

- **chain of responsibility [pattern]** *n.* the behavioral object design pattern that allows messages to be implicitly sent to an object via a chain of intermediate objects that may either fulfill the associated responsibility or further delegate it down the chain. [Gamma, Helm, Johnson, and Vlissides]

- **command [pattern]** *n.* the behavioral object design pattern that objectifies a request as an object, thereby allowing clients to be parameterized with different requests. [Gamma, Helm, Johnson, and Vlissides] *Synonym:* ACTION, TRANSACTION.

- **iterator [pattern]** *n.* the behavioral object design pattern that provides a way to sequentially access the components of an aggregate without exposing its underlying implementation. [Gamma, Helm, Johnson, and Vlissides]

Synonym: CURSOR.

- **mediator [pattern]** *n.* the behavioral object design pattern that avoids unnecessary coupling between collaborating objects by introducing a mediator object between them. [Gamma, Helm, Johnson, and Vlissides]

- **memento [pattern]** *n.* the behavioral object design pattern that objectifies another object's encapsulated state so that the other object can be later returned to that state. [Gamma, Helm, Johnson, and Vlissides]

Synonym: TOKEN.

- **observer [pattern]** *n.* the behavioral object design pattern that allows one object to notify its dependents when it changes state so that they can be updated. [Gamma, Helm, Johnson, and Vlissides]

Synonym: DEPENDENTS, PUBLISH-SUBSCRIBE.

Example: Smalltalk's model/view/controller user interface framework.

- **state [pattern]** *n.* the behavioral object design pattern that stores state as an encapsulated pointer to instances of subclasses of a state class. [Gamma, Helm, Johnson, and Vlissides]

Commentary: This pattern uses inheritance and polymorphism to eliminate the need for case statements based on state as well as the need for most state-based preconditions and postconditions.

- **strategy [pattern]** *n.* the behavioral object design pattern that defines and encapsulates a family of objectified algorithms, allowing the algorithms to vary independently of the clients that use them. [Gamma, Helm, Johnson, and Vlissides]

- **visitor [pattern]** *n.* the behavioral object design pattern that encapsulates behavior that would otherwise be distributed across classes by allowing a visitor object to traverse an object structure, visiting each node. [Gamma, Helm, Johnson, and Vlissides]

behaviorally compatible descendant *n.* any descendant that can be used any where that its ancestors can. [Firesmith, Jacobson]

Synonym: SUBTYPE.

behaviored class *n.* any class that has one parent that is a behavioral class, and one or more parents that are conventional (i.e., unbehaviored) classes. The class inherits its functionality from its "sequential parents" and its behavior from its behavioral parent. [Atkinson]

See also: BEHAVIOR, BEHAVIORAL CLASS.

belong to an environment *adj.* the objects belonging to an environment *env* are the following:

– any persistent object of *env* belongs to *env*;

– any object created while *env* is open belongs to *env*;

– any dependent of an object belonging to *env* belongs to *env*. [Eiffel]

bidirectional association *n.* any logical association that represents two unidirectional associations that are coupled so that each is semantically the inverse of the other. [Firesmith]

Antonym: UNIDIRECTIONAL ASSOCIATION.

bidirectional interaction *n.* any pair of unidirectional interactions going in opposite directions that are so closely related that they are considered to be a single interaction. [Embley]

bidirectional link *n.* any logical link that represents two unidirectional links that are coupled so that each is semantically the inverse of the other. [Firesmith]
Antonym: UNIDIRECTIONAL LINK.

bidirectional relationship *n.* any logical relationship that represents two unidirectional relationships that are coupled so that each is semantically the inverse of the other. [Firesmith]
Antonym: UNIDIRECTIONAL RELATIONSHIP.
Kinds:
- BIDIRECTIONAL ASSOCIATION
- BIDIRECTIONAL LINK

- **bidirectional association** *n.* any logical association that represents two unidirectional associations that are coupled so that each is semantically the inverse of the other. [Firesmith]
Antonym: UNIDIRECTIONAL ASSOCIATION.

- **bidirectional link** *n.* any logical link that represents two unidirectional links that are coupled so that each is semantically the inverse of the other. [Firesmith]
Antonym: UNIDIRECTIONAL LINK.

binary association *n.* any association between two classes or types. [Firesmith, Rumbaugh]
Contrast with: TERNARY ASSOCIATION.

binary large object (BLOB) *n.* any large, typically unstructured, unit of data stored in databases in binary form. [Firesmith, Martin]

binary message *n.* any message with one argument whose selector is made up of one or two special characters. [Smalltalk]
Contrast with: KEYWORD MESSAGE, UNARY MESSAGE.

binary relationship *n.* any relationship between two things. [Firesmith]

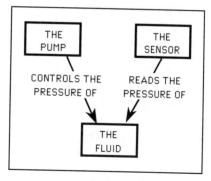

Binary Relationships

Contrast with: TERNARY RELATIONSHIP.
Kinds:
- BINARY ASSOCIATION
- BINARY LINK

- **binary association** *n.* any association between two classes or types. [Firesmith, Rumbaugh]
Contrast with: TERNARY ASSOCIATION.

- **binary link** *n.* any link between two objects. [Firesmith]
Contrast with: TERNARY LINK.

bind a name *v.* -*ed*, -*ing* to create a name binding in a given context. [OMG]

binding *n.* **1.** any selection of the appropriate method for an operation on receipt of a corresponding message and selecting those properties to be accessed by that method. [Firesmith, Jacobson, OMG] **2.** (a) any attachment of a link (e.g., reference or pointer) to the appropriate object. [Firesmith] (b) determining what item is pointed to by a pointer. [Martin] **3.** any attachment of a variable attribute name to an appropriate object or class. [Firesmith]
Synonym: **1** METHOD BINDING, METHOD RESOLUTION, **2** ATTACHMENT.

Kinds:
- COMPILE-TIME BINDING
- DELAYED BINDING
- DYNAMIC BINDING
- EARLY BINDING
- LANGUAGE BINDING
- LATE BINDING
- OVERLOADING RESOLUTION
- RUN-TIME BINDING
- STATIC BINDING
- VIRTUAL BINDING

- **compile-time binding** *n.* any binding that takes place statically before run-time when the associated message is sent. [Firesmith, Lorenz, Martin/Odell, OMG]
  Synonyms: EARLY BINDING, STATIC BINDING.
  Antonyms: DELAYED BINDING, DYNAMIC BINDING, LATE BINDING, RUN-TIME BINDING.

- **delayed binding** *n.* any binding that takes place at run-time after the message is received due to compile-time ambiguities caused by inheritance and polymorphism. [Booch, Coad, Firesmith, Martin/Odell, Jacobson, OMG]
  Synonyms: DYNAMIC BINDING, LATE BINDING, RUN-TIME BINDING, VIRTUAL BINDING.
  Antonyms: COMPILE-TIME BINDING, EARLY BINDING, STATIC BINDING.
  See also: DYNAMICALLY TAGGED.
  Commentary: Delayed binding allows the system to dynamically decide what method to use, based on the type of the current object. [Firesmith, Lorenz] Delayed binding of operations is typically implemented via a hash or jump table. [Firesmith]

- **dynamic binding** *n.* any binding that takes place at run-time after the message is received due to compile-time ambiguities caused by inheritance and polymorphism. [Booch, Coad, Firesmith, Martin/Odell, Jacobson, OMG]
  Synonyms: DELAYED BINDING, LATE BINDING, RUN-TIME BINDING, VIRTUAL BINDING.
  Antonyms: COMPILE-TIME BINDING, EARLY BINDING, STATIC BINDING.
  See also: DYNAMICALLY TAGGED.
  Commentary: Dynamic binding allows the system to dynamically decide what method to use, based on the type of the current object. [Firesmith, Lorenz] Dynamic binding of operations is typically implemented via a hash or jump table. [Firesmith]

- **early binding** *n.* any binding that takes place statically before run-time when the associated message is sent. [Firesmith, Lorenz, Martin/Odell, OMG]
  Synonyms: COMPILE-TIME BINDING, STATIC BINDING.
  Antonyms: DELAYED BINDING, DYNAMIC BINDING, LATE BINDING, RUN-TIME BINDING, VIRTUAL BINDING.

- **language binding** *n.* the means and conventions by which a programmer writing in a specific programming language accesses ORB capabilities. [OMG]
  Synonym: LANGUAGE MAPPING.

- **late binding** *n.* any binding that takes place at run-time after the message is received due to compile-time ambiguities caused by inheritance and polymorphism. [Booch, Coad, Firesmith, Martin/Odell, Jacobson, OMG]
  Synonyms: DELAYED BINDING, DYNAMIC BINDING, RUN-TIME BINDING, VIRTUAL BINDING.
  Antonyms: COMPILE-TIME BINDING, EARLY BINDING, STATIC BINDING.

Commentary: Late binding of operations is typically implemented via a hash or jump table.

- **overloading resolution** *n.* the binding of a message requesting an overloaded operation to the right method based on differences in operation signatures (e.g., number and types of arguments, type of returned value). [Firesmith]

- **run-time binding** *n.* any binding that takes place at run-time after the message is received due to compile-time ambiguities caused by inheritance and polymorphism. [Booch, Coad, Firesmith, Martin/Odell, Jacobson, OMG]
Synonyms: DELAYED BINDING, DYNAMIC BINDING, LATE BINDING, VIRTUAL BINDING.
Antonyms: COMPILE-TIME BINDING, EARLY BINDING, STATIC BINDING.
Commentary: Run-time binding of operations is typically implemented via a hash or jump table.

- **static binding** *n.* **1.** any binding that takes place statically before run-time when the associated message is sent. [Firesmith, Lorenz, Martin/Odell, OMG] **2.** any binding in which the name/class association is made when the name is declared (at compile time) but before the creation of the object that the name designates. [Booch]
Synonyms: EARLY BINDING, COMPILE-TIME BINDING.
Antonyms: DELAYED BINDING, DYNAMIC BINDING, LATE BINDING, RUN-TIME BINDING, VIRTUAL BINDING.
Commentary: Static binding allows the system to decide what method to use, based on the type of object *declared* as being dealt with. [Lorenz]

- **virtual binding** *n.* any binding that

takes place at run-time after the message is received due to compile-time ambiguities caused by inheritance and polymorphism. [Booch, Coad, Firesmith, Martin/Odell, Jacobson, OMG]
Synonyms: DELAYED BINDING, DYNAMIC BINDING, LATE BINDING, RUN-TIME BINDING.
Antonyms: COMPILE-TIME BINDING, EARLY BINDING, STATIC BINDING.
See also: DYNAMICALLY TAGGED.
Commentary: Virtual binding allows the system to dynamically decide what method to use, based on the type of the current object. [Firesmith, Lorenz] Virtual binding of operations is typically implemented via a hash or jump table. [Firesmith]

blackbox *adj.* describing any thing, the implementation of which is hidden. [Firesmith]
n. any thing, the implementation of which is hidden. [Firesmith]
Antonym: WHITEBOX.
Examples: Objects and classes are software blackboxes. [Firesmith]
Commentary: A blackbox can be viewed only from the outside. Treating something as a black box means that you don't care how it works, only that it works. [Firesmith]

blackbox testing *n.* any testing based on the visible interface of the thing being tested, which is treated as a blackbox by the test. [Firesmith]
Examples: Boundary value testing of an operation based on its arguments (i.e., its signature), protocol testing of a class based on its public features, testing of a cluster of classes based on its protocol of visible classes, and testing of an application based on its externally accessible objects. [Firesmith]

blackbox interaction diagram (BID) *n.* any interaction diagram in which the documented objects and classes are treated as blackboxes. [Firesmith]
Antonym: WHITEBOX INTERACTION DIAGRAM.

blackbox timing diagram (BTD) *n.* any timing diagram that documents the absolute or relative timing of interactions (e.g., messages, exception flows) between blackbox objects and classes. [Firesmith]
Antonym: WHITEBOX TIMING DIAGRAM.

block *n.* **1.** any object representing a deferred sequence of actions used in many of the control structures in Smalltalk. [Smalltalk] **2.** any design-level object, as opposed to an analysis-level object. [Jacobson]
Commentary: A single block often implements a single analysis object and in turn is often implemented by a single class at the programming level. However, a block may be implemented by several classes. [Jacobson]

• **public block** *n.* any block that is exported by a subsystem. [Jacobson]
See also: SERVICE PACKAGE, SUBSYSTEM.
Commentary: The interface of public blocks forms the interface of their subsystem. [Jacobson]

block expression *n.* any expression that describes an object representing deferred activities. [Smalltalk]
Contrast with: LITERAL, MESSAGE EXPRESSION, VARIABLE NAME.
See also: BLOCK.
Commentary: A block expression consists of a sequence of expressions separated by periods and delimited by square brackets.

blocking object *n.* any sequential object whose semantics are guaranteed in the presence of multiple threads of control. [Booch]

Blue Book *n.* the informal name of the book *Smalltalk-80: The Language and its Implementation* by Adele Goldberg and Dave Robson.
Commentary: This is the book that documents the original definition of Smalltalk.

body *n.* **1.** the hidden implementation details of a program unit, which generally contains two parts: a declarative part, which defines the logical entities to be used in the program unit, and a sequence of statements, which defines the execution of the program unit. [Ada95] **2.** the features hidden within the implementation of something. [Firesmith]
Synonym: IMPLEMENTATION.
Antonym: SPECIFICATION [OF A PROGRAM UNIT].
See also: PROGRAM UNIT.

bounded *adj.* having dynamic, yet limited, object code size. [Booch]
Antonym: UNBOUNDED.

bound slot *n.* any slot that does not have a value. [CLOS]
Antonym: UNBOUND SLOT.

box diagram *n.* any diagram that shows generalization hierarchies of types in terms of boxes within boxes. [Martin]
See also: COMPOSED-OF DIAGRAM.
Commentary: Box diagrams showing subtypes are useful as a component of other diagrams showing object relationships. [Martin]

branch class *n.* any class with one or more children and one or more parents. [Firesmith]
Contrast with: LEAF CLASS, ROOT CLASS.

bridge *n.* the usage of mechanisms and capabilities that one domain makes of another. [Shlaer/Mellor]

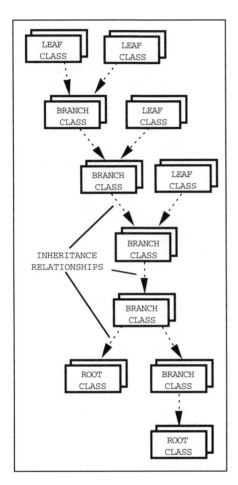

Branch Class

bridge [pattern] *n.* the structural object design pattern that decouples an interface from its implementation so that the two can vary independently. [Gamma, Helm, Johnson, and Vlissides]
Synonym: HANDLE/BODY.

browser *n.* **1.** any interactive tool that allows users to view the classes in a library and their characteristics. [Eiffel, Firesmith, Smalltalk] **2.** any view that allows you to access hierarchically organized and indexable information. [Smalltalk]
Commentary: Browsers are typically implemented as an aggregate presentation object that allows developers to scroll through the class structure and edit the features of the classes. [Firesmith] The class browser is a way to present a hierarchical index of classes and messages. Browsers are set up to help one find classes either by name or by category. [Smalltalk]

build *n.* **1.** any major increment of development that (1) implements a major subset of the requirements and (2) is used to break up the development of large, complex systems into major, manageable increments. [Firesmith] **2.** any minor iteration within the production portion of the iterative development process. This is the cycle in which developers are submitting work completed on scheduled line items to be put into the group software base. [Lorenz]
Contrast with: ITERATION, RELEASE.
Commentary: **1** The software part of a build typically consists of one or more, possibly partial, clusters. [Firesmith] **2** This definition of the term *build* and its associated definition of the term iteration are the opposite of standard industry terminology whereby a build is a major multimonth increment and an iteration is often a minor multiweek increment. [Firesmith]

• **release** *n.* any build that is delivered to the customer or user. [Firesmith]
Contrast with: BUILD.
Commentary: Releases are used to provide a significant increment of capabilities or for purposes of test and evaluation. [Firesmith]

builder [pattern] *n.* the creational object

design pattern that separates the instantiation of a complex object from its implementation so that the same instantiation process can be used to create different implementations. [Gamma, Helm, Johnson, and Vlissides]

built-in class *n.* **1.** any class that is defined as part of the object-oriented programming language. [Firesmith] **2.** any class that is an instance of *built-in class* and that has a special implementation with restricted capabilities. [CLOS]
Contrast with: USER-DEFINED CLASS.
Examples: Typical built-in classes include Boolean, character, integer, float, and real.

built-in type *n.* any type that is defined as part of the [object-oriented] programming language. [C++, Firesmith]
Contrast with: USER-DEFINED TYPE.
Examples: Typical built-in types include Boolean, character, integer, float, and real.

Business Area Analysis (BAA) *n.* the analysis stage of *information engineering*, which builds an object-oriented model of a business area or value stream, identifies business area objects, identifies business events and operations,
and expresses business policies as rules. [Martin]

business class *n.* any essential class of model objects that captures a key abstraction of the application domain (business).
Synonyms: APPLICATION CLASS, CORE CLASS, DOMAIN CLASS, KEY CLASS, MODEL CLASS.
Contrast with: CONTROLLER CLASS, KEY ABSTRACTION, PRESENTATION CLASS, SUPPORT CLASS, VIEW CLASS.

business logic object type *n.* any object type that provides the functionality of the application. [OADSIG]

business object *n.* any object that models some essential aspect of the application domain.
Synonyms: CORE OBJECT, DOMAIN OBJECT, KEY ABSTRACTION, MODEL OBJECT.

busy waiting *n.* the repeated sending of the same message to another object or class requesting a service that is frequently unavailable. [Firesmith]
Synonyms: EXCESSIVE POLLING, UNNECESSARY POLLING.
Commentary: The term *excessive polling* is more intuitive.

C

C

call *v.* *-ed, -ing* **1.** to send a message. **2.** to evaluate a postfix expression identifying an object and associated function followed by parentheses containing a possibly empty, comma-separated list of expressions, which constitute the actual arguments to the function. [C++] **3.** to invoke the method function of a method object. [CLOS] **4.** to apply a certain feature to a certain object, possibly with arguments. A call has three components:
– the target of the call, an expression whose value is attached to the object;
– the feature of the call, which must be a feature of the base class of the object's type;
– an actual argument list. [Eiffel]
Synonyms: **1** MAKE A REQUEST, SEND A MESSAGE **3** INVOKE A METHOD.

call-by-reference *n.* any message passing in which a reference to (e.g., the address of) each argument is passed rather than its value. [Rumbaugh]

call-by-value *n.* any message passing in which a copy of the value of each argument is passed rather than a reference (e.g., its address). [Rumbaugh]
Synonym: PASS-BY-REFERENCE.
Antonym: CALL-BY-REFERENCE.

Commentary: If an argument is modified, its new value will not take effect outside of the operation that modifies it. [Rumbaugh]

call-through *n.* the implementation technique for simulating inheritance in languages that do not support it by means of delegation via calls from modules representing children to calls representing parents in an inheritance hierarchy. [Firesmith, Jacobson]
See also: INHERITANCE, PROTOTYPE.
Commentary: In languages that do not support inheritance, some mechanism must be used to simulate it. This technique may cause maintenance problems and performance problems, especially for deep inheritance hierarchies. [Firesmith, Jacobson]

candidate key *n.* any minimal set of properties that uniquely identifies an instance or link. [Rumbaugh]

cardinality *n.* the *actual* number of things. [Firesmith]
Synonym: ARITY.
Contrast with: MULTIPLICITY.
Rationale: It is often (but not always) important to distinguish between the *actual* and the *potential* number of things.

Commentary: Although they have different meanings, the closely related terms *cardinality* and *multiplicity* are often confused in practice.
Kinds:
- CARDINALITY OF A GIVEN AGGREGATE
- CARDINALITY OF A GIVEN CLASS
- CARDINALITY OF A GIVEN CLUSTER
- CARDINALITY OF A GIVEN RELATIONSHIP

- **cardinality [of a given aggregate]** *n.* the *actual* number of component parts in the aggregate. [Firesmith]
Example: The current number of wheels on a car. [Firesmith]
- **cardinality [of a given class]** *n.* the *actual* number of instances of the class (i.e., the size of the extent of the class). [Booch, Firesmith]
- **cardinality [of a given cluster]** *n.* the *actual* number of classes and subclusters in the cluster. [Firesmith]
- **cardinality [of a given relationship]** *n.* **1.** the *actual* number of objects or classes that participate in the relationship. [Firesmith, Henderson-Sellers] **2.** (a) the *permitted* number of classes that may participate in a relationship. [Coleman] (b) the *expected* number of objects or classes that participate in a relationship. [Lorenz] (c) the number of instances that *may* be associated with each instance of the associating class. [Jacobson]
Commentary: Definition **2** uses the term *cardinality* to mean *multiplicity.*

cardinality constraint *n.* any structural constraint that restricts the cardinality of something. [Firesmith]
Kinds:
- AGGREGATION CARDINALITY CONSTRAINT
- CLASS CARDINALITY CONSTRAINT
- CLUSTER CARDINALITY CONSTRAINT
- CO-OCCURRENCE CONSTRAINT
- OBJECT-CLASS CARDINALITY CONSTRAINT
- RELATIONSHIP CARDINALITY CONSTRAINT

- **aggregation cardinality constraint** *n.* any cardinality constraint that restricts the cardinality of an aggregate. [Firesmith]
- **class cardinality constraint** *n.* any cardinality constraint that restricts the size of the extent of a class. [Firesmith]
Synonym: OBJECT-CLASS CARDINALITY CONSTRAINT.
- **cluster cardinality constraint** *n.* any cardinality constraint that restricts the cardinality of a cluster.
- **co-occurrence constraint** *n.* a constraint that specifies the minimum and maximum number of times an object or combination of objects can co-occur in the relationships of a relationship set with another object or combination of objects. [Embley]
Synonym: RELATIONSHIP CARDINALITY CONSTRAINT.
- **object-class cardinality constraint** *n.* A constraint used to restrict the number of objects in an object class. [Embley]
Synonym: CLASS CARDINALITY CONSTRAINT.
- **relationship cardinality constraint** *n.* any cardinality constraint that restricts the cardinality of a relationship. [Embley, Firesmith, Martin/Odell]
Synonym: CO-OCCURRENCE CONSTRAINT.
Examples: Common unidirectional relationship cardinality constraints

are *0 or 1, 1, 0, or more*, and *1 or more*. Common bidirectional relationship cardinality constraints are *1 to 1, 1 to many*, and *many to many*. More specific constraints are also possible.

Commentary: Relationship cardinality constraints can be unidirectional (i.e., restricting the number on the end that is pointed to) or bidirectional (i.e., restricting the number at both ends of the relationship).

carve [out the objects] *v. -ed, -ing* an early approach to identifying objects from data flow diagrams whereby an object or class was identified for each data store and its associated processes (i.e., data transforms).

Rationale: If an object is considered to be data and associated operations, then the data store provides the data and the processes provide the operations. This technique was originally popularized by David Bulman.

Commentary: Although briefly popular before the advent of object-oriented analysis methods, this approach has been largely abandoned by the object community because of the many problems associated with it (e.g., objects are more than just data and operations, data-flow diagrams promote functional decomposition, the "objects" tend to be scattered across numerous data flow diagrams, processes do not map well to operations that must be allocated to classes, etc.). [Firesmith]

cascaded message expression *n.* any message expression that consists of one description of the receiver followed by several messages separated by semicolons. [Smalltalk]

cascading messages *n. pl.* any series of messages performed one after the oth-

er written as a single statement with the destination object only written once. [Smalltalk]

Example: receiver message1; message2.

cast *n.* the C++ term for an explicit type conversion. [C++]

v. -ed, -ing to change the type of an object. [C++, Firesmith]

See also: CHANGE CLASS FUNCTION.

Commentary: A pointer to a derived class may be implicitly converted to a pointer to a base class, but a pointer to a base class may not be implicitly converted to point to a derived class. [C++, Firesmith]

Kinds:
- DOWNCAST
- UPCAST

- **downcast** *v. -ed, -ing* to change the type of an object to that of a descendant type. [C++, Firesmith]
  Rationale: The descendant type is lower in the inheritance hierarchy when the root class is drawn at the top. [Firesmith]

- **upcast** *v. -ed, -ing* to change the type of an object to that of an ancestor type. [C++, Firesmith]
  Rationale: The ancestor type is higher in the inheritance hierarchy when the root class is drawn at the top. [Firesmith]

catch [an exception] *v. caught, -ing* to recognize a thrown exception and execute the associated block of code designed to deal with the it. [C++]

Contrast with: HANDLE [AN EXCEPTION].

See also: EXCEPTION HANDLING.

Commentary: C++ chose the term *catch* in preference to *handle* because handle is a common identifier in C programs for PC and Mac computers. [C++] The term *handle* is ambiguous, also meaning object identifier. [Firesmith]

C-Eiffel Call-In Library (Cecil) *n.* a library of C functions. [Eiffel, Meyer]
Commentary: Cecil is used by developers who wish to write C routines that create Eiffel objects and apply features to these objects, without relying on features explicitly passed by the Eiffel side. [Eiffel, Meyer]

central interface object *n.* any interface object that contains other interface objects. [Jacobson]
Example: a window containing buttons, menus, and scroll bar interface objects. [Jacobson]

chain of responsibility [pattern] *n.* the behavioral object design pattern that allows messages to be implicitly sent to an object via a chain of intermediate objects that may either fulfill the associated responsibility or further delegate it down the chain. [Gamma, Helm, Johnson, and Vlissides]

change-class function *n.* the function that changes the class of an instance from its current class, C_{from} to a different class, C_{to}. [CLOS]
See also: CAST.

check-correct *adj.* describing an effective routine r in which, for every check instruction c in r, any execution of c (as part of an execution of r) satisfies all its assertions. [Eiffel]
Contrast with: EXCEPTION-CORRECT, LOOP CORRECT.
See also: ASSERTION, EFFECTIVE ROUTINE.

child class [of a given class] *n.* any class that is directly derived via inheritance from the given class. [Firesmith, Jacobson]
Synonyms: DIRECT DERIVED CLASS, DIRECT DESCENDANT, DIRECT SUBCLASS, HEIR CLASS, IMMEDIATE DERIVED CLASS, IMMEDIATE DESCENDANT, IMMEDIATE SUBCLASS.

Antonyms: DIRECT ANCESTOR, DIRECT BASE CLASS, DIRECT SUPERCLASS, IMMEDIATE ANCESTOR, IMMEDIATE BASE CLASS, IMMEDIATE SUPERCLASS, PARENT.
Contrast with: ANCESTOR, BASE CLASS, DERIVED CLASS, DESCENDANT CLASS, SUBCLASS, SUPERCLASS.
Commentary: The given class is called the *parent* class of the child class. This term is preferred because it is simpler, more intuitive, and more popular than its synonyms. [Firesmith]

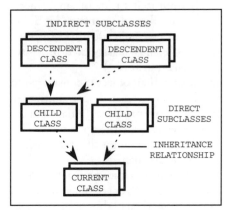

Child Class

- **repeated child class [of a given class]** *n.* any child class that multiply inherits from the given parent class. [Firesmith]
Antonym: REPEATED PARENT CLASS.

child type [of a given type] *n.* any type that is directly derived via subtyping from the given type. [Firesmith]
Synonyms: DERIVED TYPE, HEIR TYPE, SUBTYPE.
Antonym: PARENT TYPE.
Contrast with: CHILD CLASS.
Commentary: The given type is called the *parent* type of the child type. [Firesmith]

class *n.* **1.** (a) any uniquely-identified abstraction (i.e., model) of a *set* of logically-related instances that share the same or similar characteristics. [Firesmith, Lorenz, Rumbaugh] (b) any concept that has members. [Henderson-Sellers] **2.** any possibly generic factory for the instantiation of instances. [Firesmith, Lorenz, Jacobson, OMG, Wirfs-Brock] **3.** the unit of class inheritance; an encapsulation of features (possibly class-level) that may be reused by other classes via inheritance. [CLOS, Firesmith] **4.** (a) the combination of a type interface and associated type implementation. [Firesmith, Henderson-Sellers, ODMG, OMG, Smalltalk] (b) any implementation of a type of objects, all of the same kind. [Martin/Odell, Smalltalk] (c) any description of a set of objects that have identical responsibilities. [Coad] (d) any object that determines the structure and behavior of a set of other objects: its instances. [CLOS] **5.** any set of objects that share the same or similar features. [Booch, Coleman, Embley] **6.** any user-defined type. [C++] **7.** the unit of modularity, data hiding, and encapsulation. [C++] **8.** any modular unit that describes the properties of a set of possible objects, when viewed as a type. [Eiffel, Meyer] **9.** any set of types that is closed under derivation. If a given type is in the class, then all types derived from that type are also in the class. [Ada95]

Synonym: **5** EXTENT, **6** TYPE.

Contrast with: EXTENT, GENERALIZATION, SPECIALIZATION, TYPE.

Commentary: The instances of clusters are collections of objects, the instances of framework classes are frameworks, the instances of object classes are objects, and the instances of scenario classes are scenarios. [Firesmith] Definition **5** confuses the terms *class* and *extent*. Definition **6** confuses the terms *class* and *type*. Definition **7** ignores the fact that clusters are also units of modularity, data hiding, and encapsulation.

Kinds:
- ABSTRACT CLASS
  - DEFERRED CLASS
    + FULLY DEFERRED CLASS
    + PARTIALLY DEFERRED CLASS
  - MIXIN CLASS
- AGGREGATE CLASS
  - COLLECTION CLASS
  - CONTAINER CLASS
  - STRUCTURE CLASS
- ANCESTOR CLASS
  - DIRECT ANCESTOR
  - IMMEDIATE ANCESTOR
  - INDIRECT ANCESTOR
  - PARENT CLASS
    + REPEATED PARENT
  - PROPER ANCESTOR CLASS
  - REPEATED ANCESTOR
  - ULTIMATE ANCESTOR
- ANONYMOUS CLASS
- ASSOCIATION
  - BASE ASSOCIATION
  - DERIVED ASSOCIATION
- ASSOCIATIVE CLASS
- ATOMIC CLASS
- ATTRIBUTE CLASS
- BASE CLASS
- BASE CLASS [OF A GIVEN CLASS]
  - DIRECT BASE CLASS
  - INDIRECT BASE CLASS
  - VIRTUAL BASE CLASS
- BASE CLASS [OF A GIVEN CATEGORY]
- BASE CLASS [OF A GIVEN INHERITANCE STRUCTURE]
- BEHAVIORAL CLASS

- BEHAVIORED CLASS
- BRANCH CLASS
- CLASS OBJECT
- CLASS ROOTED AT A GIVEN TYPE
- CLUSTER
  - AGGREGATE CLUSTER
  - ATOMIC CLUSTER
  - COMPONENT CLUSTER
- COMPLETE CLASS
- COMPLEX CLASS
- COMPONENT CLASS
- COMPOSITE CLASS
- CONCRETE CLASS
- CONCURRENT CLASS
  - ACTIVE CLASS
  - GUARDED CLASS
  - SYNCHRONOUS CLASS
- CONSISTENT CLASS
- CORRUPTIBLE CLASS
- DERIVATION CLASS
- DERIVED CLASS
  - DIRECT DERIVED CLASS
  - INDIRECT DERIVED CLASS
  - MOST DERIVED CLASS
- DESCENDANT CLASS
  - BEHAVIORALLY COMPATIBLE DESCENDANT
  - CHILD CLASS
    + REPEATED CHILD
  - DIRECT DESCENDANT
  - HEIR CLASS
    + REPEATED HEIR
  - INDIRECT DESCENDANT
  - PROPER DESCENDANT
  - REPEATED DESCENDANT
- DESCRIPTOR CLASS
- DOMAIN CLASS
  - APPLICATION CLASS
  - BUSINESS CLASS
  - CONTROLLER CLASS
  - CORE CLASS
  - KEY CLASS
  - MODEL CLASS

- VIEW CLASS
  + PRESENTATION CLASS
  + PROXY CLASS
- EQUIVALENCE CLASS
- EXECUTABLE CLASS
- EXECUTION SUPPORT CLASS
- EXPANDED CLASS
- EXPANDED CLIENT
- FRAMEWORK CLASS
- FRIEND CLASS
- GENERATING CLASS
- GUARDABLE CLASS
- HIGH-LEVEL OBJECT CLASS
  - DOMINANT HIGH-LEVEL OBJECT CLASS
  - INDEPENDENT HIGH-LEVEL OBJECT CLASS
- JOIN CLASS
- LEAF CLASS
- LOCAL CLASS
- MEMBER CLASS
- METACLASS
  - GENERIC CLASS
  - PARAMETERIZED CLASS
  - POWER CLASS
    + DISCRIMINATOR CLASS
  - STANDARD CLASS
  - TEMPLATE CLASS
- NESTED CLASS
- OBJECT CLASS
- ORIGIN CLASS
  - DECLARING CLASS
  - IMPLEMENTATION CLASS
- PASSIVE CLASS
- PERIPHERAL CLASS
- PERSISTENT CLASS
- REACHABLE CLASS
- RELATIONAL OBJECT CLASS
- ROLE CLASS
- ROOT CLASS
- SCENARIO CLASS
  - USE CASE
    + ABSTRACT USE CASE

+ CONCRETE USE CASE
- SEQUENTIAL CLASS
- SET CLASS
- SINGLETON OBJECT CLASS
- STANDARD-OBJECT [CLASS]
- STORAGE CLASS
  - AUTOMATIC CLASS
  - STATIC CLASS
- SUBCLASS
  - DIRECT SUBCLASS
  - INDIRECT SUBCLASS
- SUBPART CLASS
- SUPERCLASS
  - DIRECT SUPERCLASS
  - INDIRECT SUPERCLASS
- SUPERPART CLASS
- SUPPORT CLASS
  - BUILT-IN CLASS
  - CLASS
  - T CLASS
- TRANSIENT CLASS
  - DYNAMIC CLASS
  - STATIC CLASS
- UNIVERSE
- USER-DEFINED CLASS
- VIRTUAL NODE CLASS

- **abstract class** *n.* **1.** (a) any incomplete class that cannot therefore be used to instantiate semantically meaningful objects. [Firesmith, Henderson-Sellers, Smalltalk, Wirfs-Brock] (b) any class that cannot have direct instances but whose descendants can have instances. [Rumbaugh] (c) any class that should not have instances. [Wirfs-Brock] **2.** any class with no instances. [Booch, Coad, Lorenz] **3.** (a) any class that can only be used as a parent class from which to derive other classes. [Coleman, C++, Firesmith, Henderson-Sellers, Jacobson] (b) a base class that declares the existence of one or more features (e.g., at-

tributes, operations) that must be implemented by its derived classes prior to instantiation. [C++]
Synonym: **3** DEFERRED CLASS.
Antonym: CONCRETE CLASS.
Contrast with: **1** DEFERRED CLASS.
Example: In a graphics application, a concrete circle class can inherit from an abstract shape class.
Commentary: An abstract class is used as a base class to provide common features, provide a minimal protocol for polymorphic substitution, or declare missing (i.e., deferred) common features that its derived classes must supply prior to instantiation. [Firesmith, Lorenz] Definition **2** is questionable because even concrete classes have no instances before they are instantiated or after all instances have been destroyed. Definition **3b** ignores the distinction between abstract and deferred classes.
Kinds:
- DEFERRED CLASS
- MIXIN CLASS

- **deferred class** *n.* **1.** any abstract class that declares the existence of one or more features (e.g., attributes, operations) that must be implemented by its descendants prior to instantiation. [Firesmith] **2.** any base class that declares the existence of one or more features (e.g., attributes, operations) that must be implemented by its derived classes prior to instantiation. [C++, Henderson-Sellers]
Contrast with: ABSTRACT CLASS, CONCRETE CLASS, EFFECTIVE CLASS.
Commentary: All deferred classes are abstract, but all abstract classes need not be deferred because an abstract class need not declare any fea-

C

ture(s) as deferred (i.e., missing implementations). Although the human designer may know that such abstract classes are incomplete abstractions, the compiler does not understand the application domain and therefore requires the clues provided by a deferred class. A deferred class should be used if one or more polymorphic features are required to implement a complete abstraction. [Firesmith] Deferred classes describe a group of implementations of an abstract data type rather the just a single implementation. A deferred class describes an incompletely implemented abstraction, which its proper descendants will use as a basis for further refinement. Declare a class as deferred if you plan to include one or more features that are specified but not implemented, with the expectation that proper descendants of the class will provide the implementations. A class that is declared deferred but has no deferred features is invalid. [Eiffel, Meyer] *Kinds:*

+ FULLY DEFERRED CLASS

+ PARTIALLY DEFERRED CLASS

+ **fully deferred class** *n.* any deferred class, all of whose features are deferred. [Eiffel, Firesmith, Meyer] *Antonym:* PARTIALLY DEFERRED CLASS.

+ **partially deferred class** *n.* any deferred class, some of whose features are not deferred. [Firesmith] *Antonym:* FULLY DEFERRED CLASS.

- **mixin [class]** *n.* any abstract class that embodies a single abstraction and is used to augment the capabilities of other base classes by providing common features to its children via multiple inheritance. [Coleman, Firesmith] *Example:* An abstract class is used to provide persistence to other classes via multiple inheritance. [Firesmith] *Commentary:* A mixin is typically combined via multiple inheritance with a generalization to form a specialization, the characteristics of which have been augmented with that of the mixin. The abstraction of a mixin (e.g., persistence) is usually orthogonal to the abstraction of the class(es) with which it is combined. [Firesmith]

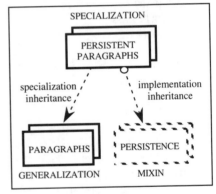

Mixin Class

• **aggregate class** *n.* **1.** any class, the instances of which are aggregate objects. [Coleman, Firesmith] **2.** any class that contains one or more classes as component parts. [Firesmith] **3.** any class that is constructed primarily by inheritance from other classes and rarely adds its own properties or behaviors. [Booch] *Synonym:* COMPOSITE CLASS. *Antonym:* ATOMIC CLASS. *Contrast with:* CONTAINER CLASS, NESTED CLASS.

Example: A class of traffic signals, each of which contains traffic light objects. [Firesmith]

Rationale: Definition **1** is the most popular and is the recommended usage. Definition **3** is ambiguous.

Kinds:
- COLLECTION CLASS
- CONTAINER CLASS
- STRUCTURE CLASS

- **collection [class]** *n.* any homogeneous aggregate class of collection objects (i.e., aggregate objects, the purpose of which are to hold component objects of a single type and its subtypes). [Firesmith]

Contrast with: CONTAINER CLASS, STRUCTURE CLASS.

Examples: Classes of arrays, bags, dictionaries, lists, queues, sets, and stacks are collection classes. [Firesmith]

Commentary: Collections enforce strong typing. Collection classes are often generic with the parameter designating the (super)type of the component objects. [Firesmith]

- **container [class]** *n.* any heterogeneous aggregate class of container objects (i.e., aggregate objects, the purpose of which are to hold unrelated component objects of multiple unrelated types). [Booch, Firesmith, Rumbaugh]

Contrast with: COLLECTION CLASS, STRUCTURE CLASS.

Example: Aclass of car trunks is a container class. [Firesmith]

Commentary: Containers allow more freedom by violating strong typing. [Firesmith]

- **structure [class]** *n.* any aggregate class of structure objects (i.e., aggregate objects, the component parts of which are interrelated). [Firesmith]

Contrast with: COLLECTION CLASS, CONTAINER CLASS.

Example: a class of car engines. [Firesmith]

- **ancestor [class of a given class]** *n.* **1.** any class from which the given class is directly or indirectly derived via inheritance. [Firesmith, Jacobson, Rumbaugh] **2.** either the given class or any class from which the given class is directly or indirectly derived via inheritance. [Eiffel, Meyer]

Synonym: **1** BASE CLASS, SUPERCLASS.

Antonym: **1** DESCENDANT CLASS, DERIVED CLASS, SUBCLASS, **2** DESCENDANT CLASS.

Contrast with: CHILD CLASS, HEIR, PARENT CLASS.

Rationale: The term *ancestor* is preferred over the older and more popular Smalltalk term *superclass* because of the potential for confusion between inheritance and aggregation when the term *superclass* is used. The term *ancestor* is preferred over the C++ term *base class* because base class often implies direct inheritance. The term *ancestor* is relatively common without being language-specific. [Firesmith]

Commentary: **2** In keeping with common usage, a class should not be allowed to be its own ancestor. [Firesmith]

Kinds:
- DIRECT ANCESTOR
- IMMEDIATE ANCESTOR
- INDIRECT ANCESTOR
- PARENT CLASS
  + REPEATED PARENT
- PROPER ANCESTOR CLASS
- REPEATED ANCESTOR
- ULTIMATE ANCESTOR

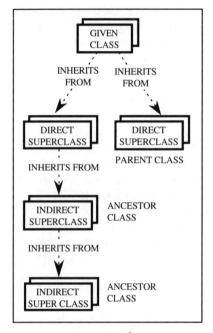

Ancestor Class

- **direct ancestor [class of a given class]** *n.* any ancestor class from which the given class is directly derived via inheritance. [Firesmith, Jacobson]

Synonyms: DIRECT BASE CLASS, DIRECT SUPERCLASS, IMMEDIATE ANCESTOR, IMMEDIATE BASE CLASS, IMMEDIATE SUPERCLASS, PARENT CLASS.

Antonyms: CHILD CLASS, IMMEDIATE DESCENDANT, IMMEDIATE DERIVED CLASS, IMMEDIATE SUBCLASS.

Contrast with: ANCESTOR CLASS.

Commentary: The term *parent* is preferred over the term *direct ancestor* because of its common usage in English and in biological inheritance. [Firesmith]

- **immediate ancestor [class of a given class]** *n.* any class from which the given class is directly derived via inheritance. [Jacobson]

Synonyms: DIRECT ANCESTOR, DIRECT BASE CLASS, IMMEDIATE BASE CLASS, IMMEDIATE SUPERCLASS, PARENT CLASS.

Antonyms: CHILD CLASS, IMMEDIATE DERIVED CLASS, IMMEDIATE DESCENDANT, IMMEDIATE SUBCLASS.

Contrast with: ANCESTOR CLASS.

Commentary: The term *parent* is preferred over the term *immediate ancestor* because of its common usage in English and in biological inheritance. [Firesmith]

- **indirect ancestor [class of a given class]** *n.* any ancestor class from which the given class is indirectly derived via inheritance. [Firesmith]

Synonyms: INDIRECT BASE CLASS, INDIRECT SUPERCLASS.

Antonyms: CHILD CLASS, DIRECT DESCENDANT, DIRECT DERIVED CLASS, DIRECT SUBCLASS.

Rationale: The term *indirect ancestor* is preferred over the terms *indirect base class* and *indirect superclass* because of the preference of the term *ancestor* over the terms *base class* and *superclass*. [Firesmith]

- **parent [class of a given class]** *n.* any class from which the given class is directly derived via inheritance. [Firesmith]

Synonyms: DIRECT BASE CLASS, DIRECT SUPERCLASS, IMMEDIATE ANCESTOR, IMMEDIATE BASE CLASS, IMMEDIATE SUPERCLASS.

Antonyms: CHILD CLASS, DIRECT DERIVED CLASS, DIRECT DESCENDANT, DIRECT SUBCLASS, HEIR, IMMEDIATE DERIVED CLASS, IMMEDIATE DESCENDANT, IMMEDIATE SUBCLASS.

Contrast with: ANCESTOR CLASS, DESCENDANT CLASS.

Rationale: The term *parent* is preferred over the term *direct ancestor* because of its common usage in English and in biological inheritance. The term *direct ancestor* is in turn preferred over the terms *direct base class* and *direct superclass* because of the preference of the term *ancestor* over the terms *base class* and *superclass.* [Firesmith]

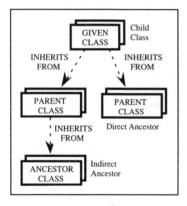

Parent Class

+ **repeated parent [class of a given class]** *n.* any parent class from which the given class multiply inherits. [Eiffel, Firesmith, Meyer]

Synonyms: INDIRECT BASE CLASS, INDIRECT SUPERCLASS.

Antonym: REPEATED CHILD CLASS, REPEATED HEIR CLASS.

Contrast with: CHILD CLASS, HEIR, INDIRECT DERIVED CLASS, INDIRECT SUBCLASS, PARENT CLASS, PROPER DESCENDANT.

- **proper ancestor [class of a given class]** *n.* any ancestor of the given class other than itself. [Eiffel, Meyer]

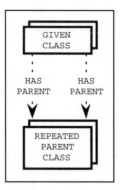

Repeated Parent Class

Commentary: Meyer's proper ancestor is the same as Firesmith's ancestor. [Firesmith]

- **repeated ancestor [of a given class]** *n.* any ancestor class from which the given class is multiply derived via multiple inheritance. [Eiffel, Firesmith, Meyer]

Antonym: REPEATED DESCENDANT

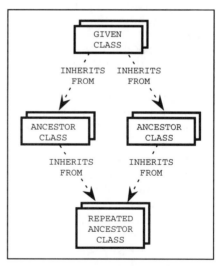

Repeated Ancestor Class

- **ultimate ancestor [class of a of a**

given class] *n.* any ancestor of the given class that is not a descendant of any other ancestor. [Firesmith]
Contrast with: ROOT CLASS.

- **anonymous class [of a given object]** *n.* the unspecified class of the given object, the class of which is not relevant to the current discussion. [Firesmith].

- **association** *n.* **1.** (a) any semantic relationship between two or more classes or types. [Firesmith] (b) any class of links between the instances of two or more classes or types. [Firesmith] **2.** any object class whose instances are sets. [Embley]
Synonym: SET CLASS.
Antonyms: MEMBER CLASS, UNIVERSE.
Contrast with: ASSOCIATIVE CLASS, LINK.
See also: IS-MEMBER-OF RELATIONSHIP SET.
Commentary: Links may also be implemented as simple pointers or as associative objects. [Firesmith]
Kinds:
  - BASE ASSOCIATION
  - DERIVED ASSOCIATION
- **base association** *n.* **1.** any association that cannot be defined in terms of other associations. [Firesmith] **2.** any association of base links. [Firesmith]
Antonym: DERIVED ASSOCIATION.
- **derived association** *n.* **1.** any association that is defined in terms of other associations. [Firesmith, Rumbaugh] **2.** any association of derived links. [Firesmith]
Antonym: BASE ASSOCIATION.
- **associative class** *n.* **1.** any class that is a reification of an association. [Firesmith] **2.** any class of associative ob-

jects. [Firesmith]
Commentary: Not every association need be implemented as a class of associative objects.

- **atomic class** *n.* **1.** any class, the instances of which are atomic objects. [Firesmith] **2.** any class that does not contain any classes as component parts. [Firesmith]
Antonym: AGGREGATE CLASS.

- **attribute class** *n.* any class of objects used as attributes. [Firesmith]
Contrast with: ATTRIBUTE TYPE.

- **base class** *n.* any class that is not application-specific, but instead is used to support those classes that are. [Lorenz]
Synonym: SUPPORT CLASS.
Antonym: DOMAIN CLASS.
Commentary: This definition is ambiguous and is not as intuitive as the term support class.

- **base class [of a given class]** *n.* **1.** the C++ term for any ancestor class of the given class (i.e., a class from which the given class has been derived). [C++, Firesmith]. **2.** any class that is not derived via inheritance from any other class. [Booch] **3.** the class from which the type of a category is derived. [Eiffel, Meyer]
Synonyms: **2** ROOT CLASS [Booch], **3** SUPPORT CLASS [Lorenz], **4** ANCESTOR CLASS.
Commentary: Definition **1** is by far the most popular. Definitions **2** and **3** are ambiguous (especially on C++ projects) and are not as intuitive as the terms *root class* and *support class.*
Kinds:
  - DIRECT BASE CLASS
  - INDIRECT BASE CLASS
  + VIRTUAL BASE CLASS

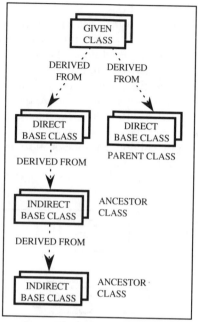

Base Class of a Given Class
(Definition 1)

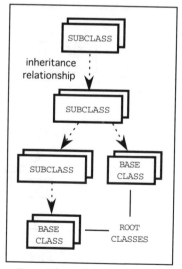

Base Class of a Given Class
(Definition 2)

- **direct base class [of a given class]** *n.* the C++ term for any parent class of the given class. [C++, Firesmith] *Synonyms:* DIRECT ANCESTOR, DIRECT SUPERCLASS, IMMEDIATE ANCESTOR, IMMEDIATE BASE CLASS, IMMEDIATE SUPERCLASS, PARENT CLASS. *Antonyms:* CHILD CLASS, DIRECT DESCENDANT, DIRECT DERIVED CLASS, DIRECT SUBCLASS.
Commentary: The term *parent* is preferred. A direct base class of the given class is also a parent ancestor class. [Firesmith]
- **indirect base class [of a given class]** *n.* the C++ term for any indirect ancestor class of the given class. [C++. Firesmith]
Synonyms: INDIRECT ANCESTOR, INDIRECT SUPERCLASS.
Antonyms: INDIRECT DERIVED CLASS, INDIRECT DESCENDANT, INDIRECT SUBCLASS.
Contrast with: DIRECT BASE CLASS, DIRECT SUPERCLASS.
Rationale: The term *indirect ancestor* is preferred.
Commentary: An indirect base class is an ancestor class that is not also a parent class. [Firesmith]
- **virtual base class** *n.* the C++ term for any base class whose members are *shared* by all of its child classes, which declare the base class as virtual. [C++]
Contrast with: ABSTRACT CLASS, BASE CLASS.
Example:
```
class VBC {};
class C1 : virtual public VBC {};
class C2 : virtual public VBC {};
class C12 : public C1, public C2
   {};
```

The child classes C1 and C2 share the information defined in the virtual base class VBC. Therefore, the ancestor derived class C12 does not inherit the members of VBC twice, which it would have if C1 and C2 had not declared VBC as virtual. [C++]

Commentary: A virtual base class provides a local point for sharing information, a statically typed interface to the information shared by its derived classes. One can cast from a derived class to a virtual base class. Casting from a virtual base class to a derived class is disallowed to avoid requiring an implementation to maintain pointers to enclosing objects. [C++]

- **base class [of a given category]** *n.* the class from which the type of a category is derived. [Eiffel, Meyer]
- **base class [of a given inheritance structure]** *n.* any class that is not derived via inheritance from any other class. [Booch].

Synonym: ROOT CLASS.

Antonym: LEAF CLASS.

Contrast with: BRANCH CLASS.

Commentary: This definition is ambiguous (especially on C++ projects) and is not as intuitive as the term *root class*. [Firesmith]

- **behavioral class** *n.* any class that defines an abstract behavior in terms of Boolean expressions over "history" functions. [Atkinson]

See also: BEHAVIOR, BEHAVIORED CLASS, MIXIN.

Commentary: A behavioral class is not a class in the normal sense because it cannot be directly instantiated, but it is called a class to emphasize the fact that it may serve as a parent. [Atkinson]

- **behaviored class** *n.* any class that has one parent that is a behavioral class, and one or more parents that are conventional (i.e., unbehaviored) classes. The class inherits its functionality from its "sequential parents" and its behavior from its behavioral parent. [Atkinson]

See also: BEHAVIOR, BEHAVIORAL CLASS.

- **branch class** *n.* any class with one or more children and one or more parents. [Firesmith]

Contrast with: LEAF CLASS, ROOT CLASS.

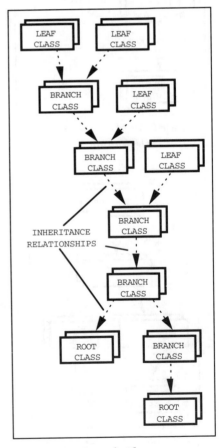

Branch Class

- **class object** *n*. any object that is also a class. [Firesmith]
  Contrast with: FACTORY, METACLASS.
  See also: OBJECT CLASS.
  Examples: All classes in Smalltalk are also objects.
  Commentary: Class objects are instances of metaclasses. Any class with class characteristics is a class object. [Firesmith]
- **class rooted at a given type** *n*. the derivation class of types for type *T*, which is the set consisting of *T* (the *root type* of the class) and all types derived from *T* (directly or indirectly) plus any associated universal or class-wide types. [Ada95]
  See also: ROOT TYPE, TYPE.
- **cluster** *n*. any encapsulation of classes or clusters that are typically analyzed, designed, coded, tested, and integrated as a small increment of development. A cluster has an interface exporting its protocol of visible features and an implementation containing its hidden features. [Firesmith]
  Contrast with: ATTRIBUTE CLASS, CLUSTER INSTANCE, FRAMEWORK CLASS, METACLASS, OBJECT CLASS.
  Rationale: Term popularized by the Eiffel language. A cluster is not necessarily a category of classes. Unlike a true subsystem, a cluster does not contain hardware, wetware (i.e., persons), and paperware (i.e., documentation). [Firesmith]
  Commentary: New clusters can be derived from existing clusters via cluster inheritance. Clusters can be instantiated to construct groups of objects. Clusters should have high cohesion and low coupling to other clusters. [Firesmith]

Kinds:
- AGGREGATE CLUSTER
- ASSEMBLY
- ATOMIC CLUSTER
- COMPONENT CLUSTER
- SUBCLUSTER

- **aggregate cluster** *n*. any cluster that contains one or more clusters (i.e., subclusters) as component parts. [Firesmith]
  Antonym: ATOMIC CLUSTER.
- **assembly** *n*. **1.** any cluster that is not contained within any other cluster. An application typically consists of multiple component clusters. An assembly has an interface exporting its protocol of visible component clusters and an implementation containing its hidden component clusters. [Firesmith] **2.** formerly, any logical collection of objects, classes, and component subassemblies. [Firesmith]
  Synonym: **2** CLUSTER.
  Contrast with: **1** CLUSTER.
  See also: **1** ASSEMBLY DIAGRAM.
  Commentary: **1** An assembly usually is a major software configuration item and often corresponds to an entire program. A large application may have multiple assemblies. Assemblies are decomposed into clusters, which in turn are decomposed into classes. [Firesmith] **2** Firesmith has abandoned this usage of the term *assembly* in favor of the more popular term *cluster* and restricted the term *assembly* to mean definition **1** above. [Firesmith]
- **atomic cluster** *n*. any cluster that does not contain any subclusters as component parts. [Firesmith]
  Antonym: AGGREGATE CLUSTER.

C

- **component [cluster]** *n.* any cluster that is contained within another cluster as a component part. [Firesmith] *Contrast with:* COMPONENT CLASS, COMPONENT OBJECT.
- **subcluster** *n.* any cluster that is derived from the given cluster via cluster inheritance. [Firesmith]
- **complete class** *n.* any class capturing all of the responsibilities and features needed to both accurately implement the associated abstraction and meet its current requirements. [Firesmith] *Commentary:* Where practical, a complete class should also implement all features required to support reusability and user-friendliness. [Firesmith]
- **complex class** *n.* any class other than Boolean, character, integer, real, and double. [Eiffel]
- **component class** *n.* any class that is contained within another class as a component part. [Firesmith] *Synonym:* SUBCLASS. *Contrast with:* COMPONENT CLUSTER, COMPONENT OBJECT, LOCAL CLASS, NESTED CLASS. *Rationale:* The term *component class* is far less ambiguous that the term *subclass,* which has another, more popular meaning. [Firesmith]
- **composite class** *n.* any class that is composed of other classes. [Wirfs-Brock] *Synonym:* AGGREGATE CLASS, NESTED CLASS. *Antonym:* ATOMIC CLASS. *Contrast with:* AGGREGATE CLASS, CONTAINER CLASS.
- **concrete class** *n.* **1.** (a) any complete class that can be instantiated to produce semantically meaningful instances. [Booch, Coad, Firesmith, Rumbaugh, Wirfs-Brock] (b) any class, the main purpose of which is to create instances. [Jacobson] **2.** any class with instances. [Lorenz] *Antonym:* ABSTRACT CLASS. *Commentary:* Definition 2 is questionable because concrete classes have no instances before they are instantiated or after all instances have been destroyed.
- **concurrent class** *n.* **1.** any class whose instances are concurrent objects. [Firesmith] **2.** any class containing a concurrent class feature (e.g., operation or object). [Firesmith] *Antonym:* SEQUENTIAL CLASS. *Kinds:*
  - ACTIVE CLASS
  - GUARDED CLASS
  - SYNCHRONOUS CLASS
- **active class** *n.* **1.** any concurrent class of active objects that execute without the need for incoming messages. [Firesmith] **2.** any concurrent class. [Booch] **3.** any class that is generated by an object that has a separate state machine for each instance. [Shlaer/Mellor] *Synonym:* 2 CONCURRENT CLASS. *Antonym:* PASSIVE CLASS. *Rationale:* Definition 1 is consistent with the traditional use of the term to describe Ada tasks without entries.
- **guarded class** *n.* **1.** any concurrent class, the instances of which provide and enforce mutually exclusive access in a concurrent environment. [Firesmith] **2.** any class whose semantics are guaranteed in the presence of multiple threads of control if all clients properly collaborate to achieve mutual exclusion. [Booch] *Synonym:* 1 SYNCHRONOUS CLASS.

Contrast with: **1** CORRUPTIBLE CLASS, GUARDABLE CLASS, **2** SEQUENTIAL CLASS, SYNCHRONOUS CLASS.

- **synchronous class** *n.* any class whose instances guarantee their semantics via mutual exclusion in the presence of multiple threads of control. [Booch]
Synonym: GUARDED CLASS.
Contrast with: GUARDED CLASS, SEQUENTIAL CLASS.

- **consistent class** *n.* any class, the instances of which are instantiated in a state satisfying all invariants and having only operations which if started in a state satisfying the precondition and the invariants also terminate in a state satisfying the postcondition and the invariants. [Firesmith]

- **corruptible class** *n.* any class, the instances of which do not provide any mechanism for ensuring mutually exclusive access in a concurrent environment. [Firesmith]
Contrast with: GUARDABLE CLASS, GUARDED CLASS.

- **derivation class** *n.* any class that is not defined by the language but is instead derived from another class. [Ada95]
Synonym: DERIVED CLASS.

- **derived class [of a given class]** *n.* the C++ term for any descendant class of the given class. [C++, Firesmith]
Synonyms: CHILD CLASS, DESCENDANT, SUBCLASS.
Antonyms: ANCESTOR CLASS, BASE CLASS, PARENT CLASS.
Rationale: The term *derived* was chosen over the term *subclass* because the term *subclass* is often confusing and ambiguous as it might imply either inheritance or aggregation. [C++, Firesmith]
Commentary: The derived class can

override virtual functions of its parent(s) and declare additional data members, functions, and so on. A pointer to a derived class may be implicitly converted to a pointer to a parent, but a pointer to a parent class may not be implicitly converted to point to a derived class. [C++, Firesmith]

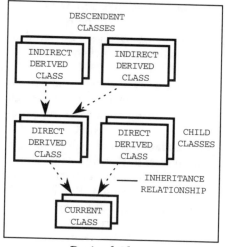

Derived Classes

Kinds:
- DIRECT DERIVED CLASS
- INDIRECT DERIVED CLASS
- MOST DERIVED CLASS

- **direct derived class [of a given class]** *n.* any child class of the given class. [Ada95, C++, Firesmith]
Synonyms: CHILD CLASS, DIRECT SUBCLASS, HEIR CLASS.
Antonym: INDIRECT DERIVED CLASS.
Contrast with: ANCESTOR, INDIRECT BASE CLASS.
Commentary: A direct derived class of a given class is a descendant class that is also a child descendant class. [Firesmith]

- **indirect derived class [of a given class]** *n.* any derived class that is indirectly derived via intermediate base classes from a given class. [Ada95, C++, Firesmith]

Synonyms: ANCESTOR CLASS, INDIRECT SUPERCLASS.

Antonyms: DIRECT DERIVED CLASS, INDIRECT BASE CLASS.

Contrast with: DESCENDANT CLASS.

Commentary: An indirect derived class of a given class is a descendant class that is not a child class. [Firesmith]

- **most derived class** *n.* the derived class of a *complete object* (i.e., an object that is not a subobject representing a base class). [C++]

• **descendant [class of a given class]** *n.*
1. any class that inherits, either directly or indirectly, from the given class. [Firesmith, Jacobson, Rumbaugh] 2. either the given class or any class that inherits, either directly or indirectly, from the given class. [Eiffel, Meyer]

Synonyms: 1 DERIVED CLASS, SUBCLASS.

Antonyms: ANCESTOR, BASE CLASS, SUPERCLASS.

Contrast with: CHILD CLASS, HEIR, PARENT CLASS.

Commentary: Definition 1 follows the normal usage of the word and does not allow a class to be its own descendant, especially because a class cannot inherit from itself. However, definition 2 allows a class to be its own descendant.

Kinds:
- BEHAVIORALLY COMPATIBLE DESCENDANT
- CHILD
  + REPEATED CHILD CLASS
- DIRECT DESCENDANT

- HEIR
  + REPEATED HEIR
- INDIRECT DESCENDANT
- PROPER DESCENDANT
- REPEATED DESCENDANT

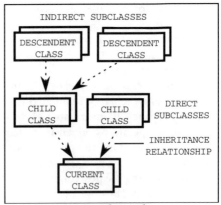

Descendant Class

- **behaviorally compatible descendant** *n.* any descendant that can be used anywhere that its ancestor can. [Firesmith, Jacobson]

Synonym: SUBTYPE.

- **child [class of a given class]** *n.* any class that is directly derived via inheritance from the given class. [Firesmith, Jacobson]

Synonyms: DIRECT DERIVED CLASS, DIRECT DESCENDANT, DIRECT SUBCLASS, HEIR CLASS, IMMEDIATE DERIVED CLASS, IMMEDIATE DESCENDANT, IMMEDIATE SUBCLASS.

Antonyms: DIRECT ANCESTOR, DIRECT BASE CLASS, DIRECT SUPERCLASS, IMMEDIATE ANCESTOR, IMMEDIATE BASE CLASS, IMMEDIATE SUPERCLASS, PARENT.

Contrast with: ANCESTOR, BASE CLASS, DERIVED CLASS, DESCENDANT, SUBCLASS, SUPERCLASS.

Commentary: The given class is called the *parent* class of the child class. This term is preferred because it is simpler, more intuitive, and more popular than its synonyms. [Firesmith]

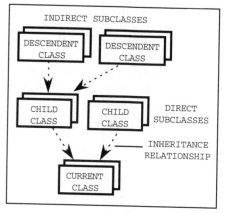

Child Class

+ repeated child class [of a given class] *n.* any child class that multiply inherits from a given parent class. [Eiffel, Firesmith, Meyer]
Synonym: REPEATED HEIR.
Antonym: REPEATED PARENT CLASS.

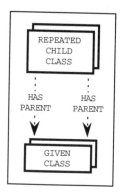

Repeated Child Class

C

- direct descendant [class of a given class] *n.* any descendant that inherits directly from the given class. [Firesmith]
Synonyms: CHILD CLASS, DIRECT DERIVED CLASS, DIRECT SUBCLASS.
Antonym: INDIRECT ANCESTOR CLASS, INDIRECT DERIVED CLASS, INDIRECT SUPERCLASS.
Commentary: A direct descendant of a given class is a descendant class that is also a child class. [Firesmith]
- heir [class of a given class] *n.* any direct (i.e., immediate) derived class of a given class. [Eiffel, Meyer]
Synonyms: CHILD CLASS, DIRECT DERIVED CLASS.
Antonym: PARENT.
Contrast with: DESCENDANT.
+ repeated heir [of a given class] *n.* any heir class that multiply inherits from a given parent class. [Eiffel, Meyer]
Synonym: REPEATED CHILD CLASS.
Antonym: REPEATED PARENT CLASS.

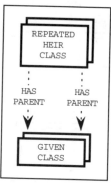

Repeated Heir Class

- indirect descendant [class of a given class] *n.* any descendant that inherits indirectly from the given class

via intermediate classes. [Firesmith]
Synonyms: INDIRECT DERIVED CLASS, INDIRECT SUBCLASS.
Antonym: DIRECT ANCESTOR CLASS, DIRECT DERIVED CLASS, DIRECT DESCENDANT, DIRECT SUPERCLASS.
Commentary: An indirect descendant of a given class is a descendant class that is not a child class. [Firesmith]

- **proper descendant** [of a given class] *n.* any descendant other than the given class itself. [Eiffel, Meyer]
Antonym: PROPER ANCESTOR.
- **repeated descendant** [of a given class] *n.* any descendant that multiply inherits from a given ancestor class. [Eiffel, Firesmith, Meyer]
Antonym: REPEATED ANCESTOR.

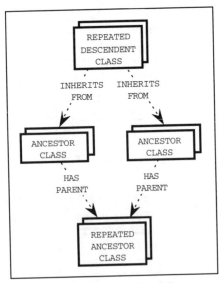

Repeated Descendant Class

• **descriptor class** *n.* any standard class used by a language environment to store useful information about classes.

Commentary: Compilers may then allocate one object (a.k.a., the descriptor object) of the descriptor class for each class in the program. The compiler can then provide an operation that, when applied to a given object, will return a pointer to the descriptor object for the class of that object.

• **domain class** *n.* any class that is application-domain specific. [Firesmith]
Antonym: SUPPORT CLASS.
Commentary: The primary partition of domain classes is consistent with the Smalltalk model/view/controller pattern. [Firesmith]
Kinds:
  - APPLICATION CLASS
  - BUSINESS CLASS
  - CONTROLLER CLASS
  - CORE CLASS
  - KEY CLASS
  - MODEL CLASS
  - VIEW CLASS
    + PRESENTATION CLASS
    + PROXY

- **application class** *n.* **1.** (a) any class of objects that model and interface with an end-user application. [OMG] (b) any class of objects encapsulating entire applications. [ODMG] **2.** any essential class of model objects that captures a key abstraction of the application domain. [Lorenz]
Synonyms: **1** WRAPPER, **2** BUSINESS CLASS, CORE CLASS, KEY CLASS, MODEL CLASS.
Contrast with: CONTROLLER CLASS, KEY ABSTRACTION, PRESENTATION CLASS, SUPPORT CLASS, VIEW CLASS.
Example: An *Account* class would be an application class for the banking industry. [Lorenz]
- **business class** *n.* any essential class

of model objects that captures a key abstraction of the application domain (business).

Synonyms: APPLICATION CLASS, CORE CLASS, DOMAIN CLASS, KEY CLASS, MODEL CLASS.

Contrast with: CONTROLLER CLASS, KEY ABSTRACTION, PRESENTATION CLASS, SUPPORT CLASS, VIEW CLASS.

- **controller [class]** *n.* any domain class of controller objects that exist to either control one or more objects or to capture user input as in the model-view-controller (MVC) framework. [Firesmith]

Contrast with: CONTROLLER OBJECT, MODEL CLASS, VIEW CLASS.

See also: CONTROLLER OBJECT.

Commentary: Controller classes are often either model classes that model input devices (e.g., mice) or are presentation classes allowing the user to control the model object. [Firesmith]

- **core class** *n.* any essential class of model objects that captures a key abstraction of the application domain.

Synonyms: APPLICATION CLASS, BUSINESS CLASS, KEY CLASS, MODEL CLASS.

Contrast with: CONTROLLER CLASS, KEY ABSTRACTION, PRESENTATION CLASS, SUPPORT CLASS, VIEW CLASS.

- **key class** *n.* any essential class of model objects that captures a key abstraction of the application domain. [Lorenz]

Synonyms: APPLICATION CLASS, BUSINESS CLASS, CORE CLASS, MODEL CLASS.

Commentary: A key class is central to the business domain being automated (i.e., it is one of the primary classes necessary to provide solu-

tions to users' needs in a particular area of the business).

- **model [class]** *n.* any domain class of model objects that model individual application-domain things. [Firesmith]

Synonyms: APPLICATION CLASS, BUSINESS CLASS, CORE CLASS, KEY CLASS.

Contrast with: CONTROLLER CLASS, VIEW CLASS.

See also: MODEL OBJECT.

Commentary: A model class may have more than one view class. [Firesmith]

- **view class** *n.* any domain class of view objects that exist to provide a user view of (i.e., information about and control over) one or more model objects. [Firesmith]

Contrast with: MODEL OBJECT, PRESENTATION OBJECT.

Commentary: A view class may also be a controller class of its model class(es). Most view classes are also presentation classes. [Firesmith]

Kinds:
  + PRESENTATION CLASS
  + PROXY CLASS

+ **presentation [class]** *n.* any specialized view class of presentation objects that exist to provide a *formatted* view of (i.e., information about and control over) one or more model or view classes. [Firesmith]

Contrast with: PRESENTATION OBJECT, PROXY CLASS.

Example: A model or view class may have more than one presentation class, and a presentation class may also be a controller class of its model or view class(es). [Firesmith]

+ **proxy [class]** *n.* any local view class

of proxy objects, each of which represents (i.e., acts as a processor-specific variant of and communicates with) its remote model object. [Firesmith]

Contrast with: PRESENTATION CLASS, PROXY OBJECT.

Commentary: A proxy provides the local protocol of (and communicates with) its model on a remote processor. Proxies are used to create a single virtual address space across multiple processors. [Firesmith]

- **executable class** *n.* any class that has one parent that is an "execution support" class, and one or more parents that are normal (nonexecution support) classes. The class inherits its functionality from its normal parents, and the ability to execute on a particular type of machine from its execution support parent. [Atkinson]

See also: EXECUTION SUPPORT CLASS.

Commentary: An executable class corresponds to a fully linked, executable object module. [Atkinson]

- **execution support class** *n.* any class that exports methods providing idiosyncratic services of a particular kind of execution environment, and endows its subclasses with the ability to execute in that kind of environment. [Atkinson]

See also: EXECUTABLE CLASS.

- **expanded class** *n.* any class, the entities of whose corresponding type will have objects as their run-time values. [Eiffel, Meyer]

Contrast with: EXPANDED TYPE.

- **expanded client** *n.* any class C is an expanded client of type S if S is an expanded type and some entity of C is of type S. [Eiffel, Meyer]

- **framework class** *n.* any class of frameworks. [Firesmith]

Contrast with: CLUSTER.

- **friend class** *n.* **1.** any class whose implementation has been granted permission by another class to reference its hidden parts in violation of information hiding. [C++, Firesmith] **2.** any class that either invokes an internal operation of another class or makes direct access of the data of the other class. [Shlaer/Mellor]

Contrast with: FRIEND FUNCTION, FRIEND OPERATION.

Commentary: The class whose internals are being accessed by the friend class must explicitly grant permission to the friend class to do so. [Firesmith]

- **generating class** *n.* the base class of any generating type. [Eiffel]

Synonym: GENERATOR.

- **guardable class** *n.* any class, the instances of which provide a mechanism for ensuring (but do not enforce) mutually exclusive access in a concurrent environment. [Firesmith]

Contrast with: CORRUPTIBLE CLASS, GUARDED CLASS.

Examples: Any class that uses semaphores that are locked and unlocked by the client.

Commentary: Guardable classes rely on their clients to use them safely (e.g., by requiring the client to remember to lock and unlock them).

- **high-level object class** *n.* any class that is created at a high level of abstraction to group a set of objects at lower-levels of abstraction. [Embley]

Kinds:
- DOMINANT HIGH-LEVEL OBJECT CLASS
- INDEPENDENT HIGH-LEVEL

OBJECT CLASS
- **dominant high-level object class** *n.* any high-level object class representing a set of objects that is named after the most important object class in the set. [Embley]
Antonym: INDEPENDENT HIGH-LEVEL OBJECT CLASS.
- **independent high-level object class** *n.* any high-level object class representing a set of objects that is not named after the most important object class in the set. [Embley]
Antonym: DOMINANT HIGH-LEVEL OBJECT CLASS.
- **join class** *n.* any class that multiply inherits from more than one parent class. [Rumbaugh]
Rationale: A join class is analogous to the joins that occur between tables in a relational database.

JOIN CLASS

INHERITS FROM   INHERITS FROM

PARENT CLASS   PARENT CLASS

Join Class

- **leaf class** *n.* any class with no descendants. [Firesmith, Rumbaugh]
Contrast with: BRANCH CLASS, ROOT CLASS.
- **local class** *n.* **1.** any class that is declared within a method [or block]. [Firesmith] **2.** any class that is declared within a function definition. [C++]

Contrast with: COMPONENT CLASS.
Commentary: A local class is in the scope of the enclosing scope. [C++]

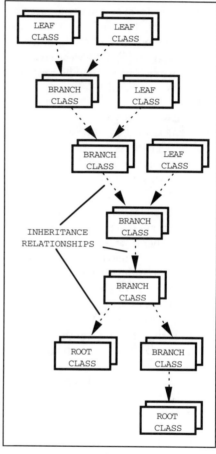

Leaf Class

- **member class** *n.* any object class whose instances are members of sets. [Embley]
Synonym: UNIVERSE.
Antonyms: ASSOCIATION, SET CLASS.
See also: IS-MEMBER-OF RELATIONSHIP SET.
- **metaclass** *n.* any class, the instances

of which are themselves classes. [Booch, CLOS, Firesmith, Jacobson, Rumbaugh, Smalltalk]

See also: CLASS OBJECT.

Commentary: The metaclass determines the form of inheritance used by the classes that are its instances and the representation of the instances of those classes. [CLOS] Metaclasses are used when classes are to be treated as objects. [Firesmith]

Kinds:
- GENERIC CLASS
- PARAMETERIZED CLASS
- POWER CLASS
  + DISCRIMINATOR CLASS
- STANDARD CLASS
- TEMPLATE CLASS

- **generic class** *n.* any abstract metaclass that is parameterized with formal generic parameters (e.g., classes, attributes, messages, operations, exceptions, invariants) that must be supplied prior to instantiation. Its instances vary, depending on the actual parameters that were supplied. [Booch, Eiffel, Firesmith, Meyer]

  Synonym: PARAMETERIZED CLASS, TEMPLATE CLASS.

  Rationale: Original term used by Ada 83 and Eiffel.

- **parameterized class** *n.* any abstract metaclass that is parameterized with formal generic parameters (e.g., classes, attributes, messages, operations, exceptions, invariants) that must be supplied as part of the instantiation process. [Booch, Firesmith, Rumbaugh]

  Synonym: GENERIC CLASS, TEMPLATE CLASS.

  Commentary: Its instances vary, depending on the actual parameters

that were supplied. GENERIC CLASS was the original term used by Ada83 and Eiffel. The parameters are often attributes, classes, or types.

- **power class** *n.* any metaclass, the instances of which are child classes of another class. [Firesmith]

  Contrast with: DISCRIMINATOR, DISCRIMINATOR CLASS, PARTITION.

  Example: The class *Item_Type* is the power class of the class *Item* and consists of all of the children of *Item*. [Firesmith]

  Commentary: Instances of power classes are often used as attributes of other classes. [Firesmith]

  + **discriminator class** *n.* any power class whose instances partition another class (i.e., whose instances form a disjoint cover of the class being partitioned). [Firesmith]

    Example: The class of *genders* is a discriminator class for the class *persons,* partitioning it into the derived classes *males* and *females.* [Firesmith]

- **standard-class** *n.* the default metaclass, defined by *defclass,* that is appropriate for most programs. [CLOS]

  See also: METACLASS, STANDARD-OBJECT.

- **template class** *n.* the C++ term for a generic class. [C++]

  Synonyms: GENERIC, GENERIC CLASS, PARAMETERIZED CLASS.

  Commentary: A class template specifies how individual classes can be constructed much as a class declaration specifies how individual objects can be constructed. [C++]

• **nested class** *n.* any class declared within another class. [C++]

  Contrast with: SUBCLASS.

Commentary: Simply declaring a class nested in another does not mean that the enclosing class contains an object of the enclosed class. Nesting expresses scoping, not containment of component objects. [C++]

- **[object] class** *n.* any class of objects. [Embley, Firesmith]
  Contrast with: ATTRIBUTE CLASS, CLASS OBJECT, CLUSTER CLASS, FRAMEWORK CLASS, METACLASS.
  Commentary: The instances of some classes (e.g., metaclasses, clusters) need not be objects. [Firesmith]

- **origin [class of a given feature]** *n.* the class in which the given feature was originally declared or last implemented. [Eiffel, Firesmith, Meyer]
  Contrast with: SEED OF A GIVEN FEATURE.
  Commentary: The origin class is the most distant ancestor in which the feature exists. The feature may have been overridden in an ancestor of the current class. [Firesmith]
  Kinds:
  - DECLARING CLASS
  - IMPLEMENTATION CLASS

- **declaring class [of a given feature]** *n.* the origin class in which the given feature was originally declared. [Firesmith]
  Antonym: IMPLEMENTION CLASS.
  Example: The declaring class of an operation is the class in which the signature of the given operation first appeared. [Firesmith]

- **implementation class [of a given feature]** *n.* the origin class in which the given feature was last implemented. [Firesmith]
  Antonym: DECLARING CLASS.
  Example: The implementation class is

the nearest class (either ancestor or current) in which a method for the given operation appeared. [Firesmith]

- **passive class** *n.* **1.** any class of passive objects that cannot execute instance operations without the need for incoming messages. [Firesmith] **2.** any class that cannot execute class operations without the need for incoming messages. [Firesmith] **3.** that which is generated by an object that does not have a separate state machine for each instance [Shlaer/Mellor]
  Antonym: ACTIVE CLASS.
  Commentary: A passive class need not be sequential, although it usually is. [Firesmith]

- **peripheral class** *n.* any class that provides part of the supporting framework for the business' key classes. [Lorenz]
  Example: User interface classes are always peripheral support classes.
  Synonym: BASE CLASS, SUPPORT CLASS.
  Contrast with: KEY CLASS.

- **persistent class** *n.* any class, the instances of which are persistent objects (i.e., objects that exist after the execution of the program, process, or thread that created them).
  Antonym: TRANSIENT CLASS.
  Example: Any class of objects stored in an objectbase.
  Commentary: A persistent object typically survives the process or thread that created it, existing until explicitly deleted. A persistent object also typically exists outside of the address space in which it was created. Persistent objects can be stored in object-oriented databases, extended relational databases, relational databases, Smalltalk images, files, etc. [Firesmith]

- **reachable class** *n.* any class that can

be accessed by a given class.

Commentary: This term is due to Desfray.

- **relational object class** *n.* any object class whose instances are relationships. [Embley]

  See also: RELATIONSHIP, RELATION-SHIP OBJECT.

- **role class** *n.* any class of role model objects or view role objects. [Firesmith]

  Contrast with: ROLE, ROLE OBJECT.

- **root class** *n.* **1.** any class that does not inherit from any other class. [Firesmith, Smalltalk] **2.** the master class in a system of classes that depends on (i.e., is a direct or indirect client or heir of) all of the other classes in the system. [Eiffel, Meyer]

  Synonym: **1** BASE CLASS. **2** MASTER CLASS.

  See also: **2** SYSTEM.

  Contrast with: BASE CLASS, BRANCH CLASS, LEAF CLASS.

  Example: The class Object in Smalltalk is a root class.

  Rationale: This class is at the root of the inheritance tree. The term *base class* is used by C++ with a different meaning. [Firesmith]

  Commentary: Definition **1** is based on inheritance, whereas definition **2** is based on inheritance and client/server dependencies.

- **scenario class** *n.* any definition of a set of related scenarios.

  Contrast with: USE CASE.

  Kinds:
    - USE CASE
      + ABSTRACT USE CASE
      + CONCRETE USE CASE

  - **use case** *n.* **1.** any description of a single way of using a system or application; any scenario class of top-level usage scenarios that captures

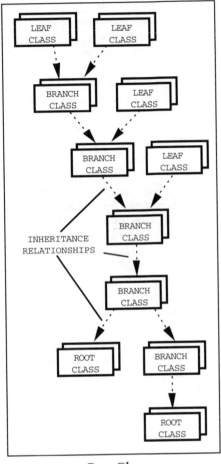

Root Class

how a blackbox application is used by its client terminators. [Firesmith, Henderson-Sellers, Jacobson] **2.** (a) any behaviorally related sequence of transactions performed by a single actor in a dialogue with a system, the purpose of which is to provide some measurable value to the actor. [Jacobson] (b) any class of top-level usage scenarios that captures how a system or application is used by its

client terminators (actors). (c) any description of the system actions upon receipt of one type of user request. [Lorenz] **3.** (formerly) any sequence of events that occur during one particular execution of an application. [Henderson-Sellers]
Synonym: SCENARIO SCRIPT.
Contrast with: USAGE SCENARIO.
Rationale: The term *use case* was introduced and initially popularized by Ivar Jacobson. [Firesmith]
Commentary: Use cases are used to document user requirements in terms of user dialogs with a system that provides some measurable value to the user. [Firesmith]
Kinds:
  + ABSTRACT USE CASE
  + CONCRETE USE CASE

+ abstract use case *n.* any use case that will not be instantiated on its own, but is meaningful only to describe parts shared among other use cases. [Jacobson]
Antonym: CONCRETE USE CASE.

+ concrete use case *n.* any use case that is meaningful and will be instantiated on its own. [Jacobson]
Antonym: ABSTRACT USE CASE.

• **sequential class** *n.* **1.** any class whose instances are sequential objects. [Firesmith] **2.** any class that does not contain any concurrent class features (e.g., operations or objects). [Firesmith] **3.** any class whose semantics are guaranteed only in the presence of a single thread of control. [Booch]
Antonym: CONCURRENT CLASS.
Contrast with: GUARDED CLASS, SYNCHRONOUS CLASS.

• **set class** *n.* any object class whose instances are sets. [Embley]

Synonym: ASSOCIATION.
Antonyms: MEMBER CLASS, UNIVERSE.
See also: IS-MEMBER-OF RELATIONSHIP SET.

• **singleton [object] class** *n.* any object class that has one and only one instance. [Embley, Firesmith]

• **standard-object [class]** *n.* any instance of the metaclass *standard-class* and the superclass of every class that is an instance of *standard-class* except itself. [CLOS]
See also: META-OBJECT, STANDARD-CLASS.

• **storage class** *n.* either any automatic or any static class. [C++]
Commentary: A named object has a storage class that determines its lifetime. [C++]
Kinds:
  - AUTOMATIC CLASS
  - STATIC CLASS

  - **automatic class** *n.* any class of automatic objects (i.e., objects that are local to each invocation of a block). [C++]
Contrast with: STATIC CLASS.

  - **static class** *n.* any class with only static members [C++]
Rationale: A static class provides a facility akin to what is called a *module* in many languages: a named collection of objects and functions in their own name space. [C++]

• **subclass [of a given class]** *n.* **1.** any class that is derived, either directly or indirectly, from the given class via inheritance. [Booch, CLOS, Firesmith, Jacobson, Smalltalk, Wirfs-Brock] **2.** (a) any specialization of a base class. [Lorenz, Rumbaugh] (b) any class that is a subtype of the given class. [Martin/Odell] **3.** any class that is a

component part of the given aggregate class.
Synonyms: **1** DERIVED CLASS, DESCENDANT CLASS. **3** COMPONENT CLASS.
Antonyms: **1** ANCESTOR CLASS, BASE CLASS, SUPERCLASS. **3** CONTAINER CLASS.
Contrast with: SUBTYPE, SUPERCLASS.
Example: Car is a subclass of *vehicle*. [Firesmith, Lorenz].
Commentary: This term is potentially confusing and ambiguous because it could refer to either inheritance or aggregation. Similarly to substates and subsystems, the term *subclass* may be ambiguously misinterpreted to mean a component class rather than a *derived class*. On the other hand, the term *derived class* is unambiguous. Definition 1 is by far the most common definition. Definition **2** restricts inheritance to subtyping. Definition **3** is ambiguous, misleading, and only rarely used because it confuses aggregation with inheritance. [Firesmith]
Kinds:
- DIRECT SUBCLASS
- INDIRECT SUBCLASS

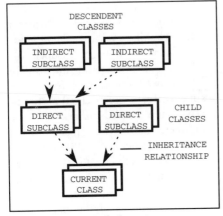

DESCENDENT CLASSES

INDIRECT SUBCLASS

INDIRECT SUBCLASS

DIRECT SUBCLASS

DIRECT SUBCLASS

CHILD CLASSES

INHERITANCE RELATIONSHIP

CURRENT CLASS

Subclass

- **direct subclass [of a given class]** *n.* the Smalltalk term for any parent class of the given class. [CLOS, Firesmith]
Synonyms: CHILD CLASS, DIRECT DERIVED CLASS, HEIR CLASS.
Antonyms: INDIRECT SUBCLASS, DIRECT SUPERCLASS.
Contrast with: ANCESTOR CLASS, INDIRECT BASE CLASS.
Commentary: If class C_2 explicitly designates C_1 as a superclass in its definition, then C_2 is a *direct subclass* of C_1. [CLOS] A direct subclass is a descendant class that is also a child class. [Firesmith]

- **indirect subclass [of a given class]** *n.* the Smalltalk term for any indirect descendant class of the given class. [Firesmith]
Synonyms: DESCENDANT CLASS, INDIRECT BASE CLASS.
Contrast with: CHILD CLASS, DIRECT BASE CLASS, DIRECT SUBCLASS.
Commentary: An indirect subclass is a descendant class that is not a child class. [Firesmith]

• **subpart class** *n.* any object class whose instances are subparts. [Embley]
Synonym: COMPONENT CLASS.
Antonym: SUPERPART CLASS.
See also: SUBPART, IS-PART-OF RELATIONSHIP SET.

• **superclass [of a given class]** *n.* **1.** any class from which the given class is derived, either directly or indirectly, via inheritance. [Booch, CLOS, Firesmith, Jacobson, Smalltalk, Wirfs-Brock] **2.** (a) any generalization from which features are inherited. [Lorenz, Rumbaugh] (b) a class that is a supertype of the given class. [Martin/Odell]
Synonym: BASE CLASS.
Antonym: SUBCLASS.

Kinds:
- DIRECT SUPERCLASS
- INDIRECT SUPERCLASS

- **direct superclass [of a given class]** *n.* any superclass from which a given derived class directly inherits. [CLOS, Firesmith]
Synonyms: DIRECT BASE CLASS, PARENT CLASS.
Antonym: INDIRECT SUPERCLASS.
Contrast with: ANCESTOR, INDIRECT DERIVED CLASS.
Commentary: If class C_2 explicitly designates C_1 as a superclass in its definition, then C_1 is a *direct superclass* of C_2. [CLOS] A direct superclass is an ancestor class that is also a parent class. [Firesmith]

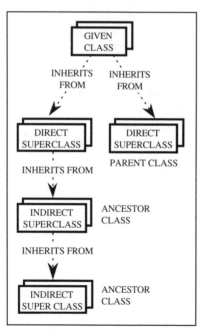

Superclass

- **indirect superclass [of a given class]** *n.* any superclass from which a given subclass indirectly inherits via intermediate superclasses. [Firesmith]
Synonyms: ANCESTOR CLASS, INDIRECT BASE CLASS.
Contrast with: DIRECT BASE CLASS, DIRECT SUPERCLASS, INDIRECT DERIVED CLASS.
Commentary: An indirect superclass is an ancestor class that is not a parent class.

- **superpart class** *n.* any object class the instances of which are superparts (i.e., aggregates). [Embley]
Synonym: AGGREGATE CLASS.
Antonym: SUBPART CLASS.
See also: SUPERPART, IS-PART-OF RELATIONSHIP SET.

- **support class** *n.* **1.** any class of support objects. [Firesmith] **2.** any class that is not application specific, but instead is used to support those classes that are. [Firesmith, Lorenz]
Synonyms: BASE CLASS, PERIPHERAL CLASS.
Antonym: DOMAIN CLASS.
Kinds:
- BUILT-IN CLASS
- CLASS
- T CLASS

- **built-in class** *n.* **1.** any class that is defined as part of the object-oriented programming language. [Firesmith] **2.** any class that is an instance of class *built-in class* and that has a special implementation with restricted capabilities. [CLOS]
Antonym: USER-DEFINED CLASS.
Examples: **1** Typical built-in classes include Boolean, character, integer, float, and real.

- **Class** *n.* the abstract superclass of all classes other than metaclasses.

[Smalltalk]

- **t [class]** *n.* the superclass of every class except itself. [CLOS]
  Synonym: OBJECT [Smalltalk]

• **transient class** *n.* any class, all instances of which are transient objects (i.e., objects that do not exist except during the execution of the program, process, or thread in which it was created). [Firesmith]
  Antonym: PERSISTENT CLASS.
  Kinds:
  - DYNAMIC CLASS
  - STATIC CLASS

- **dynamic class** *n.* any transient class, all instances of which are dynamic objects that are instantiated and destroyed at run-time. [Firesmith]
  Antonym: STATIC CLASS.
  Commentary: A dynamic object has its memory allocated (e.g., from the heap) and deallocated during program execution. Dynamic objects are usually referenced via pointers. [Firesmith]

- **static class** *n.* any transient class, all instances of which are static objects that are instantiated and whose memory is allocated at compile-time and remains allocated until the program terminates. [Firesmith]
  Antonym: DYNAMIC CLASS.
  Commentary: A static object lasts for the duration of program execution, but not after a program ceases to execute. [Firesmith]

• **universe** *n.* any object class whose instances are members of sets. [Embley]
  Synonym: MEMBER CLASS.
  Antonyms: ASSOCIATION, SET CLASS.
  See also: IS-MEMBER-OF RELATIONSHIP SET.
  Commentary: The term *universe* is an often-used mathematical notation that denotes the set of objects from which subsets may be formed. [Embley]

• **user-defined class (UDC)** *n.* any class that is defined by the user rather than built into the language. [Firesmith]
  Antonym: BUILT-IN CLASS.
  Contrast with: USER-DEFINED TYPE.

• **virtual node class** *n.* any class that conforms to a set of rules designed to ensure that its instances do not communicate with other objects by exchanging references. [Atkinson]
  Commentary: Virtual node classes are suitable for execution on the separate nodes of a loosely-coupled network. [Atkinson]

Class *n.* the abstract superclass of all classes other than metaclasses. [Smalltalk]

class abstracter *n.* any tool that produces an interface version of a class, providing client programmers with a specification of the exported features. [Meyer]
See also: INTERFACE.

class abstraction *n.* any model of a set of related object abstractions. [Firesmith]

class aggregation diagram *n.* any Object-Oriented Design Notation (OODN) diagram documenting aggregation relationships between classes.

class-&-object *n.* any class and the objects in that class. [Coad]

class association *n.* any association linking two classes. [Jacobson]
Antonym: INSTANCE ASSOCIATION.
Contrast with: META ASSOCIATION.
Example: The inherit association is a *class association*, that is, an association between classes. [Jacobson]
Commentary: Class associations are drawn with dashed arrows. [Jacobson]

• **inheritance association** *n.* any class association, meaning that the defini-

tion of the operations and attributes of one class is also used in the inheriting class which might do additions and redefinitions. [Jacobson]
See also: INHERITANCE.

class attribute *n.* **1.** any attribute of a class as a whole. [Firesmith, Jacobson] **2.** any attribute whose value is common to a class of objects. [Rumbaugh]
Synonyms: CLASS VARIABLE, COMMON INSTANCE ATTRIBUTE.
Contrast with: COMMON INSTANCE PROPERTY, INSTANCE ATTRIBUTE, EXTENT ATTRIBUTE.
Kinds:
- CLASS CONSTANT
- CLASS VARIABLE

- **class constant** *n.* any constant class attribute. [Firesmith]
Antonym: CLASS VARIABLE.

- **class variable** *n.* any variable class attribute. [Firesmith]
Antonym: CLASS CONSTANT.

class-based *adj.* describing something based on the following concepts:
  - ENCAPSULATION
  - OBJECT:
    - IDENTITY
    - PROPERTIES
    - OPERATIONS
  - MESSAGE PASSING
  - CLASSES [Firesmith]
Contrast with: OBJECT-BASED, OBJECT-ORIENTED.
Commentary: The following concepts required for full object-oriented status are missing from the definition of the term *class-based*:
  - INHERITANCE
  - POLYMORPHISM
  - DYNAMIC BINDING

class-based development *n.* any development that primarily consists of defining and instantiating classes of objects, the objects of which are then integrated and tested. [Firesmith, Lorenz]
Contrast with: COMPONENT-BASED DEVELOPMENT, INSTANCE-BASED DEVELOPMENT.

class body *n.* the detailed, hidden implementation of the class. [OADSIG]
Synonym: CLASS IMPLEMENTATION.
Antonym: CLASS INTERFACE.

class card *n.* any index card, based on a Class/Responsibility/Collaboration (CRC) card, that is used to informally document information about a class. [Wirfs-Brock]
Contrast with: CLASS-RESPONSIBILITY-COLLABORATOR CARD, CLASS SPECIFICATION.

class cardinality constraint *n.* any cardinality constraint that restricts the size of the extent of a class. [Firesmith]

class category *n.* **1.** any logical collection of classes, some of which are visible to other class categories and others of which are hidden. The classes in a class category collaborate to provide a set of services. [Booch] **2.** any container for elements of the logical model, consisting of classes, objects, other class categories, as well as class and object diagrams. [Booch]
Synonyms: ASSEMBLY, CLUSTER, KIT, SUBSYSTEM.
Contrast with: SUBJECT.

class-category diagram *n.* any Booch class diagram that documents class categories and the use relationships among them. [Booch]
Contrast with: DESIGN-CLASS DIAGRAM, INHERITANCE DIAGRAM, KEY-ABSTRACTION DIAGRAM.

class cluster *n.* any small group of classes that collaborate a great deal with each other. [Lorenz]

Synonym: CLUSTER.

Commentary: Clustering classes simplifies the amount of work required to test the functionality. [Lorenz]

class cohesion *n.* the degree of relatedness of the responsibilities within a class. [Coad]

Contrast with: OBJECT COUPLING.

Commentary: A class has strong cohesion if the attributes and services work well together and are well described by the name of the class itself. Strong class cohesion is desirable; it indicates good object partitioning and greater resiliency to change over time. [Coad]

class communication diagram *n.* **1.** any diagram documenting the communication among classes. [Martin] **2.** any Object-Oriented Design Notation (OODN) diagram documenting message passing between objects. [Page-Jones]

Synonyms: COLLABORATION DIAGRAM, INTERACTION DIAGRAM.

class constant *n.* any constant class attribute. [Firesmith]

Antonym: CLASS VARIABLE.

class declaration *n.* the complete specification of the interfaces provided by any class. [C++]

Synonym: CLASS-SPECIFIER.

Commentary: A class declaration introduces a new type including the class name into the scope where it is declared. A class declaration also hides any class, object, function, or other declaration of that name in the enclosing scope. C++ does not directly support the concepts of *interface definition* and *implementation module.* [C++]

class description *n.* any informal specification of a class including its external interface, hidden attributes, and inheritance relationships. [Coleman]

class descriptor *n.* **1.** any object representing a class that documents its features as well as the values of any class properties. [Rumbaugh] **2.** any instance of a *metaclass.*

Rationale: Class descriptors are implemented in some, but not all, OOPLs.

class diagram *n.* **1.** any diagram used to show the existence of classes, class categories, and their relationships. [Booch] **2.** any diagram that illustrates potential objects and their relationships in terms of their associated classes and the relationships between the classes. [Rumbaugh] **3.** any diagram that depicts the external view of a single class. [Shlaer/Mellor]

Commentary: A class diagram may represent all or part of the class structure of a system. Class diagrams are used during analysis to indicate the common roles and responsibilities of the entities that provide the system's behavior. Class diagrams are used during design to capture the structure of the classes that form the system's architecture.

Kinds:
- CLASS-CATEGORY DIAGRAM
- DESIGN-CLASS DIAGRAM
- INHERITANCE DIAGRAM
- KEY-ABSTRACTION DIAGRAM
  - DESIGN-CLASS DIAGRAM

- **class-category diagram** *n.* any Booch class diagram that documents class categories and the *uses* relationships among them. [Booch]

  Contrast with: DESIGN-CLASS DIAGRAM, INHERITANCE DIAGRAM, KEY-ABSTRACTION DIAGRAM.

- **design-class diagram** *n.* any Booch key-abstraction diagram that has been updated during design. [Booch]

  Contrast with: CLASS-CATEGORY DIAGRAM, INHERITANCE DIAGRAM, KEY-

ABSTRACTION DIAGRAM.

- **inheritance diagram** *n.* any Booch class diagram that documents the inheritance hierarchies. [Booch] *Contrast with:* CLASS-CATEGORY DIAGRAM, DESIGN-CLASS DIAGRAM, KEY-ABSTRACTION DIAGRAM.

- **key-abstraction diagram** *n.* any Booch class diagram that documents the key classes and the uses relationships between them. [Booch] *Contrast with:* CLASS-CATEGORY DIAGRAM, DESIGN-CLASS DIAGRAM, INHERITANCE DIAGRAM.

- **design-class diagram** *n.* any Booch key-abstraction diagram that has been updated during design. [Booch]

class dictionary *n.* **1.** any comprehensive dictionary defining all object-oriented entities (e.g., objects, classes, clusters, properties, operations, exceptions) in an application. **2.** any comprehensive dictionary defining all of the classes in an application.
Synonyms: DATA DICTIONARY, OBJECT DICTIONARY, PROJECT DICTIONARY.
Rationale: The term *data dictionary* has historically implied only data (i.e., attributes), and the term *class dictionary* may be interpreted too limitedly (e.g., definition **2**). The term *project dictionary* with definition **1** above is recommended as being least subject to misinterpretation.

class exception *n.* any exception of a class as a whole. [Firesmith]
Contrast with: EXTENT EXCEPTION, INSTANCE EXCEPTION.
Examples: Instantiation failed, class invariant violated, and precondition or postcondition of class operation violated, class operation failed are all class exceptions.

class flattener *n.* any tool that produces an inheritance-free version of a class, with all inherited features brought into the class itself, taking care of redefinition, renaming, and invariant accumulation. [Firesmith, Meyer]

class hierarchy *n.* **1.** any hierarchy of classes that results from a single inheritance. [Firesmith, Lorenz] **2.** any hierarchy that results when generalization is replaced by inheritance in an object-type generalization hierarchy. [Martin]
Synonyms: INHERITANCE HIERARCHY.
Contrast with: CLASS LATTICE, CLASS STRUCTURE, GENERALIZATION HIERARCHY.
Commentary: The use of multiple inheritance may result in structures that are not true hierarchies. [Firesmith]

class hierarchy nesting *n.* the number of levels of inheritance from the root(s) of the class hierarchy. [Lorenz]
Contrast with: HIERARCHY NESTING.

class inheritance *n.* **1.** any inheritance among classes in which a new class (a.k.a., the *child*) is defined in terms of one or more existing classes (a.k.a., its *parents*), whereby the child inherits the features of its parents. [Firesmith] **2.** any implementation of generalization using inheritance. [Martin/Odell]
Synonym: SUBCLASSING.
Contrast with: TYPE INHERITANCE.
Examples: Subclasses inherit slots, methods, and some defclass operations from their superclasses. [CLOS]

class-inheritance diagram *n.* any Object-Oriented Design Notation (OODN) diagram documenting inheritance relationships between classes.

class-instance inheritance *n.* any inheritance whereby instances inherit default attribute values from their class. [Martin]

Example: The class *Device* may have an attribute *state* and each instance of the Device class is instantiated with the state attribute having the value *Disabled*.

class interface *n.* the interface of any class. [Firesmith, OADSIG]
Antonym: CLASS IMPLEMENTATION.
Contrast with: CLASS PROTOCOL.

class invariant *n.* any invariant of a class as a whole. [Firesmith]
Contrast with: EXTENT INVARIANT, INSTANCE INVARIANT.
Example: An invariant relationship between generic formal parameters is a class invariant.

class lattice *n.* any lattice of classes connected by [multiple] inheritance relationships.
Synonym: CLASS STRUCTURE.

class-level validity *n.* any call to a feature of a class exhibits class-level validity (i.e., is class-valid) if the class has the feature, the feature is available to the caller, and the feature has the required signature. [Eiffel, Meyer]
Contrast with: CLASS-VALID, SYSTEM-LEVEL VALIDITY.

class librarian *n.* any person responsible for the maintenance of a class library. [Firesmith]

class library *n.* any collection of compatible, reusable classes. [Firesmith, Martin]
Contrast with: FRAMEWORK.
Commentary: Its intent should be to achieve the maximum degree of reusability in software development. Class-library software should help developers find, adapt, and use the classes they need. [Martin]

class name *n.* **1.** any name that uniquely refers to a single class within the scope of the definition of the name. [Firesmith] **2.** any name that describes the type of component represented by the instances of the class. [Smalltalk]
Contrast with: OBJECT NAME, TYPE NAME.
Examples: The names of classes used in object declarations are class names. [Firesmith]
Commentary: A class name serves two fundamental purposes: it is a simple way for instances to identify themselves, and it provides a way to refer to the class in expressions. [Smalltalk]

class object *n.* any object that is also a class. [Firesmith]
Contrast with: FACTORY, METACLASS.
See also: OBJECT CLASS.
Examples: All classes in Smalltalk are also objects. [Firesmith]
Commentary: Class objects are instances of metaclasses. Any class with class characteristics is a class object. [Firesmith]

class operation *n.* any operation on a class as a whole. [Booch, Firesmith, Jacobson, Rumbaugh]
Contrast with: EXTENT OPERATION, INSTANCE OPERATION.
Example: A constructor or an operation that operates on class properties is a class operation. [Firesmith, Jacobson]

class owner *n.* the individual software engineer who (or team of engineers that) is responsible for the development and maintenance of a specific class. [Firesmith]

class pool *n.* any pool that is only available to the instances of the class and that contains the class variables. [Smalltalk]

class precedence [of a given class] *n.* the total ordering from the most specific to the least specific of the set containing the given class and its superclasses. [CLOS]
Commentary: Each class has a *class precedence list*, which contains its class precedence. [CLOS]

class property *n.* any property that characterizes the class as a whole. [Firesmith, ODMG]
Contrast with: EXTENT PROPERTY, INSTANCE PROPERTY.
Kinds:
- CLASS ATTRIBUTE
  - CLASS CONSTANT
  - CLASS VARIABLE
- CLASS EXCEPTION
- CLASS INVARIANT
- COMPONENT CLASS

- **class attribute** *n.* **1.** any attribute of a class as a whole. [Firesmith, Jacobson] **2.** any attribute whose value is common to a class of objects. [Rumbaugh]
Synonyms: CLASS VARIABLE, COMMON INSTANCE ATTRIBUTE.
Contrast with: COMMON INSTANCE ATTRIBUTE, EXTENT ATTRIBUTE, INSTANCE ATTRIBUTE.
Kinds:
  - CLASS CONSTANT
  - CLASS VARIABLE

- **class constant** *n.* any constant class attribute. [Firesmith]
Antonym: CLASS VARIABLE.

- **class variable** *n.* **1.** any variable attribute of a class as a whole. [Firesmith] **2.** any variable whose value is shared by all instances of a class. [Rumbaugh, Smalltalk] **3.** any attribute of a class descriptor object. [Rumbaugh]
Antonym: CLASS CONSTANT.
Synonyms: CLASS ATTRIBUTE, COMMON INSTANCE ATTRIBUTE.
Example: In C++, a class variable is declared as a static member. [Booch]

- **class exception** *n.* any exception of a class as a whole. [Firesmith]
Contrast with: EXTENT EXCEPTION, INSTANCE EXCEPTION.

Examples: Instantiation failed, class invariant violated, and precondition or postcondition of class operation violated are all examples of class exceptions. [Firesmith]

- **class invariant** *n.* any invariant of a class as a whole. [Firesmith]
Contrast with: EXTENT INVARIANT, INSTANCE INVARIANT.
Example: An invariant relationship between generic formal parameters is a class invariant. [Firesmith]

- **component [class]** *n.* any class that is contained within another class as a component part. [Firesmith]
Synonym: SUBCLASS.
Contrast with: COMPONENT CLUSTER, COMPONENT OBJECT.
Rationale: The term *component class* is far less ambiguous that the term *subclass,* which has another more popular meaning. [Firesmith]

class protocol *n.* the protocol of any class, consisting of all messages that it can send and receive as well as all exceptions it can raise and handle. [Firesmith]
Contrast with: CLASS INTERFACE.

Class/Responsibility/Collaborator (CRC) card *n.* any index card, used as a simple, manual upperCASE tool for brainstorming about the classes and mechanisms. A CRC card documents the class name, lists the responsibilities allocated to the class, and lists those classes with which it must collaborate. [Booch, Firesmith, Wirfs-Brock]
Contrast with: CLASS CARD, CLASS SPECIFICATION, NODE CARD.
See also: CLASS, COLLABORATION, RESPONSIBILITY.
Rationale: Term introduced by Kent Beck and Ward Cunningham and popularized by Rebecca Wirfs-Brock.

C

class rooted at a given type *n.* the derivation class of types for a given type *T* which is the set consisting of *T* (the *root type* of the class) and all types derived from *T* (directly or indirectly) plus any associated universal or class-wide types. [Ada95]
See also: ROOT TYPE, TYPE.

class specification *n.* any specification formally documenting a class. [Wirfs-Brock]
Contrast with: CLASS CARD, CLASS/RESPONSIBILITY/COLLABORATION CARD, CONTRACT SPECIFICATION.

class-specifier *n.* any complete specification of the interfaces provided by some class. [C++]
Synonym: CLASS DECLARATION.

class structure *n.* any graph whose vertices represent classes and whose arcs represent relationships among these classes. The class structure of a system is represented by a set of class diagrams. [Booch, Firesmith]
Synonym: CLASS LATTICE.
Contrast with: CLASS DIAGRAM.

class-structure chart *n.* any diagram that is used to show the internal structure of the code of the operations of the class as well as the flow of data and control within the class. [Shlaer/Mellor]
Contrast with: CLASS DIAGRAM.
Commentary: A separate class structure chart is produced for each class. [Shlaer/Mellor]

Class Structure Design (CSD) *n.* the Object Structure facet of the System Design stage of information engineering, involving class identification and methods, inheritance and class hierarchies, data structures, and database design. [Martin]

class utility *n.* **1.** any logical or physical grouping of related operations, not encapsulated within any class. [Booch] **2.** any abstract class used to contain a logical or physical grouping of related operations rather than to capture an object abstraction. **3.** any C++ class used only to group related static data members and/or static member functions. [Booch]
Examples: A class utility of related functions used as a wrapper around a nonobject-oriented application (e.g., relational database or C program).
Rationale: Term introduced by Booch. Term comes from *utility* packages of functions.

class-valid call *n.* any call to a feature of a class is class valid if the class has the feature, the feature is available to the caller, and the feature has the required signature. [Eiffel, Meyer]
Contrast with: SYSTEM-VALID CALL.
Commentary: A class-valid call is not necessarily system valid.

class variable *n.* **1.** any variable attribute of a class as a whole. [Firesmith] **2.** any variable whose value is shared by all instances of a class. [Rumbaugh, Smalltalk] **3.** any attribute of a class descriptor object. [Rumbaugh]
Synonyms: CLASS ATTRIBUTE, COMMON INSTANCE PROPERTY.
Antonym: CLASS CONSTANT.
Example: In C++, a class variable is declared as a static member. [Booch]

class-wide programming *n.* any programming with classes of related abstractions that may be handled in a unified fashion so that the programmer may systematically ignore their differences when appropriate. [Ada95]
Contrast with: VARIANT PROGRAMMING.
See also: CLASS-WIDE TYPE, POLYMORPHISM.

class-wide type *n.* any type that is de-

fined for (and belongs to) a derivation class rooted at a tagged type. [Ada95]
See also: CLASS-WIDE PROGRAMMING, DERIVATION CLASS.
Rationale: Such a type called *class-wide* because when a formal parameter is defined to be of class-wide type *T'*Class, and actual parameter of any type in the derivation class rooted at *T* is acceptable. [Ada95]

classification *n.* **1.** the *is-a* relationship between an instance and the class(es) that define it. [Firesmith] **2.** (a) the organization of objects into classes that capture a common abstraction [Embley, Firesmith, Henderson-Sellers] (b) the organization of classes into metaclasses that capture a common abstraction. [Firesmith] **3.** the determination of the type that applies to a specific object. [Martin/Odell]
Example: My dog Spot *is a* (i.e., is classified as a) dog. [Firesmith]
Commentary: Each object is an instance of its class(es). [Firesmith]
Kinds:

- DYNAMIC CLASSIFICATION
- HIERARCHICAL CLASSIFICATION
- KEYWORD-BASED CLASSIFICATION
- MULTIPLE CLASSIFICATION
- SINGLE CLASSIFICATION
- STATIC CLASSIFICATION

- **dynamic classification** *n.* **1.** any classification whereby the class(es) of an instance vary over time. [Firesmith] **2.** any changing of the class of an object. [Martin/Odell]
Antonym: STATIC CLASSIFICATION.
See also: DISCRIMINATOR, POWER TYPE.
Commentary: Dynamic classification is sometimes used for the same purpose as states and role objects. Dynamic classification is typically not

supported by implementation languages and may have negative performance impacts. [Firesmith]

- **hierarchical classification** *n.* any classification of reusable components based on inheritance. [Jacobson]
Antonym: KEYWORD-BASED CLASSIFICATION.
Commentary: Searching begins at the root. The properties that the component should have are indicated at various locations in the hierarchy. [Jacobson]

- **keyword-based classification** *n.* any classification of reusable components by keywords. [Jacobson]
Antonym: HIERARCHICAL CLASSIFICATION.
Commentary: Searching the database is based on keywords describing the components. [Jacobson]

- **multiple classification** *n.* any classification whereby an instance simultaneously has more than one class. [Firesmith, Martin/Odell]
Antonym: SINGLE CLASSIFICATION.

- **single classification** *n.* any classification whereby an instance may only have one class at a time. [Firesmith]
Antonym: MULTIPLE CLASSIFICATION.

- **static classification** *n.* any classification whereby the class(es) of an instance may not vary over time. [Firesmith]
Antonym: DYNAMIC CLASSIFICATION.

classification coupling *n.* the coupling dependency of an instance on its class(s). [Firesmith]
Commentary: The class usually does not depend on its instances. [Firesmith]

classification structure *n.* an obsolete term for generalization-specialization (Gen-Spec) Structure. [Coad]

Synonym: GENERALIZATION-SPECIAL-IZATION STRUCTURE.

classify *v. -ed, -ing* to identify the type(s) or class(es) of a given object. [Firesmith] *Contrast with:* GENERALIZE, SPECIALIZE.

client *n.* **1.** relative to a given unidirectional relationship, any thing that depends on something else (a.k.a., a *server*). [Booch, Firesmith] **2.** any node at a starting end of a unidirectional relationship that depends on (i.e., requires exported features of) one or more servers. *Antonyms:* SERVER, SUPPLIER. *Contrast with:* AUDIENCE.

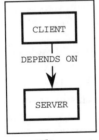

Client

Examples: any code or process that invokes an operation on an object. [OMG] any domain that depends on another domain via a bridge [Shlaer/Mellor] any requester of services. [Lorenz, Rumbaugh] any object that makes a request. [Wirfs-Brock] any module that requests an operation. [Martin] any class C is a client of a type S if some ancestor of C is a simple client, an expanded client or a generic client of S. [Eiffel, Meyer]

Commentary: Clients can be many things including objects, classes, clusters, subsystems, etc. There can be many unidirectional dependency relationships from clients to servers in-cluding aggregation, association, col-laboration, and inheritance.

Kinds:
- EXPANDED CLIENT [OF AN EXPANDED TYPE]
- GENERIC CLIENT
- SIMPLE CLIENT [OF A GIVEN REFERENCE TYPE]

- **expanded client [of an expanded type]** *n.* any class, some entity of which is of the type. [Eiffel, Meyer]
- **generic client** *n.* any class C is a generic client of a type S if for some generically derived type T of the form B [..., S, ...] one of the following holds:
  - C is a client of T.
  - One of the parent clauses of C, or of a proper ancestor of C, lists T as a parent. [Eiffel, Meyer]
- **simple client [of a given reference type]** *n.* any class, some entity of which is of the given type. [Eiffel, Meyer]

client interface *n.* that part of an interface that declares all exported (i.e., public, protected, and restricted) features that are visible to clients. [Firesmith] *Antonym:* SERVER INTERFACE. *Contrast with:* CLIENT PROTOCOL. *Example:* The client interface of an object consists of its client protocol of messages and exceptions as well as any of its exported properties. [Firesmith] *Commentary:* The client interface provides the server role (i.e., visible, outside, user viewpoint). Because most object-oriented methods and programming languages do not explicitly support the server interface, they therefore use the term *interface* when they mean *client interface*. No clients will be impacted by a change to the implementation if the client interface does not change. [Firesmith]

client object *n.* any object that issues a

request for a service. [OMG]

Antonym: SERVER OBJECT.

Commentary: A given object may be a client for some requests and a server for other requests.

client protocol *n.* the set of all potential interactions with clients, consisting of the union of the inbound message protocol and the outbound exception protocol. [Firesmith]

Antonym: SERVER PROTOCOL.

Contrast with: CLIENT INTERFACE.

client-server *n.* the broad term used to capture the dependency relationships of clients on servers. [Firesmith, Henderson-Sellers]

clock event *n.* any special type of event in which a clock time is reached and triggers some operation. [Martin]

clone *v. -ed, -ing* to create a new object by duplicating an existing one. [Eiffel, Firesmith, Meyer]

Antonym: COPY.

Commentary: Cloning involves the creating of new object(s) and the copying of properties from the original object(s) to the new object(s) that make up the clone. [Firesmith]

Kinds:
- DEEP CLONE
- SHALLOW CLONE

- **deep clone** *v. -ed, -ing* to recursively clone an entire object, starting at the source object and creating new objects as needed. [Eiffel, Meyer]

  Antonym: SHALLOW CLONE.

  Contrast with: DEEP COPY.

  Commentary: Deep cloning usually has a slower performance than shallow cloning because more creating and copying is usually required. [Firesmith]

- **shallow clone** *v. -ed, -ing* to clone by

copying fields of the source object as they appear. [Eiffel, Meyer]

Synonym: CLONE.

Antonym: DEEP CLONE.

Contrast with: SHALLOW COPY.

Commentary: Shallow cloning is less reliable than deep cloning because it may result in incomplete clones with dangling references. [Firesmith]

cloning *n.* the creation of a new object by duplicating an existing object. [Eiffel, Firesmith, Meyer]

cluster *n.* **1.** any encapsulation of classes or clusters that are typically analyzed, designed, coded, tested, and integrated as a small increment of development. New clusters can be derived from existing clusters via cluster inheritance. Clusters can be instantiated to construct groups of objects. A cluster has an interface exporting its protocol of visible features and an implementation containing its hidden features. [Firesmith] **2.** any set of semantically or pragmatically related classes. [Eiffel, Henderson-Sellers, Lorenz, Meyer] **3.** any group of objects that are interconnected with one another by many relationships. [Shlaer/Mellor]

Synonyms: CLASS CATEGORY, CLASS CLUSTER, KIT, SUBSYSTEM.

Contrast with: SUBJECT, SUBSYSTEM.

Rationale: The term *cluster* was popularized by the Eiffel language. A cluster is not necessarily a category of classes. Unlike a true subsystem, a cluster does not contain hardware, wetware (i.e., persons), and paperware (i.e., documentation). [Firesmith]

Commentary: Clusters should have high cohesion and low coupling to other clusters. [Firesmith, Lorenz] Clustering classes simplifies the amount of work required to test the functionality. [Lorenz]

Kinds:
- AGGREGATE CLUSTER
- ASSEMBLY
- ATOMIC CLUSTER
- COMPONENT CLUSTER
- SUBCLUSTER

- **aggregate cluster** *n.* any cluster that contains one or more clusters (i.e., subclusters) as component parts. [Firesmith]
  Antonym: ATOMIC CLUSTER.

- **assembly** *n.* **1.** any cluster that is not contained within any other cluster. An application typically consists of multiple component clusters. An assembly has an interface exporting its protocol of visible component clusters and an implementation containing its hidden component clusters. [Firesmith] **2.** formerly, any logical collection of objects, classes, and component subassemblies. [Firesmith]
  Synonym: 2 CLUSTER.
  Contrast with: 1 CLUSTER.
  See also: 1 ASSEMBLY DIAGRAM.
  Commentary: 1 An assembly usually is a major software configuration item and often corresponds to an entire program. A large application may have multiple assemblies. Assemblies are decomposed into clusters, which in turn are decomposed into classes. 2 Firesmith has abandoned this usage of the term *assembly* in favor of the more popular term *cluster* and restricted the term *assembly* to mean definition 1 above.

- **atomic cluster** *n.* any cluster that does not contain any subclusters as component parts. [Firesmith]
  Antonym: AGGREGATE CLUSTER.

- **component [cluster]** *n.* any cluster that is contained within another cluster as a component part. [Firesmith]
  Contrast with: COMPONENT CLASS, COMPONENT OBJECT.

- **subcluster** *n.* any cluster that is derived from the given cluster via cluster inheritance. [Firesmith]

cluster abstraction *n.* any model of a set of related class abstractions. [Firesmith]
Commentary: A cluster abstraction is captured by a cluster rather than an aggregate class or parent class.

cluster instance *n.* any collection of objects instantiated by a cluster. [Firesmith]

cluster interface *n.* the interface of a cluster. [Firesmith]
Antonym: CLUSTER IMPLEMENTATION.
Contrast with: CLASS INTERFACE, CLUSTER PROTOCOL, OBJECT INTERFACE, TYPE INTERFACE.
Commentary: The client cluster interface declares all visible objects, classes, and subclusters that it provides to its clients whereas the server cluster interface declares all exported features of its servers on which it depends. [Firesmith]

cluster protocol *n.* the protocol of any cluster, consisting of all messages and exceptions that can pass across its boundaries. [Firesmith]
Contrast with: CLUSTER INTERFACE.
Commentary: Clusters do not directly interact, but their component classes may. [Firesmith]

cluster testing *n.* the integration testing of any cluster of classes. [Firesmith]
Synonym: SUBSYSTEM TESTING.
Contrast with: UNIT TESTING.

code bloat *n.* **1.** any uncontrolled growth of object code size whereby global optimization does not delete dead code (e.g., unused operations). [Firesmith] **2.** any uncontrolled growth of source code size due to the use of extensive class libraries, many of whose classes are not needed for the current application.

Commentary: Object technology may exacerbate code bloat because inheritance increases the number of unused operations and optimizers have been immature. [Firesmith]

coherence *n.* any property of something indicating that it is consistently organized so that all its parts fit together to achieve a common purpose. [Rumbaugh]

cohesion *n.* 1. (a) the degree to which something models a single abstraction, localizing only features and responsibilities related to that abstraction. [Firesmith] (b) the degree to which something's responsibilities are related. [Coad] 2. the degree to which something's component parts are coupled.

Contrast with: COUPLING.

Rationale: The first definition is preferred, capturing a different concept than local coupling. [Firesmith]

- **class cohesion** *n.* the degree of relatedness of the responsibilities within a class. [Coad]

  Contrast with: OBJECT COUPLING.

  Commentary: A class has strong cohesion if the attributes and services work well together and are well-described by the name of the class itself. Strong class cohesion is desirable; it indicates good object partitioning and greater resiliency to change over time. [Coad]

collaborate *v.* *-ed, -ing* 1. to interact for some common purpose. [Firesmith] 2. to work together to achieve a goal. [Lorenz]

Commentary: Objects collaborate via message passing (primarily) and exception handling. The intelligence and responsibilities of an application are usually distributed among a group of collaborating objects and classes, rather than being concentrated within a single object or class as in a military chain of command. [Firesmith]

collaboration *n.* 1. the cooperative interaction of two or more objects or classes for some common purpose (e.g., to provide some higher-level behavior). [Booch, Firesmith] 2. the embodiment of a contract between a client and a server. 3. the embodiment of any request from a client to a server. [Wirfs-Brock]

Contrast with: 1 INTERACTION, 3 MESSAGE.

See also: 1 CONTRACT, MECHANISM.

Rationale: Term popularized by Wirfs-Brock.

Commentary: Collaboration implies that the whole is more than the sum of the parts in that the common purpose is achieved and visible not in the individual collaborators but only in their collaborative effort. [Firesmith]

collaboration diagram *n.* any diagram that graphically depicts classes, subsystems, contracts, and relationships between classes and subsystems. [Lorenz]

Synonyms: COLLABORATIONS GRAPH, INTERACTION DIAGRAM.

Contrast with: HIERARCHY DIAGRAM, MESSAGE-FLOW DIAGRAM.

Commentary: These diagrams are used during the analysis and design to document the system under development. The information on the diagrams can also be used to automate portions of the development process, such as the creation of class definition code as well as method selectors and comments. [Lorenz]

collaborations graph *n.* any graph showing the classes, subsystems, contracts, and collaboration and inheritance relationships. [Wirfs-Brock]

Synonyms: COLLABORATION DIAGRAM, INTERACTION DIAGRAM.

collaborator *n.* the CRC term for any server of some object or class. [Firesmith, Martin]

See also: CLIENT, SERVER

Rationale: Term popularized by Beck, Cunningham, and Wirfs-Brock.

collaborator object *n.* any object (on an object interaction graph) that provides some functionality as a server to implement a system operation. [Coleman]

collapsed view *n.* any standard system view that displays only its label part, but can be selected and expanded to show the entire view. [Smalltalk]

Contrast with: ACTIVE VIEW, BROWSER, STANDARD SYSTEM VIEW, SUBVIEW.

colleague *n.* anything that is both a client and server of the same thing. [Firesmith]

Synonym: PEER.

Contrast with: CLIENT, SERVER.

Commentary: Colleagues depend on one another. The term *colleague* is preferred because it implies collaboration whereas the term *peer* does not. [Firesmith]

collection [class] *n.* any homogeneous aggregate class of collection objects (i.e., aggregate objects, the purpose of which are to hold component objects of a single type and its subtypes). [Firesmith]

Contrast with: CONTAINER CLASS, STRUCTURE CLASS.

Examples: A class of arrays, bags, dictionaries, lists, queues, sets, or stacks. [Firesmith]

Commentary: Collections enforce strong typing. Collection classes are often generic, with the parameter designating the (super)type of the component objects. [Firesmith]

collection [object] *n.* **1.** any homogeneous aggregate object, the purpose of which is to hold component objects of a single type and its subtypes. [Firesmith, ODMG] **2.** any instance of a collection class. [Firesmith]

Contrast with: CONTAINER OBJECT, STRUCTURE OBJECT.

Examples: Any individual array, bag, dictionary, list, queue, set, or stack. [Firesmith]

Commentary: Collections enforce strong typing. Collections often provide appropriate operations to access and iterate over their contents. [Firesmith]

collection type *n.* **1.** any type of collection objects. [Firesmith] **2.** any instantiation of a collection type generator. [ODMG]

command [pattern] *n.* the behavioral object design pattern that objectifies a request as an object, thereby allowing clients to be parameterized with different requests. [Gamma, Helm, Johnson, and Vlissides]

Synonym: ACTION, TRANSACTION.

Common Facilities (CF) *n.* any collection of classes and objects that provide general purpose CORBA capabilities, which are commonly useful in many applications. [OMG]

Synonym: CORBA FACILITIES.

Contrast with: APPLICATION FACILITIES.

Commentary: Common facilities are made available through OMA-compliant class interfaces. [OMG]

Kinds:

• HORIZONTAL COMMON FACILITIES
  - SYSTEM MANAGEMENT FACILITIES
• VERTICAL COMMON FACILITIES

• **horizontal common facilities** *n.* any CORBA facilities that include functions shared by many or most systems, regardless of application domain.

Examples: User interface, information management, systems management, task management.

Antonym: VERTICAL COMMON FACILITIES.

- **system management facilities** *n.* any horizontal CORBA facilities that provide a set of interfaces that abstract basic system administration functions (e.g., control, monitoring, security management, configuration, and policy. [OMG]

• **vertical common facilities** *n.* any CORBA facilities that support a vertical market such as health care, retailing, CAD, or financial systems. [OMG]

Antonym: HORIZONTAL COMMON FACILITIES.

common global data *n.* any nonobject-oriented data that is not encapsulated within an object. [Firesmith]

Contrast with: COMMON GLOBAL OPERATION.

common global object *n.* any object that is globally visible to other objects (i.e., not encapsulated within a cluster). [Firesmith]

Contrast with: COMMON GLOBAL DATA, ENVIRONMENTAL OBJECT.

common global operation *n.* any non-object-oriented operation that is not encapsulated within a class. [Firesmith]

Synonym: FREE SUBPROGRAM.

Contrast with: COMMON GLOBAL DATA.

common instance attribute *n.* any instance attribute that has the same value for all instances of the same class. [Firesmith].

Synonym: CLASS ATTRIBUTE.

Contrast with: CLASS ATTRIBUTE, EXTENT ATTRIBUTE, INSTANCE ATTRIBUTE, OPERATION ATTRIBUTE.

Example: The interest rate for a type of

savings account is a common instance attribute. [Firesmith]

Commentary: Common instance attributes are usually stored once in the class rather than redundantly in each instance. [Firesmith]

common instance property *n.* any instance property that has the same value for all instances of the same class. [Firesmith]

Contrast with: INSTANCE PROPERTY.

Commentary: Common instance properties are usually stored once in the class rather than redundantly in each instance. [Firesmith]

• **common instance attribute** *n.* any instance attribute that has the same value for all instances of the same class. [Firesmith].

Synonym: CLASS ATTRIBUTE.

Contrast with: CLASS ATTRIBUTE, EXTENT ATTRIBUTE, INSTANCE ATTRIBUTE, OPERATION ATTRIBUTE.

Example: The interest rate for a type of savings account is a common instance attribute. [Firesmith]

Commentary: Common instance attributes are usually stored once in the class rather than redundantly in each instance. [Firesmith]

Common Object Methodology Metamodel Architecture (COMMA) *n.* an object-oriented metamodel architecture that identifies core concepts in methodologies, represents these by a metamodel, and provides the core to methodologists to elaborate for specific domains and to CASE tool vendors. [Henderson-Sellers]

communication association *n.* any association that models the communication of one object with another. [Jacobson]

Synonym: DYNAMIC ASSOCIATION.

Antonym: STATIC ASSOCIATION.

Commentary: The communication association does not show what kind of stimuli is sent between the objects; this is a level of detail that is saved for interaction diagrams. Communication associations are not named because they are dynamic. [Jacobson]

communication layer *n.* the layer that provides communication across processors. [Firesmith]

Commentary: The communication layer typically consists of communication objects and classes (e.g., proxies). The communication layer is typically built on top of the environment layer. [Firesmith]

communicator [object] *n.* any support object that allows communication between processors in a multiprocessor application. Communicator objects are used with proxies to provide a single virtual address space across multiple processors. [Firesmith]

Synonym: INTERFACER.

Contrast with: PROXY OBJECT.

Examples: Converters, data buses, network objects, and ORB objects are communicator objects. [Firesmith]

community *n.* any set of classes and objects connected by collaboration in a single application. [Firesmith]

Contrast with: FAMILY.

compatibility *n.* the ease with which something (e.g., software) may be combined with something else (e.g., other software). [Firesmith]

compile-time binding *n.* any binding that takes place statically before run-time when the associated message is sent. [Firesmith, Martin/Odell, OMG]

Synonyms: EARLY BINDING, STATIC BINDING.

Antonyms: DYNAMIC BINDING, LATE BINDING, RUN-TIME BINDING.

Rationale: Compile-time binding allows the compiler to decide what method to use, based on the declared class of the object. The term *static binding* is preferred because binding could also take place at link time. [Firesmith]

complete class *n.* any class capturing all of the responsibilities and features needed to both accurately implement the associated abstraction and meet its current requirements. [Firesmith]

Commentary: Where practical, a complete class should also implement all features required to support reusability and user-friendliness. [Firesmith]

complete model *n.* 1. any model that captures all the meaningful abstractions in the scope of the model in sufficient detail for the goals of the current iteration. [Coleman, Firesmith] 2. any model is *complete with respect to another model* if it captures all of the relevant information of the other model. [Coleman, Firesmith] 3. any model is *complete with respect to the requirements* if it implements all of the requirements. [Firesmith]

completeness *n.* the degree to which something has all of the characteristics necessary to:

– accurately implement an abstraction;
– meet its current requirements and responsibilities;
– be reusable and user-friendly. [Firesmith]

complete object *n.* any object that is not a subobject representing a base class. [C++]

Contrast with: SUBOBJECT.

complex class *n.* any class other than Boolean, character, integer, real, and double. [Eiffel, Meyer]

complex object *n.* **1.** any aggregate object containing one or more objects as component parts [Martin/Odell] **2.** any instance of a complex type. [Eiffel]
Synonyms: **1** AGGREGATE OBJECT, COMPOSITE OBJECT.
See also: COMPOSITION.

complex type *n.* any type whose base class is complex. [Eiffel]

component *n.* (a) any entity that can be used in a number of different programs. [Firesmith, Wirfs-Brock] (b) any standard, reusable, previously-implemented unit that is used to enhance the programming language constructs and to develop applications. [Jacobson]
See also: (b) CLASSIFICATION.
Commentary: A complex component that is easy to use raises the *abstraction* level for the developer. Sufficient operations must be included so that all reasonable use of the component is satisfied. [Jacobson]
Kinds:
- • COMPONENT CLASS
- • COMPONENT CLUSTER
  - - DATA MANAGEMENT COMPONENT
  - - HUMAN INTERACTION COMPONENT
  - - "NOT THIS TIME" COMPONENT
  - - PROBLEM DOMAIN COMPONENT
  - - SYSTEM INTERACTION COMPONENT
  - - TASK MANAGEMENT COMPONENT
- • COMPONENT OBJECT
  - - STATE COMPONENT

• **component [class]** *n.* any class that is contained within another class as a component part. [Firesmith]
Contrast with: COMPONENT CLUSTER, COMPONENT OBJECT.
Rationale: The term *component class* is far less ambiguous that the term *subclass*, which has another more popular meaning. [Firesmith]

• **component [cluster]** *n.* **1.** any cluster that is contained within another cluster as a component part. [Firesmith] **2.** (a) any grouping of classes that separates domain objects from technology-specific objects. [Coad] (b) the result of conceptually partitioning classes into meaningful, loosely-coupled subsets. [Coad]
Synonym: **2** MODEL COMPONENT.
Contrast with: COMPONENT CLASS, COMPONENT OBJECT.
Kinds:
- - DATA MANAGEMENT COMPONENT
- - HUMAN INTERACTION COMPONENT
- - NOT THIS TIME COMPONENT
- - PROBLEM DOMAIN COMPONENT
- - SYSTEM INTERACTION COMPONENT
- - TASK MANAGEMENT COMPONENT

- **data management (DM) component** *n.* the component that contains objects that provide an interface between problem domain objects and a database or file management system. It provides two major capabilities: storing and restoring. [Coad]
See also: "DM OBJECT SERVER" OBJECT.
- **human interaction (HI) component** *n.* the component which contains objects that provide an interface between problem domain objects and people. [Coad]
- **"not this time" (NT) component** *n.* a component used to indicate that a class or concept is outside the scope of the system. [Coad]
- **problem domain (PD) component** *n.* the component that contains the technology-neutral objects that directly correspond to the problem being modeled. [Coad]
Commentary: Theses objects have

little (or no) knowledge about objects in the other components (human interaction, data management, and system interaction). [Coad]

- **system interaction (SI) component** *n.* the component which contains system interaction objects that provide an interface between problem domain objects and other systems or devices. [Coad]
  Commentary: A system interaction object encapsulates communication protocol, keeping its companion problem domain object free of such low-level, implementation-specific detail. [Coad]
- **task management (TM) component** *n.* a component containing objects responsible for handling multitasking and related issues. [Coad]

• **component [object]** *n.* any object that is contained within another object as a component part. [Embley, Firesmith, OMG]
  Synonyms: PART, SUBPART.
  Contrast with: COMPONENT CLASS, COMPONENT CLUSTER.
  Kinds:
  - STATE COMPONENT
  - VARIABLE COMPONENT
- **state component [object]** *n.* any component object the state of which helps determine the state of its aggregate object or class. [Firesmith]
  Contrast with: STATE ATTRIBUTE, STATE LINK.
- **variable component [object]** *n.* any component object, at least one property of which can change its value. [Firesmith]
  Contrast with: VARIABLE ATTRIBUTE, VARIABLE LINK.

component-based development *n.* any

development that primarily consists of integrating instances of previously defined classes of objects. [Firesmith]
Synonym: INSTANCE-BASED DEVELOPMENT.
Contrast with: CLASS-BASED DEVELOPMENT.

component [class] *n.* any class that is contained within another class as a component part. [Firesmith]
Synonym: SUBCLASS.
Commentary: The term *component class* is far less ambiguous that the term *subclass,* which has another more popular meaning. [Firesmith]

composed-of diagram *n.* any diagram that documents *composed-of* relationships. [Martin]
Contrast with: BOX DIAGRAM.

composed-of relationship *n.* the *has-part* relationship between a composite object and its component parts. [Martin]
Contrast with: PARTOF RELATIONSHIP.

composite class *n.* any class that is composed of other classes. [Wirfs-Brock]
Synonym: AGGREGATE CLASS

composite object *n.* **1.** any aggregate object containing one or more objects as component parts [Martin/Odell] **2.** any complex object with complex subobjects. [Eiffel, Meyer]
Synonyms: AGGREGATE OBJECT, COMPLEX OBJECT.
Contrast with: SUBOBJECT.

composite [pattern] *n.* the structural object design pattern that composes objects into tree-like whole-part hierarchies. [Gamma, Helm, Johnson, and Vlissides]

composite type *n.* any type that has components. [Ada95]
Antonym: ELEMENTARY TYPE.
See also: DISCRIMINANT.
Examples: Composite types include ar-

ray and record types. [Ada95]

composition *n.* the process or result of forming an aggregate object from other objects as its component parts. [Firesmith, Martin/Odell]
Synonym: AGGREGATION.
Antonym: DECOMPOSITION.
See also: AGGREGATE OBJECT, COMPLEX OBJECT, COMPOSITE OBJECT.

compound key *n.* any key that consists of multiple properties. [ODMG]
Antonym: SIMPLE KEY.

compound name *n.* any name with multiple components. [OMG]
Antonym: SIMPLE NAME.

compound object *n.* any object with subobjects. [Eiffel, Meyer]
Synonym: AGGREGATE OBJECT.
Antonym: ATOMIC OBJECT.

compound trigger *n.* any conditions included in Boolean expressions with event monitors. [Embley]

computational state *n.* any state that describes the current status of execution, as well as potential future execution. [Jacobson]
Antonym: INTERNAL STATE.
Commentary: In principle, object behavior should only be described in terms of computational states. [Jacobson]

computed function *n.* any function whose mapping is derived or computed. [Martin/Odell]
Antonym: BASE FUNCTION.

concept *n.* **1.** anything used to describe an aspect of a subject area of object analysis and design. [OADSIG] **2.** any idea or notion people share that applies to certain things (i.e., objects) in their awareness. [Martin/Odell]
Synonym: **2** OBJECT TYPE.
Commentary: **2** A person has a concept if the person understands when the concept applies and when it does not. [Martin/Odell]
Kinds:
- ARCHITECTURE CONCEPT
- GROUP-AND-VIEW CONCEPT
- OBJECT-BEHAVIOR CONCEPT
- OBJECT-STRUCTURE CONCEPT

- **architecture concept** *n.* any concept that is a framework of functional components, embracing a set of standards, conventions, rules, and processes that support the integration of a wide range of information technology, enabling them to be used effectively within an enterprise. [OADSIG]

- **group-and-view concept** *n.* any concept that describes how a set of object types are grouped into a schema and/or viewed in a diagram. [OADSIG]

- **object-behavior concept** *n.* any concept that describes some aspect of the dynamic behavior of the object types identified during object analysis and design. These concepts include operation, state, requests, and messages. [OADSIG]

- **object-structure concept** *n.* any concept that identifies some aspect of the object types, the attribute types, and the relationship types identified during object analysis and design. [OADSIG]

concrete class *n.* **1.** (a) any complete class that can be instantiated to produce semantically meaningful instances. [Booch, Coad, Firesmith, Rumbaugh, Wirfs-Brock] (b) any class, the main purpose of which is to create instances. [Jacobson] **2.** any class with instances. [Lorenz]
Antonym: ABSTRACT CLASS.
Commentary: Definition **2** is questionable because concrete classes have no instances before they are instantiated or after all instances have been destroyed.

concrete use case *n.* any use case that is meaningful and will be instantiated on its own. [Jacobson]
Antonym: ABSTRACT USE CASE.

concurrency *n.* the property of encapsulating one or more intrinsic threads of control. [Booch, Firesmith, OADSIG]
Kinds:
- INTEROBJECT CONCURRENCY
- INTRAOBJECT CONCURRENCY

- **interobject concurrency** *n.* the ability of individual objects to behave concurrently. [Embley]
  Antonym: INTRAOBJECT CONCURRENCY.
  See also: STATE NET.
  Example: A robot might be moving to a container at the same time a packager is filling an order. [Embley]
  Commentary: OSA behavior models support interobject concurrency by associating a different state-net instance with every object. [Embley]

- **intraobject concurrency** *n.* the ability of an object to be in more than one state at the same time or to exhibit combinations of states and transitions at the same time. [Embley]
  Antonym: INTEROBJECT CONCURRENCY.
  See also: STATE NET.
  Commentary: When an object exits a final transition it ceases to exist unless the object is concurrently in some other state or transition. [Embley]

concurrency control service *n.* any service, the purpose of which is to mediate concurrent access to objects so that the consistency of the objects is not compromised when concurrently accessed. [OMG]

concurrent *adj.* **1.** containing one or more intrinsic thread(s) of control (i.e., tasks

or calls to tasks). [Firesmith] **2.** describing two or more threads of control whose execution may overlap in time. [Firesmith Rumbaugh]
Antonym: SEQUENTIAL.

concurrent class *n.* **1.** any class whose instances are concurrent objects. [Firesmith] **2.** any class that encapsulates one or more concurrent class features (e.g., operation or object). [Firesmith]
Antonym: SEQUENTIAL CLASS.
Kinds:
- ACTIVE CLASS
- GUARDED CLASS

- **active class** *n.* any concurrent class of active objects that may execute without the need for incoming messages. [Firesmith]
  Antonym: PASSIVE CLASS.

- **guarded class** *n.* any concurrent class, the instances of which provide and enforce mutually exclusive access in a concurrent environment. [Firesmith]
  Contrast with: CORRUPTIBLE CLASS, GUARDABLE CLASS.

concurrent object *n.* any object that encapsulates one or more intrinsic threads of control (e.g., concurrent operations or nested concurrent objects). [Booch, Firesmith]
Antonym: SEQUENTIAL OBJECT.
Kinds:
- ACTIVE OBJECT
- GUARDED OBJECT

- **active object** *n.* any concurrent object that executes without the need for incoming messages. [Firesmith]
  Antonym: PASSIVE OBJECT.

- **guarded object** *n.* any concurrent object that provides and enforces mutually exclusive access in a concurrent environment.
  Contrast with: CORRUPTIBLE OBJECT,

GUARDABLE OBJECT.

concurrent operation *n.* any operation that contains one or more intrinsic threads of control. [Firesmith]

Antonym: SEQUENTIAL OPERATION.

Commentary: A concurrent operation may be able to handle more than one message at a time. [Firesmith]

concurrent states *n.* any two or more states that an object or class is in simultaneously. [Firesmith]

condition *n.* **1.** (a) any Boolean (or enumeration-valued) expression involving the values of one or more properties. [Firesmith] (b) any Boolean function of object values that is valid over an interval of time. [Rumbaugh] **2.** any logical statement about the current state of an object, the current state of the system environment, the existence or absence of an object, or the existence or absence of relationships among objects. [Embley]

Contrast with: **1** ASSERTION, CONSTRAINT **2** EVENT.

See also: **2** CONDITION-BASED TRIGGER, STATE, TRIGGER.

Commentary: The distinction between events and conditions is that an event triggers an enabled transition only at the instant the event occurs, whereas a condition triggers an enabled transition during the entire time the condition holds. [Embley]

Kinds:

- ASSERTION
  - INVARIANT
    + CLASS INVARIANT
    + EXTENT INVARIANT
    + INSTANCE INVARIANT
    + MESSAGE INVARIANT
    + SCENARIO INVARIANT
  - POSTCONDITION
  - PRECONDITION

- CONTROL CONDITION
- GUARD CONDITION
- TERMINATE CONDITION
- TRIGGER CONDITION

- **assertion** *n.* **1.** any Boolean condition or relationship that must be true at certain points during execution. [Booch, Firesmith, Rumbaugh] **2.** any rule stated as a predicate that is part of the definition of an object type. **3.** any element of formal specification expressing a correctness condition. [Eiffel, Meyer]

Contrast with: CONSTRAINT.

Commentary: Assertions are typically written as expressions involving the properties of an object or class. Assertions involving multiple objects or classes are typically encapsulated in a single class, the instances of which have visibility of all of the objects and classes involved in the assertion. [Firesmith]

Kinds:

- INVARIANT
  + CLASS INVARIANT
  + EXTENT INVARIANT
  + INSTANCE INVARIANT
  + MESSAGE INVARIANT
- POSTCONDITION
- PRECONDITION

- **invariant** *n.* any assertion, the scope of which is the entire life cycle of the associated thing. [Firesmith]

Contrast with: PRECONDITION, POST-CONDITION.

Example: The length times the width of a rectangle must equal the rectangle's area. [Firesmith]

Commentary: Invariants are used to ensure that abstractions are never violated. Many equate the term *invariant* with the term *instance in-*

variant. [Firesmith]
Kinds:
+ CLASS INVARIANT
+ EXTENT INVARIANT
+ INSTANCE INVARIANT
+ MESSAGE INVARIANT
+ SCENARIO INVARIANT

+ **class invariant** *n.* any invariant involving the properties of a class that must be true upon elaboration, prior to the execution of each class operation, and after execution of each class operation. [Firesmith]
Example: Any invariant involving generic formal parameters is a class invariant. [Firesmith]

+ **extent invariant** *n.* any invariant involving the properties of an extent that must be true prior to the execution of each constructor and after execution of each destructor. [Firesmith]
Example: The maximum number of instances is an extent invariant. [Firesmith]

+ **instance invariant** *n.* any invariant involving the properties of an instance that must be true upon instantiation, prior to the execution of each instance operation, after execution of each instance operation, and prior to destruction. [Firesmith, Meyer, Rumbaugh]
Examples: The length times the width of a rectangle must equal the rectangle's area. [Firesmith] The age of a person cannot be less than zero. If the due date on a book is later than today's date, then the book is overdue. [OADSIG]

+ **message invariant** *n.* any invariant that must evaluate to true after execution of the associated operation(s) if it holds prior to receipt of the message. [Firesmith]
Contrast with: PRECONDITION, POSTCONDITION.

+ **scenario invariant** *n.* any invariant that must evaluate to true after execution of each associated operation and exception handler if it holds prior to the start of the scenario. [Firesmith]

- **postcondition** *n.* **1.** (a) any assertion on an operation or scenario that must be true immediately following the execution if all preconditions were true immediately prior to execution. [Coad, Eiffel, Firesmith, Meyer] (b) any condition that describes the correct effect of its associated operation or scenario. [Coleman, Firesmith] (c) any constraint that guarantees the results when the operation is executed. [Martin] (d) any condition that the operation itself agrees to achieve. [Rumbaugh] **2.** an invariant satisfied by an operation. [Booch]
Synonym: OPERATION POSTCONDITION RULE.
Contrast with: INVARIANT, PRECONDITION.
See also: ASSERTION.
Example: A postcondition of the push operation on a stack is that the stack not be empty. [Firesmith]
Commentary: Postconditions are "guarantees" that are used to ensure that the associated operation or scenario was correctly executed. [Firesmith] Definition **2** uses the term *invariant* instead of the more appropriate term *assertion.*

- **precondition** *n.* **1.** (a) any assertion

on an operation or scenario that must evaluate to true prior to execution. [Coad, Firesmith] (b) any predicate that characterizes the conditions under which an operation may be invoked. [Coleman] (c) any predicate that characterizes the conditions under which an operation may be invoked. [Coleman] (d) any requirement that clients must satisfy whenever they call a routine. [Eiffel, Meyer, Rumbaugh] (e) any constraint that guarantees the results when the operation is executed. [Martin] **2.** any invariant assumed by an operation. [Booch]
Synonym: OPERATION PRECONDITION RULE.
Contrast with: INVARIANT, POST-CONDITION.
See also: ASSERTION.
Example: A precondition of the push operation on a stack is that the stack not be full. [Firesmith]
Commentary: Preconditions are used to ensure that the associated operation may be correctly executed. Definition 1 (d) makes the client rather than the server responsible for satisfying the precondition. Definition 2 uses the term *invariant* instead of the more appropriate term *assertion*. [Firesmith]

- **control condition** *n.* (a) any Boolean expression that must evaluate to true prior to the execution of its associated operation. [Coad] (b) any predicate that characterizes the conditions under which an operation may be invoked. [Coleman, Martin]
Synonym: PRECONDITION.
See also: OPERATION.
Rationale: Term introduced by Martin.

- **guard condition** *n.* (a) any condition that must be true (or have the proper enumeration value) for a trigger to cause the associated transition to fire. [Booch, Firesmith, Rumbaugh] (b) any condition on the receiver of a synchronous message that must be true for the message to be received. [Firesmith]
Contrast with: PRECONDITION, POST-CONDITION.

- **terminate condition** *n.* any condition that identifies the circumstances on which a service stops itself. [Coad]
Commentary: When applicable, a terminate condition is specified in a service specification. [Coad]

- **trigger condition** *n.* any condition that identifies the circumstances on which a service starts itself. [Coad]
Commentary: A trigger condition, when applicable, is specified in a service specification. [Coad]

condition-based trigger *n.* any trigger that causes an enabled transition to fire when its logical statement is true. [Embley, Firesmith]
See also: CONDITION.
Commentary: The distinction between events and conditions is that an event triggers an enabled transition only at the instant the event occurs, whereas a condition triggers an enabled transition during the entire time the condition holds. [Embley] A condition-based trigger can be implemented as a concurrent operation that constantly checks the value of the condition and causes the state change when the value of the condition changes to true while in the appropriate state. [Firesmith]

conferred behavior *n.* the behavior that a class/object obtains through interaction with behaviored clients. [Atkinson]

See also: DELEGATION.

configuration diagram (CND) *n.* any static architecture diagram documenting the configuration management view of an assembly or system in terms of its component clusters or subsystems, their visibility, their component objects and classes (whitebox diagrams only), and the dependency relationships among them. [Firesmith]
Kinds:
- ASSEMBLY DIAGRAM
- SYSTEM DIAGRAM

- **assembly diagram (AD)** *n.* any configuration diagram documenting the static architecture of an assembly in terms of its component clusters and the dependency relationships between them. [Firesmith]
Antonym: SYSTEM DIAGRAM.

- **system diagram (SD)** *n.* any configuration diagram documenting the static architecture of a system in terms of its component subsystems and the dependency relationships between them. [Firesmith]
Antonym: ASSEMBLY DIAGRAM.

configuration model *n.* the static architecture model that documents a configuration management view of a system (or universe). The configuration model consists of one or more configuration diagrams and specifications for a system or universe. [Firesmith]
Contrast with: INTERACTION MODEL, INTERFACE MODEL, LANGUAGE MODEL, PRESENTATION MODEL, SEMANTIC MODEL, STATE MODEL.

confirmability *n.* the ability to readily determine whether software is correct, reliable, and robust.

conform [to a given signature] *v. -ed, -ing* any signature S is said to conform to the given signature if every argument of S corresponds to the same type as the corresponding argument in the given signature, and the return type of S (if any) corresponds to the return type of the given signature (if any).

conform [to a given type] *v. -ed, -ing* any type T is said to conform to the given type if any instance of type T can be used any place an instance of the given type can be used (i.e., if the protocol of type T is a superset of the protocol of the given type and if the semantics of the features that type T and the given type have in common are the same). [Firesmith]
Commentary: Conformity is a relationship between types (i.e., interfaces), whereas inheritance is a relationship between classes (i.e., interfaces and implementations). Subtypes must conform to their supertypes, whereas derived classes should usually, but need not, conform to the interfaces of their base classes. [Firesmith]

conformance [of a class] *n.* any relationship between classes, based solely on the form of their interfaces, which guarantees that instances of one class will be able to service all the method calls that instances of another will. [Atkinson]
Commentary: Conformance is a necessary, but not sufficient, condition for type compatibility. [Atkinson]

conformance [of a type] *n.* any mechanism for determining type consistency.
Kinds:
- DIRECT CONFORMANCE
- EXPRESSION CONFORMANCE
- GENERAL CONFORMANCE
- INDIRECT CONFORMANCE
- SIGNATURE CONFORMANCE
- TYPE CONFORMANCE

- **direct conformance** *n.* any immediate conformance of one class or type to a different class or type through no intermediary. [Eiffel, Firesmith, Meyer]
Antonym: INDIRECT CONFORMANCE.
Example: A subtype conforms to its parent type. [Firesmith]

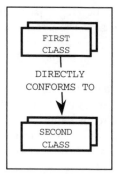

Direct Conformance

- **expression conformance** *n.* any conformance of one expression to another expression, which occurs when the type returned by the first expression conforms to the type returned by the second expression. [Eiffel, Firesmith, Meyer]

- **indirect conformance** *n.* any conformance of one class or type to a different class or type through one or more intermediary classes or types. [Eiffel, Firesmith, Meyer]
Antonym: DIRECT CONFORMANCE.
Example: The subtype of a given type conforms to the parent type of the given type. [Firesmith]

- **signature conformance** *n.* any conformance of one signature to another, whereby all arguments, return type, and exceptions of the first signature conform to the corresponding arguments, return type, and exceptions of

the second signature. [Eiffel, Firesmith, Meyer]

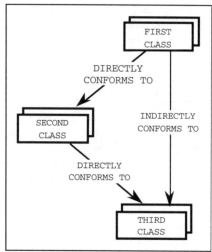

Indirect Conformance

- **type conformance** *n.* (a) any conformance of one type to another, whereby the protocol of the first type is a superset of the protocol of the second type and the semantics of the features they have in common are the same. [Eiffel, Firesmith, Meyer] (b) any relation defined over types such that type X conforms to type Y if any value that satisfies type X also satisfies type Y. [OMG]
Contrast with: SIGNATURE CONFORMANCE.
Commentary: Conformance is used as a mechanism for determining when a type is compatible with another for assignment, argument passing, or signature redefinition. If one type conforms to another, then instances of the first type can be used anywhere that instances of the second type can be used. [Eiffel, Firesmith, Meyer]

connection *n.* **1.** any coupling between processors, devices, or between processors and devices that is documented on processor diagrams. [Booch, Firesmith] **2.** any problem domain association or mapping between objects that represents what one object needs to know about some number of other objects in order to fulfill its responsibilities. [Coad]
Synonym: **2** OBJECT CONNECTION.
Example: **1** any hardware or fiberoptic cable, an Ethernet connection, or a microwave link. [Firesmith]
Commentary: **2** There are two reasons for this: (1) to know to whom to send a message and (2) to support basic querying capabilities. [Coad]
Kinds:
- MESSAGE CONNECTION
- WHOLE-PART OBJECT CONNECTION

- **message connection** *n.* any connection that models the processing dependency of an object, indicating a need for services in order to fulfill its responsibilities. [Coad]
  See also: MESSAGE.
- **whole-part object connection** *n.* any connection that carries the added meaning of container-content, group-member, or assembly-part. [Coad]
  See also: WHOLE-PART STRUCTURE.

consistent class *n.* any class that is instantiated in a state satisfying all invariants and having only operations, which, if started in a state satisfying the precondition and the invariants, also terminate in a state satisfying the postcondition and the invariants. [Eiffel, Firesmith, Meyer]

consistent models *n.* any set of models that do not contradict each other, either explicitly or implicitly. [Coleman, Firesmith]

consistsOf association *n.* any acquaintance association from an aggregate object to an object of which it consists. [Jacobson]
Antonym: PARTOF ASSOCIATION.
See also: AGGREGATE, ACQUAINTANCE ASSOCIATION.
Example: A food order consists of a dish and a beverage. [Jacobson]
Commentary: The association consistsOf is used to express that an aggregate object is a compound of other objects. [Jacobson]

const *adj.* describing any object that cannot have its value changed through an expression involving the name being declared const unless an explicit type conversion is used to remove the *constness.* [C++]
Contrast with: VOLATILE.
Commentary: The term *const* does not simply mean *store in read-only memory* nor does it mean *compile-time constant.* Fundamentally, saying *const* obliges and enables the compiler to prevent accidental updates of the value of an object using a specific name. The words *const* and *volatile* may be added to any legal *type-specifier* in the declaration of an object. [C++]

constant *adj.* describing anything, the values of which cannot change at run time. [Firesmith]
Synonym: IMMUTABLE.
Antonym: VARIABLE.
Example: The term *constant* is more popular and preferred over the term *immutable.* [Firesmith]

constant aggregate *n.* any aggregate, the aggregation structure of which and the component parts of which cannot change. [Firesmith]
Contrast with: FIXED AGGREGATE, VARI-

ABLE AGGREGATE.

constant attribute *n.* **1.** any attribute the value of which cannot change at run time. [Firesmith] **2.** any attribute whose value is the same for every instance and cannot be changed at run-time. [Eiffel, Meyer]

Antonym: VARIABLE ATTRIBUTE.

constant component *n.* any component object that is a constant object. [Firesmith]

Antonym: VARIABLE ATTRIBUTE.

constant object *n.* any object whose properties cannot change value at run-time. [Firesmith]

Antonym: VARIABLE OBJECT.

constant link *n.* any link that cannot change at run-time. [Firesmith]

Antonym: VARIABLE LINK.

Commentary: Although the values of the properties of the server may change, a constant link always points to the same server. [Firesmith]

constant property *n.* any property, the value of which cannot change at run-time.

Antonym: VARIABLE PROPERTY.

Kinds:
- CONSTANT ATTRIBUTE
- CONSTANT COMPONENT
- CONSTANT LINK

- **constant attribute** *n.* **1.** any attribute the value of which cannot change at run-time. [Firesmith] **2.** any attribute whose value is the same for every instance and cannot be changed at run-time. [Eiffel, Meyer]

  Antonym: VARIABLE ATTRIBUTE.

- **constant component** *n.* any component object that is a constant object. [Firesmith]

  Antonym: VARIABLE ATTRIBUTE.

- **constant link** *n.* any link that cannot

be created, destroyed, or changed in value at run-time. [Firesmith]

Antonym: VARIABLE LINK.

Commentary: Although the values of the properties of the server may change, a constant link always points to the same server. [Firesmith]

constrained object *n.* any object whose actual subtype is constrained. [Ada95]

constrained subtype *n.* any subtype whose type has neither unknown discriminants nor allows range, index, or discriminant constraints. [Ada95]

Rationale: The subtype is called a *constrained* subtype because it has no unconstrained characteristics. [Ada95]

constraint *n.* **1.** any required condition or semantic relationship. [Booch, Firesmith, Rumbaugh] **2.** (a) any rule stated as a restriction or requirement concerning instances of an object type. [OADSIG] (b) any restriction on the membership of one or more object classes or relationship sets. [Embley] (c) any restriction on the set of possible values for an object of a given type. [Ada95]

Contrast with: ASSERTION, CONDITION.

Examples: The object type *Position* has the instances of *on* and *off*. The attribute *part id* on the object type *Part* must take a value. [OADSIG]

Commentary: Definition **2** is implied by definition **1** as a special subcase.

Kinds:
- BEHAVIORAL CONSTRAINT
  - REAL-TIME CONSTRAINT
- STRUCTURAL CONSTRAINT
  - ANTISYMMETRIC CONSTRAINT
  - ASYMMETRIC CONSTRAINT
  - CARDINALITY CONSTRAINT
    + AGGREGATION CARDINALITY CONSTRAINT
    + CLASS CARDINALITY CONSTRAINT

+ CLUSTER CARDINALITY
  CONSTRAINT
+ OBJECT-CLASS CARDINALITY
  CONSTRAINT
+ OBJECT CONNECTION
  CONSTRAINT
+ PARTICIPATION CONSTRAINT
  > CO-OCCURENCE CONSTRAINT
+ RELATIONSHIP CARDINALITY
  CONSTRAINT
- INHERITANCE CONSTRAINT
+ COVER CONSTRAINT
+ DISJOINT CONSTRAINT
+ MUTUAL-EXCLUSION CONSTRAINT
+ PARTITION CONSTRAINT
+ UNION CONSTRAINT
- IRREFLEXIVE CONSTRAINT
- NONTRANSITIVE CONSTRAINT
- REFLEXIVE CONSTRAINT
- SET CONSTRAINT
- SYMMETRIC CONSTRAINT
- TRANSITIVE CONSTRAINT

- **behavioral constraint** *n.* any constraint that limits the behavior of objects or classes. [Firesmith]
  Antonym: STRUCTURAL CONSTRAINT.
  - **real-time constraint** *n.* **1.** any behavioral constraint specifying temporal requirements. [Firesmith] **2.** on a state net, any constraint specifying timing requirements on a trigger, action, state, or state-transition path. [Embley]
  Commentary: Analysts should add real-time constraints whenever time is important. [Embley, Firesmith]
- **structural constraint** *n.* any constraint that limits the way objects may be linked, classes may be associated, or objects may be classified into classes. [Firesmith]
  Antonym: BEHAVIORAL CONSTRAINT.
  Kinds:

- ANTISEMMETRIC CONSTRAINT
- ASYMMETRIC CONSTRAINT
- CARDINALITY CONSTRAINT
  + AGGREGATION CARDINALITY
    CONSTRAINT
  + CLASS CARDINALITY CONSTRAINT
  + CLUSTER CARDINALITY
    CONSTRAINT
  + OBJECT-CLASS CARDINALITY
    CONSTRAINT
  + OBJECT CONNECTION
    CONSTRAINT
  + PARTICIPATION CONSTRAINT
    > CO-OCCURRENCE CONSTRAINT
  + RELATIONSHIP CARDINALITY
    CONSTRAINT
- INHERITANCE CONSTRAINT
  + COVER CONSTRAINT
  + DISJOINT CONSTRAINT
  + MUTUAL-EXCLUSION
    CONSTRAINT
  + PARTITION CONSTRAINT
  + UNION CONSTRAINT
- IRREFLEXIVE CONSTRAINT
- NONTRANSITIVE CONSTRAINT
- REFLEXIVE CONSTRAINT
- SET CONSTRAINT
- SYMMETRIC CONSTRAINT
- TRANSITIVE CONSTRANT

- **antisymmetric constraint** *n.* any structural constraint that permits a symmetric relationship between two things only if those two things are the same. [Firesmith]
  Contrast with: ASYMMETRIC CONSTRAINT, SYMMETRIC CONSTRAINT.
  Example: The *is identical to* link and association are antisymmetric. A is identical to B only if A and B are the same. [Firesmith]
- **asymmetric constraint** *n.* any structural constraint that does not permit symmetry. [Firesmith]

Contrast with: ANTISYMMETRIC CONSTRAINT, SYMMETRIC CONSTRAINT.
Example: The *is-parent-of* link and association are asymmetric. The existence of an *is-parent-of* link from A to B implies that no *is-parent-of* link can exist from B to A. [Firesmith]

- **cardinality constraint** *n.* any structural constraint that restricts the cardinality of something.
Kinds:
  + AGGREGATION CARDINALITY CONSTRAINT
  + CLASS CARDINALITY CONSTRAINT
  + CLUSTER CARDINALITY CONSTRAINT
  + OBJECT-CLASS CARDINALITY CONSTRAINT
  + OBJECT CONNECTION CONSTRAINT
  + PARTICIPATION CONSTRAINT
    > CO-OCCURRENCE CONSTRAINT
  + RELATIONSHIP CARDINALITY CONSTRAINT

+ **aggregation cardinality constraint** *n.* any cardinality constraint that restricts the cardinality of an aggregate. [Firesmith]

+ **class cardinality constraint** *n.* any cardinality constraint that restricts the cardinality of a class. [Firesmith]
Synonym: OBJECT-CLASS CARDINALITY CONSTRAINT.

+ **cluster cardinality constraint** *n.* any cardinality constraint that restricts the cardinality of a cluster. [Firesmith]

+ **object-class cardinality constraint** *n.* any constraint used to restrict the number of objects in an object class. [Embley]
Synonym: CLASS CARDINALITY CONSTRAINT.

+ **object connection constraint** *n.* any constraint that indicates the number of objects that an object knows. [Coad]
Synonyms: PARTICIPATION CONSTRAINT, RELATIONSHIP CARDINALITY CONSTRAINT.
See also: OBJECT CONNECTION.
Commentary: Coad's graphical placement of this constraint is just the opposite of the entity-relationship convention for what the approach calls *multiplicities*. [Coad]

+ **participation constraint** *n.* any constraint that defines the number of times an object in an object class can participate in a connected relationship set. Participation constraints restrict the number of relationships in which an object can appear in a relationship set. [Embley]
Synonyms: OBJECT CONNECTION CONSTRAINT, RELATIONSHIP CARDINALITY CONSTRAINT.
Commentary: Every connection of a relationship set to an object class must have a participation constraint. The basic form for a participation constraint is a par: *min:max*. [Embley]

  > **co-occurrence constraint** *n.* any constraint that specifies the minimum and maximum number of times an object or combination of objects can co-occur in the relationships of a relationship set with another object or combination of objects. [Embley]

+ **relationship cardinality constraint** *n.* any cardinality constraint that restricts the cardinality of a rela-

tionship. [Firesmith, Martin/Odell]
Synonyms: OBJECT CONNECTION CONSTRAINT, PARTICIPATION CONSTRAINT.

Examples: Common unidirectional relationship cardinality constraints are *0 or 1*, *1*, *0, or more*, and *1 or more*. Common bidirectional relationship cardinality constraints are *1 to 1*, *1 to many*, and *many to many*. More specific constraints are also possible. [Firesmith]

Commentary: Relationship cardinality constraints can be unidirectional (i.e., restricting the number on the end that is pointed to) or bidirectional (i.e., restricting the number at both ends of the relationship). [Firesmith]

- **inheritance constraint** *n.* any structural constraint that restricts the relationships among children or between the children and their parent(s). [Firesmith]

Kinds:
 + COVER CONSTRAINT
 + DISJOINT CONSTRAINT
 + MUTUAL EXCLUSION CONSTRAINT
 + PARTITION CONSTRAINT
 + UNION CONSTRAINT

+ **cover constraint** *n.* the inheritance constraint that requires that the extent of the parent be a subset of the union of the extents of the children. [Firesmith]
Synonym: UNION CONSTRAINT.
Rationale: The term *cover* comes from set theory. [Firesmith]
Commentary: This constraint ensures that each instance of the parent is also an instance of at least one child. [Firesmith]

+ **disjoint constraint** *n.* the inheritance constraint that requires that the extents of the children be pairwise disjoint. [Firesmith]
Synonym: MUTUAL-EXCLUSION CONSTRAINT.
Rationale: The term *disjoint* comes from set theory. [Firesmith]
Commentary: This constraint ensures that no object will be an instance of two children. [Firesmith]

+ **mutual-exclusion constraint** *n.* any inheritance constraint that declares that a group of children of a parent are pairwise disjoint. [Embley]
Synonym: DISJOINT CONSTRAINT.

+ **partition constraint** *n.* the inheritance constraint that requires that the extents of the children form a disjoint cover that partitions the parent. [Embley, Firesmith]
Commentary: The partition constraint is the conjunction of the cover constraint and the disjoint constraint. [Firesmith] A partition requires that partitioning sets be pairwise disjoint and that their union constitute the partitioned set. A partition constraint is the combination of a mutual-exclusion constraint and a union constraint. [Embley]

+ **union constraint** *n.* any inheritance constraint that declares that the union of a group of specializations of a generalization constitutes the entire membership of the generalization. [Embley]
Synonym: COVER CONSTRAINT.
Commentary: A union constraint implies that every member of a generalization is also a member of

at least one specialization in the group. [Embley]

- **irreflexive constraint** *n.* any structural constraint that prohibits objects from being related to themselves. [Firesmith]
Antonym: REFLEXIVE CONSTRAINT.
Example: The *is-parent-of* link and association are irreflexive. One cannot be one's own parent. [Firesmith]

- **nontransitive constraint** *n.* the structural constraint on a given relationship R that requires if A is related by R to B and B is related by R to C, then A need not be related by R to C. [Firesmith]
ANTONYM: TRANSITIVE CONSTRAINT.
Example: The *has-visibility-of* link and association are nontransitive. [Firesmith]

- **reflexive constraint** *n.* any structural constraint on a relationship that requires objects or classes to be related to themselves. [Firesmith]
Antonym: IRREFLEXIVE CONSTRAINT.
Example: The *is-as-old-as* link and association are reflexive. Something can be as old as other things, but must be as old as itself.

- **set constraint** *n.* any structural constraint on an extent that prohibits duplicates. [Firesmith]

- **symmetric constraint** *n.* any structural constraint on a relationship that requires the relationship to work in both directions. [Firesmith]
Contrast with: ANTISYMMETRIC CONSTRAINT, ASYMMETRIC CONSTRAINT.
Example: The *is-spouse-of* link and association are symmetric. The existence of an *is-spouse-of* link from A to B implies the existence of an *is-spouse-of* link from B to A. [Firesmith]

- **transitive constraint** *n.* any structural constraint that requires if A is related to B and B is related to C, then A is related to C. [Firesmith]
Antonym: NONTRANSITIVE CONSTRAINT.
Example: The *is-greater-than* link and association are transitive. [Firesmith]

construction interface *n.* any interface that defines the operations used to communicate between the core of an Object Service and related objects that must participate in providing the service. [OMG]
Contrast with: FUNCTIONAL INTERFACES, SYSTEM MANAGEMENT INTERFACES.
See also: AUDIENCE.
Commentary: A construction interface is typically defined by the service and is inherited and implemented by participants in the service. Objects that participate in a service must support its construction interfaces. [OMG]

constructor [operation] *n.* any class or metaclass operation that constructs (i.e., instantiates) an instance (i.e., an object or class respectively), allocates memory to dynamic objects, creates the binding of messages to [inherited] operations (e.g., via a virtual method table), and initializes the values of the properties. [Booch, Coleman, Firesmith, Rumbaugh]
Synonyms: CREATE ACCESSOR, CREATE OPERATION.
Antonym: DESTRUCTOR OPERATION.
Commentary: Constructors turn raw memory into an object for which the rules of the type system hold. Constructors typically initialize the object before it can be used. [Firesmith]
Kinds:

- COPY CONSTRUCTOR
- DEFAULT CONSTRUCTOR

copy constructor *n.* any constructor that makes a copy an object of its class. [C++, Firesmith]

Example: In C++:

    X::X(const X&);

default constructor *n.* any constructor that can be called without arguments. [C++, Firesmith]

Examples: In C++:

    X::X();
    X::X(int=0);

Commentary: A default constructor may have default arguments. [Firesmith]

consumer *n.* any object role that process[es] event data. [OMG]

Contrast with: SUPPLIER.

container [class] *n.* any heterogeneous aggregate class of container objects (i.e., aggregate objects, the purpose of which are to hold unrelated component objects of multiple unrelated types). [Booch, Firesmith, Rumbaugh]

Contrast with: COLLECTION CLASS, STRUCTURE CLASS.

Example: A class of car trunks is a container class. [Firesmith]

Commentary: Containers allow more freedom by violating strong typing. [Firesmith]

container [object] *n.* **1.** (a) any heterogeneous aggregate object, the purpose of which is to hold unrelated component objects of multiple unrelated types. [Firesmith] (b) any instance of a container class. [Firesmith] **2.** any object that exists to contain other objects and that provides appropriate operations to access and iterate over its contents. [Rumbaugh]

Contrast with: COLLECTION OBJECT, STRUCTURE OBJECT.

Example: Any individual car trunk can be modeled a container object. [Firesmith]

Commentary: Containers allow freedom by violating strong typing. Definition **2** does not clearly distinguish between collection, container, and structure objects. [Firesmith]

containment hierarchy *n.* any hierarchy created by constructing an object from other objects via *consistsOf* relations. [Jacobson]

Synonyms: AGGREGATION HIERARCHY, PARTITION HIERARCHY.

See also: AGGREGATE, CONSISTSOF ASSOCIATION.

context *n.* **1.** the terminators of something. [Firesmith] **2.** (a) any object representing organizational structures for classes and methods that help the programmer keep track of the system. [Smalltalk] (b) any object representing histories of software modification that help interface with the efforts of other programmers. [Smalltalk]

Example: The execution state of a method is represented by a context object. [Smalltalk]

Commentary: These objects are classed as contexts and are analogous to stack frames or activation records in other systems. Even the execution state of a method is represented by an object. [Smalltalk]

context-dependent operation *n.* any operation, the effect of which depends on the context of the receiver of the associated message. [Firesmith, OMG]

Antonym: CONTEXT-INDEPENDENT OPERATION.

Example: The effect may depend on the identity or location of the client object sending the message (i.e., issuing the request). [Firesmith]

context diagram (CD) *n.* any specialized semantic net used to document a system or assembly and the semantic relationships between it and its terminators. [Firesmith]

context-independent operation *n.* any operation, the effect of which is independent of the context of the receiver of the associated message. [Firesmith, OMG]
Antonym: CONTEXT-DEPENDENT OPERATION.

context object *n.* any collection of name-value pairs that provides environmental or user-preference information. [OMG]

continuous interaction *n.* any interaction that is continuous. This is common particularly for analog sensors in systems. [Embley]
Synonym: CONTINUOUS MESSAGE.
Examples: Interactions from analog sensors. [Embley]

continuous message *n.* any message that is not discrete. [Firesmith]
Synonym: CONTINUOUS INTERACTION.
Examples: Messages from analogue sensors can be modeled as continuous messages. [Firesmith]
Commentary: All major object-oriented programming languages only support discrete messages.

contract *n.* **1.** (a) any semiformal agreement offered by a server to one or more of its clients. Contracts consist of a cohesive set of the server's public responsibilities on one or more messages that the clients can send to the server that implement a cohesive set of public responsibilities on which the clients can depend. [Firesmith, Henderson-Sellers, Jacobson, Martin, Wirfs-Brock] (b) any

simplifying abstraction for a *group* of related public responsibilities that are to be provided by subsystems and classes to their clients. [Lorenz] **2.** (a) any "formal" agreement between a server and its clients that is implemented by any *single* message constrained by assertions (e.g., preconditions, postconditions, and invariants). [Coleman, Eiffel, Henderson-Sellers, Meyer] (b) the goal that any *single* message or operation is meant to achieve. [Eiffel, Meyer]
Synonyms: **1** INTERFACE CONTRACT [Henderson-Sellers], ROLE (of the server), **2** SERVICE CONTRACT [Henderson-Sellers].
See also: CLIENT, MESSAGE, PUBLIC RESPONSIBILITY, REQUEST, RESPONSIBILITY, SERVER.
Example: Maintain account balances may be a contract for the *Account* class (and all its derived classes) and may be implemented by methods such as *deposit:, withdraw:,* and *balance.* [Lorenz]
Rationale: Credit for the term *contract* should be given to Bertrand Meyer (and Rebecca Wirfs-Brock), who introduced and popularized the concept. [Firesmith]
Commentary: Contracts are enforced via server assertions (i.e., invariants of the server as well as preconditions and postconditions of the operations of the server) and corresponding exceptions that the server may raise to the client as a result of the execution of these operations. Note that the defensive design style of the Firesmith method allocates all contract responsibilities to the server, whereas Meyer's Design by Contract method places the responsibilities on both the sender and the receiver. This has efficiency and robustness con-

sequences (e.g., should the sender have to query the receiver as to the receiver's state before sending the intended message and can the receiver's response be trusted in a concurrent environment? [Firesmith]

contract specification *n.* the formal specification documenting any given contract. [Wirfs-Brock]
Contrast with: CLASS SPECIFICATION.

contractual model *n.* any programming model in which the specification of a method is viewed as a contract between the client, which must supply a satisfied precondition, and the server, which must then deliver a satisfied postcondition. [Coleman]

control *n.* **1.** the overall behavior of something in terms of message passing, operation execution, and exception raising and handling. [Firesmith] **2.** the description of the sequences of operations that occur in response to stimuli. [Rumbaugh]

control condition *n.* **1.** any Boolean expression that must evaluate to true prior to the execution of its associated operation. [Coad] **2.** any predicate that characterizes the conditions under which an operation may be invoked. [Coleman, Martin]
Synonym: PRECONDITION.
See also: OPERATION.
Rationale: Term introduced by Martin.

control flow *n.* **1.** the transfer or synchronization of control via message passing, operation invocation, and exception raising and handling. [Firesmith] **2.** any Boolean value that affects whether a process in a DFD is executed. [Rumbaugh] **3.** any graphic representation of a constraint on the order of process execution. [Shlaer/Mellor]

Antonym: DATA FLOW.

controlled type *n.* any type that supports user-defined assignment and finalization. [Ada95]

controller [class] *n.* **1.** any domain class that exists to either control one or more classes or capture user input as in the model-view-controller (MVC) framework. [Firesmith, Smalltalk] **2.** any class of controller objects. [Firesmith, Jacobson]
Contrast with: MODEL CLASS, PRESENTATION CLASS, VIEW CLASS.
Commentary: Controller classes are often either model classes that model input devices (e.g., mice) or are presentation classes allowing the user to control the model object. [Firesmith]

controller object *n.* **1.** (a) any domain object that exists to either control one or more objects or capture user input as in the model-view-controller (MVC) framework. [Firesmith] (b) any instance of a controller class. [Firesmith] **2.** any object (on an object interaction graph) responsible for responding to a system operation request. [Coleman]
Synonym: DISPATCHER OBJECT.
Contrast with: CONTROLLER CLASS, CONTROL OBJECT, MODEL OBJECT, PRESENTATION OBJECT, VIEW OBJECT.
Example: An object that captures mouse events may be a controller object. [Firesmith]
Commentary: Controller objects are often either model objects that model input devices (e.g., mice) or are presentation objects allowing the user to control the model object. [Firesmith]

controlling operand *n.* any operand in a call on a dispatching operation of a tagged type whose corresponding formal parameter is of the type or is of an anonymous access type with the designated type. [Ada95]

See also: DISPATCHING.

control manager *n.* the system object that maintains a list of screen views, allowing one to point to a view and interact with either the view itself or with information inside the view. [Smalltalk]

control object *n.* **1.** any object that encapsulates functionality specific to one or a few use cases in an information system. [Jacobson] **2.** any object that represents a set of tasks in a business. [Jacobson]

Contrast with: CONTROLLER OBJECT, ENTITY OBJECT, INTERFACE OBJECT.

Commentary: **1** The control objects model functionality that is not naturally tied to any other object. Typically such behavior consists of operating on several different entity objects, doing some computations, and then returning the result to an interface object. [Jacobson] **2** These tasks should be performed by one resource instance, which typically is a specialist or a routine worker, not dealing directly with the customer. [Jacobson]

conversion function *n.* any function that specifies a type conversion between a class object and another type. [C++]

Contrast with: CAST, CONSTRUCTOR.

Commentary: Conversion functions can do two things that cannot be specified by constructors:
– define a conversion from a class to a basic type;
– define a conversion from one class to another without modifying the declaration for the other class. [C++]

co-occurrence constraint *n.* any constraint that specifies the minimum and maximum number of times an object or combination of objects can co-occur in the relationships of a relationship set

with another object or combination of objects. [Embley]

Contrast with: OBJECT-CLASS CARDINALITY CONSTRAINT.

coordinator object *n.* any object that coordinates other objects by passing client requests to objects that can provide the associated services.

copy *v.* **-ed, -ing** to copy the contents of an existing object into those of another existing object. [Eiffel, Firesmith, Meyer]

Contrast with: CLONE.

Kinds:
• DEEP COPY
• SHALLOW COPY

• **deep copy** *v.* **-ed, -ing** to recursively copy an entire object into another existing object, starting at the source object and creating new objects as needed. [Eiffel, Firesmith, Meyer]

Antonym: SHALLOW COPY.

Contrast with: DEEP CLONE.

• **shallow copy** *v.* **-ed, -ing** to copy properties of the source object into the existing object as they appear. [Eiffel, Firesmith, Meyer]

Antonym: DEEP COPY.

Contrast with: SHALLOW CLONE.

copy constructor *n.* any constructor that makes a copy an object of its class. [C++, Firesmith]

Contrast with: DEFAULT CONSTRUCTOR.

Example: In C++:
```
X::X(const X&);
```

CORBA™ Facilities (CF) *n.* any collection of classes and objects that provide general purpose CORBA capabilities, commonly useful in many applications. [OMG]

Synonym: COMMMON FACILITIES.

Contrast with: APPLICATION FACILITIES.

Commentary: Common facilities are made available through OMA-compliant class interfaces. [OMG]

Kinds:
- HORIZONTAL COMMON FACILITIES
  - SYSTEM MANAGEMENT FACILITIES
- VERTICAL COMMON FACILITIES

- **horizontal common facilities** *n.* any CORBA facilities that include functions shared by many or most systems, regardless of application domain.
Examples: User interface, information management, systems management, task management.
Antonym: VERTICAL COMMON FACILITIES.

  - **system management facilities** *n.* any horizontal CORBA facilities that provide a set of interfaces that abstract basic system administration functions (e.g., control, monitoring, security management, configuration, and policy. [OMG]

- **vertical common facilities** *n.* any CORBA facilities that support a vertical market such as health care, retailing, CAD, or financial systems. [OMG]
Antonym: HORIZONTAL COMMON FACILITIES.

core class *n.* any essential class of model objects that captures a key abstraction of the application domain.
Synonyms: APPLICATION CLASS, BUSINESS CLASS, DOMAIN CLASS, KEY CLASS, MODEL CLASS.
Contrast with: CONTROLLER CLASS, KEY ABSTRACTION, PRESENTATION CLASS, SUPPORT CLASS, VIEW CLASS.

correct *adj.* describing any class that is consistent and whose every routine is check-correct, loop-correct and exception-correct. [Eiffel, Meyer]
Kinds:
- CHECK-CORRECT
- EXCEPTION-CORRECT
- LOOP-CORRECT

- **check-correct** *adj.* describing any effective routine r in which, for every Check instruction c in r, any execution of c (as part of an execution of r) satisfies all its assertions. [Eiffel, Meyer]
See also: EFFECTIVE ROUTINE.

- **exception-correct** *adj.* describing any routine satisfying the following conditions:
  - the rescue block must be such that any branch terminating with a Retry ensures the precondition and the invariant;
  - any other branch ensures the invariant. [Eiffel, Meyer]

- **loop-correct** *adj.* describing any routine in which the loops maintain their invariant and every iteration decreases the variant. [Eiffel, Meyer]

correctability *n.* the ease with which errors can be found and corrected in the software. [Firesmith]

correctness *n.* **1.** the degree to which software meets its specified requirements. [Firesmith] **2.** the degree to which requirements meet their associated needs. [Firesmith] **3.** the ability of a valid component to operate properly at runtime. [Eiffel, Meyer]

corruptible class *n.* any class providing no support for mutual exclusion in a concurrent environment. [Firesmith]
Contrast with: GUARDABLE CLASS, GUARDED CLASS.

corruptible object *n.* any object providing no support for mutual exclusion in a concurrent environment. [Firesmith]
Contrast with: GUARDABLE OBJECT, GUARDED OBJECT.

coterminous_with_procedure *adj.* describing an object that is created when the operation (a.k.a., procedure) is invoked and destroyed when the operation returns. [ODMG]

Contrast with: TRANSIENT.

coupling *n.* **1.** the degree to which one thing depends on another. [Firesmith, Wirfs-Brock] **2.** the amount of relationships and interactions between things (e.g., operations, objects, classes, clusters, and modules).

Contrast with: CLASS COHESION.

Commentary: Low coupling is desirable because it produces better encapsulation, maintainability, and extensibility with fewer objects needlessly affected during iteration. [Firesmith]

Kinds:
- ABSTRACT COUPLING
- AGGREGATION COUPLING
- CLASSIFICATION COUPLING
- EXCEPTION COUPLING
- FRIENDSHIP COUPLING
- IMPLEMENTATION COUPLING
- INHERITANCE COUPLING
- INTERFACE COUPLING
- INTERNAL COUPLING
- MESSAGE COUPLING
- OBJECT COUPLING

- **abstract coupling** *n.* any coupling dependency of a class on another abstract class.

- **aggregation coupling** *n.* **1.** any coupling dependency of an aggregate on its component parts. [Firesmith] **2.** any coupling dependency between component parts within an aggregate. [Firesmith]

  Example: An internal combustion engine is built from its component parts (e.g., pistons, spark plugs, valves), which in turn depend on one another for proper functioning. [Firesmith]

  Commentary: Whereas the aggregate depends on and is defined in terms of its component parts, the component parts should usually not depend on the aggregate. Definition 1 applies to all aggregates, whereas definition 2 applies to structures, but not to collections and containers. [Firesmith]

- **classification coupling** *n.* any coupling dependency of an instance on its class(s). [Firesmith]

  Commentary: The class usually does not depend on its instances. [Firesmith]

- **exception coupling** *n.* any coupling dependency of a client on its servers due to exception raising. [Firesmith]

- **friendship coupling** *n.* the high coupling dependency of any friend on the class that declares it a friend. [Firesmith]

- **implementation coupling** *n.* any coupling via features in the implementation. [Firesmith]

  Antonym: INTERFACE COUPLING.

  Example: Any implementation inheritance or coupling due to friends is an example of implementation coupling.

- **inheritance coupling** *n.* the coupling dependency of any new definition on its parent definitions due to the inheritance relationship between them. [Firesmith]

  Example: The coupling dependency of a child on its parent(s) is an example of inheritance coupling.

- **interface coupling** *n.* **1.** (a) any coupling via features in the interface. [Firesmith] (b) any coupling in which the client object only has direct access to features exported by the server object. [Berard] **2.** any interclass coupling via message passing. [Lorenz]

  Antonym: IMPLEMENTATION COUPLING, INTERNAL COUPLING.

  Example: Any coupling due to the

use of types in signatures is interface coupling.

Commentary: The client object specifically refers to the server object and makes direct references to one or more items contained in its public interface. The public interface of the server may contain items other than operations (method selectors) such as constants, variables, exportable definitions, and exceptions. [Berard]

- **internal coupling** *n.* any coupling in which the client object has direct access to the underlying implementation of the server object. [Berard]
  Antonym: INTERFACE COUPLING.

- **message coupling** *n.* the coupling dependency of a client on its servers due to message passing. Message coupling is measured in terms of the number of messages, the number of arguments in the messages, the type of message (e.g., asynchronous implies less coupling than synchronous), and the frequency of the messages. [Firesmith]
  See also: LAW OF DEMETER.

- **object coupling** *n.* the degree of interdependence between two objects (e.g., the number of messages, the frequency of messages, and the number of arguments making values visible to other objects). [Coad]
  Contrast with: CLASS COHESION.
  Commentary: Low coupling is desirable because it produces better encapsulation and fewer objects needlessly affected when making changes. [Coad]

course [of a use case] *n.* any generic series of interactions with actors that is part of the use case. [Jacobson]
See also: USE CASE.
Kinds:

- ALTERNATIVE COURSE
- BASIC COURSE

- **alternative course [of a use case]** *n.* any variant of a basic course, possibly including errors that can occur. [Jacobson]
  Antonym: BASIC COURSE.
  Commentary: Robustness is increased as more alternative courses are described (i.e., as the more sequences have been anticipated). [Jacobson]

- **basic course [of a use case]** *n.* the most common or important sequence in the use case that gives the best understanding of the use case. [Jacobson]
  Antonym: ALTERNATIVE COURSE.
  See also: USE CASE.
  Commentary: Variants of the basic course and errors that can occur are described in *alternative courses*. The basic course is always designed before the alternative courses. [Jacobson]

cover constraint *n.* the inheritance constraint which requires that the extent of the parent be a subset of the union of the extents of the children. [Firesmith]
Rationale: The term *cover* comes from set theory. [Firesmith]
Commentary: This constraint ensures that each instance of the parent is also an instance of at least one child. [Firesmith]

create accessor *n.* any accessor operation that creates a new instance of an object. [Shlaer/Mellor]
Synonyms: CONSTRUCTOR, CREATE OPERATION.
Antonym: DELETE ACCESSOR.
Contrast with: READ ACCESSOR, WRITE ACCESSOR.

create operation *n.* any operation that allocates storage for the representation of the object, assigns an OID, and re-

turns that OID as the value of the operation. [ODMG]
Synonyms: CONSTRUCTOR OPERATION, CREATE ACCESSOR.
Antonyms: DELETE ACCESSOR, DESTRUCTOR OPERATION.

creation instruction *n.* the principal mechanism used to produce new objects in Eiffel. [Eiffel, Meyer]
Contrast with: CLONING.

creation state *n.* any state in which an instance first comes into existence. [Shlaer/Mellor]
Synonym: INITIAL STATE.
Contrast with: CURRENT STATE, FINAL STATE.

creation type *n.* either the base type of the target or the optional type appearing in the creation instruction. [Eiffel, Meyer]

creational pattern *n.* any design pattern that is primarily concerned with instantiation. [Gamma, Helm, Johnson, and Vlissides]
Kinds:
- • CREATIONAL CLASS PATTERN
  - FACTORY METHOD
- • CREATIONAL OBJECT PATTERN
  - ABSTRACT FACTORY
  - BUILDER
  - PROTOTYPE
  - SINGLETON

• **creational class pattern** *n.* any creational design pattern that uses inheritance to vary the class that is instantiated. [Gamma, Helm, Johnson, and Vlissides]
  - **factory method [pattern]** *n.* the creational class design pattern that defines an interface for creating an object, but defers instantiation of the object to subclasses. [Gamma, Helm, Johnson, and Vlissides]

Synonym: VIRTUAL CONSTRUCTOR.

• **creational object pattern** *n.* any creational design pattern that delegates instantiation to another object. [Gamma, Helm, Johnson, and Vlissides]
Kinds:
  - ABSTRACT FACTORY
  - BUILDER
  - PROTOTYPE
  - SINGLETON

- **abstract factory [pattern]** *n.* the creational object design pattern that provides an interface for creating families of related or dependent objects without specifying their concrete classes. [Gamma, Helm, Johnson, and Vlissides]
Synonym: KIT.

- **builder [pattern]** *n.* the creational object design pattern that separates the instantiation of a complex object from its implementation so that the same instantiation process can be used to create different implementations. [Gamma, Helm, Johnson, and Vlissides]

- **prototype [pattern]** *n.* the creational object design pattern that creates new objects by copying a prototypical instance. [Gamma, Helm, Johnson, and Vlissides]

- **singleton [pattern]** *n.* the creational object design pattern that ensures that a class has only a single instance and also provides a global access point to the instance. [Gamma, Helm, Johnson, and Vlissides]

critical region *n.* any contiguous piece of code that is guaranteed to execute to completion without interruption. [Firesmith]

Current *n.* the Eiffel term for the pseudo-variable that refers to the current object. [Eiffel, Firesmith, Meyer]

Synonyms: SELF, THIS.

current name [of a given feature] *n.* the name of the feature in a specified class, which is defined as follows:

- the original name of the feature if the feature is not inherited (i.e., if the specified class is the class of origin.)
- the inherited name of the given feature if the feature is inherited and not renamed in the specified class.
- the new name if the given feature is inherited and renamed in the specified class. [Firesmith]

current object *n.* the object to which the latest noncompleted routine call applies at some time during execution. [Eiffel, Meyer]

Contrast with: CURRENT ROUTINE.

current routine *n.* the routine to which the latest noncompleted routine call applies at some time during execution. [Eiffel, Meyer]

Contrast with: CURRENT OBJECT.

current state *n.* any of the states an object or class currently is in. [Firesmith, Shlaer/Mellor]

Contrast with: CREATION STATE, FINAL STATE.

D

dangling link *n.* any link to an object that does not exist. [Firesmith]
Contrast with: ATTACHED LINK, VOID LINK.
Commentary: The link may be to an object that does not yet exist or to an object that no longer exists. Dangling links are common bugs in languages that support manual garbage collection. [Firesmith]
Kinds:
- DANGLING POINTER
- DANGLING REFERENCE

- **dangling pointer** *n.* any pointer that points to an object that does not exist. [Firesmith]
  Contrast with: ATTACHED POINTER, VOID POINTER.

- **dangling reference** *n.* any reference to an object that does not exist. [Firesmith]
  Contrast with: ATTACHED REFERENCE, VOID REFERENCE.

data abstraction *n.* any abstraction (i.e., model) of a characteristic, property, trait, quantity, or quality of some object or class. [Firesmith]
Contrast with: ABSTRACT DATA TYPE.

data dictionary *n.* **1.** any comprehensive dictionary defining all object-oriented entities (e.g., objects, classes, clusters, properties, operations, exceptions) in

an application. [Rumbaugh] **2.** any comprehensive dictionary defining all of the classes in an application. [Booch] **3.** any comprehensive dictionary defining all of the data in an application. **4.** any central repository of definitions of terms and concepts. [Coleman]
Synonyms: CLASS DICTIONARY, PROJECT DICTIONARY.
Commentary: The term *project dictionary* is less subject to misinterpretation. The term *data dictionary* has historically implied only data (i.e., attributes), and the term *class dictionary* may be interpreted too limitedly (e.g., definition **2**). [Firesmith]

data flow *n.* **1.** the flow of the values of properties within objects. [Firesmith] **2.** the flow of the parameters of messages between objects and classes. [Firesmith] **3.** the connection between the output of one object or process and the input of another. [Rumbaugh]
Antonym: CONTROL FLOW.
Commentary: Definition **3** does not clearly distinguish between data and control flow and between data and messages. [Firesmith]

data-flow diagram (DFD) *n.* any graphical representation of the functional model, showing dependencies between values and the computation of output values from input values without regard for when or if the functions are executed. [Rumbaugh]

Commentary: Rumbaugh and Shlaer/ Mellor are the main proponents of DFDs in the object community. DFDs have a very questionable reputation in the object community, with most other methodologists considering them inappropriate for use with objects. [Firesmith]

data-management (DM) component *n.* the component that contains objects that provide an interface between problem domain objects and a database or file management system. It provides two major capabilities: storing and restoring. [Coad]

See also: DM "OBJECT SERVER" OBJECT.

data model *n.* any model of a collection of entities, operators, and consistency rules. [OMG]

Contrast with: BEHAVIORAL MODEL, CONFIGURATION MODEL, DYNAMIC MODEL, FUNCTIONAL MODEL, INTERACTION MODEL, INTERFACE MODEL, LANGUAGE MODEL, LIFE-CYCLE MODEL, OBJECT MODEL, OPERATION MODEL, PRESENTATION MODEL, SEMANTIC MODEL, STATE MODEL, STRUCTURAL MODEL, USE-CASE MODEL.

data object *n.* any object used as an attribute. [Lorenz]

Synonym: ATTRIBUTE.

data store *n.* any passive object documented in a DFD that stores data for later access. [Rumbaugh]

data type *n.* any categorization of values or operation arguments, typically covering both behavior and representation (i.e., the traditional non-OO programming language notion of type). [OMG]

deactivate *v.* **-ed, -ing** to store a persis-

tent object in the database and delete it from active memory.

Antonym: ACTIVATE.

deactivation *n.* return of any persistent object to the database and deletion of it from active memory. [Firesmith, OMG]

Antonym: ACTIVATION.

deadlock *n.* the situation in which two or more concurrent threads (e.g., objects, operations) are waiting on each other to execute so that neither can execute. [Firesmith]

declaration *n.* **1.** any line of code that introduces one or more names into a program and specifies the types of the names (which determines how those names are to be interpreted). [C++, Firesmith] **2.** any language construct that associates a name with a view of an entity. [Ada95]

Contrast with: CLASS, DEFINITION, IDENTIFIER, NAME, TYPE.

Commentary: Although declarations specify the interpretation given to each identifier; they do not usually reserve storage associated with the identifier. [C++, Firesmith]

Kinds:

- CLASS DECLARATION
- EXPLICIT DECLARATION
- HOMOGRAPH DECLARATIONS
- IMPLICIT DECLARATION

- **class declaration** *n.* the complete specification of the interfaces provided by a class. [C++]

Synonym: CLASS SPECIFIER.

Commentary: A class declaration introduces a new type. A class declaration introduces the class name into the scope where it is declared and hides any class, object, function, or other declaration of that name in an enclosing scope. C++ provides a single declaration for a class that acts as the interface to both users and implementors of the member functions. There is no direct support for the notions of interface definition and implementation module. [C++]

- **explicit declaration** *n.* any declaration that appears explicitly in the program text. [Ada95]
  Antonym: IMPLICIT DECLARATION.
  See also: OVERRIDE.

- **homograph [declarations]** *n.* any two declarations that have the same defining name and whose profiles are type conformant if both are overloadable. [Ada95]
  Commentary: An inner declaration hides any outer homograph from direct visibility. [Ada95]

- **implicit declaration** *n.* any declaration that does not appear explicitly in the program text, but rather implicitly occurs at a given place in the text as a consequence of the semantics of another construct. [Ada95]
  Antonym: EXPLICIT DECLARATION.
  Commentary: Implicit declarations are typically those inherited in a derived type.

declarator *n.* anything that declares a single object, function, or type, within a declaration. [C++]
Contrast with: DECLARATION.

declared type *n.* the type given by the associated declaration or redeclaration. [Eiffel, Firesmith, Meyer]

declaring class [of a given feature] *n.* the origin class in which the given feature was originally declared. [Firesmith]
Example: The class in which the signature of the given operation first appeared. [Firesmith]

decorator [pattern] *n.* the structural object design pattern that dynamically attaches additional responsibilities to an object.

[Gamma, Helm, Johnson, and Vlissides]
Synonym: WRAPPER.

deep clone *v. -ed, -ing* to recursively clone an entire object, starting at the source object and creating new objects as needed. [Eiffel, Firesmith, Meyer]
Antonym: SHALLOW CLONE.
Contrast with: DEEP COPY.
Commentary: Deep cloning usually has slower performance than shallow cloning because more creating and copying is usually required. [Firesmith]

deep copy *v. -ed, -ing* to recursively copy an entire object into an existing object, starting at the source object and creating new objects as needed. [Eiffel, Firesmith, Meyer]
Antonym: SHALLOW COPY.
Contrast with: DEEP CLONE.

deep equal objects *n.* any objects OX and OY that satisfy the following three conditions:

- the objects obtained by setting all the reference fields of OX and OY (if any) to void references are equal;
- for every void reference field of OX, the corresponding field of OY is void;
- for every non-void reference field of OX, attached to an object PX, the corresponding field of OY is attached to an object PY, and it is possible (recursively) to show, under the assumption that OX is deep equal to OY, that PX is deep equal to PY. [Eiffel, Meyer]

Antonym: SHALLOW EQUAL OBJECTS.

deep equal references *n.* any references that are either both void or attached to deep-equal objects. [Eiffel, Meyer]
Antonym: SHALLOW EQUAL REFERENCES.

default constructor *n.* any constructor that can be called without arguments. [C++, Firesmith]
Contrast with: COPY CONSTRUCTOR.

Examples: In C++:
```
X::X();
X::X(int=0);
```
Commentary: A default constructor may have default arguments. [C++, Firesmith]

deferment *n.* any design strategy in which designers specify deferred features that must be supplied by derived classes before instantiation. [Firesmith]
Commentary: Deferment is used to impose a degree of uniformity on derived classes to make effective use of polymorphism. [Firesmith, Shlaer/Mellor]

deferred class *n.* **1.** any abstract class that declares the existence of one or more features (e.g., attributes, operations) that must be implemented by its descendants prior to instantiation. [Firesmith] **2.** any base class that declares the existence of one or more features (e.g., attributes, operations) that must be implemented by its derived classes prior to instantiation. [C++, Henderson-Sellers]
Contrast with: ABSTRACT CLASS, CONCRETE CLASS, EFFECTIVE CLASS.
Commentary: All deferred classes are abstract, but all abstract classes need not be deferred because an abstract class need not declare any feature(s) as deferred (i.e., missing implementations). Although the human designer may know that such abstract classes are incomplete abstractions, the compiler does not understand the application domain and therefore requires the clues provided by a deferred class. A deferred class should be used if one or more polymorphic features are required to implement a complete abstraction. [Firesmith] Deferred classes describe a group of implementations of an abstract data type rather the just a single imple-

mentation. A deferred class describes an incompletely implemented abstraction, which its proper descendants will use as a basis for further refinement. Declare a class deferred if you plan to include one or more features that are specified but not implemented, with the expectation that proper descendants of the class will provide the implementations. A class that is declared deferred but has no deferred features is invalid. [Eiffel, Meyer]
Kinds:
- FULLY DEFERRED CLASS
- PARTIALLY DEFERRED CLASS

• **fully deferred class** *n.* any deferred class, all of whose features are deferred. [Eiffel, Firesmith, Meyer]
Antonym: PARTIALLY DEFERRED CLASS.

• **partially deferred class** *n.* any deferred class, some of whose features are effective (i.e., not deferred).
Antonym: FULLY DEFERRED CLASS.

deferred feature *n.* any feature that does *not* have a complete implementation. [Eiffel, Firesmith, Meyer]
Antonym: EFFECTIVE FEATURE.
Commentary: A *deferred feature* must be made effective in a descendant before that descendant may be instantiated.
Kinds:
- DEFERRED METHOD
- DEFERRED OPERATION
- DEFERRED PROPERTY
- DEFERRED ROUTINE

• **deferred method** *n.* any incomplete method that therefore does not implement a complete functional abstraction and that must therefore be made effective prior to execution. [Firesmith]
Antonym: CONCRETE METHOD.
Commentary: A deferred method often has preconditions and postconditions defined, but may include a TBD

(i.e., to be determined) statement or be missing its executable statements. Deferred methods are used during analysis and design, but must be made effective prior to execution. [Firesmith]

• **deferred operation** *n.* **1.** any operation that is declared but does not have an associated method (i.e., implementation). [Firesmith] **2.** the operation that supplies the implementation missing in its associated deferring operation. [Shlaer/Mellor]
Synonym: 1 DEFERRED ROUTINE, PURE VIRTUAL MEMBER FUNCTION. [C++] 2 EFFECTIVE OPERATION.
Antonym: EFFECTIVE OPERATION.
Contrast with: 2 DEFERRING OPERATION.
Rationale: The implementation of the operation is deferred until the descendant supplies the implementation. [Firesmith]
Commentary: All deferred operations must be made effective in a descendant before the descendant may be instantiated. An implementation of the deferred operation must be included (either directly or indirectly via inheritance) in any concrete derived class that encapsulates the operation. [Firesmith]

• **deferred property** *n.* any property that does not have an associated type. [Firesmith]
Antonym: EFFECTIVE PROPERTY.

• **deferred routine** *n.* any routine that is declared as deferred, meaning that the class introducing it only gives its specification, leaving it for descendants to provide implementations. [Eiffel, Meyer]
Synonym: DEFERRED OPERATION.
Antonym: EFFECTIVE ROUTINE.

deferred synchronous request *n.* any re-quest in which the client does not wait for completion of the request, but does intend to accept results later. [OMG]
Contrast with: ASYNCHRONOUS REQUEST, ONE-WAY REQUEST, SYNCHRONOUS MESSAGE, SYNCHRONOUS REQUEST.

deferring operation *n.* any operation that is declared, but not implemented, in an abstract class. [Shlaer/Mellor]
Synonym: DEFERRED OPERATION.
Contrast with: DEFERRED OPERATION.
Commentary: An implementation of the deferring operation must be included (either directly or indirectly via inheritance) in any concrete derived class that encapsulates the operation. [Shlaer/Mellor]

definite subtype *n.* any subtype that provides enough information to create an object without an additional constraint or explicit initial expression. [Ada95]
Antonym: INDEFINITE SUBTYPE.
Examples: All elementary subtypes are definite subtypes. [Ada95]

definition *n.* the specification of the implementation of something.
Contrast with: DECLARATION
Commentary: Although declarations can be repeated, there must be exactly one definition of each object, function, class, and enumerator used in a program. [C++]

• **inline definition** *n.* any definition of a member function in the class declaration [C++]

delayed binding *n.* any binding that takes place at run-time after the message is received due to compile-time ambiguities caused by inheritance and polymorphism. [Booch, Coad, Firesmith, Jacobson, Martin/Odell, OMG]
Synonyms: DYNAMIC BINDING, LATE BINDING, RUN-TIME BINDING, VIRTUAL BINDING.
Antonyms: COMPILE-TIME BINDING, EAR-

LY BINDING, STATIC BINDING.
See also: DYNAMICALLY TAGGED.
Commentary: Delayed binding allows the system to dynamically decide what method to use, based on the type of the current object. [Firesmith, Lorenz] Delayed binding of operations is typically implemented via a virtual method table. The term *dynamic binding* is preferred. [Firesmith]

delegate *v. -ed, -ing* **1.** to subcontract all or part of one's responsibilities to one or more server objects via message passing. [Firesmith] **2.** in classless languages that support prototypes instead of inheritance, to forward messages from one's clients to one's associated prototype object (which acts as one's class) for execution on one's behalf by operations of one's prototype. [Firesmith] **3.** to transfer responsibility for a subsystem contract to a class within the subsystem for actual implementation. [Wirfs-Brock]
Contrast with: INHERIT.

delegation *n.* **1.** the implementation technique whereby an object or operation subcontracts all or part of its responsibilities to one or more server objects via message passing. [Booch, Firesmith, Lorenz] **2.** in classless languages that support prototypes instead of inheritance, the forwarding of messages from one's clients to one's associated prototype object (which acts as one's class) for execution on one's behalf by operations of one's prototype. [Firesmith, Rumbaugh] **3.** the transfer of responsibility for a subsystem contract to a class within the subsystem for actual implementation. [Wirfs-Brock] **4.** the ability of an operation to send a message in such a way that self-reference in the operation performing the request

returns the same object(s) as self-reference in the operation sending the message. [OMG] **5.** any object-object inheritance that transfers the *state* of one object to another. [Martin/Odell]
Synonyms: **5** OBJECT-OBJECT INHERITANCE.
Contrast with: CLASS, INHERITANCE, SELF-REFERENCE.
Commentary: Unlike inheritance, which typically uses a virtual method table for operation resolution, delegation uses a chain of instance pointers to perform binding of messages to operations. [Firesmith, Rumbaugh]

delete *v. -ed, -ing* to remove an object from the database, free the storage used by its representation, and remove it from any relationships in which it participated. [Firesmith]

delete accessor *n.* any accessor operation that deletes an instance of an object. [Shlaer/Mellor]
Synonyms: DELETE OPERATION, DELETE OPERATOR, DESTRUCTOR.
Antonym: CREATE ACCESSOR.
Contrast with: READ ACCESSOR, WRITE ACCESSOR.

delete operation *n.* any operation that removes an object from the database, frees the storage used by its representation, and removes it from any relationships in which it participated. [Firesmith, ODMG]
Synonyms: DELETE ACCESSOR, DELETE OPERATOR.
Contrast with: DESTRUCTOR, DESTRUCTOR OPERATION.
Commentary: The OID of a deleted object is not reused. [Firesmith, ODMG]

delete operator *n.* the operator that destroys an object created by the new operator. [C++]

Synonyms: DELETE ACCESSOR, DELETE OPERATION, DESTRUCTOR.
Contrast with: NEW OPERATOR.

Denotable_Object *n.* the root type of the hierarchy of object types. [ODMG]

depend *v.* *-ed, -ing* any class C is said to depend on a class A if one of the following holds:
– C is an heir of A;
– C is a client of A;
– recursively, there is a class B such that C depends on B and B depends on A. [Eiffel, Meyer]

dependency [relationship] *n.* **1.** the client/server relationship representing reliance of the client on the server. [Firesmith] **2.** the object-oriented analog of coupling in structured design. [Shlaer/Mellor]
Examples: Message passing in which the client sends messages to the server, aggregation in which the aggregate (client) depends on its component parts (servers) for its definition, inheritance in which the derived class (client) depends on its base classes (servers) for its inherited features. [Firesmith]
Commentary: Dependency implies coupling, visibility, and reference. Dependency relationships usually imply message passing. [Firesmith]
Kinds:
• IMPLEMENTATION DEPENDENCY
• INTERFACE DEPENDENCY
• METHOD DEPENDENCY

• **implementation dependency** *n.* any dependency of the implementation (but not the interface) of the client on its server(s). [Firesmith]
Contrast with: INTERFACE DEPENDENCY, METHOD DEPENDENCY.
Example: A with clause in an Ada package body creates an implementa-

tion dependency. [Firesmith]
Commentary: Implementation dependency implies that the interface of the server is visible to only those features in the implementation of the client. [Firesmith]

• **interface dependency** *n.* any dependency of the interface (as well as the implementation) of the client on its server(s). [Firesmith]
Contrast with: IMPLEMENTATION DEPENDENCY, METHOD DEPENDENCY.
Examples: The use of types in signatures and a with clause in an Ada package specification both create interface dependencies. [Firesmith]
Commentary: Interface dependency implies that the interface of the server is visible to every feature of the client. [Firesmith]

• **method dependency** *n.* any dependency of only a single specified method of the client on its server(s). [Firesmith]
Contrast with: IMPLEMENTATION DEPENDENCY, INTERFACE DEPENDENCY.
Examples: A with clause in an Ada subprogram body creates a method dependency. [Firesmith]

dependency diagram *n.* any diagram that depicts the client/server (invocation) and friend relationships that hold between the classes. [Shlaer/Mellor]

dependent [object of a given object] *n.* **1.** any object that is either directly or indirectly visible to and referenced by the current object at some time during execution. [Firesmith] **2.** the dependents of an object are the object itself and (recursively) the dependents of its direct dependents. [Eiffel, Meyer] **3.** any access object that has been declared as a dependent of another object. [Smalltalk]

See also: DEPENDENCY.
Kinds:
- DIRECT DEPENDENT
- INDIRECT DEPENDENT

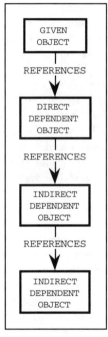

Dependent Objects

- **direct dependent** *n.* **1.** any object that is explicitly visible to and referenced by the current object at some time during execution. [Firesmith] **2.** the direct dependents of an object O, at some time during the execution of a system, are the objects attached to the reference field of O. [Eiffel, Meyer] *Antonym:* INDIRECT DEPENDENT.
- **indirect dependent** *n.* any object that is either a direct dependent of a direct dependent or recursively a direct dependent of an indirect dependent. [Firesmith]

Antonym: DIRECT DEPENDENT.

dependsOn association *n.* any association from one subsystem to another that means that objects in the first subsystem will use, in some way, objects in the second subsystem. [Jacobson]

derivation class *n.* any class that is not defined by the language but that is instead derived from another class. [Ada95] *Synonym:* DERIVED CLASS.

derived association *n.* (a) any association that is defined in terms of other associations. [Firesmith, Rumbaugh] (b) any association of derived links. [Firesmith] *Antonym:* BASE ASSOCIATION. *Contrast with:* BASE LINK. *See also:* DERIVED LINK.

derived attribute *n.* any attribute that is calculated in terms of other properties. A derived attribute is calculated by an operation rather than stored. [Firesmith, Rumbaugh] *Antonym:* BASE ATTRIBUTE. *Example:* Age can be calculated from date of birth and current date. [Firesmith]

derived class *n.* (a) the C++ term for any descendant class of the given class. [Firesmith] (b) any class that inherits from one or more base classes. [C++] *Synonym:* DERIVATION CLASS, DESCENDANT CLASS, SUBCLASS. *Antonym:* BASE CLASS. *Rationale:* The term *derived* was chosen over the term *subclass* because the term *subclass* is often confusing and ambiguous as it might imply either inheritance or aggregation. [Firesmith] *Commentary:* The derived class can override virtual functions of its bases and declare additional data members, functions and so on. A pointer to a derived class may be implicitly converted to a pointer to a base class, but a pointer to a base class may not be implicitly converted to point to a derived class. [C++, Firesmith]

Kinds:
- DIRECT DERIVED CLASS
- INDIRECT DERIVED CLASS

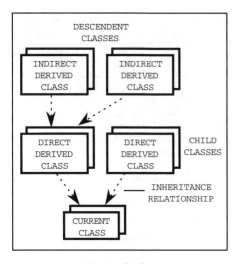

Derived Class

- **direct derived class [of a given class]** *n.* (a) the C++ term for any child class of the given class. [Firesmith] (b) any derived class that is immediately derived via inheritance from a given class. [C++]

Synonyms: CHILD CLASS, DIRECT SUPERCLASS, HEIR CLASS.

Antonyms: INDIRECT DERIVED CLASS, INDIRECT SUBCLASS.

Commentary: A direct derived class of a given class is a descendant class that is also a child descendant class. [Firesmith]

- **indirect derived class [of a given class]** *n.* (a) the C++ term for any derived class that is indirectly derived

via intermediate base classes from a given class. [Firesmith] (b) any derived class that is indirectly derived via intermediate base classes from a given class. [C++]

Synonyms: ANCESTOR CLASS, INDIRECT SUPERCLASS.

Antonyms: DIRECT DERIVED CLASS, INDIRECT BASE CLASS.

Contrast with: DESCENDANT CLASS.

Commentary: An indirect derived class of a given class is a descendant class that is not a child class. [Firesmith]

derived link *n.* (a) any indirect link that is the product of other links. [Firesmith] (b) any instance of a derived association. [Firesmith]

Antonym: BASE LINK.

Contrast with: DERIVED ASSOCIATION.

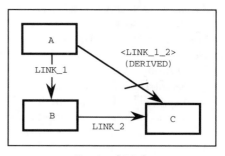

Derived Link

derived operation *n.* any operation that is directly executed by calls to other operations.

Antonym: BASE OPERATION.

derived relationship *n.* any relationship defined in terms of other relationships. [Coleman, Firesmith]

Antonym: BASE RELATIONSHIP.

Kinds:
- DERIVED ASSOCIATION
- DERIVED LINK

- **derived association** *n.* (a) any association that is defined in terms of other associations. [Firesmith, Rumbaugh] (b) any association of derived links. [Firesmith]
  Antonym: BASE ASSOCIATION.
  Contrast with: BASE LINK.
- **derived link** *n.* **1.** any indirect link that is the product of other links. [Firesmith] **2.** any instance of a derived association. [Firesmith]
  Antonym: BASE LINK.
  Contrast with: DERIVED ASSOCIATION.

derived type *n.* **1.** the C++ term for any subtype that is derived from a base type. [C++, Firesmith] **2.** the Ada95 term for any new, incompatible type that is derived from another type. [Ada95]
Synonyms: CHILD TYPE, DESCENDANT TYPE, SUBTYPE.
Antonyms: ANCESTOR TYPE, BASE TYPE, PARENT TYPE, SUPERTYPE.
Contrast with: DERIVED CLASS.
See also: TYPE EXTENSION.
Commentary: **2** Each class containing the parent type also contains the derived type. The derived type inherits properties such as components and primitive operations from the parent. A type together with the types derived from it (directly or indirectly) form a derivation class. [Ada95]

descendant class [of a given class] *n.* **1.** any class that inherits, either directly or indirectly, from the given class. [Firesmith, Jacobson, Rumbaugh] **2.** Class B is a descendant of class A if and only if A is an ancestor of B, in other words if B is A or (recursively) a descendant of one of its heirs. [Eiffel]
Synonym: **1** DERIVED CLASS, SUBCLASS.
Antonym: ANCESTOR, BASE CLASS, SUPERCLASS.

Commentary: Definition **1** follows the normal usage of the word and does not allow a class to be its own descendant, especially because a class cannot inherit from itself. However, definition **2** allows a class to be its own descendant. [Firesmith]

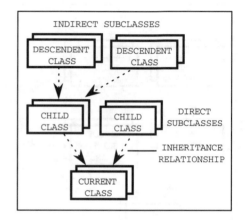

Descendant Class

Kinds:
- BEHAVIORALLY COMPATIBLE DESCENDANT
- CHILD
  - REPEATED CHILD CLASS
- DIRECT DESCENDANT
- INDIRECT DESCENDANT
- PROPER DESCENDANT
- REPEATED DESCENDANT

- **behaviorally compatible descendant** *n.* any descendant that can be used anywhere that its ancestors can. [Firesmith, Jacobson]
  Contrast with: SUBTYPE.
- **child [class of a given class]** *n.* any class that is directly derived via inheritance from the given class. [Firesmith]
  Synonyms: DIRECT DERIVED CLASS, DIRECT DESCENDANT, DIRECT SUBCLASS,

HEIR CLASS, IMMEDIATE DERIVED CLASS, IMMEDIATE DESCENDANT, IMMEDIATE SUBCLASS.
Antonyms: DIRECT ANCESTOR, DIRECT BASE CLASS, DIRECT SUPERCLASS, IMMEDIATE ANCESTOR, IMMEDIATE BASE CLASS, IMMEDIATE SUPERCLASS, PARENT.
Contrast with: CHILD TYPE.

DESCENDANT, IMMEDIATE SUBCLASS.
Antonyms: DIRECT ANCESTOR, DIRECT BASE CLASS, DIRECT SUPERCLASS, IMMEDIATE ANCESTOR, IMMEDIATE BASE CLASS, IMMEDIATE SUPERCLASS, PARENT.
Contrast with: ANCESTOR, BASE CLASS, DERIVED CLASS, SUBCLASS, SUPERCLASS.

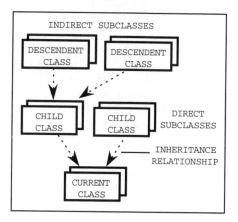

Child Class

Commentary: The given class is called the *parent* class of the child class. This term is simpler, more intuitive, and more popular than its synonyms. [Firesmith]

- **repeated child class [of a given class]** *n.* any child class that multiply inherits from a given parent class. [Eiffel, Firesmith, Meyer]
  Synonym: REPEATED HEIR CLASS.
  Antonym: REPEATED PARENT CLASS.

• **direct descendant [class of a given class]** *n.* any descendant that inherits directly from the given class. [Firesmith, Jacobson]
  Synonyms: CHILD, DIRECT DERIVED CLASS, DIRECT SUBCLASS, HEIR CLASS, IMMEDIATE DERIVED CLASS, IMMEDIATE

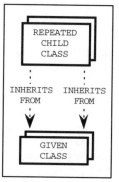

Repeated Child Class

• **indirect descendant [class of a given class]** *n.* any descendant that inherits indirectly from the given class via intermediate classes. [Firesmith]
  Synonyms: DIRECT ANCESTOR, DIRECT BASE CLASS, DIRECT SUPERCLASS, IMMEDIATE ANCESTOR, IMMEDIATE BASE CLASS, IMMEDIATE SUPERCLASS, PARENT.
  Antonyms: CHILD, DIRECT DERIVED CLASS, DIRECT SUBCLASS, HEIR CLASS, IMMEDIATE DERIVED CLASS, IMMEDIATE DESCENDANT, IMMEDIATE SUBCLASS.
  Commentary: An indirect descendant of a given class is a descendant class that is not a child class. [Firesmith]

• **proper descendant [of a given class]** *n.* any descendants other than the given class itself. [Eiffel]
  Antonym: PROPER ANCESTOR.

- **repeated descendant [of a given class]** *n.* any descendant that multiply inherits from a given ancestor class. [Eiffel, Firesmith, Meyer]
Antonym: REPEATED ANCESTOR.

descendant type [of a given type] *n.* **1.** any type that inherits, either directly or indirectly, from the given type. [Firesmith] **2.** any class-wide type that is either the same as the given type or that is derived, either directly or indirectly, from the given type. [Ada95]
Synonyms: DERIVED TYPE, SUBTYPE.
Antonyms: ANCESTOR, BASE TYPE, SUPERTYPE.
Contrast with: CHILD TYPE, PARENT TYPE.
Kinds:
  - CHILD
    - REPEATED CHILD
  - DIRECT DESCENDANT
  - INDIRECT DESCENDANT
  - REPEATED DESCENDANT

- **child [type of a given type]** *n.* any type that is directly derived via inheritance from the given type. [Firesmith]
Synonyms: DIRECT DERIVED TYPE, DIRECT DESCENDANT, DIRECT SUBTYPE, HEIR TYPE, IMMEDIATE DERIVED TYPE, IMMEDIATE DESCENDANT, IMMEDIATE SUBTYPE.
Antonyms: DIRECT ANCESTOR, DIRECT BASE TYPE, DIRECT SUPERTYPE, IMMEDIATE ANCESTOR, IMMEDIATE BASE TYPE, IMMEDIATE SUPERTYPE, PARENT.
Contrast with: CHILD CLASS.
Commentary: The given type is called the *parent* type of the child type. This term is preferred because it is simpler, more intuitive, and more popular than its synonyms. [Firesmith]
  - **repeated child [type of a given type]** *n.* any child type that multiply inherits from the given parent type. [Firesmith]
Antonym: REPEATED PARENT TYPE.

- **direct descendant [type of a given type]** *n.* any descendant type that inherits directly from the given type. [Firesmith]
Synonyms: CHILD TYPE, DIRECT DERIVED TYPE, DIRECT SUBTYPE.
Antonym: INDIRECT ANCESTOR TYPE, INDIRECT DERIVED TYPE, INDIRECT SUPERTYPE.
Commentary: A direct descendant of a given type is a descendant type that is also a child type. [Firesmith]

- **indirect descendant [class of a given class]** *n.* any descendant type that inherits indirectly from the given type via intermediate types. [Firesmith]
Synonyms: INDIRECT DERIVED TYPE, INDIRECT SUBTYPE.
Antonym: DIRECT ANCESTOR TYPE, DIRECT DESCENDANT, DIRECT DERIVED TYPE, DIRECT SUPERTYPE.
Commentary: An indirect descendant of a given type is a descendant type that is not a child type. [Firesmith]

- **repeated descendant [of a given type]** *n.* any descendant type that multiply inherits from the given ancestor type. [Firesmith]
Antonym: REPEATED ANCESTOR.

descriptive attribute *n.* any attribute that provides facts intrinsic to each instance of the object. [Shlaer/Mellor]
Examples: The altitude, latitude, and longitude of an airplane, the current and desired state of a valve, and the address and salary of an employee are all descriptive attributes.

descriptor class *n.* any standard class used by a language environment to store useful information about classes.

Commentary: Compilers may then allocate one object (a.k.a., the descriptor object) of the descriptor class for each class in the program. The compiler can then provide an operation that, when applied to a given object, will return a pointer to the descriptor object for the class of the given object.

descriptor object *n.* any instance of the descriptor class that stores useful information about its associated class.

Commentary: Compilers may then allocate one object (a.k.a., the descriptor object) of the descriptor class for each class in the program. The compiler can then provide an operation that, when applied to a given object, will return a pointer the descriptor object for the class of the given object.

Design by Contract *n.* Bertrand Meyer's design method, which views software construction as based on contracts between clients (callers) and suppliers (routines), relying on mutual obligations and advantages made explicit by the associated assertions (e.g., invariants, preconditions, and postconditions). [Firesmith, Meyer]

design-class diagram *n.* any key-abstraction diagram that has been updated during design. [Booch]

Contrast with: CLASS-CATEGORY DIAGRAM, INHERITANCE DIAGRAM, KEY-ABSTRACTION DIAGRAM.

design component *n.* any set of object types that implements a cohesive set of functionality. [OADSIG]

design modeling *n.* the activity that produces rigorous specifications of the interfaces provided by a set of object types. The purpose of design modeling is to specify the external view of a set of object types. [OADSIG]

design module *n.* any design component consisting of a collection of design components that are integrated together. [OADSIG]

design model object type *n.* any object type that is used in a design model. [OADSIG]

design pattern *n.* any pattern that systematically names, motivates, and explains a general design that addresses a recurring design problem in OO systems. [Gamma, Helm, Johnson, and Vlissides]

Commentary: A design pattern describes the problem, a solution to the problem consisting of a general arrangement of objects and classes, when to apply the solution, and the consequences of applying the solution. It should also give implementation hints and examples. [Gamma, Helm, Johnson, and Vlissides] The term *design* may be too restrictive because although patterns deal with architectural issues, they can also be used during requirements analysis. [Firesmith]

Kinds:
- BEHAVIORAL PATTERN
  - BEHAVIORAL CLASS PATTERN
    + INTERPRETER
    + TEMPLATE METHOD
  - BEHAVIORAL OBJECT PATTERN
    + CHAIN OF RESPONSIBILITY
    + COMMAND
    + ITERATOR
    + MEDIATOR
    + MEMENTO
    + OBSERVER
    + STATE
    + STRATEGY
    + VISITOR
- CREATIONAL PATTERN

- CREATIONAL CLASS PATTERN
  + FACTORY METHOD
- CREATIONAL OBJECT PATTERN
  + ABSTRACT FACTORY
  + BUILDER
  + PROTOTYPE
  + SINGLETON
- • STRUCTURAL PATTERN
  - STRUCTURAL CLASS PATTERN
    + ADAPTER
  - STRUCTURAL OBJECT PATTERN
    + ADAPTER
    + BRIDGE
    + COMPOSITE
    + DECORATOR
    + FACADE
    + FLYWEIGHT
    + PROXY

• **behavioral pattern** *n.* any design pattern that is primarily concerned with behavior, the assignment of responsibilities among objects, and the patterns of collaboration between objects. [Gamma, Helm, Johnson, and Vlissides]
Kinds:
- BEHAVIORAL CLASS PATTERN
  + INTERPRETER
  + TEMPLATE METHOD
- BEHAVIORAL OBJECT PATTERN
  + CHAIN OF RESPONSIBILITY
  + COMMAND
  + ITERATOR
  + MEDIATOR
  + MEMENTO
  + OBSERVER
  + STATE
  + STRATEGY
  + VISITOR

- **behavioral class pattern** *n.* any behavioral design pattern that uses inheritance to distribute behavior among classes. [Gamma, Helm,

Johnson, and Vlissides]
Kinds:
  + INTERPRETER
  + TEMPLATE METHOD

+ **interpreter [pattern]** *n.* the behavioral class design pattern that models a grammar as a class hierarchy and implements an interpreter as an operation on instances of grammar classes. [Gamma, Helm, Johnson, and Vlissides]

+ **template method [pattern]** *n.* the behavioral class design pattern that models an abstract algorithm in which each step invokes either an abstract or primitive algorithm. [Gamma, Helm, Johnson, and Vlissides]

- **behavioral object pattern** *n.* any behavioral design pattern that uses aggregation to distribute behavior among objects. [Gamma, Helm, Johnson, and Vlissides]
Kinds:
  + CHAIN OF RESPONSIBILITY
  + COMMAND
  + ITERATOR
  + MEDIATOR
  + MEMENTO
  + OBSERVER
  + STATE
  + STRATEGY
  + VISITOR

+ **chain of responsibility [pattern]** *n.* the behavioral object design pattern that allows messages to be implicitly sent to an object via a chain of intermediate objects that may either fulfill the associated responsibility or further delegate it down the chain. [Gamma, Helm, Johnson, and Vlissides]

+ **command [pattern]** *n.* the be-

havioral object design pattern that objectifies a request as an object, thereby allowing clients to be parameterized with different requests. [Gamma, Helm, Johnson, and Vlissides]
Synonym: ACTION, TRANSACTION.

+ **iterator [pattern]** *n.* the behavioral object design pattern that provides a way to sequentially access the components of an aggregate without exposing its underlying implementation. [Gamma, Helm, Johnson, and Vlissides]
Synonym: CURSOR.

+ **mediator [pattern]** *n.* the behavioral object design pattern that avoids unnecessary coupling between collaborating objects by introducing a mediator object between them. [Gamma, Helm, Johnson, and Vlissides]

+ **memento [pattern]** *n.* the behavioral object design pattern that objectifies another object's encapsulated state so that the other object can be later returned to that state. [Gamma, Helm, Johnson, and Vlissides]
Synonym: TOKEN.

+ **observer [pattern]** *n.* the behavioral object design pattern that allows one object to notify its dependents when it changes state so that they can be updated. [Gamma, Helm, Johnson, and Vlissides]
Synonym: DEPENDENTS, PUBLISH-SUBSCRIBE.
Example: Smalltalk's model/view/controller user interface framework.

+ **state [pattern]** *n.* the behavioral object design pattern that stores state as an encapsulated pointer to instances of subclasses of a state class. [Gamma, Helm, Johnson, and Vlissides]
Commentary: This pattern uses inheritance and polymorphism to eliminate the need for case statements based on state as well as the need for most state-based preconditions and postconditions.

+ **strategy [pattern]** *n.* the behavioral object design pattern that defines and encapsulates a family of objectified algorithms, allowing the algorithms to vary independently of the clients that use them. [Gamma, Helm, Johnson, and Vlissides]

+ **visitor [pattern]** *n.* the behavioral object design pattern that encapsulates behavior that would otherwise be distributed across classes by allowing a visitor object to traverse an object structure, visiting each node. [Gamma, Helm, Johnson, and Vlissides]

• **creational pattern** *n.* any design pattern that is primarily concerned with instantiation. [Gamma, Helm, Johnson, and Vlissides]
Kinds:
  - CREATIONAL CLASS PATTERN
    + FACTORY METHOD
  - CREATIONAL OBJECT PATTERN
    + ABSTRACT FACTORY
    + BUILDER
    + PROTOTYPE
    + SINGLETON

- **creational class pattern** *n.* any creational design pattern that uses inheritance to vary the class that is instantiated. [Gamma, Helm, Johnson, and Vlissides]

Kinds:

+ FACTORY METHOD

+ **factory method [pattern]** *n.* the creational class design pattern that defines an interface for creating an object, but defers instantiation of the object to subclasses. [Gamma, Helm, Johnson, and Vlissides]

Synonym: VIRTUAL CONSTRUCTOR.

- **creational object pattern** *n.* any creational design pattern that delegates instantiation to another object. [Gamma, Helm, Johnson, and Vlissides]

Kinds:

+ ABSTRACT FACTORY

+ BUILDER

+ PROTOTYPE

+ SINGLETON

+ **abstract factory [pattern]** *n.* the creational object design pattern that provides an interface for creating families of related or dependent objects without specifying their concrete classes. [Gamma, Helm, Johnson, and Vlissides]

Synonym: KIT.

+ **builder [pattern]** *n.* the creational object design pattern that separates the instantiation of a complex object from its implementation so that the same instantiation process can be used to create different implementations. [Gamma, Helm, Johnson, and Vlissides]

+ **prototype [pattern]** *n.* the creational object design pattern that creates new objects by copying a prototypical instance. [Gamma, Helm, Johnson, and Vlissides]

+ **singleton [pattern]** *n.* the cre-

ational object design pattern that ensures that a class has only a single instance and also provides a global access point to the instance. [Gamma, Helm, Johnson, and Vlissides]

• **structural pattern** *n.* any design pattern that is primarily concerned with how larger structures are composed out of classes and objects. [Gamma, Helm, Johnson, and Vlissides]

Kinds:

- STRUCTURAL CLASS PATTERN

  + ADAPTER

- STRUCTURAL OBJECT PATTERN

  + ADAPTER

  + BRIDGE

  + COMPOSITE

  + DECORATOR

  + FACADE

  + FLYWEIGHT

  + PROXY

- **structural class pattern** *n.* any structural design pattern that uses inheritance to compose interfaces of implementations. [Gamma, Helm, Johnson, and Vlissides]

Kinds:

+ ADAPTER

+ **adapter [pattern]** *n.* the structural class/object design pattern that converts the interface of a class into one that clients expect, thereby allowing classes to work together that otherwise could not because of incompatible interfaces. [Gamma, Helm, Johnson, and Vlissides]

Synonym: WRAPPER.

- **structural object pattern** *n.* any structural design pattern that documents ways to compose larger structures out of objects. [Gamma,

Helm, Johnson, and Vlissides]
Kinds:
+ ADAPTER
+ BRIDGE
+ COMPOSITE
+ DECORATOR
+ FACADE
+ FLYWEIGHT
+ PROXY

+ **adapter [pattern]** *n.* the structural class/object design pattern that converts the interface of a class into one that clients expect, thereby allowing classes to work together that otherwise could not because of incompatible interfaces. [Gamma, Helm, Johnson, and Vlissides]
Synonym: WRAPPER.

+ **bridge [pattern]** *n.* the structural object design pattern that decouples an interface from its implementation so that the two can vary independently. [Gamma, Helm, Johnson, and Vlissides]
Synonym: HANDLE/BODY.

+ **composite [pattern]** *n.* the structural object design pattern that composes objects into tree-like whole-part hierarchies. [Gamma, Helm, Johnson, and Vlissides]

+ **decorator [pattern]** *n.* the structural object design pattern that dynamically attaches additional responsibilities to an object. [Gamma, Helm, Johnson, and Vlissides]
Synonym: WRAPPER.

+ **facade [pattern]** *n.* the structural object design pattern that provides a unified subsystem interface to a set of objects. [Gamma, Helm, Johnson, and Vlissides]

+ **flyweight [pattern]** *n.* the structural object design pattern that allows a shared object (the flyweight) to be simultaneously used in multiple contexts. [Gamma, Helm, Johnson, and Vlissides]

+ **proxy [pattern]** *n.* the structural object design pattern that provides control over an object via a surrogate or placeholder. [Gamma, Helm, Johnson, and Vlissides]
Synonym: SURROGATE.

destructor [operation] *n.* **1.** any operation that destroys an instance including maintaining referential integrity and deallocating its associated memory. [Booch, Coleman, Firesmith, Rumbaugh] **2.** any operation that cleans up the values of an object before it is destroyed. [C++]
Synonym: DELETE OPERATION.
Antonym: CONSTRUCTOR.
Commentary: Destructors are used during garbage collection (i.e., memory reclamation). [Firesmith]

determinant attribute *n.* any attribute other than the current state attribute on which the events generated by an action depend. [Shlaer/Mellor]
Rationale: Such attributes are known as determinant attributes, because they determine how a thread of control develops as it passes through the action.

device *n.* any piece of hardware without significant software or computational resources. [Booch, Firesmith]
Examples: Actuators, motors, sensors, and valves are all devices. [Firesmith]

diagram *n.* any pictorial representation of something, having a name, a notation, a graphical representation, and semantics. [Firesmith, OADSIG]
Kinds:

- ACTION DIAGRAM
- ACTIVITY SCHEMA
- BOX DIAGRAM
- CLASS-AGGREGATION DIAGRAM
- CLASS-COMMUNICATION DIAGRAM
- CLASS DIAGRAM
  - CLASS-CATEGORY DIAGRAM
  - INHERITANCE DIAGRAM
  - KEY-ABSTRACTION DIAGRAM
  - + DESIGN-CLASS DIAGRAM
- CLASS-INHERITANCE DIAGRAM
- CLASS-STRUCTURE CHART
- COLLABORATION DIAGRAM
- COLLABORATIONS GRAPH
- COMPOSED-OF DIAGRAM
- CONFIGURATION DIAGRAM
  - ASSEMBLY DIAGRAM
  - SYSTEM DIAGRAM
- DATA-FLOW DIAGRAM
  - ACTION-DATA-FLOW DIAGRAM
- DEPENDENCY DIAGRAM
- DISTRIBUTION DIAGRAM
- EVENT DIAGRAM
- EVENT-TRACE DIAGRAM
- FERN DIAGRAM
- GENERALIZATION–SPECIALIZATION DIAGRAM
- HIERARCHY DIAGRAM
- HIERARCHY GRAPH
- INFORMATION-STRUCTURE DIAGRAM
- INHERITANCE DIAGRAM
- INHERITANCE GRAPH
- INSTANCE DIAGRAM
- INTERACTION DIAGRAM
  - BLACKBOX-INTERACTION DIAGRAM
  - FORK DIAGRAM
  - STAIR DIAGRAM
  - WHITEBOX-INTERACTION DIAGRAM
- MESSAGE-FLOW DIAGRAM
- MODULE DIAGRAM
- OBJECTCHART
- OBJECT DIAGRAM
  - DESIGN OBJECT DIAGRAM
  - OBJECT-SCENARIO DIAGRAM
  - + DESIGN–OBJECT-SCENARIO DIAGRAM
- OBJECT-FLOW DIAGRAM
- OBJECT-INTERACTION GRAPH
- OBJECT-MODEL VIEW
  - GLOBAL OBJECT VIEW
  - LOCAL OBJECT VIEW
  - USE-CASE VIEW
  - VIEW OF PARTICIPATING OBJECTS
- OBJECT–RELATIONSHIP DIAGRAM
- OBJECT–STATE DIAGRAM
- OBJECT STRUCTURE
- PRESENTATION DIAGRAM
- PROCESS DIAGRAM
- SCENARIO LIFE-CYCLE DIAGRAM
- SEMANTIC NET
  - AGGREGATION DIAGRAM
  - CONTEXT DIAGRAM
  - GENERAL SEMANTIC NET
  - INHERITANCE DIAGRAM
  - MODEL-VIEW–CONTROLLER DIAGRAM
- STATE DIAGRAM
- STATE NET
- STATE-TRANSITION DIAGRAM
- TIME LINE DIAGRAM
- TIMING DIAGRAM
  - BLACKBOX-TIMING DIAGRAM
  - WHITEBOX-TIMING DIAGRAM
- USE-CASE MODEL
- VENN DIAGRAM

- **action diagram** *n.* any diagram that organizes procedural code into components surrounded by brackets. [Martin/Odell]
- **activity schema** *n.* any diagram showing a sequence of operations [Martin/Odell]
- **box diagram** *n.* any diagram that shows generalization hierarchies of types in terms of boxes within boxes. [Martin]

Synonyms: CLASS-INHERITANCE DIAGRAM, GENERALIZATION HIERARCHY, GENERALIZATION-SPECIALIZATION DIAGRAM, HIERARCHY DIAGRAM, HIERARCHY GRAPH, INHERITANCE DIAGRAM, INHERITANCE GRAPH, SUBTYPING DIAGRAM.
Contrast with: COMPOSED-OF DIAGRAM.
Commentary: Box diagrams showing subtypes are useful as a component of other diagrams showing object relationships. [Martin]

- **class-aggregation diagram** *n.* any OODN diagram documenting aggregation relationships between classes.

- **class-communication diagram** *n.* **1.** any diagram documenting the communication among classes. [Martin] **2.** any OODN diagram documenting message passing between objects. [Page-Jones]
Synonyms: INSTANCE DIAGRAM, INTERACTION DIAGRAM, MESSAGE-FLOW DIAGRAM, OBJECT DIAGRAM, OBJECT-INTERACTION GRAPH.

- **class diagram** *n.* **1.** any diagram used to show the existence of classes and their relationships. [Booch] **2.** any diagram that illustrates potential objects and their relationships in terms of their associated classes and the relationships between the classes. [Rumbaugh] **3** any diagram that depicts the external view of a single class. [Shlaer/Mellor]
Commentary: A class diagram may represent all or part of the class structure of a system. Class diagrams are used during analysis to indicate the common roles and responsibilities of the entities that provide the system's behavior. Class diagrams are used during design to capture the structure

of the classes that form the system's architecture.
Kinds:
- CLASS-CATEGORY DIAGRAM
- INHERITANCE DIAGRAM
- KEY-ABSTRACTION DIAGRAM

- **class-category diagram** *n.* any Booch class diagram that documents class categories and the uses relationships among them. [Booch]
Contrast with: DESIGN-CLASS DIAGRAM, INHERITANCE DIAGRAM, KEY-ABSTRACTION DIAGRAM.

- **inheritance diagram** *n.* any Booch class diagram that documents the inheritance hierarchies. [Booch]
Synonyms: BOX DIAGRAM, CLASS-INHERITANCE DIAGRAM, GENERALIZATION-SPECIALIZATION DIAGRAM, HIERARCHY DIAGRAM, HIERARCHY GRAPH, INHERITANCE GRAPH.
Contrast with: CLASS-CATEGORY DIAGRAM, DESIGN-CLASS DIAGRAM, KEY-ABSTRACTION DIAGRAM.

- **key-abstraction diagram** *n.* any Booch class diagram that documents the key classes and the uses relationships between them. [Booch]
Contrast with: CLASS-CATEGORY DIAGRAM, DESIGN-CLASS DIAGRAM, INHERITANCE DIAGRAM.

+ **design-class diagram** *n.* any Booch key-abstraction diagram that has been updated during design. [Booch]
Contrast with: CLASS-CATEGORY DIAGRAM, INHERITANCE DIAGRAM, KEY-ABSTRACTION DIAGRAM.

- **class-inheritance diagram** *n.* any OODN diagram documenting inheritance relationships between classes.

- **class-structure chart** *n.* any diagram that is used to show the internal structure of the code of the operations of the class as well as the flow of data and control within the class. [Shlaer/Mellor]

Contrast with: CLASS DIAGRAM.

Commentary: A separate class structure chart is produced for each class. [Shlaer/Mellor]

- **collaboration diagram** *n.* any diagram that graphically depicts classes, subsystems, contracts, and relationships between classes and subsystems. [Lorenz]

  Synonyms: COLLABORATIONS GRAPH, INTERACTION DIAGRAM, MESSAGE-FLOW DIAGRAM.

  Contrast with: HIERARCHY DIAGRAM.

  Commentary: These diagrams are used during the analysis and design to document the system under development. The information on the diagrams can also be used to automate portions of the development process, such as the creation of class definition code as well as method selectors and comments. [Lorenz]

- **collaborations graph** *n.* any graph showing the classes, subsystems, contracts, and collaboration and inheritance relationships. [Wirfs-Brock]

  Synonyms: COLLABORATION DIAGRAM, INTERACTION DIAGRAM, MESSAGE DIAGRAM.

- **composed-of diagram** *n.* any diagram that documents *composed-of* relationships. [Martin]

  Synonym: AGGREGATION DIAGRAM.

  Contrast with: BOX DIAGRAM.

- **configuration diagram (CND)** *n.* any static architecture diagram documenting the configuration management view of an assembly or system in terms of its component clusters or

subsystems, their visibility, their component objects and classes (whitebox diagrams only), and the dependency relationships among them. [Firesmith]

Kinds:
- ASSEMBLY DIAGRAM
- SYSTEM DIAGRAM

- **assembly diagram (AD)** *n.* any configuration diagram documenting the static architecture of an assembly in terms of its component clusters and the dependency relationships between them. [Firesmith]

  Antonym: SYSTEM DIAGRAM.

- **system diagram (SD)** *n.* any configuration diagram documenting the static architecture of a system in terms of its component subsystems and the dependency relationships between them. [Firesmith]

  Antonym: ASSEMBLY DIAGRAM.

- **data-flow diagram** *n.* any graphical representation of the functional model, showing dependencies between values and the computation of output values from input values without regard for when or if the functions are executed. [Rumbaugh]

  Commentary: Rumbaugh and Shlaer/Mellor are the main proponents of DFDs in the object community. DFDs have a very questionable reputation in the object community, with most other methodologists considering them inappropriate for use with objects.

- **action-data-flow diagram (AD-FD)** *n.* any data-flow diagram that provides a graphic representation of the units of processing (a.k.a., processes) within an action and the intercommunication between them. [Shlaer/Mellor]

- **dependency diagram** *n.* any diagram that depicts the client–server (invocation) and friend relationships that hold between the classes. [Shlaer/Mellor]
- **distribution diagram (DD)** *n.* any diagram documenting processors, devices, the connections between them, and the static allocation of software (e.g., clusters, objects, classes, modules, processes) to processors. [Firesmith]
- **event diagram** *n.* any diagram that documents events and the sequence of operations triggered by the events. [Martin]
- **event-trace [diagram]** *n.* any diagram that shows the sender and receiver of events and the sequence of events. [Rumbaugh]
  Synonyms: CLASS-COMMUNICATION DIAGRAM, EVENT-FLOW DIAGRAM, INSTANCE DIAGRAM, INTERACTION DIAGRAM, MESSAGE-FLOW DIAGRAM, OBJECT DIAGRAM, OBJECT-INTERACTION GRAPH.
  Commentary: The term *interaction diagram* was used first and is less restricted to state modeling.
- **fern diagram** *n.* any diagram documenting inheritance relationships, drawn with subclasses to the left of superclasses. [Martin]
  See also: CLASS HIERARCHY, INHERITANCE.
- **generalization-specialization diagram** *n.* any diagram documenting a subtyping hierarchy. [Martin]
  Synonyms: BOX DIAGRAM, CLASS-INHERITANCE DIAGRAM, HIERARCHY DIAGRAM, HIERARCHY GRAPH, INHERITANCE DIAGRAM, INHERITANCE GRAPH.
- **hierarchy diagram** *n.* any graph of an OO system, including classes, sub-

systems groupings, and contract usage. [Lorenz]
Synonyms: BOX DIAGRAM, CLASS-INHERITANCE DIAGRAM, GENERALIZATION-SPECIALIZATION DIAGRAM, HIERARCHY GRAPH, INHERITANCE DIAGRAM, INHERITANCE GRAPH.
Contrast with: COLLABORATION DIAGRAM, MESSAGE-FLOW DIAGRAM.
- **hierarchy graph** *n.* any graph showing the inheritance relationships between classes. [Wirfs-Brock]
  Synonyms: BOX DIAGRAM, CLASS-INHERITANCE DIAGRAM, GENERALIZATION-SPECIALIZATION DIAGRAM, HIERARCHY DIAGRAM, INHERITANCE DIAGRAM, INHERITANCE GRAPH.
- **information-structure diagram** *n.* any graphic representation of the information model. [Shlaer/Mellor]
  Synonym: ENTITY-RELATIONSHIP DIAGRAM, INFORMATION MODEL.
  Commentary: The information structure diagram is concerned only with declaring the objects, attributes, and relationships of the model. [Shlaer/Mellor]
- **inheritance diagram (INHD)** *n.* **1.** any specialized semantic net that documents an inheritance structure showing the relevant classes, the inheritance relationships between the derived classes and their base classes, and where useful and practical, the generic parameters of generic classes, the interfaces and implementations of classes, their instances, and the classification relationships between instances and their classes. [Firesmith] **2.** any class diagram that documents the inheritance hierarchies. [Booch] **3.** any diagram that shows the inheritance relationships between the

classes. [Shlaer/Mellor]

Synonyms: BOX DIAGRAM, CLASS-IN-HERITANCE DIAGRAM, GENERALIZA-TION-SPECIALIZATION DIAGRAM, HI-ERARCHY DIAGRAM, HIERARCHY GRAPH, INHERITANCE GRAPH.

Contrast with: CLASS-CATEGORY DIA-GRAM, DESIGN-CLASS DIAGRAM, KEY-ABSTRACTION DIAGRAM.

Commentary: The purpose of the in-heritance diagram is to depict the in-heritance relationships between the classes of a single program, library, or environment. [Shlaer/Mellor]

• **inheritance graph** *n.* a synonym for INHERITANCE DIAGRAM. [Coleman]

• **instance diagram** *n.* an object dia-gram documenting a particular set of instances and their relationships. [Rumbaugh]

Synonyms: CLASS-COMMUNICATION DIAGRAM, INTERACTION DIAGRAM, MESSAGE-FLOW DIAGRAM, OBJECT DIA-GRAM, OBJECT-INTERACTION GRAPH.

Contrast with: CLASS DIAGRAM.

• **interaction diagram (ID)** *n.* **1.** any diagram that documents the dynamic behavior of a set of collaborating ob-jects and classes in terms of their ex-istence, the interactions among them, and optionally the control and data flows within them. [Booch, Colbert, Embley, Firesmith] **2.** any diagram that documents the sequencing of message passing between objects, classes, or blocks in a scenario or use case. [Booch, Jacobson]

Synonyms: 1 CLASS-COMMUNICATION DIAGRAM, INSTANCE DIAGRAM, INTER-ACTION DIAGRAM, MESSAGE-FLOW DI-AGRAM, OBJECT DIAGRAM, OBJECT-IN-TERACTION GRAPH, **2** TIMING DIAGRAM.

See also: OBJECT-INTERACTION MODEL.

Kinds:
- BLACKBOX-INTERACTION DIAGRAM
- FORK DIAGRAM
- STAIR DIAGRAM
- WHITEBOX-INTERACTION DIAGRAM

- **blackbox-interaction diagram (BID)** *n.* any interaction diagram in which the documented objects and classes are treated as blackboxes. [Fire-smith]

Antonym: WHITEBOX-INTERACTION DIAGRAM.

- **fork diagram** *n.* any interaction diagram that exhibits an extreme structure in which one object sends messages to numerous other ob-jects. [Jacobson]

Antonym: STAIR DIAGRAM.

Rationale: The message arcs from the central control object look like the tines on a fork.

Commentary: By looking for fork or stair structures, the interaction diagram can be used to assess how decentralized an architecture is. [Ja-cobson]

- **stair diagram** *n.* any interaction di-agram indicating a decentralized structure with extensive delegation of responsibilities. [Jacobson]

Antonym: FORK DIAGRAM.

- **whitebox-interaction diagram (WID)** *n.* any interaction diagram in which the documented objects and classes are treated as whitebox-es, showing their interfaces and im-plementations. [Firesmith]

Antonym: BLACKBOX-INTERACTION DIAGRAM.

• **message-flow diagram** *n.* any dia-gram documenting a time-ordered sequence of message sends between a group of classes or subsystems. The message-flow diagram shows a set of classes across the top and a time sequence from top to bottom. Shown within this table are message sends between classes, in the order that they would occur according to the system design. [Lorenz]

Synonyms: CLASS-COMMUNICATION DIAGRAM, EVENT-FLOW DIAGRAM, INSTANCE DIAGRAM, INTERACTION DIAGRAM, OBJECT DIAGRAM, OBJECT-INTERACTION GRAPH.

Contrast with: COLLABORATION DIAGRAM, HIERARCHY DIAGRAM.

Commentary: Message-flow diagrams can be used for more than one purpose, including use case, method, and test-case documentation. [Lorenz] The messages shown should be the key application-related messages and not every message sent to accomplish the function. Focus on messages that are part of contracts. [Lorenz]

- **module diagram (MD)** *n.* any programming-language-level diagram that documents the modules (i.e., their identification, interface, implementation) in a cluster or cluster instance and the static dependency relationships between them. A module diagram is used to show the allocation of objects and classes to modules in the physical design of an application. [Booch, Firesmith]

- **objectchart** *n.* any extension of a statechart (a.k.a. state transition diagram) useful in describing the dynamics of class behavior. [Henderson-Sellers]

- **object diagram** *n.* **1.** any diagram used to show the existence of object and their relationships in the logical

design of a system. An object diagram may represent all or part of the object structure of a system. A single object diagram represents a snapshot in time of an otherwise transitory event or configuration of objects. [Booch] **2.** any graphical representation of the object model. [Rumbaugh]

Synonyms: CLASS-COMMUNICATION DIAGRAM, EVENT-FLOW DIAGRAM, INSTANCE DIAGRAM, INTERACTION DIAGRAM, MESSAGE-FLOW DIAGRAM, OBJECT-INTERACTION GRAPH.

Commentary: Booch object diagrams are used during analysis to indicate the semantics of primary and secondary scenarios that provide a trace of the system's behavior. Object diagrams are used during design to illustrate the semantics of mechanisms in the logical design of a system.

Kinds:
- OBJECT-SCENARIO DIAGRAM
  + DESIGN-OBJECT SCENARIO
    DIAGRAM

- **object-scenario diagram** *n.* any object diagram that documents a single scenario during domain analysis. [Booch]
  + **design–object-scenario diagram** *n.* any object-scenario diagram updated during design. [Booch]

- **object-flow diagram (OFD)** *n.* any diagram that documents the objects that flow from activity to activity. [Martin]

Commentary: Object-flow diagrams are similar to data-flow diagrams (DFDs), because they depict activities interfacing with other activities. [Martin]

- **object-interaction graph** *n.* any graph providing a visual representation of

D

diagram: object-interaction graph
144
diagram: object structure

how functionality is distributed across the objects of a system, showing the run-time messaging of objects to support a system operation. [Coleman]
Synonyms: CLASS-COMMUNICATION DIAGRAM, EVENT-FLOW DIAGRAM, INSTANCE DIAGRAM, INTERACTION DIAGRAM, MESSAGE-FLOW DIAGRAM, OBJECT DIAGRAM.
Contrast with: TIMING DIAGRAM.

- **object-model view** *n.* any object diagram of a subset of an object model. [Jacobson]
Kinds:
  - GLOBAL OBJECT VIEW
  - LOCAL OBJECT VIEW
  - USE CASE VIEW
  - VIEW OF PARTICIPATING OBJECTS

- **global object view** *n.* any object model view that shows either the entire object model or a subsystem of the object model. [Jacobson]
Antonym: LOCAL OBJECT VIEW.
Contrast with: VIEW OF PARTICIPATING OBJECTS.

- **local object view** *n.* any object-model view that shows an object with all of its relations to and from other objects. [Jacobson]
Antonym: GLOBAL OBJECT VIEW.
Contrast with: VIEW OF PARTICIPATING OBJECTS.

- **use case view** *n.* any object-model view that shows the objects and associations that participate in a specific use case. [Jacobson]
Synonym: VIEW OF PARTICIPATING OBJECTS.
Contrast with: GLOBAL OBJECT VIEW, LOCAL OBJECT VIEW.
See also: USE CASE.
Commentary: The purpose of this type of view is to illustrate how the behavior of a use case is distributed over the objects and how the objects interact to realize the course of events in a use case. The union of all views of participating objects is the global object view. [Jacobson]

- **view of participating objects** *n.* any object model view that shows the objects and associations that participate in a specific use case. [Jacobson]
Synonym: USE-CASE VIEW.
Contrast with: GLOBAL-OBJECT VIEW, LOCAL OBJECT VIEW.
See also: USE CASE.
Commentary: The purpose of this type of view is to illustrate how the behavior of a use case is distributed over the objects and how the objects interact to realize the course of events in a use case. The union of all views of participating objects is the global object view. [Jacobson]

- **object-relationship diagram** *n.* any diagram that maps the relationships among object types. [Martin]
Commentary: An object-relationship diagram is similar to an entity-relationship diagram. [Martin]

- **object-state diagram** *n.* any diagram that documents the states or modes of an object over time and the transitions between them. [Coad]
Synonyms: STATE DIAGRAM, STATE NET, STATE-TRANSITION DIAGRAM.
See also: OBJECT STATE.

- **object structure** *n.* any graph whose vertices represent objects and whose arcs represent relationships among those objects. The object structure of a system is represented by a set of object diagrams. [Booch]

- **presentation diagram (PRD)** *n.* any diagram showing the format and contents of a presentation object or class. [Firesmith]
- **process diagram (PD)** *n.* a diagram used to show the allocation of processes to processors in the physical design of an application. [Booch] *Contrast with:* DISTRIBUTION DIAGRAM.
- **scenario life-cycle diagram (SLD)** *n.* any diagram documenting all top-level scenarios and the transitions between them. SLDs document all valid orders of these scenarios during the life cycle of a system or cluster. [Firesmith]
- **semantic net (SN)** *n.* any diagram using a graph structure to represent knowledge in which the nodes represent things and the arcs represent relationships between things. [Firesmith]
  Synonym: SEMANTIC NETWORK.
  Contrast with: ENTITY-RELATIONSHIP DIAGRAM, INFORMATION MODEL.
  Kinds:
    - AGGREGATION DIAGRAM
    - CONTEXT DIAGRAM
    - GENERAL SEMANTIC NET
    - INHERITANCE DIAGRAM
    - MODEL VIEW CONTROLLER DIAGRAM
  - **aggregation diagram (AGD)** *n.* any specialized semantic net that documents all or part of an aggregation hierarchy.
    Synonyms: COMPOSED-OF DIAGRAM.
    Contrast with: INHERITANCE DIAGRAM.
  - **context diagram (CD)** *n.* any specialized semantic net used to document a system or assembly and the semantic relationships between it and its terminators. [Firesmith]
  - **general semantic net (GSN)** *n.* any semantic net that documents a collection of related objects, classes, subsystems or clusters, terminators, and the important semantic relationships (primarily links or associations) between them. [Firesmith]
  - **inheritance diagram (INHD)** *n.* any specialized semantic net that documents all or part of an inheritance structure showing the relevant classes, the inheritance relationships between the derived classes and their base classes, and where useful and practical, the generic parameters of generic classes, the interfaces and implementations of classes, their instances, and the classification relationships between instances and their classes. [Firesmith]
    Synonyms: BOX DIAGRAM, CLASS-INHERITANCE DIAGRAM, GENERALIZATION-SPECIALIZATION DIAGRAM, HIERARCHY DIAGRAM, HIERARCHY GRAPH, INHERITANCE GRAPH.
    Contrast with: AGGREGATION DIAGRAM.
  - **model-view–controller diagram (MVCD)** *n.* any semantic net documenting the dependency relationships between models, views, and controllers.
- **state diagram** *n.* any directed graph in which nodes represent states and arcs represent transitions between states. [Rumbaugh]
  Synonyms: OBJECT-STATE DIAGRAM, STATE NET, STATE-TRANSITION DIAGRAM.
- **state net** *n.* **1.** any diagram represent-

ing states and state transitions for all objects in a particular object class. **2.** any "behavior template" that specifies the expected behavior for instances of an object class. [Embley]
Synonyms: OBJECT-STATE DIAGRAM, STATE DIAGRAM, STATE-TRANSITION DIAGRAM.
See also: OBJECT-BEHAVIOR MODEL.
Commentary: In OSA, state nets are used to model object behavior. When a state net is associated with an object class, every instance of the object class has the behavior described by the state net. [Embley]
Synonyms: STATE DIAGRAM, STATE TRANSITION DIAGRAM.

- **state-transition diagram (STD)** *n.* **1.** any diagram that documents the states of an object or class, the triggers (e.g., operations and terminators) that cause the transitions between the states, and the corresponding operations. [Booch, Firesmith, Jacobson] **2.** any diagram that documents the sequence of states of an object. [Martin]
Synonyms: OBJECT-STATE DIAGRAM, STATE DIAGRAM, STATE NET.
Rationale: This is the traditional term.
Commentary: When a class is instantiated, the instance created follows a path in this diagram throughout its lifetime. [Jacobson] Although individual objects have their own state machines, all direct instances of the same class have equivalent state machines and therefore conform to the same state-transition diagram. However, if the class itself also has state properties, it typically has a different state-transition diagram than its instances. [Firesmith]

- **timeline diagram** *n.* any diagram doc-

umenting a scenario in terms of the temporal ordering of system operations and the events that flow to agents. [Coleman]

- **timing diagram (TD)** *n.* any diagram documenting the temporal aspects of a scenario or thread of control in terms of the associated objects, classes, and possibly their operations and the sequencing of their behavior in terms of interactions and the execution of operations. [Firesmith]
Synonym: SCENARIO DIAGRAM.
Commentary: One should use the term *timing diagram* rather than the term *interaction diagram*, because of its emphasis on the timing involved and the fact that the term *interaction diagram* has historically been used by Colbert, Booch, and Firesmith to summarize the possible interactions prior to Jacobson's use of the term *interaction diagram* for this purpose. [Firesmith]
Kinds:
  - BLACKBOX-TIMING DIAGRAM
  - WHITEBOX-TIMING DIAGRAM

- **blackbox-timing diagram (BTD)** *n.* any timing diagram that documents the absolute or relative timing of interactions (e.g., messages, exception flows) between blackbox objects and classes. [Firesmith]
Antonym: WHITEBOX-TIMING DIAGRAM.

- **whitebox-timing diagram (WTD)** *n.* any timing diagram that documents the duration of operation execution and the transfer of control (message or call). [Firesmith]
Antonym: BLACKBOX-TIMING DIAGRAM.

- **use case model** *n.* any diagram that

documents a system's behavior as a set of use cases, actors, and the communication arcs between them. [Jacobson]

• **Venn diagram** *n.* a diagram from set theory used to show the intersection and union relationships among sets. [Wirfs-Brock]

Commentary: Used to show the inheritance relationships between classes and types by showing the intersection and union relationships among their extents. Venn diagrams have sometimes been misused to show aggregation relationships. [Firesmith]

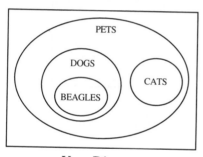

Venn Diagram

dialog object type *n.* any user interface object type that maintains the state of the interface and from the user's perception controls its overall behavior. [OADSIG]

Example: The open file dialogue provided by a word processor can be modeled as a dialog object type. [OADSIG]

direct ancestor [of a given class] *n.* any ancestor class from which the given class is directly derived via inheritance. [Firesmith, Jacobson]

Synonyms: DIRECT BASE CLASS, DIRECT SUPERCLASS, IMMEDIATE ANCESTOR, IMMEDIATE BASE CLASS, IMMEDIATE SUPERCLASS, PARENT CLASS.

Antonyms: CHILD CLASS, IMMEDIATE DESCENDANT, IMMEDIATE DERIVED CLASS, IMMEDIATE SUBCLASS.

Contrast with: ANCESTOR CLASS.

direct base class [of a given class] *n.* any base class from which the given class is immediately derived. [C++, Firesmith]

Synonyms: DIRECT ANCESTOR, DIRECT SUPERCLASS, PARENT CLASS.

Contrast with: ANCESTOR, INDIRECT BASE CLASS.

Commentary: A direct base class of a given class is also a parent ancestor class. [Firesmith]

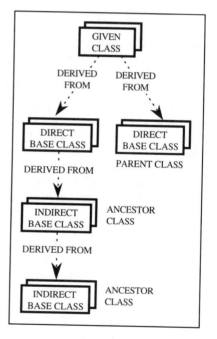

Direct Base Class

direct conformance *n.* any immediate conformance of one type to another type through no intermediary. [Eiffel, Firesmith, Meyer]

Antonym: INDIRECT CONFORMANCE.

Example: A subtype conforms to its parent type. [Firesmith]

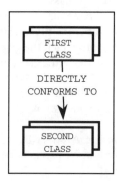

Direct Conformance

direct dependent [of a given object]
n. **1.** any object visible to and referenced by the current object at some time during execution. [Firesmith] **2.** the direct dependents of an object O, at some time during the execution of a system, are the objects attached to the reference field of O. [Eiffel, Meyer]
Antonym: INDIRECT DEPENDENT.

direct derived class [of a given class]
n. any derived class that is immediately derived from a given class. [Ada95, C++, Firesmith]
Synonyms: CHILD CLASS, DIRECT SUBCLASS, HEIR, IMMEDIATE DERIVED CLASS, IMMEDIATE DESCENDANT, IMMEDIATE SUBCLASS.
Antonyms: DIRECT ANCESTOR, DIRECT BASE CLASS, DIRECT SUPERCLASS, IMMEDIATE ANCESTOR, IMMEDIATE BASE CLASS, IMMEDIATE SUPERCLASS, PARENT CLASS.
Contrast with: ANCESTOR, DESCENDANT.
Commentary: A direct derived class of a given class is a descendant class that is also a child descendant class. [Firesmith]

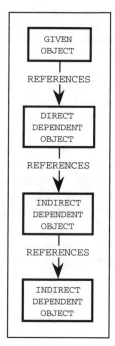

Direct Dependent

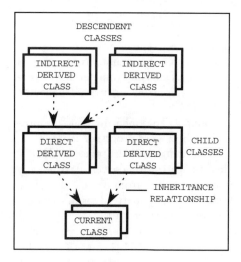

Direct Derived Class

direct descendant [class of a given class] *n.* any descendant class that is directly derived via inheritance from the given class. [Firesmith, Jacobson]

Synonyms: CHILD CLASS, DIRECT DERIVED CLASS, DIRECT SUBCLASS, HEIR CLASS, IMMEDIATE DERIVED CLASS, IMMEDIATE DESCENDANT, IMMEDIATE SUBCLASS.

Antonyms: DIRECT ANCESTOR, DIRECT BASE CLASS, DIRECT SUPERCLASS, IMMEDIATE ANCESTOR, IMMEDIATE BASE CLASS, IMMEDIATE SUPERCLASS, PARENT CLASS.

Contrast with: ANCESTOR, BASE CLASS, DERIVED CLASS, DESCENDANT, SUBCLASS, SUPERCLASS.

Commentary: A direct descendant of a given class is a descendant class that is also a child class. [Firesmith]

direct instance [of a class] *n.* **1.** any object that has been explicitly instantiated using a constructor of the given class. [Eiffel, Firesmith, Meyer] **2.** any object that is an instance of a class but is not an instance of any subclass of the class. [Rumbaugh]

Antonym: INDIRECT INSTANCE.

Commentary: Only concrete classes can have direct instances. A direct instance of a given class is not an instance of any specialized descendant of the given class and is only an indirect instance of all generalized ancestors of the given class. [Firesmith]

direct repeated inheritance [of a given class] *n.* any repeated inheritance in which a parent class of the given class is then multiply inherited. [Eiffel, Firesmith, Meyer]

Antonym: INDIRECT REPEATED INHERITANCE.

See also: REPEATED PARENT CLASS.

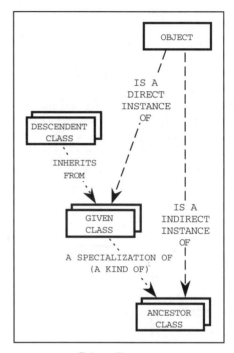

Direct Instance

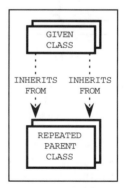

Direct Repeated Inheritance

direct subclass [of a given class] *n.* any child class of the given class. [CLOS, Firesmith]

Synonyms: CHILD CLASS, DIRECT DE-

RIVED CLASS, DIRECT DESCENDANT, HEIR CLASS.

Antonyms: DIRECT SUPERCLASS, INDIRECT SUBCLASS.

Contrast with: ANCESTOR CLASS, INDIRECT BASE CLASS.

Commentary: If class C_2 explicitly designates C_1 as a superclass in its definition, then C_2 is a *direct subclass* of C_1. [CLOS] A direct subclass is a descendant class that is also a child class. [Firesmith]

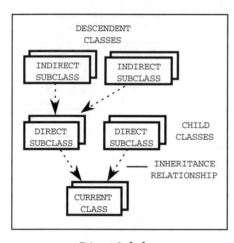

Direct Subclass

direct superclass [of a given class] *n.* any superclass from which a given derived class directly inherits. [CLOS, Firesmith]

Synonyms: DIRECT ANCESTOR, DIRECT BASE CLASS, PARENT CLASS.

Antonym: INDIRECT SUPERCLASS.

Contrast with: ANCESTOR, INDIRECT DERIVED CLASS.

Commentary: If class C_2 explicitly designates C_1 as a superclass in its definition, then C_1 is a *direct superclass* of C_2. [CLOS] A direct superclass is an ances-

tor class that is also a parent class. [Firesmith]

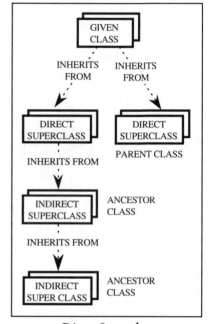

Direct Superclass

discriminant *n.* any parameter of a composite type. [Ada95]

See also: COMPOSITE TYPE, GENERIC.

Examples: A discriminant can control the bounds of a component of the type if that type is an array type. A discriminant of a task type can be used to pass data to a task of the type upon creation. [Ada95]

discriminator *n.* (a) any attribute that indicates which property of the base class is used to differentiate a set of its child classes (i.e., to differentiate the members of a partition). [Firesmith, Rumbaugh] (b) any attribute that is an instance of a discriminator class. [Firesmith]

Contrast with: POWER TYPE.
Example: The engine type of a car can be used as a discriminator to partition cars into disjoint derived classes or types. For example, cars can be subtyped as either diesel, electric, gas, or solar powered. [Firesmith]

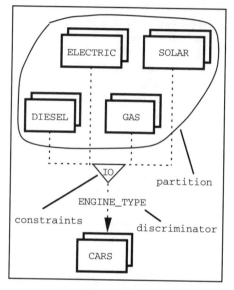

Discriminator

discriminator class *n.* any power class whose instances partition another class (i.e., whose instances form a disjoint cover of the class being partitioned). [Firesmith]
Example: The class of *genders* is a discriminator class for the class *persons,* partitioning it into the derived classes *males* and *females.* [Firesmith]
Commentary: A discriminator class is often implemented as an enumeration type whose values are the names of the derived classes in the partition. [Firesmith]

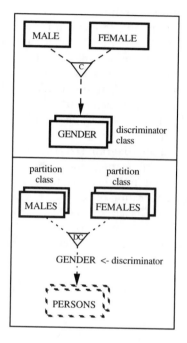

Discriminator Class

disjoint constraint *n.* the inheritance constraint that requires that the extents of the children be pair-wise disjoint. [Firesmith]
Rationale: The term *disjoint* comes from set theory. [Firesmith]
Commentary: This constraint ensures that no object will be an instance of two children. [Firesmith]
dispatch *v.* **-ed, -ing** to use a tag to control which body to execute. [Ada95]
Synonyms: METHOD LOOKUP.
See also: BINDING, CONTROLLING OPERAND, TAGGED, TAGGED TYPE.
dispatcher object *n.* any object that captures user input.
SYNONYM: CONTROLLER OBJECT.
Example: Any object that captures mouse events is an example dispatcher object.

distribution architecture *n.* the architecture of any application in terms of processors, devices, the connections between them, and the static allocation of processes to processors. [Firesmith] *Commentary:* The distribution architecture is documented by one or more related distribution diagrams. [Firesmith]

distribution diagram (DD) *n.* any diagram documenting processors, devices, the connections between them, and the static allocation of software (e.g., clusters, objects, classes, modules, processes) to processors. [Firesmith]

"DM object server" object *n.* any single object, whose purpose is to create DM objects for each supported class, to maintain a collection of DM objects, and to provide a single point of access to get a DM object for a specific class. [Coad] *See also:* DATA MANAGEMENT COMPONENT.

doesNotUnderstand *n.* any standard message used to report to the user that the receiver does not understand the message. [Smalltalk]

domain *n.* 1. (a) any subject area of expertise used to decompose an application. [Firesmith, Lorenz] (b) any separate real, hypothetical, or abstract world inhabited by a distinct set of objects that behave according to rules and policies characteristic of the domain. [Shlaer/Mellor] 2. any scope or name space. [ODMG] 3. any set of classes, connected by inheritance relationships. *Synonyms:* 1 PROBLEM DOMAIN, 3 FAMILY. *Example:* 1 Examples include application domain, banking, command and control, insurance, retail, telecommunications, and user interfaces. [Firesmith]

Kinds:
- APPLICATION DOMAIN
- ARCHITECTURAL DOMAIN
- IMPLEMENTATION DOMAIN
- PROBLEM DOMAIN
- SERVICE DOMAIN
- SOLUTION DOMAIN

- **application domain** *n.* the subject matter of the system from the perspective of the end user of the system. [Shlaer/Mellor] *Synonym:* PROBLEM DOMAIN.

- **architectural domain** *n.* the domain that provides generic mechanisms and structures for managing data and control for the system as a whole. [Shlaer/Mellor]

- **implementation domain** *n.* the domain providing the conceptual entities in which the entire system will be implemented. [Shlaer/Mellor] *Examples:* Programming languages, networks, operating systems, and common class libraries are example implementation domains. [Shlaer/Mellor]

- **problem domain** *n.* 1. the real world. 2. the overall area of the business with which the application under development is concerned. [Firesmith, Lorenz] 3. the domain of the problem as opposed to the solution. [Firesmith] 4. a separate real, hypothetical, or abstract world inhabited by a distinct set of objects that behave according to rules and policies characteristic of the domain. [Shlaer/Mellor] *Synonym:* APPLICATION DOMAIN, PROBLEM SPACE. *Contrast with:* SOLUTION DOMAIN, SOLUTION SPACE. *Example:* The area of a bank's business that has to do with automated teller machines (ATMs) is the problem domain for an ATM application. [Lorenz]

Commentary: Unlike the solution space, the problem domain is usually a part of the real world or business in which specific rules and policies apply. [Firesmith]

- **service domain** *n.* the domain that provides generic mechanisms and utility functions as required to support the application domain. [Shlaer/Mellor]

- **solution domain** *n.* **1.** the world of software design and implementation. **2.** the targeted implementation hardware and software platform. [Lorenz]

Synonym: SOLUTION SPACE.

Contrast with: APPLICATION DOMAIN, PROBLEM DOMAIN, PROBLEM SPACE.

Example: A solution domain could be concerned with implementing an application in Smalltalk under OS/2, running on a 386-based processor with 8 MB of memory and 60 MB of disk space. [Lorenz]

domain [of a given attribute] *n.* the set of values the given attribute can take on. [Shlaer/Mellor]

Synonym: ATTRIBUTE DOMAIN.

domain [of a given function] *n.* the set of all objects mapped by the given function (i.e., the range of the return type of the function). [Martin/Odell]

domain chart *n.* any chart that provides a concise graphic representation of the domains and bridges required by a system. [Shlaer/Mellor]

domain class *n.* any class that is application-domain specific.

Synonyms: APPLICATION CLASS, BUSINESS CLASS, CORE CLASS, KEY CLASS.

Antonyms: BASE CLASS, SUPPORT CLASS.

Contrast with: KEY ABSTRACTION, PRE-

SENTATION CLASS.

Commentary: The partition of domain classes is based on the Smalltalk model-view-controller pattern. [Firesmith]

Kinds:
- CONTROLLER CLASS
- MODEL CLASS
- VIEW CLASS
  - PRESENTATION CLASS
  - PROXY CLASS

- **controller [class]** *n.* any domain class of controller objects that exist to either control one or more classes or capture user input as in the model-view-controller (MVC) framework. [Firesmith]

Contrast with: CONTROLLER OBJECT, MODEL CLASS, VIEW CLASS.

See also: CONTROLLER OBJECT.

Commentary: Controller classes are often either model classes that model input devices (e.g., mice) or are presentation classes allowing the user to control the model object. [Firesmith]

- **model [class]** *n.* any domain class of model objects that model application-domain things. [Firesmith]

Contrast with: CONTROLLER CLASS, MODEL OBJECT, VIEW CLASS.

Commentary: A model class may have more than one view class. [Firesmith]

- **view [class]** *n.* any domain class of view objects that exist to provide a user view of (i.e., information about and control over) one or more model classes. [Firesmith]

Contrast with: CONTROLLER CLASS, MODEL CLASS, VIEW OBJECT.

Commentary: A view class may also be a controller class of its model class(es). Most view classes are also presentation classes. [Firesmith]

D

Kinds:
- PRESENTATION CLASS
- PROXY CLASS
- **presentation [class]** *n.* any specialized view class of presentation objects that exist to provide a *formatted* view of (i.e., information about and control over) one or more model or view classes. [Firesmith]
Contrast with: PRESENTATION OBJECT, PROXY CLASS.
Example: A model or view class may have more than one presentation class, and a presentation class may also be a controller class of its model or view class(es). [Firesmith]
- **proxy [class]** *n.* any local view class of proxy objects that represent (i.e., acts as a processor-specific variant of and communicates with) its remote model class. [Firesmith]
Contrast with: PRESENTATION CLASS, PROXY OBJECT.
Commentary: A proxy provides the local protocol of (and communicates with) its model on a remote processor. Proxies are used to create a single virtual address space across multiple processors. [Firesmith]
domain object *n.* (a) any object that is application domain-specific. [Firesmith] (b) any instance of a domain class. [Firesmith]
Antonym: SUPPORT OBJECT.
Kinds:
- CONTROLLER OBJECT
- MODEL OBJECT
- VIEW OBJECT
  - PRESENTATION OBJECT
  - PROXY OBJECT
- **controller [object]** *n.* (a) any domain object that exists to either control one or more objects or capture user input as in the model-view-controller (MVC) framework. [Firesmith] (b) any instance of a controller class. [Firesmith]
Contrast with: CONTROLLER CLASS, MODEL OBJECT, PRESENTATION OBJECT, VIEW OBJECT.
Example: (a) An object that captures mouse events is an example controller object. [Firesmith]
Commentary: Controller objects are often either model objects that model input devices (e.g., mice) or are presentation objects allowing the user to control the model object. [Firesmith]
- **model [object]** *n.* (a) any domain object that models an application-domain thing. [Firesmith] (b) any instance of a model class. [Firesmith]
Contrast with: CONTROLLER OBJECT, MODEL CLASS, VIEW OBJECT.
Examples: A concept, document, event, device, financial instrument, interaction, location, organization, role, software, standard, substance, or system is a model object. [Firesmith]
- **view [object]** *n.* (a) any domain object that exists to provide a user view of (i.e., information about and control over) one or more model objects. [Firesmith] (b) any instance of a view class. [Firesmith]
Contrast with: CONTROLLER OBJECT, MODEL OBJECT, VIEW CLASS.
Commentary: A model object may have more than one view object, and a view object may also be a controller object of its model object(s). Most view objects are also presentation objects. [Firesmith]
Kinds:
- PRESENTATION OBJECT
- PROXY OBJECT

- **presentation [object]** *n.* (a) any specialized view object that exists to provide a *formatted* view of (i.e., information about and control over) one or more model or view objects. [Firesmith] (b) any instance of a presentation class. [Firesmith]
Contrast with: PRESENTATION CLASS, PROXY OBJECT.
Commentary: A model or view object may have more than one presentation object, and a presentation object may also be a controller object of its model or view object(s). [Firesmith]

- **proxy [object]** *n.* (a) any local view object that represents (i.e., acts as a processor-specific variant of and communicates with) its remote model object. [Firesmith] (b) any instance of a proxy class. [Firesmith]
Contrast with: PRESENTATION OBJECT, PROXY CLASS.
Commentary: A proxy provides the local protocol of (and communicates with) its model on a remote processor. Proxies are used to create a single virtual address space across multiple processors. [Firesmith]

domain object model *n.* any object model that consists of problem domain objects and serves as a support for the development of the requirements model. [Jacobson]
See also: USE-CASE VIEW.
Commentary: A logical and surveyable domain object model is used to communicate with the potential users, and also to get a stable basis for the descriptions of the use cases. [Jacobson]

dominance [of a name] *n.* if a feature of a derived class overrides an inherited feature of its ancestor, then the full name of the feature is said to have dominance over (a.k.a., dominate) the full name of the inherited feature from the ancestor. [C++]
Example: If B is a derived class of A, then B::f has dominance over A::f. [C++]
Commentary: If one name dominates another, then no ambiguity exists between the two; the feature associated with the dominant name will be used when there is a choice. [Firesmith]

dominant high-level object class *n.* any high-level object class representing a set of objects that is named after the most important object class in the set. [Embley]
Antonym: INDEPENDENT HIGH-LEVEL OBJECT CLASS.

downcast *v.* *-ed, -ing* the C++ term for changing the type of an object to that of a descendant type. [C++, Firesmith]
Antonym: UPCAST.
Rationale: The descendant type is lower in the inheritance hierarchy when the root class is drawn at the top. [Firesmith]

dwell time *n.* the time any instance remains in the state after completion of the associated action. [Shlaer/Mellor]
Antonym: ACTION TIME.

dynamic architecture *n.* the logical or physical partitioning of some dynamic behavior. [Firesmith]
Antonym: STATIC ARCHITECTURE.
Examples: The partitioning of an application's dynamic behavior into multiple mechanisms, scenarios, or concurrent threads of control. [Firesmith]

dynamic association *n.* any association that captures a dynamic interaction. [Jacobson]
Antonym: STATIC ASSOCIATION.

D

● **communication association** *n.* any association that models the communication of one object with another. [Jacobson]
Synonym: DYNAMIC ASSOCIATION.
Antonym: STATIC ASSOCIATION.
Commentary: The communication association does not show what kind of stimuli is sent between the objects; this is a level of detail that is saved for interaction diagrams. Communication associations are not named because they are dynamic. [Jacobson]

dynamic binding *n.* any binding that takes place at run-time after the message is received due to compile-time ambiguities caused by inheritance and polymorphism. [Booch, Coad, Firesmith, Jacobson, Martin/Odell, OMG]
Synonyms: DELAYED BINDING, LATE BINDING, RUN-TIME BINDING, VIRTUAL BINDING.
Antonyms: COMPILE-TIME BINDING, EARLY BINDING, STATIC BINDING.
See also: DYNAMICALLY TAGGED.
Commentary: Dynamic binding allows the system to dynamically decide what method to use, based on the type of the current object. [Firesmith, Lorenz] Dynamic binding of operations is typically implemented via a virtual method table. [Firesmith]

dynamic class *n.* any class, all instances of which are dynamic objects that are instantiated and destroyed at run-time. [Firesmith]
Antonym: STATIC CLASS.
Commentary: A dynamic object has its memory allocated (e.g., from the heap) and deallocated during program execution. Dynamic objects are usually referenced via pointers. [Firesmith]

dynamic class set [of an entity] *n.* the set of base classes of all types that the entity may take on at run-time, as a result of polymorphic reattachments and creation instructions. [Eiffel, Meyer]
Contrast with: DYNAMIC TYPE SET.

dynamic classification *n.* (a) any classification whereby the class(es) of an instance vary over time. [Firesmith] (b) any changing of the class of an object. [Martin/Odell]
Antonym: STATIC CLASSIFICATION.
Commentary: Dynamic classification is sometimes used for the same purpose as states and role objects. Dynamic classification is typically not supported by commercial implementation languages and may negatively impact performance. [Firesmith]

dynamic inheritance *n.* any inheritance that requires dynamic binding (e.g., to support polymorphism). [Firesmith]
Antonym: STATIC INHERITANCE.

dynamic invocation *n.* constructing and issuing a request whose signature is possibly not known until runtime. [OMG]
Antonym: STATIC INVOCATION.

dynamic method *n.* any method that may be dynamically bound to an object at run-time. [Firesmith]
Synonym: VIRTUAL METHOD
Antonym: STATIC METHOD.

dynamic model *n.* any model describing those aspects of a system concerned with control, including time, sequencing of operations, and interactions of objects. [Rumbaugh]
Contrast with: BEHAVIORAL MODEL, CONFIGURATION MODEL, DATA MODEL, FUNCTIONAL MODEL, INTERACTION MODEL, INTERFACE MODEL, LANGUAGE MODEL, LIFE-CYCLE MODEL, OBJECT MODEL, OPERATION MODEL, PRESENTATION

MODEL, SEMANTIC MODEL, STATE MODEL, STRUCTURAL MODEL, USE-CASE MODEL.

dynamic object *n.* any object that is instantiated and destroyed at run-time. [Firesmith]

Contrast with: PERSISTENT OBJECT, STATIC OBJECT.

Commentary: A dynamic object has its memory allocated (e.g., from the heap) and deallocated during program execution. Dynamic objects are usually referenced via pointers. [Firesmith]

dynamic object-based application *n.* **1.** one or more programs consisting of a collection of interacting objects. **2.** the end-user functionality provided by one or more programs consisting of a collection of interacting objects. [OMG]

Synonyms: PROCESS, PROGRAM, RUNNING APPLICATION.

Contrast with: STATIC OBJECT-BASED APPLICATION.

dynamic state *n.* any state of a persistent or distributed object, which is stored in memory and is not likely to exist for the whole lifetime of the object. [OMG]

Antonym: PERSISTENT STATE.

dynamic type [of a given expression] *n.* the run-time type of the value returned by the given expression. [Eiffel, Firesmith, Meyer]

Antonym: STATIC TYPE.

See also: POLYMORPHISM.

dynamic type [of a given property] *n.* the run-time type of the value of the given property. [Eiffel, Firesmith, Meyer]

Antonym: STATIC TYPE.

See also: POLYMORPHISM.

dynamic type set [of an entity or expression] *n.* the set of possible dynamic types for the entity or expression. [Eiffel, Meyer]

Contrast with: DYNAMIC CLASS SET.

dynamic typing *n.* any typing that occurs at run-time. [Firesmith, Wirfs-Brock]

Antonym: STATIC TYPING.

dynamically tagged *adj.* describing any name or expression of tagged type whose tag is determined dynamically at run time. [Ada95]

Antonym: STATICALLY TAGGED.

D

E

early binding *n.* any binding that takes place statically before run-time when the associated message is sent. [Firesmith, Martin/Odell, OMG]
Synonyms: COMPILE-TIME BINDING, STATIC BINDING.
Antonyms: DYNAMIC BINDING, LATE BINDING, RUN-TIME BINDING.
Commentary: Early binding allows the compiler (or linker) to decide what method to use, based on the declared class of the object. The term *static binding* is preferred. [Firesmith]

effecting *n.* the process of making a feature effective by providing a definition of a deferred feature. [Eiffel, Firesmith, Meyer]

effective feature *n.* any feature that has a complete implementation. [Eiffel, Firesmith, Meyer]
Antonym: DEFERRED FEATURE.
See also: EFFECTING.
Commentary: Either the origin class of the feature may have supplied both the interface and complete implementation of the feature or else some descendant of the origin class may have supplied or completed the missing implementation. [Firesmith]

Kinds:
- EFFECTIVE METHOD
- EFFECTIVE OPERATION
- EFFECTIVE PROPERTY
- EFFECTIVE ROUTINE

- **effective method** *n.* **1.** any method that has been completely implemented. [Firesmith] **2.** the code that is executed for particular arguments of any generic function. [CLOS]
Antonym: DEFERRED METHOD.

- **effective operation** *n.* any operation that has an associated effective method. [Firesmith]
Synonym: EFFECTIVE ROUTINE.
Antonym: DEFERRED OPERATION.

- **effective property** *n.* any property that has an associated type. [Firesmith]
Antonym: DEFERRED PROPERTY.

- **effective routine** *n.* any inherited deferred routine that has been completed by a descendant. [Eiffel, Meyer]
Synonym: EFFECTIVE OPERATION.
Antonym: DEFERRED ROUTINE.

effective method *n.* **1.** any method that has been completely implemented. [Firesmith] **2.** the code that is executed for particular arguments of any generic function. [CLOS]

Antonym: DEFERRED METHOD.

effective operation *n.* any operation that has an associated effective method. [Firesmith]

Synonym: EFFECTIVE ROUTINE.

Antonym: DEFERRED OPERATION.

effective property *n.* any property that has an associated type. [Firesmith]

Antonym: DEFERRED PROPERTY.

effective routine *n.* any inherited deferred routine that has been completed by a descendant. [Eiffel, Meyer]

Synonym: EFFECTIVE OPERATION.

Antonym: DEFERRED ROUTINE.

Eiffel shelf *n.* the distribution mechanism that makes reusable classes from various sources accessible to Eiffel users worldwide. [Eiffel, Meyer]

elaboration *n.* the process by which declarations take effect. [Firesmith]

elementary type *n.* any type that does not have components. [Ada95]

Antonym: COMPOSITE TYPE.

Examples: Enumeration, numeric, and access types are all elementary types. [Ada95]

embed *v.* *-ed, -ing* to create an object out of a nonobject entity by encapsulating it in an appropriate wrapper. [Firesmith, OMG]

Contrast with: REIFY, WRAPPER.

enabled transition *n.* any transition from a current state. [Embley, Firesmith]

Commentary: Triggers cannot cause transitions to fire unless the transitions are enabled. [Embley, Firesmith]

encapsulation *n.* **1.** (a) the physical localization of features (e.g., properties, behaviors) into a single blackbox abstraction that hides their implementation (and associated design decisions) behind a public interface. [Booch, Firesmith, Jacobson] (b) the packaging of operations and data together into an object type such that the data are only accessible through its interface. [OADSIG] (c) the hiding of data inside an object so that they are only accessible though messages to the object. [Lorenz] (d) the hiding of individual design decisions in modules that reveal as little as possible about their inner workings. [Coad] (e) a means of defining objects and operations that hides their implementation details behind an abstract interface. [Ada95, Martin/Odell] **2.** the physical localization of features. [Berard, Henderson-Sellers, Wirfs-Brock]

Synonym: 1 INFORMATION HIDING, 2 LOCALIZATION.

Contrast with: INFORMATION HIDING, LOCALIZATION.

Example: 1 The packaging of operations and data together into an object type such that the data are only accessible through its interface. [Firesmith, OADSIG]

Commentary: Definition 1 is the combination of localization and information hiding. [Firesmith] Definition 2 does not require information hiding so that features can be encapsulated within a transparent capsule.

ensure *n.* the Eiffel keyword used to introduce a postcondition of a routine that expresses those conditions that the routine guarantees on return, if the precondition was satisfied on entry (i.e., if the routine was called in a state satisfying the precondition). [Eiffel, Meyer]

Contrast with: REQUIRE.

entity *n.* any name used by a class text to refer to values that may at run-time become associated in some way to the instances of the class. In a class context, four kinds of entities may appear:

– attributes of the class;
– local entities of routines, including the redefined entity Result for functions;
– formal routine arguments;
– current, the predefined entity used to represent a reference to the current object. [Eiffel, Meyer]

entity object *n.* **1.** any object in a business system that represents occurrences that are handled in the business. [Jacobson] **2.** any object in an information system that manages either (1) some piece of information that should be held for a significant time and that typically should survive a use case or (2) some resource and its access. [Jacobson]
Contrast with: CONTROL OBJECT, INTERFACE OBJECT.
Examples: **1** Products, deliverables, documents, and other things that are handled in the business can be modeled as entity objects.
Commentary: The object types used in the analysis model are *entity objects, interface objects* and *control objects.* Most entity objects are found early and are obvious. These "obvious" entity objects are often identified in the problem domain object model. Entity objects usually correspond to some concept in real life, outside the system, although this is not always the case. [Jacobson]

entry operation *n.* any state-dependent operation that executes upon transition into a state. [Firesmith]
Antonym: EXIT OPERATION.
Kinds:
• GENERAL ENTRY OPERATION
• SPECIFIC ENTRY OPERATION
• **general entry operation** *n.* any entry operation that does not depend on the incoming transition. [Firesmith]

Antonym: SPECIFIC ENTRY OPERATION.
• **specific entry operation** *n.* any entry operation that depends on the incoming transition. [Firesmith]
Antonym: GENERAL ENTRY OPERATION.

enumeration [type] *n.* any developer-defined type whose instances are named literal objects. [Firesmith]

environment *n.* **1.** the set of direct and indirect terminators of an application. [Coleman, Firesmith] **2.** the local operating system and processor. [Firesmith] **3.** any instance of class Environment that represents a set of objects that is always complete under dependency. In other words, if an object belongs to an environment, all of its dependents, direct or indirect, also belong to the environment. [Eiffel, Meyer]

environment layer *n.* the layer that provides independence of the underlying operating system and hardware. [Firesmith]
Contrast with: COMMUNICATION LAYER, MODEL LAYER, PERSISTENCE LAYER, USER-INTERFACE LAYER.
Commentary: The environment layer is typically built directly on top of the operating system and hardware. [Firesmith]

environmental [object] *n.* any support object that provides independence of the underlying environment (i.e., the processor and operating system). [Firesmith]

equal objects *n.* two objects are equal if and only if they are instances of the same class and the values of their corresponding properties are equal. [Eiffel, Firesmith, Meyer]
Contrast with: IDENTICAL OBJECTS.
See also: EQUAL REFERENCES.
Kinds:
• DEEP EQUAL OBJECTS
• SHALLOW EQUAL OBJECTS

- **deep equal objects** *n.* any objects OX and OY that satisfy the following three conditions:
  - the objects obtained by setting all the reference fields of OX and OY (if any) to void references are equal;
  - for every void reference field of OX, the corresponding field of OY is void;
  - for every non-void reference field of OX, attached to an object PX, the corresponding field of OY is attached to an object PY, and it is possible (recursively) to show, under the assumption that OX is deep equal to OY, that PX is deep equal to PY. [Eiffel, Meyer]

  Antonym: SHALLOW EQUAL OBJECTS.
- **shallow equal objects** *n.* any objects that are field-by-field identical. [Eiffel, Meyer]

  Antonym: DEEP EQUAL REFERENCES.

equal references *n.* two references are equal if and only if they are both void or are attached to equal objects. [Eiffel, Firesmith, Meyer]

Contrast with: IDENTICAL REFERENCES.

See also: EQUAL OBJECTS

Kinds:
  - DEEP EQUAL REFERENCES
  - SHALLOW EQUAL REFERENCES
- **deep equal references** *n.* any references that are either both void or attached to deep-equal objects. [Eiffel, Meyer]

  Antonym: SHALLOW EQUAL REFERENCES.
- **shallow equal references** *n.* any references that are either void or attached to shallow-equal objects.

  Antonym: DEEP EQUAL OBJECTS.

equality expression *n.* any expression that serves to test equality (with the = symbol) or inequality (with the ≠ symbol) of values. The expression e=f has two possible meanings:
  - If both e and f are of reference types, the expression denotes reference equality.
  - If either e or f is of an expanded type, the expression denotes object equality. [Eiffel, Meyer]

equivalence class *n.* any set of property values that cause an object or class to behave in an equivalent manner. [Firesmith, Jacobson]

Contrast with: STATE.

Example: An equivalence class is any set of values of a state attribute that define the state. [Firesmith]

See also: INTERNAL STATE.

Commentary: This is not a true class in the object-oriented sense.

error *n.* **1.** the violation of an assertion. [Eiffel, Meyer] **2.** the violation of a precondition. [Coleman]

essential *adj.* anything (1) whose existence and capabilities are required, (2) that is typically known and understood by the customer or application-domain specialist, and (3) that is identified during requirements analysis and specified in the appropriate requirements specification document, either as a required capability or as a design constraint. [Firesmith]

event *n.* **1.** (a) any significant incident or occurrence that for all practical purposes occurs instantaneously and that must be modeled in the application. [Firesmith] (b) an incident that requires some response [OADSIG] (c) any change within a system. [Embley] (d) anything that occurs instantaneously at some point in time. [Rumbaugh] **2.** in state modeling, (a) any occurrence that

E

causes a state transition. [Booch, Shlaer/ Mellor] (b) the abstraction of any occurrence in the real world that tells us that something is moving to a new state. [Shlaer/Mellor] (c) any change in state. [Martin, OADSIG] **3.** (a) any instantaneous and atomic unit of asynchronous communication between an application and its environment. [Coleman] (b) the sending of any message from one object to another. [Rumbaugh]

Synonyms: **2** (a) TRIGGER, (b) TRANSITION **3** (a) SIGNAL, (b) MESSAGE.

Contrast with: CONDITION.

Commentary: The primary differences between these definitions is whether or not the term *event* should be restricted to state modeling and either cause or be a state transition. Events may be modeled as objects, messages, or triggers. Events are typically modeled in the application by an object, message, exception, or trigger. Events often, but not always, cause state transitions and are therefore often modeled during state modeling. [Firesmith]

Kinds:
- CLOCK EVENT
- EXTERNAL EVENT
  - SOLICITED EVENT
  - UNSOLICITED EVENT
- INTERNAL EVENT

- **clock event** *n.* any special type of event in which a clock time is reached and triggers some operation. [Martin]

- **external event** *n.* (a) any event, the source of which is *outside* the current scope (e.g., application, cluster, object). [Firesmith, Martin/Odell, OADSIG] (b) any event that is generated by an external activity (terminator). [Shlaer/Mellor]

  Antonym: INTERNAL EVENT.

Kinds:
- SOLICITED EVENT
- UNSOLICITED EVENT

- **solicited event** *n.* any external event that was generated in response to some previous operation within the current scope. [Firesmith, Shlaer/ Mellor]

  Antonym: UNSOLICITED EVENT.

- **unsolicited event** *n.* any external event that was not caused to occur by some previous operation within the current scope. [Shlaer/Mellor]

  Antonym: SOLICITED EVENT.

- **internal event** *n.* **1.** any event, the source of which is *inside* the current scope (e.g., application, cluster, object). [Firesmith, Martin/Odell, OADSIG] **2.** any event that is generated by a state model within the system. [Shlaer/Mellor]

  Antonym: EXTERNAL EVENT.

event attribute *n.* **1.** any attribute of an event object. [Firesmith] **2.** the parameters of a message. [Rumbaugh]

Contrast with: PARAMETER.

event channel *n.* any intervening object that allows multiple suppliers to communicate with multiple consumers asynchronously. [OMG]

event data flow *n.* any data flow on an action data flow diagram (ADFD) pointing into a process from nowhere. [Shlaer/Mellor]

event diagram *n.* any diagram that documents events and the sequence of operations triggered by the events. [Martin]

event generator *n.* any process that produces exactly one event as output. [Shlaer/Mellor]

Contrast with: ACCESSOR, EVENT TAKER, TEST, TRANSFORMATION.

event inheritance *n.* any inheritance whereby event subtypes inherit trigger rules and control conditions from their event supertypes. [Martin]

Commentary: If different kinds of events are implemented as instances of different classes of event objects, then there is no need to have a special kind of inheritance for events. [Firesmith]

event instance *n.* any particular unspecified occurrence of an event. [Shlaer/Mellor]

event list *n.* any listing of all the events that have been defined for all the state models. [Shlaer/Mellor]

event model *n.* any model that shows O/Cs and a particular sequence of messages passed among them. [Henderson-Sellers]

Synonym: INTERACTION MODEL.

event monitor *n.* the component of a trigger that detects event occurrences. [Embley]

See also: EVENT, TRIGGER.

Commentary: Event monitors are conceptual devices that *observe* a certain type of event in a system. [Embley]

event service *n.* any service, the purpose of which is to decouple the communication among objects. [OMG]

Commentary: The event service defines the supplier role and the consumer role for objects. [OMG]

event subtype *n.* any subtype of events that inherit trigger rules and control conditions from event supertypes. [Martin]

Antonym: EVENT SUPERTYPE.

event supertype *n.* any supertype of events from which event subtypes can inherit trigger rules and control conditions. [Martin]

Antonym: EVENT SUBTYPE.

event taker *n.* any published operation

corresponding to each event generator that is shown in the state process table as having been assigned to the object under consideration. [Shlaer/Mellor]

Contrast with: EVENT GENERATOR.

event trace [diagram] *n.* any diagram that shows the sender and receiver of events and the sequence of events. [Rumbaugh]

Synonyms: COLLABORATION DIAGRAM, INTERACTION DIAGRAM, MESSAGE-FLOW DIAGRAM.

Commentary: The term *interaction diagram* was originally used for this concept and is less restricted to state modeling.

event type *n.* any type of event that defines the common trigger rules and control conditions for a set of related events. [Martin]

exception *n.* **1.** (a) any abstraction of an exceptional or error condition that is identified and raised by an operation. [Firesmith] (b) any indication that an operation request was not performed successfully. [Eiffel, Meyer] **2.** (a) any exceptional situation. [Ada95] (b) a system event or condition that is not part of normal system behavior. [Embley] **3.** (a) the violation of an assertion. [Booch, Eiffel, Meyer] (b) any violation of a contract. [Eiffel, Meyer] **4.** any object representing an error condition.

Synonym: CONTRACT VIOLATION.

See also: CATCH, EXCEPTION HANDLER, RAISE, RESCUE BLOCK, THROW, TRANSITION.

Examples: Contract violations, the violation of assertions (e.g., invariants, preconditions, postconditions), failure of related hardware, and failure of an operation (e.g., due to arithmetic overflow, lack of memory) are all examples of exceptions. [Eiffel, Firesmith, Meyer]

Commentary: **1** Exceptions should be

used to notify the client that the associated operation could not be performed successfully. Exceptions can be used to produce robust, reliable, and correct objects and classes. An exception should be implemented by an object so that associated properties may be defined and inheritance can be used to capture specialization relationships between classes of exceptions. [Firesmith] 2(b) When an exception arises, it takes precedence over any normal exit transition. [Embley]
Kinds:

- CLASS EXCEPTION
- EXTENT EXCEPTION
- INSTANCE EXCEPTION

- **class exception** *n.* any exception of a class as a whole. [Firesmith]
  Contrast with: EXTENT EXCEPTION, INSTANCE EXCEPTION.
  Example: Instantiation failed is a class exception.

- **extent exception** *n.* any exception of the extent of a class. [Firesmith]
  Contrast with: CLASS EXCEPTION, INSTANCE EXCEPTION.

- **instance exception** *n.* any exception of an individual instance.
  Contrast with: CLASS EXCEPTION, EXTENT EXCEPTION.

exception abstraction *n.* any model of an error condition. [Firesmith]

exception-correct *adj.* describing any routine satisfying the following conditions:
– the rescue block must be such that any branch terminating with a Retry ensures the precondition and the invariant
– any other branch ensures the invariant. [Eiffel, Meyer]

exception coupling *n.* the coupling dependency of any client on its servers due to exception raising. [Firesmith]
Contrast with: AGGREGATION COUPLING, CLASSIFICATION COUPLING, FRIENDSHIP COUPLING, IMPLEMENTATION COUPLING, INHERITANCE COUPLING, INTERFACE COUPLING, MESSAGE COUPLING.

exception handler *n.* any part of an operation to which an exception is propagated and that subsequently deals with the exception. [Firesmith]
Contrast with: EXCEPTION SIGNALER.

exception handling *n.* the management of the detection, raising (a.k.a. throwing), propagation, catching, and dealing with exceptions. [Firesmith]
Commentary: Exception handling provides a way of transferring control and information to an unspecified caller that has expressed willingness to handle exceptions of a given type. The operation that raises the exception abandons execution, and control is transferred to the local exception handler if it exists. Otherwise, the calling operation (possibly in a client object or class) is automatically notified so that it can properly handle the exception (i.e., control is transferred to its exception handler). [Firesmith]

exception occurrence *n.* any occurrence of an exception at run-time. [Ada95]
See also: EXCEPTION, HANDLE, RAISE.

exception protocol *n.* the union of the inbound exception protocol and the outbound exception protocol. [Firesmith]
Antonym: MESSAGE PROTOCOL.
Commentary: The exception protocol consists of all exceptions that can be raised to clients and all server exceptions that must be handled. [Firesmith]

exception signaler *n.* any operation that raises an exception. [Firesmith]
Contrast with: EXCEPTION HANDLER.

exceptional trigger *n.* any trigger that occurs during the abnormal execution of an object or class (e.g., during exception handling). [Firesmith]
Contrast with: NORMAL TRIGGER.

exchange format *n.* the form of a description used to import and export objects. [OMG]

executable class *n.* any class that has one parent that is an "execution support" class, and one or more parents that are normal (non-execution support) classes. The class inherits its functionality from its normal parents, and the ability to execute on a particular type of machine from its execution support parent. [Atkinson]
See also: EXECUTION SUPPORT CLASS.
Commentary: An executable class corresponds to a fully linked, executable object module. [Atkinson]

execution engine *n.* any abstract machine (not a program) that can interpret methods of certain formats, causing the described computations to be performed. [OMG]
Contrast with: METHOD FORMAT.

execution support class *n.* any class that exports methods providing services idiosyncratic of a particular kind of execution environment, and endows its subclasses with the ability to execute in that kind of environment. [Atkinson]
See also: EXECUTABLE CLASS.

exit operation *n.* any state-dependent operation that executes upon transition out of a state. [Firesmith]
Antonym: ENTRY OPERATION.
Kinds:
- GENERAL EXIT OPERATION
- SPECIFIC EXIT OPERATION

- **general exit operation** *n.* any exit operation that does not depend on the outgoing transition. [Firesmith]
Antonym: SPECIFIC EXIT OPERATION.

- **specific exit operation** *n.* any exit operation that depends on the outgoing transition. [Firesmith]
Antonym: GENERAL EXIT OPERATION.

expanded class *n.* any class, the entities of whose corresponding type will have objects as their run-time values. [Eiffel, Meyer]

expanded client [of an expanded type] *n.* any class, some entity of which is of the type. [Eiffel, Meyer]

expanded type *n.* any type T where one of the following conditions holds:
- T is a Class_type whose base class C is an expanded class;
- T is of the form expanded CT;
- T is of the form BIT M for some non-negative integer M. [Eiffel, Meyer]
Contrast with: EXPANDED CLASS.

explicit declaration *n.* any declaration that appears explicitly in the program text. [Ada95]
Antonym: IMPLICIT DECLARATION.
See also: OVERRIDE.

exploded view *n.* any view modeled in its detailed form, making the subsumed components (relationship sets, states, and transitions) of the dominant high-level components explicit or visible. [Embley]
Antonym: IMPLODED VIEW.

export [a feature] *v.* *-ed, -ing* **1.** to declare a feature in the interface and thereby make that feature visible (and therefore accessible) to all clients and colleagues within the scope of the declaration. [Firesmith] **2.** to make available to all classes. [Eiffel, Meyer]
Synonym: MAKE PUBLIC.
Antonym: IMPORT.

export [an object] *v.* *-ed, -ing* to transmit a description of an object to an external entity. [OMG]

exported feature *n.* **1.** any feature that was declared in the interface and thereby made visible and accessible to all clients and colleagues within the scope of the declaration. [Firesmith] **2.** any feature that is available to all classes. [Eiffel, Meyer]

Synonym: 1 SELECTIVELY AVAILABLE, FEATURE 2 GENERALLY AVAILABLE FEATURE.

Antonym: PRIVATE FEATURE.

Kinds:
- PROTECTED FEATURE
- PUBLIC FEATURE
- RESTRICTED FEATURE

- **protected feature** *n.* any feature that is exported to all children, but not to any other clients. [Firesmith]
  Contrast with: PUBLIC FEATURE.

- **public feature** *n.* any feature that is exported to all children and all other potential clients within the scope of the encapsulating object or class. [Firesmith]
  Contrast with: PROTECTED FEATURE.

- **restricted feature** *n.* any feature that is exported to all children as well as to only certain other explicitly declared clients. [Firesmith]
  Contrast with: PROTECTED FEATURE, PUBLIC FEATURE.
  See also: FRIEND.
  Example: All features in a role are restricted to only those clients that need to use the role. [Firesmith]
  Commentary: Restricting a feature's visibility to only certain specified clients allows the designer to restrict visibility of the feature to only those clients that need to (or should) see and access the feature. Restriction in-

creases information hiding at the expense of reuse because it explicitly couples the feature to those clients that see it. Whereas only exported features may be restricted features, C++ unfortunately allows both protected and private features to be made visible via friends. [Firesmith]

expression *n.* any sequence of characters that describes an object that is the *value of the expression.* [Smalltalk]

Kinds:
- BLOCK EXPRESSION
- LITERAL CONSTANT
- MESSAGE EXPRESSION
  - CASCADED MESSAGE EXPRESSION
- VARIABLE NAME

- **block expression** *n.* any expression that describes an object representing deferred activities. [Smalltalk]
  See also: BLOCK.
  Commentary: A block expression consists of a sequence of expressions separated by periods and delimited by square brackets.

- **literal [constant]** *n.* any expression that describes a constant object. [Smalltalk]
  Example: Numbers and strings are literals. [Smalltalk]
  Synonyms: CONSTANT, LITERAL.

- **message expression** *n.* any expression that describes messages to receivers. [Smalltalk]
  Commentary: The value of a message expression is determined by the method the message invokes. That method is found in the class of the receiver. A message expression describes a receiver, selector, and possibly some arguments. [Smalltalk]

  - **cascaded message expression** *n.* any message expression that consists of one description of the receiver followed by several messages separated by semicolons. [Smalltalk]

- **variable name** *n.* any expression that describes the current value of an accessible variable. The value of a variable name is the current value of the variable with that name. [Smalltalk]

expression conformance *n.* any conformance of one expression to another expression, which occurs when the type returned by the first expression conforms to the type returned by the second expression. [Eiffel, Firesmith, Meyer]

extend *v.* -*ed, -ing* to add new features or modify existing features via inheritance. [Firesmith]
See also: EXTENSION.

extend association *n.* any association from one use case to another, specifying how the first use case description extends (i.e., is inserted into) the second use case description. [Jacobson]
Contrast with: USES ASSOCIATION.
See also: PROBE.
Commentary: When performing a use case, it might be performed either with or without the extended description according to some condition. The description of the second use case should be completely independent and unknowing of first use case. Ideally, the first use case should take the initiative and insert itself into the second use case. [Jacobson]

extended relational DBMS *n.* any relational database management system to which object-oriented features (e.g., object identifiers, stored procedures, user-defined types) have been added. [Firesmith, Jacobson]

extensibility *n.* the ease with which the software can be modified to implement

new or changed requirements. [Firesmith, Rumbaugh]
Commentary: Object technology supports extensibility primarily via encapsulation, inheritance, and polymorphism. [Firesmith] Extensibility is increased if new requirements can be implemented by new software without having to change the existing software.

extensible *adj.* describing software that is easy to modify to implement new or changed requirements, especially without modification to existing modules. [Firesmith]
Examples: Classes may easy be extended via subclasses. [Firesmith]

extension [of a given class or type] *n.* **1.** either the addition of new features or the modification of existing features by a child of the given class or type. [Firesmith, Rumbaugh] **2.** (a) the set of all instances of a given type or class (and its ancestors). [Firesmith, Henderson-Sellers, Martin/Odell] (b) the set of values that satisfy the type at any particular time. [OMG] **3.** short for type extension, a tagged type that has been derived type from some ancestor type. [Ada95]
Synonym: **2** EXTENT.
Antonym: **2** INTENSION.
Examples: **3** Every type extension is a tagged type, and is either a *record extension* or a *private extension* of some other tagged type. [Ada95]
Commentary: The first definition is more popular. The term *extent* is more popular if the second definition is intended.
Kinds:
- PRIVATE EXTENSION
- RECORD EXTENSION

- **private extension** *n.* any record type

E

extension that extends another type by adding additional components that are hidden from its clients. [Ada95]
Antonym: RECORD EXTENSION.

- **record extension** *n.* any type extension that extends another type by adding additional components. [Ada95]
Antonym: PRIVATE EXTENSION.

extent [of a given class or type] *n.* **1.** the set of all instances of a given class or type. [Firesmith] **2.** the lifetime of an object (i.e., the period during which storage is bound to the object.
Synonym: **1** EXTENSION. **2** LIFETIME.
Antonym: **1** INTENSION.
Commentary: Definition **1** is by far more popular than definition **2**. The term *lifetime* can be used to avoid confusion if definition **2** is intended.

extent attribute *n.* any attribute that describes an extent rather than an instance or a class. [Firesmith]
Contrast with: CLASS ATTRIBUTE, INSTANCE ATTRIBUTE, PARAMETER.
Example: The current, maximum, and minimum number of instances are all extent attributes. [Firesmith]

extent exception *n.* any exception of the extent of a class. [Firesmith]
Contrast with: CLASS EXCEPTION, INSTANCE EXCEPTION.
Example: Extent assertion failed is an extent exception. [Firesmith]

extent invariant *n.* any invariant of an extent as a whole (e.g., the maximum number of instances). [Firesmith]
Contrast with: CLASS INVARIANT, INSTANCE INVARIANT, MESSAGE INVARIANT.
Example: The current number of instances must never exceed the maximum number of instances. [Firesmith]

extent operation *n.* any operation that operates only on the properties of the

extent of some class or type. [Firesmith]
Contrast with: INSTANCE OPERATION, CLASS OPERATION.
Example: Update and access an extent attribute are extent operations. [Firesmith]

extent property *n.* any property that characterizes the extent of a class as a wholes, rather than the class or any of its individual instances. [Firesmith]
Contrast with: CLASS PROPERTY, INSTANCE PROPERTY.
Kinds:
- EXTENT ATTRIBUTE
- EXTENT EXCEPTION
- EXTENT INVARIANT

- **extent attribute** *n.* any attribute that describes an extent of some class or type. [Firesmith]
Contrast with: CLASS ATTRIBUTE, INSTANCE ATTRIBUTE.
Example: The current, maximum, and minimum number of instances are all extent attributes. [Firesmith]

- **extent exception** *n.* any exception of the extent of some class or type. [Firesmith]
Contrast with: CLASS EXCEPTION, INSTANCE EXCEPTION.
Example: Extent assertion failed is an extent exception. [Firesmith]

- **extent invariant** *n.* any invariant involving only properties of the extent of some class or type. [Firesmith]
Contrast with: CLASS INVARIANT, INSTANCE INVARIANT, MESSAGE INVARIANT.
Example: The current number of instances must never exceed the maximum number of instances. [Firesmith]

external event *n.* (a) any event, the source of which is *outside* the current scope (e.g., application, cluster, object). [Fire-

smith, Martin/Odell, OADSIG] (b) any event that is generated by an external activity (terminator). [Shlaer/Mellor]
Antonym: INTERNAL EVENT.
Kinds:
- SOLICITED EVENT
- UNSOLICITED EVENT
- **solicited event** *n.* any external event that was generated in response to some previous operation within the current scope. [Firesmith, Shlaer/Mellor]
Antonym: UNSOLICITED EVENT.
- **unsolicited event** *n.* any external event that was not caused to occur by some previous operation within the current scope. [Shlaer/Mellor]
Antonym: SOLICITED EVENT.

external-event list *n.* any concise list of the events that occur just outside the automation boundary and require action to take place inside the automated portion of the system. [Shlaer/Mellor]

external object *n.* any object that is external to the system, yet nevertheless affects the system. [Martin]

external operation *n.* **1.** any operation that sends messages directly to other objects or classes. [Firesmith] **2.** any operation that is external to the system, yet nevertheless affects the system. [Martin]
Antonym: INTERNAL OPERATION.
Contrast with: EXTERNAL ROUTINE.

external routine *n.* any foreign routine as viewed from the text of the current language. [Eiffel, Meyer]
Synonyms: CONCRETE OPERATION, EFFECTIVE OPERATION.
Antonym: INTERNAL ROUTINE.
Contrast with: EXTERNAL OPERATION.
See also: FOREIGN ROUTINE.

externalized object reference *n.* any object reference expressed as an ORB-specific string, suitable for storage in files or other external media. [OMG]

E

F

facade [pattern] *n.* the structural object design pattern that provides a unified subsystem interface to a set of objects. [Gamma, Helm, Johnson, and Vlissides]

factor *v.* *-ed, -ing* to move common features from two or more descendants into their common ancestor. [Firesmith]
See also: INHERITANCE, POLYMORPHISM.
Commentary: Factoring avoids redundancy, but should probably not be used if it would violate specialization inheritance or if the ancestor would become a poor abstraction. Improper factoring can decrease understandability and maintainability. [Firesmith]

factory *n.* **1.** any object that creates other objects. [OMG] **2.** that part of any class that creates new instances. [Firesmith]
Synonyms: **1** CLASS, **2** CONSTRUCTOR.
Commentary: Each factory has a well-defined IDL interface and implementation in some programming language. Factories provide the client with specialized operations to naturally create and initialized new instances. [OMG]

factory method [pattern] *n.* the creational class design pattern that defines an interface for creating an object, but defers instantiation of the object to subclasses.

[Gamma, Helm, Johnson, and Vlissides]
Synonym: VIRTUAL CONSTRUCTOR.

family *n.* the set of classes in a single inheritance structure. [Firesmith]
Contrast with: COMMUNITY.
Example: The graphical shapes classes developed for a drawing application form a family. [Firesmith]

feature *n.* **1.** any resource (e.g., attribute, link, message, exception, operation, invariant, cluster) localized within something else. Features are either exported by the interface or hidden in the implementation. [Firesmith] **2.** any feature is either an attribute, describing information stored with each instance, or a routine, describing an algorithm. The features of a class include its inherited features and its immediate features. [Eiffel, Meyer, Rumbaugh] **3.** any entity named in a class interface. [Coleman]
Synonyms: CHARACTERISTIC, MEMBER.
Commentary: Objects, classes, clusters, assemblies, scenarios, and systems can have features. [Firesmith] The term *feature* was popularized by Eiffel.
Kinds:
- DEFERRED FEATURE
  - DEFERRED METHOD

- DEFERRED OPERATION
- DEFERRED PROPERTY
• EFFECTIVE FEATURE
  - EFFECTIVE METHOD
  - EFFECTIVE OPERATION
  - EFFECTIVE PROPERTY
• EXPORTED FEATURE
  - PROTECTED FEATURE
  - PUBLIC FEATURE
    + AVAILABLE FEATURE
      > GENERALLY AVAILABLE
        FEATURE
      > SELECTIVELY AVAILABLE
        FEATURE
  - RESTRICTED FEATURE
• FLUID FEATURE
• FROZEN FEATURE
• IMMEDIATE FEATURE
• INHERITED FEATURE
• NEW FEATURE
• POTENTIALLY AMBIGUOUS FEATURF
• PRECURSOR
• PRIVATE FEATURE
• REPLICATED FEATURE
• SECRET FEATURE
• SHARED FEATURE

• **deferred feature** *n.* any feature that does *not* have a complete implementation. [Eiffel, Firesmith, Meyer]
Antonym: EFFECTIVE FEATURE.
See also: DEFERRMENT.
Commentary: A *deferred feature* must be made effective in a descendant before that descendant may be instantiated. [Firesmith]
Kinds:
  - DEFERRED METHOD
  - DEFERRED OPERATION
  - DEFERRED PROPERTY

- **deferred method** *n.* any incomplete method that therefore does not implement a complete functional abstraction and that must

therefore be made effective prior to execution. [Firesmith]
Antonym: CONCRETE METHOD.
Commentary: A deferred method often has preconditions and post-conditions defined, but may include a TBD (to be determined) statement or be missing its executable statements. Deferred methods are used during analysis and design, but must be made effective prior to execution. [Firesmith]

- **deferred operation** *n.* any operation that does not have an associated method. [Firesmith]
Antonym: EFFECTIVE OPERATION.
Rationale: The implementation of the operation is deferred until the descendant supplies the implementation.
Commentary: All deferred operations must be made effective in a descendant before the descendant may be instantiated. [Firesmith]

- **deferred property** *n.* any property that does not have an associated type. [Firesmith]
Antonym: EFFECTIVE PROPERTY.

• **effective feature** *n.* any feature that has a complete implementation. [Firesmith]
Antonym: DEFERRED FEATURE.
See also: EFFECTING.
Commentary: Either the origin class of the feature may have supplied both the interface and complete implementation of the feature or else some descendant of the origin class may have supplied or completed the missing implementation. [Firesmith]
Kinds:
  - EFFECTIVE METHOD
  - EFFECTIVE OPERATION
  - EFFECTIVE PROPERTY

- **effective method** *n.* any method that has been completely implemented. [Firesmith]
  Antonym: DEFERRED METHOD.
- **effective operation** *n.* any operation that has an associated method. [Firesmith]
  Antonym: DEFERRED OPERATION.
- **effective property** *n.* any property that has an associated type. [Firesmith]
  Antonym: DEFERRED PROPERTY.
- **exported feature** *n.* **1.** any feature that was declared in the interface and thereby made visible and accessible to all clients and colleagues within the scope of the declaration. [Firesmith] **2.** any feature that is available to all classes. [Eiffel, Meyer]
  Synonym: **1** SELECTIVELY AVAILABLE FEATURE, **2** GENERALLY AVAILABLE FEATURE.
  Antonym: PRIVATE FEATURE.
  Kinds:
  - PROTECTED FEATURE
  - PUBLIC FEATURE
    + AVAILABLE FEATURE
      > GENERALLY AVAILABLE FEATURE
      > SELECTIVELY AVAILABLE FEATURE
  - RESTRICTED FEATURE
- **protected feature** *n.* any feature that is exported to all children and hidden from all other potential clients within the scope of the encapsulating object or class. [Firesmith]
  Contrast with: PUBLIC FEATURE.
  Commentary: In C++, protected members are typically declared in the interface (i.e., header file) but implemented in the body (e.g., cpp file). [Firesmith]

- **public feature** *n.* any feature that is exported to all children and to all other potential clients within the scope of the encapsulating object or class. [Firesmith]
  Contrast with: PROTECTED FEATURE.
  Kinds:
  + AVAILABLE FEATURE
    > GENERALLY AVAILABLE FEATURE
    > SELECTIVELY AVAILABLE FEATURE
+ **available feature** *n.* any public feature that is either exported to all classes or selectively exported to specific classes and their descendants [Eiffel, Meyer]
  Contrast with: SECRET FEATURE.
  > **generally available feature** *n.* a public feature that is exported to all classes. [Eiffel, Meyer]
    Synonym: EXPORTED FEATURE.
    Antonym: SELECTIVELY AVAILABLE FEATURE.
  > **selectively available feature** *n.* any feature that is only available to specific classes and their descendants. [Eiffel, Meyer]
    Antonym: GENERALLY AVAILABLE FEATURE.
- **restricted feature** *n.* any feature that is exported to all children as well as to only certain other explicitly declared clients. [Firesmith]
  Contrast with: PROTECTED FEATURE, PUBLIC FEATURE.
  See also: FRIEND.
  Example: All features in a role are restricted to only those clients that need to use the role. [Firesmith]
  Commentary: Restricting a feature's visibility to only certain specified

clients allows the designer to restrict visibility of the feature to only those clients that need to (or should) see and access the feature. Restriction increases information hiding at the expense of reuse because it explicitly couples the feature to those clients that see it. [Firesmith]

- **fluid feature** *n.* any feature that may be redefined by descendants of the origin class.

Antonym: FROZEN FEATURE.

See also: VIRTUAL.

Commentary: Because designers cannot usually foresee all possible legitimate extensions of their classes, features should by default be fluid in order to allow polymorphism. Note that Eiffel takes this recommended approach, whereas C++ takes the opposite approach as default. [Firesmith]

- **frozen feature** *n.* any feature that may *not* be redefined by descendants of the origin class.

Antonym: FLUID FEATURE.

Commentary: Because features should by default be fluid in order to support polymorphism, frozen features should be explicitly declared as frozen. Frozen features are used by the designer to restrict the possible extensions of the origin class. [Firesmith]

- **immediate feature** *n.* any new feature not obtained from ancestors via inheritance. [Eiffel, Meyer]

Synonym: NEW FEATURE.

Antonym: INHERITED FEATURE.

- **inherited feature** *n.* **1.** any feature obtained from ancestors via inheritance. [Firesmith] **2.** any feature obtained by a class from its parents, if any. [Eiffel, Meyer]

See also: PRECURSOR [OF AN INHERITED FEATURE], SEED [OF A GIVEN FEATURE].

Antonym: IMMEDIATE FEATURE.

- **new feature** *n.* any feature not obtained from ancestors via inheritance.

Synonym: IMMEDIATE FEATURE.

Antonym: INHERITED FEATURE.

- **potentially ambiguous feature** *n.* any feature that is potentially ambiguous in a repeated descendant because it may be dynamically bound in multiple ways. [Eiffel, Firesmith, Meyer]

See also: REPEATED INHERITANCE.

- **precursor [of an inherited feature]** *n.* the version of the feature in the parent from which it was inherited. [Firesmith]

See also: REDEFINITION.

- **private feature** *n.* **1.** any feature that is hidden from both external clients and descendants. [Firesmith] **2.** any feature that is hidden from external clients. [Eiffel, Henderson-Sellers]

Contrast with: PROTECTED FEATURE, PUBLIC FEATURE.

Commentary: Definition 1 follows the popular C++ distinction between the terms *private* and *protected*. A *private feature* must be used with care as it may violate subtyping, specialization inheritance, and polymorphic substitutability. An exported *feature* may be transformed into a *private feature* in derived classes by the use of *private inheritance*. In C++, private features (e.g., members functions) are typically declared in the interface (i.e., header file) but implemented in the body (e.g., cpp file). [Firesmith]

- **replicated feature** *n.* any feature, multiple copies of which exist because of repeated replicated inheritance.

Contract with: SHARED FEATURE.

See also: REPEATED REPLICATED INHERITANCE.

- **secret feature** *n.* any feature whose Feature_clause has an empty Clients list, that is to say, begins with feature [] and is therefore not available to any classes. [Eiffel, Meyer]
Synonym: PRIVATE FEATURE.
Contrast with: AVAILABLE FEATURE.

- **shared feature** *n.* any multiply inherited feature, only one copy of which exists because of shared repeated inheritance.
Contrast with: REPLICATED FEATURE.
See also: SHARED REPEATED INHERITANCE.

feature name *n.* any name that uniquely refers to a single feature within a specified class. [Eiffel, Firesmith, Meyer]
Commentary: Because a feature may be renamed in a derived class, the name of a feature is relative to a specified class. [Firesmith]
Kinds:
  - CURRENT NAME
  - FINAL NAME
  - INHERITED NAME
  - OPERATION NAME
  - ORIGINAL NAME
  - PROPERTY NAME

- **current name [of a given feature]** *n.* the name of the given feature in a specified class, which is defined as follows:
  - the original name of the feature if the feature is not inherited (i.e., if the specified class is the class of origin).
  - the inherited name of the given feature if the feature is inherited and not renamed in the specified class.
  - the new name if the given feature is inherited and renamed in the specified class. [Firesmith]

Synonym: FINAL NAME.

- **final name [of a given feature]** *n.* the name of the given feature in a specified class. The final feature name is:
  - the original feature name if the feature is not inherited (i.e., if the specified class is the class of origin.)
  - the inherited feature name if the feature is inherited and not renamed in the specified class.
  - the new name if the feature is inherited and renamed in the specified class. [Eiffel, Meyer]
Synonym: CURRENT NAME.

- **inherited name [of a given feature]** *n.* the name of the given feature in its parent class. [Eiffel, Firesmith, Meyer]
Contrast with: FINAL NAME [OF A GIVEN FEATURE], ORIGINAL NAME.

- **operation name** *n.* **1.** any name that uniquely refers to a single operation within a specified class. [Firesmith] **2.** any name used in a request to identify an operation. [OMG]
Synonym: OPERATION IDENTIFIER.
Examples: the name used in the signature of any operation and the name used in the corresponding messages. [Firesmith]

- **original name [of a given feature]** *n.* the name of the given feature as declared in its class of origin. [Eiffel, Firesmith, Meyer]

- **property name** *n.* any name that uniquely refers to a single property within a specified class. [Firesmith]

feature redefinition *n.* the redefinition of the interface or implementation of an inherited feature. [Eiffel, Firesmith, Meyer]
See also: EFFECTING, PRECURSOR, REDECLARATION.
Commentary: A redeclaration is a re-

definition if and only if it is not an effecting (i.e., if it does not make a deferred feature effective). [Firesmith]

feature type *n.* (a) the type of a property or the return type of an operation (if any). [Firesmith] (b) the declared type of a feature. [Eiffel, Meyer]

Kinds:

- CURRENT TYPE
- INHERITED TYPE
- ORIGINAL TYPE

- **current type [of a given feature]** *n.* the type of the feature in a specified class, which is defined as follows:
  - the original type of the feature if the feature is neither inherited nor cast to a new type (i.e., if the specified class is the class of origin).
  - the inherited type of the given feature if the feature is inherited and not cast to a new type in the specified class.
  - the new type if the type of the given feature has been cast in the specified class. [Firesmith]
- **inherited type [of a given feature]** *n.* the current type of the given feature in its parent class. [Firesmith]
- **original type [of a given feature]** *n.* the type of the given feature as declared in its class of origin. [Firesmith]

fern diagram *n.* any diagram documenting inheritance relationships, drawn with subclasses to the left of superclasses. [Martin]

See also: CLASS HIERARCHY, INHERITANCE.

field *n.* **1.** any encapsulated property of its enclosing object, class, or extent. **2.** any part of an aggregate object. [Booch] **3.** the OOPL implementation of an attribute type. [Martin/Odell]

Synonyms: **1** ATTRIBUTE, DATA MEMBER, INSTANCE ATTRIBUTE, PROPERTY, SLOT.

Rationale: Term originally used for parts of records.

Commentary: The terms *property* or *attribute* may be used instead to avoid the many preobject-oriented connotations of the term *field*.

final name [of a given feature] *n.* the name of the given feature in a specified class. The final feature name is:

- the original feature name if the feature is not inherited (i.e., if the specified class is the class of origin);
- the inherited feature name if the feature is inherited and not renamed in the specified class;
- the new name if the feature is inherited and renamed in the specified class. [Eiffel, Meyer]

Synonym: CURRENT NAME.

final name set *n.* the final names of all the features of a class. [Eiffel, Meyer]

Contrast with: ORIGINAL FEATURE NAME.

final state *n.* (a) any terminal state from which its object or class cannot transition. [Firesmith] (b) any state that serves as the end of the life cycle for an instance. [Shlaer/Mellor]

Synonym: END STATE, STOP STATE.

Antonym: INITIAL STATE.

final transition *n.* any transition with no subsequent states. [Embley]

Antonym: INITIAL TRANSITION.

fire [a transition] *v.* *-ed, -ing* to cause a state transition. [Embley, Firesmith, Rumbaugh]

fixed aggregate *n.* **1.** any aggregate, the aggregation structure of which cannot change, but the component parts of which can change. [Firesmith] **2.** any aggregate with a predefined number and types of component parts. [Rumbaugh]

Contrast with: CONSTANT AGGREGATE, VARIABLE AGGREGATE.

flatten (a derived class in an inheritance structure) *v. -ed, -ing* to determine and document the effects of inheritance resulting in the given descendant class by means of a stand alone class that includes all of the features inherited from the ancestors of the descendant class. [Firesmith]

Commentary: A flattened class is used (1) to fake inheritance in languages that do not support it and (2) to display to people the end result of inheritance, especially if multiple inheritance or deep inheritance structures are involved. [Firesmith]

flexibility *n.* the ease with which the software can be used in different ways to accomplish the same overall purpose. [Firesmith]

fluid feature *n.* any feature that may be redefined by descendants of the origin class. [Firesmith]

Antonym: FROZEN FEATURE.

See also: VIRTUAL.

Commentary: Because designers cannot usually foresee all possible legitimate extensions of their classes, features should by default be fluid in order to allow polymorphism. Note that Eiffel takes this recommended approach, whereas C++ takes the opposite approach as default. [Firesmith]

• **fluid operation** *n.* any operation that may be redefined by descendants of the origin class.

Antonym: FROZEN OPERATION.

See also: VIRTUAL.

Commentary: Because designers cannot usually foresee all possible legitimate extensions of their classes, operations should by default be fluid in

order to allow polymorphism. Note that Eiffel takes this recommended approach, whereas C++ takes the opposite approach as default.

flyweight [pattern] *n.* the structural object design pattern that allows a shared object (the flyweight) to be simultaneously used in multiple contexts. [Gamma, Helm, Johnson, and Vlissides]

foreign module *n.* any module on a class structure chart that does not belong to the class being depicted. [Shlaer/Mellor]

Example: A foreign module may be either a module of another class, a utility function, or a friend function that is not a member of any class. [Firesmith]

foreign operation *n.* any operation imported from another language. [Firesmith]

Contrast with: EXTERNAL OPERATION.

foreign routine *n.* any routine imported from another language. [Eiffel, Meyer]

Contrast with: EXTERNAL ROUTINE.

fork diagram *n.* any interaction diagram that exhibits an extreme structure in which one object sends messages to numerous other objects. [Jacobson]

Antonym: STAIR DIAGRAM.

See also: INTERACTION DIAGRAM.

Rationale: The message arcs from the central control object look like the tines on a fork.

Commentary: By looking for fork or stair structures, the interaction diagram can be used to assess how decentralized an architecture is. [Jacobson]

formal argument *n.* any argument that specifies the actual value to be supplied by the client. [Firesmith]

Synonym: FORMAL PARAMETER.

Antonym: ACTUAL ARGUMENT.

Commentary: Actual arguments must be supplied for each formal argument prior to execution or instantiation. The specification of a formal argument may include its name, its mode (e.g., in, out, or in and out), its type, and any default value). [Firesmith]

- **generic formal argument** *n.* any formal argument of a generic that must be supplied by the client as part of the instantiation process. [Firesmith]

Synonym: GENERIC FORMAL PARAMETER.

Commentary: Actual arguments must be supplied for each generic formal argument prior to instantiation. [Firesmith]

formal parameter *n.* **1.** the specification of a parameter of a message, operation, or generic whose actual value must be supplied prior to execution or instantiation. [Firesmith] **2.** any object directly visible within a subprogram body that represents the actual parameter passed to the subprogram in a call. [Ada95]

Synonym: FORMAL ARGUMENT.

Antonym: ACTUAL PARAMETER.

Commentary: The specification of a formal parameter may include its name, its mode (e.g., in, out, or in and out), its type, and any default value). [Firesmith]

- **generic formal parameter** *n.* any formal parameter of a generic that must be supplied by the client as part of the instantiation process. [Firesmith]

Synonym: GENERIC FORMAL ARGUMENT.

Commentary: Actual parameters must be supplied for each generic formal parameter prior to instantiation. [Firesmith]

fountain model *n.* the iterative, incremental, parallel object-oriented development cycle popularized by the MOSES method that continues the wa-

ter metaphor of the waterfall model. [Henderson-Sellers]

Commentary: The fountain lifecycle model is a high level visualization of an iterative and recursive development process that permits visualization of a seamless transition and reuse. [Henderson-Sellers]

frame *n.* any object in a knowledgebase that has a collection of rules associated with it. [Martin]

See also: RULE.

framework *n.* **1.** (a) any large reusable, generic specification, design, code, and test pattern of part of an application, consisting primarily of classes (possibly organized into clusters and subframeworks) that implement common capabilities. [Firesmith] (b) any portion of a software system that is designed to provide some useful services through refinement and extension by client developers. [Lorenz] **2.** (a) any set of prebuilt classes and methods that define the basic structure of some end user functions, leaving the application-specific details to be filled in by developers. [Booch, Henderson-Sellers, Lorenz, Wirfs-Brock] (b) any set of reusable classes in a block that have a well-defined protocol, that are used to build other blocks, and that provide a skeleton on which to build an application. [Jacobson] c) at an implementation level, any set of classes that cooperate to achieve the goal of providing some functionality. [Lorenz] **3.** any implementation of a design pattern. [Lorenz]

Contrast with: CLASS LIBRARY, IDIOM, MECHANISM, PATTERN.

Examples: Both GUI frameworks and relational database wrapper frame-

F

works are popular domain-independent frameworks.

Commentary: A framework is a kind of pattern that provides reuse in the large by capturing reusable strategic analysis and design decisions that provide a skeleton on which to build multiple applications. A framework exports a number of individual classes and mechanisms that clients can use or adapt. [Booch, Firesmith]

framework class *n.* any class of frameworks. [Firesmith]

Contrast with: CLUSTER.

free operation *n.* any operation that is not encapsulated within a class; (i.e. a non-object-oriented operation). [Firesmith]

Synonym: FREE SUBPROGRAM.

free subprogram *n.* any operation that is not encapsulated within a class; (i.e. a nonobject-oriented operation). [Booch]

Synonym: FREE OPERATION.

Commentary: The term *free operation* can be used instead to avoid the Ada-specific connotation of the term *subprogram.*

freeze *v.* -*froze,* -*freezing* **1.** to declare a feature to be frozen and therefore not redefinable via inheritance in the descendants). [Eiffel, Firesmith, Meyer] **2.** to store a persistent object in a database.

Synonym: PICKLE.

friend *n.* the C++ term for an *external* entity whose implementation may reference the hidden members (a.k.a. features) of another class, which permits the violation of information hiding. [Booch, C++, Firesmith]

See also: ACCESS CONTROL.

Example: Because encapsulation hides state properties, a class may grant an associated test class access to its hidden

features in order to simplify state-based testing. [Firesmith]

Commentary: The *friend* mechanism provides a way for a class to grant other classes and individual functions access to its hidden members. Friendship, like all other access, is granted by the class—*not* unilaterally grabbed by the friend. [C++] C++ is the only popular OOPL that allows friends to touch the private parts of classes. Such intimate access is a source of many bugs and should only be used with great care and justification. [Firesmith]

Kinds:

- FRIEND CLASS
- FRIEND FUNCTION
- FRIEND MODULE
- FRIEND OPERATION

- **friend class** *n.* **1.** the C++ term for any external class whose implementation has been granted permission by another class to reference its hidden properties and operations in violation of information hiding. [C++, Firesmith] **2.** any class that either invokes an internal operation of another class or makes direct access of the data of the other class. [Shlaer/Mellor]

  Contrast with: FRIEND FUNCTION, FRIEND OPERATION.

- **friend function** *n.* the C++ term for any external function, the implementation of which may reference the hidden members of another class which permits the violation of information hiding. [C++, Firesmith]

  Synonym: FRIEND OPERATION.

  Contrast with: FRIEND CLASS.

- **friend module** *n.* any module that has been granted permission by a class to either invoke an internal operation of the class or make direct access of the data of the class. [Shlaer/ Mellor]

Contrast with: FRIEND CLASS, FRIEND FUNCTION, FRIEND OPERATION.

- **friend operation** *n.* any external operation that has been granted permission by another class to reference the hidden properties and operations of the granting class in violation of its encapsulation. [Firesmith]

Synonym: FRIEND FUNCTION.

Contrast with: FRIEND CLASS.

friendship coupling *n.* the high coupling dependency of any friend on the class that declares it a friend. [Firesmith]

Contrast with: AGGREGATION COUPLING, CLASSIFICATION COUPLING, EXCEPTION COUPLING, IMPLEMENTATION COUPLING, INHERITANCE COUPLING, INTERFACE COUPLING, MESSAGE COUPLING.

frozen feature *n.* any feature that may *not* be redefined by descendants of the origin class. [Eiffel, Firesmith, Meyer]

Antonym: FLUID FEATURE.

Commentary: Because features should by default be fluid in order to support polymorphism, frozen features should be explicitly declared as frozen. Frozen features are used by the designer to restrict the possible extensions of the origin class. [Firesmith]

frozen operation *n.* any operation that may *not* be redefined by descendants of the origin class. [Firesmith]

Antonym: FLUID OPERATION.

Commentary: Because operations should by default be fluid in order to support polymorphism, frozen operations should be explicitly declared as frozen. Frozen operations are used by the designer to restrict the possible extensions of the origin class. [Firesmith]

fully deferred class *n.* any deferred class,

all of whose features are deferred. [Eiffel, Firesmith, Meyer]

Antonym: PARTIALLY DEFERRED CLASS

function *n.* **1.** any sequential operation that returns a value. [Ada95, C++, Eiffel, Firesmith] **2.** (a) any input/output mapping resulting from some object's behavior. [Booch] (b) any operation that maps an object of one set into a set of objects in the same or different set. [Martin/Odell]

Synonym: **1** METHOD, OPERATION, SERVICE. **2** ATTRIBUTE TYPE.

Contrast with: **2** PROCESS.

Kinds:

- BASE FUNCTION
- CHANGE-CLASS FUNCTION
- COMPUTED FUNCTION
- FRIEND FUNCTION
- GENERIC FUNCTION
- MEMBER FUNCTION
  - VIRTUAL MEMBER FUNCTION
    + PURE VIRTUAL FUNCTION
- VIRTUAL FUNCTION

- **base function** *n.* any function whose mapping is fixed by assertion. [Martin/Odell]

Antonym: COMPUTED FUNCTION.

- **change-class function** *n.* the function *change-class* changes the class of an instance from its current class, C_{from} to a different class, C_{to}. [CLOS]

- **computed function** *n.* any function whose mapping is derived or computed. [Martin/Odell]

Antonym: BASE FUNCTION.

- **friend function** *n.* the C++ term for any external function whose implementation may reference the hidden members of another class which permits the violation of information hiding. [C++, Firesmith]

Synonym: FRIEND OPERATION.

Contrast with: FRIEND CLASS.

- **generic function** *n.* **1.** (a) a parameterized function encapsulated within an object or class. [Ada, Firesmith] (b) any function whose behavior depends on the classes or identities of the arguments supplied to it. [CLOS] **2.** any function that may be redefined by derived classes. [Booch] **3.** a function object that contains a set of methods, a lambda-list, a method combination type, and other information. [CLOS]

  Synonyms: **1** GENERIC OPERATION. **2** VIRTUAL MEMBER FUNCTION.

  See also: LAMBDA-LIST.

  Commentary: Definition 1 is far more traditional and popular than definitions 2 and 3.

- **member function** *n.* the C++ term for any function encapsulated within an object or class. [Booch, C++, Firesmith]

  - **virtual member function** *n.* any C++ member function that may be dynamically bound to an object at run-time. [C++, Firesmith]

    Synonyms: DYNAMIC OPERATION, VIRTUAL FUNCTION, VIRTUAL OPERATION.

    Contrast with: STATIC OPERATION.

    + **pure virtual function** *n.* the C++ term for any virtual function whose implementation is deferred and must be supplied by a descendant base class before the descendant class can be instantiated. [Firesmith]

      Contrast with: ABSTRACT.

      Commentary: Pure virtual functions are used to create deferred classes. [Firesmith]

- **virtual function** *n.* any function that

may be dynamically bound to an object at run-time. [Booch]

Synonyms: DYNAMIC OPERATION, VIRTUAL MEMBER FUNCTION, VIRTUAL OPERATION.

Contrast with: STATIC OPERATION.

functional *n.* any operation that has other operations as arguments. [Firesmith]

functional abstraction *n.* any model of a sequential operation. [Firesmith]

Contrast with: PROCESS ABSTRACTION.

functional cohesion *n.* the degree to which something implements a single functional abstraction. [Firesmith]

functional decomposition *n.* the traditional development method in which functional abstractions are decomposed into their subfunctions. [Firesmith]

Commentary: Functional decomposition is generally considered to be a relatively poor and obsolete technique within the object community (and by its original proponents) because it destroys the localization of objects and increasing data coupling due to the scattering of their attributes and operations throughout the software. Although only rarely necessary due to the small average size of operations within objects, functional decomposition may still be appropriate *within an object* or *class* if an operation should be decomposed because it is too large. [Firesmith]

functional interface *n.* any interface that defines the operations invoked by users of an object service. The audience for these interfaces is the service consumer, the user of the service. These interfaces present the functionality (the useful operations) of the service. [OMG]

Contrast with: CONSTRUCTION INTERFACES, SYSTEM MANAGEMENT INTERFACES.

See also: AUDIENCE.

functional model *n.* any model describing those aspects of a system that transform values using functions, mappings, constraints, and functional dependencies. The emphasis is on processing inputs into outputs and operations rather than on objects and state. [OADSIG, Rumbaugh]

Contrast with: DYNAMIC MODEL, INTERACTION MODEL, OBJECT MODEL.

Examples: Data flow diagrams (DFDs), functional decomposition diagrams, and HIPO charts are used in functional models. [Firesmith]

Commentary: Rumbaugh's functional model is controversial in the object community because it primarily consists of data-flow diagrams. [Firesmith]

function call *n.* **1.** the C++ term for sending a message. [Firesmith] **2.** any postfix expression consisting of the name of a function followed by parentheses containing a possibly empty, comma-separated list of expressions that constitute the actual arguments to the function. [C++]

Synonym: SEND A MESSAGE.

function overloading *n.* the use of a single name for several member functions of the same class. [C++]

See also: OVERLOADING.

functor [object] *n.* any object that models an operation.

See also: REIFY.

fundamental pattern *n.* the collection-worker pattern, of which all others are variations. [Coad]

future [object] *n.* **1.** any object that transparently takes the place of another object that cannot yet be instantiated. [Firesmith] **2.** any asynchronous computation that will result, when completed, in the desired object.

Contrast with: PROXY.

See also: LAZY INITIALIZATION.

Example: Futures are used as temporary incomplete proxies in GUI interfaces when users would have to wait too long for the desired view object to appear. [Firesmith]

F

G

garbage collection *n.* **1.** that part of memory management concerned with heap compaction and the reclaiming of the memory of dynamic objects that should be deallocated (e.g., that are no longer referenced or pointed to). [Firesmith] **2.** any language mechanism for automatically deallocating data structures that can no longer be accessed and are therefore not needed. [Rumbaugh]
Kinds:
- AUTOMATIC GARBAGE COLLECTION
- MANUAL GARBAGE COLLECTION
- **automatic garbage collection** *n.* the language mechanism for automatically performing heap compaction and deallocating the memory of objects (and data structures) that can no longer be accessed and that is therefore no longer needed. [Firesmith] *Commentary:* Eiffel and Smalltalk provide automatic garbage collection. [Firesmith]
- **manual garbage collection** *n.* the manual use of destructors to deallocate the memory of objects that are no longer needed. [Firesmith] *Commentary:* C++ requires the programmer to manually perform gar-

bage collection. [Firesmith]
garbage collector *n.* any software tool that automatically reclaims the storage associated with unused or unreachable objects, relieving programmers from this tedious and error-prone task. [Eiffel, Firesmith, Meyer]
gateway product *n.* any product that provides a wrapper to nonobject software.
Example: A product that provides interfaces to relational databases is a gateway product.
general entry operation *n.* any entry operation that does not depend on the incoming transition. [Firesmith]
Antonym: SPECIFIC ENTRY OPERATION.
general exit operation *n.* any exit operation that does not depend on the outgoing transition. [Firesmith]
Antonym: SPECIFIC EXIT OPERATION.
general semantic net (GSN) *n.* any general semantic net that documents a collection of related objects, classes, subsystems or clusters, terminators, and the important semantic relationships (primarily links or associations) between them. [Firesmith]
Contrast with: AGGREGATION DIAGRAM, CONTEXT DIAGRAM, INHERITANCE DI-

AGRAM, MODEL–VIEW–CONTROLLER DIAGRAM.

generalization *n.* **1.** the process of creating a generalization from one or more specializations. [Firesmith, Henderson-Sellers, Jacobson, Martin] **2.** the result of using the generalization process. [Fire-smith] **3.** any relationship from a specialization to one or more of its generalizations. [Firesmith]

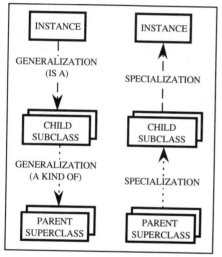

Generalization

Antonym: SPECIALIZATION, SUBTYPING.
Examples: **1** creating a new generalized class or type by factoring out common characteristics and responsibilities from one or more existing classes or types (e.g., the specializations). [Firesmith] **2** (a) any ancestor of a given type or class. For example, vehicles are generalizations of cars, boats, and aircraft. [Firesmith] b) any class or type of a given instance. [Firesmith] **3** (a) the *a-kind-of* relationship from a specialization to its more general parent. [Coleman, Firesmith, Rumbaugh] (b) the *is-a* relationship from an instance to its more general type or class. [Firesmith]

Commentary: The extent of a generalized (class or type) is a superset of the union of the extents of its specializations. [Firesmith]

Kinds:

- A-KIND-OF RELATIONSHIP
- IS-A RELATIONSHIP
- MULTIPLE GENERALIZATION
- SINGLE GENERALIZATION

- **a-kind-of relationship** *n.* the relationship between a specialization and its generalization(s). [Firesmith]
  Contrast with: IS-A RELATIONSHIP.
  Examples: A-kind-of relationships include the subtyping relationship from a subtype to its supertype and the specialization inheritance relationship from a derived class to its base class whereby instances of the derived class are a kind of the base class. A car is a kind of vehicle. [Firesmith]
  Commentary: Many developers confuse the *a-kind-of* relationship between types or classes with the *is-a* relationship between objects and their types or classes. [Firesmith]

- **is-a relationship** *n.* **1.** the classification relationship from an object to its class or type. [Firesmith] **2.** the specialization relationship from a derived class to its base class or from a subtype to its supertype. [Lorenz]
  Synonym: CLASSIFICATION.
  Contrast with: A-KIND-OF RELATIONSHIP.
  Examples: **1** Spot is a dog. My car is a car. [Firesmith] **2** A car is a [kind of] vehicle.
  Commentary: Instances are more specific that their more general class-

es and types. Many developers (e.g., Definition 2) confuse the *a-kind-of* relationship between types or classes with the *is-a* relationship between objects and their types or classes. [Firesmith]

- **multiple generalization** *n.* any generalization whereby a parent has more than one child. [Firesmith]
  Antonym: MULTIPLE CLASSIFICATION.
  Contrast with: SINGLE GENERALIZATION, SINGLE INHERITANCE.

- **single generalization** *n.* any generalization whereby a parent has only a single child. [Firesmith]
  Antonym: SINGLE CLASSIFICATION.
  Contrast with: MULTIPLE GENERALIZATION, MULTIPLE INHERITANCE.

generalization hierarchy *n.* (a) any hierarchy organized by generalization relationships from specializations to generaliza-tions. [Firesmith] (b) the result of organizing a mass of knowledge into a hierarchy arranged from the general to the more specific. [Martin]
Contrast with: CLASS HIERARCHY, INHERITANCE HIERARCHY.
See also: GENERALIZATION-SPECIALIZATION DIAGRAM.
Commentary: The use of multiple generalization may result in structures that are not true hierarchies. [Firesmith]

generalization–specialization diagram *n.* any diagram documenting a subtyping hierarchy. [Martin]
Synonym: GENERALIZATION HIERARCHY, INHERITANCE HIERARCHY, SUBTYPING DIAGRAM. [MARTIN]

generalization–specialization (gen-spec) structure *n.* any structure produced by *is-a-kind-of* relationships between classes. [Coad]
Contrast with: WHOLE-PART STRUCTURE.

See also: INHERITANCE.
Example: An example is the generalization Vehicle, and the specialization TruckVehicle. A TruckVehicle is a kind of Vehicle.
Commentary: A specialization class inherits the responsibilities of its generalization class(es).

generalize *v.* *-ed, -ing* to create a generalization from one or more specializations. [Firesmith]
Synonym: CLASSIFY.
Contrast with: SPECIALIZE.
Examples: (a) to create a new generalized class or type by factoring out common characteristics and responsibilities from one or more existing classes or types (e.g., the specializations). (b) to classify an object as an instance of a class or type. [Firesmith]

generally available feature *n.* any public feature that is exported to all classes. [Eiffel, Meyer]
Synonym: EXPORTED.
Contrast with: SELECTIVELY AVAILABLE.

generating class [of a given object] *n.* the class from which the given object is a direct instance. [Firesmith]
Contrast with: GENERATING TYPE.

generating class [of a given type] *n.* the base class of the given generating type. [Eiffel]
Synonym: GENERATOR.

generating type [of a given object] *n.* the type from which the given object is a direct instance. [Eiffel, Firesmith, Meyer]
Contrast with: GENERATING CLASS.

generator [of a given type] *n.* the base class of the given generating type. [Eiffel]
Synonym: GENERATING CLASS.

generic *adj.* parameterized with generic formal parameters. [Firesmith]
n. anything that has been parameter-

ized with generic formal parameters. [Firesmith]

Synonym: adj. PARAMETERIZED.

Rationale: Original term used by Ada-83 and Eiffel.

Commentary: The term *generic* is more popular than the term *parameterized* because of its use by the Ada and Eiffel languages. [Firesmith]

Kinds:
- GENERIC CLASS
- GENERIC CLIENT
- GENERIC FUNCTION
- GENERIC OBJECT
- GENERIC OPERATION
- GENERIC PROGRAM UNIT
- GENERIC TYPE

● **generic class** *n.* any metaclass that is parameterized with generic formal parameters that must be supplied as part of the instantiation process. [Booch, Eiffel, Firesmith, Meyer]

Synonym: PARAMETERIZED CLASS, TEMPLATE [CLASS].

Contrast with: GENERIC OPERATION, GENERIC TYPE.

Examples: Container classes parameterized by size or the type of the stored objects. [Firesmith]

Commentary: The instances of a generic class vary, depending on the actual parameters that were supplied. [Firesmith]

● **generic client** *n.* any class C is a generic client of a type S if for some generically derived type T of the form B [..., S, ...] one of the following holds:
  – C is a client of T.
  – one of the Parent clauses of C, or of a proper ancestor of C, lists T as a parent. [Eiffel, Meyer]

● **generic function** *n.* **1.** (a) a parameterized function encapsulated within an object or class. [Ada, Firesmith] (b) any function whose behavior depends on the classes or identities of the arguments supplied to it. [CLOS] **2.** any function that may be redefined by derived classes. [Booch] **3.** a function object that contains a set of methods, a lambda-list, a method combination type, and other information. [CLOS]

Synonyms: **1** GENERIC OPERATION, PARAMETERIZED OPERATION. **2** VIRTUAL MEMBER FUNCTION.

See also: LAMBDA-LIST.

Commentary: Definition **1** is far more traditional and popular than definitions **2** and **3**.

● **generic object** *n.* any object (relative to some given Object Service) whose primary purpose for existence is unrelated to the Object Service. [OMG]

● **generic operation** *n.* **1** any polymorphic operation that is parameterized with generic formal parameters that must be supplied as part of the instantiation process. [Firesmith] **2** any operation that can be bound to more than one method. [OMG]

Synonym: GENERIC FUNCTION.

Contrast with: GENERIC CLASS, GENERIC TYPE.

● **generic program unit** *n.* any parameterized template for the creation of a nongeneric program unit; the template can be parameterized by objects, types, subprograms, and packages, allowing general algorithms and data structures to be defined that are applicable to all types of a given class. [Ada95]

See also: PROGRAM UNIT.

Commentary: An instance of a generic unit is created by a generic_instan-

G

tiation. The rules of the language are enforced when a generic unit is compiled, using a generic contract model; additional checks are performed on instantiation to verify the contract is met. That is, the declaration of a generic unit represents a contract between the body of the generic and instances of the generic. Generic units can be used to perform the role that macros sometimes play in other languages. [Ada95]

• **generic type** *n.* any abstract type that is parameterized with generic formal parameters that must be supplied as part of the instantiation process. [Firesmith]
Synonym: PARAMETERIZED TYPE.
Contrast with: GENERIC CLASS, GENERIC OPERATION.
Commentary: The instances of a generic type vary, depending on the actual parameters that were supplied. [Firesmith]

generic actual [argument] *n.* any actual argument of a generic that was supplied by the client as part of the instantiation process. [Firesmith]
Synonym: GENERIC FORMAL PARAMETER.
Commentary: Actual arguments must be supplied for each generic formal argument prior to instantiation. [Firesmith]

generic actual [parameter] *n.* **1.** any actual parameter of a generic that was supplied by the client as part of the instantiation process. [Firesmith] **2.** either the explicit_generic_actual_parameter given in a generic_parameter_association for each formal, or the corresponding default_expression or default_name if no generic_parameter_association is given for the formal. [Ada95]

Synonym: ACTUAL, GENERIC ACTUAL, GENERIC ACTUAL ARGUMENT.
Antonym: FORMAL PARAMETER.

generic formal *adj.* describing any function, object, package, procedure, subtype, or type that has been declared by using a generic_formal_parameter_declaration so that it can be used as a parameter of a generic. [Ada95]
Synonyms: FORMAL.
Antonym: GENERIC ACTUAL.
See also: FORMAL PARAMETER.
Examples: A generic formal procedure and a formal integer type declaration are examples of *generic formals.* [Ada95]

generic formal [argument] *n.* any formal argument of a generic that must be supplied by the client as part of the instantiation process. [Firesmith]
Synonym: GENERIC FORMAL PARAMETER.
Commentary: Actual arguments must be supplied for each generic formal argument prior to instantiation. [Firesmith]

generic formal [parameter] *n.* any formal parameter of a generic that must be supplied by the client as part of the instantiation process. [Firesmith]
Synonym: GENERIC FORMAL ARGUMENT.
Commentary: Actual parameters must be supplied for each generic formal parameter prior to instantiation. [Firesmith]

genericity *n.* the ability to parameterize something (e.g., a class, operation, type, or cluster). [Eiffel, Firesmith, Henderson-Sellers, Meyer]
Synonym: PARAMETRIC POLYMORPHISM.

global *n.* any name in Smalltalk other than that of a class or pool. [Smalltalk]

globally overloaded operation *n.* any overloaded operation, the variants of which occur in different contexts or

scopes unrelated by inheritance. [Firesmith]
Antonym: LOCALLY OVERLOADED OPERATION.
See also: GLOBAL OVERLOADING.
Rationale: Global overloading occurs *globally* across classes that are unrelated by inheritance. [Firesmith]

global object view *n.* any object model view that shows either the entire object model or a subsystem of the object model. [Jacobson]
Antonym: LOCAL OBJECT VIEW.
Contrast with: VIEW OF PARTICIPATING OBJECTS.

global recursion *n.* any recursion across more than one development activity (e.g., requirements analysis, design, coding, integration, and testing). [Firesmith]
Contrast with: LOCAL RECURSION.

global variable *n.* any variable shared by all instances of all classes. [Smalltalk]
Contrast with: CLASS VARIABLE, INSTANCE VARIABLE, POOL VARIABLE, TEMPORARY VARIABLE.
Commentary: In spite of being a part of the archetypical pure object-oriented programming language Smalltalk, global variables implement common global data and are definitely not object-oriented in that they violate the encapsulation of objects and classes.

graphical user interface (GUI) *n.* any user interface that primarily uses graphical icons for communicating with the user. [Firesmith]

group-and-view concept *n.* any concept that describes how a set of object types are grouped into a schema and/or viewed in a diagram. [OADSIG]
Contrast with: ARCHITECTURE CONCEPT, OBJECT-BEHAVIOR CONCEPT, OBJECT STRUCTURE CONCEPT.

group transition *n.* any transition involving an aggregate state in which substates are treated equally in some sense because they are specializations of the more general superstate. [Firesmith]
Kinds:
- GROUP-EXTERNAL TRANSITION
- GROUP-INTERNAL TRANSITION

- **group-external transition** *n.* any group transition from an aggregate superstate that fires regardless of the current substate. [Firesmith]
Antonym: GROUP-INTERNAL TRANSITION.

- **group-internal transition** *n.* any group transition to an aggregate superstate that is forwarded to a specific substate. [Firesmith]
Antonym: GROUP-EXTERNAL TRANSITION.

guard [condition] *n.* **1.** any condition that must be true (or have the proper enumeration value) for a trigger to cause the associated transition to fire. [Booch, Firesmith, Rumbaugh] **2.** any condition on the receiver of a synchronous message that must be true for the message to be received. [Firesmith]
Contrast with: POSTCONDITION, PRECONDITION.

guardable *adj.* providing, but not enforcing, support for mutual exclusion in a concurrent environment. [Firesmith]
Contrast with: CORRUPTIBLE, GUARDED.

guardable class *n.* any class, the instances of which provide a mechanism for ensuring (but do not enforce) mutually exclusive access in a concurrent environment. [Firesmith]
Contrast with: CORRUPTIBLE CLASS, GUARDED CLASS.

G

guarded *adj.* **1.** providing and enforcing support for mutual exclusion in a concurrent environment. [Firesmith] **2.** providing, but not enforcing, support for mutual exclusion in a concurrent environment. [Booch]

Synonym: **2** GUARDABLE.

Contrast with: **1** CORRUPTIBLE, GUARDABLE.

guarded class *n.* **1.** any class, the instances of which provide and enforce mutually exclusive access in a concurrent environment. [Firesmith] **2.** any class whose semantics are guaranteed in the presence of multiple threads of control if all clients properly collaborate to achieve mutual exclusion. [Booch]

Contrast with: CORRUPTIBLE CLASS, GUARDABLE CLASS.

guarded object *n.* any concurrent object that provides and enforces mutually exclusive access in a concurrent environment. [Firesmith]

Contrast with: CORRUPTIBLE OBJECT, GUARDABLE OBJECT.

guarded transition *n.* any state transition that occurs only if the trigger fires while its associated guard condition evaluates to true (or to the enumeration value associated with the transition). [Firesmith, Rumbaugh]

Antonym: UNGUARDED TRANSITION.

H

handle *n.* **1.** any client's value that uniquely identifies a [server] object. [Firesmith, OMG] **2.** any pointer or other reference to the data structure containing data describing an instance. [Shlaer/Mellor]
Contrast with: IDENTIFIER, KEY, OBJECT NAME.
See also: IDENTITY.
Commentary: Although the handle may be equal to the server's identifier or the value of a server key, the client need not know or use the server's identifier or key(s). [Firesmith]

handle [an exception] *v.* *-ed, -ing* to perform an operation designed to deal with the problem upon catching an exception. [Ada95, C++, Firesmith]
Contrast with: CATCH AN EXCEPTION, RAISE AN EXCEPTION, THROW AN EXCEPTION.

[exception] handler *n.* any part of an operation to which an exception is propagated and that subsequently deals with the exception. [Firesmith]
Contrast with: EXCEPTION SIGNALER.

handling case *n.* any specific flow through an enterprise or organization that provides a way for it to function in order to attain a goal. [Jacobson]

Contrast with: USE CASE.
Examples: New Development and *Further Development*, as well as the handling cases *Give a tender* and *Handle errors* in an enterprise where computer systems are developed. [Jacobson]
Commentary: The actual handling cases to be included in an enterprise are determined by the goals of the enterprise. [Jacobson]

has-a *n.* the relationship from any source class to one or more instances of the target class that it contains or with which it collaborates. [Lorenz]

heir [class of a given class] *n.* any class that is directly derived via inheritance from

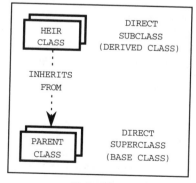

Heir Class

a given class, its parent. [Eiffel, Meyer]
Synonym: CHILD CLASS.
Antonym: PARENT.
Contrast with: DESCENDANT.

- **repeated heir [of a given class]** *n.* any heir class that multiply inherits from a given parent class. [Eiffel, Firesmith, Meyer]
Synonym: REPEATED CHILD CLASS.
Contrast with: REPEATED PARENT CLASS.

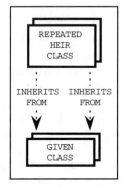

Repeated Heir Class

hierarchical classification *n.* any classification of reusable components based on inheritance. [Jacobson]
Antonym: KEYWORD-BASED CLASSIFICATION.
Commentary: Searching begins at the root and the properties the component should have are indicated at various locations in the hierarchy. [Jacobson]

hierarchy *n.* any ranking or ordering of abstractions into a tree-like structure. [Booch, Firesmith, Lorenz]
Kinds:
- AGGREGATION HIERARCHY
- CLASS HIERARCHY
- CONTAINMENT HIERARCHY
- GENERALIZATION HIERARCHY
- INHERITANCE HIERARCHY
- PARTITION HIERARCHY
- SPECIALIZATION HIERARCHY
- TYPE HIERARCHY

- **aggregation hierarchy** *n.* any hierarchy consisting of an aggregate, its component parts, the component parts of these component parts, etc. and the aggregation relationships between them. [Firesmith]
Synonyms: ASSEMBLY STRUCTURE, CONTAINMENT HIERARCHY, PARTITION HIERARCHY, WHOLE-PART STRUCTURE.

- **class hierarchy** *n.* (a) any hierarchy of classes that results from single inheritance. [Firesmith, Lorenz] (b) any hierarchy that results when generalization is replaced by inheritance in an object-type generalization hierarchy. [Martin]
Synonyms: INHERITANCE HIERARCHY.
Contrast with: GENERALIZATION HIERARCHY.
Commentary: The use of multiple inheritance may result in structures that are not true hierarchies. [Firesmith]

- **containment hierarchy** *n.* any hierarchy created by constructing an object from other objects via *consistsOf* relations. [Jacobson]
Synonyms: AGGREGATION HIERARCHY, ASSEMBLY STRUCTURE, PARTITION HIERARCHY, WHOLE-PART STRUCTURE.
See also: CONSISTSOF ASSOCIATION, AGGREGATE.

- **generalization hierarchy** *n.* the result of organizing a mass of knowledge into a hierarchy arranged from the general to the more specific. [Martin]
Contrast with: CLASS HIERARCHY, INHERITANCE HIERARCHY.
See also: GENERALIZATION-SPECIALIZATION DIAGRAM.

- **inheritance hierarchy** *n.* a hierarchy consisting of classes or types and the single inheritance relationships between them. [Firesmith]
Synonym: CLASS HIERARCHY.
Contrast with: GENERALIZATION HIERARCHY.
Commentary: The use of multiple inheritance may result in structures that are not true hierarchies.

- **partition hierarchy** *n.* any hierarchy created by partitioning an object into other objects via *consistsOf* relations. [Jacobson]
Synonyms: AGGREGATION HIERARCHY, ASSEMBLY STRUCTURE, CONTAINMENT HIERARCHY, WHOLE-PART STRUCTURE.
See also: CONSISTSOF ASSOCIATION, AGGREGATE.

- **specialization hierarchy** *n.* any hierarchy consisting of classes or types and the single specialization relationships between them. [Firesmith]
Contrast with: INHERITANCE HIERARCHY.
Commentary: The use of multiple specialization may result in structures that are not true hierarchies. [Firesmith]

- **type hierarchy** *n.* any hierarchy of types related by subtyping. [Firesmith]
Contrast with: CLASS HIERARCHY.
Commentary: The use of multiple subtyping may result in structures that are not true hierarchies. [Firesmith]

hierarchy diagram *n.* any graph of an OO system, including classes, subsystem groupings, and contract usage. [Lorenz]
Synonym: HIERARCHY GRAPH, INHERITANCE DIAGRAM.
Contrast with: COLLABORATION DIAGRAM, MESSAGE-FLOW DIAGRAM.

hierarchy graph *n.* any graph showing the inheritance relationships between classes. [Wirfs-Brock]
Synonym: HIERARCHY DIAGRAM, INHERITANCE DIAGRAM.

hierarchy nesting *n.* the number of levels of derived classes in the class hierarchy. [Lorenz]

high level of abstraction *n.* any level of abstraction that is relatively close to the root and far from the leaves of the hierarchy. [Firesmith]
Antonym: LOW LEVEL OF ABSTRACTION.
Examples: An aggregate is at a higher level of abstraction than its parts in an aggregation hierarchy. An ancestor is at a higher level of abstraction than its descendants in an inheritance structure. [Firesmith]
Commentary: A high level of abstraction typically implies either more abstract (inheritance) or closer to the masters (message passing). [Booch, Firesmith]

high-level interaction *n.* any abstract interaction representing and subsuming several detailed interactions. [Embley]

high-level modeling component *n.* any component at a high level of abstraction that groups lower-level-like components. [Embley]
Kinds:
- HIGH-LEVEL RELATIONSHIP SET
- HIGH-LEVEL STATE
- HIGH-LEVEL TRANSITION

- **high-level relationship set** *n.* any relationship set that groups and subsumes object classes, relationship sets, constraints, and notes. [Embley]

- **high-level state** *n.* any state that groups and subsumes lower-level states, transitions, constraints, and notes. [Embley]
Synonyms: AGGREGATE STATE, SUPERSTATE.

H

- **high-level transition** *n.* any transition that groups and subsumes lower-level transitions, states, constraints, and notes. [Embley]

high-level object class *n.* any class that is created at a high level of abstraction to group a set of objects at lower-levels of abstraction. [Embley]

Kinds:
- DOMINANT HIGH-LEVEL OBJECT CLASS
- INDEPENDENT HIGH-LEVEL OBJECT CLASS

- **dominant high-level object class** *n.* any high-level object class representing a set of objects that is named after the most important object class in the set. [Embley]
  Antonym: INDEPENDENT HIGH-LEVEL OBJECT CLASS.

- **independent high-level object class** *n.* any high-level object class representing a set of objects that is not named after the most important object class in the set. [Embley]
  Antonym: DOMINANT HIGH-LEVEL OBJECT CLASS.

high-level relationship set *n.* any relationship set that groups and subsumes object classes, relationship sets, constraints, and notes. [Embley]

high-level state *n.* any state that groups and subsumes lower-level states, transitions, constraints, and notes. [Embley]

high-level transition *n.* any transition that groups and subsumes lower-level transitions, states, constraints, and notes. [Embley]

Hillside [Generative Patterns] Group, the *n.* a group of methodologists devoted to the study and applications of patterns.

homogeneous composite object *n.* any composite object that is *conceptually* composed of component objects that are all *conceptually* of the same type. [Berard]

homogenize [stimuli] *v.* -*ed*, -*ing* to limit the number of stimuli while keeping the remaining stimuli as reusable and easy to work with as possible. [Jacobson]
See also: STIMULUS.
Commentary: Use cases (and stimuli) are normally designed in parallel and by several designers who can work more or less independently of one another. Homogenization is necessary to avoid redundancy. [Jacobson]

homograph [declarations] *adj.* describing two declarations that have the same defining name and whose profiles are type conformant if both are overloadable. [Ada95]
Commentary: An inner declaration hides any outer homograph from direct visibility. [Ada95]

homonymic [types] *n.* any two or more types that have the same protocol, but different semantics. [Firesmith]
Commentary: One homonymic type typically has a more restricted functionality than another. [Firesmith]

horizontal common facilities *n.* any CORBA facilities that include functions shared by many or most systems, regardless of application domain.
Examples: User interface, information management, systems management, task management.
Antonym: VERTICAL COMMON FACILITIES.

- **system management facilities** *n.* any horizontal CORBA facilities that provide a set of interfaces that abstract basic system administration functions (e.g., control, monitoring, security management, configuration, and policy). [OMG]

human interaction (HI) component
n. the component that contains objects that provide an interface between problem domain objects and people. [Coad]

hybrid object-oriented programming language *n.* any object-oriented programming language that has both object-oriented types (types implemented by classes) and nonobject-oriented types (primitive data types). [Firesmith, Rumbaugh, Wirfs-Brock]

Examples: The Ada95, C++, CLOS, Object COBOL, Objective C, and Object Pascal languages are all hybrid OOPLs.

Commentary: A hybrid OOPL also supports nonobject-oriented development. [Firesmith]

H

I

ideal design *n.* the development of any ideal-object model. [Jacobson]
See also: IDEAL-OBJECT MODEL.

ideal object *n.* **1.** any information-system object that is developed independently of the implementation environment. **2.** any business object that operates in the best possible way. **3.** any object in an ideal-object model. [Jacobson]
Antonym: REAL OBJECT.
See also: IDEAL-OBJECT MODEL.

ideal-object models *n.* **1.** any object model of a business that contains only those objects required to perform the use cases to run the business in the best possible way. [Jacobson] **2.** any object-model of an information system that is independent of the implementation environment. [Jacobson]
Antonym: REAL-OBJECT MODEL.
See also: IDEAL DESIGN, IDEAL OBJECT.

identical objects *n.* any objects that have the same identifier. [Firesmith]
Contrast with: EQUAL OBJECTS.

identical references *n.* any references that are attached to identical objects.
Contrast with: EQUAL REFERENCES.

[object] identifier *n.* **1.** the single identifier permanently assigned to each ob-ject that is:
– unique within some specified scope or domain (e.g., an application)
– independent of the instance's:
  - properties
  - state
  - [possibly dynamic] classification
– constant during the existence of the object. [Firesmith]
2. any set of one or more attributes whose values uniquely distinguish each instance of an object. [Shlaer/Mellor] **3.** any category of variable tokens that describe symbolic names denoting various Eiffel components such as classes, features, or entities. [Eiffel, Meyer]
Synonyms: OBJECT REFERENCE, OID.
Contrast with: HANDLE, KEY, OBJECT NAME.
Commentary: An identifier is typically implemented as a unique arbitrary bit pattern generated strictly for the purpose of uniquely identifying a specific object. Although some languages (e.g., C++) use the address of an object as its identifier, this does not work in a distributed system. Definitions 1 and 2 are inconsistent. Definition 2 is controversial in the object community. [Firesmith].

Kinds:
- LOCAL IDENTIFIER
- UNIVERSAL IDENTIFIER
- **local identifier (LID)** *n.* any object identifier that is local to a specific processor or process. [Firesmith]
Antonym: UNIVERAL IDENTIFIER.
- **universal identifier (UID)** *n.* any system-wide object identifier. [Firesmith]
Antonym: LOCAL IDENTIFIER.
Commentary: UIDs are required in distributed applications with multiple address spaces in which using the local address does not uniquely identify an object, especially if that object is to be moved around the system. [Firesmith]

identity *n.* the use of identifiers rather than keys to uniquely identify objects. [Firesmith]

idiom *n.* any reusable pattern, smaller than a mechanism, that is usually specific to a particular programming language or application culture, representing a generally accepted convention for use of the language. [Booch, Firesmith, Lorenz]
Contrast with: FRAMEWORK, MECHANISM, PATTERN.
Commentary: Idioms may exist within or across cluster boundaries. [Firesmith] An idiom has proven useful multiple times in the past and is therefore recommended as a starting point for similar endeavors. [Lorenz]

[Smalltalk] image *n.* an integrated in-memory object repository consisting of a bound set of tightly interrelated objects. [Smalltalk]
Synonym: SMALLTALK IMAGE.

immediate feature *n.* any new feature not obtained from ancestors via inheritance. [Eiffel, Meyer]
Antonym: INHERITED FEATURE.

immutable object *n.* any object having a fixed structure and constant properties that cannot change their intrinsic values. [Coleman, Firesmith, Martin/Odell, ODMG]
Antonym: MUTABLE OBJECT.
Contrast with: CONSTANT, LITERAL.

impedance mismatch *n.* the inconsistencies due to mixing paradigms on the same project. [Firesmith]
Synonym: IMPEDANCE PROBLEM.
Example: Using a relational database on a object-oriented project causes an impedance mismatch between the code and the database (i.e., different type system, conceptual basis, languages). [Firesmith]
Rationale: The word *impedance* comes from its use in electrical engineering (i.e., the total opposition offered by an electric circuit to the flow of an alternating current of a single frequency). [Firesmith, Jacobson]
Commentary: The term is often used to describe the difficulties that occur when one mixes procedural and object-oriented software on the same project. [Firesmith]

impedance problem *n.* the inconsistencies due to mixing paradigms on the same project. [Jacobson]
Synonym: IMPEDANCE MISMATCH.
Example: Using a relational database on a object-oriented project causes an impedance mismatch between the code and the database (i.e., different type system, conceptual basis, languages). [Firesmith]
Rationale: The word *impedance* comes from its use in electrical engineering (i.e., the total opposition offered by an

electric circuit to the flow of an alternating current of a single frequency). [Firesmith, Jacobson]

Commentary: The term is often used to describe the difficulties that occur when one mixes procedural and object-oriented software on the same project. [Firesmith]

implementation *n.* **1.** (a) the specification of the hidden features of something. [Firesmith] b) the hidden attributes and operations of an object. [Booch, Jacobson] **2.** the coding or programming activity. [Firesmith]

Synonym: 1 BODY, 2 CODING, PROGRAMMING.

Antonym: 1 INTERFACE, PROTOCOL.

Contrast with: 1 BODY.

Example: The implementation of an object includes its hidden properties, hidden operations, and methods. A class is an implementation of a type. [Firesmith]

Commentary: An implementation typically includes a description of the data structure used to represent the core state associated with an object, as well as definitions of the methods that access the data structure. It also typically includes information about the intended type of the object.

implementation class [of a given feature] *n.* the origin class in which the given feature was last implemented. [Firesmith]

Antonym: DECLARING CLASS.

Example: The implementation class is the nearest class (either ancestor or current) in which a method for the given operation appeared. [Firesmith]

implementation coupling *n.* the coupling via features in the implementation of the client on their server(s). [Firesmith]

Contrast with: AGGREGATION COUPLING, CLASSIFICATION COUPLING, EXCEPTION COUPLING, FRIENDSHIP COUPLING, INHERITANCE COUPLING, INTERFACE COUPLING, MESSAGE COUPLING.

Examples: Coupling due to implementation inheritance and friends are both types of implementation coupling. [Firesmith]

implementation-defined behavior *n.* any vendor-specific behavior of a product such as a compiler or object database. [ODMG]

implementation definition language *n.* a notation for describing implementations, that may be vendor specific or adapter specific. [OMG]

implementation dependency *n.* any dependency of the implementation (but not the interface) of the client on its server(s). [Firesmith]

Contrast with: INTERFACE DEPENDENCY, METHOD DEPENDENCY.

Example: Any dependency provided by a with clause in an Ada package body is a form of implementation dependency. [Firesmith]

Commentary: Implementation dependency implies that the interface of the server is visible to only those features in the implementation of the client. [Firesmith]

implementation description *n.* any description of a class that shows how the functionality described in the protocol description is implemented in terms of the private memory of the class's instances and the set of methods that describe how instances perform their operations. [Smalltalk]

Contrast with: PROTOCOL DESCRIPTION, SYSTEM BROWSER.

implementation domain *n.* the domain

providing the conceptual entities in which the entire system will be implemented. [Shlaer/Mellor]
Contrast with: APPLICATION DOMAIN, ARCHITECTURAL DOMAIN, SERVICE DOMAIN.
Examples: Programming languages, networks, operating systems, and common class libraries are all implementation domains.

implementation inheritance *n.* **1.** any inheritance whereby a new *implementation* is incrementally defined in terms of existing implementations. [Firesmith] **2.** any inheritance used merely for the purpose of reusing [some of] the implementation of the base class(es). [Henderson-Sellers]
Antonym: INTERFACE INHERITANCE.
Contrast with: SPECIALIZATION INHERITANCE.
See also: SIGNATURE CONFORMANCE, TYPE CONFORMANCE.
Commentary: The use of implementation inheritance is controversial in the object community because it is typically used merely for code (i.e., implementation) reuse rather than to capture an *a-kind-of* taxonomy. Implementation inheritance neither implies any semantic relationship nor conformity of interfaces. Many methodologists consider it not to be as good as specialization or interface inheritance because it need support neither specialization nor polymorphic substitutability. The use of implementation inheritance is often a sign that aggregation or delegation should have been used instead of inheritance. [Firesmith]

implementation method *n.* any method that implements specific computations on fully specified arguments, but does not make context-dependent decisions. [Rumbaugh]
Contrast with: POLICY METHOD

implementation object *n.* any object that serves as an implementation definition and resides in an implementation repository. [OMG]

implementation repository *n.* any storage place for object implementation information; a service that allows the ORB to locate and activate implementations of objects. [OMG]
Contrast with: INTERFACE REPOSITORY.

implicit declaration *n.* any declaration that does not appear explicitly in the program text, but rather implicitly occurs at a given place in the text as a consequence of the semantics of another construct. [Ada95]
Antonym: EXPLICIT DECLARATION.
Commentary: Implicit declarations are typically those inherited in a derived type.

imploded view *n.* any view modeled in its summary form, making the subsumed components (relationship sets, states, and transitions) of the dominant high-level components implicit or invisible, while leaving the high-level component explicit or visible. [Embley]
Synonym: COLLAPSED VIEW.
Antonym: EXPLODED VIEW.

import *v.* *-ed, -ing* to create any object based on a description of an object transmitted from an external entity. [OMG]
Contrast with: EXPORT.

imported reference *n.* any reference stored in an object's instance variable that was not generated by the object itself through invocation of a *create* method. [Atkinson]
Antonym: INGENERATE REFERENCE.

inbound protocol *n.* the set of all inbound interactions, consisting of the union of the inbound message protocol and the inbound exception protocol. [Firesmith]
Antonym: OUTBOUND PROTOCOL.
Contrast with: INBOUND INTERFACE.
Kinds:
- INBOUND EXCEPTION PROTOCOL
- INBOUND MESSAGE PROTOCOL

- **inbound exception protocol** *n.* the set of all server exceptions that must be handled. [Firesmith]
Contrast with: INBOUND MESSAGE PROTOCOL, OUTBOUND EXCEPTION PROTOCOL, OUTBOUND MESSAGE PROTOCOL.

- **inbound message protocol** *n.* the set of all inbound messages. [Firesmith]
Contrast with: INBOUND EXCEPTION PROTOCOL, OUTBOUND EXCEPTION PROTOCOL, OUTBOUND MESSAGE PROTOCOL.

incident *n.* an abstraction of any happening or occurrence. [Shlaer/Mellor]

incident object *n.* any object used to represent an occurrence or event: something that happens at a specific time. [Shlaer/Mellor]
Examples: Accidents, events (in a nuclear physics experiment, flight, performance (of a play, etc.), service calls (appliance repair), and system crashes can all be modeled as incident objects.

inclusion polymorphism *n.* any polymorphism in which a single inherited operation may be dynamically bound to different methods in different descendants of the same ancestor.
Synonym: INHERENT POLYMORPHISM.
Contrast with: AD HOC POLYMORPHISM, OVERLOADING, PARAMETRIC POLYMORPHISM.

Commentary: Inclusion polymorphism requires the use of either specialization or interface inheritance so that the same message can be sent to instances of the different derived classes. Inclusion polymorphism also requires dynamic binding so that this common message can be bound to the correct associated polymorphic operation, even if the class of the associated instance is not known at compile time. The operation is called *polymorphic* (i.e., having *many forms*) because the implementation of the operation may be different in different derived classes.

incremental, iterative, parallel (IIP) development cycle *n.* any powerful object-oriented development cycle that is:
- *Incremental* in that the system and software are developed in small and large increments;
- *Iterative* in that intermediate products are iterated (e.g., as errors are discovered);
- *Parallel* in that different teams work on different increments in parallel. [Firesmith]

incremental process *n.* the developmental steps that result in a piecemeal delivery of application functions over the life of the project. [Lorenz]
Commentary: A set of end-user functions are delivered in prerelease 1, some additional end-user functions are delivered in prerelease 2, and so on until the entire application has been built. [Lorenz]

indefinite subtype *n.* any subtype that does not by itself provide enough information to create an object without an additional constraint or explicit initial expression. [Ada95]

Antonym: DEFINITE SUBTYPE.

Examples: An unconstrained array subtype is an indefinite subtype, as is a subtype with unknown discriminants or unconstrained discriminants without default. [Ada95]

Commentary: The object's *actual subtype* can be more restrictive than the nominal subtype of the view; it always is if the nominal subtype is an *indefinite subtype*. [Ada95]

independence *n.* the degree to which something does not rely on anything else. [Firesmith]

See also: COUPLING.

Commentary: Where practical, objects and classes should be independent of the underlying hardware and the operating system. [Firesmith]

independent high-level object class *n.* any high-level object class representing a set of objects that is not named after the most important object class in the set. [Embley]

Antonym: DOMINANT HIGH-LEVEL OBJECT CLASS.

index *n.* any data structure that maps one or more attribute values into the objects or database table rows that hold the values, usually for optimization purposes. [Rumbaugh]

indexed instance variable *n.* any instance variable that is not accessed by name. [Smalltalk]

Antonym: NAMED INSTANCE VARIABLE.

Example: names at: 1 [Smalltalk]

Commentary: An object can have indexed instance variables only if all instances of its class can have indexed instance variables. [Smalltalk]

indirect ancestor [type of a given type] *n.* any ancestor type from which the given type is indirectly derived via inheri-

tance. [Firesmith]

Synonyms: INDIRECT BASE CLASS, INDIRECT SUPERCLASS.

Antonyms: CHILD TYPE, DIRECT DESCENDANT, DIRECT DERIVED CLASS, DIRECT SUBCLASS.

Rationale: The term *indirect ancestor* is preferred over the terms *indirect base class* and *indirect superclass* because of the preference of the term *ancestor* over the terms *base class* and *superclass*. [Firesmith]

indirect base class [of a given class] *n.* any base class from which a given class is indirectly derived via intermediate base classes. [C++]

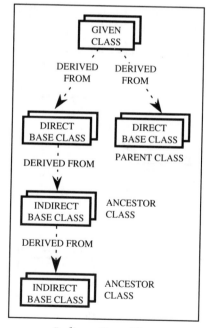

Indirect Base Class

Synonyms: INDIRECT ANCESTOR, INDIRECT SUPERCLASS.

Antonyms: INDIRECT DERIVED CLASS, IN-

DIRECT DESCENDANT, INDIRECT SUB-CLASS.
Contrast with: DIRECT BASE CLASS, DIRECT SUPERCLASS.
Commentary: An indirect base class of a given class is an ancestor class that is not a parent class. The term *indirect ancestor* is preferred as being more general and less language dependent. [Firesmith]

indirect conformance *n.* conformance of one class or type to a different class or type through one or more intermediary classes or types. [Eiffel, Firesmith, Meyer]
Antonym: DIRECT CONFORMANCE.
Example: The subtype of a given type conforms to the parent type of the given type. [Firesmith]

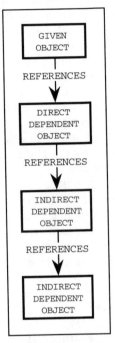

Indirect Conformance

indirect dependent [of a given object] *n.* any object that is either a direct dependent of a direct dependent or recursively a direct dependent of an indirect

dependent. [Firesmith]
Antonym: DIRECT DEPENDENT.

Indirect Dependent

indirect derived class [of a given class] *n.* any derived class that is indirectly derived via intermediate base classes from a given class. [Ada95, C++]
Synonyms: ANCESTOR CLASS, INDIRECT SUPERCLASS.
Contrast with: DIRECT BASE CLASS, DIRECT SUPERCLASS.
Commentary: An indirect derived class of a given class is a descendant class that is not a child class. [Firesmith]

indirect instance [of a given class] *n.* any object that is a direct instance of some specialized descendant of the given class. [Firesmith, Rumbaugh]
Antonym: DIRECT INSTANCE.

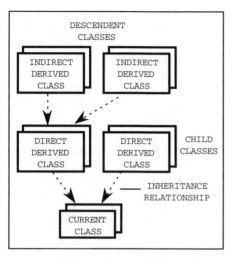

Indirect Derived Class

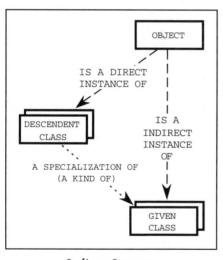

Indirect Instance

indirect repeated inheritance [of a given class] *n.* any repeated inheritance in which an ancestor class of a given class is the parent of two or more descendants of the given class. [Eiffel, Firesmith, Meyer] *See also:* REPEATED ANCESTOR CLASS.

Contrast with: DIRECT REPEATED INHERITANCE.

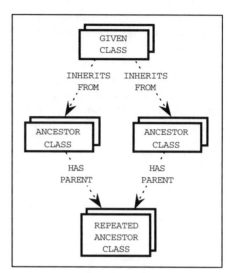

Indirect Repeated Inheritance

indirect subclass [of a given class] *n.* any subclass that indirectly inherits from a given superclass via one or more intermediary superclasses. [Firesmith]

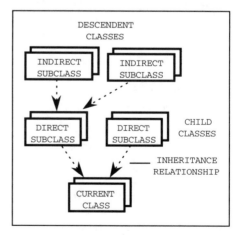

Indirect Subclass

Synonyms: DESCENDANT CLASS.
Contrast with: CHILD CLASS, DIRECT BASE CLASS, DIRECT SUBCLASS.
Commentary: An indirect subclass is a descendant class that is not a child class. [Firesmith]

indirect superclass [of a given class] *n.* any superclass from which a given subclass indirectly inherits via intermediate superclasses. [Firesmith]
Synonyms: ANCESTOR CLASS, INDIRECT BASE CLASS.
Antonyms: DIRECT BASE CLASS, DIRECT SUPERCLASS, INDIRECT DERIVED CLASS.
Commentary: An indirect superclass is an ancestor class that is not a parent class. [Firesmith]

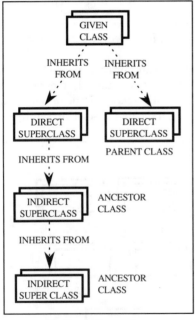

Indirect Superclass

information hiding *n.* (a) the deliberate and enforced hiding of information (e.g., design decisions, implementation details) from clients. [Booch, Firesmith, Jacobson, Wirfs-Brock] (b) the limiting of scope so that some information is invisible outside of the boundary of the scope. [Henderson-Sellers]
Contrast with: ENCAPSULATION.
See also: INTERFACE.
Example: An object typically hides the implementation of its properties and operations. [Booch, Firesmith, Jacobson]
Commentary: Information hiding is used to promote abstraction, support incremental top-down development, protect against accidental corruption, and promote the achievement of software engineering goals. Designers of suppliers use information hiding to protect clients from later changes in design. Information hiding is thus concerned with the separation of interface from implementation. Information hiding is combined with localization to create encapsulation. [Firesmith]

information holder *n.* any object that primarily exists to hold information about which other objects may inquire.

information management object type *n.* any object type that provides persistent storage for the application. [OADSIG]
Example: A record definition in a logical database design can be modeled as an information management object type. [OADSIG]

information model *n.* any organization and graphical notation suitable for describing and defining the vocabulary and conceptualization of a problem domain. [Shlaer/Mellor]

information-structure diagram *n.* any graphic representation of the information model. [Shlaer/Mellor]
Synonyms: ENTITY-RELATIONSHIP DIA-

GRAM, INFORMATION MODEL.
Commentary: The information structure diagram is concerned only with declaring the objects, attributes, and relationships of the model. [Shlaer/Mellor]

ingenerate reference *n.* any reference stored in an object's instance variable that was generated by the object itself through invocation of a *create* method. [Atkinson]
Antonym: IMPORTED REFERENCE.

inherent polymorphism *n.* **1.** any polymorphism in which a single inherited operation may be dynamically bound to different methods in different descendants of the same ancestor. [Firesmith] **2.** any polymorphism whereby operations are inherited by every subtype. [OADSIG]
Synonym: INHERENT POLYMORPHISM.
Rationale: An instance of a specialization is also an instance of its generalization because the extent of the specialization is *included* (i.e., is a subset of) the extent of its generalization. [Firesmith]
Commentary: Inclusion polymorphism requires the use of either specialization or interface inheritance so that the same message can be sent to instances of the different derived classes. Inclusion polymorphism also requires dynamic binding so that this common message can be bound to the correct associated polymorphic operation of the correct instance, even if the class of the instance is not known at compile time. The operation is called *polymorphic* (i.e., having *many forms*) because it has different methods in different descendants. Together with dynamic binding, inclusion polymorphism usually makes type-specific coding unnecessary and eliminates most case statements based on type. Unlike local overloading, in-

clusion polymorphism must often be resolved at run-time. [Firesmith]

inherently concurrent objects *n.* any two objects that can receive messages at the same time without interacting. [Rumbaugh]
Commentary: Note that the use of the term *inherently* has nothing to do with inheritance. [Firesmith]

inherently polymorphic operation *n.* any polymorphic operation that occurs in different descendants of the same ancestor whereby each variant has the same name, functional abstraction, and signature, but has a different method. [Firesmith]
See also: INHERENT POLYMORPHISM.

inherit *v.* *-ed, -ing* to obtain the declarations and definitions of features via inheritance. [Firesmith]
Example: Child classes inherit features from their parent classes. [Firesmith]

inheritance *n.* **1.** (a) the incremental construction of a new definition in terms of existing definitions without disturbing the original definitions and their clients. [Ada95, Firesmith] (b) the construction of a definition by incremental modification of other definitions. [Jacobson, OMG] **2.** the definition of a derived class in terms of one or more base classes. [Booch, Coleman, Embley, Jacobson, Wirfs-Brock] **3.** (a) a mechanism for expressing commonality between classes so that new classes inherit responsibilities from existing classes. [Coad] (b) a mechanism that permits classes to share characteristics. [Rumbaugh] **4.** (a) the organization of similar types of classes of objects into categories. [Lorenz] (b) the taxonomic relationship between *parents* and *children,* possibly over many *generations.* [Henderson-Sellers]

Contrast with: SPECIALIZATION, SUBTYPING.

See also: GENERALIZATION-SPECIALIZATION STRUCTURE, INHERITANCE STRUCTURE.

Examples: The definition of a derived class in terms of the features defined in its base classes, the definition of a subtype in terms of the features defined in its supertypes, and the definition of a derived cluster in terms of its base clusters. For example, *Savings* accounts are types of general *Account,* and *IRA* accounts are types of Savings accounts. The *Savings* account inherits the capability to handle deposits from the *Account* class. [Lorenz]

Rationale: Inheritance should be defined generally enough to include both class and type inheritance. However, there is a consensus in the object community that the definition of inheritance should be restrictive enough to disallow the derived typing mechanism of Ada83. Even though an Ada derived type is a new data type that inherits all of the attributes and operations of its parent type, it is not usually considered an example of true single inheritance because a derived type may only restrict the range of the parent type and may not add new features, which greatly restricts its value and is why true inheritance was added to Ada95. Definition 1 above meets these criteria, whereas definition 2 does not.

Commentary: 1 A new definition may (1) add new features, (2) modify or replace some of the inherited features, (3) define deferred inherited features, or (4) delete inherited features. Because of the inherent dangers involved, few methodologists or languages allow the deletion of inherited features. Definition 2 unnecessarily restricts inheritance to classes (a.k.a. class inheritance). Definition 3 discusses points out that inheritance can be used (and misused) as a mechanism for expressing commonality and sharing characteristics. Definition 4 unnecessarily restricts inheritance to specialization inheritance. Inheritance plays a key role in the development of an object-oriented type system. [Firesmith]

Kinds:

- CLASS INHERITANCE
- CLASS-INSTANCE INHERITANCE
- DYNAMIC INHERITANCE
- EVENT INHERITANCE
- IMPLMENTATION INHERITANCE
- INTERFACE INHERITANCE
  - SPECIALIZATION INHERITANCE
  - STRICT INHERITANCE
- INVERTED INHERITANCE
- MULTIPLE INHERITANCE
  - MIXIN INHERITANCE
  - REPEATED INHERITANCE
    + DIRECT REPEATED INHERITANCE
    + INDIRECT REPEATED INHERITANCE
    + REPLICATED REPEATED INHERITANCE
    + SHARED REPEATED INHERITANCE
    + VIRTUAL INHERITANCE
- OBJECT–OBJECT INHERITANCE
- PRIVATE INHERITANCE
- PROTECTED INHERITANCE
- PUBLIC INHERITANCE
- SELECTIVE INHERITANCE
- SINGLE INHERITANCE
- SINGLE INHERITANCE
- SPECIFICATION INHERITANCE
- TYPE INHERITANCE

- **class inheritance** *n.* **1.** any inheritance among classes in which a new class (a.k.a. the *parent*) is defined in terms of one or more existing classes (a.k.a. its parent[s]), whereby the child inherits the features of its parents. [Firesmith] **2.** any implementation of generalization using inheritance. [Martin/Odell]
  Synonym: SUBCLASSING.
  Contrast with: TYPE INHERITANCE.
  Examples: Subclasses inherit slots, methods, and some defclass operations from their superclasses. [CLOS]
  Commentary: Definition **2** unnecessarily restricts class inheritance to specialization inheritance.
- **class-instance inheritance** *n.* any inheritance whereby instances inherit default attribute values from their class. [Martin]
  Example: The class *Device* may have an attribute *state* and each instance of the Device class is instantiated with the state attribute having the value *Disabled.*
- **dynamic inheritance** *n.* any inheritance that requires dynamic binding (e.g., to support polymorphism). [Firesmith]
  Antonym: STATIC INHERITANCE.
- **event inheritance** *n.* any inheritance whereby event subtypes inherit trigger rules and control conditions from their event supertypes. [Martin]
- **implementation inheritance** *n.* **1.** any inheritance whereby a new *implementation* is incrementally defined in terms of existing implementations. [Firesmith] **2.** any inheritance used merely for the purpose of reusing [some of] the implementation of the base class(es). [Henderson-Sellers]

Antonym: INTERFACE INHERITANCE.
Contrast with: SPECIALIZATION INHERITANCE.
See also: SIGNATURE CONFORMANCE, TYPE CONFORMANCE.
Commentary: The use of implementation inheritance is controversial in the object community because it is typically used merely for code (i.e., implementation) reuse rather than to capture an *a-kind-of* taxonomy. Implementation inheritance neither implies any semantic relationship nor conformity of interfaces. Many methodologists consider it not to be as good as specialization or interface inheritance because it need support neither specialization nor polymorphic substitutability. The use of implementation inheritance is often a sign that aggregation or delegation should have been used instead of inheritance. [Firesmith]

- **interface inheritance** *n.* any inheritance whereby the new definition conforms to the existing definition(s). [Firesmith, Henderson-Sellers]
  Synonym: SPECIFICATION INHERITANCE, SUBTYPING.
  Antonym: IMPLEMENTATION INHERITANCE.
  Contrast with: SPECIALIZATION INHERITANCE.
  Commentary: Interface inheritance implies that the protocol of the child is a superset of the union of the protocols of its parents. Interface inheritance allows polymorphic substitution of instances of the derived class for instances of any of its base classes, even if the derived class is not a specialization of its base class(es). [Firesmith]
  Kinds:

I

- SPECIALIZATION INHERITANCE
- STRICT INHERITANCE
- **specialization inheritance** *n.* any inheritance that implements the *a-kind-of* relationship so that the child is a specialization of its parents. [Firesmith, Henderson-Sellers]
Synonym: SUBTYPING.
Contrast with: IMPLEMENTATION INHERITANCE, INTERFACE INHERITANCE.
Example: Cars are specializations of (a kind of) vehicles. [Firesmith]
Commentary: Specialization inheritance implies interface inheritance because an instance of a specialization can be used anywhere that an instance of its generalization can be used. [Firesmith]
- **strict inheritance** *n.* any interface inheritance whereby the new definition only adds new features to the old definition(s) but neither deletes nor redefines inherited features from the old definition(s). [Firesmith]
- **inverted inheritance** *n.* any inheritance whereby the parent defines *all* of the features needed by *all* of its children and these individual children *delete* the unnecessary features of the parent rather than add new features or override inherited features. [Firesmith]
Synonym: SELECTIVE INHERITANCE.
Commentary: Inverted inheritance is generally rejected in the object community. It produces inheritance structures that are neither extensible nor maintainable. The parent does not capture a meaningful abstraction and is not restricted to the definition of common features. Contrary to ex-

pectations, the children are neither more abstract nor more detailed. Instead of being extensions that can do more than their parents, they can only do less. Inverted inheritance is therefore a source of confusion and not recommended. [Firesmith]
- **multiple inheritance** *n.* **1.** the incremental construction of a new definition in terms of *multiple* existing definitions, whereby the new definition may both add new features and modify existing inherited features. [Firesmith] **2.** the construction of a definition by incremental modification of more than one definition. [OMG] c) inheritance from several distinct parents. [Ada94, Coleman, Firesmith, Jacobson, Martin, Rumbaugh, Wirfs-Brock]
Antonym: SINGLE INHERITANCE.
Example: Inheritance whereby a single class is simultaneously a child class of more than one parent class. [Firesmith]

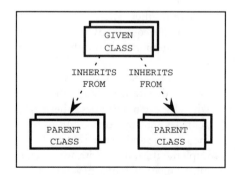

Multiple Inheritance

Commentary: The extent of the child is a subset of the intersection of the extents of the parents. [Embley, Firesmith]
Kinds:

- MIXIN INHERITANCE
- REPEATED INHERITANCE
  + DIRECT REPEATED INHERITANCE
  + INDIRECT REPEATED
    INHERITANCE
  + REPLICATED REPEATED
    INHERITANCE
  + SHARED REPEATED INHERITANCE
  + VIRTUAL INHERITANCE
- **mixin inheritance** *n.* any multiple inheritance involving a mixin, an abstract parent class that exists only to provide a set of properties for classes to inherit. [Ada95]
- **repeated inheritance** *n.* any multiple inheritance in which a given child inherits the same feature, either directly or indirectly, from the same ancestor class multiple times. [Eiffel, Firesmith, Jacobson, Meyer] *See also:* REPLICATED FEATURE, SHARED FEATURE.
Commentary: In the majority of programming languages that support multiple inheritance, the user is forced to redefine the name of each replicated feature so that it becomes unique. This is the most acceptable solution, as only the user has sufficient knowledge to solve this conflict. If an operation is replicated, the selection of which version does not matter unless the original operation has been overridden. Then the problem is to know which one to select. [Jacobson]
Kinds:
  + DIRECT REPEATED INHERITANCE
  + INDIRECT REPEATED
    INHERITANCE
  + REPLICATED REPEATED
    INHERITANCE
  + SHARED REPEATED INHERITANCE

+ VIRTUAL INHERITANCE

+ **direct repeated inheritance [of a given class]** *n.* any repeated inheritance in which a parent class of the given class is multiply inherited. [Eiffel, Firesmith, Meyer] *Antonym:* INDIRECT REPEATED INHERITANCE.

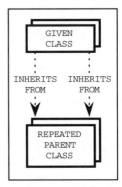

Direct Repeated Inheritance

+ **indirect repeated inheritance [of a given class]** *n.* any repeated in-

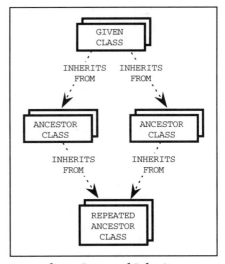

Indirect Repeated Inheritance

heritance in which an ancestor class of the given class is the parent of two or more descendants of the given class. [Eiffel, Firesmith, Meyer]

Antonym: DIRECT REPEATED INHERITANCE.

+ **replicated repeated inheritance** *n.* any repeated inheritance from a common ancestor of a single feature under different names yielding two features in the current class. [Eiffel, Firesmith, Meyer]

Antonym: SHARED REPEATED INHERITANCE.

Commentary: The inherited feature is thus replicated and occurs multiple times in the current class or type. In the majority of programming languages that support multiple inheritance, the developer is required to redefine the name of each replicated feature so that it becomes unique. This is the most acceptable solution, as only the developer has sufficient knowledge to resolve this conflict. If an operation is repeated, the selection of which version does not matter unless the original operation has been overridden. Then the problem is to know which one to select. [Firesmith]

+ **shared repeated inheritance** *n.* any repeated inheritance from a common ancestor of a single feature under the same final name yielding a single feature in the current class. [Eiffel, Firesmith, Meyer]

Synonym: VIRTUAL INHERITANCE.

Antonym: REPLICATED REPEATED INHERITANCE.

Commentary: The inherited feature is thus shared and occurs only once in the current class. [Firesmith]

+ **virtual inheritance** *n.* any repeated inheritance whereby the features of repeated base classes (or supertypes) are only inherited once in the derived class (or subtype).

Synonym: SHARED REPEATED INHERITANCE.

See also: SHARED FEATURE.

• **object–object inheritance** *n.* any inheritance that transfers the *state* of one object to another. [Martin/Odell]

Synonym: DELEGATION.

• **private inheritance** *n.* any inheritance in which all inherited features become private, regardless of their visibility in the parents. [Firesmith]

Contrast with: PROTECTED INHERITANCE, PUBLIC INHERITANCE.

Commentary: The use of private inheritance supports information hiding and the maintainability of inheritance structures because it allows developers to change the implementation of ancestors without impacting their descendants. However, private inheritance must be used with care as it may also prevent the child from conforming to its parents by hiding their visible features, thus violating subtyping, specialization inheritance, and polymorphic substitutability. [Firesmith]

• **protected inheritance** *n.* any inheritance in which all inherited private and protected features have the same visibility in the child as they did in the parent(s), but all inherited public features become protected in the

child. [Firesmith]
Contrast with: PRIVATE INHERITANCE,
PUBLIC INHERITANCE.
- **public inheritance** *n.* any inheritance
in which all inherited features have
the same visibility in the child as they
did in the parent(s). [Firesmith]
Contrast with: PRIVATE INHERITANCE,
PROTECTED INHERITANCE.
- **selective inheritance** *n.* any inheritance
whereby the parent defines *all* of
the features needed by *all* of its children
and these individual children *delete* the
unnecessary features of the parent rather
than add new features or override inherited
features. [Firesmith]
Synonym: INVERTED INHERITANCE.
Commentary: Inverted inheritance is
generally rejected in the object community.
It produces inheritance structures
that are neither extensible nor
maintainable. The parent does not
capture a meaningful abstraction and
is not restricted to the definition of
common features. Contrary to expectations,
the children are neither
more abstract nor more detailed. Instead
of being extensions that can do
more than their parents, they can
only do less. Inverted inheritance is
therefore a source of confusion and
not recommended. [Firesmith]
- **single inheritance** *n.* **1.** any inheritance
in which the definition of the
child is constructed in terms of the
definition of only a *single* parent.
[Coleman, Firesmith, Martin, OMG,
Rumbaugh, Smalltalk, Wirfs-Brock]
2. inheritance using only a single Parent
clause. [Eiffel, Meyer]
Antonym: MULTIPLE INHERITANCE.
Contrast with: MULTIPLE GENERALIZATION,
SINGLE GENERALIZATION.

Example: In single inheritance, a single
class is a child class of only a single
parent class. [Firesmith]

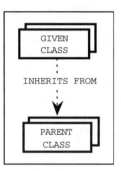

Single Inheritance

- **specification inheritance** *n.* any inheritance
whereby the specification
of the new definition conforms to
those of the existing definition(s).
[Henderson-Sellers]
Synonym: INTERFACE INHERITANCE,
SUBTYPING.
Antonym: IMPLEMENTATION INHERITANCE.
Contrast with: SPECIALIZATION INHERITANCE.
Commentary: Specification inheritance
allows polymorphic substitution
of instances of the derived class for instances
of any of its base classes, even
if the derived class is not a specialization
of its base class(es). [Firesmith]
- **static inheritance** *n.* any inheritance
that does not require dynamic binding.
[Firesmith]
Antonym: DYNAMIC INHERITANCE.
- **type inheritance** *n.* any inheritance
among types in which a new type
(a.k.a. the *subtype*) is defined in terms
of one or more existing types (a.k.a. its
supertypes), whereby the subtype is a

specialization of its supertypes, conforms to their interfaces, and inherits their features. [Firesmith, ODMG]
Synonym: SUBTYPING.
Contrast with: CLASS INHERITANCE.
See also: TYPE CONFORMANCE.

inheritance association *n.* any class association, meaning that the definition of the operations and attributes of one class is also used in the inheriting class which might do additions and redefinitions. [Jacobson]
See also: INHERITANCE.

inheritance constraint *n.* any structural constraint which restricts the relationships among children or between the children and their parent(s). [Firesmith]
Kinds:
• COVER CONSTRAINT
• DISJOINT CONSTRAINT
• PARTITION CONSTRAINT

• **cover constraint** *n.* the inheritance constraint which requires that the extent of the parent be a subset of the union of the extents of the children. [Firesmith]
Rationale: The term *cover* comes from set theory.
Commentary: This constraint ensures that each instance of the parent is also an instance of at least one child. [Firesmith]

• **disjoint constraint** *n.* the inheritance constraint which requires that the extents of the children be pair-wise disjoint. [Firesmith]
Rationale: The term *disjoint* comes from set theory. [Firesmith]
Commentary: This constraint ensures that no object will be an instance of two children. [Firesmith]

• **partition constraint** *n.* the inheritance constraint which requires that

the extents of the children form a disjoint cover of the parent. [Firesmith]
Commentary: The partition constraint is the conjunction of the disjoint constraint and the cover constraint. [Firesmith]

inheritance coupling *n.* the coupling dependency of a new definition on its parent definitions due to the inheritance relationship between them. [Firesmith, Henderson-Sellers]
Contrast with: AGGREGATION COUPLING, CLASSIFICATION COUPLING, EXCEPTION COUPLING, FRIENDSHIP COUPLING, IMPLEMENTATION COUPLING, INTERFACE COUPLING, MESSAGE COUPLING.
Example: The coupling dependency of a derived class on its base classes is an example of inheritance coupling. [Firesmith]

inheritance diagram (INHD) *n.* **1.** any specialized semantic net that documents an inheritance structure showing the relevant classes, the inheritance relationships between the derived classes and their base classes, and where useful and practical, the generic parameters of generic classes, the interfaces and implementations of classes, their instances, and the classification relationships between instances and their classes. [Firesmith] **2.** any class diagram that documents the inheritance hierarchies. [Booch] **3.** any diagram that shows the inheritance relationships that pertain between the classes. [Shlaer/Mellor]
Synonym: INHERITANCE GRAPH.
Contrast with: CLASS-CATEGORY DIAGRAM, DESIGN-CLASS DIAGRAM, KEY-ABSTRACTION DIAGRAM.
Commentary: The purpose of the inheritance diagram is to depict the inheritance relationships that pertain between

the classes of a single program, library, or environment. [Shlaer/Mellor]

inheritance forest *n.* any group of inheritance trees. [Firesmith]
Contrast with: INHERITANCE TREE.
Commentary: Languages like Smalltalk place all classes within a single inheritance tree, whereas languages like C++ allow classes to be in multiple inheritance trees within an inheritance forest. [Firesmith]

inheritance graph *n.* any inheritance diagram. [Coleman]
Synonym: INHERITANCE DIAGRAM.

inheritance hierarchy *n.* any hierarchy consisting of classes or types and the single inheritance relationships between them. [Firesmith]
Synonym: CLASS HIERARCHY, INHERITANCE TREE.
Contrast with: GENERALIZATION HIERARCHY.
Commentary: The use of multiple inheritance may result in graph structures that are not true hierarchies (i.e., tree structures). [Firesmith]

inheritance model *n.* any model that graphically describes the class hierarchy. [Henderson-Sellers]
Synonym: INTERACTION MODEL.
Commentary: It may be either generalization or implementation inheritance. It is distinct from the O/C model. [Henderson-Sellers]

inheritance structure *n.* any structure consisting of a connected graph of base classes and derived classes connected by their inheritance relationships. [Firesmith]

inheritance tree *n.* any hierarchical tree-shaped structure consisting of a connected graph of base classes and derived classes connected by single inheritance relationships. [Firesmith]
Synonyms: CLASS HIERARCHY, INHERITANCE HIERARCHY.
Contrast with: INHERITANCE FOREST.
Example: Smalltalk classes belong to a single large tree, whereas C++ often produces forests of smaller trees when restricted to single inheritance. [Firesmith]
Rationale: A single inheritance structure is similar to a tree, with a root class, branch classes, and leaf classes. Inheritance trees grow with time like real trees, extending new branches and growing new leaves. [Firesmith]
Commentary: Languages like Smalltalk place all classes within a single inheritance tree, whereas languages like C++ allow classes to be in multiple inheritance trees within an inheritance forest. [Firesmith]

inherited feature *n.* **1.** any feature obtained from ancestors via inheritance. [Firesmith] **2.** the features obtained by a class from its parents, if any. [Eiffel, Meyer]
See also: PRECURSOR [OF AN INHERITED FEATURE], SEED [OF A GIVEN FEATURE].
Antonym: IMMEDIATE FEATURE.
Commentary: Definition **2** unnecessarily restricts the term to classes and ignores types and clusters. [Firesmith]

inherited name [of a given feature] *n.* the name of the given feature in its parent class. [Eiffel, Firesmith, Meyer]
Contrast with: FINAL NAME, ORIGINAL NAME.

initial state *n.* the first atomic state of an object or class upon instantiation. [Firesmith]
Synonyms: BEGIN STATE, CREATION STATE, START STATE.
Antonyms: FINAL STATE.

Commentary: The term *initial state* is preferred. [Firesmith]

initial transition *n.* a state transition that has no prior state and that is always enabled. Initial transitions have no prior states and are always enabled. [Embley]
Antonym: FINAL TRANSITION.
Contrast with: BEGIN STATE, INITIAL STATE, START STATE.
Commentary: Every complete state net must have an initial transition, which fires whenever its trigger is satisfied. [Embley]

initialization argument list *n.* the list of alternating initialization argument names and values that follows a class or the name of a class in the call of a generic function. [CLOS]

inline operation *n.* any operation, the method of which is directly compiled into each point the program where it is used. [Firesmith]
Synonym: INLINE FUNCTION. [C++]
Commentary: Inlining implies static binding and avoids the overhead of message passing. Inlining is usually used to trade space for speed. [Firesmith]

instance *n.* **1.** anything created from or corresponding to a definition. [Firesmith] **2.** an example of something [Coad]
Kinds:
- • INSTANCE OF A GIVEN ASSOCIATION
- • INSTANCE OF A GIVEN CLASS
  - - DIRECT INSTANCE OF A GIVEN CLASS
  - - INDIRECT INSTANCE OF A GIVEN CLASS
- • INSTANCE OF A GIVEN CLUSTER
- • INSTANCE OF A GIVEN GENERIC
- • INSTANCE OF A GIVEN IMPLEMENTATION
- • INSTANCE OF A GIVEN METACLASS
- • INSTANCE OF A GIVEN TYPE

• **instance [of a given association]** *n.* a link instantiated from the association. [Firesmith, Rumbaugh]

• **instance [of a given class]** *n.* **1.** (a) any object instantiated according to the definition provided by the given class. [Booch, CLOS, Firesmith, Shlaer/Mellor, Smalltalk] (b) an object behaving in the manner specified by the given class. [Rumbaugh, Wirfs-Brock] c) any object created to conform to the description of the given class. [Jacobson] **2.** any single real-world thing. [Shlaer/Mellor] **3.** any actual object, waiting to perform services or holding some state data. [Lorenz] **4.** any object whose type is that of the given class or a subtype of it. [Coleman, Martin/Odell]
Synonyms: **1** DIRECT INSTANCE, OBJECT.
Commentary: An instance of a class is also a member of the extent of the class. [Embley, Firesmith]
Kinds:
- - DIRECT INSTANCE [OF A GIVEN CLASS]
- - INDIRECT INSTANCE [OF A GIVEN CLASS]

- **direct instance [of a given class]** *n.* **1.** any object that has been explicitly instantiated using a constructor of the given class. [Eiffel, Firesmith, Meyer] **2.** any object that is an instance of a class but not an instance of any subclass of the class. [Rumbaugh]
Antonym: INDIRECT INSTANCE.
Commentary: Only concrete classes can have direct instances. A direct instance of a given class is not an instance of any specialized descendant of the given class and is only an indirect instance of all generalized ancestors of the given class. [Eiffel, Firesmith, Meyer]

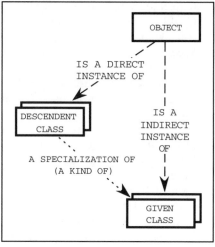

Direct Instance

- **indirect instance [of a given class]** *n.* any object that is a direct instance of some descendant of the given class whereby the descendant class is a specialization of the given class. [Firesmith, Rumbaugh]
Antonym: DIRECT INSTANCE.
- **instance [of a given cluster]** *n.* any collection of objects instantiated from the cluster. [Firesmith]
- **instance [of a given generic]** *n.* any instance created by supplying actual parameters for the formal parameters of the given generic. [Firesmith]
- **instance [of a given implementation]** *n.* any object whose behavior is provided by that implementation. [OMG]
- **instance [of a given metaclass]** *n.*

any class instantiated from the metaclass. [Firesmith]
- **instance [of a given type]** *n.* **1.** any object that conforms to the type. [Eiffel, Firesmith, Meyer] **2.** an object that is a member of the extent of the type. [Firesmith]

Indirect Instance

instance association *n.* any association linking two instances. [Jacobson]
Antonym: CLASS ASSOCIATION.
Contrast with: META ASSOCIATION.
instance attribute *n.* any attribute of an individual instance. [Firesmith, Jacobson]
Synonym: INSTANCE VARIABLE.
Contrast with: CLASS ATTRIBUTE, EXTENT ATTRIBUTE.
Commentary: All instance attributes are protected in Smalltalk, whereas C++ also allows instance attributes (a.k.a., data members) to be public or protected. [Firesmith]
Kinds:
 • INSTANCE VARIABLE

    - INDEXED INSTANCE VARIABLE

    - NAMED INSTANCE VARIABLE

• **instance variable** *n.* **1.** any variable attribute of an individual instance. [Firesmith, Rumbaugh, Smalltalk] **2.** any place to store and refer to an object's state data. [Booch, Lorenz] **3.** any name that allows one object (instance) to refer to another one. [Lorenz] **4.** the OOPL implementation of any attribute type [Martin/Odell]

Synonym: 1 INSTANCE ATTRIBUTE, 2 FIELD, MEMBER OBJECT, SLOT.

Commentary: All instance variables are protected in Smalltalk, whereas C++ also allows instance variables (a.k.a. data members) to be public or protected. Instance variables in Eiffel have read-only semantics.

Kinds:

    - INDEXED INSTANCE VARIABLE

    - NAMED INSTANCE VARIABLE

- **indexed instance variable** *n.* any instance variable that is not accessed by name. [Smalltalk]

Antonym: NAMED INSTANCE VARIABLE.

Example: `names at: 1` [Smalltalk]

Commentary: An object can have indexed instance variables only if all instances of its class can have indexed instance variables. [Smalltalk]

- **named instance variable** *n.* an instance variable that is accessed by its instance variable name. [Smalltalk]

Antonym: INDEXED INSTANCE VARIABLE.

Commentary: All instances of a class have the same number of named instance variables and use the same names to refer to them. [Smalltalk]

instance-based development *n.* any development that primarily consists of integrating instances of previously defined classes of objects. [Firesmith, Lorenz]

Synonym: COMPONENT-BASED DEVELOPMENT.

Contrast with: CLASS-BASED DEVELOPMENT.

instance component *n.* any logical component that is implemented as a separate element of the instance's data structure. [Shlaer/Mellor]

Example: an element of member data in C++.

instance diagram *n.* any object diagram documenting a particular set of instances and their relationships. [Rumbaugh]

Contrast with: CLASS DIAGRAM.

instance exception *n.* any exception of an individual instance.

Contrast with: CLASS EXCEPTION, EXTENT EXCEPTION.

instance invariant *n.* any invariant of an individual instance defined in terms of the properties of the instance. An instance invariant must evaluate to true for each instance whenever the instance is accessible: after instantiation and after the completion of each visible operation. [Booch, Coleman, Eiffel, Firesmith, Meyer, Rumbaugh]

Example: The age of a person cannot be less than zero. [Firesmith]

Commentary: Invariants may (and sometimes must) be temporarily violated during execution, but such violations must never be detectable outside of the instance. Concurrency and mutual exclusion influences the practical implementations of invariant checks. [Firesmith]

instance operation *n.* any operation that operates on an individual instance. [Firesmith]
Contrast with: CLASS OPERATION, EXTENT OPERATION.

instance property *n.* any property that characterizes the individual instance. [Firesmith, ODMG]
Contrast with: CLASS PROPERTY, EXTENT PROPERTY, TYPE PROPERTY.
Kinds:
- • COMPONENT OBJECT
- • INSTANCE ATTRIBUTE
  - - INSTANCE VARIABLE
    - + INDEXED INSTANCE VARIABLE
    - + NAMED INSTANCE VARIABLE
- • INSTANCE EXCEPTION
- • INSTANCE INVARIANT
- • LINK
  - - BASE LINK
  - - BIDIRECTIONAL LINK
  - - BINARY LINK
  - - DERIVED LINK
  - - POINTER
    - + ATTACHED POINTER
    - + IMPORTED REFERENCE
    - + INGENERATE REFERENCE
    - + VOID POINTER
  - - REFERENCE
    - + ATTACHED REFERENCE
    - + IMPORTED REFERENCE
    - + INGENERATE REFERENCE
    - + VOID REFERENCE
  - - STATE LINK
  - - TERNARY LINK
  - - UNIDIRECTIONAL LINK
- • **component [object]** *n.* any object that is contained within another object as a component part. [Firesmith]
  Contrast with: COMPONENT CLASS, COMPONENT CLUSTER.
- • **instance attribute** *n.* any attribute of an individual instance. [Firesmith, Ja-

cobson]
Synonym: INSTANCE VARIABLE.
Contrast with: CLASS ATTRIBUTE, EXTENT ATTRIBUTE.
Commentary: All instance attributes are protected in Smalltalk, whereas C++ also allows instance attributes (a.k.a. data members) to be public or protected. [Firesmith]
Kinds:
- - INSTANCE VARIABLE
  - + INDEXED INSTANCE VARIABLE
  - + NAMED INSTANCE VARIABLE
- - **instance variable** *n.* **1.** any variable attribute of an individual instance. [Firesmith, Rumbaugh, Smalltalk] **2.** any place to store and refer to an object's state data. [Booch, Lorenz] **3.** any name that allows one object (instance) to refer to another one. [Lorenz] **4.** the OOPL implementation of any attribute type [Martin/Odell]
  Synonym: **1** INSTANCE ATTRIBUTE, **2** FIELD, MEMBER OBJECT, SLOT.
  Commentary: All instance variables are protected in Smalltalk, whereas C++ also allows instance variables (a.k.a. data members) to be public or protected. Instance variables in Eiffel have read-only semantics.
  Kinds:
  - + INDEXED INSTANCE VARIABLE
  - + NAMED INSTANCE VARIABLE
- + **indexed instance variable** *n.* any instance variable that is not accessed by name. [Smalltalk]
  Antonym: NAMED INSTANCE VARIABLE.
  Example: names at: 1 [Smalltalk]
  Commentary: An object can have indexed instance variables only if all instances of its class can have in-

dexed instance variables. [Smalltalk]

+ **named instance variable** *n.* an instance variable that is accessed by its instance variable name. [Smalltalk]

Antonym: INDEXED INSTANCE VARIABLE.

Commentary: All instances of a class have the same number of named instance variables and use the same names to refer to them. [Smalltalk]

• **instance exception** *n.* any exception of an individual instance. [Firesmith]

Contrast with: CLASS EXCEPTION.

• **instance invariant** *n.* any invariant of an individual instance defined in terms of the properties of the instance. An instance invariant must evaluate to true for each instance whenever the instance is accessible: after instantiation and after the completion of each visible operation. [Booch, Coleman, Eiffel, Firesmith, Meyer, Rumbaugh]

Example: The age of a person cannot be less than zero. [Firesmith]

Commentary: Invariants may (and sometimes must) be temporarily violated during execution, but such violations must never be detectable outside of the instance. Concurrency and mutual exclusion influences the practical implementations of invariant checks. [Firesmith]

• **link** *n.* **1.** during analysis and logical design, any instance of an association that captures a named semantic relationship between objects. [Firesmith, OMG, Rumbaugh] **2.** during implementation design and coding, any feature that contains one or more values, each of which reliably points to a

server object. [Firesmith]

Contrast with: ASSOCIATION.

Commentary: Links imply visibility and enable message passing. Links are the roads, whereas messages are the traffic on those roads. [Firesmith]

Kinds:

- BASE LINK
- BIDIRECTIONAL LINK
- BINARY LINK
- DERIVED LINK
- POINTER
    + ATTACHED POINTER
    + VOID POINTER
- REFERENCE
    + ATTACHED REFERENCE
    + IMPORTED REFERENCE
    + INGENERATE REFERENCE
    + VOID REFERENCE
- STATE LINK
- TERNARY LINK
- UNIDIRECTIONAL LINK

- **base link** *n.* any link that cannot be derived from other links. [Firesmith]

Antonym: DERIVED LINK.

- **bidirectional link** *n.* any logical link that represents two unidirectional links that are coupled whereby each is the inverse of the another. [Firesmith]

Antonym: UNIDIRECTIONAL LINK.

- **binary link** *n.* any link between two objects. [Firesmith]

Contrast with: TERNARY LINK.

- **derived link** *n.* (a) any indirect link that is the product of other links. [Firesmith] (b) any instance of a derived association. [Firesmith]

Antonym: BASE LINK.

Contrast with: DERIVED ASSOCIATION.

- **pointer [to a given object]** *n.* **1.** any link, the value of which should

be the address of the given server object. [Firesmith] **2.** an attribute of one object that contains an explicit reference to another object. [Rumbaugh]
Contrast with: IDENTIFIER, LINK, REFERENCE.
Commentary: Unless changed, a pointer will identify the same object each time the pointer is used (subject to certain pragmatic limits of space and time). An object may be denoted by multiple, distinct pointers. [Firesmith]
Kinds:
+ ATTACHED POINTER
+ VOID POINTER
+ **attached pointer** *n.* any pointer that currently points to an object. [Firesmith]
Antonym: VOID POINTER.
Commentary: The pointer is said to be attached to the object, and the object is also said to be attached to the pointer. [Firesmith]
+ **void pointer** *n.* any pointer that does not currently point to an object. [Firesmith]
Synonym: NULL POINTER.
Antonym: ATTACHED POINTER.
- **reference [to a given object]** *n.* (a) any constant value that is used as an alias for the OID of the given server object. [Firesmith] (b) any value that refers to an object. [Eiffel, Meyer]
Contrast with: IDENTIFIER, LINK, POINTER.
Commentary: References are used as links and as arguments in messages and operations. Unless changed, a reference will identify the same object each time the reference is used

(subject to certain pragmatic limits of space and time). An object may be denoted by multiple, distinct references. [Firesmith]
Contrast with: VALUE.
Kinds:
+ ATTACHED REFERENCE
+ IMPORTED REFERENCE
+ INGENERATE REFERENCE
+ VOID REFERENCE
+ **attached reference** *n.* any reference that currently refers to an object. [Eiffel, Firesmith, Meyer]
Antonym: VOID REFERENCE.
Commentary: The reference is said to be attached to the object, and the object is also said to be attached to the reference. [Eiffel, Firesmith, Meyer]
+ **imported reference** *n.* any reference stored in an object's instance variable that was not generated by the object itself through invocation of a *create* method. [Atkinson]
Antonym: INGENERATE REFERENCE.
+ **ingenerate reference** *n.* any reference stored in an object's instance variable that was generated by the object itself through invocation of a *create* method. [Atkinson]
Antonym: IMPORTED REFERENCE.
+ **void reference** *n.* (a) any reference that does not currently refer to an object. [Firesmith] (b) any reference about which no further information is available. [Eiffel, Meyer]
Antonym: ATTACHED REFERENCE.
- **state link** *n.* any link whose existence helps determine the state of its

client object or class. [Firesmith]
Contrast with: STATE ATTRIBUTE, STATE COMPONENT.

- **ternary link** *n.* any link among three objects. [Firesmith]
Contrast with: BINARY LINK.

- **unidirectional link** *n.* any link directed from the client(s) to the server(s). [Firesmith]
Antonym: BIDIRECTIONAL LINK.
Commentary: Unidirectional links are typically implemented by one or more attributes acting as pointers or messages requesting services. [Firesmith]

instance variable *n.* **1.** any variable attribute of an individual instance. [Firesmith, Rumbaugh, Smalltalk] **2.** any place to store and refer to an object's state data. [Booch, Lorenz] **3.** any name that allows one object (instance) to refer to another one. [Lorenz] **4.** the OOPL implementation of any attribute type [Martin/Odell]
Synonym: 1 INSTANCE ATTRIBUTE, 2 FIELD, MEMBER OBJECT, SLOT.
Commentary: All instance variables are protected in Smalltalk, whereas C++ also allows instance variables (a.k.a. data members) to be public or protected. Instance variables in Eiffel have read-only semantics.
Kinds:

instantiate *v.* *-ed, -ing* to construct an instance. [Firesmith]

instantiation *n.* **1.** the process of constructing a new instance from its definition using a constructor. [Firesmith, Henderson-Sellers, Martin, Rumbaugh] **2.** the process of constructing a new instance from its generic definition by supplying actual generic parameters for its formal generic parameters. [Booch,

Firesmith]
Contrast with: CLASSIFICATION.

intangible object *n.* any object that models something that is not tangible in the real world. [Firesmith]
Examples: Objects that model events, interactions, or states are all intangible objects. [Firesmith]
Antonym: TANGIBLE OBJECT.

integration *n.* **1.** the coupling together of multiple classes via inheritance and aggregation. [Firesmith] **2.** the coupling together of multiple objects via message passing and reference. [Firesmith] **3.** the coupling together of multiple attributes and operations within a single class.
Examples: 1 the integration via inheritance of classes within a class library. 2 the integration via dependency of objects within a cluster instance. [Firesmith]

integration testing *n.* **1.** the testing of the multiple integrated classes or objects to find integration errors. [Firesmith] **2.** the testing of the multiple integrated features to find integration errors.
See also: INTEGRATION.
Commentary: Integration errors occur when things behave correctly in isolation, but do not behave correctly when coupled with other things during integration. [Firesmith]

integrity *n.* the degree to which the enforcement of abstractions (e.g., via assertions) is achieved. Firesmith]
Kinds:
• REFERENTIAL INTEGRITY
• STATE INTEGRITY

• **referential integrity** *n.* **1.** the degree to which each identifier refers to a unique object. [Firesmith] **2.** the degree to which links (especially bidirectional links) are maintained. [Firesmith]

- **state integrity** *n.* the degree to which the state of an object or class cannot be corrupted (e.g., via messages from clients). [Firesmith]

integrity rule *n.* any rule that states that something must be true. [Martin]

Synonym: ASSERTION.

Examples: A value must be within a certain range, an object relationship must have a stated cardinality, and a precondition must hold before an operation is executed are all examples of integrity rules. [Martin]

intension [of a given abstraction] *n.* **1.** the complete definition of the given abstraction. [Firesmith, Martin/Odell] **2.** the description of a template/model representing some concept. [Henderson-Sellers]

Antonym: EXTENSION.

Examples: The intension defines when a abstraction applies (and does not apply) to an instance. For example, an intension for Man could be stated as an adult Person of the male gender. [Firesmith, Martin/Odell]

Rationale: The word *intension* is used rather than *intention* because intension reflects more than intent: it implies a thorough and *intensive* definition. [Firesmith, Martin/Odell]

interact *v.* *-ed*, *-ing* to communicate via message passing, exception raising, or the visibility of public properties.

interaction *n.* **1.** the mechanisms by which two objects interact. [Firesmith] **2.** the sending of a message. [Embley] **3.** an object that results from associations between other objects. [Shlaer/Mellor]

Synonym: **3** INTERACTION OBJECT.

Examples: A message pass or the raising of an exception are both forms of interactions. [Firesmith]

Commentary: Objects interact in order to collaborate. Definition **1** is the most general. Definition **2** is most popular, but ignores exceptions. Definition **3** is not widely used. [Firesmith]

Kinds:

- ACCESS INTERACTION
- ASYNCHRONOUS INTERACTION
- BIDIRECTIONAL INTERACTION
- CONTINUOUS INTERACTION
- HIGH-LEVEL INTERACTION
- MODIFY INTERACTION
- SYNCHRONOUS INTERACTION

- **access interaction** *n.* any interaction that obtains information about objects. [Embley]

- **asynchronous interaction** *n.* any interaction via an intermediate. [Embley]

  Synonym: ASYNCHRONOUS MESSAGE, ASYNCHRONOUS REQUEST, SIGNAL.

  Antonym: SYNCHRONOUS INTERACTION, SYNCHRONOUS MESSAGE, SYNCHRONOUS REQUEST.

  Examples: Communication via mail objects. [Embley]

- **bidirectional interaction** *n.* any pair of unidirectional interactions going in opposite directions that are so closely related that they are considered to be a single interaction. [Embley]

- **continuous interaction** *n.* any interaction that is continuous. [Embley]

  Examples: Interactions from analogue sensors may be modeled as continuous interactions. [Embley]

  Commentary: This is common particularly for analogue sensors in systems. [Embley]

- **high-level interaction** *n.* any abstract interaction representing and subsuming several detailed interactions. [Embley]

- **modify interaction** *n.* any interaction that alters existing objects. [Embley]
  Synonym: MODIFIER OPERATION.

- **synchronous interaction** *n.* any interaction used to synchronize interacting objects. [Embley]
  Synonym: SYNCHRONOUS MESSAGE, SYNCHRONOUS REQUEST.
  Antonym: ASYNCHRONOUS INTERACTION, ASYNCHRONOUS MESSAGE, ASYNCHRONOUS REQUEST, SIGNAL.
  Commentary: Usually, the sender and receiver understand that certain conditions must be met so that communication can take place, and they see to it that these conditions are met. [Embley]

interaction diagram (ID) *n.* **1.** any diagram that documents the dynamic behavior of a set of collaborating objects and classes in terms of their existence, the interactions among them, and optionally the control and data flows within them. [Booch, Colbert, Embley, Firesmith] **2.** any diagram that documents the sequencing of message passing between objects, classes, or blocks in a scenario or use case. [Booch, Jacobson]
Synonym: **1** EVENT-TRACE DIAGRAM, **2** TIMING DIAGRAM.
See also: OBJECT-INTERACTION MODEL.
Kinds:
- BLACKBOX INTERACTION DIAGRAM
- WHITBOX INTERACTION DIAGRAM

- **blackbox interaction diagram (BID)** *n.* any interaction diagram in which the documented objects and classes are treated as blackboxes. [Firesmith]
  Antonym: WHITEBOX INTERACTION DIAGRAM.

- **whitebox interaction diagram (WID)** *n.* any interaction diagram in which the documented objects and classes are treated as whiteboxes, showing their interfaces and implementations. [Firesmith]
  Antonym: BLACKBOX INTERACTION DIAGRAM.

interaction model *n.* the object-oriented dynamic-behavior model that documents the dynamic behavior of objects and classes in terms of the interactions between them, their operations, and optionally their attributes and the data flows between the operations and attribute stores. The interaction model consists of scenarios, scenario lifecycles, scenario life cycle diagrams, interaction diagrams, timing diagrams, class lifecycle diagrams, and their OOSDL specifications. [Firesmith]
Synonym: EVENT MODEL.
Contrast with: CONFIGURATION MODEL, DATA MODEL, LANGUAGE MODEL, PRESENTATION MODEL, SEMANTIC MODEL, STATE MODEL.

interaction object *n.* any object that relates to two or more other objects in the model and that generally has a *transaction* or *contract* quality. [Shlaer/Mellor]
Synonym: ASSOCIATIVE OBJECT
Contrast with: INCIDENT OBJECT, ROLE OBJECT, SPECIFICATION OBJECT, SUBTYPE OBJECT, SUPERTYPE OBJECT, TANGIBLE OBJECT.
Examples: A purchase (related to buyer, seller, and thing purchased) and marriage (related to man and women), an electrical network, the piping in a refinery, and the tracks of a railroad are all examples of interaction objects. [Shlaer/Mellor]

interaction pattern *n.* any pattern of interaction, which is overlaid on players in other patterns. [Coad]

iterative development process (IDP) *n.* the sequence of phases within the build stage of the product life cycle of the MOSES method. [Henderson-Sellers] *Commentary:* The IDP provides a heuristic framework for the iterative nature of the process life cycle. [Henderson-Sellers]

interface *n.* **1.** (a) any specification of the boundary of something in terms of the possible interactions or properties that are visible across that boundary. [Firesmith] (b) the visible outside, user view of something. [Booch] **2.** the messages to which an object can respond. [Smalltalk]
Synonym: **2** PROTOCOL.
Antonym: IMPLEMENTATION.
Contrast with: **1** PROTOCOL.
Commentary: The interface determines the entire external view of something, what it is, and how it will acts and reacts. The interface of something documents what it does, not how it does it. Definition **1** is more general than definition **2**. [Firesmith]
Kinds:
- CLASS INTERFACE
- CLIENT INTERFACE
- CLUSTER INTERFACE
- CONSTRUCTION INTERFACE
- FUNCTIONAL INTERFACE
- MESSAGE INTERFACE
- OBJECT INTERFACE
- OPERATION INTERFACE
- ORB INTERFACE
- PRINCIPAL INTERFACE
- SERVER INTERFACE
- SYSTEM INTERFACE
- TYPE INTERFACE
- **class interface** *n.* the interface of any

class. [Firesmith, OADSIG]
Antonym: CLASS IMPLEMENTATION.
Contrast with: CLASS PROTOCOL, CLUSTER INTERFACE, OBJECT INTERFACE, TYPE INTERFACE.

- **client interface** *n.* that part of an interface that declares all exported (i.e., public, protected, and restricted) features that are visible to clients. [Firesmith]
Antonym: SERVER INTERFACE.
Contrast with: CLIENT PROTOCOL.
Example: The client interface of an object consists of its client protocol of messages and exceptions as well as any of its exported properties. [Firesmith]
Commentary: The client interface provides the server role (i.e., visible, outside, user viewpoint). Because most object-oriented methods and programming languages do not explicitly support the server interface, they therefore use the term *interface* when they mean *client interface.* No clients will be impacted by a change to the implementation if the client interface does not change. [Firesmith]

- **cluster interface** *n.* the interface of a cluster. [Firesmith]
Synonym: CLUSTER PROTOCOL.
Antonym: CLUSTER IMPLEMENTATION.
Contrast with: CLASS INTERFACE, OBJECT INTERFACE, TYPE INTERFACE.
Commentary: The client cluster interface declares all visible objects, classes, and subclusters that it provides to its clients whereas the server cluster interface declares all exported features of its servers on which it depends. [Firesmith]

- **construction interface** *n.* any interface that defines the operations used to communicate between the core of an Object Service and related objects that must participate in providing the service. [OMG]

Contrast with: FUNCTIONAL INTER-FACE.

Commentary: A construction interface is typically defined by the service and inherited and implemented by participants in the service. Objects that participate in a service must support its construction interfaces. [OMG]

- **functional interface** *n.* any interface that defines the operations invoked by users of an object service. [OMG]

Contrast with: CONSTRUCTION INTER-FACE.

Commentary: The audience for these interfaces is the service consumer, the user of the service. These interfaces present the functionality (the useful operations) of the service. [OMG]

- **message interface** *n.* any message declaration or signature.

- **object interface** *n.* **1.** the interface of any individual object. [Firesmith] **2.** any description of a set of possible uses of any object; specifically, a set of potential requests in which an object can meaningfully participate. [Jacobson, OMG] **3.** any listing of the operations and attributes that any object provides. This includes the signatures of the operations, and the types of the attributes. An interface definition ideally includes the semantics as well. [OMG] **4.** the union of the object's type interfaces. [OMG]

Antonym: OBJECT IMPLEMENTATION.

Contrast with: CLASS INTERFACE, CLUSTER INTERFACE, OBJECT PROTOCOL, TYPE INTERFACE.

Commentary: The client interface of an object includes the union of all vis-

ible instance features declared in the type(s) of the object. The client object interface includes the signatures of all messages in its protocol, thereby providing a description of its possible uses. Many methodologists do not consider the attributes to be a part of the interface because they should be hidden, encapsulated in the implementation. [Firesmith]

- **operation interface** *n.* any operation declaration or signature.

- **ORB interface** *n.* the interface that goes directly to the ORB which is the same for all ORBs and does not depend on the object's interface or object adapter. [OMG]

- **principal interface** *n.* the interface that describes all requests in which an object is meaningful. [OMG]

- **server interface** *n.* that part of an interface that declares all features that are required of servers. [Firesmith]

Antonym: INBOUND INTERFACE.

Contrast with: OUTBOUND PROTOCOL.

Example: The server interface of an object consists of the messages it sends to its servers, all exceptions that servers may raise to it, and any visible server properties on which it depends. [Firesmith]

Commentary: Most programming languages do not explicitly support the server part of the interface. No contract with servers will be impacted by a change to the implementation if the server interface does not change. [Firesmith]

- **system interface** *n.* **1.** the interface of any system. [Firesmith] **2.** the set of system operations to which a system can respond and the set of events that it can output. [Coleman]

Commentary: The interface of a system declares its visible features (e.g., objects, classes, clusters, and subsystems). [Firesmith]

- **type interface** *n.* **1.** the interface of any type, declaring its visible features (i.e., the set of operation signatures defined on the type). [Martin, OMG] **2.** the interface that defines the requests in which instances of this type can meaningfully participate as a parameter. [OMG]
Synonym: TYPE PROTOCOL.
Antonym: TYPE IMPLEMENTATION.
Contrast with: CLASS INTERFACE, CLUSTER INTERFACE, CONSTRUCTION INTERFACE, FUNCTIONAL INTERFACE, MESSAGE INTERFACE, OBJECT INTERFACE, OPERATION INTERFACE, ORB INTERFACE, PRINCIPLE INTERFACE, SYSTEM INTERFACE.
Example: If the interface to document type comprises edit and print and the interface to product type comprises set price and check inventory, then the object interface of a particular document which is also a product comprises all four requests. [OMG]

interface coupling *n.* **1.** any coupling due to any dependencies of the interface of the client on its server(s). [Firesmith] **2.** (a) any coupling in which the client object only has direct access to features exported by the server object. [Berard] (b) any interclass coupling via message passing. [Henderson-Sellers, Lorenz]
Antonym: IMPLEMENTATION COUPLING, INTERNAL COUPLING.
Contrast with: AGGREGATION COUPLING, CLASSIFICATION COUPLING, EXCEPTION COUPLING, FRIENDSHIP COUPLING, IMPLEMENTATION COUPLING, INHERITANCE COUPLING, MESSAGE COUPLING.

Examples: Coupling due to the use of types in signatures is a form of interface coupling. [Firesmith]
Commentary: The client object specifically refers to the server object and makes direct references to one or more items contained in its public interface. The public interface of the server may contain items other than operations (method selectors) such as constants, variables, exportable definitions, and exceptions. [Berard] Clients that directly access the implementation of servers (e.g., via friends) clearly exhibit high coupling. Less well known is that coupling is also increased if the interface of the client accesses the server. [Firesmith]

Interface Definition Language™ (IDL) *n.* the language used by applications to specify the various interfaces they intend to offer to other applications via the ORB layer. It describes the interfaces that client objects call and object implementations provide. [OMG]

interface dependency *n.* any dependency of the interface (as well as the implementation) of the client on its server(s). [Firesmith]
Contrast with: IMPLEMENTATION DEPENDENCY, METHOD DEPENDENCY.
Examples: Any dependency due to the use of types in signatures and any dependency provided by a with clause in an Ada package specification are forms of interface dependency. [Firesmith]
Commentary: Interface dependency implies that the interface of the server is visible to every feature of the client. [Firesmith]

interface inheritance *n.* any inheritance whereby the new definition conforms to the existing definition(s). [Firesmith]
Contrast with: IMPLEMENTATION INHER-

ITANCE, SPECIALIZATION INHERITANCE.

Example: Class inheritance in which the protocol of the child is a superset of the union of the protocols of its parents is an example of interface inheritance. [Firesmith]

Commentary: Interface inheritance produces consistent interfaces because the protocol of the child is a superset of the union of the protocols of its parents. Interface inheritance thus allows polymorphic substitution of instances of the child for instances of any of its parent(s), even if the child is not strictly a specialization of its parents. [Firesmith]

- **strict inheritance** *n.* any interface inheritance whereby the new definition only adds new features to the existing definition(s), but neither deletes nor redefines inherited features from the existing definition(s). [Firesmith]

interface model *n.* 1. any model that defines the input and output communication of the system. 2. any model composed of a life-cycle model and an operation model. [Coleman]

Contrast with: BEHAVIORAL MODEL, CONFIGURATION MODEL, DATA MODEL, DYNAMIC MODEL, FUNCTIONAL MODEL, INTERACTION MODEL, LANGUAGE MODEL, LIFE-CYCLE MODEL, OBJECT MODEL, OPERATION MODEL, PRESENTATION MODEL, SEMANTIC MODEL, STATE MODEL, STRUCTURAL MODEL, USE-CASE MODEL.

interface object *n.* 1. any object that serves to describe an interface. [OMG] an object in a business system that represents a set of business operations that should be performed by a single object that communicates with the environment of the business. [Jacobson] 2. any object in an information system that communi-

cates with one or more actors in the environment of the information system.

Commentary: Interface objects reside in an interface repository. [OMG] Interface objects encapsulate all of the functionality specified in use cases that is directly dependent on the system environment. [Jacobson]

- **central interface object** *n.* any interface object that contains other interface objects. [Jacobson]

  Commentary: A window containing buttons, menus, and scroll bar interface objects are all examples of central interface objects. [Jacobson]

interface repository *n.* 1. any storage place for interface information. [OMG] 2. any service that provides persistent objects that represent the IDL information in a form available at runtime. [OMG]

Contrast with: IMPLEMENTATION REPOSITORY.

interface type *n.* 1. any type that is satisfied by any object (literally, by any value that identifies an object) that satisfies a particular interface. [OMG] 2. any type of interface objects.

Contrast with: OBJECT TYPE.

interfacer *n.* any object that supports communication between other objects and external systems or users.

Synonym: COMMUNICATOR.

Contrast with: PROXY.

internal coupling *n.* any coupling in which the client object has direct access to the underlying implementation of the server object. [Berard]

Antonym: INTERFACE COUPLING.

internal event *n.* 1. any event, the source of which is *inside* the current scope (e.g., application, cluster, object). [Firesmith, Martin/Odell, OADSIG] 2. any

event that is generated by an a state model within the system. [Shlaer/Mellor]
Antonym: EXTERNAL EVENT.

internal operations *n.* an operation that does not directly send messages to other objects or classes. [Firesmith]
Synonym: INTERNAL ROUTINE.
Antonym: EXTERNAL OPERATION.

internal routine *n.* any routine written in the current language and therefore accessible to language processing tools. [Eiffel, Meyer]
Synonym: INTERNAL OPERATION.
Antonym: EXTERNAL ROUTINE.

internal state *n.* any state that is characterized by the values of all of the relevant variables. [Jacobson]
Antonym: COMPUTATIONAL STATE.

interobject concurrency *n.* the ability of individual objects to behave concurrently. [Embley]
Antonym: INTRAOBJECT CONCURRENCY.
See also: STATE NET.
Example: A robot might be moving to a container at the same time a packager is filling an order. [Embley]
Commentary: OSA behavior models support interobject concurrency by associating a different state-net instance with every object. [Embley]

interoperability *n.* **1.** the ability for two or more ORBs to cooperate to deliver requests to the proper object. Interoperating ORBs appear to a client as a single ORB. [OMG] **2.** the ability to exchange requests using the ORB in conformance with the OMG Architecture Guide. Objects interoperate if the methods of one object request services of another. [OMG]

interpreter [pattern] *n.* the behavioral class design pattern that models a grammar as a class hierarchy and implements an interpreter as an operation on instances of grammar classes. [Gamma, Helm, Johnson, and Vlissides]

interruptible action *n.* any action associated with a state that may be suspended before it finishes executing and may resume execution at a later time. [Embley]
Synonym: ACTIVITY, INTERRUPTIBLE OPERATION.
Antonym: NONINTERRUPTIBLE ACTION.

interruptible operation *n.* any operation that may be suspended before it finishes executing and may resume execution at a later time. [Firesmith]
Synonym: INTERRUPTIBLE ACTION.
Antonym: NONINTERRUPTIBLE OPERATION.
Commentary: Interruptible operations do not contain any critical regions that must execute to completion without interruption. [Firesmith]

intersubsystem relationship *n.* any relationship that associates objects in different subsystems. [Shlaer/Mellor]
Synonym: SPANNING RELATIONSHIP.

intraobject concurrency *n.* the ability of an object to be in more than one state at the same time or to exhibit combinations of states and transitions at the same time. [Embley]
Antonym: INTEROBJECT CONCURRENCY.
See also: STATE NET.
Commentary: When an object exits a final transition it ceases to exist unless the object is concurrently in some other state or transition. [Embley]

invariant *n.* any assertion, the scope of which is the entire life cycle of the associated thing. [Booch, Coleman, Eiffel, Firesmith, Meyer, Rumbaugh]
Contrast with: PRECONDITION, POSTCONDITION.
Examples: The length times the width

of any given rectangle must equal the rectangle's area. The age of something cannot be less than zero. [Firesmith]
Commentary: Invariants are used to ensure that abstractions are never violated in any detectable way. Although invariants may (and sometimes must) be temporarily violated during execution, such violations must never be detectable from the outside. Concurrency and mutual exclusion influence the practical implementations of invariant checks. [Firesmith]
Kinds:
- CLASS INVARIANT
- EXTENT INVARIANT
- INSTANCE INVARIANT
- MESSAGE INVARIANT
- SCENARIO INVARIANT
- **class invariant** *n.* any invariant involving the properties of a class that must be true on elaboration, prior to the execution of each class operation, and after execution of each class operation. [Firesmith]
Contrast with: EXTENT INVARIANT, INSTANCE INVARIANT, MESSAGE INVARIANT.
Example: Any invariant involving generic formal parameters is a class invariant. [Firesmith]
- **extent invariant** *n.* any invariant involving the properties of an extent that must be true prior to the execution of each constructor and after execution of each destructor. [Firesmith]
Contrast with: CLASS INVARIANT, INSTANCE INVARIANT, MESSAGE INVARIANT, SCENARIO INVARIANT.
Example: The current number of instances must never exceed the maximum number of instances. [Firesmith]
- **instance invariant** *n.* any invariant

involving the properties of an instance that must be true on instantiation, prior to the execution of each instance operation, after execution of each instance operation, and prior to destruction. [Booch, Coleman, Eiffel, Firesmith, Meyer, Rumbaugh]
Contrast with: CLASS INVARIANT, EXTENT INVARIANT, MESSAGE INVARIANT, SCENARIO INVARIANT.
Examples: The length times the width of any given rectangle must equal the rectangle's area. The age of something cannot be less than zero. [Firesmith]
- **message invariant** *n.* any invariant that must evaluate to true after execution of the associated operation if it holds prior to receipt of the message. [Firesmith]
Contrast with: CLASS INVARIANT, EXTENT INVARIANT, INSTANCE INVARIANT, SCENARIO INVARIANT.
- **scenario invariant** *n.* any invariant that must evaluate to true after execution of each associated operation and exception handler if it holds prior to the start of the scenario. [Firesmith]
Contrast with: CLASS INVARIANT, EXTENT INVARIANT, INSTANCE INVARIANT, MESSAGE INVARIANT.

inverted inheritance *n.* any inheritance whereby the parent class defines *all* of the features needed by *all* of its child classes and these individual derived classes *delete* the unnecessary features of the base class rather than add new features or override inherited features. [Firesmith]
Synonym: SELECTIVE INHERITANCE.
Commentary: Inverted inheritance is generally rejected in the object community. It produces inheritance structures that are neither extensible nor

maintainable. The parent does not capture a meaningful abstraction and is not restricted to the definition of common features. Contrary to expectations, the children are neither more abstract nor more detailed. Instead of being extensions that can do more than their parents, they can only do less. Inverted inheritance is therefore a source of confusion and not recommended. [Firesmith]

invoke [a method] *v.* *-ed, -ing* to call the method function of a method object. [CLOS]
Synonym: CALL.

invoked operation *n.* any *instance* of an operation. [Martin]

irreflexive constraint *n.* the structural constraint on a given relationship that prohibits objects or classes to be related to themselves. [Firesmith]
Antonym: REFLEXIVE CONSTRAINT.
Example: The *is parent of* link and association are irreflexive. No one can be its own parent. [Firesmith]

is-a relationship *n.* **1.** the classification relationship from an object to its class or type. [Firesmith] **2.** the specialization relationship from a derived class to its base class or from a subtype to its supertype. [Lorenz]
Synonym: CLASSIFICATION.
Contrast with: A-KIND-OF RELATIONSHIP.
Examples: **1** My dog Spot is a dog. My car is a car. **2** A car *is-a* [kind of] vehicle.
Commentary: Many developers confuse the *a-kind-of* relationship between types or classes with the *is-a* relationship between objects and their types or classes. Definition **2** confuses *is-a* with *a-kind-of.* [Firesmith]

is-a relationship set *n.* any relationship set of relationships between specializations and generalizations. [Embley]
Synonym: GENERALIZATION-SPECIALIZATION.
See also: SPECIALIZATION.
Commentary: This definition confuses *is-a* (classification) with *a-kind-of* (specialization).

is-kind-of relationship *n.* a synonym for *a-kind-of relationship, specialization inheritance, subtyping.* [Wirfs-Brock]

is-member-of relationship set *n.* any relationship set that forms a set object out of a group of members objects. [Embley]
Synonym: ASSOCIATION.
Contrast with: IS-PART-OF RELATIONSHIP SET.
See also: MEMBER CLASS, SET CLASS.
Commentary: The is-member-of relationship set forms a *set*, whereas the is-part-of relationship set forms an *aggregate.* [Embley]

is-part-of relationship *n.* **1.** the relationship from a component part to its aggregate. [Firesmith] **2.** any relationship set that forms an aggregate object out of a group of component parts. [Embley]
Synonym: AGGREGATION.
Contrast with: IS-MEMBER-OF RELATIONSHIP SET.
See also: AGGREGATE, COMPONENT, SUBPART CLASS, SUPERPART CLASS.
Commentary: The is-member-of relationship set forms a *set*, whereas the is-part-of relationship set forms an *aggregate.* [Embley]

iteration *n.* **1.** the repetition of some or all of a development method's steps to modify existing product(s) at the current level of abstraction. [Firesmith] **2.** any single cycle of an iterative development process (IDP), consisting of plan-

ning, production, and assessment phases over a multimonth effort to work on a set of product line items. [Lorenz]
Synonym: **2** MAJOR ITERATION.
Contrast with: 1 BUILD.
Rationale: **2** This is also called a major iteration, to distinguish it from a build cycle, which is a minor iteration of the system. [Lorenz]
Commentary: **1** Iteration is typically used to fix mistakes, but may be used to extend the capabilities of existing objects, classes, (sub)clusters, or frameworks. Firesmith] **2** These definitions of the term *iteration* and *build* are the reverse of standard industry terminology whereby a build is a major multimonth increment and an iteration is often a minor multi-week increment. [Firesmith]

Iterative Development Process (IDP) *n.* a technique for developing software in an evolutionary, discovery mode, with each major iteration providing inputs to the next. [Lorenz]
Commentary: Iterative development is not incremental development. In iterative development, the same portion of the system is reworked based on increased understanding of the task and related requirements. [Lorenz]

iterative process *n.* any developmental steps that result in multiple deliveries of the same application functions over the life of the project. [Lorenz]
Commentary: Most end-user functions are delivered in multiple drivers, with each delivery better than the last. [Lorenz]

iterator operation *n.* **1.** any operation that operates on multiple instances of a class. [Firesmith] **2.** (a) any operation that operates on multiple properties of

a single object or class. [Firesmith] (b) any operation that reads or writes to multiple attributes of an object or class. [Booch] **3.** any operation that systematically accesses some, or all, of the nodes in a homogeneous composite object and performs some method (most often a selector) at each node. [Berard]
Antonym: NONITERATOR OPERATION.
Example: Paying all employees in a division is an iterator operation.
Commentary: Iteration continues until every node in the composite object has been visited, or until some predetermined condition(s) have been met. [Berard]
Kinds:
- ACTIVE ITERATOR
- PASSIVE ITERATOR

- **active iterator** *n.* any iterator that consists of multiple low-level methods whereby the user has the ability to decide which methods(s) are to be performed at each node. [Berard]
Antonym: PASSIVE ITERATOR.
See also: HOMOGENEOUS COMPOSITE OBJECT.
Commentary: Although users of active iterators have a great deal of control, they must be careful to ensure that all nodes have been accessed and to avoid unintentional changes in the object during iteration. [Berard]

- **passive iterator** *n.* any iterator that consists of a single atomic method. [Berard]
Antonym: ACTIVE ITERATOR.
See also: HOMOGENEOUS COMPOSITE OBJECT.
Commentary: Although users of passive iterators have less control, they need not concern themselves with the

low-level methods necessary to accomplish the iteration. [Berard]

iterator [pattern] *n.* the behavioral object design pattern that provides a way to sequentially access the components of an aggregate without exposing its underlying implementation. [Gamma, Helm, Johnson, and Vlissides]

Synonym: CURSOR.

I

J

join class *n.* any class that multiply in-
herits from more than one parent class.
[Firesmith, Rumbaugh]
Rationale: A join class is analogous to

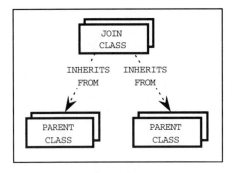

Join Class

the joins that occur between tables in a
relational database. [Firesmith]

joint application design (JAD) *n.* the joint
design of an application using OO-
CASE tools and CRC cards. Based on
the OO enterprise model, the design is
generated from rules, directly linked to
a code generator, and end users sign off
on a computer-validated OO design in
the repository. [Martin]

joint enterprise modeling (JEM) *n.* the
joint modeling of an enterprise using
OO techniques such as an intelligent
enterprise model, OO model, object-
structure diagrams and event diagrams,
and rules linked to OO diagrams that
reflect the business policies. [Martin]

K

key *n.* **1.** any set of one or more properties, the values of which uniquely identify a member of an extent (i.e., a specific instance of a type or class). [Firesmith, ODMG] **2.** any attribute whose values uniquely identify a single object. [Booch]
Contrast with: HANDLE, IDENTIFIER.
Kinds:
- AGGREGATE KEY
- ATOMIC KEY
- CANDIDATE KEY
- COMPOUND KEY
- SIMPLE KEY

- **aggregate key** *n.* any key that consists of multiple properties. [Firesmith]
  Antonym: ATOMIC KEY.
- **atomic key** *n.* any key that consists of a single property. [Firesmith]
  Antonym: AGGREGATE KEY.
  Rationale: An employee's social security number (i.e., a single attribute) can be used to uniquely identify specific employees in a relational database. [Firesmith]
- **candidate key** *n.* any minimal set of properties that uniquely identifies an instance or link. [Rumbaugh]

- **compound key** *n.* any key that consists of multiple properties. [ODMG]
  Antonym: SIMPLE KEY.
- **simple key** *n.* any key that consists of a single property. [ODMG]
  Antonym: COMPOUND KEY.
  Rationale: An employee's social security number (i.e., a single attribute) can be used to uniquely identify specific employees in an object database. [Firesmith]

key abstraction *n.* any essential abstraction that forms a part of the vocabulary of the application domain. [Booch, Firesmith]
Synonyms: BUSINESS OBJECT, CORE OBJECT, MODEL OBJECT.
Contrast with: KEY CLASS.
Commentary: Not every essential abstraction is an object or class. [Firesmith]

key-abstraction diagram *n.* any Booch class diagram that documents the key classes and the uses relationships between them. [Booch]
Contrast with: CLASS-CATEGORY DIAGRAM, DESIGN-CLASS DIAGRAM, INHERITANCE DIAGRAM.

key class *n.* any essential class of model

objects that captures a key abstraction of the application domain. [Lorenz]
Synonyms: APPLICATION CLASS, BUSINESS CLASS, CORE CLASS, DOMAIN CLASS, MODEL CLASS.
Contrast with: CONTROLLER CLASS, KEY ABSTRACTION, PERIPHERAL CLASS, PRESENTATION CLASS, SUPPORT CLASS, VIEW CLASS.
Example: For an automated teller machine application at a bank, classes such as *Account*, *Transaction*, and *Customer* are central to the functions being provided, whereas other support classes, such as *TransactionLog* and *Receipt*, are not as important to providing these functions. [Lorenz]
Commentary: A key class is central to the business domain being automated (i.e., it is one of the primary classes necessary to provide solutions to users' needs in a particular area of the business). Key classes tend to be more stable than other parts of the system. [Lorenz]

key mechanism *n.* any essential mechanism that forms a part of the vocabulary of the application domain. [Booch, Firesmith]
Contrast with: MECHANISM.

keyword-based classification *n.* any classification of reusable components by keywords. [Jacobson]
Antonym: HIERARCHICAL CLASSIFICATION.
Commentary: Searching the database is based on keywords describing the components. [Jacobson]

keyword message *n.* any message with one or more arguments whose selector is made up of one or more keywords. [Smalltalk]
Contrast with: BINARY MESSAGE, UNARY MESSAGE.
Commentary: A keyword is an identifier with a trailing colon. [Smalltalk]

kit *n.* any cohesive collection of objects, classes, metaclasses, unencapsulated operations, and kits that support a single, large object-oriented concept. [Berard]

L

Lace *n.* Language for Assembling Classes in Eiffel. [Eiffel, Meyer]

Examples: Lace is used to write an Assembly of Classes in Eiffel (Ace). [Eiffel, Meyer]

laissez-faire initialization *n.* the initialization technique whereby instance variables are initialized only as they are needed. [Firesmith, Lorenz]

Commentary: This technique is sometimes used for very large objects. [Firesmith] It allows for more self-managing objects and system robustness, with a cost in additional overhead. [Lorenz]

lambda-list *n.* any list that specifies names for the *parameters* of associated functions. [CLOS]

See also: GENERIC FUNCTION.

language binding *n.* the means and conventions by which a programmer writing in a specific programming language accesses ORB capabilities. [OMG]

Synonym: LANGUAGE MAPPING.

language mapping *n.* the means and conventions by which a programmer writing in a specific programming language accesses ORB capabilities. [OMG]

Synonym: LANGUAGE BINDING.

language model *n.* the implementation-level model that documents a language-specific view of the modules and clusters used to implement the objects, classes, and clusters. The language model consists of one or more module diagrams and the source code for the modules and clusters. [Firesmith]

Contrast with: CONFIGURATION MODEL, INTERACTION MODEL, PRESENTATION MODEL, SEMANTIC MODEL, STATE MODEL.

late binding *n.* any binding that takes place at run-time after the message is received due to compile-time ambiguities caused by inheritance and polymorphism. [Firesmith, Jacobson, Martin/Odell, OMG]

Synonyms: DEFERRED, DYNAMIC BINDING, RUN-TIME BINDING, VIRTUAL BINDING.

Antonyms: COMPILE-TIME BINDING, EARLY BINDING, STATIC BINDING.

Commentary: Late binding allows the system to dynamically decide what method to use, based on the class of the current object. Late binding of methods is typically implemented via a method binding table. The term *dynamic binding* is preferred.

Law of Demeter *n.* the guideline for minimizing message coupling that states that an object should only send messages to objects that are immediately referenced (e.g., only send messages to itself, its object-valued properties, and the arguments of its messages). [Firesmith]

layer *n.* **1.** any logically related collection of clusters or cluster instances at the same level of abstraction. [Firesmith] **2.** any collection of class categories or subsystems at the same level of abstraction. [Booch] **3.** any subsystem that provides multiple services, all of which are at the same level of abstraction, built on subsystems at a lower level of abstraction. [Rumbaugh]

Contrast with: ABSTRACTION LEVEL, PARTITION.

Examples: Examples include the user-interface layer, application domain layer, database-independence layer, processor-communication layer, and environment-independence layer.

Commentary: Layers are horizontal slices of an application, whereas partitions are vertical slices through an application. [Firesmith]

Kinds:
- COMMUNICATION LAYER
- ENVIRONMENT LAYER
- MODEL LAYER
- PERSISTENCE LAYER
- USER-INTERFACE LAYER

- **communication layer** *n.* the layer that provides communication across processors. [Firesmith]
Commentary: The communication layer typically consists of communication objects and classes (e.g., proxies). The communication layer is typically built on top of the environment layer. [Firesmith]
- **environment layer** *n.* the layer that provides independence of the under-

lying operating system and hardware. [Firesmith]
Commentary: The environment layer is typically built directly on top of the operating system and hardware. [Firesmith]
- **model layer** *n.* the layer that contains model objects and classes. [Firesmith]
Commentary: The model layer typically consists of model and controller objects and classes. The model layer is typically built on top of the communication, persistence, and environment layers. [Firesmith]
- **persistence layer** *n.* the layer that provides independence of any databases or object bases. [Firesmith]
Commentary: The persistence layer is typically built on top of the environment layer. [Firesmith]
- **user-interface layer** *n.* the layer that provides the interface to the user. [Firesmith]
Commentary: The user-interface layer is typically built on top of the model layer and contains view and controller objects and classes. [Firesmith]

layout *n.* **1.** how something (e.g., an object), is represented and sequenced in memory. [C++] **2.** how subviews are arranged in a view (i.e., screen layout). [Henderson-Sellers]
Commentary: An object of a class is typically represented by a contiguous region of memory. [C++]

lazy initialization *n.* the initialization technique whereby instance variables are initialized only as they are needed.
Synonym: LAISSEZ-FAIRE INITIALIZATION.
See also: FUTURE [OBJECT].
Commentary: This technique is sometimes used for very large objects.

leaf class *n.* any class with no descen-

dants. [Firesmith, Rumbaugh]
Antonym: ROOT CLASS.
Contrast with: BRANCH CLASS.

Leaf Class

legacy software *n.* any preexisting software that must be replaced by, incorporated into, or interfaced with software that is currently being developed. [Firesmith]
Commentary: Legacy software is typically not object-oriented, and the use of legacy software on projects developing object-oriented software can cause problems due to the impedance mismatch between the different structures of the software. [Firesmith]

legacy system object type *n.* any object type that encapsulates an existing non-object-oriented application or application component, by defining an object-oriented interface so that it can be re-used. [OADSIG]

level of abstraction *n.* **1.** any collection of logically related abstractions at the same level in some ordered structure. [Booch, Firesmith] **2.** the relative ranking of abstractions in a class structure, object structure, module architecture, or process architecture. [Booch]
Synonym: ABSTRACTION LEVEL.
See also: LAYER.
Examples: Classes at the same level in an inheritance structure and objects at the same level in a collaboration structure form levels of abstraction. [Firesmith]
Kinds:
- HIGH LEVEL OF ABSTRACTION
- LOW LEVEL OF ABSTRACTION

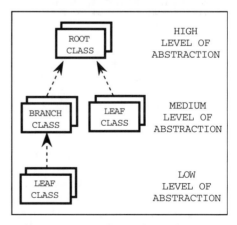

Abstraction Level Based on Inheritance

- **high level of abstraction** *n.* any level of abstraction that is relatively near to the root and far from the leaves of a hierarchy of abstractions. [Firesmith]

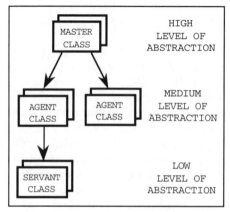

Abstraction Level Based on Messaging

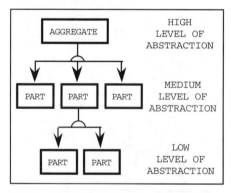

Abstraction Level Based on Aggregation

Antonym: LOW LEVEL OF ABSTRACTION. *Examples:* An *aggregate* is at a higher level of abstraction than its *parts* in an *aggregation hierarchy.* An *ancestor* is at a higher level of abstraction than its *descendants* in an *inheritance structure.* [Firesmith]

Commentary: A high level of abstraction typically implies an abstraction that is either more complete (aggregation), more abstract (inheritance), or closer to the masters (message passing). [Booch, Firesmith]

- **low level of abstraction** *n.* any level of abstraction that is relatively far from the root and near to the leaves of a hierarchy of abstractions. [Firesmith] *Antonym:* HIGH LEVEL OF ABSTRACTION. *Examples:* A *part* is at a lower level of abstraction than its *aggregate* in an *aggregation hierarchy.* A *descendant* is at a lower level of abstraction than its *ancestors* in an *inheritance hierarchy.* [Firesmith] *Commentary:* A low level of abstraction typically implies an abstraction that is either less complete (aggregation), less abstract (inheritance), or closer to the servants (message passing). [Booch, Firesmith]

life cycle [of an object or relationship] *n.* any orderly pattern of behavior of an object or a relationship in OOA. [Shlaer/Mellor]

life-cycle expression *n.* the definition of the allowable sequences of interactions that a system may participate in during its lifetime. [Coleman]

life-cycle model *n.* any model that characterizes the allowable sequencing of system operations and events. [Coleman] *Kinds:*
- BASEBALL MODEL
- FOUNTAIN MODEL
- INCREMENTAL, ITERATIVE, PARALLEL DEVELOPMENT CYCLE

- **baseball model** *n.* the Coad object-oriented development cycle implying both iteration and concurrent devel-

opment. [Coad]
Contrast with: FOUNTAIN MODEL.
Commentary: This is represented by a graphic resembling a baseball showing bidirectional interactions between OOA, OOD, and OOP.

- **fountain model** *n.* the iterative, incremental, parallel object-oriented development cycle popularized by the MOSES method that continues the water metaphor of the waterfall model. [Henderson-Sellers]
  Commentary: The fountain life-cycle model is a high-level visualization of an iterative and recursive development process that permits visualization of a seamless transition and reuse. [Henderson-Sellers]

- **incremental, iterative, parallel (IIP) development cycle** *n.* any powerful object-oriented development cycle that is:
  - *Incremental* in that the system and software are developed in small and large increments;
  - *Iterative* in that intermediate products are iterated (e.g., as errors are discovered);
  - *Parallel* in that different teams work on different increments in parallel. [Firesmith]

Life-Cycle Service *n.* the ORB service that provides operations, services, and conventions for managing object creation, deletion, copy, moving, and equivalence. [OMG]

lifetime [of an object] *n.* the period during which storage is bound to the object.

limited polymorphism *n.* polymorphism that is restricted to the instances of specific classes. [Jacobson]

limited type *n.* any type (or view of a type) for which the assignment operation is not allowed. [Ada95]
Antonym: NONLIMITED TYPE.

link *n.* **1.** during analysis and logical design, any instance of an association that captures a named semantic relationship between objects. [Firesmith, OMG, Rumbaugh] **2.** during implementation design and coding, any feature that contains one or more values, each of which reliably points to a server object. [Firesmith]
Contrast with: ASSOCIATION.
Commentary: Links imply visibility and enable message passing. If links are viewed as roads, then messages form the traffic on those roads. Links are often implemented as either a pointer or reference. [Firesmith]
Kinds:

- ATTACHED LINK
  - ATTACHED POINTER
  - ATTACHED REFERENCE
- BASE LINK
- BIDIRECTIONAL LINK
- BINARY LINK
- CONSTANT LINK
- DANGLING LINK
  - DANGLING POINTER
  - DANGLING REFERENCE
- DERIVED LINK
- POINTER
  - ATTACHED POINTER
  - DANGLING POINTER
  - VOID POINTER
- REFERENCE
  - ATTACHED REFERENCE
  - DANGLING REFERENCE
  - IMPORTED REFERENCE
  - INGENERATE REFERENCE
  - VOID REFERENCE
- STATE LINK
- STATE-DEPENDENT LINK
- STATE-INDEPENDENT LINK

L

- TERNARY LINK
- UNIDIRECTIONAL LINK
- VARIABLE LINK
- VOID LINK
  - VOID POINTER
  - VOID REFERENCE
- **attached link** *n.* any link to an existing object. [Firesmith]
Contrast with: DANGLING LINK, VOID LINK.
Commentary: Even though links are typically unidirectional, the link is said to be attached to the object, and the object is also said to be attached to the link. [Firesmith]
Kinds:
  - ATTACHED POINTER
  - ATTACHED REFERENCE
- **attached pointer** *n.* any pointer that points to an existing object. [Firesmith]
Contrast with: DANGLING POINTER, VOID POINTER.
Commentary: The pointer is said to be attached to the object, and the object is also said to be attached to the pointer. [Firesmith]
- **attached reference** *n.* any reference that refers to an existing object. [Eiffel, Firesmith, Meyer]
Contrast with: DANGLING REFERENCE, VOID REFERENCE.
Commentary: The reference is said to be attached to the object, and the object is also said to be attached to the reference. [Eiffel, Firesmith, Meyer]
- **base link** *n.* any link that cannot be derived from other links. [Firesmith]
Antonym: DERIVED LINK.
- **bidirectional link** *n.* any logical link that represents two unidirectional links that are coupled whereby each is the inverse of the another. [Firesmith]

Antonym: UNIDIRECTIONAL LINK.
- **binary link** *n.* any link between two objects. [Firesmith]
Contrast with: TERNARY LINK.
- **constant link** *n.* any link that cannot be created, destroyed, or changed in value at run-time. [Firesmith]
Antonym: VARIABLE LINK.
Commentary: A constant link always points to the same server. [Firesmith]
- **dangling link** *n.* any link to an object that does not exist. [Firesmith]
Contrast with: ATTACHED LINK, VOID LINK.
Commentary: The link may be to an object that does not yet exist or to an object that no longer exists. Dangling links are common bugs in languages that support manual garbage collection. [Firesmith]
Kinds:
  - DANGLING POINTER
  - DANGLING REFERENCE
- **dangling pointer** *n.* any pointer that points to an object that does not exist. [Firesmith]
Contrast with: ATTACHED POINTER, VOID POINTER.
- **dangling reference** *n.* any reference to an object that does not exist. [Firesmith]
Contrast with: ATTACHED REFERENCE, VOID REFERENCE.
- **derived link** *n.* (a) any indirect link that is the product of other links. [Firesmith] (b) any instance of a derived association. [Firesmith]
Antonym: BASE LINK.
Contrast with: DERIVED ASSOCIATION.
- **pointer [to a given object]** *n.* **1.** any link, the value of which is the identifier of the given server object. [Firesmith] **2.** any attribute of one object

that contains an explicit reference to another object. [Rumbaugh]

Contrast with: IDENTIFIER, LINK, REFERENCE.

Commentary: Unless changed, a pointer will identify the same object each time the pointer is used (subject to certain pragmatic limits of space and time). An object may be denoted by multiple, distinct pointers. [Firesmith]

Kinds:
- ATTACHED POINTER
- DANGLING POINTER
- VOID POINTER

- **attached pointer** *n.* any pointer that currently points to an object. [Firesmith]

Contrast with: DANGLING POINTER, VOID POINTER.

Commentary: The pointer is said to be attached to the object, and the object is also said to be attached to the pointer. [Firesmith]

- **dangling pointer** *n.* any pointer that points to an object that does not exist. [Firesmith]

Contrast with: ATTACHED POINTER, VOID POINTER.

- **void pointer** *n.* any pointer that does not point to an object. [Firesmith]

Synonym: NULL POINTER.

Contrast with: ATTACHED POINTER, DANGLING POINTER.

- **reference [to a given object]** *n.* (a) any constant value that is used as an alias for the OID of the given server object. [Firesmith] (b) any value that refers to an object. [Eiffel, Meyer]

Contrast with: IDENTIFIER, LINK, POINTER.

Commentary: References are used as links and as arguments in messages and operations. Unless changed, a reference will identify the same object each time the reference is used (subject to certain pragmatic limits of space and time). An object may be denoted by multiple, distinct references. [Firesmith]

Contrast with: VALUE.

Kinds:
- ATTACHED REFERENCE
- DANGLING REFERENCE
- IMPORTED REFERENCE
- INGENERATE REFERENCE
- VOID REFERENCE

- **attached reference** *n.* any reference that refers to an existing object. [Eiffel, Firesmith, Meyer]

Contrast with: DANGLING REFERENCE, VOID REFERENCE.

Commentary: The reference is said to be attached to the object, and the object is also said to be attached to the reference. [Eiffel, Firesmith, Meyer]

- **dangling reference** *n.* any reference that refers to an object that does not exist. [Firesmith]

Contrast with: ATTACHED REFERENCE, VOID REFERENCE.

- **imported reference** *n.* any reference stored in an object's instance variable that was not generated by the object itself through invocation of a *create* method. [Atkinson]

Antonym: INGENERATE REFERENCE.

- **ingenerate reference** *n.* any reference stored in an object's instance variable that was generated by the object itself through invocation of a *create* method. [Atkinson]

Antonym: IMPORTED REFERENCE.

- **void reference** *n.* (a) any reference that does not refer to an object. [Firesmith] (b) any reference about

L

which no further information is available. [Eiffel, Meyer]
Contrast with: ATTACHED REFERENCE, DANGLING REFERENCE.

- **state link** *n.* any link, the existence (or value) of which helps determine the state of its client object or class. [Firesmith]
Contrast with: STATE ATTRIBUTE, STATE COMPONENT.

- **state-dependent link** *n.* any link that has meaning only during specific states. [Firesmith]
Antonym: STATE-INDEPENDENT LINK.
Contrast with: STATE-DEPENDENT ATTRIBUTE.

- **state-independent link** *n.* any link that has meaning during all states. [Firesmith]
Antonym: STATE-DEPENDENT LINK.
Contrast with: STATE-INDEPENDENT ATTRIBUTE.

- **ternary link** *n.* any link among three objects.
Contrast with: BINARY LINK.

- **unidirectional link** *n.* any link directed from the client(s) to the server(s). [Firesmith]
Antonym: BIDIRECTIONAL LINK.
Commentary: Unidirectional links are typically implemented by one or more attributes acting as pointers or messages requesting services. [Firesmith]

- **variable link** *n.* any link that can change at run-time. [Firesmith]
Antonym: CONSTANT LINK.
Commentary: A link can change by pointing to another server. [Firesmith]

- **void link** *n.* any link to nothing. [Firesmith]
Contrast with: ATTACHED LINK, DANGLING LINK.
Kinds:

- VOID POINTER
- VOID REFERENCE

- **void pointer** *n.* any pointer that does not point to an existing object. [Firesmith]
Synonym: NULL POINTER.
Contrast with: ATTACHED POINTER, DANGLING POINTER.

- **void reference** *n.* **1.** any reference that does not refer to an existing object. [Firesmith] **2.** any reference about which no further information is available. [Eiffel, Meyer]
Contrast with: ATTACHED REFERENCE, DANGLING REFERENCE.

link attribute *n.* any attribute of each link in an association. [Rumbaugh]
Contrast with: ASSOCIATION ATTRIBUTE.

link signature *n.* the signature of any link, declaring its:
– name
– mutability (i.e., constant or variable)
– the type of the object referred to or pointed at
– initial value (if any)
– qualifier (if any). [Firesmith]
Contrast with: ATTRIBUTE SIGNATURE, MESSAGE SIGNATURE, OPERATION SIGNATURE, RELATIONSHIP SIGNATURE.

literal [object] *n.* **1.** any constant primitive object having no properties but only a value equal to its name. [Firesmith] **2.** any immutable (i.e., constant) object. [ODMG] **3.** any value that identifies an entity that is not an object. [OMG] **4.** any expression that describes a constant object. [Smalltalk]
Synonym: CONSTANT.
Contrast with: IMMUTABLE, OBJECT, OBJECT NAME.
Examples: Numbers, characters, and the Boolean objects *true* and *false* are each literals.

Kinds:
- ATOMIC LITERAL
- STRUCTURED LITERAL
- **atomic literal** *n.* any literal having no structure (i.e., containing no objects). [ODMG]
  Contrast with: ATOMIC OBJECT, STRUCTURED LITERAL.
  Example: An integer, a float, a Boolean, and a character are each atomic literals.
- **structured literal** *n.* any literal that is either an immutable collection or an immutable structure. [ODMG]
  Contrast with: ATOMIC LITERAL.

local class *n.* any class that is declared locally within a method or block. [Firesmith, C++]
Commentary: A local class is within the scope of the enclosing class. [C++]

localization *n.* the logical and physical grouping of related things (e.g., requirements and resources). [Firesmith]
Contrast with: ENCAPSULATION, INFORMATION HIDING.
Commentary: Localization is used to build abstractions, increase their cohesion, and decrease coupling. [Firesmith]

locally overloaded operation *n.* any overloaded operation that occurs multiple times in the same class whereby each variant has the same name and functional abstraction, but each has a different signature and method. [Firesmith]
Antonym: GLOBALLY OVERLOADED OPERATION.
See also: LOCAL OVERLOADING.
Examples: Constructors are often overloaded with the simple default constructor having the same name but fewer parameters than more complex constructors. [Firesmith]
Rationale: Local overloading occurs *locally* within a single class. [Firesmith]

Commentary: Local overloading allows multiple operations with the same name to be defined provided their signatures differ sufficiently for calls to be resolved. The resolution of local overloading may be based on different numbers of parameters, parameters of different types, different return types, different exceptions raised, or different message type (e.g., sequential, synchronous, asynchronous). Unlike inherent polymorphism, local overloading is usually resolved at compile time. [Firesmith]

local identifier (LID) *n.* any object identifier that is local to a specific processor or process. [Firesmith]
Antonym: UNIVERAL IDENTIFIER.

local object view *n.* any object-model view that shows an object with all of its relations to and from other objects. [Jacobson]
Antonym: GLOBAL OBJECT VIEW.
Contrast with: VIEW OF PARTICIPATING OBJECTS.

local precedence order *n.* the precedence order given by any list consisting of the class followed by its direct superclasses in the order mentioned in the defining form. [CLOS]
See also: CLASS PRECEDENCE.

local recursion *n.* any recursion limited to within a single developmental activity (i.e., requirements analysis, design, coding, integration, and testing). [Firesmith]
Antonym: GLOBAL RECURSION.

local slot *n.* any slot that is visible to exactly one instance, namely the one in which the slot is allocated. [CLOS]

local type name *n.* any type name defined within a class declaration. [C++]
Commentary: A local type name cannot

L

be used outside the class in which it was defined without qualification. [C++]

loop-correct *adj.* describing any routine in which the loops maintain their invariant and every iteration decreases the variant. [Eiffel, Meyer]

low level of abstraction *n.* any level of abstraction that is relatively far from the root and near to the leaves of a hierarchy of abstractions. [Firesmith]

Antonym: HIGH LEVEL OF ABSTRACTION.

Examples: A *part* is at a lower level of abstraction than its *aggregate* in an *ag-*gregation hierarchy. A *descendant* is at a lower level of abstraction than its *ancestors* in an *inheritance hierarchy.* [Firesmith]

Commentary: A low level of abstraction typically implies either less complete (aggregation), less abstract (inheritance), or closer to the servants (message passing). [Booch, Firesmith]

lvalue *n.* any expression referring to an object or function. [C++]

Example: The name of an object is an lvalue.

M

maillon [object] *n.* any object that allows either a local reference or remote reference for implementation. [Firesmith]
See also: FUTURE.

major iteration *n.* any multi-month effort to work on a set of product line items in an iterative development process (IDP). [Lorenz]

managed object *n.* any client of System Management services, including the installation and activation service and the operational control service (dynamic behavior). These clients may be application objects, common facilities objects, or other object services. [OMG]
Commentary: The term is used for compatibility with system management standards (the X/Open GDMO specification and ISO/IEC 10164 System Management Functions parts 1 to 4). [OMG]

manager object *n.* any object that manages the work of several subordinate objects. [Coad]
Commentary: Challenge any class name that ends in *-er.* If it has no parts, change the name of the class to what each object is managing. If it has parts, put as much work in the parts that the parts know enough to do themselves. [Coad]

manual garbage collection *n.* the manual use of destructors to deallocate the memory of objects that are no longer needed. [Firesmith]
Commentary: C++ typically requires the programmer to manually perform garbage collection, although destructors are automatically activated in C++. [Firesmith]

master *n.* any client that is not also a server. At either the system level or the software level, masters control agents and servants, but are not controlled by others. [Firesmith]
Antonym: SERVANT.
Contrast with: AGENT.

- **master object** *n.* any object that sends messages to other objects, but does not receive messages. [Firesmith]
Contrast with: AGENT, SERVANT.

meaningful message *n.* any message in which signature correctly matches a signature in the interface of the receiver. [Firesmith]
Synonym: MEANINGFUL REQUEST.

meaningful request *n.* any request in which the actual parameters satisfy the signature of the named operation. [OMG]
Synonym: MEANINGFUL MESSAGE.

mechanism *n.* any mid-sized pattern of collaborating objects or classes whose cooperative behavior provides one or more capabilities. [Booch, Firesmith]
Contrast with: FRAMEWORK, IDIOM.
Example: Any control loop consisting of a model object with attribute(s) to be controlled and its associated actuators, sensors, and views is a mechanism. [Firesmith]
Commentary: A mechanism captures tactical analysis and design decisions. [Booch, Firesmith] A mechanism is larger than an idiom and smaller than a framework. [Firesmith]
• **key mechanism** *n.* any essential mechanism that forms a part of the vocabulary of the application domain. [Booch, Firesmith]
mediator [pattern] *n.* the behavioral object design pattern that avoids unnecessary coupling between collaborating objects by introducing a mediator object between them. [Gamma, Helm, Johnson, and Vlissides]
member *n.* the C++ term for a characteristic of a class or object. [Coleman, C++, Firesmith]
Synonyms: CHARACTERISTIC, FEATURE.
Examples: Data, functions, classes, enumerations, bit-fields, friends, and type names can all be members. [C++, Firesmith]
member class *n.* any object class whose instances are members of sets. [Embley]
Synonym: UNIVERSE.
Antonyms: ASSOCIATION, SET CLASS.
See also: IS-MEMBER-OF RELATIONSHIP SET.
member function *n.* 1. the C++ term for an operation encapsulated within an object or class. [Coleman, C++, Firesmith] 2. any operation on an object,

defined as part of the declaration of a class. [Booch]
Contrast with: GENERIC FUNCTION, VIRTUAL FUNCTION.
member object *n.* 1. any object that is a component part of an aggregate object. [C++] 2. any repository for part of the state of an object. [Booch]
Synonyms: ATTRIBUTE, FIELD, INSTANCE VARIABLE, SLOT.
Contrast with: DATA MEMBER, MEMBER FUNCTION.
Commentary: The terms *attribute* and *part* are more specific and popular.
member [of an extent] *n.* any instance of the corresponding class or type. [Firesmith]
Contrast with: INSTANCE.
member [of a type] *n.* any value that satisfies a type. [OMG]
Contrast with: SATISFY [A TYPE].
membership condition [for an object class] *n.* any condition that is a conjunction of all the constraints imposed by an object-relationship model on the object class. [Embley]
See also: OBJECT, OBJECT CLASS.
Commentary: An object that satisfies the conditions for membership in an object class is a member of the object class. [Embley]
membership condition [for a relationship set] *n.* any condition that is a conjunction of all the constraints imposed by an object-relationship model on the relationship set. [Embley]
See also: RELATIONSHIP, RELATIONSHIP SET.
Commentary: A relationship that satisfies the conditions for membership in a relationship set is a member of the relationship set. [Embley]
memento [pattern] *n.* the be˙   ɔral ob-

ject design pattern that objectifies another object's encapsulated state so that the other object can be later returned to that state. [Gamma, Helm, Johnson, and Vlissides]

Synonym: TOKEN.

memory leakage *n.* any reference to memory that is allocated during execution, but that is not released when the requesting process completes execution. [Firesmith]

Commentary: Memory leakage is a major source of bugs in languages (e.g., C++) that do not provide automatic garbage collection. This is not typically a problem with Smalltalk and Eiffel, which provide automatic garbage collection. [Firesmith]

message *n.* **1.** (a) the normal unit of communication that is sent to an object or class. [Firesmith] (b) any communication sent or received by an object. [OADSIG] **2.** (a) a request for a service that is sent to an object or class. [Coad, Henderson-Sellers, Lorenz, Smalltalk] (b) any request for an operation that is sent to an object or class to perform an operation. [Martin] (c) the invocation of any operation. [Rumbaugh] **3.** any name of an operation and any required arguments. [Wirfs-Brock] **4.** any intra-process stimulus. [Jacobson]

Synonyms: **2** CALL, OPERATION INVOCATION, REQUEST.

Antonym: **4** SIGNAL.

Contrast with: METHOD, OPERATION.

See also: INTERFACE, STIMULUS.

Rationale: Term popularized by Smalltalk.

Commentary: Unlike a subroutine call, a message may possibly be bound at run-time. A message may be used to (1) request a service, (2) provide data, (3)

provide notification of an event, or (4) synchronize two threads of control. A message usually invokes a single operation in sequential languages. A message may not map one-to-one due to concurrency and information hiding purposes. [Firesmith] Definition 1(b) seems both too limited (e.g., classes may also send and receive messages) and too broad (e.g., objects may also communicate via exceptions). Definition 2(a) seems too limited because messages can be sent for other purposes than to make a request. Definition 2(b) seems too limited because it implies a one-to-one mapping between messages and operations, which may not hold (especially in a concurrent environment). Definition **3** ignores the destination of the message, its return type, its priority, associated exceptions, etc. and says more about how messages are implemented in popular languages rather than what they are. [Firesmith]

v. **-ed, -ing** to send a message. [Coleman, Firesmith]

Kinds:

- ASYNCHRONOUS MESSAGE
- BINARY MESSAGE
- BROADCAST
- CONTINUOUS
- DIRECTED MESSAGE
- DISCRETE
- KEYWORD MESSAGE
- MEANINGFUL MESSAGE
- PRESERVER MESSAGE
- REQUEST
  - ASYNCHRONOUS REQUEST
  - DEFERRED SYNCHRONOUS REQUEST
  - MEANINGFUL REQUEST
  - STATE-MODIFYING REQUEST
  - SYNCHRONOUS REQUEST
- SEQUENTIAL MESSAGE
  - SIMPLE SEQUENTIAL MESSAGE

M

- SYNCHRONOUS MESSAGE
  - BALKING MESSAGE
  - GUARDED MESSAGE
  - TIMED MESSAGE
  - TIMEOUT MESSAGE
- TEST MESSAGE
- UNARY MESSAGE.

- **asynchronous message** *n.* any message involving two threads of control that do not synchronize during message passing so that neither the sender nor the receiver of the message is blocked, waiting for the other. [Booch, Firesmith]
  Synonyms: ASYNCHRONOUS REQUEST, SIGNAL.

- **binary message** *n.* any message with one argument whose selector is made up of one or two special characters. [Smalltalk]
  Contrast with: KEYWORD MESSAGE, UNARY MESSAGE.

- **broadcast message** *n.* any message that is sent to all servers in a given scope. [Firesmith]
  Antonym: DIRECTED MESSAGE.
  Commentary: Most languages only support directed messages. Broadcast messages are often decomposed into a series of directed messages during implementation. [Firesmith]

- **continuous message** *n.* any message that is logically or physically continuous. [Firesmith]
  Antonym: DISCRETE MESSAGE.
  Examples: Messages from analog sensors. [Firesmith]
  Commentary: Most languages only support discrete messages. Continuous messages are often decomposed into a series of discrete messages during implementation. [Firesmith]

- **directed message** *n.* any message that is directed to a single specified receiver. [Firesmith]
  Antonym: BROADCAST MESSAGE.

- **discrete message** *n.* any message that is neither logically nor physically continuous.
  Antonym: CONTINUOUS MESSAGE.
  Examples: Messages as implemented by most programming languages are discrete. [Firesmith]
  Commentary: Most languages only support discrete messages. Continuous messages are often decomposed into a series of discrete messages during implementation. [Firesmith]

- **keyword message** *n.* any message with one or more arguments whose selector is made up of one or more keywords. [Smalltalk]
  Contrast with: BINARY MESSAGE, UNARY MESSAGE.
  Commentary: A keyword is an identifier with a trailing colon. [Smalltalk]

- **meaningful message** *n.* any message whose signature correctly matches a signature in the interface of the receiver. [Firesmith]

- **preserver message** *n.* any message that does not result, either directly or indirectly, in the modification of the value of any properties. [Firesmith]
  Antonym: MODIFIER MESSAGE.

- **request** *n.* **1.** any message requesting a server to provide a service to the client. [Firesmith] **2.** (a) any message from one object to another, in which an operation of the first object requests the invocation of a specified operation of the other object. [Martin] (b) any invocation of an operation on an object or class, comprising an operation name, a list of zero or more actual parameters, and the results to be returned to the client. [OMG, OADSIG]

Synonym: MESSAGE, OPERATION INVO-CATION.

Contrast with: OPERATION DISPATCH-ING.

See also: CLIENT, SERVER, SERVICE.

Commentary: Not every message is a request for a service. Messages can also be used to send information (e.g., data), notify the receiver of the occurrence of an event, or to synchronize a concurrent thread of the sender with a thread of the receiver. With most languages, a request is implemented in the form of a visible operation requested by the message. [Firesmith]

Kinds: **2**

- ASYNCHRONOUS REQUEST
- DEFERRED SYNCHRONOUS REQUEST
- MEANINFUL REQUEST
- ONE-WAY REQUEST
- STATE-MODIFYING REQUEST
- SYNCHRONOUS REQUEST

- **asynchronous request** *n.* any request involving two threads of control that do not synchronize so that neither the sender nor the receiver of the request is blocked, waiting for the other. [OMG]
Contrast with: ASYNCHRONOUS MES-SAGE, SYNCHRONOUS REQUEST.

- **deferred synchronous request** *n.* any request in which the client does not wait for completion of the request, but does intend to accept results later. [OMG]
Contrast with: ASYNCHRONOUS RE-QUEST, ONE-WAY REQUEST, SYN-CHRONOUS MESSAGE, SYNCHRONOUS REQUEST.
Commentary: Note that this is a

poor choice of terms because a *deferred synchronous request* is not a kind of *synchronous request.*

- **meaningful request** *n.* any request in which the actual parameters satisfy the signature of the named operation. [OMG]

- **one-way request n.** any request in which the client does not wait for completion of the request, nor does it intend to accept results. [OMG]
Contrast with: ASYNCHRONOUS RE-QUEST, DEFERRED SYNCHRONOUS REQUEST, SYNCHRONOUS REQUEST.

- **state-modifying request** *n.* any request whereby performing the service alters the results of future requests. [OMG]

- **synchronous request** *n.* any request in which the client object pauses to wait for completion of the request. [OMG]
Contrast with: ASYNCHRONOUS RE-QUEST, DEFERRED SYNCHRONOUS REQUEST, ONE-WAY REQUEST, SYN-CHRONOUS MESSAGE.

M

- **sequential message** *n.* **1.** any message involving only one thread of control that is temporarily passed from the client to the server, thereby blocking the client until the server's operation(s) are completed. [Firesmith] **2.** a message whose semantics are guaranteed only in the presence of a single thread of control. [Booch]

- **simple sequential message** *n.* a message whose semantics are guaranteed only in the presence of a single thread of control. [Booch]
Synonym: SEQUENTIAL MESSAGE.

- **synchronous message** *n.* **1.** any message that synchronizes two threads of control, thereby potentially blocking either the sender or the receiver until both are ready to communicate. [Booch, Firesmith] **2.** any message in which the thread of control passes from the originating instance to the receiving instance—as would happen where both instances were part of the one overall process. [OADSIG]

Rationale: Definition **2** appears to confuse synchronous and sequential messages.

Kinds:
- BALKING MESSAGE
- GUARDED MESSAGE
- TIMED MESSAGE
- TIMEOUT MESSAGE

- **balking message** *n.* any synchronous message that can be passed only if the receiver is immediately ready to accept the message. [Booch, Firesmith]

- **guarded message** *n.* any synchronous message that requires an associated guard condition to evaluate to true for the message to be passed. [Booch]

- **timed message** *n.* any synchronous message that allows a caller to pass a message while waiting at most a limited amount of time. [Firesmith]
Synonym: TIMEOUT MESSAGE.

- **timeout message** *n.* any synchronous message that allows a caller to pass a message while waiting at most a limited amount of time. [Booch]
Synonym: TIMED MESSAGE.

• **test message** *n.* any message including associated parameters that is sent to find errors. [Firesmith]
Contrast with: TEST CASE, TEST SUITE.

• **unary message** *n.* any message without arguments. [Smalltalk]
Contrast with: BINARY MESSAGE, KEY-

WORD MESSAGE.

message argument *n.* **1.** any argument of a message. [Firesmith] **2.** any object that specifies additional information for an operation. [Smalltalk]
Commentary: The value returned by the message is typically not considered an argument. [Firesmith]

message category *n.* in a class description, any named group of messages that invoke similar operations. [Smalltalk]
Commentary: The name of a category indicates the common functionality of the messages in the category.

message category name *n.* the name of a category indicating the common functionality of the messages in the category [Smalltalk]

message connection *n.* any connection that models the processing dependency of an object, indicating a need for services in order to fulfill its responsibilities. [Coad]
See also: MESSAGE.

message coupling *n.* the coupling dependency of a client on its servers due to message passing. Message coupling is measured in terms of the number of messages, the number of arguments in the messages, the type of message (e.g. asynchronous implies less coupling than synchronous), and the frequency of the messages. [Firesmith]

message expression *n.* any expression that describes messages to receivers. [Smalltalk]
Commentary: The value of a message expression is determined by the method the message invokes. That method is found in the class of the receiver. A message expression describes a receiver, selector, and possibly some arguments.

• **cascaded message expression** *n.* any

message expression that consists of one description of the receiver followed by several messages separated by semicolons. [Smalltalk]

message-flow diagram *n.* any diagram documenting a time-ordered sequence of message sends between a group of classes or subsystems. The message-flow diagram shows a set of classes across the top and a time sequence from top to bottom. Shown within this table are message sends between classes, in the order they would occur according to the system design. [Lorenz]
Synonyms: INTERACTION DIAGRAM, TIMING DIAGRAM.
Contrast with: COLLABORATION DIAGRAM, HIERARCHY DIAGRAM.
Commentary: Message-flow diagrams can be used for more than one purpose, including use-case, method, and test-case documentation. [Lorenz] The messages shown should be the key application-related messages and not every message sent to accomplish the function. Focus on messages that are part of contracts. [Lorenz]

message interface *n.* any message declaration or signature.

message invariant *n.* any invariant that must evaluate to true after execution of the associated operation(s) if the expression evaluates to true prior to receipt of the message. [Firesmith]
Contrast with: CLASS INVARIANT, EXTENT INVARIANT, INSTANCE INVARIANT, SCENARIO INVARIANT.

message name *n.* the name of the operation requested by the message. [Wirfs-Brock]

message pattern *n.* the declaration of a message, specifying the message selector and a set of argument names, one for each argument, which a message with this selector must have. [Smalltalk]
Synonyms: MESSAGE INTERFACE, MESSAGE SIGNATURE.
Commentary: A message pattern matches any messages that have the same selector. A class will have only one method with a given selector in its message pattern. [Smalltalk]

message protocol *n.* the union of the inbound message protocol and the outbound message protocol. [Firesmith]
Antonym: EXCEPTION PROTOCOL.
Commentary: The message protocol consists of all messages that can be either sent to servers or received from clients. [Firesmith]

message queue *n.* any object-specific or class-specific queue in which messages to the object or class are queued before being bound to the associated encapsulated operation(s). [Firesmith]
Rationale: Messages may need to be queued because they may arrive at a concurrent object or class simultaneously or faster than the associated operations may execute. [Firesmith]
Commentary: An object or class may have more than one message queue, in which case the message queue implements a role of its object or class. Message queues should probably be priority based. [Firesmith]

message quiescence *n.* any terminating method in a sequence of method executions linked by messages, which does not issue any further messages of its own.

message selector *n.* the name of the type of operation a message requests of its receiver. [Smalltalk]
See also: INTERFACE, MESSAGE, OPERATION.

M

Commentary: The selector of a message determines which of the receiver's operations will be invoked. A class has one method for each selector in its interface. [Smalltalk]

message send *n.* the sending of a message to an object. [Firesmith, Smalltalk]
Commentary: In a view of an interrupted process, the term *message send* usually refers to a message from which a response has not yet been received. [Smalltalk]

message signature *n.* the signature of any message, declaring its:
– name;
– destination (possibly including role, message queue, and target operation, if different);
– parameters including their names, modes, types, and order;
– the type of the value returned by the message;
– any assertions (e.g., preconditions, postconditions, or message invariants);
– the names and types of any exceptions raised by the message;
– the category of the message (e.g., sequential, synchronous, asynchronous);
– the priority of the message (if any). [Firesmith]
Synonyms: MESSAGE DECLARATION, MESSAGE INTERFACE, MESSAGE PATTERN.
Contrast with: ATTRIBUTE SIGNATURE, LINK SIGNATURE, OPERATION SIGNATURE, RELATIONSHIP SIGNATURE.

meta association *n.* any association linking a class to an instance or vice versa. [Jacobson]
Contrast with: CLASS ASSOCIATION, INSTANCE ASSOCIATION.

metaclass *n.* any class, the instances of which are themselves classes. [Booch,

CLOS, Firesmith, Jacobson, Rumbaugh, Smalltalk]
Commentary: The metaclass determines the form of inheritance used by the classes that are its instances and the representation of the instances of those classes. [CLOS] Metaclasses are used when classes are to be treated as objects. [Firesmith]
Kinds:
• GENERIC CLASS
• PARAMETERIZED CLASS
• POWER CLASS
  - DISCRIMINATOR CLASS
• TEMPLATE CLASS

• **generic class** *n.* any abstract metaclass that is parameterized with formal generic parameters (e.g., classes, attributes, messages, operations, exceptions, invariants) that must be supplied prior to instantiation. Its instances vary, depending on the actual parameters that were supplied. [Booch, Eiffel, Firesmith, Meyer]
Synonym: PARAMETERIZED CLASS, TEMPLATE CLASS.
Rationale: Original term used by Ada-83 and Eiffel.

• **parameterized class** *n.* any abstract metaclass that is parameterized with formal generic parameters (e.g., classes, attributes, messages, operations, exceptions, invariants) that must be supplied as part of the instantiation process. [Booch, Firesmith, Rumbaugh]
Synonym: GENERIC CLASS, TEMPLATE CLASS.
Commentary: Its instances vary, depending on the actual parameters that were supplied. Generic class was the original term used by Ada83 and Eiffel. The parameters are often attributes, classes, or types.

• **power class** *n.* any metaclass, the instances of which are child classes of another class. [Firesmith]
Contrast with: DISCRIMINATOR, DISCRIMINATOR CLASS, PARTITION.
Example: The class *Item_Type* is the power class of the class *Item* and consists of all of the children of *Item*. [Firesmith]
Commentary: Instances of power classes are often used as attributes of other classes. [Firesmith]
- **discriminator class** *n.* any power class whose instances partition another class (i.e., whose instances form a disjoint cover of the class being partitioned). [Firesmith]
Example: The class of *genders* is a discriminator class for the class *persons*, partitioning it into the derived classes *males* and *females*. [Firesmith]
• **template class** *n.* the C++ term for a generic class. [C++]
Synonyms: GENERIC, GENERIC CLASS, PARAMETERIZED CLASS.
Commentary: A class template specifies how individual classes can be constructed much as a class declaration specifies how individual objects can be constructed. [C++]

metaobject *n.* **1.** any object that represents a type, operation, class, method, or other object model entity that describes objects. [OMG] **2.** The metaobject protocol specifies a set of generic functions that are defined by methods on classes and whose behavior defines the behavior of the Object System. Metaobjects are the instances of the classes on which those methods are defined. [CLOS]
See also: METACLASS, METHOD-COMBINATION OBJECT, STANDARD OBJECT.

Commentary: **2** The Object System supplies a standard set of metaobjects, called *standard metaobjects* which include the class *standard object* and instances of the classes *standard method, standard generic function,* and *method combination.* [CLOS]

method *n.* **1.** (a) the hidden implementation of an associated operation. [Coleman, Firesmith, Martin, ODMG, OMG, Rumbaugh, Smalltalk, Wirfs-Brock] (b) an implementation of a responsibility. [Lorenz] **2.** a discrete activity, action, or behavior that (1) implements a functional (i.e., sequential) or process (i.e., concurrent) abstraction, (2) is performed by, belongs to, and is encapsulated in an object or class, and (3) usually implements a service requested by a message. [Booch, Henderson-Sellers, Lorenz] **3.** any object that contains a method function, a sequence of *parameter specializers* that specify when the given method is applicable, a lambda-list, and a sequence of *qualifiers* that are used by the method combination facility to distinguish among methods. A method object is not a function and cannot be invoked as a function. [CLOS] **4.** any systematic and well-documented set of developmental activities coupled with associated standards, procedures, and guidelines that is used to perform requirements analysis, design, coding, testing, or integration. [Coleman, Firesmith, Jacobson]
Synonyms: **2** MESSAGE, OPERATION.
See also: **3** METHOD-COMBINATION OBJECT, PARAMETER SPECIALIZER.
Contrast with: ATTRIBUTE SIGNATURE, LINK SIGNATURE, OPERATION SIGNATURE.
Rationale: **1** The term *method* was

M

popularized by Smalltalk.

Commentary: Definition **2** confuses the term *method*, which is the implementation of an operation with the term *operation*. [Firesmith] A Smalltalk method is executed when a message matching its message pattern is sent to an instance of the class in which the method is found. [Smalltalk] A method object is not a function and cannot be invoked as a function. [CLOS]

Kinds:

- ABSTRACT METHOD
- AUXILIARY METHOD
  - :AFTER METHOD
  - :AROUND METHOD
  - :BEFORE METHOD
- BASE METHOD
- DEFAULT METHOD
- DEFERRED METHOD
- DYNAMIC METHOD
- EFFECTIVE METHOD
- EXTERNAL METHOD
- IMPLEMENTATION METHOD
- INTERNAL METHOD
- POLICY METHOD
- PRIMARY METHOD
- PRIMITIVE METHOD
- PRIVATE METHOD
- PUBLIC METHOD
- SAFE METHOD
- STATIC METHOD
- TEMPLATE METHOD
- UNSAFE METHOD
- VIRTUAL METHOD

- **abstract method** *n.* any method that provides default behavior that subclasses are expected to override. [Wirfs-Brock]

  Synonym: DEFAULT METHOD.
  Antonym: BASE METHOD.

- **auxiliary method** *n.* any method that modifies the main, primary action of

effective methods. [CLOS]

Kinds:

- :AFTER METHOD
- :AROUND METHOD
- :BEFORE METHOD

- **:after method** *n.* any auxiliary method that specifies code that is to be run after primary methods. [CLOS]

  Antonym: :BEFORE METHOD.
  Contrast with: :AROUND METHOD.
  Commentary: An :after method has the keyword *:after* as its only qualifier. [CLOS]

- **:around method** *n.* any auxiliary method that specifies code that is to be run instead of other applicable methods, but that is able to cause some of them to be run. [CLOS]

  Contrast with: :AFTER METHOD, :BEFORE METHOD.
  Commentary: An *:around* method has the keyword *:around* as its only qualifier. [CLOS]

- **:before method** *n.* any auxiliary method that specifies code that is to be run before primary methods. [CLOS]

  Antonym: :AFTER METHOD.
  Contrast with: :AROUND METHOD.
  Commentary: A :before method has the keyword *:before* as its only qualifier. [CLOS]

- **base method** *n.* any method that provides behavior that is generally useful to subclasses. [Wirfs-Brock]

  Antonym: ABSTRACT METHOD.

- **default method** *n.* any method that provides default behavior that descendants are expected to override. [Firesmith]

  Synonym: ABSTRACT METHOD.

- **deferred method** *n.* any incomplete method that therefore does not implement a complete functional abstraction method. [Firesmith]

Antonym: EFFECTIVE METHOD.

Commentary: A deferred method often has preconditions and postconditions defined, but may include a TBD statement or be missing its executable statements. Deferred methods are used during analysis and design, but must be made effective prior to execution. [Firesmith]

- **dynamic method** *n.* any method that may be dynamically bound to an object at run-time. [Firesmith]

Synonym: VIRTUAL METHOD.

Antonym: STATIC METHOD.

- **effective method** *n.* **1.** any method written and compiled in another language. [Firesmith] **2.** the code that is executed for particular arguments of a generic function. [CLOS]

Antonym: **1** DEFERRED METHOD.

- **external method** *n.* any method written and compiled in another language. [Firesmith]

Antonym: INTERNAL METHOD.

- **implementation method** *n.* any method that implements specific computations on fully specified arguments, but does not make context-dependent decisions. [Rumbaugh]

Contrast with: POLICY METHOD.

- **internal method** *n.* any method written and compiled in the current language and therefore accessible to language processing tools. [Firesmith]

Antonym: EXTERNAL ROUTINE.

- **policy method** *n.* any method that makes context-dependent decisions, switches control among other methods, combines and parameterizes calls to lower-level methods, and checks for status and error, but which calls

on other methods for detailed computations. [Rumbaugh]

Contrast with: IMPLEMENTATION METHOD.

- **primary method** *n.* a method that defines the main action of the effective method. [CLOS]

Commentary: A primary method has no method qualifiers. [CLOS]

- **primitive method** *n.* **1.** any method provided by the programming language that is performed directly by the language run-time (i.e., virtual machine) and is not expressed as a sequence of expressions in that language. [Firesmith, Smalltalk] **2.** any method that *cannot* be accomplished simply, reliably, and efficiently without knowledge of the underlying implementation. [Berard]

- **private method** *n.* any hidden method that exists to help this class get its work done. [Lorenz]

Antonym: PUBLIC METHOD.

Commentary: The term *operation* was probably intended, because all methods (i.e., implementations of operations) are hidden. [Firesmith]

- **public method** *n.* any method that is made available to other classes (clients). [Lorenz]

Antonym: PRIVATE METHOD.

Commentary: The term *operation* was probably intended, because all methods (i.e., implementations of operations) are hidden. [Firesmith] Public methods are grouped into contracts. [Lorenz]

- **safe method** *n.* any method that has no parameters of a class type or an access type. [Atkinson]

Antonym: UNSAFE METHOD.

Commentary: All of the parameters

M

of the method are thus of a static type. [Atkinson]

- **static method** *n.* any method that is statically bound to an object at compile-time. [Firesmith]
Antonyms: DYNAMIC METHOD, DYNAMIC METHOD.

- **template method** *n.* any method that provides step-by-step algorithms. [Wirfs-Brock]
Commentary: The steps of the algorithm may be abstract methods that the subclass must define, base methods, other template methods, or some combination of these. [Wirfs-Brock]

- **unsafe method** *n.* any method that contains one or more parameters of a class or access type, and may thus be used to exchange references. [Atkinson]
Antonym: SAFE METHOD.

- **virtual method** *n.* any C++ method in a base class that can be redefined in a derived class. [Coleman]
Synonym: DYNAMIC METHOD.

method activation *n.* the execution of any method. [OMG]

method binding *n.* (a) any selection of the appropriate method for an operation on receipt of a corresponding message and selecting those properties to be accessed by that method. [Firesmith] (b) the programming language process of selecting and binding the method to a message that is appropriate to the class. [Martin/Odell, OMG]
Synonym: METHOD RESOLUTION.
Commentary: Method resolution is often implemented via a virtual-method table. [Firesmith]

method caching *n.* a technique for optimizing method binding in which the address of a method is found the first

time an operation is executed and then stored in a table attached to the associated class. [Firesmith, Rumbaugh]

method-combination facility *n.* a facility that controls the selection of methods, the order in which they are run, and the values that are returned by the generic function. [CLOS]

method-combination object *n.* any object that encapsulates the method combination type and options specified by the *:method-combination* option to forms that specify generic function options. [CLOS]
See also: METAOBJECT, METHOD-COMBINATION FACILITY, METHOD OBJECT.

method dependency *n.* any dependency of only a single specified method of the client on its server(s). [Firesmith]
Contrast with: IMPLEMENTATION DEPENDENCY, INTERFACE DEPENDENCY.
Examples: Any dependency provided by a *with* clause in a subprogram body is a method dependency. [Firesmith]

Method Design *n.* the Object Behavior facet of the System Design stage of object-oriented information engineering, involving operation identification, method creation, procedural logic, nonprocedural code, input to code generators, screen and dialog design, and prototyping. [Martin]

method format *n.* any immutable attribute of a method that defines the set of execution engines that can interpret the method. [OMG]

method/message path (MM-Path) *n.* any sequence of method executions linked by messages.
Commentary: Term used during object-oriented testing.

method object *n.* any object that contains a method function, a sequence of

parameter specializers that specify when the given method is applicable, a lambda-list, and a sequence of *qualifiers* that are used by the method-combination facility to distinguish among methods. [CLOS]
See also: METHOD-COMBINATION OBJECT, PARAMETER SPECIALIZER.
Commentary: A method object is not a function and cannot be invoked as a function. [CLOS]

method overriding *n.* to override the method of an operation in an ancestor by creating a method of an operation in a child class with the same signature. [Lorenz]
See also: OVERRIDING.
Commentary: This results in different behavior for the same message. [Lorenz]

method resolution *n.* the programming language process of selecting and binding the method to a message that is appropriate to the class. [OMG, Rumbaugh]
Synonym: METHOD BINDING.
Commentary: Method resolution is often implemented via a virtual-method table. [Firesmith]

microarchitecture *n.* the patterns from which any well-structured object-oriented system is composed. [Booch]
See also: PATTERN.

Miller limit *n.* named after the psychologist George Miller, the natural limitation on human understanding resulting from complexity which becomes significant at approximately seven plus or minus two. [Ada, Firesmith]
Commentary: Quality and productivity decreases when the Miller limit is violated. The number of nodes on a diagram should be typically less than the Miller limit in order to maximize understand-

ability. Often called the hrair limit in the Ada community. [Firesmith]

mixin [class] *n.* an abstract class that embodies a single abstraction that is used to augment the protocol or functionality of other classes by providing common characteristics by means of multiple inheritance. [Booch, Coleman, Firesmith]
Example: an abstract class used to provide persistence to other classes via multiple inheritance. [Firesmith]
Commentary: The abstraction of a mixin (e.g., persistence) is usually orthogonal to the abstraction of the class(es) with which it is combined. [Booch, Firesmith]

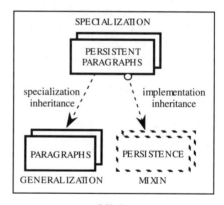

Mixin

mixin inheritance *n.* any inheritance involving a mixin, an abstract parent class that exists only to provide a set of properties for classes to inherit. [Ada94]

mode [of a given argument] *n.* the direction of data flow of the given argument. [Firesmith]
Synonym: PARAMETER PASSING MODE.
Examples: The modes in Ada are *in, out,* and *inout.*

Commentary: Mode *in* means that the argument goes in the same direction as the message (i.e., data and control flows in the same direction). Mode *out* means that the argument goes in the opposite direction as the message (i.e., data and control flows in opposite directions). Mode inout means that the argument goes both directions (i.e., read/write). [Firesmith]

mode [of a given object or class] *n.* the status, situation, condition, state, or phase of the given object or class during a specific period that determines its overall behavior (e.g., response to messages). [Firesmith]
Examples: a state of a GUI during which the user's actions are interpreted in a specific way. [Firesmith]

model *n.* **1.** any abstraction that includes all essential capabilities, properties, or aspects of what is being modeled without any extraneous details. [Firesmith, Henderson-Sellers] **2.** any cohesive set of requirements or design information, typically consisting largely of object-oriented diagrams and supporting information. [Firesmith]
Kinds:
- BEHAVIORAL MODEL
- CONFIGURATION MODEL
- DATA MODEL
- DYNAMIC MODEL
- EVENT MODEL
- FUNCTIONAL MODEL
- IDEAL-OBJECT MODEL
- INHERITANCE MODEL
- INTERACTION MODEL
- INTERFACE MODEL
- LANGUAGE MODEL
- LIFE-CYCLE MODEL
  - BASEBALL MODEL
  - FOUNTAIN MODEL

  - INCREMENTAL, ITERATIVE, PARALLEL DEVELOPMENT CYCLE
- OBJECT-BEHAVIOR MODEL
- OBJECT-INTERACTION MODEL
- OBJECT MODEL
- OBJECT-RELATIONSHIP MODEL
- OPERATION MODEL
- PRESENTATION MODEL
- SEMANTIC MODEL
- SERVICE-STRUCTURE MODEL
- STATE MODEL
- STRUCTURAL MODEL
- USE-CASE MODEL.

- **behavioral model** *n.* any model that describes the dynamics of the object types within the problem domain. [OADSIG]
Contrast with: FUNCTIONAL MODEL, STRUCTURAL MODEL.
Examples: Behavioral models are captured using event lists, state transition diagrams, life-cycle diagrams, event diagrams, event traces, scenarios, use cases, or object request diagrams.

- **configuration model** *n.* the static architecture model that documents a configuration management view of any system (or universe). The configuration model consists of one or more configuration diagrams and specifications for a system or assembly. [Firesmith]

- **data model** *n.* any collection of entities, operators, and consistency rules. [OMG]

- **dynamic model** *n.* any model describing those aspects of a system concerned with control, including time, sequencing of operations, and interactions of objects. [Rumbaugh]
Contrast with: FUNCTIONAL MODEL, OBJECT MODEL.

- **event model** *n.* any model that shows

O/Cs and a particular sequence of messages passed among them. [Henderson-Sellers]
Synonym: INTERACTION MODEL.

- **functional model** *n.* any model describing those aspects of a system that transform values using functions, mappings, constraints, and functional dependencies. [Rumbaugh]
Commentary: Rumbaugh's functional model is controversial in the object community because it primarily consists of data-flow diagrams.

- **ideal-object model** *n.* 1 any object model of a business that contains only those objects required to perform the use cases to run the business in the best possible way. [Jacobson] 2 any object-model of an information system that is independent of the implementation environment. [Jacobson]
Antonym: REAL-OBJECT MODEL.
See also: IDEAL OBJECT, IDEAL DESIGN, SEMANTIC GAP.

- **inheritance model** *n.* any model that graphically describes the class hierarchy. [Henderson-Sellers]
Contrast with: INTERACTION MODEL.
Commentary: It may be either generalization or implementation inheritance. It is distinct from the O/C model. [Henderson-Sellers]

- **interaction model** *n.* the object-oriented dynamic-behavior model that documents the dynamic behavior of objects and classes in terms of the interactions between them, their operations, and optionally their attributes and the data flows between the operations and attribute stores. The interaction model consists of scenarios, scenario life cycles, scenario life-cycle diagrams, interaction diagrams, tim-

ing diagrams, class life-cycle diagrams, and their specifications (e.g., in OOSDL). [Firesmith]
Synonym: EVENT MODEL.

- **interface model** *n.* **1.** any model that defines the input and output communication of the system. **2.** any model composed of a life-cycle model and an operation model. [Coleman]

- **language model** *n.* the implementation-level model that documents a language-specific view of the modules and clusters used to implement the objects, classes, and clusters. The language model consists of one or more module diagrams and the source code for the modules and clusters. [Firesmith]

- **life-cycle model** *n.* any model that characterizes the allowable sequencing of system operations and events. [Coleman]
Kinds:
  - BASEBALL MODEL
  - FOUNTAIN MODEL
  - INCREMENTAL, ITERATIVE, PARALLEL DEVELOPMENT CYCLE

- **baseball model** *n.* the Coad object-oriented development cycle implying both iteration and concurrent development. [Coad]
Contrast with: FOUNTAIN MODEL.
Commentary: This is represented by a graphic resembling a baseball showing bidirectional interactions between OOA, OOD, and OOP.

- **fountain model** *n.* the iterative, incremental, parallel object-oriented development cycle popularized by the MOSES method that continues the water metaphor of the waterfall model. [Henderson-Sellers]
Commentary: The fountain life-

M

cycle model is a high-level visualization of an iterative and recursive development process that permits visualization of a seamless transition and reuse. [Henderson-Sellers]

- **incremental, iterative, parallel (IIP) development cycle** *n.* any powerful object-oriented development cycle that is:
  - *Incremental* in that the system and software are developed in small and large increments;
  - *Iterative* in that intermediate products are iterated (e.g., as errors are discovered);
  - *Parallel* in that different teams work on different increments in parallel. [Firesmith]

- **object-behavior model** *n.* any object-oriented systems-analysis model consisting of state nets used to model the behavior of an object in terms of its perceived states, the conditions and events that cause it to change from one state to another, the actions it performs, the actions performed on it, exceptions to normal behavior, and real-time constraints. [Embley]
  See also: STATE NET.

- **object-interaction model** *n.* any model that allows an analyst to describe the interaction among objects. [Embley]
  Synonym: INTERACTION MODEL.
  See also: INTERACTION.

- **object model** *n.* **1.** any model defining the static structure of an application, used to capture the concepts that exist in the problem domain and the relationships between them. It can represent classes, attributes, and relationships between classes. [Coleman] **2.** the collection of principles

that form the foundation of object-oriented design. [Booch] **3.** any software engineering paradigm emphasizing the principles of abstraction, encapsulation, modularity, hierarchy, typing, concurrency, and persistence. [Booch] **4.** any description of the structure of the objects in a system including their identity, relationships to other objects, attributes, and operations. [Rumbaugh]

- **object-relationship model (ORM)** *n.* any model consisting of objects and relationships, object classes and relationship sets, constraints, and notes. [Embley]
  Synonym: SEMANTIC MODEL.

- **operation model** *n.* the Coleman model that defines the semantics (i.e., effect) of each system operation in the system interface in terms of change of state and the events that are output. [Coleman]

- **presentation model** *n.* the implementation-level model that documents a physical view of the user interface objects and classes (e.g., windows, dialog boxes). The presentation model may contain one or more presentation diagrams, prototype windows, and model-view-controller diagrams. [Firesmith]

- **semantic model** *n.* the object-oriented static model that documents the context of a system (or cluster) and the architecture of its component subsystems (or subclusters) in terms of the existence, abstraction, and visibility of their component objects and classes, the terminators with which these individual objects and classes directly (and indirectly) interface, and the important semantic rela-

tionships (e.g., links and associations, inheritance, classification, aggregation) between them. The semantic model consists of one or more context diagrams, general semantic nets, inheritance diagrams, aggregation diagrams, and OOSDL specifications. [Firesmith]
Synonym: OBJECT-RELATIONSHIP MODEL.

- **service-structure model** *n.* any model that documents the procedural design of a single service. [Henderson-Sellers]
- **state model** *n.* the object-oriented dynamic model that documents the behavior of the objects and classes in terms of their states and the transitions between these states. [Firesmith]
- **structural model** *n.* any model that describes the structure of the object types in the problem domain. [OAD-SIG]
Contrast with: BEHAVIORAL MODEL, FUNCTIONAL MODEL.
Examples: Object-relationship diagrams, type hierarchies, whole-part diagrams, subject-area-relationship diagrams are structural models.
- **use-case model** *n.* any diagram that documents a system's behavior as a set of use cases, actors, and the communication arcs between them. [Jacobson]

model class *n.* any domain class of model objects that model application-domain things. [Firesmith]
Synonyms: APPLICATION CLASS, BUSINESS CLASS, CORE CLASS, DOMAIN CLASS, KEY CLASS.
Contrast with: CONTROLLER CLASS, KEY ABSTRACTION, PRESENTATION CLASS, SUPPORT CLASS, VIEW CLASS.

See also: MODEL OBJECT.
Commentary: A model class may have more than one view class. [Firesmith]

model component *n.* **1.** any grouping of classes that separates domain objects from technology-specific objects. [Coad] **2.** the result of conceptually partitioning classes into meaningful, loosely coupled subsets. [Coad]
Synonym: COMPONENT.
Kinds: 3
- DATA-MANAGEMENT COMPONENT
- HUMAN-INTERACTION COMPONENT
- "NOT-THIS-TIME" COMPONENT
- PROBLEM-DOMAIN COMPONENT
- SYSTEM-INTERACTION COMPONENT
- TASK-MANAGEMENT COMPONENT.

- **data-management (DM) component** *n.* the component that contains objects that provide an interface between problem-domain objects and a database or file-management system. It provides two major capabilities: storing and restoring. [Coad]
See also: DM "OBJECT SERVER" OBJECT.
- **human-interaction (HI) component** *n.* the component that contains objects that provide an interface between problem-domain objects and people. [Coad]
- **"not-this-time" (NT) component** *n.* a component used to indicate that a class or concept is outside of the scope of the system. [Coad]
- **problem-domain (PD) component** *n.* the component that contains the technology-neutral objects that directly correspond to the problem being modeled. [Coad]
Commentary: Theses objects have little (or no) knowledge about objects in the other components (human interaction, data management, and sys-

M

tem interaction). [Coad]

- **system-interaction (SI) component** *n.* the component that contains system-interaction objects that provide an interface between problem-domain objects and other systems or devices. [Coad]
Commentary: A system interaction component encapsulates its communication protocol, keeping its companion problem domain object free of such low-level, implementation-specific detail. [Coad]

- **task-management (TM) component** *n.* the component that contains objects responsible for handling multitasking and related issues. [Coad]

model layer *n.* the layer that contains model objects and classes. [Firesmith]
Commentary: The model layer typically consists of model and controller objects and classes. The model layer is typically built on top of the communication, persistence, and environment layers. [Firesmith]

model object *n.* **1.** (a) any domain object that models an application-domain thing. [Firesmith] (b) any instance of a model class. [Firesmith] **2.** an object that simulates something in the problem domain of a business. [Lorenz]
Synonyms: APPLICATION OBJECT, BUSINESS OBJECT, CORE OBJECT, DOMAIN OBJECT, KEY OBJECT.
Contrast with: PRESENTATION OBJECT, VIEW OBJECT.
Examples: 1 A concept, document, event, device, financial instrument, interaction, location, organization, role, software, standard, substance, or system. [Firesmith] 2 An account is a model object for a bank. [Lorenz]
Commentary: Classes of model objects

are relatively stable, because they are fundamental to the way the business works. [Lorenz]

model-view-controller (MVC) *n.* an architectural pattern, originally from the Smalltalk community, in which GUIs are divided into model classes, view classes, and controller classes.
Rationale: This framework separates the concerns of user input and output from the information stored.

model-view-controller diagram (MVCD) *n.* any semantic net documenting the dependency relationships between models, views, and controllers.

modifiability *n.* the ease with which the software can be changed. [Firesmith]

modifier [operation] *n.* **1.** (a) any operation that modifies the value of properties. [Firesmith] (b) any fundamental field operation that changes the value of a field. [Martin/Odell] **2.** any operation that modifies the state of an object or class. [Booch, Martin/Odell]
Synonym: MODIFY INTERACTION.
Antonym: PRESERVER OPERATION.

modify interaction *n.* any interaction that alters existing objects. [Embley]
Synonym: MODIFIER OPERATION.

module *n.* **1.** the basic unit of source code that serves as the basic building block of the physical architecture. A module typically consists of a separately compilable interface and implementation. [Booch, Firesmith, Jacobson] **2.** the lowest-level cluster consisting of one or more classes and capturing the relationships between them. [Rumbaugh] **3.** any piece of code that is invoked and, when complete, returns control to the caller. [Shlaer/Mellor]
Synonym: OBJECT MODULE [Jacobson].
Commentary: Modules are usually classes

in pure object-oriented languages such as Smalltalk and Eiffel. [Firesmith]
Kinds:
- FOREIGN MODULE
- PRIMARY MODULE
- PRIVATE-OBJECT MODULE
- PUBLIC-OBJECT MODULE

- **foreign module** *n.* on a class structure chart, a module that does not belong to the class being depicted. [Shlaer/Mellor]
  Example: A foreign module may be either a module of another class, a utility function, or a friend function that is not a member of any class.

- **primary module** *n.* the unit of code that receives control when a published operation is invoked. [Shlaer/Mellor]

- **private-object module** *n.* any object module that is hidden within, and therefore cannot be accessed from the outside of, its enclosing block. [Jacobson]
  Antonym: PUBLIC-OBJECT MODULE.

- **public-object module** *n.* any object module that is exported from, and therefore can be accessed from the outside of, its enclosing block. [Jacobson]
  Antonym: PRIVATE-OBJECT MODULE.

module diagram (MD) *n.* any programming-language-level diagram that documents the modules (e.g., their identification, interface, implementation) in a cluster or cluster instance and the static dependency relationships between them. A module diagram is used to show the allocation of objects and classes to modules in the physical design of an application. [Booch, Firesmith]
Synonyms: BOOCHGRAM, GRADYGRAM.

modularity *n.* the logical and physical decomposition of things (e.g., responsibilities and software) into small, simple groupings (e.g., requirements and classes, respectively), which increase the achievement of software-engineering goals. [Booch, Firesmith]

monolithic object *n.* any *nonprimitive object* that conceptually has no *externally* discernible structure. [Berard]
Commentary: Internally, monolithic objects may be implemented using any appropriate objects. [Berard]

monomorphism *n.* the restriction that a name may only refer to things that all have the same form. [Booch, Firesmith]
Antonym: POLYMORPHISM.
Example: Monomorphism occurs when a variable declaration may only denote objects of a single type.

most-derived class *n.* the derived class of a *complete object* (i.e., an object that is not a subobject representing a base class). [C++]

MOO *n.* any multi-user dungeon (MUD) that is object-oriented.
Example: LambdaMOO.

Methodology for Object-oriented Software Engineering of Systems (MOSES) *n.* the full life-cycle development method developed by Henderson-Sellers et al.
Commentary: MOSES focuses on business issues, quality, reuse, and process support. [Henderson-Sellers]

multiple classification *n.* any classification whereby an instance simultaneously has more than one class. [Firesmith, Martin/Odell]
Antonym: SINGLE CLASSIFICATION.
Commentary: Some methodologists may consider the same concept to apply to types as well as to classes.

M

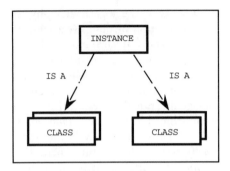

Multiple Classification

multiple generalization *n.* any generalization whereby a child has multiple parents. [Firesmith]
Antonym: SINGLE GENERALIZATION.
Contrast with: MULTIPLE CLASSIFICATION, SINGLE GENERALIZATION, SINGLE INHERITANCE.

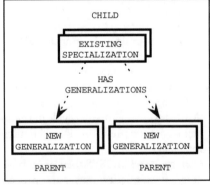

Multiple Generalization

multiple inheritance *n.* (a) the incremental construction of a new definition in terms of *multiple* existing definitions, whereby the new definition may both add new features and modify existing inherited features. [Firesmith] (b) the construction of a definition by incre-

mental modification of more than one definition. [OMG] (c) inheritance from several distinct parents. [Ada94, Coleman, Firesmith, Jacobson, Martin, Rumbaugh, Wirfs-Brock]
Antonym: SINGLE INHERITANCE.
Example: Multiple inheritance is any inheritance whereby a single class is simultaneously a child class of more than one base class. [Firesmith]
Commentary: The extent of the derived type is a subset of the intersection of the extents of the parent base types [Embley]
Kinds:
• MIXIN INHERITANCE
• REPEATED INHERITANCE
  - DIRECT REPEATED INHERITANCE
  - INDIRECT REPEATED INHERITANCE
  - REPLICATED REPEATED INHERITANCE
  - SHARED REPEATED INHERITANCE
  - VIRTUAL INHERITANCE

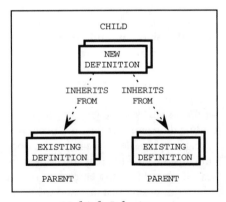

Multiple Inheritance

• **mixin inheritance** *n.* any multiple inheritance involving a mixin, an abstract parent class that exists only to provide a set of properties for classes to inherit. [Ada95]

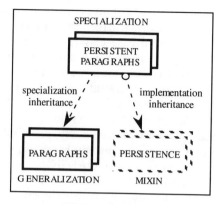

Mixin Inheritance

• **repeated inheritance** *n.* any multiple inheritance in which a given child inherits the same feature, either directly or indirectly, from the same ancestor class multiple times. [Eiffel, Firesmith, Jacobson, Meyer]
See also: REPLICATED FEATURE, SHARED FEATURE.
Commentary: In the majority of programming languages that support multiple inheritance, the user is forced to redefine the name of each replicated feature so that it becomes unique. This is the most acceptable solution, as only the user has sufficient knowledge to solve this conflict. If an operation is replicated, it does not matter which version is selected unless the original operation has been overridden. Then the problem is to know which one to select. [Jacobson]
Kinds:

- DIRECT REPEATED INHERITANCE
- INDIRECT REPEATED INHERITANCE
- REPLICATED REPEATED INHERITANCE
- SHARED REPEATED INHERITANCE
- VIRTUAL INHERITANCE

- **direct repeated inheritance [of a given class]** *n.* any repeated inheritance in which a parent class of the given class is the multiply inherited [Eiffel, Firesmith, Meyer]
Antonym: INDIRECT REPEATED INHERITANCE.

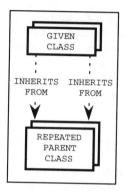

Direct Repeated Inheritance

- **indirect repeated inheritance [of a given class]** *n.* any repeated inheri-

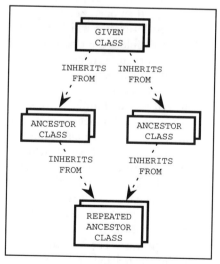

Indirect Repeated Inheritance

tance in which an ancestor class of the given class is the parent of two or more descendants of the given class. [Eiffel, Firesmith, Meyer]

Antonym: DIRECT REPEATED INHERITANCE.

- **replicated repeated inheritance** *n.* any repeated inheritance from a common ancestor of a single feature under different names yielding two features in the current class. [Eiffel, Firesmith, Meyer]

Antonym: SHARED REPEATED INHERITANCE.

Commentary: The inherited feature is thus replicated and occurs multiple times in the current class or type. In the majority of programming languages that support multiple inheritance, the developer is required to redefine the name of each replicated feature so that it becomes unique. This is the most acceptable solution, as only the developer has sufficient knowledge to resolve this conflict. If an operation is repeated, it does not matter which version is selected unless the original operation has been overridden. Then the problem is to know which one to select. [Firesmith]

- **shared repeated inheritance** *n.* any repeated inheritance from a common ancestor of a single feature under the same final name yielding a single feature in the current class. [Eiffel, Firesmith, Meyer]

Synonym: VIRTUAL INHERITANCE.

Antonym: REPLICATED REPEATED INHERITANCE.

Commentary: The inherited feature is thus shared and occurs only once in the current class. [Firesmith]

- **virtual inheritance** *n.* any repeated inheritance whereby the features of repeated base classes (or supertypes) are only inherited once in the derived class (or subtype).

Synonym: SHARED REPEATED INHERITANCE.

See also: SHARED FEATURE.

multiple specialization *n.* any specialization whereby a parent has multiple children. [Coleman, OADSIG]

Antonym: SINGLE SPECIALIZATION.

Contrast with: MULTIPLE GENERALIZATION, SINGLE GENERALIZATION.

Commentary: The extent of the parent is a superset of the union of the extents of the children.

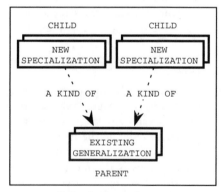

Multiple Specialization

multiplicity *n.* the *potential* number of things. [Firesmith]

Contrast with: CARDINALITY.

Commentary: Although they have different meanings, the terms *cardinality* and *multiplicity* are often confused in practice.

Kinds:

• MULTIPLICITY OF A GIVEN AGGREGATE
• MULTIPLICITY OF A GIVEN CLASS

- MULTIPLICITY OF A GIVEN CLUSTER
- MULTIPLICITY OF A GIVEN
  RELATIONSHIP
- **multiplicity [of a given aggregate]** *n.* the *potential* number of component parts in the given aggregate. [Firesmith] *Example:* The number of wheels on a car (including spares in the trunk) is the multiplicity of the wheels. [Firesmith]
- **multiplicity [of a given class]** *n.* the *potential* number of instances of the given class (i.e., the size of the extent of the class). [Firesmith]
- **multiplicity [of a given cluster]** *n.* the *potential* number of classes and subclusters in the given cluster. [Firesmith[
- **multiplicity [of a given relationship]** *n.* **1.** the *potential* number of objects that participate in each instance of the given relationship. [Firesmith, Rumbaugh] **2.** the number of instances of the objects that participate in each instance of the relationship. [Shlaer/Mellor]

mutability *n.* access permission given to the properties of an object. [Coleman]

mutable object *n.* any object that can change the intrinsic values of its properties. [Firesmith, ODMG]
Synonym: VARIABLE OBJECT.
Antonym: IMMUTABLE OBJECT, LITERAL.
Commentary: The values of the properties of a mutable object may change, although the identity of the object remains invariant across these changes. [Firesmith]

mutual-exclusion constraint *n.* any inheritance constraint that declares that a group of children of a parent are pairwise disjoint. [Embley]
Synonym: DISJOINT CONSTRAINT.

- **partition constraint** *n.* the inheritance constraint that requires that the extents of the children form a disjoint cover that partitions the parent. [Embley, Firesmith]
Commentary: The partition constraint is the conjunction of the cover constraint and the disjoint constraint. [Firesmith] A partition requires that partitioning sets be pairwise disjoint and that their union constitute the partitioned set. A partition constraint is the combination of a mutual-exclusion constraint and a union constraint. [Embley]

M

N

name *n.* **1.** any developer-provided name that uniquely identifies something within the scope of the name. [Firesmith] **2.** an ordered sequence of components. [OMG]

Contrast with: HANDLE, IDENTIFIER, KEY, OBJECT IDENTIFIER.

Examples: Names that are used for types, classes, and objects. [Firesmith]

Commentary: Names provide a way for people to refer to things both in documentation and in code. A name is introduced into a program via a declaration. Although a name is not an attribute, a name may have a type that determines its use. Unlike an OID, a name need not be constant and something may have multiple names. [Firesmith]

Kinds:
- AGGREGATE NAME
- ARGUMENT NAME
- ATOMIC NAME
- CLASS NAME
- COMPOUND NAME
- FEATURE NAME
  - CURRENT NAME
  - FINAL NAME
  - INHERITED NAME
  - MESSAGE NAME
  - OPERATION NAME
  - ORIGINAL NAME
  - PROPERTY NAME
- MESSAGE-CATEGORY NAME
- OBJECT NAME
- PARAMETER NAME
- PSEUDOVARIABLE NAME
- ROLE NAME
- SIMPLE NAME
- TYPE NAME
- VARIABLE NAME

- **aggregate name** *n.* any name with multiple components. [Firesmith]
  Synonym: COMPOUND NAME.
  Antonym: ATOMIC NAME.

- **argument name** *n.* (a) the name of any pseudovariable that holds a argument. [Firesmith] (b) the name of a pseudovariable available to a method only for the duration of that method's execution; the value of the argument names are the arguments of the message that invoked the method. [Smalltalk]

- **atomic name** *n.* any name with only a single component. [Firesmith]
  Antonym: AGGREGATE NAME.

- **class name** *n.* **1.** the name of any class. [Firesmith] **2.** any name that describes the type of component represented by

the instances of the class. [Smalltalk]
Contrast with: OBJECT NAME, TYPE NAME.
Commentary: A class name serves two fundamental purposes; it is a simple way for instances to identify themselves, and it provides a way to refer to the class in expressions. [Smalltalk]

- **compound name** *n.* any name with multiple components. [OMG]
Synonym: AGGREGATE NAME.
Antonym: SIMPLE NAME.

- **feature name** *n.* any name that uniquely refers to a single feature within a specified class. [Eiffel, Meyer]
Commentary: Because a feature may be renamed in a derived class, the name of a feature is relative to a specified class. [Firesmith]
Kinds:
    - CURRENT NAME [OF A GIVEN FEATURE]
    - FINAL NAME [OF A GIVEN FEATURE]
    - INHERITED NAME [OF A GIVEN FEATURE]
    - MESSAGE NAME
    - OPERATION NAME
    - ORIGINAL NAME [OF A GIVEN FEATURE]
    - PROPERTY NAME

- **current name [of a given feature]** *n.* the name of the feature in a specified class, which is defined as follows:
    - the original name of the feature if the feature is not inherited (i.e., if the specified class is the class of origin);
    - the inherited name of the given feature if the feature is inherited and not renamed in the specified class;
    - the new name if the given feature is inherited and renamed in the

specified class. [Firesmith]

- **final name [of a given feature]** *n.* the name of the feature in a specified class, which is defined as follows:
    - the original feature name if the feature is not inherited (i.e., if the specified class is the class of origin);
    - the inherited feature name if the feature is inherited and not renamed in the specified class;
    - the new name if the feature is inherited and renamed in the specified class. [Eiffel, Meyer]

- **inherited name [of a given feature]** *n.* the current name of the given feature in its parent class. [Eiffel, Firesmith, Meyer]

- **message name** *n.* the name of the operation requested by the message. [Wirfs-Brock]

- **operation name** *n.* (a) the name of any operation. [Firesmith] (b) any name used in a request to identify an operation. [OMG]
Synonym: OPERATION IDENTIFIER.
Examples: The method selector used in a message and in the signature of an operation are both operation names [Firesmith]

- **original name [of a given feature]** *n.* the name of the given feature as declared in its class of origin. [Eiffel, Firesmith, Meyer]

- **property name** *n.* any name that uniquely refers to a single property within a specified class. [Firesmith]

- **message-category name** *n.* the name of any category indicating the common functionality of the messages in the category [Smalltalk]

- **object name** *n.* the name of any object. [Firesmith, ODMG, OMG]

N

Contrast with: CLASS NAME, OBJECT IDENTIFIER, TYPE NAME.

Commentary: A name is not explicitly defined as an attribute of an object. Unlike an OID, a name need not be constant during the existence of the object, and an object may have one or more names. [ODMG, OMG]

- **parameter name** *n.* the name of any pseudovariable that holds a parameter. [Firesmith]
- **pseudovariable name** *n.* any expression similar to a variable name that cannot be changed by an assignment. [Smalltalk]
- **role name** *n.* any name that uniquely identifies a role. [Firesmith]
  Example: The name of one end of an association is a role name. [Firesmith]
- **simple name** *n.* any name with a single component. [OMG]
  Contrast with: COMPOUND NAME.
- **type name** *n.* any name that uniquely refers to a single type within the scope of the definition of the name. [C++]
  Contrast with: CLASS NAME, OBJECT NAME.
- **variable name** *n.* any expression that describes the current value of an accessible variable. [Smalltalk]
  Commentary: The value of a variable name is the current value of the variable with that name. [Smalltalk]

name binding *n.* any name-to-object association defined relative to a *naming context.* [OMG]

name clash *n.* the use of the same name for two different things within the same scope in such a manner that the name is ambiguous. [Firesmith]
Contrast with: OVERLOADING, POLYMORPHISM.
Commentary: Commonly occurs when

classes from different development efforts (e.g., vendors) are integrated on the same application. [Firesmith]

named instance variable *n.* any instance variable that is accessed by its instance variable name. [Smalltalk]
Antonym: INDEXED INSTANCE VARIABLE.
Commentary: All instances of a class have the same number of named instance variables and use the same names to refer to them. [Smalltalk]

naming attribute *n.* any attribute that provides facts about the arbitrary labels and names carried by each instance of an object. [Shlaer/Mellor]
Examples: The aircraft ID and name of an airplane, the code of a valve, and the name and ID of an employee are all naming attributes.

naming context *n.* any object that contains a set of name bindings in which each name is unique. [OMG]

navigation *n.* the movement from one view/presentation object to a second view/presentation object by selecting (e.g., double clicking on) the reference to the second object in the presentation of the first. [Firesmith]

nest *v.* *-ed, -ing* to declare something in the declaration of the same kind of thing. [C++]
See also: NESTED CLASS.

nested class *n.* any class declared within another class. [C++, Firesmith]
Contrast with: AGGREGATE CLASS, COMPOSITE CLASS, SUBCLASS.
Commentary: Simply declaring a class nested in another does not mean that the enclosing class contains an object of the enclosed class. Nesting expresses scoping, not containment of component objects. [C++]

new feature *n.* any feature not obtained

from ancestors via inheritance. [Firesmith]

Antonym: INHERITED FEATURE.

new [operator] *n.* any operator that creates an object of the *type-name* to which it is applied. [C++]

Synonym: CONSTRUCTOR.

Contrast with: DELETE OPERATOR.

nil *n.* **1.** any pseudovariable name that refers to an object used as the value of a variable when no other object is appropriate. Variables that have not been otherwise initialized refer to nil. [Smalltalk] **2.** any pseudovariable that specifies the empty set. [CLOS]

Synonym: NULL.

Commentary: The only instance of class UndefinedObject, nil is typically the value of variables that have not been assigned as yet. [Smalltalk]

node card *n.* any card taped to a whiteboard and used to represent a node on an object-oriented diagram. [Firesmith]

Contrast with: CLASS CARD, CLASS RESPONSIBILITY CARD, CLASS SPECIFICATION.

Commentary: Node cards are used to simplify the iteration of diagrams by making it easier to move the nodes. Node cards can be annotated with responsibilities.

nominal subtype *n.* the subtype that is associated with the view when a view of an object is defined. [Ada94]

Contrast with: ACTUAL SUBTYPE.

Commentary: The object's *actual subtype* can be more restrictive than the nominal subtype of the view; it always is if the nominal subtype is an *indefinite subtype.* [Ada95]

NONE *n.* the kernel library class that is considered to inherit from all classes assuming appropriate renaming to remove any resulting name clashes. [Eiffel, Meyer]

Commentary: NONE does not actually exist as a class text in the library, but serves as a convenient fiction to make the class structure and the type system complete. NONE has no instances and does not export any features. [Eiffel, Meyer]

noninterruptible action *n.* any action associated with the state transition that the analyst expects to run to completion unless exceptions or system failures occur. [Embley]

Antonym: INTERRUPTIBLE ACTION.

noninterruptible operation *n.* any operation that may not be suspended before it finishes executing. [Firesmith]

Antonym: INTERRUPTIBLE OPERATION.

Commentary: Noninterruptible operations contain at least one critical region that must execute to completion without interruption. [Firesmith]

non-iterator operation *n.* any operation that neither operates on multiple instances of a class nor on multiple properties. [Firesmith]

Antonym: ITERATOR OPERATION.

nonlimited type *n.* any type (or view of a type) for which the assignment operation is allowed. [Ada94]

Antonym: LIMITED TYPE.

nonobject *n.* any thing that is not an object [OMG]

Example: The basic and constructed values as defined in the CORBA specification are nonobjects.

Commentary: Each nonobject belongs to a type of values called a non-object type. [OMG]

nonobject type *n.* the type of any nonobject. [OMG]

nonprimitive value *n.* any value that is

N

also an object. [Firesmith]

Antonym: PRIMITIVE VALUE.

nonspontaneous transition *n.* any transition that only fires when triggered by an incoming message. [Firesmith]

Antonym: SPONTANEOUS TRANSITION.

Commentary: A nonspontaneous transition most often results from the execution of a sequential modifier operation. [Firesmith]

nontransitive constraint *n.* the structural constraint on a given relationship R that requires if A is related by R to B and B is related by R to C, then A need not be related by R to C. [Firesmith]

Antonym: TRANSITIVE CONSTRAINT.

Example: The *has-visibility-of* link and association are nontransitive. [Firesmith]

normal trigger *n.* any trigger that occurs during the normal execution of an object or class. [Firesmith]

Antonym: EXCEPTIONAL TRIGGER.

"not this time" (NT) component *n.* the component used to indicate that a class or concept is outside of scope of the system. [Coad]

null *n.* the pseudovariable name that refers to an object used as the value of a variable when no other object is appropriate. Variables that have not been otherwise initialized refer to null. [C++]

Synonym: NIL.

O

Obj *n.* the set of all object identifiers (OIDs) in the OMG Core Model. [OMG]

object *n.* **1.** (a) any abstraction that models a *single* thing. [Coad, Coleman, Eiffel, Firesmith, Lorenz, Meyer, OMG, Rumbaugh] (b) during design, any abstraction of a real-world thing. [Shlaer/Mellor] (c) any real or abstract thing about which we store data and the operations to manipulate those data. [Martin/Odell] **2.** (a) any identifiable, encapsulated entity that provides one or more services that can be requested by a client. [Jacobson, OMG] (b) any encapsulation of properties (e.g., data, state) and behavior (e.g., operations). [Booch, Coad, Firesmith, Lorenz, Jacobson, OMG, Smalltalk, Wirfs-Brock] **3.** anything with identity. [Booch, Embley, Firesmith, Jacobson, OMG, OADSIG] **4.** anything that can send and/or receive messages. **5.** (a) any instance of one or more (possibly anonymous) classes or types. [Booch, CLOS, Eiffel, Firesmith, Henderson-Sellers, Martin/Odell, Meyer, Rumbaugh, Wirfs-Brock] (b) during analysis, any typical but unspecified instance. [Shlaer/Mellor] (c) any member

of an extent (a.k.a. extension). [Firesmith, Henderson-Sellers] (d) anything to which a type applies. [Martin/Odell] **6.** the primary root type of the inheritance structure. [OMG] **7.** any region of storage. [C++] **8.** during analysis, any abstraction of a set of real-world things such that all of the real-world things in the set (the instances) have the same characteristics and all instances are subject to and conform to the same rules. [Shlaer/Mellor] **9.** any person, place, or thing. [Embley] **10.** any run-time entity of a given type that has a value of that type. [Ada95]

Synonym: INSTANCE.

Examples: Individual numbers, character strings, queues, dictionaries, rectangles, file directories, text editors, programs, compilers, computational processes, financial histories, and views of information can all be modeled as objects. [Smalltalk]

Commentary: As a model of a single thing, objects must have an *identifier* that is unique within their scope. As a complete model, an object encapsulates *responsibilities* and the *features* necessary to implement them. These features typically include both *properties* (e.g., attributes, links to other objects, component objects, and invariants) and *behavior* (e.g., messages that may be received, exceptions that may be raised, operations that execute). An object collaborates with others by sending and/or receiving messages. Objects may occur as part of either the system or software requirements, design, and/or implementation. Objects may be discovered in the real-world during requirements analysis or invented as part of the solution space during design. [Firesmith] In definition **8** Shlaer/Mellor appear to use the term *object* to mean *class*, and the term *instance* to mean *object*. However, Mellor has stated that this view is incorrect and that an object during analysis should rather be considered to be a representative, but unspecified, instance.

Kinds:

- ACTOR
- AGGREGATE OBJECT
  - COLLECTION OBJECT
  - CONTAINER OBJECT
  - STRUCTURE OBJECT
- ASSOCIATIVE OBJECT
- ATOMIC OBJECT
- AUTOMATIC OBJECT
- BINARY LARGE OBJECT
- CLASS DESCRIPTOR
- CLASS OBJECT
- CLIENT OBJECT
- COLLABORATOR OBJECT
- COMPLETE OBJECT
- COMPLEX OBJECT
- COMPONENT OBJECT
- COMPOSITE OBJECT
  - HOMOGENEOUS COMPOSITE OBJECT
- COMPOUND OBJECT
- CONCURRENT OBJECT

- ACTIVE OBJECT
- GUARDED OBJECT
- CONSTRAINED OBJECT
- CONTEXT OBJECT
- CONTROL OBJECT
- COORDINATOR OBJECT
- CURRENT OBJECT
- DEPENDENT OBJECT
  - DIRECT DEPENDENT OBJECT
  - INDIRECT DEPENDENT OBJECT
- DESCRIPTOR OBJECT
- DISPATCHER OBJECT
- SERVER OBJECT
- "DM OBJECT SERVER" OBJECT
- DOMAIN OBJECT
  - APPLICATION OBJECT
  - BUSINESS OBJECT
  - CONTROLLER OBJECT
  - ENTITY OBJECT
  - MODEL OBJECT
  - PROBLEM-DOMAIN OBJECT
  - VIEW OBJECT
    + PANE OBJECT
    + PRESENTATION OBJECT
    + PROXY
- EXTERNAL OBJECT
- FRAME
- FUNCTOR OBJECT
- FUTURE OBJECT
- GENERIC OBJECT
- IDEAL OBJECT
- IMMUTABLE OBJECT
- IMPLEMENTATION OBJECT
- INCIDENT OBJECT
- INSTANCE OF A GIVEN CLASS
  - DIRECT INSTANCE OF A GIVEN CLASS
  - INDIRECT INSTANCE OF A GIVEN CLASS
- INTANGIBLE OBJECT
- INTERACTION OBJECT
- INTERFACE OBJECT
  - CENTRAL INTERFACE OBJECT
- LITERAL OBJECT

- MAILLON OBJECT
- MANAGED OBJECT
- MANAGER OBJECT
- MASTER OBJECT
- METAOBJECT
- METHOD-COMBINATION OBJECT
- METHOD OBJECT
- MONOLITHIC OBJECT
- MUTABLE OBJECT
- PASSIVE OBJECT
  - BLOCKING OBJECT
  - SEQUENTIAL OBJECT
- PERSISTENT OBJECT
- PRIMITIVE OBJECT
- REAL OBJECT
- RECEIVER
- RELATIONSHIP OBJECT
- REPLICANT OBJECT
- RESILIENT OBJECT
- ROLE OBJECT
- ROOT OBJECT
- SERVER OBJECT
- SPECIAL OBJECT
- SPECIFICATION OBJECT
- STANDARD OBJECT
- STATE-CONTROLLED OBJECT
- STATE-DEPENDENT OBJECT
- STATE-INDEPENDENT OBJECT
- STIMULUS-CONTROLLED OBJECT
- STRATEGY
- SUBOBJECT
- SUBPART OBJECT
- SUBTYPE OBJECT
- SUPERPART OBJECT
- SUPERTYPE OBJECT
- SUPPORT OBJECT
  - UTILITY OBJECT
- TANGIBLE OBJECT
- TRANSACTION OBJECT
- TRANSIENT OBJECT
  - DYNAMIC OBJECT
    + ORPHANED OBJECT
  - STATIC OBJECT
- TYPE OBJECT

- USER-INTERFACE OBJECT
- **actor** *n.* **1.** (a) any object that models a role that a perspective user plays. [Booch, Henderson-Sellers, Jacobson, Rumbaugh] (b) any person, an organization, or some other thing that participates in one or more ways over time. [Coad] **2.** any object in the Actor language. [Firesmith] **3.** any object with one or more threads of control. [Booch] **4.** any object that sends messages to other objects, but does not receive messages. [Booch]

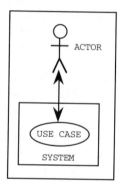

Actor (Definition 1)

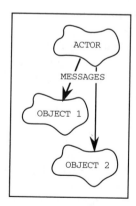

Actor (Definition 4)

Synonyms: **1** TERMINATOR; **3** ACTIVE OBJECT, CONCURRENT OBJECT; **4** MASTER OBJECT.

Commentary: Originally introduced by Jacobson's Objectory method, definition **1**(a) has become popular with several other methods. [Henderson-Sellers] Definitions **1** and **2** are the most popular. Using the term *master* instead of the term *actor* for definition **4** avoids ambiguity. [Firesmith]

- **aggregate object** *n.* (a) any object that contains one or more objects as component parts. [Booch, Embley, Firesmith, Rumbaugh] (b) any instance of an aggregate class. [Firesmith]
Synonym: COMPOSITE OBJECT, SUPERPART.
Antonym: ATOMIC OBJECT, SUBPART.
Example: A paragraph object contains one or more sentence objects. [Firesmith]
Commentary: The term *aggregate object* is preferred over the term *composite object*. [Firesmith]
Kinds:
  - COLLECTION OBJECT
  - CONTAINER OBJECT
  - STRUCTURE OBJECT

- **collection [object]** *n.* (a) any homogeneous aggregate object, the purpose of which is to hold component objects of a single type and its subtypes. [Firesmith] (b) any instance of a collection class. [Firesmith]
Contrast with: CONTAINER OBJECT, STRUCTURE OBJECT.
Examples: Any individual array, bag, dictionary, list, queue, set, or stack can be modeled as a collection object. [Firesmith]
Commentary: Collections enforce strong typing. Collections often

provide appropriate operations to access and iterate over their contents. [Firesmith]

- **container [object]** *n.* (a) any heterogeneous aggregate object, the purpose of which is to hold unrelated component objects of multiple unrelated types. [Firesmith, Rumbaugh] (b) any instance of a container class. [Firesmith]
Contrast with: COLLECTION OBJECT, STRUCTURE OBJECT.
Example: Any individual car trunk. [Firesmith]
Commentary: Compared with collections, containers allow more freedom by violating strong typing. [Firesmith]

- **structure [object]** *n.* (a) any aggregate object, the component parts of which are interrelated. [Firesmith] (b) any instance of a structure class. [Firesmith]
Contrast with: COLLECTION OBJECT, CONTAINER OBJECT.
Example: A car engine can be modeled as a structure object, the component parts of which are interrelated.
Commentary: A car engine is more than the mere sum of its parts; it must be whole to function.

- **associative object** *n.* (a) any object that is a reification of a link (i.e., an instance of an association). [Firesmith, Shlaer/Mellor] (b) any instance of an associative class. [Firesmith]
Synonym: INTERACTION OBJECT.

- **atomic object** *n.* any object that does not contain any objects as component parts. [Firesmith]
Antonym: AGGREGATE OBJECT.
Commentary: An atomic object may,

however, contain one or more objects *as attributes* or *links* to one or more objects. [Firesmith]

- **automatic object** *n.* any object that is local to each invocation of a block. [C++]
  Contrast with: STATIC OBJECT.

- **binary large object (BLOB)** *n.* any large, typically unstructured, unit of data stored in databases in binary form. [Firesmith, Martin]

- **class descriptor** *n.* **1.** any object representing a class, documenting its features as well as the values of any class properties. [Rumbaugh] **2.** any instance of a *metaclass*.
  Rationale: Class descriptors are implemented in some, but not all, OOPLs.

- **class object** *n.* (a) any object that is also a class. [Firesmith] (b) any object that serves as a factory for instantiating objects. [OMG]
  Contrast with: FACTORY.
  See also: METACLASS, POWER CLASS.
  Commentary: Class objects are instances of metaclasses. [Firesmith]

- **client object** *n.* any object that issues a request for a service. [OMG, Wirfs-Brock]
  Antonym: SERVER OBJECT.
  Commentary: A given object may be a client for some requests and a server for other requests. [Firesmith]

- **collaborator object** *n.* any object (on an object-interaction graph) that provides some functionality as a server to implement a system operation. [Coleman]

- **complete object** *n.* any object that is not a subobject representing a base class. [C++]
  Contrast with: SUBOBJECT.

- **complex object** *n.* **1.** any aggregate

object containing one or more objects as component parts [Martin/Odell] **2.** any instance of a complex type. [Eiffel]
Synonyms: **1** AGGREGATE OBJECT, COMPOSITE OBJECT.
See also: COMPOSITION.

- **component [object]** *n.* any object that is contained within another object as a component part. [Embley, Firesmith, OMG]
  Synonym: SUBPART.
  Antonyms: AGGREGATE, SUPERPART.
  Contrast with: COMPONENT CLASS, SUBPART CLASS.

- **composite object** *n.* **1.** any aggregate object containing one or more objects as component parts [Martin/Odell] **2.** any complex object with complex subobjects. [Eiffel, Meyer]
  Synonym: AGGREGATE OBJECT, COMPLEX OBJECT.
  Contrast with: SUBOBJECT.

  - **homogeneous composite object** *n.* any composite object that is *conceptually* composed of component objects that are all *conceptually* of the same type. [Berard]

- **compound object** *n.* any object that contains one or more objects as component parts. [OMG]
  Synonym: AGGREGATE OBJECT.

- **concurrent object** *n.* **1.** any object that contains one or more threads of control (e.g., concurrent operations or nested concurrent objects). [Firesmith] **2.** any active object whose semantics are guaranteed in the presence of multiple threads of control. [Booch]
  Antonym: SEQUENTIAL OBJECT.
  Kinds:
  - ACTIVE OBJECT
  - GUARDED OBJECT

O

- **active object** *n.* **1.** any concurrent object that executes without the need for incoming messages. [Firesmith] **2.** any object that sends messages to other objects, but does not receive messages. **3.** any concurrent object. [Booch]
  Synonyms: ACTOR, CONCURRENT OBJECT, MASTER OBJECT.
  Antonym: PASSIVE OBJECT.
- **guarded object** *n.* any concurrent object that provides and enforces mutually exclusive access in a concurrent environment.
  Contrast with: CORRUPTIBLE OBJECT, GUARDABLE OBJECT.
- **constrained object** *n.* any object whose actual subtype is constrained. [Ada95]
- **context object** *n.* any collection of name-value pairs that provides environmental or user-preference information. [OMG]
- **control object** *n.* **1.** any object that encapsulates functionality specific to one or a few use cases in an information system. [Jacobson] **2.** any object that represents a set of tasks in a business. [Jacobson]
  Contrast with: ENTITY OBJECT, INTERFACE OBJECT.
  Commentary: **1** The control objects model functionality that is not naturally tied to any other object. Typically such behavior consists of operating on several different entity objects, doing some computations, and then returning the result to an interface object. [Jacobson] **2** These tasks should be performed by one resource instance, which typically is a specialist or a routine worker, not dealing directly with the customer. [Jacobson]

- **coordinator object** *n.* any object that coordinates other objects by passing client requests to objects that can provide the associated services.
- **current object** *n.* the object to which the latest noncompleted routine call applies at some time during execution. [Eiffel, Meyer]
  Contrast with: CURRENT ROUTINE.

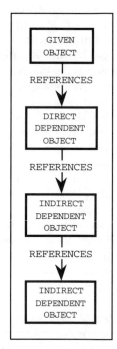

Dependent Objects

- **dependent object** *n.* **1.** any object that is either directly or indirectly visible to and referenced by the current object at some time during execution. [Firesmith] **2.** the dependents of an object are the object itself and (recursively) the dependents of its direct dependents. [Eiffel, Meyer]
  Commentary: Clients depend on

their servers.
Kinds:
- DIRECT DEPENDENT OBJECT
- INDIRECT DEPENDENT OBJECT
- **direct dependent object** *n.* **1.** any
object visible to and referenced by
the current object at some time
during execution. [Firesmith] **2.**
the direct dependents of an object
O, at some time during the execution of a system, are the objects attached to the reference field of O.
[Eiffel, Meyer]
Contrast with: INDIRECT DEPEN-
DENT OBJECT.
- **indirect dependent object** *n.* any
object that is either a direct dependent of a direct dependent or recursively a direct dependent of an
indirect dependent. [Firesmith]
Contrast with: DIRECT DEPENDENT
OBJECT.
• **descriptor object** *n.* any instance of
the descriptor class that stores useful
information about its associated class.
Commentary: Compilers may then
allocate one object (a.k.a. the descriptor object) of the descriptor class for
each class in the program. The compiler can then provide an operation
that, when applied to a given object,
will return a pointer to the descriptor
object for the class of that object.
• **dispatcher object** *n.* any object that
captures user input.
Synonym: CONTROLLER OBJECT.
Example: an object that captures
mouse events.
• **"DM object server" object** *n.* any
single object, whose purpose is: to
create DM objects for each supported
class, to maintain a collection of DM
objects, and to provide a single point

of access to get a DM object for a spe-
cific class. [Coad]
See also: DATA MANAGEMENT (DM)
COMPONENT.
• **domain object** *n.* (a) any object that
is application domain-specific. [Fire-
smith] (b) any instance of a domain
class. [Firesmith]
Antonym: SUPPORT OBJECT.
Kinds:
- APPLICATION OBJECT
- BUSINESS OBJECT
- CONTROLLER OBJECT
- ENTITY OBJECT
- MODEL OBJECT
- PROBLEM-DOMAIN OBJECT
- VIEW OBJECT
  + PANE
  + PRESENTATION OBJECT
  + PROXY OBJECT
- **application object (AO)** *n.* **1.** any
object that models and interfaces
with an end-user application.
[OMG] **2.** any object encapsulating an entire application. [ODMG]
Commentary: 1 Example operations on such objects are open, install, move, and remove. [OMG]
- **business object** *n.* any object that
models some essential aspect of the
application domain.
Synonyms: CORE OBJECT, DOMAIN
OBJECT, KEY ABSTRACTION, MODEL
OBJECT.
- **controller [object]** *n.* (a) any domain object that exists to either
control one or more objects or
capture user input as in the model–
view–controller (MVC) framework. [Coleman, Firesmith, Small-
talk] (b) any instance of a controller class. [Firesmith]
Contrast with: MODEL OBJECT, VIEW

OBJECT, PRESENTATION OBJECT.
Example: Any object that captures mouse events is a controller object. [Firesmith]
Commentary: Controller objects are often either model objects that model input devices (e.g., mice) or are presentation objects allowing the user to control the model object. [Firesmith]

- **entity object** *n.* **1.** any object in a business system that represents occurrences that are handled in the business. [Jacobson] **2.** any object in an information system that manages either (1) some piece of information that should be held for a significant time and that typically should survive a use case or (2) some resource and its access. [Jacobson]
Contrast with: CONTROL OBJECT, INTERFACE OBJECT.
Examples: **1** Products, deliverables, documents, and other things that are handled in the business can all be modeled as entity objects.
Commentary: The object types used in the analysis model are *entity objects, interface objects,* and *control objects.* Most entity object are found early and are obvious. These obvious entity objects are often identified in the problem-domain object model. Entity objects usually correspond to some concept in real life, outside the system, although this is not always the case. [Jacobson]

- **model [object]** *n.* **1.** (a) any domain object that models an application-domain thing. [Firesmith] (b) any instance of a model class. [Firesmith] **2.** an object that simulates

something in the problem domain of a business. [Lorenz]
Synonyms: APPLICATION OBJECT, BUSINESS OBJECT, CORE OBJECT, DOMAIN OBJECT, KEY OBJECT.
Contrast with: PRESENTATION OBJECT, VIEW OBJECT.
Examples: **1** A concept, document, event, device, financial instrument, interaction, location, organization, role, software, standard, substance, or system can each be modeled as model objects. [Firesmith] **2** An account is a model object for a bank. [Lorenz]
Commentary: Classes of model objects are relatively stable, because they are fundamental to the way the business works. [Lorenz]

- **problem-domain object** *n.* any object that has a direct counterpart in the application environment about which the system should handle information. [Jacobson]

- **view [object]** *n.* (a) any domain object that exists to provide a user view of (i.e., information about and control over) one or more model objects. [Firesmith] (b) any instance of a view class. [Firesmith]
Contrast with: MODEL OBJECT, PRESENTATION OBJECT.
Commentary: A model object may have more than one view object, and a view object may also be a controller object of its model object(s). Most view objects are also presentation objects. [Firesmith]
Kinds:
  + PANE OBJECT
  + PRESENTATION OBJECT
  + PROXY OBJECT

+ pane [object] *n.* any domain object that exists to presents a view of (i.e., information about and control over) one or more model objects.

Synonym: PRESENTATION OBJECT.

+ **presentation [object]** *n.* (a) any specialized view object that exists to provide a *formatted* view of (i.e., information about and control over) one or more model or view objects. [Firesmith] (b) any instance of a presentation class. [Firesmith]

Synonym: PANE OBJECT.

Contrast with: PRESENTATION CLASS, PROXY OBJECT.

Commentary: A model or view object may have more than one presentation object, and a presentation object may also be a controller object of its model or view object(s). [Firesmith]

+ **proxy [object]** *n.* (a) any local view object that represents (i.e., acts as a processor-specific variant of and communicates with) its remote model object. [Firesmith] (b) any instance of a proxy class. [Firesmith]

Contrast with: PRESENTATION OBJECT, PROXY CLASS.

Commentary: A proxy provides the local protocol of (and communicates with) its model on a remote processor. Proxies are used to create a single virtual address space across multiple processors. [Firesmith]

• **external object** *n.* any object that is external to the system, yet nevertheless affects the system. [Martin]

• **frame** *n.* any object in a knowledge-base that has a collection of rules as-

sociated with it. [Martin]

See also: RULE.

• **functor [object]** *n.* any object that models an operation. [Firesmith]

See also: REIFY.

• **future [object]** *n.* **1.** any object that transparently takes the place of another object that cannot yet be instantiated. [Firesmith] **2.** an asynchronous computation that will result, when completed, with a desired object.

Example: Futures are used as temporary incomplete proxies in GUI interfaces when users would have to wait too long for the desired view object to appear. [Firesmith]

• **generic object** *n.* any object (relative to some given Object Service) whose primary purpose for existence is unrelated to the Object Service. [OMG]

• **ideal object** *n.* **1.** any information-system object that is developed independently of the implementation environment. **2.** any business object that operates in the best possible way. **3.** any object in an ideal-object model. [Jacobson]

Antonym: REAL OBJECT.

See also: IDEAL-OBJECT MODEL.

• **immutable object** *n.* any object having a fixed structure and constant properties that cannot change their intrinsic values. [Firesmith, ODMG]

Synonyms: CONSTANT OBJECT.

Antonym: MUTABLE OBJECT, VARIABLE OBJECT.

Contrast with: LITERAL OBJECT.

• **implementation object** *n.* any object that serves as an implementation definition and resides in an implementation repository. [OMG]

• **incident object** *n.* any object used to represent an occurrence or event:

something that happens at a specific time. [Shlaer/Mellor]

Examples: An accident, event (in a nuclear physics experiment, flight, performance (of a play, etc.), service call (appliance repair), and system crash can each be modeled as an incident object.

- **instance [of a given class]** *n.* **1.** (a) any object instantiated according to the definition provided by the given

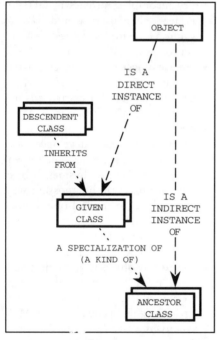

Instance

class. [Booch, CLOS, Firesmith, Shlaer/Mellor, Smalltalk] (b) any object behaving in the manner specified by the given class. [Rumbaugh, Wirfs-Brock] (c) any object created to conform to the description of the given class. [Jacobson] **2.** any object that is

a member of the extent of the class. [Embley, Firesmith] **3.** any single real-world thing. [Shlaer/Mellor] **4.** any actual object, waiting to perform services or holding some state data. [Lorenz] **5.** any object whose type is that of the class or a subtype of it. [Coleman, Martin/Odell]

Synonyms: **1** DIRECT INSTANCE, OBJECT **2** DIRECT INSTANCE, INDIRECT INSTANCE, OBJECT.

Kinds:
- DIRECT INSTANCE OF A GIVEN CLASS
- INDIRECT INSTANCE OF A GIVEN CLASS

- **direct instance [of a given class]** *n.* **1.** any object that has been explicitly instantiated using a constructor of the given class. [Eiffel, Firesmith, Meyer] **2.** any object that is an instance of a class but not an instance of any subclass of the class. [Rumbaugh]

Antonym: INDIRECT INSTANCE.

Commentary: Only concrete classes can have direct instances. A direct instance of a given class is not an instance of any specialized descendant of the given class and is only an indirect instance of all generalized ancestors of the given class. [Firesmith]

- **indirect instance [of a given class]** *n.* any object that is a direct instance of some specialized descendant of the given class. [Firesmith, Rumbaugh]

Antonym: DIRECT INSTANCE.

- **intangible object** *n.* any object that models something that is not tangible in the real world. [Firesmith]

Examples: Objects that model events, interactions, or states are all intan-

gible objects. [Firesmith]
Antonym: TANGIBLE OBJECT.

- **interaction object** *n.* any object that relates to two or more other objects in the model and that generally has a *transaction* or *contract* quality. [Shlaer/Mellor]
Synonym: ASSOCIATIVE OBJECT.
Examples: A purchase (related to buyer, seller, and thing purchased) and marriage (related to man and women), an electrical network, the piping in a refinery, and the tracks of a railroad can all be modeled as interaction objects.
- **interface object** *n.* **1.** (a) any object that serves to describe an interface. [OMG] (b) any object in a business system that represents a set of business operations that should be performed by a single object that communicates with the environment of the business. [Jacobson] **2.** any object in an information system that communicates with one or more actors in the environment of the information system.
Commentary: Interface objects reside in an interface repository. [OMG] Interface objects encapsulate all of the functionality specified in use cases that is directly dependent on the system environment. [Jacobson]
  - **central interface object** *n.* any interface object that contains other interface objects. [Jacobson]
  Commentary: A window containing buttons, menus, and scroll bar can all be modeled as interface objects. [Jacobson]
- **literal [object]** *n.* any constant primitive object having no properties but only a value equal to its name. [Firesmith]

Contrast with: IMMUTABLE OBJECT, OBJECT NAME.
Examples: Numbers, characters, and the Boolean objects *true* and *false* are all literal objects. [Firesmith]

- **maillon [object]** *n.* any object that allows either a local reference or remote reference for implementation. [Firesmith]
- **managed object** *n.* any client of System Management services, including the installation and activation service and the operational control service (dynamic behavior). These clients may be application objects, common facilities objects, or other object services. [OMG]
Commentary: The term is used for compatibility with system-management standards (the X/Open GDMO specification and ISO/IEC 10164 System Management Functions parts 1 to 4). [OMG]
- **manager object** *n.* any object that manages the work of several subordinate objects. [Coad]
Commentary: Challenge any class name that ends in *-er*. If it has no parts, change the name of the class to what each object is managing. If it has parts, put as much work in the parts that the parts know enough to do themselves. [Coad]
- **master object** *n.* any object that sends messages to other objects, but does not receive messages. [Firesmith]
Synonyms: ACTIVE OBJECT, ACTOR.
Contrast with: AGENT, SERVANT.
- **metaobject** *n.* **1.** any object that represents a type, operation, class, method, or other object-model entity that describes objects. [OMG] **2.** The metaobject protocol specifies a set of

O

generic functions that are defined by methods on classes and whose behavior defines the behavior of the Object System. Metaobjects are the instances of the classes on which those methods are defined. [CLOS]

See also: METACLASS, METHOD-COMBINATION OBJECT, STANDARD OBJECT.

Commentary: The Object System supplies a standard set of metaobjects, called *standard metaobjects,* which include the class *standard object* and instances of the classes *standard method, standard generic function,* and *method combination.* [CLOS]

- **method combination object** *n.* any object that encapsulates the method-combination type and options specified by the *:method-combination* option to forms that specify generic function options. [CLOS]

See also: METAOBJECT, METHOD-COMBINATION FACILITY, METHOD OBJECT.

- **method object** *n.* any object that contains a method function, a sequence of *parameter specializers* that specify when the given method is applicable, a lambda-list, and a sequence of *qualifiers* that are used by the method-combination facility to distinguish among methods. [CLOS]

See also: METHOD-COMBINATION OBJECT, PARAMETER SPECIALIZER.

Commentary: A method object is not a function and cannot be invoked as a function. [CLOS]

- **monolithic object** *n.* any *nonprimitive object* that conceptually has no *externally* discernible structure. [Berard]

Commentary: Internally, monolithic objects may be implemented using any appropriate objects. [Berard]

- **mutable object** *n.* any object that can

change the intrinsic values of its properties. [Firesmith, ODMG]

Antonym: IMMUTABLE OBJECT.

- **passive object** *n.* **1.** any object whose behavior must logically be triggered by an incoming message. [Firesmith] **2.** an object that does not encompass its own thread of control. [Booch]

Synonym: **2** SEQUENTIAL OBJECT.

Antonym: ACTIVE OBJECT.

Kinds:
  - BLOCKING OBJECT
  - SEQUENTIAL OBJECT

- **blocking object** *n.* any sequential (i.e., passive) object whose semantics are guaranteed in the presence of multiple threads of control. [Booch]

- **sequential object** *n.* **1.** any object that does not contain any threads of control (e.g., concurrent operations or nested concurrent objects). [Firesmith] **2.** any passive object whose semantics are guaranteed only in the presence of a single thread of control. [Booch]

Synonym: **1** PASSIVE OBJECT.

Antonym: CONCURRENT OBJECT.

Commentary: All sequential objects are passive, but not all passive objects are sequential. [Firesmith]

- **persistent object** *n.* **1.** any object that exists after the execution of the program, process, or thread that created it. [Firesmith, OMG] **2.** any object of an environment (and their dependents) that is recorded under some key in the environment. [Eiffel, Meyer]

Antonym: TRANSIENT OBJECT.

Contrast with: DYNAMIC OBJECT, STATIC OBJECT.

Example: Any object stored in an objectbase is a persistent object. [Firesmith]

Commentary: A persistent object exists until it is explicitly deleted. [OMG] A persistent object typically survives the process or thread that created it, existing until explicitly deleted. A persistent object also typically exists outside of the address space in which it was created. Persistent objects can be stored in object-oriented databases, extended relational databases, relational databases, Smalltalk images, files, etc. [Firesmith]

- **primitive object** *n.* any object that is provided by the environment, most typically by the programming language. [Berard]
Commentary: Primitive objects provide a basis for the construction of other, nonprimitive objects, and are a mechanism for communication among otherwise uncoupled objects. [Berard]

- **real object** *n.* any object in a real-object model. [Jacobson]
Antonym: IDEAL OBJECT.
See also: REAL-OBJECT MODEL.

- **receiver** *n.* the object to which a message is sent. [Smalltalk]
Synonym: SERVER.
Antonyms: CLIENT, SENDER.
Commentary: The receiver determines how to carry out the requested operation. [Smalltalk]

- **relationship object** *n.* any object modeling a relationship in a relationship set. [Embley]
See also: RELATIONSHIP, RELATIONAL OBJECT CLASS.
Example: Marriages in the relationship set *"Female Person is married to Male Person."* are relationship objects.

- **replicant object** *n.* any object that is a complete replication of another object. [Coad]

Contrast with: PROXY OBJECT.
Commentary: In a distributed architecture, use replicant objects to provide access to remote objects and a local copy of an object. [Coad]

- **resilient object** *n.* any object in a distributed application whose state is simultaneously maintained on several different nodes on the network in order that processing can continue with the preserved state, should a node containing the object become unavailable for any reason. [Berard]

- **role object** *n.* **1.** any model object that is an abstraction of a role. [Firesmith] **2.** any view object that is used to provide access to only those resources of its model object that abstracts a specific role that the model may play. [Firesmith] **3.** an abstraction of the purpose or assignment of a person, piece of equipment, or organization. [Shlaer/Mellor]
Contrast with: DYNAMIC CLASSIFICATION, ROLE, ROLE CLASS.

- **root object** *n.* **1.** a named persistent object that can be referenced by a program once it has opened the object database. [ODMG] **2.** the instance of some root class whose creation is the first act of system execution. [Eiffel, Firesmith, Meyer]
Contrast with: ROOT CLASS.

- **server [object]** *n.* an object providing response to a request for a service. [Firesmith, OMG, Wirfs-Brock]
Antonyms: CLIENT [OBJECT], SENDER.
Commentary: A given object may be a client for some requests and a server for other requests. [OMG]

- **special object** *n.* any sequence of values, all compatible with a given type. [Eiffel, Meyer]

O

Contrast with: STANDARD OBJECT.
Commentary: A special object may be a string or an array. [Eiffel, Meyer]

- **specification object** *n.* any objects that represents rules, standards, or quality criteria (as opposed to the tangible object or role that meets these standards. [Shlaer/Mellor]
Example: A recipe represents the rules for making a certain quantity of a certain food. [Shlaer/Mellor]
Commentary: Specification objects frequently show up in inventory or manufacturing applications. The have the quality of a standard or a definition. [Shlaer/Mellor]

- **standard object** *n.* any direct instance of a class that is the direct result of a Creation instruction or clone operation executed by the system. [Eiffel, Meyer]
Contrast with: SPECIAL OBJECT.

- **state-controlled object** *n.* any object that selects operations based on the current state as well as on the stimulus received. [Jacobson]
Antonym: STIMULUS-CONTROLLED OBJECT.

- **state-dependent object** *n.* any object, the behavior of which is dependent on the state as well as on the message received. [Firesmith]
Antonym: STATE-INDEPENDENT OBJECT.

- **state-independent object** *n.* any object, the behavior of which only depends on the message received. [Firesmith]
Antonym: STATE-INDEPENDENT OBJECT.

- **stimulus-controlled object** *n.* any object that will perform the same operation independent of the state in which a stimulus is received. [Jacobson]

Synonym: STATE-INDEPENDENT OBJECT.
Antonym: STATE-CONTROLLED OBJECT, STATE-DEPENDENT OBJECT.

- **strategy** *n.* any object that represents an algorithm. [Johnson]

- **subobject** *n.* **1.** any part of an object representing the data members inherited from a base class. [C++] **2.** any complex object in an enclosing complex object. [Eiffel, Meyer]
Contrast with: 1 COMPLETE OBJECT 2 COMPOSITE OBJECT.

- **subpart [object]** *n.* any object that is a component part of another (i.e., aggregate, superpart) object. [Embley]
Synonym: COMPONENT.
Antonyms: AGGREGATE, SUPERPART.
Contrast with: COMPONENT CLASS, SUBPART CLASS.

- **subtype object** *n.* any object representing a subtype. [Shlaer/Mellor]
Synonym: CHILD CLASS.

- **superpart [object]** *n.* any object that contains one or more other objects as component parts. [Embley]
Synonym: AGGREGATE.
Antonym: COMPONENT, SUBPART.
Contrast with: SUPERPART CLASS.

- **supertype object** *n.* any object representing a supertype. [Shlaer/Mellor]
Synonym: PARENT CLASS.

- **support object** *n.* any application domain-independent object that provides (1) a low-level utility or (2) application independence of the environment, database(s), or user-interface. [Firesmith]
Antonym: DOMAIN OBJECT.

- **utility object** *n.* any support object that provides a low-level utility. [Firesmith]
Commentary: Any queue, linked-list, set, stack, transporter, relay, etc.,

can be modeled as a utility object. [Firesmith]

• **tangible object** *n.* **1.** any object that models something tangible in the real world. [Firesmith] **2.** any abstraction of the actual existence of some thing in the physical world. [Shlaer/Mellor] *Examples:* Any pipe, pump, valve, and tank in a juice bottling plant can be modeled as a tangible object.

• **transaction object** *n.* any object that models a transaction (i.e., a recording or logging of any event of significance). A *transaction object* knows about a significant event, knows who the players are in that event, and calculates things pertaining to that event. [Coad] *See also:* TRANSACTION PATTERN.

• **transient object** *n.* any object that does not exist except during the execution of the program, process, or thread in which it was created. [Firesmith, Martin/Odell, OMG] *Antonym:* PERSISTENT OBJECT. *Kinds:*
  - DYNAMIC OBJECT
    + ORPHANED OBJECT
  - STATIC OBJECT

- **dynamic object** *n.* any object that is instantiated and destroyed at run-time. [Firesmith] *Antonym:* STATIC OBJECT. *Commentary:* A dynamic object has its memory allocated (e.g., from the heap) and deallocated during program execution. Dynamic objects are usually referenced via pointers. [Firesmith]

  + **orphaned object** *n.* any dynamic object that continues to use memory even though it is no longer referenced (e.g., via pointers). [Firesmith]

Commentary: Orphaned objects are a common bug in languages (C++) that do not support automatic garbage collection. [Firesmith]

- **static object** *n.* **1.** any object that is instantiated and whose memory is allocated at compile time and remains allocated until the program terminates. [Firesmith] **2.** any object that exists and retains the values of its properties throughout the execution of the entire program. [C++] *Antonym:* 1 DYNAMIC OBJECT, 2 AUTOMATIC OBJECT. *Commentary:* A static object lasts for the duration of program execution, but not after a program ceases to execute. [Firesmith]

• **type object** *n.* any object that serves as a type. [OMG]

• **user-interface (UI) object** *n.* any object that provides an interface between the end user and the system's model objects. [Lorenz] *Contrast with:* MODEL OBJECT. *Example:* An automatic teller machine (ATM) function menu window is a UI object for the ATM model object in a bank. [Lorenz] *Commentary:* The UI object classes change relatively frequently, as new technology, screen layouts, report formats, and usability studies require. [Lorenz]

Object *n.* (a) the single-system class that describes the similarities of all objects in the system, so every class will at least be a subclass of Object. (b) the single root class; it is the only class without a superclass. [Smalltalk] *Synonym:* ANY. [Eiffel]

O

Commentary: Every class is ultimately a subclass of class Object, except for Object itself, which has no superclass. [Smalltalk]

object abstraction *n.* any model of a single thing from the problem space (i.e., real world) or solution space. [Firesmith]

object-access model (OAM) *n.* the model that provides the complementary view to the object-communication model: a summary of the synchronous communication between state models and object instance data. [Shlaer/Mellor]

object-access-model document *n.* a one page document containing the object-access model. [Shlaer/Mellor]

object-and-attribute description document *n.* any document that lists each object and attribute in the model and provides an organized collection of the object, attribute, and domain descriptions. [Shlaer/Mellor]

object adapter *n.* the ORB component that provides object reference, activation, and state-related services to an object implementation (i.e., the primary way that an object implementation accesses services provided by the ORB). [OMG]

objectbase *n.* any database management system that stores objects rather than mere data. [Firesmith]

Synonym: OBJECT-DATABASE MANAGEMENT SYSTEM, OBJECT-ORIENTED DATABASE.

object-based *adj.* describing something based on the following concepts:
- ENCAPSULATION
- OBJECT
- IDENTITY
- PROPERTIES
- OPERATIONS
- MESSAGE PASSING [Firesmith]

Contrast with: CLASS-BASED, OBJECT-ORIENTED.

Commentary: The following important concepts that are required for full OO status are missing:
- CLASSES
- INHERITANCE
- POLYMORPHISM
- DYNAMIC BINDING [Firesmith]

object-based programming *n.* **1.** any programming resulting in programs that consist of collections of collaborating objects, which have a unique identity, encapsulate properties and operations, and communicate via message passing. [Firesmith] **2.** any form of programming in which programs are organized as cooperative collections of objects, each of which represents an instance of some type, and whose types are all members of a hierarchy of types united via other than inheritance relationships. [Booch]

Commentary: In such programs, types are generally viewed as static, whereas objects typically have a much more dynamic nature, somewhat constrained by the existence of static binding and monomorphism. [Booch]

Object-Behavior Analysis (OBA) *n.* that part of object-oriented analysis concerned with behavior, resulting in the specification of object-flow diagrams, event schemas, operation diagrams, states, trigger rules, and control conditions. [Martin]

Commentary: the term Object Behavior Analysis has also been used for the ParcPlace method developed by Goldberg and Rubin.

object-behavior concept *n.* any concept that describes some aspect of the dynamic behavior of the object types identified during object analysis and design. These concepts include operation, state, requests, and messages. [OADSIG]

Contrast with: ARCHITECTURE CONCEPT, GROUP-AND-VIEW CONCEPT, OBJECT-STRUCTURE CONCEPT.

Object-Behavior Design (OBD) *n.* that part of object-oriented design concerned with behavior (i.e., the design of methods). [Martin]

Synonym: METHOD DESIGN.

object-behavior model *n.* any object-oriented systems analysis model consisting of state nets used to model the behavior of an object in terms of its perceived states, the conditions and events that cause it to change from one state to another, the actions it performs, the actions performed on it, exceptions to normal behavior, and real-time constraints. [Embley]

See also: STATE NET.

objectchart *n.* any extension of a statechart (a.k.a. state transition diagram) useful in describing the dynamics of class behavior. [Henderson-Sellers]

[object] class *n.* **1.** any class of objects. [Firesmith] **2.** any set of logically-related objects having similar properties and behavior. [Embley]

Synonym: CLASS.

Contrast with: **1** ATTRIBUTE CLASS, CLUSTER CLASS, FRAMEWORK CLASS, METACLASS.

Commentary: The instances of some classes (e.g., metaclasses, clusters) need not be objects. [Firesmith]

Kinds:
- • ASSOCIATION
- • HIGH-LEVEL OBJECT CLASS
  - - DOMINANT HIGH-LEVEL OBJECT CLASS

  - - INDEPENDENT HIGH-LEVEL OBJECT CLASS
- • MEMBER CLASS
- • RELATIONAL OBJECT CLASS
- • SET CLASS
- • SINGLETON OBJECT CLASS
- • SUBPART CLASS
- • SUPERPART CLASS
- • UNIVERSE

• **association** *n.* any object class whose instances are sets. [Embley]

Synonym: SET CLASS.

Antonyms: MEMBER CLASS, UNIVERSE.

See also: IS-MEMBER-OF RELATIONSHIP SET.

• **high-level object class** *n.* any class that is created at a high level of abstraction to group a set of objects at lower levels of abstraction. [Embley]

Kinds:
- - DOMINANT HIGH-LEVEL OBJECT CLASS
- - INDEPENDENT HIGH-LEVEL OBJECT CLASS

- **dominant high-level object class** *n.* any high-level object class representing a set of objects that is named after the most important object class in the set. [Embley]

Antonym: INDEPENDENT HIGH-LEVEL OBJECT CLASS.

- **independent high-level object class** *n.* any high-level object class representing a set of objects that is not named after the most important object class in the set. [Embley]

Antonym: DOMINANT HIGH-LEVEL OBJECT CLASS.

• **member class** *n.* any object class whose instances are members of sets. [Embley]

Synonym: UNIVERSE.

Antonyms: ASSOCIATION, SET CLASS.

O

See also: IS-MEMBER-OF RELATIONSHIP SET.

- **relational object class** *n.* any object class whose instances are relationships. [Embley]
  See also: RELATIONSHIP, RELATIONSHIP OBJECT.

- **set class** *n.* any object class whose instances are sets. [Embley]
  Synonym: ASSOCIATION.
  Antonyms: MEMBER CLASS, UNIVERSE.
  See also: IS-MEMBER-OF RELATIONSHIP SET.

- **singleton object class** *n.* any object class that contains one and only one instance. [Embley]

- **subpart class** *n.* any object class whose instances are subparts. [Embley]
  Synonym: COMPONENT CLASS.
  Antonym: SUPERPART CLASS.
  See also: SUBPART, IS-PART-OF RELATIONSHIP SET.

- **superpart class** *n.* any object class whose instances are superparts. [Embley]
  Synonym: AGGREGATE CLASS.
  Antonym: SUBPART CLASS.
  See also: SUPERPART, IS-PART-OF RELATIONSHIP SET.

- **universe** *n.* any object class whose instances are members of sets. [Embley]
  Synonym: MEMBER CLASS.
  Antonyms: ASSOCIATION, SET CLASS.
  See also: IS-MEMBER-OF RELATIONSHIP SET.
  Commentary: The term *universe* is an often-used mathematical notation that denotes the set of objects from which subsets may be formed. [Embley]

object/class (O/C) *n.* a general term for objects and classes across the life cycle. [Henderson-Sellers]
Commentary: This term avoids fruit-less discussions about whether diagrams and relationships pertain to *either* objects *or* classes, when the answer is both, depending on the context. [Henderson-Sellers]

object-class cardinality constraint *n.* any constraint used to restrict the number of objects in an object class. [Embley]
Synonym: CLASS-CARDINALITY CONSTRAINT.

object communication *n.* **1.** the interaction of objects, consisting of message passing and exception raising. **2.** that which occurs when one object sends requests to other objects. [OADSIG]

object-communication model (OCM) *n.* the model that provides a graphical summary of event communication between state models and external entities, such as operators, physical devices, and objects in objects in other subsystems. [Shlaer/Mellor]
Commentary: A separate object communication model is built for each subsystem. [Shlaer/Mellor]

object connection *n.* any problem domain association or mapping between objects that represents what one object needs to know about some number of other objects in order to fulfill it responsibilities. [Coad]
See also: OBJECT-CONNECTION CONSTRAINT.
Contrast with: MESSAGE CONNECTION.
Commentary: There are two reasons for this knowing: (1) to know to whom to send a message (during a scenario); and (2) to support basic querying capabilities (given an object, tell me who the corresponding objects are). An object connection represents part of the state information needed by an object. [Coad]
Synonym: CONNECTION.

Commentary: The term *object connection* replaced the earlier term *instance connection*. [Coad]

Kinds:

- MESSAGE CONNECTION
- WHOLE-PART OBJECT CONNECTION

- **message connection** *n.* any connection that models the processing dependency of an object, indicating a need for services in order to fulfill its responsibilities. [Coad]

  See also: MESSAGE.

- **whole-part object connection** *n.* any connection that carries the added meaning of container-content, group-member, or assembly-part. [Coad]

  See also: WHOLE-PART STRUCTURE.

object-connection constraint *n.* any constraint that indicates the number of objects that an object knows. [Coad]

See also: OBJECT CONNECTION.

Commentary: Coad's graphical placement of this constraint is just the opposite of the entity-relationship convention for what the approach calls *multiplicities.* [Coad]

object coupling *n.* the degree of interdependence between two objects (e.g., the number of messages, the frequency of messages, and the number of arguments making values visible to other objects). [Coad]

Contrast with: CLASS COHESION.

Commentary: Low coupling is desirable because it produces better encapsulation and fewer objects are needlessly affected when making changes. [Coad]

object creation *n.* any event that causes an object to exist that is distinct from any other object. [OMG]

object database management system (ODBMS) *n.* any database management system that stores objects rather than mere data. [Firesmith]

Synonym: OBJECTBASE, OBJECT-ORIENTED DATABASE.

Rationale: This is the preferred term used by the object database management group. [Firesmith]

Commentary: An ODBMS logically encapsulates both data and operations within objects identified with object identifiers (OIDs) rather than key attributes. The inclusion of operations allows the storage of active objects rather than passive data. The type system of the object database is the same as the type system of the application software. An ODBMS makes persistent objects appear as programming language objects by using the object-oriented programming language (OOPL) as the data definition language (i.e., the OOPL and the objectbase share the same type schema) and data manipulation language (i.e., query language). The ODBMS extends the OOPL with transparently persistent objects, concurrency control, data recoverability, associative queries, and other database capabilities. [Firesmith]

object definition language (ODL) *n.* any specification language used to define the interfaces to object types that conform to the ODMG Object Model. [ODMG]

Contrast with: OBJECT MANIPULATION LANGUAGE.

object description *n.* any short, informative statement that allows one to tell, with certainty, whether or not a particular real-world thing is an instance of the object as conceptualized in the information model. [Shlaer/Mellor]

object-description table (ODT) *n.* any informal table used during require-

ments analysis or design for capturing information about an individual object. [Firesmith]
Contrast with: CLASS-DESCRIPTION TABLE.

object design *n.* the development activity during which the implementation of each class, association, attribute, and operation is determined. [Rumbaugh]

object destruction *n.* any event that causes an object to cease to exist and its associated resources to become available for reuse. [OMG]

object diagram *n.* **1.** any diagram used to show the existence of object and their relationships in the logical design of a system. An object diagram may represent all or part of the object structure of a system. A single object diagram represents a snapshot in time of an otherwise transitory event or configuration of objects. [Booch] **2.** any graphical representation of the object model. [Rumbaugh]
Commentary: Booch object diagrams are used during analysis to indicate the semantics of primary and secondary scenarios that provide a trace of the system's behavior. Object diagrams are used during design to illustrate the semantics of mechanisms in the logical design of a system.
Kinds:
- OBJECT-SCENARIO DIAGRAM
- DESIGN–OBJECT SCENARIO DIAGRAM

- **object-scenario diagram** *n.* any object diagram that documents a single scenario during domain analysis. [Booch]
Contrast with: DESIGN–OBJECT SCENARIO DIAGRAM.

- **design–object-scenario diagram** *n.* any object-scenario diagram updated

during design. [Booch]
Contrast with: OBJECT-SCENARIO DIAGRAM.

object-flow diagram (OFD) *n.* any diagram that documents the objects that flow from activity to activity. [Martin]
Commentary: Object-flow diagrams are similar to data-flow diagrams (DFDs), because they depict activities interfacing with other activities. [Martin]

object dictionary *n.* **1.** any comprehensive dictionary defining all object-oriented entities (e.g., objects, classes, clusters, properties, operations, exceptions) in an application. **2.** any comprehensive dictionary defining all of the objects (or classes) in an application.
Synonyms: DATA DICTIONARY, CLASS DICTIONARY, PROJECT DICTIONARY.
Rationale: The term *data dictionary* has historically implied only data (i.e., attributes), and the terms *object dictionary* and *class dictionary* may be interpreted too limitedly (e.g., definition **2**). The term *project dictionary* is least subject to misinterpretation.

object identifier (OID) *n.* the single identifier (a.k.a. handle) permanently assigned to each object that is:
- Unique within some specified scope or domain (e.g., an application)
- Independent of the instance's:
  - Properties
  - State
  - [Possibly dynamic] classification
- Constant during the existence of the object. [C++, Firesmith, Martin/ Odell, ODMG]
Synonym: IDENTIFIER, OBJECT POINTER, OBJECT REFERENCE.
Contrast with: HANDLE, KEY, OBJECT NAME.
See also: IDENTITY.

Rationale: Term used by the ODMG.
Commentary: An identifier is typically implemented as a unique arbitrary bit pattern generated strictly for the purpose of uniquely identifying a specific object. Although some languages (e.g., C++) use the address of an object as its identifier, this does not work in a distributed system. [Firesmith] An identifier may also be implemented as an arbitrarily long sequence of letters and digits. [C++].
Kinds:
- LOCAL IDENTIFIER
- UNIVERSAL IDENTIFIER

- **local identifier (LID)** *n.* any object identifier that is local to a specific processor or process. [Firesmith]
Antonym: UNIVERSAL IDENTIFIER.
- **universal identifier (UID)** *n.* any system-wide object identifier. [Firesmith]
Antonym: LOCAL IDENTIFIER.
Commentary: UIDs are required in distributed applications with multiple address spaces in which using the local address does not uniquely identify an object, especially if that object is to be moved around the system. [Firesmith]

objectification *n.* the process of reconstructing an *object* from possibly non-object-oriented components. [Berard]
Commentary: Objectification is typically used to reconstruct an object after it has been transmitted over a communication link or after it has been stored in a relational database. [Berard]

object implementation *n.* **1.** the hidden implementation of any object. [Firesmith] **2.** any implementation. [OMG]
Antonym: OBJECT INTERFACE.
Contrast with: CLASS IMPLEMENTATION,

OBJECT PROTOCOL.
Commentary: Definition **2** is too general because other things besides objects (e.g., clusters, operations) have implementations.

object-interaction graph *n.* any graph providing a visual representation of how functionality is distributed across the objects of a system, showing the run-time messaging of objects to support a system operation. [Coleman]
Synonym: INTERACTION DIAGRAM.
Contrast with: TIMING DIAGRAM.

object-interaction model *n.* any model that allows an analyst to describe the interaction among objects. [Embley]
Synonym: INTERACTION MODEL.
See also: INTERACTION.

object interface *n.* **1.** the interface of any individual object. [Firesmith] **2.** any description of a set of possible uses of an object; specifically, a set of potential requests in which an object can meaningfully participate. [Jacobson, OMG] **3.** any listing of the operations and attributes that an object provides. This includes the signatures of the operations, and the types of the attributes. An interface definition ideally includes the semantics as well. [OMG] **4.** the union of the object's type interfaces. [OMG]
Antonym: OBJECT IMPLEMENTATION.
Contrast with: CLASS INTERFACE, CLUSTER INTERFACE, OBJECT PROTOCOL, TYPE INTERFACE.
Commentary: The inbound interface of an object includes the union of all visible instance features declared in the type(s) of the object. The inbound object interface includes the signatures of all messages in its protocol, thereby providing a description of its possible

O

uses. Many methodologists do not consider the attributes to be a part of the interface because they should be hidden, encapsulated in the implementation. [Firesmith]

Object Management Group™ (OMG) *n.* the leading international trade association dedicated to maximizing the portability, reusability, and interoperability of software by producing a framework and specifications for commercially available object-oriented environments. [Firesmith]

Commentary: The OMG provides an open forum for industry discussion, education, and promotion of OMG endorsed object technology. [Firesmith]

object manipulation language (OML) *n.* the language used for retrieving objects from the objectbase and modifying them. [ODMG]

Contrast with: OBJECT DEFINITION LANGUAGE.

object model *n.* **1.** (a) any description of the structure of the objects in a system including their identity, relationships to other objects, attributes, and operations. [Rumbaugh] (b) any model described in an object-oriented language that consists of a set of classes and the associations between them. [Jacobson] (c) any model defining the static structure of an application, used to capture the concepts that exist in the problem domain and the relationships between them. It can represent classes, attributes, and relationships between classes. [Coleman] (d) any model representing objects and their responsibilities. [Coad] **2.** (a) the collection of principles that form the foundation of object-oriented design. [Booch] (b) any software engineering paradigm emphasizing the principles of abstraction, encapsulation, modularity, hierarchy, typing, concurrency, and persistence. [Booch]

Contrast with: BEHAVIORAL MODEL, CONFIGURATION MODEL, DATA MODEL, DYNAMIC MODEL, FUNCTIONAL MODEL, INTERACTION MODEL, INTERFACE MODEL, LANGUAGE MODEL, LIFE-CYCLE MODEL, OPERATION MODEL, PRESENTATION MODEL, SEMANTIC MODEL, STATE MODEL, STRUCTURAL MODEL, TIMING MODEL, USE-CASE MODEL.

Kinds:
- DOMAIN OBJECT MODEL
- IDEAL OBJECT MODEL
- PRIVATE OBJECT MODULE
- PUBLIC OBJECT MODULE
- REAL OBJECT MODEL

- **domain object model** *n.* any object model that consists of problem-domain objects and serves as a support for the development of the requirements model. [Jacobson]

  See also: USE CASE VIEW.

  Commentary: A logical and surveyable domain object model is used to communicate with the potential users, and also to get a stable basis for the descriptions of the use cases. [Jacobson]

- **ideal object model** *n.* **1.** any object model of a business that contains only those objects required to perform the use cases to run the business in the best possible way. [Jacobson] **2.** any object-model of an information system that is independent of the implementation environment. [Jacobson]

  Antonym: REAL OBJECT MODEL.

  See also: IDEAL OBJECT, IDEAL DESIGN.

- **private object module** *n.* any object module that is hidden within, and therefore cannot be accessed from the outside of, its enclosing block. [Jacobson]

Antonym: PUBLIC OBJECT MODULE.

- **public object module** *n.* any object module that is exported from, and therefore can be accessed from the outside of, its enclosing block. [Jacobson] *Antonym:* PRIVATE OBJECT MODULE.

- **real object model** *n.* **1.** any object model of a business that takes into consideration the restrictions on the business. [Jacobson] **2.** any object model of an information system that takes into consideration the implementation environment (e.g., the problems and limitations of the implementation language and database. [Jacobson]
Antonym: IDEAL OBJECT MODEL.
See also: REAL OBJECT.

object model documentation set *n.* any set of documentation consisting of an object model (usually presented with a number of views, highlighting different aspects of the model), scenario views (one for each feature of the system under consideration), attribute descriptions, and service descriptions. [Coad]

[object-model] strategy *n.* any plan of action, intended to accomplish a specific objective, with regard to an object model. [Coad]
Commentary: Object model strategies fall into four major categories, referred to as four major activities:
- Identifying system purpose and features
- Selecting objects
- Establishing responsibilities
- Working out dynamics with scenarios. [Coad]

object-model view *n.* any object diagram of a subset of an object model. [Jacobson]
Kinds:

- GLOBAL OBJECT VIEW
- LOCAL OBJECT VIEW
- USE CASE VIEW
- VIEW OF PARTICIPATING OBJECTS

- **global object view** *n.* any object model view that shows either the entire object model or a subsystem of the object model. [Jacobson]
Antonym: LOCAL OBJECT VIEW.
Contrast with: VIEW OF PARTICIPATING OBJECTS.

- **local object view** *n.* any object-model view that shows an object with all of its relations to and from other objects. [Jacobson]
Antonym: GLOBAL OBJECT VIEW.
Contrast with: VIEW OF PARTICIPATING OBJECTS.

- **use case view** *n.* any object-model view that shows the objects and associations that participate in a specific use case. [Jacobson]
Synonym: VIEW OF PARTICIPATING OBJECTS.
Contrast with: GLOBAL OBJECT VIEW, LOCAL OBJECT VIEW.
See also: USE CASE.
Commentary: The purpose of this type of view is to illustrate how the behavior of a use case is distributed over the objects and how the objects interact to realize the course of events in a use case. The union of all views of participating objects is the global object view. [Jacobson]

- **view of participating objects** *n.* any object-model view that shows the objects and associations that participate in a specific use case. [Jacobson]
Synonym: USE CASE VIEW.
Contrast with: GLOBAL OBJECT VIEW, LOCAL OBJECT VIEW.
See also: USE CASE.

O

Commentary: The purpose of this type of view is to illustrate how the behavior of a use case is distributed over the objects and how the objects interact to realize the course of events in a use case. The union of all views of participating objects is the global object view. [Jacobson]

Object Modeling Technique (OMT) *n.* the Rumbaugh et al. object-oriented development method that uses object, dynamic, and functional models throughout the development life cycle. [Rumbaugh]

object name *n.* any name that uniquely refers to a single object within the scope of the definition of the name. [Firesmith, ODMG, OMG]
Contrast with: OBJECT IDENTIFIER.
Commentary: A name is not explicitly defined as an attribute of an object. Unlike an OID, a name need not be constant during the existence of the object, and an object may have one or more names. [ODMG, OMG] An object may also be known by one or more aliases from elsewhere in the system. [Henderson-Sellers]

object-object inheritance *n.* any inheritance that transfers the *state* of one object to another. [Martin/Odell]
Synonym: DELEGATION.

object-orientation *n.* **1.** (a) the paradigm that uses objects with identity that encapsulate properties and operations, message passing, classes, inheritance, polymorphism, and dynamic binding to develop solutions that model problem domains. [Firesmith, Lorenz] (b) any technique based on the concepts of object, class, instance, and inheritance. [Jacobson] **2.** the use of objects as the atoms of modeling. [Coleman]

object-oriented (OO) *adj.* **1.** describing

something based on the following concepts:
  – ENCAPSULATION
  – OBJECT:
    - IDENTITY
    - PROPERTIES
    - OPERATIONS
  – MESSAGE PASSING
  – CLASSES
  – INHERITANCE
  – POLYMORPHISM
  – DYNAMIC BINDING [FIRESMITH]
2. describing any software development strategy that organizes software as a collection of objects that contain both data structure and behavior. [Rumbaugh]
Commentary: The term object-oriented is primarily used to describe CASE tools, databases, development methods, and programming languages. [Firesmith]

object-oriented analysis (OOA) *n.* the discovery, analysis, and specification of requirements in terms of objects with identity that encapsulate properties and operations, message passing, classes, inheritance, polymorphism, and dynamic binding. [Firesmith]
Contrast with: OBJECT-ORIENTED DESIGN (OOD).
Commentary: The requirements are typically developed and organized in increments of clusters and subsystems. [Firesmith] Booch restricts OOA to a single project, whereas Martin makes OOA enterprise wide.
Kinds:
  • OBJECT-ORIENTED DOMAIN ANALYSIS
  • OBJECT-ORIENTED REQUIREMENTS ANALYSIS
  • OBJECT-ORIENTED SYSTEMS ANALYSIS

• **object-oriented domain analysis
(OODA)** *n.* the object-oriented analysis of *application-domain-independent* requirements, typically for reuse on multiple projects within that application domain. [Firesmith]
Antonym: OBJECT-ORIENTED REQUIREMENTS ANALYSIS.
Contrast with: OBJECT-ORIENTED DOMAIN DESIGN.

• **object-oriented requirements analysis (OORA)** *n.* the object-oriented analysis of *application-domain-dependent* software requirements for use on a single project. [Firesmith]
Antonym: OBJECT-ORIENTED DOMAIN ANALYSIS.
Contrast with: OBJECT-ORIENTED DESIGN, OBJECT-ORIENTED SYSTEMS DESIGN.

• **object-oriented systems analysis (OSA)** *n.* **1.** the object-oriented analysis of *application-domain-dependent* software requirements for use on a single project. [Firesmith] **2.** the study of a specific domain of interacting objects for the purpose of understanding and documenting their essential characteristics. [Embley]
Antonym: **1** OBJECT-ORIENTED DOMAIN ANALYSIS.
Contrast with: OBJECT-ORIENTED REQUIREMENTS ANALYSIS.

object-oriented application development (OOAD) *n.* the class of object-oriented development methods used for the development of project-specific objects, classes, and clusters. [Firesmith]

object-oriented architecture *n.* **1.** any architecture consisting of objects, classes, and the collaboration and inheritance relationships among them. [Firesmith] **2.** an architecture documented using object interaction graphs, class descriptions, and the inheritance graphs. [Coleman]

object-oriented CASE (OO-CASE) tool *n.* any computer-aided software engineering (CASE) tool that supports object-oriented analysis, design, programming, or testing. [Firesmith, Martin]

object-oriented database (OODB) *n.* any database that stores objects rather than mere data. [Firesmith, Martin]
Synonym: OBJECTBASE, OBJECT DATABASE, OBJECT-ORIENTED DATABASE MANAGEMENT SYSTEM.
Commentary: Object databases logically encapsulate both data and operations within objects. Object databases use object identifiers (OIDs) rather than key attributes. The type system of the object database is the same as the types system of the application software. The object-oriented programming language is used as the data definition language and the data manipulation language. [Firesmith] The stored data are generally *active* rather than *passive*. [Martin]

object-oriented decomposition *n.* **1.** the decomposition of a system into its component objects and classes. [Booch, Firesmith] **2.** the decomposition of an aggregate object into its component objects. [Firesmith]

object-oriented design (OOD) *n.* **1.** the design of an application in terms of objects, classes, clusters, frameworks, and their interactions. [Firesmith] **2.** the design of software systems as structured collections of classes. [Eiffel, Meyer] **3.** design based on object-oriented decomposition using a notation for logical and physical as well as static and dynamic models. [Booch] **4.** the design of classes and methods. [Martin]

Contrast with: OBJECT-ORIENTED RE-
QUIREMENTS ANALYSIS (OORA), OBJECT-
ORIENTED DOMAIN DESIGN (OODD).
Kinds:
- OBJECT-ORIENTED
  IMPLEMENTATION DESIGN
- OBJECT-ORIENTED LOGICAL DESIGN
- OBJECT-ORIENTED SYSTEMS DESIGN

- **object-oriented implementation design (OOID)** *n.* the language-dependent design of application-specific objects, classes, clusters, and their static
relationships and dynamic interactions. [Firesmith]
- **object-oriented logical design
(OOLD)** *n.* the language-independent
design of application-specific objects,
classes, clusters, and their static relationships and dynamic interactions.
[Firesmith]
- **object-oriented systems design
(OSD)** *n.* **1.** any object-oriented logical and implementation design at the
systems level. [Firesmith] **2.** any object-oriented system design including
system formalization, lexicalization,
normalization, and encapsulation.
[Embley]

**Object-Oriented Design Language
(OODLE)** *n.* a language-independent
graphical notation for depicting the design of an object-oriented program, library, or environment. [Shlaer/Mellor]

object-oriented development (OOD)
n. **1.** the development of systems or software using object-orientation. [Fire-
smith] **2.** any software development
technique that uses objects as a basis for
analysis, design, and implementation.
[Rumbaugh]

**object-oriented domain design
(OODD)** *n.* the design of common objects, classes, clusters, and frameworks

from a specific application domain,
typically for reuse on multiple projects
within that application domain. [Fire-
smith]
Contrast with: OBJECT-ORIENTED DE-
SIGN.

**object-oriented domain programming
(OODP)** *n.* the programming of common objects, classes, subclusters, and
frameworks from a specific application
domain, typically for reuse on multiple
projects within that application domain. [Firesmith]
Contrast with: OBJECT-ORIENTED PRO-
GRAMMING.

**object-oriented implementation design
(OOID)** *n.* the language-dependent design of application-specific objects, classes, clusters, and their static relationships
and dynamic interactions. [Firesmith]
Contrast with: OBJECT-ORIENTED LOG-
ICAL DESIGN.

**object-oriented integration and test
(OOIT)** *n.* the integration and testing
of application-specific objects, classes,
and clusters. [Firesmith]

object-oriented logical design (OOLD)
n. the language-independent design of
application-specific objects, classes, clusters, and their static relationships and
dynamic interactions.
Contrast with: OBJECT-ORIENTED IM-
PLEMENTATION DESIGN.

object-oriented programming (OOP)
n. any application-specific programming resulting in programs that consist
of collections of collaborating objects,
which have a unique identity, encapsulate properties and operations, communicate via message passing, any are instances of classes related by inheritance,
polymorphism, and dynamic binding.
[Booch, Firesmith]

Contrast with: OBJECT-ORIENTED DO-MAIN PROGRAMMING.

object-oriented programming language (OOPL) *n.* **1.** any programming language that supports objects with identity that encapsulate properties and operations that collaborate using message passing as well as classes related by inheritance, polymorphism, and (possibly dynamic) binding. [Firesmith] **2.** any language that supports objects (combining identity, data, and operations), method resolution, and inheritance. [Rumbaugh]

Kinds:
- HYBRID OBJECT-ORIENTED PROGRAMMING LANGUAGE
- PURE OBJECT-ORIENTED PROGRAMMING LANGUAGE

- **hybrid object-oriented programming language** *n.* any object-oriented programming language that has both object-oriented types (types implemented by classes) and nonobject-oriented types (data types). [Firesmith, Rumbaugh, Wirfs-Brock]
Antonym: PURE OBJECT-ORIENTED PROGRAMMING LANGUAGE.
Examples: Ada95, C++, CLOS, object COBOL, Objective C, and object Pascal are all hybrid OOPLs. [Firesmith]
Commentary: A hybrid OOPL also supports nonobject-oriented development. [Firesmith]

- **pure object-oriented programming language** *n.* any object-oriented programming language that only has object-oriented types (types implemented by classes). [Firesmith]
Antonym: HYBRID OBJECT-ORIENTED PROGRAMMING LANGUAGE.
Examples: Eiffel and Smalltalk are pure OOPLs. [Firesmith]

Commentary: A pure OOPL only supports object-oriented development. [Firesmith]

object-oriented software engineering (OOSE) *n.* **1.** the engineering of object-oriented software. [Firesmith] **2.** the subset of the Objectory method documented in the book of the same name. [Jacobson]
Contrast with: OBJECTORY.

Object-Oriented Specification and Design Language (OOSDL) *n.* Firesmith's formal language for the specification of object-oriented requirements and designs. [Firesmith]

object-oriented systems design (OSD) *n.* **1.** any object-oriented logical and implementation design at the systems level. [Firesmith] **2.** any object-oriented system design including system formalization, lexicalization, normalization, and encapsulation. [Embley]

object-oriented systems implementation (OSI) *n.* coding and optimizing a design for a particular hardware and software environment. OSI activities involved include data and process distribution, software reuse, custom code development, optimization, and fine tuning. [Embley]

object-oriented systems specification (OSS) *n.* the formulation of a system-development contract for a client. OSS activities include system-boundary definition, rapid prototyping, performance and functional requirements specification, interface specification, and contract writing. [Embley]

Objectory *n.* the Object Factory for software development is the product and trademark of Objective Systems SF AB, and is a modern object-oriented development process consisting of four levels: architecture, method, process, and tools. [Jacobson]

Contrast with: OBJECT-ORIENTED SOFTWARE ENGINEERING.

object pointer *n.* the unique identifier of any object. [Smalltalk]

Synonym: HANDLE, IDENTIFIER, IDENTITY, OBJECT IDENTIFIER, OBJECT REFERENCE, OID.

object protocol *n.* the protocol of any object. [Firesmith]

Synonym: OBJECT INTERFACE.

Antonym: OBJECT IMPLEMENTATION.

Contrast with: CLASS PROTOCOL, CLUSTER PROTOCOL, OPERATION PROTOCOL.

Commentary: The inbound protocol of an object includes the union of all visible instance features declared in the type(s) of the object. The inbound object protocol includes the signatures of all messages in its protocol, thereby providing a description of its possible uses. Many methodologists do not consider the attributes to be a part of the protocol because they should be hidden, encapsulated in the implementation. [Firesmith]

object reference *n.* **1.** any object name that reliably denotes a particular object. **2.** the information needed to specify an object within an ORB. [OMG]

Contrast with: IDENTIFIER, OBJECT NAME.

Commentary: Specifically, an object reference will identify the same object each time the reference is used in a request (subject to certain pragmatic limits of space and time). An object may be denoted by multiple, distinct object references.

- **externalized object reference** *n.* any object reference expressed as an ORB-specific string that is suitable for storage in files or other external media. [OMG]

object-relationship diagram *n.* any diagram that maps the relationships among object types. [Martin]

Commentary: An object-relationship diagram is similar to an entity-relationship diagram. [Martin]

object-relationship model (ORM) *n.* any model consisting of objects and relationships, object classes and relationship sets, constraints, and notes. [Embley]

Synonym: SEMANTIC MODEL.

Object Request Broker™ (ORB) *n.* the means by which objects make and receive requests and responses. [OMG]

Object Services (OS) *n.* any collection of services with object interfaces that provide basic functions for object life-cycle management and storage (e.g., creation / deletion, activation / passivation, identification / location). [OMG]

Synonym: CORBA SERVICES.

object slicing *n.* the metaphor that describes how an object can be an instance in more than one OOPL class by *slicing* it into multiple *pieces*. [Martin/Odell]

Commentary: Each *piece* is implemented as an instance of one of the multiple classes. The object-slicing mechanism does this by maintaining one *whole* copy of an object as a Conceptual Object linked to its many Implementation Object *pieces*. [Martin/Odell]

object-specification document *n.* any document that presents the entire information model in text. [Shlaer/Mellor]

Commentary: It is intended to describe the reality being modeled—the real-world matter—and show how that reality has been formalized in the model.

object state *n.* **1.** (a) any status, situation,

condition, mode, or life cycle phase of an object or class during which certain rules of overall behavior (e.g., response to messages) apply. [Embley, Firesmith, Jacobson] (b) any situation or condition of the object during which certain physical laws, rules, and policies apply; a stage in the life cycle of a typical instance of the object. [Shlaer/Mellor] (c) the cumulative results of the behavior of an object or class. [Booch] (d) the information about the history of previous requests needed to determine the behavior of future requests. [OMG] **2.** the equivalence class (i.e., set of all equivalent members) of state attribute values, state links, and the states of parts that produces the same overall behavior of the associated object or class. [Firesmith, Jacobson] **3.** (a) the current value of all properties of an object or class. [Booch, Coad, Lorenz, OADSIG, Rumbaugh] (b) the time varying properties of an object that affect that object's behavior. [OMG] (c) the collection of associations that an object has with other objects. [Martin/Odell] **4.** the collection of types that apply to an object. [Martin/Odell] **5.** in the ROOM method, any quiescent point where the object is waiting for an event to trigger it back into action.
Synonym: STATE.
Contrast with: STATE ATTRIBUTE, STATE COMPONENT, STATE LINK.
Examples: Enabled and *Disabled* are often states of devices.
Commentary: The state of an object or class is typically implemented as the equivalence class of state attribute values, state links, and the states of parts that produces the same overall behavior. [Firesmith] States may be used to model a nondiscrete or long-running activity, or a continuous activity that must be interrupted to allow a response to events or conditions that affect an object. [Embley] Definitions **2** and **3** are quite different. Definition **2** is a way of implementing definition **1**, whereas definition **3** is inconsistent with definition **1**. Definition **4** implies dynamic typing in which the type of an object changes each time its state changes.
Kinds:
- AGGREGATE STATE
- ATOMIC STATE
- BEGIN STATE
- CREATION STATE
- CURRENT STATE
- END STATE
- FINAL STATE
- INITIAL STATE
- START STATE
- STOP STATE
- SUPERSTATE
- **aggregate state** *n.* any state that contains one or more substates.
Synonym: SUPERSTATE.
Antonym: ATOMIC STATE.
- **atomic state** *n.* any state that does not contain any substates
Antonym: AGGREGATE STATE.
- **begin state** *n.* **1.** any atomic state of an object or class upon instantiation or reinitialization. [Firesmith] **2.** any first state in which an instance first comes into existence. [Shlaer/Mellor]
Synonyms: CREATION STATE, INITIAL STATE, START STATE.
Antonyms: END STATE, FINAL STATE, STOP STATE.
Commentary: Use together with the term *end state.*
- **creation state** *n.* **1.** any atomic state of an object or class upon instantiation or

reinitialization. [Firesmith] **2.** any first state in which an instance first comes into existence. [Shlaer/Mellor]
Synonyms: BEGIN STATE, INITIAL STATE, START STATE.
Antonyms: END STATE, FINAL STATE, STOP STATE.
Commentary: Term used by Shlaer/Mellor.

- **current state** *n.* the state any instance is in. [Shlaer/Mellor]
- **end state** *n.* **1.** any terminal state from which the object or class cannot transition. [Firesmith] **2.** any state that serves as the end of the life cycle for an instance. [Shlaer/Mellor]
Synonyms: FINAL STATE, STOP STATE.
Antonyms: CREATION STATE, INITIAL STATE, START STATE.
Commentary: Use together with the term *begin state*.
- **final state** *n.* **1.** any terminal state from which the object or class cannot transition. [Firesmith] **2.** any state that serves as the end of the life cycle for an instance. [Shlaer/Mellor]
Synonyms: END STATE, STOP STATE.
Antonyms: CREATION STATE, INITIAL STATE, START STATE.
Commentary: Use together with INITIAL STATE.
- **initial state** *n.* **1.** any atomic state of an object or class upon instantiation or reinitialization. [Firesmith] **2.** any first state in which an instance first comes into existence. [Shlaer/Mellor]
Synonyms: BEGIN STATE, CREATION STATE, START STATE.
Antonyms: END STATE, FINAL STATE, STOP STATE.
Commentary: Use together with the term *final state*.
- **start state** *n.* **1.** any atomic state of an object or class upon instantiation or reinitialization. [Firesmith] **2.** any first state in which an instance first comes into existence. [Shlaer/Mellor]
Synonyms: BEGIN STATE, CREATION STATE, INITIAL STATE.
Antonyms: END STATE, FINAL STATE, STOP STATE.
Commentary: Term used by Firesmith. Use together with the term *stop state*.
- **stop state** *n.* **1.** any terminal state from which the object or class cannot transition. [Firesmith] **2.** any state that serves as the end of the life cycle for an instance. [Shlaer/Mellor]
Synonyms: END STATE, FINAL STATE.
Antonyms: CREATION STATE, INITIAL STATE, START STATE.
Commentary: Term used by Firesmith. Use together with the term *start state*.
- **superstate** *n.* any state that contains one or more substates.
Synonym: AGGREGATE STATE.
Antonym: ATOMIC STATE.

object state diagram *n.* any diagram that documents the states or modes of an object over time and the transitions between them. [Coad]
Synonyms: STATE CHART, STATE TRANSITION DIAGRAM.
See also: OBJECT STATE.

object structure *n.* any graph whose vertices represent objects and whose arcs represent relationships among those objects. The object structure of a system is represented by a set of object diagrams. [Booch]

Object Structure Analysis (OSA) *n.* that part of object-oriented analysis concerned with structure, including the identification of object types and associations and the development of object structure diagrams, object-relationship diagrams, and composed-of diagrams. [Martin]

object-structure concept *n.* any concept that identifies some aspect of the object types, the attribute types, and the relationship types identified during object analysis and design. [OADSIG] *Contrast with:* ARCHITECTURE CONCEPT, GROUP-AND-VIEW CONCEPT.

Object-Structure Design (OSD) *n.* that part of object-oriented design concerned with classes, methods, and inheritance. [Martin]

object tag *n.* any object name, including its value, that is for identification. [Coad] *Example:* See <name>John Doe in the following file listing:

    <ObjectDefn>
    <ClassName>Employee
    <ObjectID><id>71
    <name>John Doe
    <transaction><id>34
    <transaction><id>14
    <\ObjectDefn>

object type *n.* **1.** any type, the extension of which is a set of objects (literally, a set of values that identify objects). [OMG] **2.** any definition of some set of object instances with similar behavior. [OADSIG] **3.** any conceptual notion specifying a family of objects without stipulating how they are implemented. [Martin] *Synonym:* CONCEPT. *Contrast with:* INTERFACE TYPE. *Example:* An object type might be Invoice and a corresponding object might be Invoice #51783. [Martin] *Commentary:* A type is a semantic property. An object type is satisfied only by (values that identify) objects. The characteristics of an object type is its definition, any extension of its defi-

nition, its supertypes, and its subtypes. *Kinds:*

- ABSTRACT OBJECT TYPE
- BUSINESS LOGIC OBJECT TYPE
- DESIGN MODEL OBJECT TYPE
- DIALOG OBJECT TYPE
- INFORMATION MANAGEMENT OBJECT TYPE
- LEGACY SYSTEM OBJECT TYPE
- PRESENTATION OBJECT TYPE
- PROBLEM-DOMAIN OBJECT TYPE
- REAL-WORLD OBJECT TYPE
- USER INTERFACE METAPHOR
- USER INTERFACE OBJECT TYPE

- **abstract object type** *n.* any abstraction used to group common characteristics of real-world object types. [OADSIG]
- **business logic object type** *n.* any object type that provides the functionality of the application. [OADSIG]
- **design model object type** *n.* any object type that is used in a design model. [OADSIG]
- **dialog object type** *n.* any user interface object type that maintains the state of the interface and from the user's perception controls its overall behavior. [OADSIG] *Example:* The type of the open file dialogue provided by a word processor can be modeled as a dialog object type. [OADSIG]
- **information management object type** *n.* any object type that provides persistent storage for the application. [OADSIG] *Example:* A record definition in a logical database design can be modeled as an information management object type. [OADSIG]
- **legacy system object type** *n.* any object type that encapsulates an existing

O

nonobject-oriented application or application component, by defining an object-oriented interface so that it can be reused. [OADSIG]

- **presentation object type** *n.* any user interface object type that describes the visual appearance of the user interface. [OADSIG]
  Examples: The chart of today's stock usage, a box object, a line object, and a tree object can all be modeled as presentation object types. [OADSIG]
- **problem-domain object type** *n.* any tangible or conceptual real-world object type. [OADSIG]
- **real-world object type** *n.* any abstraction of a tangible real-world object identified during strategic modeling. [OADSIG]
- **user interface metaphor** *n.* any user interface object type that ensures that users can understand the user interface. [OADSIG]
- **user interface object type** *n.* any object used to define the user interface for the application. [OADSIG]

object veneer *n.* any thin coating of objects (e.g., a wrapper) placed around non-object-oriented software used to simplify its integration with object-oriented software by making it look object-oriented.

observer [pattern] *n.* the behavioral object design pattern that allows one object to notify its dependents when it changes state so that they can be updated. [Gamma, Helm, Johnson, and Vlissides]
Synonym: DEPENDENTS, PUBLISH-SUBSCRIBE.
Example: Smalltalk's model/view/controller user interface framework is an example usage of the observer pattern.

ODBMS profile *n.* the OMG profile for object database management systems defined in the ODMG-93 standard.

offer [a use case] *v. -ed, -ing* any set of objects offer a use case only if the objects are required in the system for the given use case to execute. [Jacobson]
See also: USE CASE.

OMA-compliant application *n.* any application consisting of a set of interacting classes and instances that interact via the ORB and that conform to the OMA protocol definitions and interface specifications outlined in the OMA Guide. [OMG]

OMG object model *n.* the OMG model that defines a common object semantics for specifying the externally visible characteristics of objects in a standard and implementation-independent way. The common semantics characterize objects that exist in an OMG-compliant system. [OMG]

one-way request *n.* any request where the client does not wait for completion of the request, nor does it intend to accept results. [OMG]
Contrast with: ASYNCHRONOUS REQUEST, DEFERRED SYNCHRONOUS REQUEST, SYNCHRONOUS REQUEST.

operation *n.* **1.** any discrete activity, action, or behavior that is performed by (i.e., belongs to) an object or class. [Ada95, Firesmith, Henderson-Sellers] **2.** any service that can be requested. [Jacobson, Martin, OMG] **3.** any work that one object performs on another in order to elicit a reaction. [Booch] **4.** any function or transformation that may be applied to objects in a class. [Rumbaugh]
Synonyms: **1** FUNCTION, METHOD, **2** SERVICE.
Contrast with: BEHAVIOR, PROPERTY.
Commentary: An operation should im-

plement a single functional (i.e., sequential) or process (i.e., concurrent) abstraction. An operation usually implements a service requested by a message and in turn is implemented by a method.
Kinds:

- ABSTRACT OPERATION
- ACCESSOR OPERATION
  - CREATE ACCESSOR
  - DELETE ACCESSOR
  - READ ACCESSOR
  - WRITE ACCESSOR
- ACTION
  - INTERRUPTIBLE ACTION
  - NONINTERRUPTIBLE ACTION
- ACTIVITY
- AGGREGATE OPERATION
- ASSOCIATOR OPERATION
- ATOMIC OPERATION
- BASE OPERATION
- CLASS OPERATION
- CONCURRENT OPERATION
- CONSTRUCTOR OPERATION
  - COPY CONSTRUCTOR
  - DEFAULT CONSTRUCTOR
- CONTEXT-DEPENDENT OPERATION
- CONTEXT-INDEPENDENT OPERATION
- CONVERSION FUNCTION
- CREATE OPERATION
- DEFAULT OPERATION
- DEFERRED OPERATION
- DELETE OPERATION
- DELETE OPERATOR
- DERIVED OPERATION
- DESTRUCTOR OPERATION
- DYNAMIC OPERATION
- EFFECTIVE OPERATION
- EXCEPTION SIGNALER
- EXTENT OPERATION
- EXTERNAL OPERATION
- FLUID OPERATION
- FOREIGN OPERATION

- FRIEND OPERATION
- FROZEN OPERATION
- FUNCTION
  - FRIEND FUNCTION
  - MEMBER FUNCTION
    + VIRTUAL MEMBER FUNCTION
      > PURE VIRTUAL FUNCTION
  - READ ACCESSOR
- FUNCTIONAL
- GENERIC OPERATION
- INSTANCE OPERATION
- INTERNAL OPERATION
- INTERRUPTIBLE OPERATION
- INVOKED OPERATION
- ITERATOR OPERATION
- MODIFIER OPERATION
- NON-INTERRUPTIBLE OPERATION
- NON-ITERATOR OPERATION
- OVERLOADED OPERATION
- POLYMORPHIC OPERATION
  - AD HOC POLYMORPHIC OPERATION
  - GENERIC OPERATION
  - INHERENTLY POLYMORPHIC OPERATION
  - OVERLOADED OPERATION
    + GLOBALLY OVERLOADED OPERATION
    + LOCALLY OVERLOADED OPERATION
- PRESERVER OPERATION
- PRIMARY OPERATION
- PRIMITIVE OPERATION
- PRIMITIVE OPERATION OF A TYPE
- PROCEDURE
- QUERY OPERATION
- REQUIRED OPERATION
- SECONDARY OPERATION
- SELECTOR OPERATION
- SEQUENTIAL OPERATION
- STATE-DEPENDENT OPERATION
  - ENTRY OPERATION
    + GENERAL ENTRY OPERATION

O

+ SPECIFIC ENTRY OPERATION
- EXIT OPERATION
  + GENERAL EXIT OPERATION
  + SPECIFIC EXIT OPERATION
- STATE-INDEPENDENT OPERATION
- STATIC OPERATION
- STUB
- SUFFERED OPERATION
- SYNCHRONIZER OPERATION
- VALUE-DEPENDENT OPERATION
- VIRTUAL OPERATION

- **abstract operation** *n.* any operation that is declared by, but not implemented in, an abstract class. [Booch, Rumbaugh]

  Synonyms: ABSTRACT METHOD, ABSTRACT SUBPROGRAM, DEFERRED OPERATION.

  Example: Each pure virtual member function in C++ is an abstract operation. [Booch]

  Commentary: The term *deferred operation* is more commonly used than the term *abstract operation*, which is inconsistent with other popular uses of the term *abstract.*

- **accessor [operation]** *n.* any typically small, simple, almost standard operation used to get or set the value of an instance attribute. [Martin/Odell, Shlaer/Mellor]

  Synonyms: ACCESSING METHOD, ACCESSING OPERATION, ACCESSOR METHOD, PRESERVER OPERATION.

  Contrast with: ACCESSOR MESSAGE, ACCESSING MESSAGE, PRESERVER MESSAGE.

  Kinds:
  - CREATE ACCESSOR
  - DELETE ACCESSOR
  - READ ACCESSOR
  - WRITE ACCESSOR

- **create accessor** *n.* any accessor operation that creates a new instance of an object. [Shlaer/Mellor]

  Antonym: DELETE ACCESSOR.

- **delete accessor** *n.* any accessor operation that deletes an instance of an object. [Shlaer/Mellor]

  Antonym: CREATE ACCESSOR.

- **read accessor** *n.* any accessor operation that returns the value of a property. [Firesmith, Shlaer/Mellor]

  Antonym: WRITE ACCESSOR.

  Commentary: A read accessor is a kind of function. [Firesmith]

- **write accessor** *n.* any accessor operation that updates the value of a property. [Firesmith, Shlaer/Mellor]

  Antonym: READ ACCESSOR.

  Commentary: A write accessor is a kind of procedure. [Firesmith]

- **action** *n.* **1.** the term used during state modeling for any operation that, for all practical purposes, takes zero time to execute. [Booch, Firesmith, Rumbaugh] **2.** any operation that must be executed upon arrival in a state. [Shlaer/Mellor] **3.** any operation performed by an object. [Embley]

  Contrast with: ACTIVITY.

  Examples: The updating of an attribute usually takes such a short time to accomplish that is may be considered an action for state modeling purposes. [Firesmith] The passing of a message, the invocation of an operation, the starting and stopping of an activity, the updating of an attribute. [Booch, Firesmith] An *action* may cause events, create or destroy objects and relationships, observe objects and relationships, and send or receive messages. [Embley]

  Rationale: Standard term used by Booch, Embley, Firesmith, Rumbaugh,

and Shlaer/ Mellor.
Commentary: Definition **1** is the most popular definition.
Kinds:

- INTERRUPTIBLE ACTION
- NONINTERRUPTIBLE ACTION

- **interruptible action** *n.* any action associated with a state that may be suspended before it finishes executing and may resume execution at a later time. [Embley]
Synonym: INTERRUPTIBLE OPERATION.
Antonym: NONINTERRUPTIBLE ACTION.

- **noninterruptible action** *n.* any action associated with a state transition that the analyst expects to run to completion unless exceptions or system failures occur. [Embley]
Synonym: INTERRUPTIBLE OPERATION.
Antonym: INTERRUPTIBLE ACTION.

● **activity** *n.* the term used during state modeling for an operation that takes significant time to execute. [Booch, Firesmith, Rumbaugh]
Antonym: ACTION.
Rationale: Standard term used by Booch, Firesmith, and Rumbaugh.

● **aggregate operation** *n.* any operation that has been functionally decomposed into two or more suboperations. [Firesmith]
Antonym: ATOMIC OPERATION.

● **associator operation** *n.* any operation that creates, destroys, or maintains the referential integrity of a link. [Firesmith]
See also: LINK, REFERENTIAL INTEGRITY.
Example: When a bidirectional link is moved from one object to another, associator operations in the three ob-

jects involved must work together to break the original link and establish the new one. [Firesmith]

● **atomic operation** *n.* **1.** any operation that either consistently updates the states of all participating objects, or does not update the state of any. [Firesmith] **2.** any operation that is not functionally decomposed into component suboperations. [Firesmith]
Antonym: AGGREGATE OPERATION.
Contrast with: NON-INTERRUPTIBLE OPERATION.

● **base operation** *n.* any operation that cannot be derived from other operations.
Antonym: DERIVED OPERATION.

● **class operation** *n.* any operation that operates on a class. [Booch, Firesmith, Jacobson, Rumbaugh]
Contrast with: EXTENT OPERATION, INSTANCE OPERATION.
Examples: A constructor and an operation that operates on class properties are both class operations. [Firesmith, Jacobson]

● **concurrent operation** *n.* any operation that contains one or more separate threads of control. [Firesmith]
Antonym: SEQUENTIAL OPERATION.
Commentary: A concurrent operation may be able to handle more than on message at a time. [Firesmith]

● **constructor [operation]** *n.* any class or metaclass operation that constructs (i.e., instantiates) an instance (i.e., an object or class, respectively), allocates memory to dynamic objects, creates the binding of messages to [inherited] operations (e.g., via a virtual-method table), and initializes the values of the properties. [Booch, Firesmith]

O

Commentary: Constructors turn raw memory into an object for which the rules of the type system hold. Constructors typically initialize the object before it can be used. [Firesmith]

Kinds:
- COPY CONSTRUCTOR
- DEFAULT CONSTRUCTOR

- **copy constructor** *n.* any constructor that makes a copy of an object of its class. [C++, Firesmith]
Example: In C++:
```
X::X(const X&);
```

- **default constructor** *n.* any constructor that does not require actual arguments. [C++, Firesmith]
Examples: In C++:
```
X::X();
X::X(int=0);
```
Commentary: A default constructor may have default arguments. [Firesmith]

● **context-dependent operation** *n.* any operation, the effect of which depends on the context of the receiver of the associated message. [Firesmith, OMG]
Antonym: CONTEXT-INDEPENDENT OPERATION.
Example: The effect may depend on the identity or location of the client object sending the message (i.e., issuing the request). [Firesmith]

● **context-independent operation** *n.* any operation, the effect of which is independent of the context of the receiver of the associated message. [Firesmith, OMG]
Antonym: CONTEXT-DEPENDENT OPERATION.

● **conversion function** *n.* any function that specifies a type conversion between a class and another type. [C++]

Contrast with: CAST, CONSTRUCTOR.
Commentary: Conversion functions can do two things that cannot be specified by constructors:
– Define a conversion from a class to a basic type
– Define a conversion from one class to another without modifying the declaration for the other class. [C++]

● **create operation** *n.* any operation that allocates storage for the representation of the object, assigns an OID, and returns that OID as the value of the operation. [ODMG]
Contrast with: CONSTRUCTOR OPERATION, DELETE OPERATION.

● **default operation** *n.* any operation that is implemented in an ancestor and that provides a default behavior that is intended to be overridden in its descendants.
Contrast with: DEFERRED OPERATION.

● **deferred operation** *n.* any operation that is declared, but not implemented, in an abstract class. [Firesmith]
Synonyms: ABSTRACT OPERATION, PURE VIRTUAL MEMBER FUNCTION [C++]
Antonym: EFFECTIVE OPERATION.
Rationale: The implementation of the operation is deferred until the derived class supplies the implementation. [Firesmith]
Commentary: All deferred operations must be made effective in a descendant before the descendant may be instantiated. [Firesmith]

● **delete operation** *n.* any operation that removes an object from the database, frees the storage used by its representation, and removes it from any relationships in which it participated.

The OID of a deleted object is not re-used. [ODMG]

Antonym: CONSTRUCTOR OPERA-TION, DESTRUCTOR OPERATION.

- **delete operator** *n.* the operator that destroys an object created by the new operator. [C++

Synonym: DESTRUCTOR.

Antonym: NEW OPERATOR.

- **derived operation** *n.* any operation that is directly executed by calls to other operations.

Antonym: BASE OPERATION.

- **destructor [operation]** *n.* **1.** any oper-ation that destroys an instance includ-ing maintaining referential integrity and deallocating its associated memo-ry. [Booch, Firesmith] **2.** any opera-tion that cleans up the values of an ob-ject before it is destroyed. [C++]

Synonym: DELETE OPERATION.

Antonym: CONSTRUCTOR.

Commentary: Destructors are used during garbage collection (i.e., mem-ory reclamation). [Firesmith]

- **dynamic operation** *n.* any operation that may be dynamically bound to an object at run-time. [Firesmith]

Synonym: VIRTUAL MEMBER FUNC-TION, VIRTUAL OPERATION.

Antonym: STATIC OPERATION.

- **effective operation** *n.* **1.** any opera-tion that has an associated effective method. [Firesmith] **2.** any inherited deferred operation that has been completed by a descendant. [Eiffel]

Antonym: DEFERRED OPERATION.

Commentary: Because an effective operation has a completed method, it can be executed.

- **exception signaler** *n.* any operation that raises an exception. [Firesmith]

Contrast with: EXCEPTION HANDLER.

- **extent operation** *n.* any operation on an extent. [Firesmith]

Contrast with: INSTANCE OPERA-TION, CLASS OPERATION.

Example: update and access an extent attribute. [Firesmith]

- **external operation** *n.* **1.** any opera-tion that sends messages (either direct-ly or indirectly) to other objects or classes. [Firesmith] **2.** any operation that is external to the system, yet nev-ertheless affects the system. [Martin]

Antonym: INTERNAL OPERATION.

Contrast with: FOREIGN ROUTINE.

- **fluid operation** *n.* any operation that may be redefined by descendants of the origin class. [Firesmith]

Antonym: FROZEN OPERATION.

See also: VIRTUAL.

Commentary: Because designers can-not usually foresee all possible legiti-mate extensions of their classes, oper-ations should by default be fluid in order to allow polymorphism. Note that Eiffel takes this recommended ap-proach, whereas C++ takes the oppo-site approach as default. [Firesmith]

- **foreign operation** *n.* any operation imported from another language. [Firesmith]

Contrast with: EXTERNAL OPERATION.

- **friend operation** *n.* any operation whose implementation may reference the private parts of another class, which permits the violation of infor-mation hiding. [C++]

- **frozen operation** *n.* any operation that may *not* be redefined by descen-dants of the origin class. [Firesmith]

Antonym: FLUID OPERATION.

Commentary: Because operations should by default be fluid in order to support polymorphism, frozen oper-

O

ations should be explicitly declared as frozen. Frozen operations are used by the designer to restrict the possible extensions of the origin class. [Firesmith]

● **function** *n.* any operation that returns a value.

Antonym: PROCEDURE.

Kinds:
- FRIEND FUNCTION
- MEMBER FUNCTION
  + VIRTUAL MEMBER FUNCTION
    > PURE VIRTUAL FUNCTION
- READ ACCESSOR

+ **friend function** *n.* the C++ term for a function whose implementation may reference the hidden members of another class which permits the violation of information hiding. [Firesmith]

Contrast with: FRIEND CLASS.

+ **member function** *n.* the C++ term for a function encapsulated within an object or class. [Firesmith]

> **virtual member function** *n.* the C++ term for any member function that may be dynamically bound to an object at run-time, thereby permitting redefinition by the derived class. [Firesmith]

Synonyms: DYNAMIC OPERATION, VIRTUAL OPERATION.

Contrast with: STATIC OPERATION.

> **pure virtual function** *n.* in C++, any virtual function whose implementation is deferred and must be supplied by a descendant base class before the descendant class can be instantiated. [Firesmith]

Contrast with: ABSTRACT.

Commentary: Pure virtual functions are used to create deferred classes. [Firesmith]

+ **read accessor** *n.* any accessor operation that returns the value of a property. [Firesmith, Shlaer/Mellor]

Antonym: WRITE ACCESSOR.

Commentary: A read accessor is a kind of function. [Firesmith]

● **functional** *n.* any operation that has other operations as arguments. [Firesmith]

● **generic operation** *n.* 1. any parameterized operation. [Firesmith] 2. any operation that can be bound to more than one method. [OMG]

Contrast with: GENERIC CLASS.

● **instance operation** *n.* any operation of an individual instance. [Firesmith, Jacobson]

Contrast with: CLASS OPERATION, EXTENT OPERATION.

Commentary: Most of the operations defined in an instance's class are instance operations.

● **internal operation** *n.* any operation that does not send messages (either directly or indirectly) to other objects or classes. [Firesmith]

Antonym: EXTERNAL OPERATION.

● **interruptible operation** *n.* any operation that may be suspended before it finishes executing and may resume execution at a later time. [Firesmith]

Antonym: NONINTERRUPTIBLE OPERATION.

Commentary: Interruptible operations do not contain any critical regions that must execute to completion without interruption. [Firesmith]

- **interruptible action** *n.* any action associated with a state that may be

suspended before it finishes executing and may resume execution at a later time. [Embley]
Synonym: INTERRUPTIBLE OPERATION.
Antonym: NONINTERRUPTIBLE ACTION.

- **invoked operation** *n.* any *instance* of an operation. [Martin]
- **iterator operation** *n.* **1.** any operation that operates on multiple instances of a class. [Firesmith] **2.** any operation that reads or writes to multiple properties. [Booch, Firesmith]
Antonym: NONITERATOR OPERATION.
- **modifier [operation]** *n.* **1.** any operation that modifies the value of properties. [Firesmith, Martin/Odell] **2.** any operation that modifies the state of an object or class. [Booch, Martin/Odell]
Antonyms: ACCESSOR, PRESERVER OPERATION.
- **noninterruptible operation** *n.* any operation that may not be suspended before it finishes executing.
Antonym: INTERRUPTIBLE OPERATION.
See also: ATOMIC OPERATION.
Commentary: Noninterruptible operations contain at least one critical region that must execute to completion without interruption.
  - **noninterruptible action** *n.* any action associated with a state transition that the analyst expects to run to completion unless exceptions or system failures occur. [Embley]
Synonym: INTERRUPTIBLE OPERATION.
Antonym: INTERRUPTIBLE ACTION.
- **noniterator operation** *n.* any operation that neither operates on multiple instances of a class nor on multiple properties. [Firesmith]
Antonym: ITERATOR OPERATION.
- **overloaded operation** *n.* any operation that occurs multiple times in the same class whereby each variant has the same abstraction and name, but each has its own signature and implementation. [Firesmith]
See also: LOCAL OVERLOADING.
- **polymorphic operation** *n.* any operation that has multiple forms (i.e., implementations) due to polymorphism. [Firesmith]
See also: POLYMORPHISM.
Kinds:
  - AD HOC POLYMORPHIC OPERATION
  - GENERIC OPERATION
  - INHERENTLY POLYMORPHIC OPERATION
  - OVERLOADED OPERATION
    + GLOBALLY OVERLOADED OPERATION
    + LOCALLY OVERLOADED OPERATION
  - **ad hoc polymorphic operation** *n.* any polymorphic operation that has a single method containing multiple implementations of the same functional abstraction, one of which is selected at run-time using a case statement, switch statement, or similar language construct. [Firesmith]
See also: AD HOC POLYMORPHISM.
  - **generic operation** *n.* **1.** any operation that is parameterized with generic formal parameters that must be supplied as part of the instantiation process. [Firesmith] **2.** any operation that can be bound to more than one method. [OMG]
Contrast with: GENERIC CLASS GENERIC TYPE.
See also: PARAMETRIC POLYMORPHISM.

O

- **inherently polymorphic operation** *n.* any polymorphic operation that occurs in different descendants of the same ancestor whereby each variant has the same name, functional abstraction, and signature, but has a different method. [Firesmith]
  See also: INHERENT POLYMORPHISM.
- **overloaded operation** *n.* any polymorphic operation whereby each variant has the same name and functional abstraction, but each has a different signature and method. [Firesmith, ODMG]
  See also: OVERLOADING.
  Kinds:
  + GLOBALLY OVERLOADED OPERATION
  + LOCALLY OVERLOADED OPERATION
+ **globally overloaded operation** *n.* any overloaded operation, the variants of which occur in different contexts or scopes unrelated by inheritance. [Firesmith]
  Antonym: LOCALLY OVERLOADED OPERATION.
  See also: GLOBAL OVERLOADING.
  Rationale: Global overloading occurs *globally* across classes that are unrelated by inheritance. [Firesmith]
+ **locally overloaded operation** *n.* any overloaded operation that occurs multiple times in the same class whereby each variant has the same name and functional abstraction, but each has a different signature and method. [Firesmith]
  Antonym: GLOBALLY OVERLOADED OPERATION.
  See also: LOCAL OVERLOADING.

Examples: Constructors are often overloaded with the simple default constructor having the same name but fewer parameters than more complex constructors. [Firesmith]
Rationale: Local overloading occurs *locally* within a single class. [Firesmith]
Commentary: Local overloading allows multiple operations with the same name to be defined provided their signatures differ sufficiently for calls to be resolved. The resolution of local overloading may be based on different numbers of parameters, parameters of different types, different return types, different exceptions raised, or different message type (e.g., sequential, synchronous, asynchronous). Unlike inherent polymorphism, local overloading is usually resolved at compile time. [Firesmith]
- **preserver [operation]** *n.* any operation that does not modify the value of any properties. [Firesmith]
  Synonym: SELECTOR OPERATION.
  Antonym: MODIFIER OPERATION.
- **primary operation** *n.* any operation that directly implements a primary responsibility of the class. [Firesmith]
  Antonym: SECONDARY OPERATION.
  Contrast with: SECONDARY METHOD.
- **primitive operation** *n.* any operation, the method of which is performed directly by the run-time of the language and therefore not expressed as a sequence of expressions in that programming language. [Firesmith]
  Contrast with: PRIMITIVE METHOD.
- **primitive operation [of a type]** *n.* either the predefined operations of the

type or any user-defined primitive subprograms. [Ada95]

See also: INHERITANCE.

Commentary: Primitive operations are the derivable (inherited) operations. [Ada95]

- **procedure** *n.* **1.** any operation that does not return a value. [Firesmith] **2.** any operation that may perform multiple actions and modify the instance to which it is applied, but does not return a value. [Eiffel, Meyer]

  Antonym: FUNCTION.

  Contrast with: ROUTINE, SUBPROGRAM.

  Example: A procedure may read data, update variables, or produce some output. [Ada95]

  Commentary: A procedure may have parameters to provide a controlled means of passing information between the procedure and the point of call. [Ada95]

- **query operation** *n.* any preserver operation that returns or computes a value. [Rumbaugh]

  Contrast with: PRESERVER OPERATION, SYNCHRONIZER OPERATION.

- **required operation** *n.* any operation that is needed by the current object and is exported by the public interface of a server of the current object. [Berard]

  Antonym: SUFFERED OPERATION.

- **secondary operation** *n.* any operation that does not directly implement a primary responsibility of the class. [Firesmith]

  Antonym: PRIMARY OPERATION.

- **selector [operation]** *n.* **1.** any operation that accesses the state of an object, but does not alter the state. [Booch] **2.** any fundamental field operation used to query the values of an

object without changing its state. [Martin/Odell]

Synonym: PRESERVER [OPERATION].

Antonym: MODIFIER [OPERATION].

Commentary: The term *preserver operation* is more intuitive.

- **sequential operation** *n.* any operation not containing one or more separate threads of control. [Firesmith]

  Antonym: CONCURRENT OPERATION.

- **state-dependent operation** *n.* any operation, the method of which is dependent on the state of the object or class. [Firesmith]

  Antonym: STATE-INDEPENDENT OPERATION.

  Contrast with: STATE-DEPENDENT PROPERTY.

  Kinds:
  - ENTRY OPERATION
    + GENERAL ENTRY OPERATION
    + SPECIFIC ENTRY OPERATION
  - EXIT OPERATION
    + GENERAL EXIT OPERATION
    + SPECIFIC EXIT OPERATION

- **entry operation** *n.* any state-dependent operation that executes on transition into a state. [Firesmith]

  Antonym: EXIT OPERATION.

  Kinds:
    + GENERAL ENTRY OPERATION
    + SPECIFIC ENTRY OPERATION

- **general entry operation** *n.* any entry operation that does not depend on the incoming transition. [Firesmith]

  Antonym: SPECIFIC ENTRY OPERATION.

- **specific entry operation** *n.* any entry operation that depends on the incoming transition. [Firesmith]

  Antonym: GENERAL ENTRY OPERATION.

- **exit operation** *n.* any state-dependent operation that executes on transition out of a state. [Firesmith]
  Antonym: ENTRY OPERATION.
  Kinds:
  + GENERAL EXIT OPERATION
  + SPECIFIC EXIT OPERATION
  + **general exit operation** *n.* any exit operation that does not depend on the outgoing transition. [Firesmith]
    Antonym: SPECIFIC EXIT OPERATION.
  + **specific exit operation** *n.* any exit operation that depends on the outgoing transition. [Firesmith]
    Antonym: GENERAL EXIT OPERATION.

- **state-independent operation** *n.* any operation, the method of which is independent of the state of the object or class. [Firesmith]
  Antonym: STATE-DEPENDENT OPERATION.
  Contrast with: STATE-INDEPENDENT PROPERTY.

- **static operation** *n.* any operation that is statically bound to an object at compile time. [Firesmith]
  Antonym: DYNAMIC OPERATION.
  Contrast with: FROZEN OPERATION.

- **stub** *n.* any local operation that sends a message to a remote object that invokes its associated operation. [Firesmith]
  Contrast with: PROXY.

- **suffered operation** *n.* any operation that is exported by the public interface of the current object. [Berard]
  Antonym: REQUIRED OPERATION.

- **synchronizer operation** *n.* any preserver operation that synchronizes two threads of control. [Firesmith]

Contrast with: PRESERVER OPERATION, QUERY OPERATION.

- **value-dependent operation** *n.* any operation whereby the behavior of the corresponding request depends on which names are used to identify object parameters (if an object can have multiple names). [OMG]

- **virtual operation** *n.* any operation that may be dynamically bound to an object at run-time. [Jacobson]
  Synonym: DYNAMIC OPERATION, VIRTUAL MEMBER FUNCTION.
  Antonym: STATIC OPERATION.

operation attribute *n.* any attribute that is local to a specific operation. [Firesmith]
Synonym: TEMPORARY ATTRIBUTE.

operation dispatching *n.* (a) any selection process whereby a specific operation implementation (method) is selected for execution when an operation request is issued. [OMG] (b) any selection of the appropriate method for an operation on receipt of a corresponding message.
Synonym: METHOD BINDING, METHOD RESOLUTION.

operation identifier *n.* the identifier or name of an operation. [Martin]
Synonym: OPERATION NAME.

operation invocation *n.* an invocation of an operation on an object or class, comprising an operation name, a list of zero or more actual parameters, and the results to be returned to the client.
Synonym: REQUEST.

operation model *n.* the Fusion model that defines the semantics (i.e., effect) of each system operation in the system interface in terms of change of state and the events that are output. [Coleman]
Contrast with: BEHAVIORAL MODEL,

CONFIGURATION MODEL, DATA MODEL, DYNAMIC MODEL, FUNCTIONAL MODEL, INTERACTION MODEL, INTERFACE MODEL, LANGUAGE MODEL, LIFE-CYCLE MODEL, OBJECT MODEL, PRESENTATION MODEL, SEMANTIC MODEL, STATE MODEL, STRUCTURAL MODEL, USE-CASE MODEL.

operation name *n.* (a) the name of any operation. [Firesmith] (b) any name used in a request to identify an operation. [OMG]
Synonym: OPERATION IDENTIFIER.
Examples: The method selector used in a message and in the signature of an operation are both operation names [Firesmith]

operation postcondition rule *n.* any constraint that must be satisfied before an operation will perform correctly. [Martin]
Synonym: POSTCONDITION.
Antonyms: OPERATION PRECONDITION RULE, PRECONDITION.
See also: CONTRACT.

operation precondition rule *n.* any constraint that guarantees the results when the operation is executed. [Martin]
Synonym: PRECONDITION.
Antonyms: POSTCONDITION, OPERATION POSTCONDITION RULE.
See also: CONTRACT

operation protocol *n.* the declaration of an operation, specifying the name of the operation, the names, modes, and types of any parameters (including the order), the name and type of any returned value, and optionally, any preconditions and postconditions, the names of any exceptions the operation can raise, and the priority of the operation. [ODMG]
Synonym: OPERATION SIGNATURE.
Contrast with: CLASS PROTOCOL, CLUSTER PROTOCOL, OBJECT PROTOCOL.

operation signature *n.* the signature of any operation, declaring:
its name;
– its parameters (including their names, modes, types, and order);
– the type of the value returned by the operation;
– any preconditions and postcondition;
– the names and types of any exceptions raised by the operation;
– the category of the operation (e.g., concurrent, sequential);
– the priority of the operation (if any). [Firesmith, ODMG]
Synonym: OPERATION PROTOCOL.
Contrast with: ATTRIBUTE SIGNATURE, LINK SIGNATURE, MESSAGE SIGNATURE, RELATIONSHIP SIGNATURE.

operation subtype *n.* any specialized type of operation derived from some parent type of operation. [Martin]

ORB core *n.* the ORB component that moves a request from a client to the appropriate adapter for the target object. [OMG]

ORB interface *n.* the interface that goes directly to the ORB, which is the same for all ORBs and does not depend on the object's interface or object adapter. [OMG]
Contrast with: CLASS INTERFACE, CLUSTER INTERFACE, CONSTRUCTION INTERFACE, FUNCTIONAL INTERFACE, MESSAGE INTERFACE, OBJECT INTERFACE, OPERATION INTERFACE, PRINCIPAL INTERFACE, SYSTEM INTERFACE, TYPE INTERFACE.

original feature name *n.* the name of the feature as declared in its class of origin. [Eiffel, Firesmith, Meyer]
Contrast with: FINAL FEATURE NAME, INHERITED FEATURE NAME.

origin [of a given feature] *n.* the class in which the given feature was originally

O

declared or last implemented. [Eiffel, Firesmith, Meyer]

Contrast with: SEED.

Commentary: The origin of a feature is the most distant ancestor in which the feature exists. The feature may have been overridden in an ancestor of the current class. [Eiffel, Firesmith, Meyer]

Kinds:
- DECLARING CLASS
- IMPLEMENTATION CLASS

- **declaring class [of a given feature]** *n.* the origin class in which the given feature was originally declared. [Firesmith]

Antonym: IMPLEMENTATION CLASS.

Example: The declaring class of an operation is the class in which the signature of the given operation first appeared. [Firesmith]

- **implementation class [of a given feature]** *n.* the origin class in which the given feature was last implemented. [Firesmith]

Antonym: DECLARING CLASS.

Example: The implementation class is the nearest class (either ancestor or current) in which a method for the given operation was appeared. [Firesmith]

orphaned object *n.* any dynamic object that continues to use memory even though it is no longer referenced (e.g., via pointers). [Firesmith]

Commentary: Orphaned objects are a common bug in languages (e.g., C++) that do not support automatic garbage collection. [Firesmith]

outbound exception protocol *n.* the set of all exceptions that may be raised to clients. [Firesmith]

Contrast with: INBOUND EXCEPTION PROTOCOL, INBOUND MESSAGE PROTOCOL, OUTBOUND MESSAGE PROTOCOL.

outbound message protocol *n.* the set of all inbound messages. [Firesmith]

Contrast with: INBOUND EXCEPTION PROTOCOL, INBOUND MESSAGE PROTOCOL, OUTBOUND EXCEPTION PROTOCOL.

outbound protocol *n.* that part of a protocol that provides the client role (i.e., hidden, inside, developer viewpoint).

Synonym: OUTBOUND INTERFACE.

Antonym: INBOUND PROTOCOL.

Example: The outbound protocol of an object consists of the messages it sends (and exceptions it raises) to other objects. [Firesmith]

Commentary: Most programming languages do not explicitly support the outbound part of the protocol. No contract with servers will be impacted by a change to the implementation if the outbound protocol does not change. [Firesmith]

overload *v.* *-ed, -ing* **1.** to use the same name for different, but analogous, things (e.g., attributes types, attributes, messages, operations, exceptions, objects, classes, and subclusters) in different contexts or scopes. [Firesmith] **2.** to use the same name, but different signatures (e.g., different numbers of parameters or parameters of different classes), for messages and operations implementing the same functional abstraction within the same class. [Firesmith] **3.** to use the same name for methods (doing logically the same thing) in different classes. [Lorenz]

Examples: Constructors are often overloaded, with a simple default constructor being used most of the time and with more complex constructors with more arguments being available when needed. [Firesmith] Balance might be a method in *CDAccount, MutualFund-*

Account, and *CheckingAccount* classes. Logically, balance means the same thing: "please give me your current balance, whatever that means to an object of your type." [Lorenz]

overloaded operation *n.* any polymorphic operation that occurs multiple times in the same class whereby each variant has the same name and functional abstraction, but each has its own signature and implementation. [Firesmith, ODMG]

See also: OVERLOADING.

Kinds:
• GLOBALLY OVERLOADED OPERATION
• LOCALLY OVERLOADED OPERATION

• **globally overloaded operation** *n.* any overloaded operation, the variants of which occur in different contexts or scopes unrelated by inheritance. [Firesmith]

Antonym: LOCALLY OVERLOADED OPERATION.

See also: GLOBAL OVERLOADING.

Rationale: Global overloading occurs *globally* across classes that are unrelated by inheritance. [Firesmith]

• **locally overloaded operation** *n.* any overloaded operation that occurs multiple times in the same class whereby each variant has the same name and functional abstraction, but each has a different signature and method. [Firesmith]

Antonym: GLOBALLY OVERLOADED OPERATION.

See also: LOCAL OVERLOADING.

Examples: Constructors are often overloaded with the simple default constructor having the same name but fewer parameters than more complex constructors. [Firesmith]

Rationale: Local overloading occurs *lo-*

cally within a single class. [Firesmith]

Commentary: Local overloading allows multiple operations with the same name to be defined provided their signatures differ sufficiently for calls to be resolved. The resolution of local overloading may be based on different numbers of parameters, parameters of different types, different return types, different exceptions raised, or different message type (e.g., sequential, synchronous, asynchronous). Unlike inherent polymorphism, local overloading is usually resolved at compile time. [Firesmith]

overloading *n.* any polymorphism whereby the same name is overloaded (i.e., is used for different, but analogous, abstractions). [Firesmith]

Contrast with: AD HOC POLYMORPHISM, INHERENT POLYMORPHISM, PARAMETRIC POLYMORPHISM.

Example: Buildings and people may both have age and height attributes with associated accessor operations, even though the building and person classes are not related by inheritance. [Firesmith]

Commentary: Overloading allows multiple operations with the same name to be defined provided their signatures differ sufficiently for calls to be resolved. Unlike inclusion polymorphism, overloading is usually resolved at compile time. This form of polymorphism applies the software engineering principle of uniformity to naming. [Firesmith]

Kinds:
• FUNCTION OVERLOADING
• GLOBAL OVERLOADING
• LOCAL OVERLOADING

• **function overloading** *n.* any use of a single name for several member func-

O

tions of the same class. [C++]

- **global overloading** *n.* any overloading in which the same name is used for abstractions in different contexts or scopes unrelated by inheritance. [Firesmith]
  Example: Buildings and people may both have age and height attributes with associated accessor operations, even though the building and person classes are not related by inheritance. [Firesmith]
  Rationale: Global overloading occurs *globally* across unrelated classes. [Firesmith]

- **local overloading** *n.* any overloading in which the same name, but different signatures, is used for messages and operations implementing the same functional abstraction within the same class. [Firesmith, Rumbaugh]
  Examples: Constructors are often overloaded with the simple default constructor having the same name but fewer parameters than more complex constructors. [Firesmith]
  Rationale: Local overloading occurs *locally* within a single class. [Firesmith]
  Commentary: Local overloading allows multiple operations with the same name to be defined provided their signatures differ sufficiently for calls to be resolved. The resolution of local overloading may be based on different numbers of parameters, parameters of different types, different return types, different exceptions raised, or different message type (e.g., sequential, synchronous, asynchronous). Unlike inherent polymorphism, local overloading is usually resolved at compile time. [Firesmith]

overloading resolution *n.* the binding of a message requesting an overloaded operation to the right method based on differences in operation signatures (e.g., number and types of arguments, type of returned value). [Firesmith]

override [a given feature] *v. overrode, -ing* **1.** to redefine the implementation of a feature in a child class that will then replace the original implementation of the feature that was inherited from the parent. [CLOS, Firesmith, Jacobson, Smalltalk] **2.** to create a method in a class that replaces a method with the same name that was inherited from one of its base classes. [Lorenz, Rumbaugh] **3.** to replace an explicit declaration with a visible explicit declaration. [Ada95]
Synonym: SHADOW. [CLOS]
Example: If a class *base* contains a *virtual* function *vf*, and a class *derived* that was derived from it also contains a function *vf* of the same type, then a call of *vf* for an object of class derived invokes *derived::vf* (even if the access is through a pointer or reference to *base*). The derived class function is said to *override* the base class function. [C++] To override the inherited method of an operation. [Firesmith]
Commentary: Overriding allows children to be and do what is appropriate for their abstraction while remaining true to their heritage. [Firesmith] If a subclass adds a method whose message pattern has the same selector as a method in the superclass, its instances will respond to messages with that selector by executing the new method. This is called overriding a method. [Smalltalk] Overriding results in different behavior for the same message. [Lorenz] Inheritance is not transitive if overriding is used. [Jacobson].

P

package *n.* any program unit that allows the specification of groups of logically related entities. [Ada95]
Commentary: Typically, a package contains the declaration of a type (often a private type or private extension) along with the declarations of primitive subprograms of the type, which can be called from outside the package, while their inner workings remain hidden from outside users. [Ada95]

pane [object] *n.* any domain object that exists to provide a view of (i.e., information about and control over) one or more model objects.
Synonym: VIEW OBJECT.
Contrast with: MODEL OBJECT, PRESENTATION OBJECT.
Commentary: A model object may have more than one view object, and a view object may also be a controller object of its model object(s). Most view objects are also presentation objects.

parameter *n.* any value that must be supplied by a client as part of a message, operation invocation, or generic instantiation. [Firesmith]
Synonym: ARGUMENT.
Kinds:

- ACTUAL PARAMETER
- FORMAL PARAMETER
  - GENERIC FORMAL PARAMETER

● **actual parameter** *n.* any parameter that contains the actual value supplied by the client. [Firesmith]
Synonym: ACTUAL ARGUMENT.
Antonym: FORMAL ARGUMENT, FORMAL PARAMETER.

● **formal parameter** *n.* any parameter that specifies the actual value to be supplied by the client. [Firesmith]
Synonym: FORMAL ARGUMENT.
Antonym: ACTUAL PARAMETER.
Commentary: Actual parameters must be supplied for each formal parameter prior to execution or instantiation. The specification of a formal parameter may include its name, its mode (e.g., in, out, or in and out), its type, and any default value). [Firesmith]

- **generic formal parameter** *n.* any formal parameter of a generic that must be supplied by the client as part of the instantiation process. [Firesmith]
Synonym: GENERIC FORMAL ARGUMENT.
Commentary: Actual parameters

P

must be supplied for each generic formal parameter prior to instantiation. [Firesmith]

parameter name *n.* the name of any pseudovariable that holds a parameter. [Firesmith]

parameter-passing mode *n.* the direction (i.e., *in, out,* and *inout*) of information (i.e., data or object) flow of a parameter. [Firesmith, OMG]

Synonym: ARGUMENT MODE.

Commentary: Mode *in* means that the argument goes in the same direction as the message (i.e., data and control flows in the same direction). Mode *out* means that the argument goes in the opposite direction as the message (i.e., data and control flows in opposite directions). Mode inout means that the argument goes in both directions (i.e., read/write). [Firesmith]

parameter specializer *n.* the part of any method that specifies when the given method is applicable. [CLOS]

See also: METHOD.

Commentary: Each required formal parameter of each method has an associated parameter specializer, and the method will invoked only on arguments that satisfy its parameter specializers. [CLOS]

parameterized class *n.* any abstract metaclass that is parameterized with formal generic parameters (e.g., classes, attributes, messages, operations, exceptions, invariants) that must be supplied as part of the instantiation process. [Booch, Firesmith, Rumbaugh]

Synonyms: GENERIC CLASS, TEMPLATE CLASS.

Commentary: The instances of a generic class vary, depending on the actual parameters supplied. The term *generic*

class is preferred over the term *parameterized class* for historical reasons. [Firesmith]

parameterized type *n.* any type that has been parameterized with generic formal parameters. [C++, Firesmith]

Synonym: GENERIC.

Contrast with: GENERIC, GENERIC CLASS, GENERIC OPERATION, PARAMETERIZED CLASS, TEMPLATE.

parametric polymorphism *n.* **1.** any polymorphism due to parameterization. [Booch, Firesmith] **2.** the overriding of an inherited feature by a subclass. [Martin]

Synonym: GENERICITY.

Examples: The parameterization of types, classes, and clusters are examples of parametric polymorphism.

Commentary: Although inherent polymorphism can simulate parametric polymorphism and the reverse is not true, parametric polymorphism provides great convenience and minimizes the number of classes needed in a class library. [Firesmith] Definition **1** is the standard definition for this term. The standard term for definition **2** is *inclusion polymorphism.*

parent [class of a given class] *n.* any ancestor class from which the given class is directly derived via inheritance. [Eiffel, Firesmith, Jacobson, Meyer]

Synonyms: DIRECT ANCESTOR, DIRECT BASE CLASS, DIRECT SUPERCLASS.

Antonyms: CHILD CLASS, DIRECT DESCENDANT, DIRECT DERIVED CLASS, DIRECT SUBCLASS.

Rationale: The term *parent* is preferred over the term *direct ancestor* because of its common usage in English and in biological inheritance. The term *direct ancestor* is in turn preferred over the terms *direct base class* and *direct super-class* because of the preference of the term *ancestor* over the terms *base class* and *superclass*. [Firesmith]

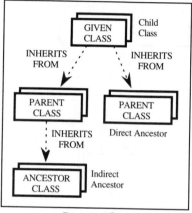

Parent Class

parent type [of a given type] *n.* **1.** any ancestor type from which the given type is directly derived via subtyping. [Firesmith] **2.** the type from which the given type was immediately derived. [Ada95] *Synonyms:* DIRECT ANCESTOR, DIRECT BASE TYPE, DIRECT SUPERTYPE.

Antonyms: CHILD TYPE, DIRECT DESCENDANT, DIRECT DERIVED TYPE, DIRECT SUBTYPE.

Rationale: The term *parent* is preferred over the term *direct ancestor* because of its common usage in English and in biological inheritance. The term *direct ancestor* is in turn preferred over the terms *direct base type* and *direct super-type* because of the preference of the term *ancestor* over the terms *base type* and *supertype*. [Firesmith]

part *n.* any component of an aggregate. [Firesmith]

Synonym: COMPONENT.

participate [in a request] *v.* *-ed, -ing* any object participates in a request if one or more of the actual parameters of the request identifies the object. [OMG]

participation constraint *n.* any constraint that defines the number of times an object in an object class can participate in a connected relationship set. Participation constraints restrict the number of relationships in which an object can appear in a relationship set. [Embley]

Commentary: Embley et al. requires that every connection of a relationship set to an object class have a participation constraint. The basic form for a participation constraint is a par: *min:max*. [Embley]

Kinds:

- MUTUAL-EXCLUSION CONSTRAINT
  - PARTITION CONSTRAINT
- UNION CONSTRAINT
  - PARTITION CONSTRAINT

- **mutual-exclusion constraint** *n.* any constraint that declares that a group of specializations of generalization are pairwise disjoint. [Embley]

  - **partition constraint** *n.* **1.** the inheritance constraint that requires that the extents of the children form a disjoint cover of the parent. [Firesmith] **2.** any constraint that declares that a group of specializations partitions a generalization. A partition requires that partitioning sets be pairwise disjoint and that their union constitute the partitioned set. [Embley]

  Commentary: A partition constraint is the combination of a mutual-exclusion constraint and a union constraint. [Embley] The partition constraint is the conjunction of the disjoint constraint and the cover constraint. [Firesmith]

● **union constraint** *n.* any constraint that declares that the union of a group of specializations of a generalization constitutes the entire membership of the generalization. [Embley]
Commentary: When we have a union constraint, we know that every member of a generalization is a member of at least one specialization in the group. [Embley]

- **partition constraint** *n.* **1.** the inheritance constraint that requires that the extents of the children form a disjoint cover of the parent. [Firesmith] **2.** any constraint that declares a group of specialization partitions to be a generalization. A partition requires that partitioning sets be pairwise disjoint and that their union constitute the partitioned set. [Embley]
Commentary: A partition constraint is the combination of a mutual-exclusion constraint and a union constraint. [Embley] The partition constraint is the conjunction of the disjoint constraint and the cover constraint. [Firesmith]

partition *n.* **1.** any set of children differentiated by a discriminator. [Firesmith, McGregor] **2.** (a) any vertical slice of the overall architecture consisting of one or more logically related clusters. [Firesmith] (b) one or more logically related clusters, class categories, or subsystems that form a part of a given level of abstraction. [Booch, Rumbaugh]
Antonym: **2** LAYER.
See also: DISCRIMINATOR.
Example: **1** The derived classes of cars based on engine type form a partition of cars. [Firesmith]

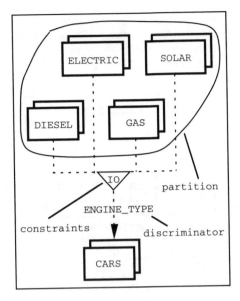

Partition

partition constraint *n.* **1.** the inheritance constraint that requires that the extents of the children form a disjoint cover of the parent. [Firesmith] **2.** any constraint that declares that a group of specializations partitions a generalization. A partition requires that partitioning sets be pairwise disjoint and that their union constitute the partitioned set. [Embley]
Commentary: A partition constraint is the combination of a mutual-exclusion constraint and a union constraint. [Embley] The partition constraint is the conjunction of the disjoint constraint and the cover constraint. [Firesmith]

partition hierarchy *n.* any hierarchy created by partitioning an object into other objects via *consistsOf* relations. [Jacobson]
Synonyms: AGGREGATION HIERARCHY, ASSEMBLY STRUCTURE, CONTAINMENT HIERARCHY, WHOLE-PART STRUCTURE.

See also: AGGREGATE, CONSISTSOF AS-
SOCIATION.

partOf association *n.* any acquaintance
association from an object to the aggregate object of which it is a part. [Ja-
cobson]

Antonym: CONSISTSOF ASSOCIATION.

See also: AGGREGATE, ACQUAINTANCE
ASSOCIATION.

Example: A dish and a beverage are parts
of a food order. [Jacobson]

Commentary: The association partOf is
used to express that an aggregate object is
a compound of other objects. [Jacobson]

pass *v.* **-ed, -ing** to send arguments with
a message. [Firesmith]

Kinds:
- PASS-BY-POINTER
- PASS-BY-REFERENCE
- PASS-BY VALUE

- **pass-by-pointer** *v.* to send a pointer
  to (e.g., the OID of) the value of an
  argument. [Firesmith]
  Contrast with: PASS-BY-REFERENCE,
  PASS-BY-VALUE.
  Example: in C++:
  ```
  void foo(X *x);
  ```
  Commentary: If the receiver modifies
  the value of an argument of the message, its new value will also take effect
  outside of the object that modifies it.
  Thus, pass-by-value is faster but less
  safe. [Firesmith]
- **pass-by-reference** *v.* to send a reference to (e.g., an alias for the OID of)
  the value of an argument. [Firesmith]
  Contrast with: PASS-BY-POINTER, PASS-
  BY-VALUE.
  Example: in C++:
  ```
  void foo(X &x);
  ```
  Commentary: If the receiver modifies
  the value of an argument of the message, its new value will also take effect

outside of the object that modifies it.
Thus, pass-by-value is typically faster but less safe. [Firesmith]

- **pass-by-value** *v.* to send a copy of
  the value of an argument. [Firesmith]
  Contrast with: CALL-BY-REFERENCE,
  PASS-BY-POINTER, PASS-BY-REFERENCE.
  Example: in C++:
  ```
  void foo(X x);
  ```
  Commentary: If the receiver modifies
  the copy of the value of an argument
  of the message, the original value will
  not be affected. Thus, pass-by-value
  is safer but typically slower because a
  new object must be created for each
  argument. [Firesmith]

passive *adj.* **1.** describing an object or
class that cannot execute except in response to an incoming message. [Fire-
smith] **2.** having no inherent thread of
control. [Booch]

Synonym: **2** SEQUENTIAL.

Antonym: ACTIVE.

Rationale: Definition **1** is consistent
with the traditional use of the term to
describe Ada tasks with entries.

passive class *n.* **1.** any class of passive objects that cannot execute instance operations without the need for incoming
messages. [Firesmith] **2.** any class that
cannot execute class operations without the need for incoming messages.
[Firesmith] **3.** any class that does not
have a separate state machine for each
instance. [Shlaer/Mellor]

Antonym: ACTIVE CLASS.

passive iterator *n.* any iterator that consists of a single atomic method. [Berard]

Antonym: ACTIVE ITERATOR.

See also: HOMOGENEOUS COMPOSITE
OBJECT.

Commentary: Although users of passive iterators have less control, they

P

need not concern themselves with the low-level methods necessary to accomplish the iteration. [Berard]

passive object *n.* **1.** any object whose behavior must be triggered by an incoming message. [Firesmith] **2.** any object that does not encompass its own thread of control. [Booch]
Antonym: ACTIVE OBJECT.
Kinds:
- BLOCKING OBJECT
- SEQUENTIAL OBJECT
- **blocking object** *n.* any sequential (i.e., passive) object whose semantics are guaranteed in the presence of multiple threads of control. [Booch]
- **sequential object** *n.* **1.** any object that does not contain any threads of control (e.g., concurrent operations or nested concurrent objects). [Firesmith] **2.** any passive object whose semantics are guaranteed only in the presence of a single thread of control. [Booch]
  Synonym: **1** PASSIVE OBJECT.
  Antonym: CONCURRENT OBJECT.
  Commentary: All sequential objects are passive, but not all passive objects are sequential. [Firesmith]

path [through a given scenario class] *n.* **1.** any instance of the given scenario class. **2.** any sequence of interactions described by the given scenario class. [Firesmith]
Kinds:
- PRIMARY PATH
- SECONDARY PATH.
- **primary path [through a given scenario class]** *n.* any of the most common or important paths through the given scenario class. [Firesmith]
  Antonym: SECONDARY PATH.
  See also: SCENARIO.
  Commentary: The description of a

scenario class is normally divided into *primary paths* and *secondary paths,* whereby the primary paths provide the best understanding of the scenario class. Primary paths are usually developed before the secondary paths. [Firesmith]

- **secondary path [through a given scenario class]** *n.* any of the less common or important paths through the given scenario class. [Firesmith]
  Antonym: PRIMARY PATH.
  See also: SCENARIO.
  Commentary: The description of a scenario class is normally divided into *primary paths* and *secondary paths,* whereby the secondary paths are variants of the primary paths that often include exception handling. Secondary paths are usually developed after the primary paths. [Firesmith]

path marker *n.* any marker used to mark begin or end times along state-transition paths. [Embley]
See also: STATE NET.

pattern *n.* **1.** any reusable architecture that experience has shown to solve a common problem in a specific context. [Firesmith] **2.** any reusable template of objects with stereotypical responsibilities and interactions. [Coad] **3.** any basic design rule that can be used to guide the development of frameworks. [Lorenz]
Commentary: Patterns are useful during analysis, design, coding, and testing. Patterns provide larger building blocks than individual classes or objects. Patterns are usually based on experience and discovery rather than on invention. [Firesmith] A pattern provides a common solution to a problem in a specific context. [Booch]
Kinds:

- DESIGN PATTERN
  - BEHAVIORAL PATTERN
    + BEHAVIORAL CLASS PATTERN
      > INTERPRETER
      > TEMPLATE METHOD
    + BEHAVIORAL OBJECT PATTERN
      > CHAIN OF RESPONSIBILITY
      > COMMAND
      > ITERATOR
      > MEDIATOR
      > MEMENTO
      > OBSERVER
      > STATE
      > STRATEGY
      > VISITOR
  - CREATIONAL PATTERN
    + CREATIONAL CLASS PATTERN
      > FACTORY METHOD
    + CREATIONAL OBJECT PATTERN
      > ABSTRACT FACTORY
      > BUILDER
      > PROTOTYPE
      > SINGLETON
  - STRUCTURAL PATTERN
    + STRUCTURAL CLASS PATTERN
      > ADAPTER
    + STRUCTURAL OBJECT PATTERN
      > ADAPTER
      > BRIDGE
      > COMPOSITE
      > DECORATOR
      > FACADE
      > FLYWEIGHT
      > PROXY
- FRAMEWORK
- FUNDAMENTAL PATTERN
- IDIOM
- MECHANISM
  - KEY MECHANISM
- MESSAGE PATTERN
- TRANSACTION PATTERN
- **design pattern** *n.* any pattern that systematically names, motivates, and

explains a general design that addresses a recurring design problem in OO systems. [Gamma, Helm, Johnson, & Vlissides]
Commentary: A design pattern describes the problem, a solution to the problem consisting of a general arrangement of objects and classes, when to apply the solution, and the consequences of applying the solution. It should also give implementation hints and examples. [Gamma, Helm, Johnson, & Vlissides] The term *design* may be too restrictive because although these patterns deal with architectural issues, they can also be used during requirements analysis. [Firesmith]
- **behavioral pattern** *n.* any design pattern that is primarily concerned with behavior, the assignment of responsibilities among objects, and the patterns of collaboration between objects. [Gamma, Helm, Johnson, & Vlissides]
Kinds:
    + BEHAVIORAL CLASS PATTERN
      > INTERPRETER
      > TEMPLATE METHOD
    + BEHAVIORAL OBJECT PATTERN
      > CHAIN OF RESPONSIBILITY
      > COMMAND
      > ITERATOR
      > MEDIATOR
      > MEMENTO
      > OBSERVER
      > STATE
      > STRATEGY
      > VISITOR
+ **behavioral class pattern** *n.* any behavioral design pattern that uses inheritance to distribute behavior among classes. [Gamma,

P

Helm, Johnson, & Vlissides]

Kinds:

> INTERPRETER

> TEMPLATE METHOD

> **interpreter [pattern]** *n.* the behavioral class design pattern that models a grammar as a class hierarchy and implements an interpreter as an operation on instances of grammar classes. [Gamma, Helm, Johnson, & Vlissides]

> **template method [pattern]** *n.* the behavioral class design pattern that models an abstract algorithm in which each step invokes either an abstract or primitive algorithm. [Gamma, Helm, Johnson, & Vlissides]

+ **behavioral object pattern** *n.* any behavioral design pattern that uses aggregation to distribute behavior among objects. [Gamma, Helm, Johnson, & Vlissides]

Kinds:

> CHAIN OF RESPONSIBILITY

> COMMAND

> ITERATOR

> MEDIATOR

> MEMENTO

> OBSERVER

> STATE

> STRATEGY

> VISITOR

> **chain of responsibility [pattern]** *n.* the behavioral object design pattern that allows messages to be implicitly sent to an object via a chain of intermediate objects that may either fulfill the associated responsibility or further delegate it down the chain. [Gamma, Helm, Johnson, & Vlissides]

> **command [pattern]** *n.* the behavioral object design pattern that objectifies a request as an object, thereby allowing clients to be parameterized with different requests. [Gamma, Helm, Johnson, & Vlissides]

Synonym: ACTION, TRANSACTION.

> **iterator [pattern]** *n.* the behavioral object design pattern that provides a way to sequentially access the components of an aggregate without exposing its underlying implementation. [Gamma, Helm, Johnson, & Vlissides]

Synonym: CURSOR.

> **mediator [pattern]** *n.* the behavioral object design pattern that avoids unnecessary coupling between collaborating objects by introducing a mediator object between them. [Gamma, Helm, Johnson, & Vlissides]

> **memento [pattern]** *n.* the behavioral object design pattern that objectifies another object's encapsulated state so that the other object can be later returned to that state. [Gamma, Helm, Johnson, & Vlissides]

Synonym: TOKEN.

> **observer [pattern]** *n.* the behavioral object design pattern that allows one object to notify its dependents when it changes state so that they can be updated. [Gamma, Helm, Johnson, & Vlissides]

Synonym: DEPENDENTS, PUBLISH-SUBSCRIBE.

Example: Smalltalk's model/view/controller user interface framework.

> state [pattern] *n.* the behavioral object design pattern that stores state as an encapsulated pointer to instances of subclasses of a state class. [Gamma, Helm, Johnson, & Vlissides]
Commentary: This pattern uses inheritance and polymorphism to eliminate the need for case statements based on state as well as the need for most state-based preconditions and post-conditions.

> strategy [pattern] *n.* the behavioral object design pattern that defines and encapsulates a family of objectified algorithms, allowing the algorithms to vary independently of the clients that use them. [Gamma, Helm, Johnson, & Vlissides]

> visitor [pattern] *n.* the behavioral object design pattern that encapsulates behavior that would otherwise be distributed across classes by allowing a visitor object to traverse an object structure, visiting each node. [Gamma, Helm, Johnson, & Vlissides]

- creational pattern *n.* any design pattern that is primarily concerned with instantiation. [Gamma, Helm, Johnson, & Vlissides]
Kinds:
+ CREATIONAL CLASS PATTERN
> FACTORY METHOD
+ CREATIONAL OBJECT PATTERN
> ABSTRACT FACTORY
> BUILDER
> PROTOTYPE
> SINGLETON

+ creational class pattern *n.* any creational design pattern that uses inheritance to vary the class that is instantiated. [Gamma, Helm, Johnson, & Vlissides]

> factory method [pattern] *n.* the creational class design pattern that defines an interface for creating an object, but defers instantiation of the object to subclasses. [Gamma, Helm, Johnson, & Vlissides]
Synonym: VIRTUAL CONSTRUCTOR.

+ creational object pattern *n.* any creational design pattern that delegates instantiation to another object. [Gamma, Helm, Johnson, & Vlissides]
Kinds:
> ABSTRACT FACTORY
> BUILDER
> PROTOTYPE
> SINGLETON

> abstract factory [pattern] *n.* the creational object design pattern that provides an interface for creating families of related or dependent objects without specifying their concrete classes. [Gamma, Helm, Johnson, & Vlissides]
Synonym: KIT.

> builder [pattern] *n.* the creational object design pattern that separates the instantiation of a complex object from its implementation so that the same instantiation process can be used to create different implementations. [Gamma, Helm, Johnson, & Vlissides]

> prototype [pattern] *n.* the creational object design pattern that creates new objects by copying a

P

prototypical instance. [Gamma, Helm, Johnson, & Vlissides]

> **singleton [pattern]** *n.* the creational object design pattern that ensures that a class has only a single instance and also provides a global access point to the instance. [Gamma, Helm, Johnson, & Vlissides]

- **structural pattern** *n.* any design pattern that is primarily concerned with how larger structures are composed out of classes and objects. [Gamma, Helm, Johnson, & Vlissides]

Kinds:
+ STRUCTURAL CLASS PATTERN
> ADAPTER
+ STRUCTURAL OBJECT PATTERN
> ADAPTER
> BRIDGE
> COMPOSITE
> DECORATOR
> FACADE
> FLYWEIGHT
> PROXY

+ **structural class pattern** *n.* any structural design pattern that uses inheritance to compose interfaces of implementations. [Gamma, Helm, Johnson, & Vlissides]

> **adapter [pattern]** *n.* the structural class/object design pattern that converts the interface of a class into one that clients expect, thereby allowing classes to work together that otherwise could not because of incompatible interfaces. [Gamma, Helm, Johnson, & Vlissides]
Synonym: WRAPPER.

+ **structural object pattern** *n.* any structural design pattern that doc-uments ways to compose larger structures out of objects. [Gamma, Helm, Johnson, & Vlissides]

Kinds:
> ADAPTER
> BRIDGE
> COMPOSITE
> DECORATOR
> FACADE
> FLYWEIGHT
> PROXY

> **adapter [pattern]** *n.* the structural class/object design pattern that converts the interface of a class into one that clients expect, thereby allowing classes to work together that otherwise could not because of incompatible interfaces. [Gamma, Helm, Johnson, & Vlissides]
Synonym: WRAPPER.

> **bridge [pattern]** *n.* the structural object design pattern that decouples an interface from its implementation so that the two can vary independently. [Gamma, Helm, Johnson, & Vlissides]
Synonym: HANDLE/BODY.

> **composite [pattern]** *n.* the structural object design pattern that composes objects into tree-like whole-part hierarchies. [Gamma, Helm, Johnson, & Vlissides]

> **decorator [pattern]** *n.* the structural object design pattern that dynamically attaches additional responsibilities to an object. [Gamma, Helm, Johnson, & Vlissides]
Synonym: WRAPPER.

> **facade [pattern]** *n.* the struc-

tural object design pattern that provides a unified subsystem interface to a set of objects. [Gamma, Helm, Johnson, & Vlissides]

>**flyweight [pattern]** *n.* the structural object design pattern that allows a shared object (the flyweight) to be simultaneously used in multiple contexts. [Gamma, Helm, Johnson, & Vlissides]

>**proxy [pattern]** *n.* the structural object design pattern that provides control over an object via a surrogate or placeholder. [Gamma, Helm, Johnson, & Vlissides]
Synonym: SURROGATE.

• **framework** *n.* **1.** any large reusable, generic specification, design, code, and test pattern of part of an application, consisting primarily of classes (possibly organized into clusters and subframeworks) that implement common capabilities. [Firesmith] **2.** any set of prebuilt classes and methods that define the basic structure of some end-user functions, leaving the application-specific details to be filled in by developers. [Booch, Lorenz, Wirfs-Brock] **3.** any portion of a software system that is designed to provide some useful services through refinement and extension by client developers. [Lorenz] **4.** at an implementation level, any set of classes that cooperate to achieve the goal of providing some functionality. [Lorenz] **5.** any implementation of a design pattern. [Lorenz] **6.** any kind of pattern that provides reuse in the large. [Booch, Firesmith]

Contrast with: CLASS LIBRARY, IDIOM, MECHANISM, PATTERN.
Examples: A GUI framework, a relational database wrapper framework.
Commentary: A framework is a kind of pattern that provides reuse in the large by capturing reusable strategic analysis and design decisions that provide a skeleton on which to build multiple applications. A framework exports a number of individual classes and mechanisms that clients can use or adapt. [Booch, Firesmith]

• **idiom** *n.* any reusable pattern, smaller than a mechanism, that is usually specific to a particular programming language or application culture, representing a generally accepted convention for use of the language. [Booch, Firesmith, Lorenz]
Contrast with: FRAMEWORK, MECHANISM, PATTERN.
Commentary: Idioms may exist within or across cluster boundaries. [Firesmith] An idiom has proven useful multiple times in the past and is therefore recommended as a starting point for similar endeavors. [Lorenz]

• **mechanism** *n.* any mid-sized pattern of collaborating objects or classes whose cooperative behavior provides one or more capabilities. [Booch, Firesmith]
Contrast with: FRAMEWORK, IDIOM, PATTERN.
Example: a control loop consisting of a model object with attribute(s) to be controlled and its associated actuators, sensors, and views. [Firesmith]
Commentary: A mechanism captures tactical analysis and design decisions. A mechanism is larger than an idiom and smaller than a framework.

P

- **key mechanism** *n.* any essential mechanism that forms a part of the vocabulary of the application domain. [Booch, Firesmith]
- **message pattern** *n.* the declaration of any message, specifying the message selector and a set of argument names, one for each argument that a message with this selector must have. [Smalltalk]
Synonyms: MESSAGE DECLARATION, MESSAGE INTERFACE, MESSAGE SIGNATURE.
Commentary: A message pattern matches any messages that have the same selector. A class will have only one method with a given selector in its message pattern. [Smalltalk]

pattern instance *n.* the outcome of applying a pattern. [Coad]
Example: A cashier-sale is a pattern instance of participant-transaction. [Coad]
See also: PATTERN.

pattern player *n.* one of the participating objects in any pattern. [Coad]
See also: PATTERN.
Example: A participant and transaction are the pattern players in the participant-transaction pattern. [Coad]

peer *n.* **1.** anything that is both a client and server of the same thing. [Firesmith] **2.** one of two or more things that depend on one another. [Rumbaugh]
Synonym: COLLEAGUE.
Contrast with: CLIENT, SUPPLIER.
Commentary: Peers depend on one another. The term *colleague* implies collaboration whereas the term *peer* does not. [Firesmith]

peripheral class *n.* any class that provides part of the supporting framework for the business" key classes. [Lorenz]
Example: User interface classes are al-

ways peripheral support classes.
Synonym: BASE CLASS, SUPPORT CLASS.
Contrast with: KEY CLASS.

persist *v.* *-ed, -ing* **1.** to exist after the execution of the program, process, or thread that created one. [Firesmith] **2.** to exist beyond the address space in which one was constructed. [Firesmith, Lorenz]
Commentary: In many OO systems, objects are created and destroyed a furious rates. Those that do remain around for fairly long times often live precariously in the latest volatile copy of the system environment. Persistent objects are saved outside the system, ready to be recreated when needed. The storage for persistent objects can be system files, OODBMSs, traditional DBMSs, or other storage techniques. [Lorenz]
See also: PICKLE.

persistence *n.* **1.** the ability of an object to continue to exist after the execution of the program, process, or thread that created it. [Booch, Firesmith, Henderson-Sellers, Jacobson, OADSIG] **2.** the ability of an object to move beyond the address space in which it was constructed. [Booch, Firesmith]
Contrast with: DYNAMIC OBJECT, PERSISTENT OBJECT, STATIC OBJECT.
Example: Persistence is the property of an object that continues to exist in an objectbase after the program that created it ceases to execute. [Firesmith]
Commentary: Persistence is often implemented by moving the object beyond the address space in which it was constructed. [Firesmith]

persistence layer *n.* the layer that provides independence of any databases or object bases. [Firesmith]
Contrast with: COMMUNICATION LAYER, ENVIRONMENT LAYER, MODEL LAY-

ER, USER-INTERFACE LAYER.

Commentary: The persistence layer is typically built on top of the environment layer. [Firesmith]

persistent-capable class *n.* any class that can have both persistent and transient instances. [ODMG]

Contrast with: TRANSIENT CLASS.

persistent class *n.* any class, the instance of which are persistent objects that exist after the execution of the program, process, or thread that created it. [Firesmith]

Antonym: TRANSIENT CLASS.

Example: any class of objects stored in an objectbase. [Firesmith]

Commentary: A persistent object typically survives the process or thread that created it, existing until explicitly deleted. A persistent object also typically exists outside of the address space in which it was created. Persistent objects can be stored in object-oriented databases, extended relational databases, relational databases, Smalltalk images, files, etc. [Firesmith]

persistent object *n.* **1.** any object that exists after the execution of the program, process, or thread that created it. [Firesmith, OMG] **2.** the persistent objects of an environment are all the objects recorded under some key in the environment, and their dependents. [Eiffel, Meyer]

Contrast with: DYNAMIC OBJECT, STATIC OBJECT.

Example: Any object stored in an objectbase is a persistent object. [Firesmith]

Commentary: A persistent object exists until it is explicitly deleted. [OMG] A persistent object typically survives the process or thread that created it, existing until explicitly deleted. A persistent

object also typically exists outside of the address space in which it was created. Persistent objects can be stored in object-oriented databases, extended relational databases, relational databases, Smalltalk images, files, etc. [Firesmith]

personification *n.* any figure of speech that gives human characteristics to inanimate objects. [Coad]

Synonym: ANTHROPOMORPHISM.

Examples: "I am an object. Here's what I know, who I know, and what I do." [Coad]

Examples: Personification helps developers think like an object (rather than remain somewhat aloof, at a distance, merely describing the data and functions that are needed in a model. [Coad]

physical pragma *n.* any construct defined in the ODL or OML used to either (1) give a programmer some direct control over the physical storage of objects, clustering, and memory management issues associated with the stored physical representation of objects, and access structures like indices used to accelerate object retrieval or (2) enable a programmer to provide *hints* to the storage management subsystem provided as part of the ODBMS run-time. [ODMG]

pickle *v.* *-ed, ing* to store a persistent object in a permanent storage (e.g., in object-oriented databases, extended relational databases, relational databases, Smalltalk images, files, etc.). [Firesmith]

Synonym: FREEZE.

See also: PERSIST.

place *n.* any object type associated by a *relation*. [Martin/Odell]

See also: RELATION.

Example: Employment is a relation between the object types *Person* and *Or-*

P

ganization. Employment, then, is a 2-place relation, where *Person* and *Organization* are its places. [Martin/Odell]

Rationale: The word *place* is used, because it refers to a specific position in a relational expression, as in Employment (Person, Organization). [Martin/Odell]

pointer [to a given object] *n.* **1.** any link, the value of which is the identifier of the given server object. [Firesmith] **2.** any attribute of one object that contains an explicit reference to another object. [Rumbaugh]

Contrast with: IDENTIFIER, KEY, LINK, REFERENCE.

Commentary: Unless changed, a pointer will identify the same object each time the pointer is used (subject to certain pragmatic limits of space and time). An object may be denoted by multiple, distinct pointers. [Firesmith]

Kinds:
- ATTACHED POINTER
- DANGLING POINTER
- VOID POINTER

- **attached pointer** *n.* any pointer that currently points to an object. [Firesmith]

  Contrast with: DANGLING POINTER, VOID POINTER.

  Commentary: The pointer is said to be attached to the object, and the object is also said to be attached to the pointer. [Firesmith]

- **dangling pointer** *n.* any pointer that points to an object that does not exist. [Firesmith]

  Contrast with: ATTACHED POINTER, VOID POINTER.

- **void pointer** *n.* any pointer that does not currently point to an object. [Firesmith]

  Synonym: NULL POINTER.

Contrast with: ATTACHED POINTER, DANGLING POINTER.

policy method *n.* any method that makes context-dependent decisions, switches control among other methods, combines and parameterizes calls to lower-level methods, and checks for status and error, but which calls on other methods for detailed computations. [Rumbaugh]

Contrast with: IMPLEMENTATION METHOD.

polling *n.* the situation that occurs when a client-concurrent operation must continually send messages to a server-concurrent operation to determine whether an event has occurred instead of being sent a message once on occurrence of the event. [Firesmith]

Commentary: Avoiding unnecessary polling is an important design heuristic, especially in real-time applications, and an important consideration when determining the direction of message passing. [Firesmith]

polymorphic invocation *n.* any invocation at design time of one of a set of instance-based published operations, where all of the published operations in the set have the same module name but differing class names. [Shlaer/Mellor]

polymorphic operation *n.* any operation that has multiple forms (i.e., implementations) due to polymorphism. [Firesmith]

See also: POLYMORPHISM.

Kinds:
- AD HOC POLYMORPHIC OPERATION
- GENERIC OPERATION
- INHERENTLY POLYMORPHIC OPERATION
- OVERLOADED OPERATION
  - GLOBALLY OVERLOADED

OPERATION
- LOCALLY OVERLOADED
OPERATION

- **ad hoc polymorphic operation** *n.* any polymorphic operation that has a single method containing multiple implementations of the same functional abstraction, one of which is selected at run-time using a case statement, switch statement, or similar language construct. [Firesmith]
See also: AD HOC POLYMORPHISM.

- **generic operation** *n.* **1.** any operation that is parameterized with generic formal parameters that must be supplied as part of the instantiation process. [Firesmith] **2.** any operation that can be bound to more than one method. [OMG]
Contrast with: GENERIC CLASS GENERIC TYPE.
See also: PARAMETRIC POLYMORPHISM.

- **inherently polymorphic operation** *n.* any polymorphic operation that occurs in different descendants of the same ancestor whereby each variant has the same name, functional abstraction, and signature, but has a different method. [Firesmith]
See also: INHERENT POLYMORPHISM.

- **overloaded operation** *n.* any polymorphic operation whereby each variant has the same name and functional abstraction, but each has a different signature and method. [Firesmith, ODMG]
See also: OVERLOADING.
Kinds:
  - GLOBALLY OVERLOADED OPERATION
  - LOCALLY OVERLOADED OPERATION

- **globally overloaded operation** *n.* any overloaded operation, the variants of which occur in different contexts or scopes unrelated by inheritance. [Firesmith]
See also: GLOBAL OVERLOADING.
Rationale: Global overloading occurs *globally* across classes that are unrelated by inheritance. [Firesmith]

- **locally overloaded operation** *n.* any overloaded operation that occurs multiple times in the same class whereby each variant has the same name and functional abstraction, but each has a different signature and method. [Firesmith]
See also: LOCAL OVERLOADING.
Examples: Constructors are often overloaded with the simple default constructor having the same name but fewer parameters than more complex constructors. [Firesmith]
Rationale: Local overloading occurs *locally* within a single class. [Firesmith]
Commentary: Local overloading allows multiple operations with the same name to be defined provided their signatures differ sufficiently for calls to be resolved. The resolution of local overloading may be based on different numbers of parameters, parameters of different types, different return types, different exceptions raised, or different message type (e.g., sequential, synchronous, asynchronous). Unlike inherent polymorphism, local overloading is usually resolved at compile time. [Firesmith]

polymorphic substitution *n.* the substitution of an instance of a child where an instance of one of its ancestors was expected. [Firesmith]

See also: INHERENT POLYMORPHISM, SPECIALIZATION INHERITANCE.

Commentary: Polymorphic substitutability requires both inherent polymorphism and the use of specialization inheritance so that messages intended for instances of the ancestor can be correctly handled by instances of the child. Thus, the protocol of the child must be a superset of the protocol of the ancestor and common messages must implement common abstractions. The ability to perform polymorphic substitutions is a major advantage of interface inheritance over implementation inheritance. [Firesmith]

polymorphism *n.* **1.** the ability of a single name to refer to different things having different forms. [Firesmith] **2.** (a) the ability of a single name (e.g., that of a variable or link) to refer to different objects (e.g., objects of different classes related by subtyping). [Booch, Coleman, Firesmith, Jacobson, Wirfs-Brock] (b) the ability of a single name to refer to different objects that fulfill some of the same message protocol responsibilities (roles). [Lorenz] (c) the ability to call a variety of operations using the same interface (i.e., signature). [Coleman, C++] **3.** the ability to have more than one dynamic type. [Eiffel, Meyer]

Antonym: MONOMORPHISM.

See also: FEATURE REDEFINITION.

Rationale: The Greek term *polymorphos* means having *many forms.* The term *polymorphism* has related meanings in biology, chemistry, and mineralogy. [Firesmith]

Commentary: Inherent polymorphism is more powerful than parametric polymorphism, which is more powerful than local overloading, which is more powerful than global overloading, which is more powerful than ad hoc polymorphism. Inherent polymorphism determines the correct method based on the type of the object, local overloading determines the correct method based on the signature of the operation, and ad hoc polymorphism determines the correct submethod based on the parameters of the operation. [Firesmith] Together with dynamic binding, polymorphism makes type-specific coding unnecessary and eliminates many case statements based on type (e.g., objects belonging to classes related by type). [Booch] Polymorphism provides a means of factoring out the differences among a collection of abstractions, so that a program may be written in terms of their common properties. [Ada95]

Kinds:
- AD HOC POLYMORPHISM
- INCLUSION POLYMORPHISM
- INHERENT POLYMORPHISM
- LIMITED POLYMORPHISM
- OVERLOADING
  - FUNCTIONAL OVERLOADING
  - GLOBAL OVERLOADING
  - LOCAL OVERLOADING
- PARAMETRIC POLYMORPHISM

• **ad hoc polymorphism** *n.* any polymorphism in which multiple implementations of a single operation are included within a single method and one of these implementations is selected at run-time (e.g. using a case statement, switch statement, or similar language construct). [Firesmith]

Contrast with: INHERENT POLYMORPHISM.

Rationale: This kind of polymorphism is *ad hoc* in that it does not make use of any of the powerful tools of object orientation. [Firesmith] *Commentary:* The implementation selected is typically dependent on either an argument of the message or the state of the receiver. This form of polymorphism is neither maintainable, extensible, nor object oriented. [Firesmith]

• **inclusion polymorphism** *n.* **1.** any polymorphism in which a single inherited message/operation may be dynamically bound to different methods in different descendants of the same ancestor. [Coad, Firesmith, Martin] **2.** any polymorphism whereby operations are inherited by every subtype. [OADSIG] *Synonym:* INHERENT POLYMORPHISM. *Rationale:* An instance of a specialization is also an instance of its generalization because the extent of the specialization is *included* (i.e., is a subset of) the extent of its generalization. [Firesmith] *Commentary:* Inclusion polymorphism requires the use of either specialization or interface inheritance so that the same message can be sent to instances of the different derived classes. Inclusion polymorphism also requires dynamic binding so that this common message can be bound to the correct associated polymorphic operation of the correct instance, even if the class of the instance is not known at compile time. The operation is called *polymorphic* (i.e., having *many forms*) because it has different methods in different descendants. Together with dynamic binding, inclusion polymorphism usually makes type-specific coding unnecessary and

eliminates most case statements based on type. Unlike local overloading, inclusion polymorphism must often be resolved at run-time. [Firesmith]

• **inherent polymorphism** *n.* **1.** any polymorphism in which a single inherited message/operation may be dynamically bound to different methods in different descendants of the same ancestor. [Coad, Firesmith, Martin] **2.** any polymorphism whereby operations are inherited by every subtype. [OADSIG]

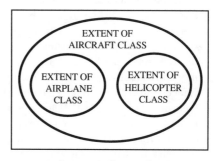

Inherent Polymorphism

Synonym: INCLUSION POLYMORPHISM. *Rationale:* Most developers mean inherent polymorphism when they say polymorphism. *Inherent* polymorphism requires the use of either specialization or interface *inheritance* so that the same message can be sent to instances of the different descendants. The term *inclusion* is ambiguous and therefore not as intuitive as the term *inherent.* [Firesmith] *Commentary:* Inherent polymorphism requires the use of either specialization or interface inheritance so that the same message can be sent to instances of the different derived classes. Inherent polymorphism also requires dynamic binding so that this common message can be bound to the correct associated polymorphic operation of the correct instance, even if the class of the instance is not known at compile time. The operation is called *polymorphic* (i.e., having *many forms*) because it has different methods in different descendants. Together with dynamic binding, inherent polymorphism usually makes type-specific coding unnecessary and eliminates most case statements based on type. Unlike local overloading, inherent polymorphism must often be resolved at run-time. [Firesmith]

• **limited polymorphism** *n.* any polymorphism that is restricted to the instances of specific classes. [Jacobson] *Contrast with:* INCLUSION POLYMORPHISM, INHERENT POLYMORPHISM.

• **overloading** *n.* any polymorphism whereby the same name is overloaded (i.e., is used for different, but analogous, abstractions). [Firesmith] *Example:* Buildings and people may both have age and height attributes with associated accessor operations, even though the building and person classes need not be related by inheritance. [Firesmith] *Commentary:* Overloading allows multiple operations with the same name to be defined provided their signatures differ sufficiently for calls to be resolved. Unlike inclusion polymorphism, overloading is usually resolved at compile time. This form of polymorphism applies the software engineering principle of uniformity to naming. [Firesmith] *Kinds:*

- FUNCTIONAL OVERLOADING
- GLOBAL OVERLOADING
- LOCAL OVERLOADING

- **functional overloading** *n.* the use of a single name for several different functions in a single scope. [C++]
- **global overloading** *n.* any overloading in which the same name is used for abstractions in different contexts or scopes unrelated by inheritance. [Firesmith] *Example:* Buildings and people may both have age and height attributes with associated accessor operations, even though the building and person classes are not related by inheritance. [Firesmith] *Rationale: Global* overloading occurs *globally* across unrelated classes. [Firesmith]
- **local overloading** *n.* any overloading in which the same name, but different signatures, is used for messages and operations implementing the same functional abstraction within the same class. [Firesmith, Rumbaugh] *Examples:* Constructors are often overloaded with the simple default constructor having the same name but fewer parameters than more complex constructors. [Firesmith] *Rationale: Local* overloading occurs *locally* within a single class. [Firesmith] *Commentary:* Local overloading allows multiple operations with the same name to be defined provided their signatures differ sufficiently for calls to be resolved. The resolution of local overloading may be based on different numbers

of parameters, parameters of different types, different return types, different exceptions raised, or different message type (e.g., sequential, synchronous, asynchronous). Unlike inherent polymorphism, local overloading is usually resolved at compile time. [Firesmith]

• **parametric polymorphism** *n.* **1.** any polymorphism due to parameterization. [Booch, Firesmith] **2.** the overriding of an inherited feature by a subclass. [Martin]
Synonym: GENERICITY.
Examples: The parameterization of types, classes, and clusters are examples of parametric polymorphism.
Commentary: Although inherent polymorphism can simulate parametric polymorphism and the reverse is not true, parametric polymorphism provides great convenience and minimizes the number of classes needed in a class library. [Firesmith] Definition 1 is the standard definition for this term. The standard term for definition 2 is *inclusion polymorphism.*

pool *n.* any group of variables that are shared by more than one object. [Smalltalk]
See also: CLASS VARIABLE, POOL VARIABLE, SMALLTALK.
Commentary: Each class has two or more pools whose variables can be accessed by its instances. [Smalltalk]
Kinds:
  • CLASS POOL
  • SMALLTALK

• **class pool** *n.* any pool that is only available to the instances of the class and that contains the class variables. [Smalltalk]

• **Smalltalk** *n.* any pool that is shared

by all classes and that contains all of the global variables. [Smalltalk]

pool variable *n.* any variable shared by the instances of a subset of the classes. [Smalltalk]
Contrast with: CLASS VARIABLE, GLOBAL VARIABLE, INSTANCE VARIABLE, TEMPORARY VARIABLE.

port variable *n.* any instance variable designed to hold imported references, and thus to refer to "external" objects. [Atkinson]

portability *n.* the ease with which software can be transitioned to another hardware or software environment. [Firesmith]

postcondition *n.* **1.** (a) any assertion on an operation or scenario that must be true immediately following the execution if all preconditions were true immediately prior to execution. [Coad, Firesmith] (b) any condition that describes the correct effect of its associated operation or scenario. [Coleman, Firesmith] (c) any requirement that the routine (server) must satisfy on return, if the precondition was satisfied on entry. [Eiffel, Meyer] (d) any constraint that guarantees the results when the operation is executed. [Martin] (e) any condition that the operation itself agrees to achieve. [Rumbaugh] **2.** any invariant satisfied by an operation. [Booch]
Synonym: OPERATION POSTCONDITION RULE.
Contrast with: INVARIANT, PRECONDITION.
See also: ASSERTION.
Example: A postcondition of the push operation on a stack is that the stack not be empty. [Firesmith]
Commentary: Postconditions are used

P

to ensure that the associated operation was correctly executed. Definition **2** uses the term *invariant* instead of the more appropriate term *assertion* (i.e., precondition or postcondition). [Firesmith]

potential version in a descendant [of a feature] *n.* any feature in the descendant that is inherited from the original feature after possible redeclarations and generic derivations. [Eiffel, Meyer] *Contrast with:* CURRENT FEATURE.

potentially ambiguous feature *n.* any feature that is potentially ambiguous in a repeated descendant because it presents more than one choice for dynamic binding. [Eiffel, Firesmith, Meyer]

power class *n.* any metaclass, the instances of which are child classes of another class. [Firesmith]
Contrast with: DISCRIMINATOR, DISCRIMINATOR CLASS, PARTITION.
Example: The class *Item_Type* is the power class of the class *Item* and its instances are the children of *Item*. [Firesmith]
Commentary: Instances of power classes are often used as attributes of other classes. [Firesmith]

- **discriminator class** *n.* any power class whose instances partition another class (i.e., whose instances form a disjoint cover of the class being partitioned). [Firesmith]
Example: The *genders* class is a discriminator class for the class *persons*, partitioning it into the child classes *males* and *females*. [Firesmith]

power type *n.* any type, the instances of which are the subtypes of another type. [Firesmith, Martin/Odell]
Contrast with: DISCRIMINATOR, DISCRIMINATOR CLASS, PARTITION.
Example: The type *Item_Type* is the

power type of the type *Item* and its instances are the children of *Item*. [Firesmith]
Commentary: Instances of power types are often used as attributes of other classes. [Firesmith] The object type *Product Type* is the power type of the object type *Product* and consists of all of the subtypes of *Product*. [Martin/Odell]

precondition *n.* **1.** (a) any assertion on an operation or scenario that must evaluate to true prior to execution. [Coad, Firesmith] (b) any predicate that characterizes the conditions under which an operation may be invoked. [Coleman] (c) any constraint that guarantees the results when the operation is executed. [Martin] (d) any requirement that clients must satisfy whenever they call a routine. [Eiffel, Meyer, Rumbaugh] **2.** any invariant assumed by an operation. [Booch]
Synonyms: CONTROL CONDITION, OPERATION PRECONDITION RULE.
Contrast with: INVARIANT, POSTCONDITION.
See also: ASSERTION.
Example: A precondition of the push operation on a stack is that the stack not be full. [Firesmith]
Commentary: Preconditions are used to ensure that the associated operation may be correctly executed. Definition 1 (d) makes the client rather than the server responsible for satisfying the precondition. Definition **2** uses a nonstandard definition of the term *invariant*. [Firesmith]

precursor [of an inherited feature] *n.* the version of the feature in the parent from which it is inherited. [Eiffel, Firesmith, Meyer]

See also: REDEFINITION.

Contrast with: ORIGIN.

predicate *n.* **1.** any Boolean conjunction or disjunction of operations supported by the object types that appear within the predicate. [ODMG] **2.** any list of clauses each of which must be true in order for the predicate to be satisfied. [Coleman]

presentation [class] *n.* **1.** any specialized view class that exists to provide a *formatted* view of (i.e., information about and control over) one or more model or view classes. [Firesmith] **2.** any class of presentation objects. [Firesmith]

Contrast with: PRESENTATION OBJECT, PROXY CLASS.

Example: A model or view class may have more than one presentation class, and a presentation class may also be a controller class of its model or view class(es). [Firesmith]

presentation [object] *n.* **1.** any specialized view object that exists to provide a *formatted* view of (i.e., information about and control over) one or more model or view objects. [Firesmith] **2.** any instance of a presentation class. [Firesmith]

Contrast with: PRESENTATION CLASS, PROXY OBJECT.

Commentary: A model or view object may have more than one presentation object, and a presentation object may also be a controller object of its model or view object(s). [Firesmith]

presentation object type *n.* any user interface object type that describes the visual appearance of the user interface. [OADSIG]

Examples: The chart of today's stock usage, a box object, a line object, and a tree object are all instances of presenta-

tion object types. [OADSIG]

presentation diagram (PRD) *n.* any diagram showing the display of a presentation object or class.

presentation model *n.* the implementation-level model that documents a physical view of the user interface objects and classes (e.g., windows, dialog boxes). The presentation model consists of one or more presentation diagrams and presentation dependency diagrams. [Firesmith]

Contrast with: CONFIGURATION MODEL, INTERACTION MODEL, LANGUAGE MODEL, SEMANTIC MODEL, STATE MODEL.

preserver message *n.* any message that does not result, either directly or indirectly, in the modification of the value of any properties. [Firesmith]

Antonym: MODIFIER MESSAGE.

preserver operation *n.* any operation that does not modify the value of any properties. [Firesmith]

Antonym: MODIFIER OPERATION.

primary actor *n.* any actors who is going to use the system directly and that will perform one or some of the main tasks of the system. [Jacobson]

Antonym: SECONDARY ACTOR

primary method *n.* any method that defines the main action of the effective method. [CLOS]

Commentary: A primary method has no method qualifiers. [CLOS]

primary module *n.* the unit of code that receives control when a published operation is invoked. [Shlaer/Mellor]

primary operation *n.* any operation that directly implements a primary responsibility of the class. [Firesmith]

Antonym: SECONDARY OPERATION.

primary path [through a given scenario class] *n.* any of the most common or

P

important paths through the given scenario class. [Firesmith]

Antonym: SECONDARY PATH.

See also: SCENARIO.

Commentary: The description of a scenario class is normally divided into *primary paths* and *secondary paths*, whereby the primary paths provide the best understanding of the scenario class. Primary paths are usually developed before the secondary paths. [Firesmith]

primary responsibility *n.* any essential responsibility. [Firesmith]

Antonym: SECONDARY OPERATION.

primary scenario *n.* any scenario that directly implements a primary requirement of the application. [Booch, Firesmith]

Antonym: SECONDARY SCENARIO.

primitive method *n.* **1.** any method performed directly by the run time of the language and therefore not expressed as a sequence of expressions in that programming language. [Firesmith, Smalltalk] **2.** any method that *cannot* be accomplished simply, reliably, and efficiently without knowledge of the underlying implementation. [Berard]

Contrast with: PRIMITIVE OPERATION.

primitive object *n.* any object that is provided by the environment, most typically by the programming language. [Berard]

Commentary: Primitive objects provide a basis for the construction of other, non-primitive objects, and are a mechanism for communication among otherwise uncoupled objects. [Berard]

primitive operation *n.* any operation, the method of which is performed directly by the run time of the language and therefore not expressed as a sequence of expressions in that program-

ming language. [Firesmith]

Contrast with: PRIMITIVE METHOD.

primitive operation [of a type] *n.* either the predefined operations of the type or any user-defined primitive subprograms. [Ada95]

See also: INHERITANCE.

Commentary: Primitive operations are the derivable (inherited) operations. [Ada95]

primitive value *n.* any value that is merely a data abstraction. [Firesmith]

Antonym: NONPRIMITIVE VALUE.

Examples: Any character, integer, or the Boolean values *true* and *false* are all primitive values. [Firesmith]

principal interface *n.* the interface that describes all requests in which an object is meaningful. [OMG]

Contrast with: CLASS INTERFACE, CLUSTER INTERFACE, CONSTRUCTION INTERFACE, FUNCTIONAL INTERFACE, MESSAGE INTERFACE, OBJECT INTERFACE, OPERATION INTERFACE, ORB INTERFACE, SYSTEM INTERFACE, TYPE INTERFACE.

priority inversion *n.* the situation that occurs when a high priority concurrent operation is blocked from execution because it is waiting on a low-priority concurrent operation that is in turn waiting on a medium priority concurrent operation. [Firesmith]

prior state *n.* any state that an object or class is in immediately preceding a specified transition. [Embley, Firesmith]

Antonyms: SUBSEQUENT STATE.

private *adj.* **1.** describing members (i.e., features) that are hidden from both external clients and descendants. [Booch, C++, Firesmith, Rumbaugh] **2.** describing inheritance in which all inherited members (i.e., features) become *private* in the derived class, regardless

of their visibility in the defining base class. [C++]
Contrast with: PROTECTED, PUBLIC.

private extension *n.* any record-type extension that extends another type by adding additional components that are hidden from its clients. [Ada95]
Antonym: RECORD EXTENSION.

private feature *n.* any feature that is hidden in the implementation from all children as well as all other clients. [Firesmith]
Antonym: EXPORTED FEATURE.
Commentary: A private feature must be used with care as it may violate subtyping, specialization inheritance, and polymorphic substitutability. An *exported feature* may be transformed into a private feature in child classes by the use of *private inheritance*. In C++, private features (a.k.a., members) are typically declared in the interface (i.e., header file) but implemented in the body (e.g., cpp file). [Firesmith]

private inheritance *n.* any inheritance in which all inherited features become private, regardless of their visibility in the parents. [Firesmith]
Contrast with: PROTECTED INHERITANCE, PUBLIC INHERITANCE.
Commentary: The use of private inheritance supports information hiding and the maintainability of inheritance structures because it allows developers to change the implementation of ancestors without impacting their descendants. However, private inheritance must be used with care as it may also prevent the child from conforming to its parents by hiding their visible features, thus violating subtyping, specialization inheritance, and polymorphic substitutability. [Firesmith]

private member *n.* any member (i.e., feature) that is hidden from both external clients and descendants. [C++]
Contrast with: PROTECTED MEMBER, PUBLIC MEMBER.
Commentary: In C++, private members are typically declared in the interface (i.e., header file) but implemented in the body (i.e., cpp file).

private method *n.* any hidden method that exists to help this class get its work done. [Lorenz]
Antonym: PUBLIC METHOD.

private-object module *n.* any object module that is hidden within, and therefore cannot be accessed from the outside of, its enclosing block. [Jacobson]
Antonym: PUBLIC-OBJECT MODULE.

private property [of an object] *n.* either any instance variable that makes up part of its private memory or a method that describes how to carry out one of its operations. [Smalltalk]

private responsibility *n.* any responsibility that is hidden in the implementation from all children as well as all other clients. [Firesmith, Martin, Wirfs-Brock]
Antonym: PUBLIC RESPONSIBILITY.
Commentary: Private responsibilities are implemented by private members. [Firesmith]

private type *n.* any partial view of a type whose full view is hidden from its clients. [Ada95]

private variable *n.* a variable that is available only to a single object. [Smalltalk]
Kinds:
- INSTANCE VARIABLE
  - INDEXED INSTANCE VARIABLE
  - NAMED INSTANCE VARIABLE
- TEMPORARY VARIABLE

- **instance variable** *n.* **1.** any attribute

P

of an individual instance. [Firesmith, Smalltalk] **2.** any place to store and refer to an object's state data. [Booch, Lorenz] **3.** any name that allows one object (instance) to refer to another one. [Lorenz]

Synonym: INSTANCE ATTRIBUTE.

Rationale: In OO systems, data are made up of object instances, hence the name *instance variable*. [Lorenz] The term *instance attribute* should probably be used instead of *instance variable* because it is less language specific and because some instance attributes are constants.

Commentary: All instance variables are protected in Smalltalk, whereas C++ also allows instance variables (a.k.a. data members) to be public or protected.

Kinds:
- INDEXED INSTANCE VARIABLE
- NAMED INSTANCE VARIABLE

- **indexed instance variable** *n.* any instance variable that is not accessed by names. [Smalltalk]

Antonym: NAMED INSTANCE VARIABLE.

Example: names at: 1 [Smalltalk]

Commentary: An object can have indexed instance variables only if all instances of its class can have indexed instance variables. [Smalltalk]

- **named instance variable** *n.* any instance variable that is accessed by its instance variable name. [Smalltalk]

Antonym: INDEXED INSTANCE VARIABLE.

Commentary: All instances of a class have the same number of named instance variables and use the same names to refer to them. [Smalltalk]

- **temporary variable** *n.* any variable created for a specific activity and available only for the duration of that activity. [Smalltalk]

Commentary: Temporary variables do not include pseudo-variables such as argument names and self. [Smalltalk]

probe *n.* any position in the description of a use case where another use case can be inserted to extend the behavior of the first use case. [Jacobson]

See also: EXTEND ASSOCIATION.

problem domain *n.* **1.** the real-world. **2.** the overall area of the business with which the application under development is concerned. [Firesmith, Lorenz] **3.** the domain of the problem as opposed to the solution. [Firesmith] **4.** any separate real, hypothetical, or abstract world inhabited by a distinct set of objects that behave according to rules and policies characteristic of the domain. [Shlaer/Mellor]

Synonyms: APPLICATION DOMAIN, PROBLEM SPACE.

Antonyms: SOLUTION DOMAIN, SOLUTION SPACE.

Example: The area of a bank's business that has to do with automated teller machines (ATMs) is the problem domain for an ATM application. [Lorenz]

Kinds:
- APPLICATION DOMAIN
- ARCHITECTURAL DOMAIN
- IMPLEMENTATION DOMAIN
- SERVICE DOMAIN

- **application domain** *n.* the subject matter of the system from the perspective of the end user of the system. [Shlaer/Mellor]

- **architectural domain** *n.* the domain that provides generic mechanisms and structures for managing data and control for the system as a whole. [Shlaer/Mellor]

- **implementation domain** *n.* the domain providing the conceptual entities in which the entire system will be implemented. [Shlaer/Mellor]
Examples: Programming languages, networks, operating systems, and common class libraries are common implementation domains.
- **service domain** *n.* the domain that provides generic mechanisms and utility functions as required to support the application domain. [Shlaer/Mellor]

problem domain (PD) component *n.* the component that contains the technology-neutral objects that directly correspond to the problem being modeled. [Coad]
Commentary: Theses objects have little (or no) knowledge about objects in the other components (human interaction, data management, and system interaction). [Coad]

problem domain object *n.* any object that has a direct counterpart in the application environment about which the system should handle information. [Jacobson]

problem domain object type *n.* any tangible or conceptual real-world object type. [OADSIG]

problem space *n.* **1.** the real-world. **2.** the domain of the problem as opposed to the solution.
Synonym: PROBLEM DOMAIN.
Antonym: SOLUTION SPACE.

procedure *n.* **1.** any operation that does not return a significant value. [Firesmith] **2.** any operation that may perform multiple actions and modify the instance to which it is applied, but does not return a value. [Eiffel, Meyer]

Antonym: FUNCTION.
Contrast with: ROUTINE, SUBPROGRAM.
Examples: Any C++ member function that returns void or most Smalltalk methods that return self may be considered to be procedures rather than functions. [Firesmith]
Commentary: A procedure may read data, update variables, or produce some output. A procedure may have parameters to provide a controlled means of passing information between the procedure and the point of call. [Ada95]

process *n.* **1.** (a) any thread of control that can logically execute concurrently with other processes. [Firesmith] (b) the activation of any single thread of control. [Booch] **2.** any operation documented on a data flow diagram that performs a data transform. [Rumbaugh] **3.** any separate unit of computation on an action data flow diagram (ADFD) that incorporates both computation or transformation of data as well as any work required to read or write data from data stores. [Shlaer/Mellor] **4.** any sequence of actions described by expressions and performed by the Smalltalk virtual machine. [Smalltalk]
Kinds: **3**

- ACCESSOR
  - CREATE ACCESSOR
  - DELETE ACCESSOR
  - READ ACCESSOR
  - WRITE ACCESSOR
- ACTIVE PROCESS
- EVENT GENERATOR
- TEST
- TRANSFORMATION

- **accessor** *n.* any typically small, simple, almost standard operation used to access the value of an attribute. [Shlaer/Mellor]

P

Synonyms: ACCESSING METHOD, AC-
CESSING OPERATION, ACCESSOR METH-
OD, PRESERVER OPERATION.
Contrast with: ACCESSOR MESSAGE,
ACCESSING MESSAGE, PRESERVER MES-
SAGE.
Kinds:
- CREATE ACCESSOR
- DELETE ACCESSOR
- READ ACCESSOR
- WRITE ACCESSOR

- **create accessor** *n.* any accessor operation that creates a new instance
of an object. [Shlaer/Mellor]
- **delete accessor** *n.* any accessor operation that deletes an instance of
an object. [Shlaer/Mellor]
- **read accessor** *n.* any accessor operation that reads attributes of an object. [Firesmith, Shlaer/Mellor]
- **write accessor** *n.* any accessor operation that updates attributes of an
object [Firesmith, Shlaer/Mellor]
- **active process** *n.* the process whose
actions are currently being carried
out. [Smalltalk]
- **event generator** *n.* any process that
produces exactly one event as output.
[Shlaer/Mellor]
Contrast with: ACCESSOR, EVENT TAK-
ER, TEST, TRANSFORMATION.
- **test** *n.* any process that tests a condition and makes one of several conditional control outputs is known as a
test. [Shlaer/Mellor]
- **transformation** *n.* any process whose
purpose is one of computation or
transformation of data: the process
exists to convert its input data into a
new form that is then output. [Shlaer/
Mellor]
process abstraction *n.* any model of a
concurrent operation. [Firesmith]

Contrast with: FUNCTIONAL ABSTRAC-
TION.
process architecture *n.* **1.** the architecture of an application in terms of processors, devices, the connections between them, and the static allocation of
processes to processors. [Booch, Fire-
smith] **2.** the architecture documented
by one or more related processor diagrams. [Booch]
Synonym: PROCESS MODEL.
Contrast with: PROCESSOR ARCHITEC-
TURE.
process-descriptions document *n.* any
compilation of any process descriptions produced, ordered by process
identifier. [Shlaer/Mellor]
process diagram (PD) *n.* any diagram
used to show the allocation of processes to processors in the physical design
of an application. [Booch]
Contrast with: PROCESSOR DIAGRAM.
process model *n.* any static architecture
model of an application in terms of
processes, the objects they contain, and
the processors they are allocated to.
Synonym: PROCESS ARCHITECTURE.
processor *n.* any piece of hardware that
has significant computational resources. [Booch, Firesmith]
processor architecture *n.* **1.** the architecture of an application in terms of processors, devices, the connections between
them, and the static allocation of processes to processors. [Firesmith] **2.** the architecture documented by one or more related processor diagrams. [Firesmith]
Contrast with: PROCESS ARCHITEC-
TURE.
processor-communication layer *n.* any
layer of communication objects and
classes providing access to objects and
classes on other processors.

Contrast with: DATABASE-INDEPENDENCE LAYER, DOMAIN LAYER, ENVIRONMENT-INDEPENDENCE LAYER, USER-INTERFACE LAYER.

profile *n.* any group of components. [OMG]

program *n.* any static object-based application consisting of a set of types and classes interrelated specific to a particular (end-user) objective. [OMG]

program unit *n.* any unit of a program consisting of a visible specification and hidden body. [Ada95]
See also: BODY, SPECIFICATION.
Kinds:
- GENERIC UNIT
- PACKAGE
- PROTECTED UNIT
- SUBPROGRAM
  - ABSTRACT SUBPROGRAM
  - FUNCTION
  - PROCEDURE
- TASK

- **generic program unit** *n.* any parameterized template for the creation of a nongeneric program unit; the template can be parameterized by objects, types, subprograms, and packages, allowing general algorithms and data structures to be defined that are applicable to all types of a given class. [Ada95]
  See also: PROGRAM UNIT.
  Commentary: An instance of a generic unit is created by a generic instantiation. The rules of the language are enforced when a generic unit is compiled, using a generic contract model; additional checks are performed on instantiation to verify the contract is met. That is, the declaration of a generic unit represents a contract between the body of the generic and in-

stances of the generic. Generic units can be used to perform the role that macros sometimes play in other languages. [Ada95]

- **package** *n.* any program unit that allows the specification of groups of logically related entities. [Ada95]
  Commentary: Typically, a package contains the declaration of a type (often a private type or private extension) along with the declarations of primitive subprograms of the type, which can be called from outside the package, while their inner workings remain hidden from outside users. [Ada95]

- **protected unit** *n.* any program unit that is the basic unit for defining protected operations for the coordinated use of data shared between tasks. [Ada95b]

- **subprogram** *n.* the basic program unit for expressing an algorithm. [Ada95]
  Commentary: An Ada subprogram is known as an operation in other languages.
  Kinds:
  - ABSTRACT SUBPROGRAM
  - FUNCTION
  - PROCEDURE.

  - **abstract subprogram** *n.* any subprogram that has no body, but is intended to be overridden at some point when inherited. [Ada95]
    Synonyms: ABSTRACT METHOD, ABSTRACT OPERATION, DEFERRED OPERATION.

  - **function** *n.* **1.** any sequential operation that returns a value. [Ada95, C++, Eiffel] **2.** any input/output mapping resulting from some object's behavior. [Booch]
    Antonym: PROCEDURE.

P

- **procedure** *n.* any operation that may perform multiple actions and modify the instance to which it is applied, but does not return a value. [Eiffel, Meyer]

Antonym: FUNCTION.

Contrast with: ROUTINE, SUBPROGRAM.

Commentary: A procedure may read data, update variables, or produce some output. A procedure may have parameters to provide a controlled means of passing information between the procedure and the point of call. [Ada95]

- **task [unit]** *n.* any program unit for defining tasks whose sequence of actions may be executed concurrently with those of other tasks. [Ada95]

See also: TASK TYPE.

Commentary: The execution of an Ada program consists of the execution of one or more *tasks*. Each task represents a separate thread of control that proceeds independently and concurrently between the points where it interacts with other tasks. [Ada95]

project *n.* any collection of views of information that takes up an entire display screen for the presentation of its views. [Smalltalk]

project dictionary *n.* any comprehensive dictionary defining all object-oriented entities (e.g., objects, classes, clusters, properties, operations, exceptions) in an application.

Contrast with: CLASS DICTIONARY, DATA DICTIONARY, OBJECT DICTIONARY.

Rationale: The term *project dictionary* is recommended as being less restrictive and less subject to misinterpretation than the terms *data dictionary*, *class dictionary*, and *object dictionary*.

project matrix *n.* any simple representation of the planning and organizational framework provided by the subsystems and by OOA. In the project matrix, each row of the matrix represents a step in the OOA method and each column represents a subsystem. [Shlaer/Mellor]

propagation *n.* the automatic application of an operation to selected objects in a network when the operation is applied to some starting object in the network. [Rumbaugh]

proper ancestor [class of a given class] *n.* any ancestor class of the given class other than itself. [Meyer]

Antonym: PROPER DESCENDANT.

Contrast with: PARENT CLASS.

Commentary: Meyer's proper ancestor is the same as Firesmith's ancestor.

proper descendant *n.* The proper descendants of class B are its descendants other than B itself. [Eiffel, Meyer]

Contrast with: PROPER ANCESTOR.

Commentary: Meyer's proper descendant is the same as Firesmith's descendant.

property *n.* **1.** any encapsulated static aspect (i.e., attribute, link, component part, exception, invariant) that characterizes an object, class, extent, or type. [Firesmith] **2.** (a) either any attribute or relationship. [ODMG] (b) the state aspect of any object or class. [Henderson-Sellers] **3.** any service that provides state information about an object or class. [Henderson-Sellers] **4.** any value that is made visible to clients via a message.

Commentary: Under definition **4**, a property may be implemented either as an attribute, link, or component part or may be calculated as necessary by an operation. [Firesmith]

Kinds:

- ATTRIBUTE
  - ASSOCIATION ATTRIBUTE
  - BASE ATTRIBUTE
  - CLASS ATTRIBUTE
  - CLASS VARIABLE
  - COMMON INSTANCE ATTRIBUTE
  - CONSTANT ATTRIBUTE
  - DERIVED ATTRIBUTE
  - DESCRIPTIVE ATTRIBUTE
  - DETERMINANT ATTRIBUTE
  - DISCRIMINATOR
  - EVENT ATTRIBUTE
  - EXTENT ATTRIBUTE
  - INSTANCE ATTRIBUTE
    + DEFAULT ATTRIBUTE
  - LINK ATTRIBUTE
  - NAMING ATTRIBUTE
  - OPERATION ATTRIBUTE
  - QUALIFIER
  - REFERENTIAL ATTRIBUTE
  - STATE ATTRIBUTE
  - STATE DEPENDENT ATTRIBUTE
  - STATE-INDEPENDENT ATTRIBUTE
  - TEMPORARY ATTRIBUTE
  - VARIABLE ATTRIBUTE
- CLASS PROPERTY
  - CLASS ATTRIBUTE
    + CLASS CONSTANT
    + CLASS VARIABLE
  - CLASS EXCEPTION
  - CLASS INVARIANT
  - COMPONENT CLASS
- CONSTANT PROPERTY
  - CONSTANT ATTRIBUTE
  - CONSTANT COMPONENT
  - CONSTANT LINK
- EXCEPTION
  - CLASS EXCEPTION
  - EXTENT EXCEPTION
  - INSTANCE EXCEPTION
- EXTENT PROPERTY
  - EXTENT ATTRIBUTE

- EXTENT EXCEPTION
- EXTENT INVARIANT
- INSTANCE PROPERTY
  - COMPONENT OBJECT
  - INSTANCE ATTRIBUTE
    + INSTANCE VARIABLE
      > INDEXED INSTANCE VARIABLE
      > NAMED INSTANCE VARIABLE
  - INSTANCE EXCEPTION
  - INSTANCE INVARIANT
  - LINK
    + ATTACHED LINK
      > ATTACHED POINTER
      > ATTACHED REFERENCE
    + BASE LINK
    + BIDIRECTIONAL LINK
    + BINARY LINK
    + DANGLING LINK
      > DANGLING POINTER
      > DANGLING REFERENCE
    + DERIVED LINK
    + POINTER
      > ATTACHED POINTER
      > DANGLING POINTER
      > VOID POINTER
    + REFERENCE
      > ATTACHED REFERENCE
      > DANGLING REFERENCE
      > IMPORTED REFERENCE
      > INGENERATE REFERENCE
      > VOID REFERENCE
    + STATE LINK
    + TERNARY LINK
    + UNIDIRECTIONAL LINK
    + VARIABLE LINK
    + VOID LINK
      > VOID POINTER
      > VOID REFERENCE
- INVARIANT
  - CLASS INVARIANT
  - EXTENT INVARIANT
  - INSTANCE INVARIANT
  - MESSAGE INVARIANT

P

- SCENARIO INVARIANT
- PRIVATE PROPERTY
- STATE-DEPENDENT PROPERTY
  - STATE-DEPENDENT ATTRIBUTE
  - STATE-DEPENDENT LINK
- STATE-INDEPENDENT PROPERTY
  - STATE-INDEPENDENT ATTRIBUTE
  - STATE-INDEPENDENT LINK
- STATE PROPERTY
  - STATE ATTRIBUTE
  - STATE COMPONENT
  - STATE LINK
- TYPE PROPERTY
- VARIABLE PROPERTY
  - VARIABLE ATTRIBUTE
  - VARIABLE COMPONENT
  - VARIABLE LINK

- **attribute** *n.* **1.** (a) any named property used as a data abstraction to describe its enclosing object, class, or extent. [Firesmith, Rumbaugh] (b) any named property of an object that takes a literal as its value, does not have an OID, defines the abstract state of its object, and appears within the interface rather than the implementation. [ODMG] (c) a data item associated with class instances. [Coad, Eiffel, Meyer] **2.** any instance of an attribute class or attribute type. [Firesmith, Jacobson] **3.** any part of an aggregate object. [Booch] **4.** (a) an identifiable link or association between the object and some other entity (e.g., object, data value) or entities that describe the object. [Martin/Odell, OMG] (b) a set of named values associated with an object, class, or relationship. [Coleman] (c) a unit of information consisting of an attribute association and an attribute type that is stored in and describes an object. [Jacobson] **5.** an abstraction of a sin-

gle characteristic possessed by all entities that were, themselves, abstracted as an object. [Shlaer/Mellor] **6.** the information that a class keeps on itself; the state data of a class. [Lorenz] **7.** something that an object *knows*. [Coad] **8.** a characteristic that can be queried. [Ada95]
Synonyms: MEMBER DATA.
Commentary: Definitions **1** and **2** are often used together. Definition **1**(b) prohibits objects as attributes, is unnecessarily restrictive, and requires a hybrid approach. Definition **3** confuses attribute and part. Definition **4** has the referent of the attribute exist independently of the object that encapsulates the attribute.
Kinds:
- ASSOCIATION ATTRIBUTE
- BASE ATTRIBUTE
- CLASS ATTRIBUTE
- CLASS VARIABLE
- COMMON INSTANCE ATTRIBUTE
- CONSTANT ATTRIBUTE
- DERIVED ATTRIBUTE
- DESCRIPTIVE ATTRIBUTE
- DETERMINANT ATTRIBUTE
- DISCRIMINATOR
- EVENT ATTRIBUTE
- EXTENT ATTRIBUTE
- INSTANCE ATTRIBUTE
  + DEFAULT ATTRIBUTE
- LINK ATTRIBUTE
- NAMING ATTRIBUTE
- OPERATION ATTRIBUTE
- QUALIFIER
- REFERENTIAL ATTRIBUTE
- STATE ATTRIBUTE
- STATE DEPENDENT ATTRIBUTE
- STATE-INDEPENDENT ATTRIBUTE
- TEMPORARY ATTRIBUTE
- VARIABLE ATTRIBUTE

- **association attribute** *n.* any attribute of an association as a whole. *Contrast with:* LINK ATTRIBUTE REFERENTIAL ATTRIBUTE.
- **base attribute** *n.* any attribute that cannot be derived from other attributes. A base attribute is stored rather than calculated by an operation. [Firesmith] *Antonym:* DERIVED ATTRIBUTE.
- **class attribute** *n.* **1.** any attribute of a class as a whole. [Firesmith, Jacobson] **2.** any attribute whose value is common to a class of objects. [Rumbaugh] *Synonyms:* **1** CLASS VARIABLE, **2** COMMON-INSTANCE ATTRIBUTE. *Contrast with:* COMMON-INSTANCE ATTRIBUTE, INSTANCE ATTRIBUTE, EXTENT ATTRIBUTE. *Examples:* **1** a generic parameter, **2** a C++ static data member.
- **class variable** *n.* **1.** any variable shared by all the instances of a single class. [Smalltalk] **2.** any variable attribute of a class descriptor object. **3.** any variable describing the class as a whole. *Example:* In C++, a class variable is declared as a static member. [Booch]. *Synonyms:* **2** CLASS ATTRIBUTE, **3** COMMON-INSTANCE ATTRIBUTE.
- **common instance attribute** *n.* an instance attribute that has the same value for all instances of the same class. Common-instance attributes are usually stored once in the class rather than redundantly in each instance. [Firesmith] *Synonym:* SHARED ATTRIBUTE. *Contrast with:* CLASS ATTRIBUTE, INSTANCE ATTRIBUTE.
- **constant attribute** *n.* **1.** any attribute whose value cannot change at run-time. [Firesmith] **2.** any attribute whose value is the same for every instance and cannot be changed at run-time. [Eiffel, Meyer] *Antonym:* VARIABLE ATTRIBUTE.
- **derived attribute** *n.* any attribute that is calculated in terms of other properties (i.e., attributes, links, or component parts). A derived attribute is calculated by an operation rather than stored. [Firesmith, Rumbaugh] *Antonym:* BASE ATTRIBUTE. *Example:* Age can be calculated from date of birth and current date. [Firesmith]
- **descriptive attribute** *n.* any attribute that provides facts intrinsic to each instance of the object. [Shlaer/Mellor] *Examples:* The altitude, latitude, and longitude of an airplane, the current and desired state of a valve, and the address and salary of an employee can all be modeled as descriptive attributes.
- **determinant attribute** *n.* any attribute other than the current state attribute on which the events generated by the an action depend. [Shlaer/Mellor] *Rationale:* Such attributes are known as determinant attributes, because they determine how a thread of control develops as it passes through the action.
- **discriminator** *n.* **1.** any attribute that indicates which property of the base class is used to differentiate a set of its direct derived classes (i.e., to differentiate the members of a partition). [Firesmith, Henderson-

P

Sellers, Rumbaugh] **2.** any attribute that is an instance of a discriminator class. [Firesmith]

See also: PARTITION.

Example: The engine type of a car can be used as a discriminator to partition cars into disjoint derived classes or types. That is, cars can be subtyped as either diesel, electric, gas, or solar powered. [Firesmith]

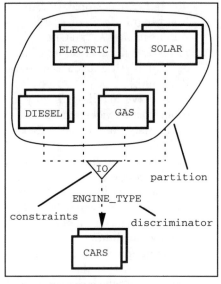

Discriminator

- **event attribute** *n.* **1.** any attribute of an event object. **2.** any parameters of a message. [Rumbaugh]
- **extent attribute** *n.* any attribute that describes an extent. [Firesmith]

  Contrast with: INSTANCE ATTRIBUTE, CLASS ATTRIBUTE.

  Example: The current, maximum, and minimum number of instances are all extent attributes. [Firesmith]
- **instance attribute** *n.* any attribute that describes an individual instance. [Firesmith, Jacobson]

  Contrast with: CLASS ATTRIBUTE, EXTENT ATTRIBUTE.
- **+ default attribute** *n.* any instance attribute the default value of which is used if not explicitly supplied. [Kim]
- **link attribute** *n.* any attribute of each link in an association. [Rumbaugh]

  Contrast with: ASSOCIATION ATTRIBUTE.
- **naming attribute** *n.* any attribute that provides facts about the arbitrary labels and names carried by each instance of an object. [Shlaer/Mellor]

  Examples: The aircraft ID and name of an airplane, the code of a valve, and the name and ID of an employee can all be modeled as naming attributes.
- **operation attribute** *n.* any attribute that is local to a specific operation. [Firesmith]

  Synonym: TEMPORARY ATTRIBUTE.
- **qualifier** *n.* any attribute of an object that distinguishes it from other objects, thereby acting as a cardinality constraint. [Firesmith, Rumbaugh]

  See also: QUALIFIED ASSOCIATION.
- **referential attribute** *n.* any attribute that captures the facts that tie an instance of one object to an instance of another object. [Shlaer/Mellor]
- **state attribute** *n.* any attribute whose value helps determine the state of its encapsulating object or class. [Firesmith]

  Contrast with: STATE COMPONENT, STATE LINK.

- **state-dependent attribute** *n.* any attribute that has meaning only during specific states. [Coad, Firesmith]
Contrast with: STATE-DEPENDENT OPERATION, STATE-INDEPENDENT ATTRIBUTE.
- **state-independent attribute** *n.* any attribute that has meaning during all states. [Firesmith]
Contrast with: STATE-DEPENDENT ATTRIBUTE, STATE-INDEPENDENT OPERATION.
- **temporary attribute** *n.* any attribute that is local to a specific operation. [Jacobson]
Synonym: OPERATION ATTRIBUTE.
- **variable [attribute]** *n.* **1.** any attribute whose value can change at run-time. [Firesmith, Jacobson] **2.** an attribute whose value associated with a particular instance can be changed by a routine. [Eiffel, Meyer]
Antonym: CONSTANT ATTRIBUTE.
• **class property** *n.* any property that characterizes the class as a whole. [Firesmith, ODMG]
Contrast with: EXTENT PROPERTY, INSTANCE PROPERTY, TYPE PROPERTY.
Kinds:
  - CLASS ATTRIBUTE
    + CLASS CONSTANT
    + CLASS VARIABLE
  - CLASS EXCEPTION
  - CLASS INVARIANT
  - COMPONENT CLASS
- **class attribute** *n.* **1.** any attribute of a class as a whole. [Firesmith, Jacobson] **2.** any attribute whose value is common to a class of objects. [Rumbaugh]
Synonyms: CLASS VARIABLE, COM-MON INSTANCE ATTRIBUTE.
Contrast with: COMMON INSTANCE ATTRIBUTE, EXTENT ATTRIBUTE, INSTANCE ATTRIBUTE.
Kinds:
  + CLASS CONSTANT
  + CLASS VARIABLE
+ **class constant** *n.* any constant class attribute. [Firesmith]
Antonym: CLASS VARIABLE.
+ **class variable** *n.* **1.** any variable attribute of a class as a whole. [Firesmith] **2.** any variable whose value is shared by all instances of a class. [Rumbaugh, Smalltalk] **3.** any attribute of a class descriptor object. [Rumbaugh]
Antonym: CLASS CONSTANT.
Synonyms: CLASS ATTRIBUTE, COMMON INSTANCE ATTRIBUTE.
Example: In C++, a class variable is declared as a static member. [Booch]
- **class exception** *n.* any exception of a class as a whole. [Firesmith]
Contrast with: EXTENT EXCEPTION, INSTANCE EXCEPTION.
Examples: Instantiation failed, class invariant violated, and precondition or postcondition of class operation violated are all class exceptions. [Firesmith]
- **class invariant** *n.* any invariant of a class as a whole. [Firesmith]
Contrast with: EXTENT INVARIANT, INSTANCE INVARIANT.
Example: Any invariant relationship between generic formal parameters is a class invariant. [Firesmith]
- **component [class]** *n.* any class that is contained within another class as a component part. [Firesmith]

P

Contrast with: COMPONENT CLUSTER, COMPONENT OBJECT.

Rationale: The term *component class* is far less ambiguous that the term *subclass,* which has another more popular meaning. [Firesmith]

- **constant property** *n.* any property, the value of which cannot change at run-time. [Firesmith]
Antonym: VARIABLE PROPERTY.
Kinds:
  - CONSTANT ATTRIBUTE
  - CONSTANT COMPONENT
  - CONSTANT LINK

  - **constant attribute** *n.* **1.** any attribute the value of which cannot change at run time. [Firesmith] **2.** any attribute whose value is the same for every instance and cannot be changed at run time. [Eiffel, Meyer]
  Antonym: VARIABLE ATTRIBUTE.
  - **constant component** *n.* any component object which is a constant object. [Firesmith]
  Antonym: VARIABLE ATTRIBUTE.
  - **constant link** *n.* any link that cannot be created, destroyed, or changed in value at run-time. [Firesmith]
  Antonym: VARIABLE LINK.
  Commentary: A constant link always points to the same server. [Firesmith]

- **exception** *n.* **1.** (a) any abstraction of an exceptional or error condition that is identified and raised by an operation. [Firesmith] (b) any indication that an operation request was not performed successfully. [Eiffel, Meyer] **2.** (a) any exceptional situation. [Ada95] (b) a system event or condition that is not part of normal system behavior. [Embley] **3.** (a) the viola-

tion of an assertion. [Booch, Eiffel, Meyer] (b) any violation of a contract. [Eiffel, Meyer] **4.** any object representing an error condition.
Synonym: CONTRACT VIOLATION.
See also: CATCH, EXCEPTION HANDLER, RAISE, RESCUE BLOCK, THROW, TRANSITION.
Examples: Contract violations, the violation of assertions (e.g., invariants, preconditions, postconditions), failure of related hardware, and failure of an operation (e.g., due to arithmetic overflow, lack of memory) are all examples of exceptions. [Eiffel, Firesmith, Meyer]
Commentary: **1** Exceptions should be used to notify the client that the associated operation could not be performed successfully. Exceptions can be used to produce robust, reliable, and correct objects and classes. An exception should be implemented by an object so that associated properties may be defined and inheritance can be used to capture specialization relationships between classes of exceptions. [Firesmith] **2(b)** When an exception arises, it takes precedence over any normal exit transition. [Embley]
Kinds:
  - CLASS EXCEPTION
  - EXTENT EXCEPTION
  - INSTANCE EXCEPTION

  - **class exception** *n.* any exception of a class as a whole. [Firesmith]
  Contrast with: EXTENT EXCEPTION, INSTANCE EXCEPTION.
  Example: Instantiation failed is a class exception.
  - **extent exception** *n.* any exception of the extent of a class. [Firesmith]
  Contrast with: CLASS EXCEPTION,

INSTANCE EXCEPTION.

- **instance exception** *n.* any exception of an individual instance. *Contrast with:* CLASS EXCEPTION, EXTENT EXCEPTION.
- **extent property** *n.* any property that characterize the extent of a class, rather than the class or any of its individual instances. [Firesmith] *Kinds:*
  - EXTENT ATTRIBUTE
  - EXTENT EXCEPTION
  - EXTENT INVARIANT
- **extent attribute** *n.* any attribute that describes an extent of some class or type. [Firesmith] *Contrast with:* CLASS ATTRIBUTE, INSTANCE ATTRIBUTE. *Example:* the current, maximum, and minimum number of instances. [Firesmith]
- **extent exception** *n.* any exception of the extent of some class or type. [Firesmith] *Contrast with:* INSTANCE EXCEPTION, CLASS EXCEPTION. *Example:* extent assertion failed. [Firesmith]
- **extent invariant** *n.* any invariant involving only properties of the extent of some class or type. [Firesmith] *Contrast with:* CLASS INVARIANT, INSTANCE INVARIANT, MESSAGE INVARIANT. *Example:* the maximum number of instances. [Firesmith]
- **instance property** *n.* any property that characterizes the an individual instance. [Firesmith, ODMG] *Contrast with:* CLASS PROPERTY, EXTENT PROPERTY, TYPE PROPERTY. *Kinds:*
  - COMPONENT OBJECT

- INSTANCE ATTRIBUTE
  + INSTANCE VARIABLE
    > INDEXED INSTANCE VARIABLE
    > NAMED INSTANCE VARIABLE
- INSTANCE EXCEPTION
- INSTANCE INVARIANT
- LINK
  + ATTACHED LINK
    > ATTACHED POINTER
    > ATTACHED REFERENCE
  + BASE LINK
  + BIDIRECTIONAL LINK
  + BINARY LINK
  + CONSTANT LINK
  + DANGLING LINK
    > DANGLING POINTER
    > DANGLING REFERENCE
  + DERIVED LINK
  + CONSTANT LINK
  + POINTER
    > ATTACHED POINTER
    > DANGLING POINTER
    > VOID POINTER
  + REFERENCE
    > ATTACHED REFERENCE
    > DANGLING REFERENCE
    > IMPORTED REFERENCE
    > INGENERATE REFERENCE
    > VOID REFERENCE
  + STATE LINK
  + TERNARY LINK
  + UNIDIRECTIONAL LINK
  + VARIABLE LINK
  + VOID LINK
    > VOID POINTER
    > VOID REFERENCE

- **component [object]** *n.* any object that is contained within another object as a component part. [Firesmith] *Contrast with:* COMPONENT CLASS, COMPONENT CLUSTER.
- **instance attribute** *n.* any attribute

P

of an individual instance. [Firesmith, Jacobson]

Contrast with: CLASS ATTRIBUTE, EXTENT ATTRIBUTE.

Commentary: All instance attributes are protected in Smalltalk, whereas C++ also allows instance attributes (a.k.a. data members) to be public or protected. [Firesmith]

Kinds:
+ INSTANCE VARIABLE
> INDEXED INSTANCE VARIABLE
> NAMED INSTANCE VARIABLE

+ **instance variable** *n.* **1.** any variable attribute of an individual instance. [Firesmith, Rumbaugh, Smalltalk] **2.** any place to store and refer to an object's state data. [Booch, Lorenz] **3.** any name that allows one object (instance) to refer to another one. [Lorenz] **4.** the OOPL implementation of any attribute type [Martin/Odell]

Synonym: INSTANCE ATTRIBUTE.

Commentary: All instance variables are protected in Smalltalk, whereas C++ also allows instance variables (a.k.a. data members) to be public or protected. Instance variables in Eiffel have read-only semantics.

Kinds:
> INDEXED INSTANCE VARIABLE
> NAMED INSTANCE VARIABLE

> **indexed instance variable** *n.* an instance variable that is not accessed by name. [Smalltalk]

Antonym: NAMED INSTANCE VARIABLE.

Example: names at: 1 [Smalltalk]

Commentary: An object can have indexed instance variables only if all instances of its class

can have indexed instance variables. [Smalltalk]

> **named instance variable** *n.* an instance variable that is accessed by its instance variable name. [Smalltalk]

Antonym: INDEXED INSTANCE VARIABLE.

Commentary: All instances of a class have the same number of named instance variables and use the same names to refer to them. [Smalltalk]

- **instance exception** *n.* any exception of an individual instance. [Firesmith]

Contrast with: CLASS EXCEPTION.

- **instance invariant** *n.* any invariant of an individual instance defined in terms of the properties of the instance. An instance invariant must evaluate to true for each instance whenever the instance is accessible: after instantiation and after the completion of each visible operation. [Booch, Coleman, Eiffel, Firesmith, Meyer, Rumbaugh]

Example: The age of a person cannot be less than zero. [Firesmith]

Commentary: Invariants may (and sometimes must) be temporarily violated during execution, but such violations must never be detectable outside of the instance. Concurrency and mutual exclusion influences the practical implementations of invariant checks. [Firesmith]

- **link** *n.* **1.** during analysis and logical design, any instance of an association that captures a named semantic relationship between objects. [Firesmith, OMG, Rumbaugh] **2.** during implementation design and coding, any feature that contains one or

more values, each of which reliably points to a server object. [Firesmith]
Contrast with: ASSOCIATION.
Commentary: Links imply visibility and enable message passing. Links are the roads, whereas messages are the traffic on those roads. [Firesmith]
Kinds:
+ ATTACHED LINK
> ATTACHED POINTER
> ATTACHED REFERENCE
+ BASE LINK
+ BIDIRECTIONAL LINK
+ BINARY LINK
+ CONSTANT LINK
+ DANGLING LINK
> DANGLING POINTER
> DANGLING REFERENCE
+ DERIVED LINK
+ CONSTANT LINK
+ POINTER
> ATTACHED POINTER
> DANGLING POINTER
> VOID POINTER
+ REFERENCE
> ATTACHED REFERENCE
> DANGLING REFERENCE
> IMPORTED REFERENCE
> INGENERATE REFERENCE
> VOID REFERENCE
+ STATE LINK
+ TERNARY LINK
+ UNIDIRECTIONAL LINK
+ VARIABLE LINK
+ VOID LINK
> VOID POINTER
> VOID REFERENCE

+ **attached link** *n.* any link to an existing object. [Firesmith]
Contrast with: DANGLING LINK, VOID LINK.
Commentary: Even though links are typically unidirectional, the link is said to be attached to the object, and the object is also said to be attached to the link. [Firesmith]
Kinds:
> ATTACHED POINTER
> ATTACHED REFERENCE

> **attached pointer** *n.* any pointer that currently points to an existing object. [Firesmith]
Contrast with: DANGLING POINTER, VOID POINTER.
Commentary: The pointer is said to be attached to the object, and the object is also said to be attached to the pointer. [Firesmith]

> **attached reference** *n.* any reference that currently refers to an existing object. [Eiffel, Firesmith, Meyer]
Contrast with: DANGLING REFERENCE, VOID REFERENCE.
Commentary: The reference is said to be attached to the object, and the object is also said to be attached to the reference. [Eiffel, Firesmith, Meyer]

+ **base link** *n.* any link that cannot be derived from other links. [Firesmith]
Antonym: DERIVED LINK.

+ **bidirectional link** *n.* any logical link that represents two unidirectional links that are coupled whereby each is the inverse of the another. [Firesmith]
Antonym: UNIDIRECTIONAL LINK.

+ **binary link** *n.* any link between two objects. [Firesmith]
Contrast with: TERNARY LINK.

+ **constant link** *n.* any link that cannot be created, destroyed, or changed in value at run-time. [Firesmith]

P

Antonym: VARIABLE LINK.

Commentary: A constant link always points to the same server. [Firesmith]

+ **dangling link** *n.* any link to an object that does not exist. [Firesmith]

Contrast with: ATTACHED LINK, VOID LINK.

Commentary: The link may be to an object that does not yet exist or to an object that no longer exists. Dangling links are common bugs in languages that support manual garbage collection. [Firesmith]

Kinds:

> DANGLING POINTER

> DANGLING REFERENCE

> **dangling pointer** *n.* any pointer that points to an object that no longer exists. [Firesmith]

Contrast with: ATTACHED POINTER, VOID POINTER.

> **attached reference** *n.* any reference to an object that no longer exists. [Firesmith]

Contrast with: ATTACHED REFERENCE, VOID REFERENCE.

+ **derived link** *n.* **1.** any indirect link that is the product of other links. [Firesmith] **2.** any instance of a derived association. [Firesmith]

Antonym: BASE LINK.

Contrast with: DERIVED ASSOCIATION.

+ **pointer [to a given object]** *n.* **1.** any link, the value of which is the identifier of the given server object. [Firesmith] **2.** any attribute of one object that contains an explicit reference to another object. [Rumbaugh]

Contrast with: IDENTIFIER, LINK,

REFERENCE.

Commentary: Unless changed, a pointer will identify the same object each time the pointer is used (subject to certain pragmatic limits of space and time). An object may be denoted by multiple, distinct pointers. [Firesmith]

Kinds:

> ATTACHED POINTER

> DANGLING POINTER

> VOID POINTER

> **attached pointer** *n.* any pointer that currently points to an object. [Firesmith]

Contrast with: DANGLING POINTER, VOID POINTER.

Commentary: The pointer is said to be attached to the object, and the object is also said to be attached to the pointer. [Firesmith]

> **dangling pointer** *n.* any pointer that points to an object that does not exist. [Firesmith]

Contrast with: ATTACHED POINTER, VOID POINTER.

> **void pointer** *n.* any pointer that does not currently point to an object. [Firesmith]

Synonym: NULL POINTER.

Contrast with: ATTACHED POINTER, DANGLING POINTER.

+ **reference [to a given object]** *n.* **1.** any constant value that is used as an alias for the OID of the given server object. [Firesmith] **2.** any value that refers to an object. [Eiffel, Meyer]

Contrast with: IDENTIFIER, LINK, POINTER.

Commentary: References are used as links and as arguments in

messages and operations. Unless changed, a reference will identify the same object each time the reference is used (subject to certain pragmatic limits of space and time). An object may be denoted by multiple, distinct references. [Firesmith]
Contrast with: VALUE.
Kinds:
> ATTACHED REFERENCE
> IMPORTED REFERENCE
> INGENERATE REFERENCE
> VOID REFERENCE

> **attached reference** *n.* any reference that refers to an existing object. [Eiffel, Firesmith, Meyer]
Antonym: VOID REFERENCE.
Commentary: The reference is said to be attached to the object, and the object is also said to be attached to the reference. [Eiffel, Firesmith, Meyer]

> **dangling pointer** *n.* any reference that refers to an object that does not exist. [Firesmith]
Contrast with: ATTACHED REFERENCE, VOID REFERENCE.

> **imported reference** *n.* any reference stored in an object's instance variable that was not generated by the object itself through invocation of a *create* method. [Atkinson]
Antonym: INGENERATE REFERENCE.

> **ingenerate reference** *n.* any reference stored in an object's instance variable that was generated by the object itself through invocation of a *create* method. [Atkinson]
Antonym: IMPORTED REFERENCE.

> **void reference** *n.* **1.** any reference that does not currently refer to an object. [Firesmith] **2.** any reference about which no further information is available. [Eiffel, Meyer]
Contrast with: ATTACHED REFERENCE, DANGLING REFERENCE.

+ **state link** *n.* any link whose existence helps determine the state of its client object or class. [Firesmith]
Contrast with: STATE ATTRIBUTE, STATE COMPONENT.

+ **ternary link** *n.* any link among three objects. [Firesmith]
Contrast with: BINARY LINK.

+ **unidirectional link** *n.* any link directed from the client(s) to the server(s). [Firesmith]
Antonym: BIDIRECTIONAL LINK.
Commentary: Unidirectional links are typically implemented by one or more attributes acting as pointers or messages requesting services. [Firesmith]

+ **variable link** *n.* any link that can change at run-time. [Firesmith]
Antonym: CONSTANT LINK.
Commentary: A link can change by pointing to another server. [Firesmith]

+ **void link** *n.* any link to nothing. [Firesmith]
Contrast with: ATTACHED LINK, DANGLING LINK.
Kinds:
> VOID POINTER
> VOID REFERENCE

> **void pointer** *n.* any pointer that does not currently point to an object. [Firesmith]
Synonym: NULL POINTER.

P

Contrast with: ATTACHED POINTER, DANGLING POINTER.

> **void reference** *n.* **1.** any reference that does not refer to an object. [Firesmith] **2.** any reference about which no further information is available. [Eiffel, Meyer]

Antonym: ATTACHED REFERENCE.

• **invariant** *n.* any assertion, the scope of which is the entire life cycle of the associated thing. [Booch, Coleman, Eiffel, Firesmith, Meyer, Rumbaugh]

Contrast with: PRECONDITION, POSTCONDITION.

Examples: The length times the width of any given rectangle must equal the rectangle's area. The age of something cannot be less than zero. [Firesmith]

Commentary: Invariants are used to ensure that abstractions are never violated in any detectable way. Although invariants may (and sometimes must) be temporarily violated during execution, such violations must never be detectable from the outside. Concurrency and mutual exclusion influence the practical implementations of invariant checks. [Firesmith]

Kinds:
- CLASS INVARIANT
- EXTENT INVARIANT
- INSTANCE INVARIANT
- MESSAGE INVARIANT
- SCENARIO INVARIANT

- **class invariant** *n.* any invariant involving the properties of a class that must be true on elaboration, prior to the execution of each class operation, and after execution of each class operation. [Firesmith]

Contrast with: EXTENT INVARIANT, INSTANCE INVARIANT, MESSAGE INVARIANT.

Example: Any invariant involving generic formal parameters is a class invariant. [Firesmith]

- **extent invariant** *n.* any invariant involving the properties of an extent that must be true prior to the execution of each constructor and after execution of each destructor. [Firesmith]

Contrast with: CLASS INVARIANT, INSTANCE INVARIANT, MESSAGE INVARIANT.

Example: The current number of instances must never exceed the maximum number of instances. [Firesmith]

- **instance invariant** *n.* any invariant involving the properties of an instance that must be true on instantiation, prior to the execution of each instance operation, after execution of each instance operation, and prior to destruction. [Booch, Coleman, Eiffel, Firesmith, Meyer, Rumbaugh]

Contrast with: CLASS INVARIANT, EXTENT INVARIANT, MESSAGE INVARIANT.

Examples: The length times the width of any given rectangle must equal the rectangle's area. The age of something cannot be less than zero. [Firesmith]

- **message invariant** *n.* any invariant that must evaluate to true after execution of the associated operation if it holds prior to receipt of the message. [Firesmith]

Contrast with: CLASS INVARIANT, EXTENT INVARIANT, INSTANCE INVARIANT, SCENARIO INVARIANT.

- **private property [of an object]** *n.* either any instance variable that makes up part of its private memory or any method that describes how to carry out one of its operations. [Smalltalk]
- **state-dependent property** *n.* any property, the meaning of which is dependent on the state of its encapsulating object or class. [Firesmith]
  Antonym: STATE-INDEPENDENT PROPERTY.
  Contrast with: STATE-DEPENDENT OPERATION.
  Kinds:
    - STATE-DEPENDENT ATTRIBUTE
    - STATE-DEPENDENT LINK
  - **state-dependent attribute** *n.* any attribute that has meaning only during specific states. [Firesmith]
    Antonym: STATE-INDEPENDENT ATTRIBUTE.
    Contrast with: STATE-DEPENDENT LINK.
  - **state-dependent link** *n.* any link that has meaning only during specific states. [Firesmith]
    Antonym: STATE-INDEPENDENT LINK.
    Contrast with: STATE-DEPENDENT ATTRIBUTE.
- **state-independent property** *n.* any property, the meaning of which is independent of the state of its encapsulating object or class. [Firesmith]
  Antonym: STATE-DEPENDENT PROPERTY.
  Contrast with: STATE-INDEPENDENT OPERATION.
  Kinds:
    - STATE-INDEPENDENT ATTRIBUTE
    - STATE-INDEPENDENT LINK
  - **state-independent attribute** *n.* any attribute that has meaning during all states. [Firesmith]
    Antonym: STATE-DEPENDENT ATTRIBUTE.
    Contrast with: STATE-DEPENDENT LINK.
  - **state-independent link** *n.* any link that has meaning during all states. [Firesmith]
    Antonym: STATE-DEPENDENT LINK.
    Contrast with: STATE-INDEPENDENT ATTRIBUTE.
- **state property** *n.* any property whose value helps determine the state of its encapsulating object or class. [Firesmith]
  Kinds:
    - STATE ATTRIBUTE
    - STATE COMPONENT
    - STATE LINK
  - **state attribute** *n.* any attribute whose value helps determine the state of its encapsulating object or class. [Firesmith]
    Contrast with: STATE COMPONENT, STATE LINK.
  - **state component** *n.* any component object the state of which helps determine the state of its aggregate object or class. [Firesmith]
    Contrast with: STATE ATTRIBUTE, STATE LINK.
  - **state link** *n.* any link whose existence helps determine the state of its client object or class. [Firesmith]
    Contrast with: STATE ATTRIBUTE, STATE COMPONENT.
- **type property** *n.* any property that characterize the type itself, rather than any of its individual instances. [Firesmith, ODMG]
- **variable property** *n.* any property whose value can change at run-time. [Firesmith]
  Antonym: CONSTANT PROPERTY.

P

Kinds:
- VARIABLE ATTRIBUTE
- VARIABLE COMPONENT
- VARIABLE LINK
- **variable attribute** *n.* **1.** any attribute whose value can change at run-time. [Firesmith, Jacobson] **2.** any attribute whose value associated with a particular instance can be changed by a routine. [Eiffel, Meyer]
  Antonym: CONSTANT ATTRIBUTE.
- **variable component** *n.* any component object, the value of whose properties that can change at run-time. [Firesmith]
  Antonym: CONSTANT LINK.
  Commentary: A link can change by pointing to another server.
- **variable link** *n.* any link that can change at run-time. [Firesmith]
  Antonym: CONSTANT LINK.
  Commentary: A link can change by pointing to another server. [Firesmith]

protected *adj.* **1.** describing features (i.e., members) that are hidden from external clients but not from descendants. [Booch, C++, Firesmith, Rumbaugh] **2.** describing inheritance in which private and protected inherited features have the same visibility as they did in the defining class, whereas public inherited members (i.e., features) become *protected* in the derived class. [C++, Firesmith]
Contrast with: PRIVATE, PUBLIC.
Commentary: In C++, private features are typically declared in the interface (i.e., header file) but implemented in the body (i.e., cpp file).

protected feature *n.* any feature that is exported to all children and hidden from all other potential clients within the scope of the encapsulating object or class. [Firesmith]
Contrast with: FRIEND FEATURE, PRIVATE FEATURE, PUBLIC FEATURE.
Commentary: In C++, protected members are typically declared in the interface (i.e., header file) but implemented in the body (e.g., cpp file). Ada95 uses the term *protected record* for the same purpose.

protected inheritance *n.* any inheritance in which private and protected inherited features have the same visibility as they did in the defining class, whereas public inherited members (i.e., features) become *protected* in the derived class. [C++, Firesmith]
Contrast with: PRIVATE INHERITANCE, PUBLIC INHERITANCE.

protected member *n.* any member (i.e., feature) that is hidden from external clients but not from descendants. [C++]
Contrast with: PRIVATE MEMBER, PUBLIC MEMBER.

protected type *n.* any composite type whose components are protected from concurrent access by multiple tasks. [Ada95]

protected unit *n.* any program unit that is the basic unit for defining protected operations for the coordinated use of data shared between tasks. [Ada95b]

protection *n.* the ability to restrict the client objects for which a requested service will be performed. [OMG]

protocol *n.* **1.** the set of interactions that can cross the boundary of something. [Firesmith] **2.** (a) the set of messages that can be received. [Wirfs-Brock] (b) the set of visible signatures of something. [Jacobson] **3.** any cohesive subset of interactions that can cross the boundary of something. [Firesmith] **4.**

any subset of the messages that can be received.

Contrast with: INTERFACE.

See also: IMPLEMENTATION, INFORMATION HIDING.

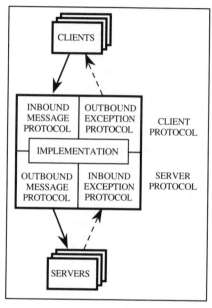

Protocols

Commentary: **1** The most general interpretation of the term *protocol* captures both all messages that something can send and receive as well as all external exceptions that something can raise and handle. The protocol therefore isolates both clients and servers from changes made to the implementation as long as the protocol is unaffected by these changes. If the protocol is completely specified, then upper and lower CASE tools can automatically determine consistency between the protocol and implementation and also determine whether clients or serv-

ers should be obsoleted by changes. Unfortunately, most current methods and languages only consider the inbound message protocol and ignore both exception and the server protocols. [Firesmith]

Kinds:
- CLASS PROTOCOL
- CLIENT PROTOCOL
- CLUSTER PROTOCOL
- EXCEPTION PROTOCOL
- INBOUND EXCEPTION PROTOCOL
- INBOUND MESSAGE PROTOCOL
- INBOUND PROTOCOL
- MESSAGE PROTOCOL
- OBJECT PROTOCOL
- OPERATION PROTOCOL
- OUTBOUND EXCEPTION PROTOCOL
- OUTBOUND MESSAGE PROTOCOL
- OUTBOUND PROTOCOL
- SERVER PROTOCOL

- **class protocol** *n.* the protocol of any class, consisting of all messages that it can send and receive as well as all exceptions it can raise and handle. [Firesmith]
Contrast with: CLASS INTERFACE.

- **client protocol** *n.* the set of all potential interactions with clients, consisting of the union of the inbound message protocol and the outbound exception protocol. [Firesmith]
Antonym: SERVER PROTOCOL.
Contrast with: CLIENT INTERFACE.

- **cluster protocol** *n.* the protocol of any cluster, consisting of all messages and exceptions that can pass across its boundaries. [Firesmith]
Contrast with: CLUSTER INTERFACE.
Commentary: Clusters do not directly interact, but their component classes may. [Firesmith]

- **exception protocol** *n.* the union of

P

the inbound exception protocol and the outbound exception protocol. [Firesmith]

Antonym: MESSAGE PROTOCOL.

Commentary: The exception protocol consists of all exceptions that can be raised to clients and all server exceptions that must be handled. [Firesmith]

- **inbound exception protocol** *n.* the set of all server exceptions that must be handled. [Firesmith]

Contrast with: INBOUND MESSAGE PROTOCOL, OUTBOUND EXCEPTION PROTOCOL, OUTBOUND MESSAGE PROTOCOL.

- **inbound message protocol** *n.* the set of all inbound messages. [Firesmith]

Contrast with: INBOUND EXCEPTION PROTOCOL, OUTBOUND EXCEPTION PROTOCOL, OUTBOUND MESSAGE PROTOCOL.

- **inbound protocol** *n.* the set of all inbound interactions, consisting of the union of the inbound message protocol and the inbound exception protocol. [Firesmith]

Antonym: OUTBOUND PROTOCOL.

Contrast with: INBOUND INTERFACE.

- **message protocol** *n.* the union of the inbound message protocol and the outbound message protocol. [Firesmith]

Antonym: EXCEPTION PROTOCOL.

Commentary: The message protocol consists of all messages that can be either sent to servers or received from clients. [Firesmith]

- **object protocol** *n.* 1. the protocol of any object, consisting of all messages and exceptions that can pass across its boundaries. [Firesmith] 2. the messages to which the object can respond. [Smalltalk]

Contrast with: OBJECT INTERFACE.

Commentary: 1 The protocol of an object captures the entire static and dynamic outside view of the ways in which it may act and react. [Booch]

- **operation protocol** *n.* 1. the declaration of an operation, specifying the name of the operation, the names, modes, and types of any parameters (including the order), the name and type of any returned value, and optionally, any preconditions and postconditions, the names of any exceptions the operation can raise, and the priority of the operation. [ODMG, Rumbaugh] 2. the protocol of any operation, consisting of all messages that it can send and receive as well as all exceptions that it can raise and handle. [Firesmith]

Synonym: 1 OPERATION SIGNATURE.

Contrast with: 2 OPERATION SIGNATURE.

Commentary: Most languages require a one-to-one mapping between messages and operation so that the inbound operation protocol is the operation signature. [Firesmith]

- **outbound exception protocol** *n.* the set of all exceptions that may be raised to clients. [Firesmith]

Contrast with: INBOUND EXCEPTION PROTOCOL, INBOUND MESSAGE PROTOCOL, OUTBOUND MESSAGE PROTOCOL.

- **outbound message protocol** *n.* the set of all inbound messages. [Firesmith]

Contrast with: INBOUND EXCEPTION PROTOCOL, INBOUND MESSAGE PROTOCOL, OUTBOUND EXCEPTION PROTOCOL.

- **outbound protocol** *n.* the set of all outbound interactions, consisting of the union of the outbound message protocol and the outbound exception protocol. [Firesmith]

Antonym: INBOUND PROTOCOL.

Contrast with: OUTBOUND INTERFACE.

- **server protocol** *n.* the set of all interactions with servers, consisting of the union of the outbound message protocol and the inbound exception protocol. [Firesmith]

Antonym: CLIENT PROTOCOL.

Contrast with: SERVER INTERFACE.

protocol description *n.* any description of a class in terms of the message interface of its instances. [Smalltalk]

Contrast with: IMPLEMENTATION DESCRIPTION, SYSTEM BROWSER.

Commentary: A protocol description lists the messages understood by instances of a particular class. Each message is accompanied by a comment describing the operation an instance will perform when it receives that type of message. [Smalltalk]

protocol role *n.* any inheritable subset of a given protocol that can be accessed as a group and used to restrict client access to only that part of the protocol that abstracts a specific role that the model may play. [Firesmith]

Contrast with: MODEL ROLE, RELATIONSHIP ROLE, VIEW ROLE.

prototype *n.* **1.** any "quick and dirty" partial implementation of part of an application. [Firesmith] **2.** any primal object from which other objects are developed in a language supporting delegation rather than class inheritance. [Firesmith]

v. **-ed, -ing** to rapidly develop non-production-quality software for the purpose of understanding requirements, comparing alternate designs, developing size or timing estimated or budgets, or

feasibility studies. [Firesmith]

Synonym: *n.* **2** ANCESTOR OBJECT, EXEMPLAR, *v.* RAPID PROTOTYPE.

Commentary: Rapid prototyping should not be confused with the incremental development of deliverable software. [Firesmith]

prototype [pattern] *n.* the creational object design pattern that creates new objects by copying a prototypical instance. [Gamma, Helm, Johnson, & Vlissides]

proxy [class] *n.* **1.** any local view class that represents (i.e., acts as a processor-specific variant of and communicates with) its remote model class. [Firesmith] **2.** any class of a proxy objects. [Firesmith]

Contrast with: PRESENTATION CLASS, PROXY OBJECT.

Commentary: A proxy provides the local protocol of (and communicates with) its model on a remote processor. Proxies are used to create a single virtual address space across multiple processors. [Firesmith]

proxy [object] *n.* **1.** any local view object that represents (i.e., acts as a processor-specific variant of and communicates with) its remote model object. [Firesmith] **2.** any instance of a proxy class. [Firesmith]

Contrast with: PRESENTATION OBJECT, PROXY CLASS.

Commentary: A proxy provides the local protocol of (and communicates with) its model on a remote processor. Proxies are used to create a single virtual address space across multiple processors. [Firesmith]

proxy [pattern] *n.* the structural object design pattern that provides control over an object via a surrogate or placeholder. [Gamma, Helm, Johnson, & Vlissides]

Synonym: SURROGATE.

P

pseudovariable name *n.* any expression similar to a variable name that cannot be changed by an assignment. [Smalltalk]

public *adj.* **1.** describing features that are visible to both external clients and descendants. [Booch, C++, Firesmith, Rumbaugh] **2.** describing inheritance in which all inherited members (i.e., features) retain their base class visibility in the derived class. [C++, Firesmith]
Contrast with: PRIVATE, PROTECTED.

public block *n.* any block that is exported by a subsystem. [Jacobson]
See also: SERVICE PACKAGE, SUBSYSTEM.
Commentary: The interface of public blocks forms the interface of their subsystem. [Jacobson]

public feature *n.* any feature that is exported to all children and to all other potential clients within the scope of the encapsulating object or class. [Booch, C++, Firesmith, Rumbaugh]
Contrast with: FRIEND FEATURE, PROTECTED FEATURE.

public inheritance *n.* any inheritance in which all inherited features have the same visibility in the child as they did in the parent(s). [C++, Firesmith]
Contrast with: PRIVATE INHERITANCE, PROTECTED INHERITANCE.

public member *n.* any member (i.e., feature) that is visible to both external clients and descendants. [C++]
Contrast with: PRIVATE MEMBER, PROTECTED MEMBER.

public method *n.* any method that is made available to other classes (clients). Public methods are grouped into contracts. [Lorenz]
Antonym: PRIVATE METHOD.

public-object module *n.* any object module that is exported from, and therefore can be accessed from the outside of, its enclosing block. [Jacobson]
Antonym: PRIVATE-OBJECT MODULE.

public responsibility *n.* any visible responsibility that is visible to clients and can be a part of a contract. [Firesmith, Martin]
Antonym: PRIVATE RESPONSIBILITY.
Commentary: Public responsibilities are implemented by public features. [Firesmith, Martin]

pull model *n.* any approach to initiating event communication that allows a consumer of events to request the event data from a supplier. [OMG]
Antonym: PUSH MODEL.

pure object-oriented programming language *n.* any object-oriented programming language that only has object-oriented types (types implemented by classes). [Firesmith, Wirfs-Brock]
Antonym: HYBRID OBJECT-ORIENTED PROGRAMMING LANGUAGE.
Examples: Eiffel and Smalltalk are pure object-oriented languages. [Firesmith]
Commentary: A pure OOPL only supports object-oriented development. [Firesmith]

pure virtual function *n.* in C++, any virtual function whose implementation is deferred and must be supplied by a descendant base class before the descendant class can be instantiated. [C++, Firesmith]
Contrast with: ABSTRACT.
Commentary: Pure virtual functions are used to create deferred classes and are inherited as pure virtual functions. [C++, Firesmith]

push model *n.* any approach to initiating event communication that allows a supplier of events to initiate the transfer of the event data to consumers. [OMG]
Antonym: PULL MODEL.

Q

qualified association *n.* **1.** any binary association from a class and a qualifier to another class. [Rumbaugh] **2.** any binary association, a cardinality of which is constrained by a qualifier. [Firesmith] *Antonym:* UNQUALIFIED ASSOCIATION. *See also:* QUALIFIER.

qualified name *n.* the name of any feature that has been qualified by the name of its enclosing class. [Firesmith] *Example:* In C++,

```
ClassName::FeatureName;
```

Commentary: Qualified names are used to prevent overriding inorder to explicitly select the correct associated implementation. As a rule of thumb, explicit qualification only should be used to access the features of parents from within a child. [C++, Firesmith]

qualifier *n.* **1.** any attribute of an object that distinguishes among a set of objects a *many* end of an association.

[Rumbaugh] **2.** any attribute of an object that distinguishes it from other objects, thereby acting as a relationship cardinality constraint. [Firesmith] *See also:* QUALIFIED ASSOCIATION.

qualify *v. -ed, -ing* to append the name of the enclosing class to the name of an inherited feature to avoid overriding in order to explicitly select the correct associated implementation. [C++, Firesmith]

query *n.* **1.** any activity that involves selecting objects from implicitly or explicitly identified collections based on a specified predicate. [Firesmith, OMG] **2.** any service that returns information (i.e., an object). [Henderson-Sellers]

query operation *n.* any preserver operation that returns or computes a value. [Rumbaugh] *Contrast with:* PRESERVER OPERATION, SYNCHRONIZER OPERATION.

Q

R

race condition *n.* the condition that may occur in a concurrent environment during which concurrency affects the order that messages are received and this ordering impacts the properties or behavior of the receiver. [Firesmith]

Rationale: During a race condition, multiple messages are *racing* each other to the server and it is important to know which is the winner. [Firesmith]

raise [an exception] *v. rose, -ing* **1.** to abandon normal execution and notify a calling operation or local exception handler of the occurrence of a developer-defined exception. [Ada95] **2.** to identify an exception, abandon local execution, and transfer execution to a local exception handler (if any) or else transfer execution to the calling operation. [Firesmith]

Synonym: THROW AN EXCEPTION [C++].
Contrast with: CATCH AN EXCEPTION, HANDLE AN EXCEPTION.

Rationale: Raise is the original Ada and Eiffel term and implies a direction of propagation, whereas the C++ term *throw* does not and may therefore support the misuse of exceptions as glorified "gotos."

Commentary: The original term *raise* is preferred over the C++ term *throw*.

range of a function *n.* the collection of all objects to which the function maps. [Martin/Odell]

Contrast with: DOMAIN, EXTENSION.
See also: FUNCTION.

rapid prototype *v. -ed, -ing* to rapidly develop non-production-quality software for the purpose of understanding requirements, comparing alternate designs, developing size or timing estimates or budgets, or feasibility studies. [Firesmith]

Synonym: PROTOTYPE.
Commentary: Rapid prototyping should not be confused with the incremental development of deliverable software. [Firesmith]

read accessor *n.* any accessor operation that returns a property of an object. [Firesmith, Shlaer/Mellor]

Antonym: WRITE ACCESSOR.
Contrast with: CREATE ACCESSOR, DELETE ACCESSOR.

real object *n.* any object in a real-object model. [Jacobson]

Antonym: IDEAL OBJECT.
See also: REAL-OBJECT MODEL.

real-object model *n.* **1.** any object model of a business that takes into consideration the restrictions on the business. [Jacobson] **2.** any object model of an information system that takes into consideration the implementation environment (e.g., the problems and limitations of the implementation language and database. [Jacobson]
Antonym: IDEAL-OBJECT MODEL.
See also: REAL OBJECT.

real-time constraint *n.* **1.** any behavioral constraint specifying temporal requirements. [Firesmith] **2.** on a state net, any constraint specifying timing requirements on a trigger, action, state, or state-transition path. [Embley]
Commentary: Analysts should add real-time constraints whenever time is important. [Embley, Firesmith]

real-world object type *n.* any abstraction of a tangible real-world object identified during strategic modeling. [OADSIG]

recipient [of an exception] *n.* the current routine in which the exception is triggered and from which the exception is raised. [Eiffel, Meyer]

receiver [of a given message] *n.* the server object to which the given message was sent. [Firesmith, Smalltalk]
Synonym: SERVER.
Antonyms: CLIENT, SENDER.
Commentary: The receiver determines how to handle the message. [Firesmith, Smalltalk]

record extension *n.* any type extension that extends another type by adding additional components. [Ada95]
Antonym: PRIVATE EXTENSION.

recursion *n.* the repetition of a development method's steps to generate an increment of new product(s). [Firesmith]

Commentary: The increment of recursion may be a build, subcluster, class hierarchy, framework, object, or class. [Firesmith]
Kinds:
- GLOBAL RECURSION
- LOCAL RECURSION

- **global recursion** *n.* any recursion across more than one development activity (i.e., requirements analysis, design, coding, integration, and testing). [Firesmith]
Antonym: LOCAL RECURSION.

- **local recursion** *n.* any recursion limited to within a single development activity (i.e., requirements analysis, design, coding, integration, and testing). [Firesmith]
Antonym: GLOBAL RECURSION.

recursive aggregate *n.* any aggregate that contains, directly or indirectly, an instance of the same kind of aggregate. [Firesmith, Rumbaugh]
Example: A document may have other documents inside it. [Firesmith]

redeclaration [of a feature] *n.* the overriding of an inherited feature due to either the redefinition of an inherited effective feature or the effecting of an inherited deferred feature. [Eiffel, Firesmith, Meyer]
Contrast with: EFFECTING, REDEFINITION.
Commentary: Redeclaration may change an inherited feature's original implementation, signature, or specification. Redeclaration never introduces a new feature, but simply overrides the original declaration of an inherited feature, deferred or not. [Eiffel, Firesmith, Meyer]

redefine [a class] *v.* *-ed, -ing* to modify the existing class object to reflect the new class definition. [CLOS]

R

Commentary: Redefining a class does not create a new class object for the class. When the class *C* is redefined, changes are propagated to its instances and to instances of any of its subclasses. Updating such an instance occurs at an implementation-dependent time, but no later than the next time a slot of that instance is read or written. Updating an instance does not change its identity as defined by the *eq* (i.e., equals) function. The updating process may change the slots of that particular instance, but it does not create a new instance. [CLOS]

redefinition [of a given feature] *n.* the overriding of the given inherited effective feature. [Eiffel, Firesmith, Meyer]
Contrast with: EFFECTING, REDECLARATION, PRECURSOR.

refactoring *n.* any behavior-preserving manipulation that changes the design of the detailed software. [Firesmith]
Examples: Either renaming instance and class attributes and changing all references, or generating accessor operations for a variable and replacing all direct references with uses of the accessors. [Firesmith]

reference [to a given object] *n.* **1.** any constant value that is used as an alias for the OID of the given server object. [Firesmith] **2.** any value that refers to an object. [Eiffel, Meyer]
Contrast with: IDENTIFIER, LINK, POINTER, VALUE.
Commentary: References are used as links and as arguments in messages and operations. Unless changed, a reference will identify the same object each time the reference is used (subject to certain pragmatic limits of space and time). An object may be denoted by multiple, distinct references. [Firesmith]

Kinds:
- ATTACHED REFERENCE
- DANGLING REFERENCE
- IMPORTED REFERENCE
- INGENERATE REFERENCE
- VOID REFERENCE

- **attached reference** *n.* any reference that currently refers to an object. [Eiffel, Firesmith, Meyer]
Contrast with: DANGLING REFERENCE, VOID REFERENCE.
Commentary: The reference is said to be attached to the object, and the object is also said to be attached to the reference. [Eiffel, Firesmith, Meyer]

- **dangling reference** *n.* any reference that refers to an object that does not exist. [Firesmith]
Contrast with: ATTACHED REFERENCE, VOID REFERENCE.

- **imported reference** *n.* any reference stored in an object's instance variable that was not generated by the object itself through invocation of a *create* method. [Atkinson]
Antonym: INGENERATE REFERENCE.

- **ingenerate reference** *n.* any reference stored in an object's instance variable that was generated by the object itself through invocation of a *create* method. [Atkinson]
Antonym: IMPORTED REFERENCE.

- **void reference** *n.* **1.** any reference that does not currently refer to an object. [Firesmith] **2.** any reference about which no further information is available. [Eiffel, Meyer]
Contrast with: ATTACHED REFERENCE, DANGLING REFERENCE.

reference [to a type] *n.* any variable that has been declared a reference to a type and that must therefore be initialized to an object of that type or to an object that

can be converted to that type [C++]
Commentary: A reference cannot be
changed to refer to another object after
initialization. This means that references are not first-class citizens in C++. In
a very real sense a reference is not an
object. [C++].

reference type *n.* any type that is not a
formal generic name and for which none
of the following conditions apply:
– T is a Class_type whose base class C
  is an expanded class.
– T is of the form expanded CT.
– T is of the form BIT M for some
  non-negative integer M.
  [Eiffel, Meyer]
Contrast with: EXPANDED TYPE.

referential attribute *n.* any attribute that
captures the facts that tie an instance of
one object to an instance of another object. [Shlaer/Mellor]
Contrast with: ASSOCIATION ATTRIBUTE,
LINK ATTRIBUTE.

referential integrity *n.* **1.** (a) the degree
to which each identifier refers to a
unique object. [Firesmith] (b) the assurance that an object reference that exists in the state associated with an object reliably identifies a single object.
[OMG] **2.** the degree to which links
(especially bidirectional links) are
maintained. [Firesmith]
Contrast with: STATE INTEGRITY.

reflexive constraint *n.* the structural constraint on any given relationship that
requires objects or classes to be related
to themselves. [Firesmith]
Antonym: IRREFLEXIVE CONSTRAINT.
Example: The *is-as-old-as* link and association are reflexive. Something can
be as old as other things, but must be as
old as itself. [Firesmith]

regeneration *n.* the automatic produc-

tion of appropriate ODL declaration in
order to establish communications or
sharing between an existing ODBMS
application and another ODMG compliant system. [ODMG]

reification *n.* the creation of an object
out of a nonobject entity. [Firesmith]
Examples: The creation of objects that
model links and operations. [Firesmith]

reify *v.* **-ed, -ing** to create an object out
of a nonobject entity. [Firesmith]
Contrast with: EMBED.

relation *n.* any object type modeling an
association whose extension is a set of
tuples. [Martin/Odell]
Contrast with: RELATIONSHIP.
See also: TUPLE, OBJECT TYPE, PLACE,
ASSOCIATION.
Example: The *Employment* association
between the *Organization* and *Person*
object types is a relation.

relational object class *n.* any object class
whose instances are relationships. [Em-
bley]
See also: RELATIONSHIP, RELATIONSHIP
OBJECT.

relationship *n.* **1.** (a) any logical static connection between two or more things.
[Firesmith] (b) any logical connection
between individual objects. [Embley]
2. any potential association between
classes. [Coleman] **3.** any characteristic
that specifies a mapping from one object to another; an instance of a relationship type. [OADSIG] **4.** any abstraction of a set of associations that
hold systematically between different
kinds of things in the real world.
[Shlaer/Mellor] **5.** any instance of a relationship set. [Embley]
Kinds:
• AGGREGATION
• ASSOCIATION

R

- ATTRIBUTE ASSOCIATION
- BASE ASSOCIATION
- BIDIRECTIONAL ASSOCIATION
- BINARY ASSOCIATION
- CLASS ASSOCIATION
  + INHERITANCE ASSOCIATION
- DEPENDSON ASSOCIATION
- DERIVED ASSOCIATION
- DYNAMIC ASSOCIATION
  + COMMUNICATION
    ASSOCIATION
- EXTEND ASSOCIATION
- FUNCTION
- INSTANCE ASSOCIATION
- META-ASSOCIATION
- QUALIFIED ASSOCIATION
- RELATION
- STATIC ASSOCIATION
  + ACQUAINTANCE ASSOCIATION
    > CONSISTSOF ASSOCIATION
    > PARTOF ASSOCIATION
  + INHERITANCE ASSOCIATION
- TERNARY ASSOCIATION
- UNIDIRECTIONAL ASSOCIATION
- UNQUALIFIED ASSOCIATION
- USES ASSOCIATION
• BASE RELATIONSHIP
- BASE ASSOCIATION
- BASE LINK
• BIDIRECTIONAL RELATIONSHIP
- BIDIRECTIONAL ASSOCIATION
- BIDIRECTIONAL LINK
• BINARY RELATIONSHIP
- BINARY ASSOCIATION
- BINARY LINK
• DEPENDENCY RELATIONSHIP
- IMPLEMENTATION DEPENDENCY
- INTERFACE DEPENDENCY
- METHOD DEPENDENCY
• DERIVED RELATIONSHIP
- DERIVED ASSOCIATION
- DERIVED LINK
• GENERALIZATION

- A-KIND-OF RELATIONSHIP
- IS-A RELATIONSHIP
- MULTIPLE GENERALIZATION
- SINGLE GENERALIZATION
• INHERITANCE
- CLASS INHERITANCE
- CLASS-INSTANCE INHERITANCE
- DYNAMIC INHERITANCE
- EVENT INHERITANCE
- IMPLEMENTATION INHERITANCE
- INTERFACE INHERITANCE
  + STRICT INHERITANCE
- INVERTED INHERITANCE
- MULTIPLE INHERITANCE
  + MIXIN INHERITANCE
  + REPEATED INHERITANCE
    > DIRECT REPEATED INHERITANCE
    > INDIRECT REPEATED
      INHERITANCE
    > REPLICATED REPEATED
      INHERITANCE
    > SHARED REPEATED
      INHERITANCE
    > VIRTUAL INHERITANCE
- OBJECT-OBJECT INHERITANCE
- PRIVATE INHERITANCE
- PROTECTED INHERITANCE
- PUBLIC INHERITANCE
- SELECTIVE INHERITANCE
- SINGLE INHERITANCE
- SPECIALIZATION INHERITANCE
- STATIC INHERITANCE
- TYPE INHERITANCE
• INTER-SUBSYSTEM RELATIONSHIP
• IS-PART-OF RELATIONSHIP
• LINK
- ATTACHED LINK
  + ATTACHED POINTER
  + ATTACHED LINK
- BASE LINK
- BIDIRECTIONAL LINK
- BINARY LINK
- CONSTANT LINK

- DANGLING LINK
  + DANGLING POINTER
  + DANGLING LINK
- DERIVED LINK
- POINTER
  + ATTACHED POINTER
  + DANGLING POINTER
  + VOID POINTER
- REFERENCE
  + ATTACHED REFERENCE
  + DANGLING REFERENCE
  + IMPORTED REFERENCE
  + INGENERATE REFERENCE
  + VOID REFERENCE
- STATE LINK
- STATE-DEPENDENT LINK
- STATE-INDEPENDENT LINK
- TERNARY LINK
- UNIDIRECTIONAL LINK
- VARIABLE LINK
- VOID LINK
  + VOID POINTER
  + VOID REFERENCE
• SPECIALIZATION
  - MULTIPLE SPECIALIZATION
  - SINGLE SPECIALIZATION
• TERNARY RELATIONSHIP
  - TERNARY ASSOCIATION
  - TERNARY LINK
• UNIDIRECTIONAL RELATIONSHIP
  - UNIDIRECTIONAL ASSOCIATION
  - UNIDIRECTIONAL LINK

• **aggregation** *n.* **1.** the whole-part relationship from an aggregate to its component parts. [Firesmith, Henderson-Sellers, Rumbaugh] **2.** any relationship such as *consistsOf, contains,* or a similar relationship between object types that defines the composition of an object type from other object types. [OADSIG] **3.** (a) any mechanism for structuring the object model whereby a new class is constructed from several other classes and relationships. [Coleman] (b) the process of forming an aggregate object from other objects as its component parts. [Firesmith, Martin/Odell] *Synonym:* COMPOSITION.

• **association** *n.* **1.** (a) any semantic relationship between two or more classes or types. [Booch, Firesmith, Henderson-Sellers, Martin/Odell, OADSIG] (b) any class of links between the instances of two or more classes or types. [Firesmith, Rumbaugh] **2.** any relationship between two objects or classes describing their interaction. [Henderson-Sellers] **3.** any *is-member-of* relationship, containing a *set class* and one or more *member classes.* [Embley] **4.** any object class whose instances are sets. [Embley] **5.** any directed binary relation between instances or classes. [Jacobson]
Synonym: **4** SET CLASS [Embley].
Contrast with: LINK.
Examples: Employer and *Employee* are relations connecting the object types *Company* and *Person.*
Commentary: An association may be unidirectional [Firesmith, Jacobson], bidirectional [Firesmith, Rumbaugh], or have an explicit inverse relation [OADSIG]. It is always the associating object that acts on and knows of the associated object, never the other way around. [Jacobson]
Kinds:
  - ATTRIBUTE ASSOCIATION
  - BASE ASSOCIATION
  - BIDIRECTIONAL ASSOCIATION
  - BINARY ASSOCIATION
  - CLASS ASSOCIATION
    + INHERITANCE ASSOCIATION
  - DEPENDSON ASSOCIATION

R

- DERIVED ASSOCIATION
- DYNAMIC ASSOCIATION
  + COMMUNICATION ASSOCIATION
- EXTEND ASSOCIATION
- FUNCTION
- INSTANCE ASSOCIATION
- META-ASSOCIATION
- QUALIFIED ASSOCIATION
- RELATION
- STATIC ASSOCIATION
  + ACQUAINTANCE ASSOCIATION
    > CONSISTSOF ASSOCIATION
    > PARTOF ASSOCIATION
  + INHERITANCE ASSOCIATION
- TERNARY ASSOCIATION
- UNIDIRECTIONAL ASSOCIATION
- UNQUALIFIED ASSOCIATION
- USES ASSOCIATION

- **attribute association** *n.* any association captures the relationship from the object to that part of its attribute that holds the value of the attribute. [Jacobson]
Contrast with: ATTRIBUTE TYPE.
See also: ATTRIBUTE.
Commentary: The attribute association represents the unit that holds the value of the attribute, whereas the attribute type shows the attributes' structure and type. The attribute association has a name that, like the name of acquaintance associations, describes the role that the attribute plays in relation to the object. The association can also have a cardinality. [Jacobson]

- **base association** *n.* **1.** any association that cannot be defined in terms of other associations. [Firesmith] **2.** any association of base links. [Firesmith]
Antonym: DERIVED ASSOCIATION.

- **bidirectional association** *n.* any logical association that represents two unidirectional associations that are coupled so that each is the inverse of the other. [Firesmith]
Antonym: UNIDIRECTIONAL ASSOCIATION.

- **binary association** *n.* any association between two classes. [Firesmith, Rumbaugh]
Contrast with: TERNARY ASSOCIATION.

- **class association** *n.* any association linking two classes. [Jacobson]
Antonym: INSTANCE ASSOCIATION.
Contrast with: META ASSOCIATION.
Example: The inherit association is a *class association*, that is, an association between classes. [Jacobson]
Commentary: Class associations are drawn with dashed arrows. [Jacobson]

  + **inheritance association** *n.* any class association, meaning that the definition of the operations and attributes of one class is also used in the inheriting class, which might do additions and redefinitions. [Jacobson]
  See also: INHERITANCE.

- **dependsOn association** *n.* any association from one subsystem to another that means that objects in the first subsystem will use, in some way, objects in the second subsystem. [Jacobson]

- **derived association** *n.* **1.** any association that is defined in terms of other associations. [Firesmith, Rumbaugh] **2.** any association of derived links. [Firesmith]
Antonym: BASE ASSOCIATION.

- **dynamic association** *n.* any association that captures a dynamic in-

teraction. [Jacobson]
Antonym: STATIC ASSOCIATION.
+ **communication association** *n.* any association that models the communication of one object with another. [Jacobson]
Synonym: DYNAMIC ASSOCIATION.
Antonym: STATIC ASSOCIATION.
Commentary: The communication association does not show what kind of stimuli is sent between the objects; this is a level of detail that is saved for interaction diagrams. Communication associations are not named because they are dynamic. [Jacobson]
- **extend association** *n.* any association from one use case to another, specifying how the first use case description extends (i.e., is inserted into) the second use case description. [Jacobson]
Contrast with: USES ASSOCIATION.
See also: PROBE.
Commentary: When performing a use case, it might be performed either with or without the extended description according to some condition. The extends association has no direct implementation technique in the common programming languages. What extends actually means is that a behavior, *b1*, shall be inserted into another behavior, *b2*. The description of behavior *b2* should be completely independent and unknowing of behavior *b1*. Ideally, *b1* itself should take the initiative and insert itself into *b2*. This will normally be implemented with a stimulus being sent from *b2* to *b1*. [Jacobson]
- **function** *n.* **1.** any operation that

returns a value. [Ada95, C++, Eiffel, Firesmith] **2.** (a) any input/output mapping resulting from some object's behavior. [Booch] b) any operation that maps an object of one set into a set of objects in the same or different set. [Martin/Odell]
Synonym: **1** METHOD, OPERATION, SERVICE.
Contrast with: **2** PROCESS.
- **instance association** *n.* any association linking two instances. [Jacobson]
Antonym: CLASS ASSOCIATION.
Contrast with: META-ASSOCIATION.
- **meta-association** *n.* any association linking a class to an instance or vice versa. [Jacobson]
Contrast with: CLASS ASSOCIATION, INSTANCE ASSOCIATION.
- **qualified association** *n.* any binary association, a cardinality of which is constrained by a qualifier. [Firesmith, Rumbaugh]
Antonym: UNQUALIFIED ASSOCIATION.
See also: QUALIFIER.
- **relation** *n.* any object type modeling an association whose extension is a set of tuples. [Martin/Odell]
Contrast with: RELATIONSHIP.
See also: ASSOCIATION, OBJECT TYPE, PLACE, TUPLE.
Example: The *Employment* association between the *Organization* and *Person* object types is a relation.
- **static association** *n.* any association that captures a static relationship. [Jacobson]
Antonym: DYNAMIC ASSOCIATION.
Kinds:
    + ACQUAINTANCE ASSOCIATION

R

> CONSISTSOF ASSOCIATION
> PARTOF ASSOCIATION
+ INHERITANCE ASSOCIATION

+ **acquaintance association** *n.* any static association between objects, in which one object knows of the existence of another. [Jacobson]
See also: ATTRIBUTE, ENTITY OBJECT.
Contrast with: STATIC ASSOCIATION.
Commentary: An acquaintance association does not give the object the right to exchange information with the other object; for that, a dynamic association is needed. Acquaintance associations are normally implemented in the same way as attributes, namely as ordinary instance references or pointer variables to instances. [Jacobson]
Kinds:
> CONSISTSOF ASSOCIATION
> PARTOF ASSOCIATION

> **consistsOf association** *n.* any acquaintance association from an aggregate object to an object of which it consists. [Jacobson]
Antonym: PARTOF ASSOCIATION.
See also: AGGREGATE, ACQUAINTANCE ASSOCIATION.
Example: A food order consists of a dish and a beverage. [Jacobson]
Commentary: The associations called consistsOf and partOf are variants of the acquaintance association. They are used to express that an object is a compound of other objects. A construction of this type is called an aggregate. [Jacobson]

> **partOf association** *n.* any ac-

quaintance association from an object to the aggregate object of which it is a part. [Jacobson]
Antonym: CONSISTSOF ASSOCIATION.
See also: AGGREGATE, ACQUAINTANCE ASSOCIATION.
Example: A dish and a beverage are parts of a food order. [Jacobson]
Commentary: The associations called consistsOf and partOf are variants of the acquaintance association. They are used to express that an object is a compound of other objects. A construction of this type is called an aggregate. [Jacobson]

+ **inheritance association** *n.* any class association whereby the definition of the operations and attributes of one class is also used in the inheriting class, which might do additions and redefinitions. [Jacobson]
See also: INHERITANCE.

- **ternary association** *n.* any association among three classes. [Firesmith, Rumbaugh]
Contrast with: BINARY ASSOCIATION.

- **unidirectional association** *n.* any association directed from the client(s) to the server(s). [Firesmith]
Antonym: BIDIRECTIONAL ASSOCIATION.
Commentary: Unidirectional associations are typically implemented by one or more attributes acting as pointers or messages requesting services. [Firesmith]

- **unqualified association** *n.* any association, no cardinality of which is constrained by a qualifier.

Antonym: QUALIFIED ASSOCIATION.
See also: QUALIFIER.

- **uses association** *n.* any association from an abstract use case to a concrete use case in which the description of the abstract use case is used in the description of the concrete use case. [Jacobson]
Contrast with: EXTEND ASSOCIATION.
See also: INHERITANCE.

• **base relationship** *n.* any relationship that cannot be derived from other relationships. [Firesmith]
Antonym: DERIVED RELATIONSHIP.
Kinds:
  - BASE ASSOCIATION
  - BASE LINK

- **base association** *n.* **1.** any association that cannot be defined in terms of other associations. [Firesmith] **2.** any association of base links. [Firesmith]
Antonym: DERIVED ASSOCIATION.

- **base link** *n.* any link that cannot be derived from other links. [Firesmith]
Antonym: DERIVED LINK.

• **bidirectional relationship** *n.* any logical relationship that represents two unidirectional relationships that are coupled so that each is the inverse of the other. [Firesmith]
Antonym: UNIDIRECTIONAL RELATIONSHIP.
Kinds:
  - BIDIRECTIONAL ASSOCIATION
  - BIDIRECTIONAL LINK

- **bidirectional association** *n.* any logical association that represents two unidirectional associations that are coupled so that each is the inverse of the other. [Firesmith]

Antonym: UNIDIRECTIONAL ASSOCIATION.

- **bidirectional link** *n.* any logical link that represents two unidirectional links that are coupled so that each is the inverse of the other. [Firesmith]
Antonym: UNIDIRECTIONAL LINK.

• **binary relationship** *n.* any relationship between two things. [Firesmith]
Contrast with: TERNARY RELATIONSHIP.
Kinds:
  - BINARY ASSOCIATION
  - BINARY LINK

- **binary association** *n.* any association between two classes or types. [Firesmith, Rumbaugh]
Contrast with: TERNARY ASSOCIATION.

- **binary link** *n.* any link between two objects. [Firesmith]
Contrast with: TERNARY LINK.

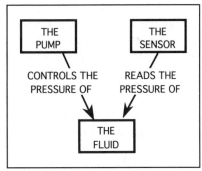

Binary Relationships

• **dependency [relationship]** *n.* **1.** the client/server relationship representing reliance of the client on the server. [Firesmith] **2.** the object-oriented analog of coupling in structured design. [Shlaer/Mellor]

Examples: Message passing in which the client sends messages to the server, aggregation in which the aggregate (client) depends on its component parts (servers) for its definition, inheritance in which the derived class (client) depends on its base classes (servers) for its inherited features. [Firesmith]

Commentary: Dependency implies coupling, visibility, and reference. Dependency relationships usually imply message passing. [Firesmith]

Kinds:
- IMPLEMENTATION DEPENDENCY
- INTERFACE DEPENDENCY
- METHOD DEPENDENCY

- **implementation dependency** *n.* any dependency of the implementation (but not the interface) of the client on its server(s). [Firesmith]

Contrast with: INTERFACE DEPENDENCY, METHOD DEPENDENCY.

Example: Any dependency provided by a *with* clause in an Ada package body is an implementation dependency. [Firesmith]

Commentary: Implementation dependency implies that the interface of the server is visible to only those features in the implementation of the client. [Firesmith]

- **interface dependency** *n.* any dependency of the interface (as well as the implementation) of the client on its server(s). [Firesmith]

Contrast with: IMPLEMENTATION DEPENDENCY, METHOD DEPENDENCY.

Examples: Any dependency due to the use of types in signatures and any dependency provided by a *with* clause in an Ada package specification is an interface dependency. [Firesmith]

Commentary: Interface dependency implies that the interface of the server is visible to every feature of the client. [Firesmith]

- **method dependency** *n.* any dependency of only a single specified method of the client on its server(s). [Firesmith]

Contrast with: IMPLEMENTATION DEPENDENCY, INTERFACE DEPENDENCY.

Example: Any dependency provided by a *with* clause in a subprogram body is a method dependency. [Firesmith]

• **derived relationship** *n.* any relationship that can be derived from other relationships. [Coleman, Firesmith]

Antonym: BASE RELATIONSHIP.

Kinds:
- DERIVED ASSOCIATION
- DERIVED LINK

- **derived association** *n.* **1.** any association that is defined in terms of other associations. [Firesmith, Rumbaugh] **2.** any association of derived links. [Firesmith]

Antonym: BASE ASSOCIATION.

Contrast with: BASE LINK.

- **derived link** *n.* **1.** any indirect link that is the product of other links. [Firesmith] **2.** any instance of a derived association. [Firesmith]

Antonym: BASE LINK.

Contrast with: DERIVED ASSOCIATION.

• **generalization** *n.* **1.** the process of creating a generalization from one or more specializations. [Firesmith, Henderson-Sellers, Jacobson, Martin] **2.** the result of using the generalization

process. [Fire-smith] **3** any relationship from a specialization to one or more of its generalizations. [Firesmith]
Antonym: SPECIALIZATION, SUBTYPING.

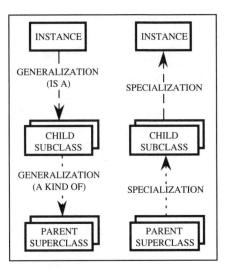

Generalization

Examples: **1** creating a new generalized class or type by factoring out common characteristics and responsibilities from one or more existing classes or types (e.g., the specializations). [Firesmith] **2** (a) any ancestor of a given type or class. For example, vehicles are generalizations of cars, boats, and aircraft. [Firesmith] (b) any class or type of a given instance. [Firesmith] **3** (a) the *a-kind-of* relationship from a specialization to its more general parent. [Coleman, Firesmith, Rumbaugh] (b) the *is-a* relationship from an instance to its more general type or class. [Firesmith]
Commentary: The extent of a generalized (class or type) is a superset of

the union of the extents of its specializations. [Firesmith]
Kinds:
- A-KIND-OF RELATIONSHIP
- IS-A RELATIONSHIP
- MULTIPLE GENERALIZATION
- SINGLE GENERALIZATION
- **a-kind-of relationship** *n.* the relationship between a specialization and its generalization(s). [Firesmith]
Contrast with: IS-A RELATIONSHIP.
Examples: Examples include the subtyping relationship from a subtype to its supertype and the specialization inheritance relationship from a derived class to its base class whereby instances of the derived class are a kind of the base class. A car is a kind of vehicle. [Firesmith]
Commentary: Many developers confuse the *a-kind-of* relationship between types or classes with the *is-a* relationship between objects and their types or classes. [Firesmith]
- **is-a relationship** *n.* **1.** the classification relationship from an object to its class or type. [Firesmith] **2.** the specialization relationship from a derived class to its base class or from a subtype to its supertype. [Lorenz]
Synonym: CLASSIFICATION.
Contrast with: A-KIND-OF RELATIONSHIP.
Examples: **1** Spot is a dog. My car is a car. [Firesmith] **2** A car is a [kind of] vehicle.
Commentary: Many developers (e.g. Definition **2**) confuse the *a-kind-of* relationship between types or classes with the *is-a* relationship between objects and their types or classes. [Firesmith]

R

- **multiple generalization** *n.* any generalization whereby a parent has more than one child. [Firesmith] *Antonym:* MULTIPLE CLASSIFICATION. *Contrast with:* SINGLE GENERALIZATION, SINGLE INHERITANCE.
- **single generalization** *n.* any generalization whereby a parent has only a single child. [Firesmith] *Antonym:* SINGLE CLASSIFICATION. *Contrast with:* MULTIPLE GENERALIZATION, MULTIPLE INHERITANCE.
- **inheritance** *n.* **1.** (a) the incremental construction of a new definition in terms of existing definitions without disturbing the original definitions and their clients. [Ada95, Firesmith] (b) the construction of a definition by incremental modification of other definitions. [Jacobson, OMG] **2.** the definition of a derived class in terms of one or more base classes. [Booch, Coleman, Embley, Jacobson, Wirfs-Brock] **3.** (a) a mechanism for expressing commonality between classes so that new classes inherit responsibilities from existing classes. [Coad] b) a mechanism that permits classes to share characteristics. [Rumbaugh] **4.** (a) the organization of similar types of classes of objects into categories. [Lorenz] (b) the taxonomic relationship between *parents* and *children*, possibly over many *generations*. [Henderson-Sellers]
Contrast with: SPECIALIZATION, SUBTYPING.
See also: GENERALIZATION–SPECIALIZATION STRUCTURE, INHERITANCE STRUCTURE.
Examples: The definition of a derived class in terms of the features defined in its base classes, the definition of a subtype in terms of the features defined in its supertypes, and the definition of a derived cluster in terms of its base clusters. For example, *Savings* accounts are types of general *Account*, and *IRA* accounts are types of Savings accounts. The *Savings* account inherits the capability to handle deposits from the *Account* class. [Lorenz]
Rationale: Inheritance should be defined generally enough to include both class and type inheritance. However, there is a consensus in the object community that the definition of inheritance should be restrictive enough to disallow the derived typing mechanism of Ada83. Even though an Ada-derived type is a new data type that inherits all of the attributes and operations of its parent type, it is not usually considered an example of true single inheritance because a derived type may only restrict the range of the parent type and may not add new features, which greatly restricts its value and is why true inheritance was added to Ada95. Definition **1** above meets these criteria, whereas definition **2** does not.
Commentary: **1** A new definition may (1) add new features, (2) modify or replace some of the inherited features, (3) define deferred inherited features, or (4) delete inherited features. Because of the inherent dangers involved, few methodologists or languages allow the deletion of inherited features. Definition **2** unnecessarily restricts inheritance to classes (a.k.a. class inheritance). Definition **3** points out that inheritance can be used (and misused) as a mechanism for express-

ing commonality and sharing characteristics. Definition **4** unnecessarily restricts inheritance to specialization inheritance. Inheritance plays a key role in the development of an object-oriented type system. [Firesmith]

Kinds:
- CLASS INHERITANCE
- CLASS-INSTANCE INHERITANCE
- DYNAMIC INHERITANCE
- EVENT INHERITANCE
- IMPLEMENTATION INHERITANCE
- INTERFACE INHERITANCE
  + STRICT INHERITANCE
- INVERTED INHERITANCE
- MULTIPLE INHERITANCE
  + MIXIN INHERITANCE
  + REPEATED INHERITANCE
    > DIRECT REPEATED INHERITANCE
    > INDIRECT REPEATED INHERITANCE
    > REPLICATED REPEATED INHERITANCE
    > SHARED REPEATED INHERITANCE
    > VIRTUAL INHERITANCE
- OBJECT-OBJECT INHERITANCE
- PRIVATE INHERITANCE
- PROTECTED INHERITANCE
- PUBLIC INHERITANCE
- SELECTIVE INHERITANCE
- SINGLE INHERITANCE
- SPECIALIZATION INHERITANCE
- STATIC INHERITANCE
- TYPE INHERITANCE

- **class inheritance** *n.* **1.** any inheritance among classes in which a new class (a.k.a. the *parent*) is defined in terms of one or more existing classes (a.k.a. its parents), whereby the child inherits the features of its parents. [Firesmith] **2.** any implementation of generalization using inheritance. [Martin/Odell]
Synonym: SUBCLASSING.
Contrast with: TYPE INHERITANCE.
Examples: Subclasses inherit slots, methods, and some defclass operations from their superclasses. [CLOS]
Commentary: Definition **2** unnecessarily restricts class inheritance to specialization inheritance.

- **class-instance inheritance** *n.* any inheritance whereby instances inherit default attribute values from their class. [Martin]
Example: If the class *Field* has several attributes—row, column, color, and so on—and the default value for color is *Green*, then every instance of the class *Field* will be created with a color value of 'Green'—unless the value is specifically changed by the user. [Martin]

- **dynamic inheritance** *n.* any inheritance that requires dynamic binding (e.g., to support polymorphism). [Firesmith]
Antonym: STATIC INHERITANCE.

- **event inheritance** *n.* any inheritance whereby event subtypes inherit trigger rules and control conditions from their event supertypes. [Martin]

- **implementation inheritance** *n.* **1.** any inheritance whereby a new definition does not conform to at least one of the existing definitions. [Firesmith] **2.** any inheritance used merely for the purpose of reusing [some of] the implementation of the base class(es). [Henderson-Sellers]
Antonym: INTERFACE INHERITANCE.
Contrast with: SPECIALIZATION INHERITANCE.

R

See also: SIGNATURE CONFORMANCE, TYPE CONFORMANCE.

Commentary: The use of implementation inheritance is controversial in the object community because it is typically used merely for code (i.e., implementation) reuse rather than to capture an *a-kind-of* taxonomy. Implementation inheritance does not imply any semantic relationship. Many methodologists consider it not to be as good as specialization or interface inheritance because it need support neither specialization nor polymorphic substitutability. The use of implementation inheritance is often a sign that aggregation or delegation should have been used instead of inheritance. [Firesmith]

- **interface inheritance** *n.* any inheritance whereby the new definition conforms to the existing definition(s). [Firesmith, Henderson-Sellers]
Synonym: SPECIFICATION INHERITANCE, SUBTYPING.
Antonym: IMPLEMENTATION INHERITANCE.
Contrast with: SPECIALIZATION INHERITANCE.
Commentary: Interface inheritance implies that the protocol of the child is a superset of the union of the protocols of its parents. Interface inheritance allows polymorphic substitution of instances of the derived class for instances of any of its base classes, even if the derived class is not a specialization of its base class(es). [Firesmith]

+ **strict inheritance** *n.* any interface inheritance whereby the new definition only adds new features to the old definition(s) but neither deletes nor redefines inherited features from the old definition(s). [Firesmith]

- **inverted inheritance** *n.* any inheritance whereby the parent defines *all* of the features needed by *all* of its children and these individual children *delete* the unnecessary features of the parent rather than add new features or override inherited features. [Firesmith]
Synonym: SELECTIVE INHERITANCE.
Commentary: Inverted inheritance is generally rejected in the object community. It produces inheritance structures that are neither extensible nor maintainable. The parent does not capture a meaningful abstraction and is not restricted to the definition of common features. Contrary to expectations, the children are neither more abstract nor more detailed. Instead of being extensions that can do more than their parents, they can only do less. Inverted inheritance is therefore a source of confusion and not recommended. [Firesmith]

- **multiple inheritance** *n.* any inheritance in which the definition of the child is constructed in terms of the definitions of *multiple* parents. [Ada95, Coleman, Firesmith, Jacobson, Martin, OMG, Rumbaugh, Wirfs-Brock]
Antonym: SINGLE INHERITANCE.
Example: Inheritance whereby a single class is simultaneously a child class of more than one parent class.
Commentary: The extent of the child is a subset of the intersection

of the extents of the parents. [Embley, Firesmith]

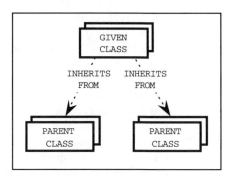

Multiple Inheritance

Kinds:
+ MIXIN INHERITANCE
+ REPEATED INHERITANCE
  > DIRECT REPEATED
    INHERITANCE
  > INDIRECT REPEATED
    INHERITANCE
  > REPLICATED REPEATED
    INHERITANCE
  > SHARED REPEATED
    INHERITANCE
  > VIRTUAL INHERITANCE
+ **mixin inheritance** *n.* any multiple inheritance involving a mixin, an abstract parent class that exists only to provide a set of properties for classes to inherit. [Ada95]
+ **repeated inheritance** *n.* any multiple inheritance in which a given child inherits the same feature, either directly or indirectly, from the same ancestor class multiple times. [Eiffel, Firesmith, Jacobson, Meyer]
See also: REPLICATED FEATURES, SHARED FEATURES.

Commentary: In the majority of programming languages that support multiple inheritance, the user is forced to redefine the name of each replicated feature so that it becomes unique. This is the most acceptable solution, as only the user has sufficient knowledge to solve this conflict. If an operation is replicated, the selection of which version does not matter unless the original operation has been overridden. Then the problem is to know which one to select. [Jacobson]
Kinds:
  > DIRECT REPEATED
    INHERITANCE
  > INDIRECT REPEATED
    INHERITANCE
  > REPLICATED REPEATED
    INHERITANCE
  > SHARED REPEATED
    INHERITANCE
  > VIRTUAL INHERITANCE
  > **direct repeated inheritance [of a given class]** *n.* any repeated inheritance in which a parent class of the given class is the multiply inherited [Eiffel, Firesmith, Meyer]
Antonym: INDIRECT REPEATED INHERITANCE.
  > **indirect repeated inheritance [of a given class]** *n.* any repeated inheritance in which an ancestor class of the given class is the parent of two or more descendants of the given class. [Eiffel, Firesmith, Meyer]
Antonym: DIRECT REPEATED INHERITANCE.

R

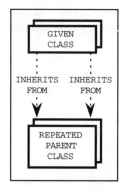

Direct Repeated Inheritance

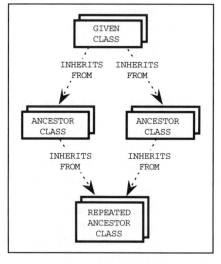

Indirect Repeated Inheritance

> **replicated repeated inheritance** *n.* any repeated inheritance from a common ancestor of a single feature under different names yielding two features in the current class. [Eiffel, Firesmith, Meyer]

Antonym: SHARED REPEATED INHERITANCE.

Commentary: The inherited feature is thus replicated and occurs multiple times in the current class or type. In the majority of programming languages that support multiple inheritance, the developer is required to redefine the name of each replicated feature so that it becomes unique. This is the most acceptable solution, as only the developer has sufficient knowledge to resolve this conflict. If an operation is repeated, the selection of which version does not matter unless the original operation has been overridden. Then the problem is to know which one to select. [Firesmith]

> **shared repeated inheritance** *n.* any repeated inheritance from a common ancestor of a single feature under the same final names yielding a single feature in the current class. [Eiffel, Firesmith, Meyer]

Synonym: VIRTUAL INHERITANCE.
Antonym: REPLICATED REPEATED INHERITANCE.

Commentary: The inherited feature is thus shared and occurs only once in the current class. [Firesmith]

> **virtual inheritance** *n.* any repeated inheritance whereby the features of repeated base classes (or supertypes) are only inherited once in the derived class (or subtype).

Synonym: SHARED REPEATED INHERITANCE.
See also: SHARED FEATURE.

- **object–object inheritance** *n.* any

inheritance that transfers the *state* of one object to another. [Martin/Odell]

Synonym: DELEGATION.

- **private inheritance** *n.* any inheritance in which all inherited features become private, regardless of their visibility in the parents. [Firesmith]

Contrast with: PROTECTED INHERITANCE, PUBLIC INHERITANCE.

Commentary: The use of private inheritance supports information hiding and the maintainability of inheritance structures because it allows developers to change the implementation of ancestors without impacting their descendants. However, private inheritance must be used with care as it may also prevent the child from conforming to its parents by hiding their visible features, thus violating subtyping, specialization inheritance, and polymorphic substitutability. [Firesmith]

- **protected inheritance** *n.* any inheritance in which all inherited private and protected features have the same visibility in the child as they did in the parent(s), whereas all inherited public features become protected in the child. [Firesmith]

Contrast with: PRIVATE INHERITANCE, PUBLIC INHERITANCE.

- **public inheritance** *n.* any inheritance in which all inherited features have the same visibility in the child as they did in the parent(s). [Firesmith]

Contrast with: PRIVATE INHERITANCE, PROTECTED INHERITANCE.

- **selective inheritance** *n.* any inheritance whereby the parent defines *all* of the features needed by *all* of its children and these individual children *delete* the unnecessary features of the parent rather than add new features or override inherited features. [Firesmith]

Synonym: INVERTED INHERITANCE.

Commentary: Inverted inheritance is generally rejected in the object community. It produces inheritance structures that are neither extensible nor maintainable. The parent does not capture a meaningful abstraction and is not restricted to the definition of common features. Contrary to expectations, the children are neither more abstract nor more detailed. Instead of being extensions that can do more than their parents, they can only do less. Inverted inheritance is therefore a source of confusion and not recommended. [Firesmith]

- **single inheritance** *n.* **1.** any inheritance in which the definition of the child is constructed in terms of the definition of only a *single* parent. [Coleman, Firesmith, Martin, OMG, Rumbaugh, Smalltalk, Wirfs-Brock] **2.** inheritance using only a single Parent clause. [Eiffel, Meyer]

R

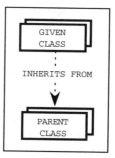

Single Inheritance

Antonym: MULTIPLE INHERITANCE.
Contrast with: MULTIPLE GENERALI-
ZATION, SINGLE GENERALIZATION.
Example: Any inheritance whereby a single class is a child class of
only a single parent class is single
inheritance. [Firesmith]

- **specialization inheritance** *n.* any
inheritance that implements the *a-
kind-of* relationship so that the child
is a specialization of its parents.
[Firesmith, Henderson-Sellers]
Synonym: SUBTYPING.
Contrast with: IMPLEMENTATION
INHERITANCE, INTERFACE INHER-
ITANCE.
Example: Cars are specializations
of (a kind of) vehicles. [Firesmith]

- **specification inheritance** *n.* any
inheritance whereby the specification of the new definition conforms to those of the existing defi-
nition(s). [Henderson-Sellers]
Synonym: INTERFACE INHERITANCE,
SUBTYPING.
Antonym: IMPLEMENTATION INHER-
ITANCE.
Contrast with: SPECIALIZATION IN-
HERITANCE.
Commentary: Specification inheritance allows polymorphic substitution of instances of the derived
class for instances of any of its base
classes, even if the derived class is
not a specialization of its base
class(es). [Firesmith]

- **static inheritance** *n.* any inheritance that does not require dynamic
binding. [Firesmith]
Antonym: DYNAMIC INHERITANCE.

- **type inheritance** *n.* any inheritance among types in which a new
type (a.k.a. the *subtype*) is defined

in terms of one or more existing
types (a.k.a. its supertypes), whereby the subtype is a specialization
of its supertypes, conforms to their
interfaces, and inherits their features. [Firesmith, ODMG]
Synonym: SUBTYPING.
Contrast with: CLASS INHERITANCE.

• **inter-subsystem relationship** *n.* any
relationship that associates objects in
different subsystems. [Shlaer/Mellor]

• **is-part-of relationship** *n.* **1.** the inverse of the aggregation relationship
from an aggregate to its component
parts. [Firesmith] **2.** any relationship
set that forms an aggregate object out
of a group of component parts. [Em-
bley]
Synonym: AGGREGATION.
Contrast with: IS-MEMBER-OF RELA-
TIONSHIP SET.
See also: AGGREGATE, COMPONENT,
SUBPART CLASS, SUPERPART CLASS.
Commentary: The is-member-of relationship set forms a *set*, whereas the
is-part-of relationship set forms an
aggregate. [Embley]

• **link** *n.* **1.** during analysis and logical
design, any instance of an association
that captures a named semantic relationship between objects. [Firesmith,
OMG, Rumbaugh] **2.** during implementation design and coding, any
feature that contains one or more values, each of which reliably points to a
server object. [Firesmith]
Contrast with: ASSOCIATION.
Commentary: Links imply visibility
and enable message passing. Links are
the roads, whereas messages are the
traffic on those roads. [Firesmith]
Kinds:
- ATTACHED LINK

+ ATTACHED POINTER
+ ATTACHED LINK
- BASE LINK
- BIDIRECTIONAL LINK
- BINARY LINK
- CONSTANT LINK
- DANGLING LINK
  + DANGLING POINTER
  + DANGLING LINK
- DERIVED LINK
- POINTER
  + ATTACHED POINTER
  + DANGLING POINTER
  + VOID POINTER
- REFERENCE
  + ATTACHED REFERENCE
  + DANGLING REFERENCE
  + IMPORTED REFERENCE
  + INGENERATE REFERENCE
  + VOID REFERENCE
- STATE LINK
- STATE-DEPENDENT LINK
- STATE-INDEPENDENT LINK
- TERNARY LINK
- UNIDIRECTIONAL LINK
- VARIABLE LINK
- VOID LINK
  + VOID POINTER
  + VOID REFERENCE

- **attached link** *n.* any link to an existing object. [Firesmith]
Contrast with: DANGLING LINK, VOID LINK.
Commentary: Even though links are typically unidirectional, the link is said to be attached to the object, and the object is also said to be attached to the link. [Firesmith]
Kinds:
  + ATTACHED POINTER
  + ATTACHED REFERENCE

+ **attached pointer** *n.* any pointer that currently points to an existing object. [Firesmith]
Contrast with: DANGLING POINTER, VOID POINTER.
Commentary: The pointer is said to be attached to the object, and the object is also said to be attached to the pointer. [Firesmith]

+ **attached reference** *n.* any reference that currently refers to an existing object. [Eiffel, Firesmith, Meyer]
Contrast with: DANGLING REFERENCE, VOID REFERENCE.
Commentary: The reference is said to be attached to the object, and the object is also said to be attached to the reference. [Eiffel, Firesmith, Meyer]

- **base link** *n.* any link that cannot be derived from other links. [Firesmith]
Antonym: DERIVED LINK.

- **bidirectional link** *n.* any logical link that represents two unidirectional links that are coupled whereby each is the inverse of the another. [Firesmith]
Antonym: UNIDIRECTIONAL LINK.

- **binary link** *n.* any link between two objects. [Firesmith]
Contrast with: TERNARY LINK.

- **constant link** *n.* any link that cannot be created, destroyed, or changed in value at run-time. [Firesmith]
Antonym: VARIABLE LINK.
Commentary: A constant link always points to the same server. [Firesmith]

- **dangling link** *n.* any link to an object that does not exist. [Firesmith]
Contrast with: ATTACHED LINK, VOID LINK.
Commentary: The link may be to an object that does not yet exist or

R

to an object that no longer exists. Dangling links are common bugs in languages that support manual garbage collection. [Firesmith]

Kinds:
+ DANGLING POINTER
+ DANGLING REFERENCE

+ **dangling pointer** *n.* any pointer that points to an object that does not exist. [Firesmith]
Contrast with: ATTACHED POINTER, VOID POINTER.

+ **dangling reference** *n.* any reference to an object that does not exist. [Firesmith]
Contrast with: ATTACHED REFERENCE, VOID REFERENCE.

- **derived link** *n.* **1.** any indirect link that is the product of other links. [Firesmith] **2.** any instance of a derived association. [Firesmith]
Antonym: BASE LINK.
Contrast with: DERIVED ASSOCIATION.

- **pointer [to a given object]** *n.* **1.** any link, the value of which is the identifier of the given server object. [Firesmith] **2.** any attribute of one object that contains an explicit reference to another object. [Rumbaugh]
Contrast with: IDENTIFIER, LINK, REFERENCE.
Commentary: Unless changed, a pointer will identify the same object each time the pointer is used (subject to certain pragmatic limits of space and time). An object may be denoted by multiple, distinct pointers. [Firesmith]

Kinds:
+ ATTACHED POINTER
+ DANGLING POINTER

+ VOID POINTER

+ **attached pointer** *n.* any pointer that currently points to an object. [Firesmith]
Contrast with: DANGLING POINTER, VOID POINTER.
Commentary: The pointer is said to be attached to the object, and the object is also said to be attached to the pointer. [Firesmith]

+ **dangling pointer** *n.* any pointer that points to an object that does not exist. [Firesmith]
Contrast with: ATTACHED POINTER, VOID POINTER.

+ **void pointer** *n.* any pointer that does not point to an object. [Firesmith]
Synonym: NULL POINTER.
Contrast with: ATTACHED POINTER, DANGLING POINTER.

- **reference [to a given object]** *n.* **1.** any constant value that is used as an alias for the OID of the given server object. [Firesmith] **2.** any value that refers to an object. [Eiffel, Meyer]
Contrast with: IDENTIFIER, LINK, POINTER.
Commentary: References are used as links and as arguments in messages and operations. Unless changed, a reference will identify the same object each time the reference is used (subject to certain pragmatic limits of space and time). An object may be denoted by multiple, distinct references. [Firesmith]
Contrast with: VALUE.

Kinds:
+ ATTACHED REFERENCE
+ DANGLING REFERENCE

+ IMPORTED REFERENCE
+ INGENERATE REFERENCE
+ VOID REFERENCE

+ **attached reference** *n.* any reference that refers to an existing object. [Eiffel, Firesmith, Meyer]
Antonym: VOID REFERENCE.
Commentary: The reference is said to be attached to the object, and the object is also said to be attached to the reference. [Eiffel, Firesmith, Meyer]

+ **dangling reference** *n.* any reference that refers to an object that does not exist. [Firesmith]
Contrast with: ATTACHED REFERENCE, VOID REFERENCE.

+ **imported reference** *n.* any reference stored in an object's instance variable that was not generated by the object itself through invocation of a *create* method. [Atkinson]
Antonym: INGENERATE REFERENCE.

+ **ingenerate reference** *n.* any reference stored in an object's instance variable that was generated by the object itself through invocation of a *create* method. [Atkinson]
Antonym: IMPORTED REFERENCE.

+ **void reference** *n.* **1.** any reference that does not currently refer to an object. [Firesmith] **2.** any reference about which no further information is available. [Eiffel, Meyer]
Contrast with: ATTACHED REFERENCE, DANGLING REFERENCE.

- **state link** *n.* any link whose existence helps determine the state of its client object or class. [Firesmith]
Contrast with: STATE ATTRIBUTE, STATE COMPONENT.

- **state-dependent link** *n.* any link that has meaning only during specific states. [Firesmith]
Antonym: STATE-INDEPENDENT LINK.
Contrast with: STATE-DEPENDENT ATTRIBUTE.

- **state-independent link** *n.* any link that has meaning during all states. [Firesmith]
Antonym: STATE-DEPENDENT LINK.
Contrast with: STATE-INDEPENDENT ATTRIBUTE.

- **ternary link** *n.* any link among three objects. [Firesmith]

- **unidirectional link** *n.* any link directed from the client(s) to the server(s). [Firesmith]
Antonym: BIDIRECTIONAL LINK.
Commentary: Unidirectional links are typically implemented by one or more attributes acting as pointers or messages requesting services. [Firesmith]

- **variable link** *n.* any link that can change at run-time. [Firesmith]
Antonym: CONSTANT LINK.
Commentary: A link can change by pointing to another server. [Firesmith]

- **void link** *n.* any link to nothing. [Firesmith]
Contrast with: ATTACHED LINK, DANGLING LINK.
Kinds:
+ VOID POINTER
+ VOID REFERENCE

+ **void pointer** *n.* any pointer that does not currently point to an object. [Firesmith]
Synonym: NULL POINTER.
Contrast with: ATTACHED POINTER, DANGLING POINTER.

R

+ **void reference** *n.* **1.** any reference that does not refer to an object. [Firesmith] **2.** any reference about which no further information is available. [Eiffel, Meyer]
Antonym: ATTACHED REFERENCE.

• **specialization** *n.* **1.** the relationship from a generalization to its more specialized child class or subtype. [Firesmith] **2.** the relationship from a class or type to its instance. **3.** a subtype of a given supertype. [OADSIG] **4.** a more specialized derived class or type of a given base class or type. [Firesmith, Martin/Odell] **5.** an instance of a given class or type. **6.** a derived class. [Embley, OMG] **7.** an extension of the behavior of a type of object. [Lorenz] **8.** the relationship between a class and its parent(s). [Coleman] **9.** (a) the creation of a specialization. [Embley, Firesmith, Martin/Odell] (b) the creation of a subclass via extension, refinement, or restriction. [Henderson-Sellers, Rumbaugh] **10.** the relationship between a parent and a descendant that has been modified by refinement or deletion so that the descendant is no longer behaviorally compatible with its parent. [Jacobson]
Synonym: SUBTYPING.
Antonym: GENERALIZATION.
Contrast with: A-KIND-OF, CLASSIFICATION, GENERALIZATION, IS-A.
Commentary: The extent of a specialization is a subset of the intersection of the extents of its generalizations. Specialization can be implemented via restriction or extension. Definition 6 incorrectly assumes that all derived classes are specialization
See also: IMPLEMENTATION INHERITANCE.

Kinds:
- MULTIPLE SPECIALIZATION
- SINGLE SPECIALIZATION

- **multiple specialization** *n.* any specialization whereby a single class or type is simultaneously a child specialization of more than one generalization. [Coleman, Firesmith]
Antonym: SINGLE SPECIALIZATION.
Contrast with: MULTIPLE GENERALIZATION, SINGLE GENERALIZATION.

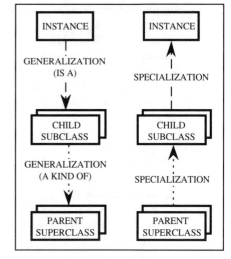

Specialization

- **single specialization** *n.* any specialization whereby a single class or type is a child specialization of only one generalization. [Firesmith]
Antonym: MULTIPLE SPECIALIZATION.
Contrast with: MULTIPLE GENERALIZATION, SINGLE GENERALIZATION.

• **ternary relationship** *n.* any relationship among three things. [Firesmith, Rumbaugh]
Kinds:

- TERNARY ASSOCIATION
- TERNARY LINK
- **ternary association** *n.* any association among three classes. [Firesmith, Rumbaugh]
- **ternary link** *n.* any link among three objects. [Firesmith]
- **unidirectional relationship** *n.* any relationship directed from the client(s) to the server(s). [Firesmith]
Antonym: BIDIRECTIONAL RELATIONSHIP.
Kinds:
   - UNIDIRECTIONAL ASSOCIATION
   - UNIDIRECTIONAL LINK
- **unidirectional association** *n.* any association directed from the client(s) to the server(s). [Firesmith]
Antonym: BIDIRECTIONAL ASSOCIATION.
Commentary: Unidirectional associations are typically implemented by one or more attributes acting as pointers or messages requesting services. [Firesmith]
- **unidirectional link** *n.* any link directed from the client(s) to the server(s). [Firesmith]
Antonym: BIDIRECTIONAL LINK.
Commentary: Unidirectional links are typically implemented by one or more attributes acting as pointers or messages requesting services. [Firesmith]

relationship cardinality constraint *n.* any cardinality constraint that restricts the cardinality of a relationship. [Embley, Firesmith, Martin/Odell]
Synonym: CO-OCCURRENCE CONSTRAINT.
Examples: Common unidirectional relationship cardinality constraints are *0 or 1, 1, 0, or more,* and *1 or more.* Common bidirectional relationship cardi-

nality constraints are *1 to 1, 1 to many,* and *many to many.* More specific constraints are also possible.
Commentary: Relationship cardinality constraints can be unidirectional (i.e., restricting the number on the end that is pointed to) or bidirectional (i.e., restricting the number at both ends of the relationship).

relationship description *n.* any description that must provide:
- the identifier of the relationship;
- a statement of the names of the relationship from the point of view of each participating object;
- the form of the relationship (its multiplicity and conditionality);
- a statement of the basis of abstraction;
- a statement of how the relationship has been formalized. [Shlaer/Mellor]

relationship-descriptions document *n.* any document that lists each relationship of the model together with its relationship description. [Shlaer/Mellor]

relationship object *n.* any object modeling a relationship in a relationship set. [Embley]
See also: RELATIONSHIP, RELATIONAL OBJECT CLASS.
Example: Marriage in the relationship set *'Female Person is married to Male Person'* is a relationship object.

relationship role *n.* any role of something in terms of a given relationship it has with something else. [Firesmith]
Contrast with: MODEL ROLE, PROTOCOL ROLE, VIEW ROLE.
See also: REFERENCE, POINTER, QUALIFIER.
Example: The *employee* class plays the *employed by* role in the *employment* association with the employer class. [Firesmith]

R

Commentary: Relationship roles are often implemented in terms of references or pointers. [Firesmith]

relationship set *n.* any set of relationships having a common meaning in which each relationship matches the same template and has as its name the text of the matched template. [Embley]
See also: MEMBERSHIP CONDITION, ROLE.
Commentary: The template for a relationship set has object classes designating slots for objects and phrases that express a logical connection among objects. [Embley]
Kinds:

- AGGREGATION
- COMPOSED-OF RELATIONSHIP
- HIGH-LEVEL RELATIONSHIP SET
- IS-A RELATIONSHIP SET
- IS-MEMBER-OF RELATIONSHIP SET
- IS-PART-OF RELATIONSHIP SET

- **aggregation [relationship set]** *n.* any relationship that declares an object, called a *superpart* or *aggregate*, to be composed of other objects, called *subparts* or *components*. [Embley]
  Synonym: AGGREGATION, IS-PART-OF RELATIONSHIP SET.
  Contrast with: IS-MEMBER-OF RELATIONSHIP SET.
  See also: RELATIONSHIP SET, SUBPART CLASS, SUPERPART CLASS.
- **composed-of relationship** *n.* the has part relationship between a composite object and its component parts. [Martin]
- **high-level relationship set** *n.* any relationship set that groups and subsumes object classes, relationship sets, constraints, and notes. [Embley]
  See also: RELATIONSHIP SET, HIGH-LEVEL.
- **is-a relationship set** *n.* any set of relationships between specializations

and generalizations. [Embley]
Synonym: GENERALIZATION–SPECIALIZATION.
See also: SPECIALIZATION.
Commentary: This definition confuses *is-a* (classification) with *a-kind-of* (specialization).

- **is-member-of relationship set** *n.* any relationship set that forms a set object out of a group of members objects. [Embley]
  Synonym: ASSOCIATION.
  Contrast with: IS-PART-OF RELATIONSHIP SET.
  See also: SET CLASS, MEMBER CLASS.
  Commentary: The is-member-of relationship set forms a *set*, whereas the is-part-of relationship set forms an *aggregate*. [Embley]
- **is-part-of relationship** *n.* **1.** the inverse of the aggregation relationship from an aggregate to its component parts. [Firesmith] **2.** any relationship set that forms an aggregate object out of a group of component parts. [Embley]
  Synonym: AGGREGATION.
  Contrast with: IS-MEMBER-OF RELATIONSHIP SET.
  See also: AGGREGATE, COMPONENT, SUBPART CLASS, SUPERPART CLASS.
  Commentary: The is-member-of relationship set forms a *set*, whereas the is-part-of relationship set forms an *aggregate*. [Embley]

relationship signature *n.* the declaration of any relationship, specifying the name of the relationship, the type of the other object or set of objects involved in the relationship, and the name of a traversal function used to refer to the related object or set of objects. [ODMG]

Contrast with: ATTRIBUTE SIGNATURE, LINK SIGNATURE, MESSAGE SIGNATURE, OPERATION SIGNATURE.

relationship type *n.* **1.** any type that specifies a mapping from one object type to another. [OADSIG] **2.** any association outside of an entity type on an entity-relationship diagram. [Martin/Odell]

Examples: Borrower defined on the type *Copy* with a range type of *Library User.*

Commentary: Characteristics of a relationship type include cardinality and optionally a range type, which identifies the object types that can participate in the relationship.

release *n.* any build that is delivered to the customer or user. [Firesmith]

Contrast with: BUILD.

Commentary: Releases are used to provide a significant increment of capabilities or for purposes of test and evaluation. A release is a major increment of development in an object-oriented development cycle. [Firesmith]

reliability *n.* the degree to which the software behaves correctly over time. [Firesmith]

renaming *n.* the mechanism enabling a class to be known to other classes within a system, under a name different than its actual class name. [Eiffel, Firesmith, Meyer]

repeated ancestor [of a given class] *n.* any ancestor class from which the given class is multiply derived via multiple inheritance. [Eiffel, Firesmith, Meyer]

Antonym: REPEATED DESCENDANT.

repeated child class [of a given class] *n.* any child class that multiply inherits from the given parent class. [Eiffel, Firesmith, Meyer]

Synonym: REPEATED HEIR CLASS.
Antonym: REPEATED PARENT CLASS.

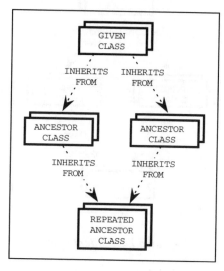

Repeated Ancestor Class

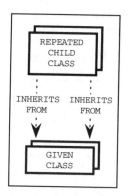

Repeated Child Class

repeated descendant [of a given class] *n.* any descendant that multiply inherits from the given ancestor class. [Eiffel, Firesmith, Meyer]

Antonym: REPEATED ANCESTOR.

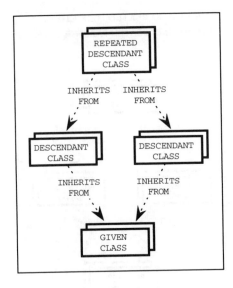

Repeated Descendant Class

repeated heir [of a given class] *n.* any heir
class that multiply inherits from a given
parent class. [Eiffel, Meyer]
Synonym: REPEATED CHILD CLASS.
Antonym: REPEATED PARENT CLASS.

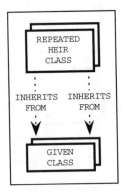

Repeated Heir Class

repeated inheritance *n.* any multiple inheritance in which a given child class

inherits the same feature, either directly or indirectly, from the same ancestor
class more than once. [Eiffel, Firesmith, Jacobson, Meyer]
See also: MULTIPLE INHERITANCE, RE-
PEATED ANCESTOR CLASS, REPLICATED
FEATURES, SHARED FEATURES.

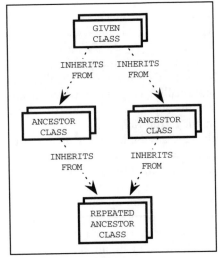

Repeated Inheritance

Commentary: In the majority of programming languages that support multiple inheritance, the user is forced to redefine the name of each replicated feature
so that it becomes unique. This is the
most acceptable solution, as only the user
has sufficient knowledge to solve this
conflict. If an operation is replicated, the
selection of which version does not matter unless the original operation has been
overridden. Then the problem is to know
which one to select. [Jacobson] C++
avoids the problem of repeated shared inheritance by only constructing virtual
base classes supplying a formula (i.e., leaf
first, left to right) for determining the

construction order of the repeated virtual base classes. [Firesmith]
Kinds:
- DIRECT REPEATED INHERITANCE
- INDIRECT REPEATED INHERITANCE
- REPLICATED REPEATED INHERITANCE
- SHARED REPEATED INHERITANCE
- VIRTUAL INHERITANCE.

- **direct repeated inheritance** *n.* any repeated inheritance in which any parent class of a given class is multiply inherited. [Eiffel, Firesmith, Meyer]
  See also: REPEATED PARENT CLASS.
  Antonym: INDIRECT REPEATED INHERITANCE.

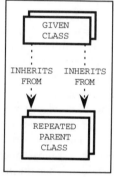

Direct Repeated Inheritance

- **indirect repeated inheritance** *n.* any repeated inheritance in which an ancestor class of a given class is the parent of two or more descendants of the given class. [Eiffel, Firesmith, Meyer]
  See also: REPEATED ANCESTOR CLASS.
  Antonym: DIRECT REPEATED INHERITANCE.

- **replicated repeated inheritance** *n.* any repeated inheritance from a common ancestor of a single feature under different names yielding two features in the current class. [Eiffel,

Firesmith, Meyer]
Antonym: SHARED REPEATED INHERITANCE

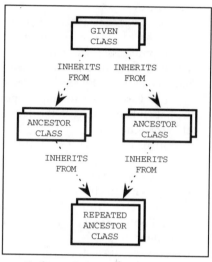

Indirect Repeated Inheritance

Commentary: The inherited feature is thus replicated and occurs multiple times in the current class or type. In the majority of programming languages that support multiple inheritance, the developer is required to redefine the name of each replicated feature so that it becomes unique. This is the most acceptable solution, as only the developer has sufficient knowledge to resolve this conflict. If an operation is repeated, the selection of which version does not matter unless the original operation has been overridden. Then the problem is to know which one to select. [Firesmith]

- **shared repeated inheritance** *n.* any repeated inheritance from a common ancestor of a single feature under the same final names yielding a single feature in the current class. [Eiffel, Firesmith, Meyer]

Synonym: VIRTUAL INHERITANCE.

Antonym: REPLICATED REPEATED INHERITANCE.

Commentary: The inherited feature is thus shared and occurs only once in the current class. [Firesmith]

- **virtual inheritance** *n.* any repeated inheritance whereby the features of repeated base classes (or supertypes) are only inherited once in the derived class (or subtype).

Synonym: SHARED REPEATED INHERITANCE.

See also: SHARED FEATURE.

repeated parent class [of a given class] *n.* any parent class from which a given class multiply inherits. [Eiffel, Firesmith, Meyer]

Contrast with: REPEATED CHILD CLASS.

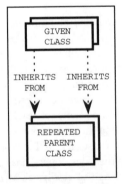

Repeated Parent Class

replicant object *n.* any object that is a complete replication of another object. [Coad]

Contrast with: PROXY OBJECT.

Commentary: In a distributed architecture, use replicant objects to provide access to remote objects and a local copy of an object. [Coad]

replicated feature *n.* any feature, multiple copies of which exist because of repeated replicated inheritance. [Firesmith]

See also: REPLICATED REPEATED INHERITANCE.

replicated repeated inheritance *n.* any repeated inheritance from a common ancestor of a single feature under different names yielding multiple versions of the feature in the current class. [Eiffel, Firesmith, Meyer]

Contrast with: SHARED REPEATED INHERITANCE.

Commentary: The inherited feature is thus replicated and occurs multiple times in the current class or type. In the majority of programming languages that support multiple inheritance, the developer is required to redefine the name of each replicated feature so that it becomes unique. This is the most acceptable solution, as only the developer has sufficient knowledge to resolve this conflict. If an operation is repeated, the selection of which version does not matter unless the original operation has been overridden. Then the problem is to know which one to select. [Firesmith]

repository *n.* any place to store information about objects, classes, clusters, features, relationships, etc. [Firesmith, OMG]

Commentary: Object-oriented CASE tools are best built around a central repository of analysis, design, coding, testing, and management information. [Firesmith]

Kinds:
- IMPLEMENTATION REPOSITORY
- INTERFACE REPOSITORY

- **implementation repository** *n.* any storage place for object implementa-

tion information; a service that allows the ORB to locate and activate implementations of objects. [OMG]
Antonym: INTERFACE REPOSITORY.

- **interface repository** *n.* **1.** any storage place for interface information. [OMG] **2.** any service that provides persistent objects that represent the IDL information in a form available at runtime. [OMG]
Antonym: IMPLEMENTATION REPOSITORY.

representation *n.* **1.** the physical implementation of all characteristics. **2.** any set of data structures. [ODMG]
Contrast with: IMPLEMENTATION.

request *n.* **1.** any message requesting a server to provide a service to the client. [Firesmith] **2.** (a) any message from one object to another, in which an operation of the first object requests the invocation of a specified operation of the other object. [Martin] (b) any invocation of an operation on an object or class, comprising an operation name, a list of zero or more actual parameters, and the results to be returned to the client. [OMG, OADSIG]
Synonym: MESSAGE, OPERATION INVOCATION.
Contrast with: OPERATION DISPATCHING.
See also: CLIENT, SERVER, SERVICE.
Commentary: Not every message is a request for a service. Messages can also be used to send information (e.g., data), notify the receiver of the occurrence of an event, or to synchronize a concurrent thread of the sender with a thread of the receiver. With most languages, a request is implemented in the form of a visible operation requested by the message. [Firesmith]
Kinds: 2

- ASYNCHRONOUS REQUEST
- DEFERRED SYNCHRONOUS REQUEST
- MEANINGFUL REQUEST
- ONE-WAY REQUEST
- STATE-MODIFYING REQUEST
- SYNCHRONOUS REQUEST

- **asynchronous request** *n.* any request involving two threads of control that do not synchronize so that neither the sender nor the receiver of the request is blocked, waiting for the other. [OMG]
Contrast with: ASYNCHRONOUS MESSAGE, SYNCHRONOUS REQUEST.

- **deferred synchronous request** *n.* any request in which the client does not wait for completion of the request, but does intend to accept results later. [OMG]
Contrast with: ASYNCHRONOUS REQUEST, ONE-WAY REQUEST, SYNCHRONOUS MESSAGE, SYNCHRONOUS REQUEST.
Commentary: Note that this is a poor choice of terms because a *deferred synchronous request* is not a kind of *synchronous request*.

- **meaningful request** *n.* any request in which the actual parameters satisfy the signature of the named operation. [OMG]

- **one-way request** *n.* any request in which the client does not wait for completion of the request, nor does it intend to accept results. [OMG]
Contrast with: ASYNCHRONOUS REQUEST, DEFERRED SYNCHRONOUS REQUEST, SYNCHRONOUS REQUEST.

- **state-modifying request** *n.* any request that by performing the service alters the results of future requests. [OMG]

- **synchronous request** *n.* any request

R

in which the client object pauses to wait for completion of the request. [OMG]

Contrast with: ASYNCHRONOUS REQUEST, DEFERRED SYNCHRONOUS REQUEST, ONE-WAY REQUEST, SYNCHRONOUS MESSAGE.

request context *n.* any context that provides additional, operation-specific information that may affect the performance of a request. [OMG]

request form *n.* any description or pattern that can be evaluated or performed multiple times to cause the issuing of requests. [OMG]

require *n.* any keyword used to introduce the precondition of the routine, which expresses the condition under which a call to the routine is correct. [Eiffel, Meyer]

Contrast with: ENSURE.

required operation *n.* any operation that is needed by the current object and is exported by the public interface of a server of the current object. [Berard]

Antonym: SUFFERED OPERATION.

resilient object *n.* any object in a distributed application whose state is simultaneously maintained on several different nodes on the network in order that processing can continue with the preserved state, should a node containing the object become unavailable for any reason. [Berard]

resolve [a given name] *v.* *-ed, -ing* to determine the object associated with the given name in a given context. [Firesmith, OMG]

responsibility *n.* **1.** any purpose, obligation, or required capability of an object or class, typically provided as a cohesive *set* of one or more services and implemented by one or more features.

[Booch, Firesmith, Henderson-Sellers, Jacobson] **2.** (a) any service provided by one object for another. [Wirfs-Brock] (b) any service that has been assigned to a class, due to client classes' needs. [Lorenz] **3.** anything that an object knows or does. [Coad, Wirfs-Brock]

Synonyms: **1** BEHAVIOR. **2** BEHAVIOR, SERVICE.

Commentary: A responsibility may either be directly implemented by the object or class or it may be delegated in whole or in part to one or more servers of the object or class. [Firesmith] An object usually has several responsibilities, one for each contract it shares. [Jacobson]

Kinds:
- PRIVATE RESPONSIBILITY
- PUBLIC RESPONSIBILITY
- STEREOTYPICAL RESPONSIBILITY

- **private responsibility** *n.* any responsibility that is hidden in the implementation from all children as well as all other clients. [Firesmith, Martin, Wirfs-Brock]

  Antonym: PUBLIC RESPONSIBILITY.

  Commentary: Private responsibilities are implemented by private members and are often derived from public responsibilities. [Firesmith] A private responsibility can neither be requested by clients nor be a part of a contract. [Wirfs-Brock]

- **public responsibility** *n.* any responsibility that is visible to clients and can be a part of a contract. [Firesmith, Martin]

  Antonym: PUBLIC RESPONSIBILITY.

  Commentary: Public responsibilities are implemented by public members. [Firesmith, Martin]

- **stereotypical responsibility** *n.* any

customary thing that a pattern player (an object within a pattern) knows and does. [Coad]

rescue block [of a routine] *n.* any sequence of exception handling instructions following the reserved word rescue that is executed if an exception is triggered during an execution of the enclosing routine. [Eiffel, Meyer]

restricted feature *n.* any feature that is exported to all children as well as to only certain other explicitly declared clients. [Firesmith]

Contrast with: PROTECTED FEATURE, PUBLIC FEATURE.

See also: FRIEND.

Example: All features in a role are restricted to only those clients who need to use the role. [Firesmith]

Commentary: Restricting a feature's visibility to only certain specified clients allows the designer to restrict visibility of the feature to only those clients who need to (or should) see and access the feature. Restriction increases information hiding at the expense of reuse because it explicitly couples the feature to those clients who see it. Whereas only exported features may be restricted features, C++ unfortunately allows both protected and private features to be made visible via friends. [Firesmith]

restriction *n.* any constraint that a derived class places on the value of an attribute contained in a base class. [Rumbaugh]

result *n.* the predefined entity that holds the results returned by functions. [Eiffel, Meyer]

results *n.* the information returned to the client by the given message or operation. [Firesmith, OMG]

Antonym: ARGUMENT, PARAMETER.

Examples: Objects, references, pointers, exceptions can all be returned as results.

Commentary: Results may include values as well as status information (e.g., exceptional conditions that were raised in attempting to perform the requested service). However, exceptions should be used instead of status flags if supported by the language. [Firesmith]

reusability *n.* the ease with which the software may be used for purposes other than originally intended. [Firesmith]

reuse *n.* the use of some preexisting product (e.g., existing requirements, design, code, test software, and documentation). [Firesmith]

v. **-ed, -ing 1.** to use some preexisting product (e.g., requirements, design, code, test software, and documentation). [Coad, Firesmith] **2.** to use existing object types during the design of a system and object classes within the implementation of a system. [OADSIG]

reuse library *n.* **1.** any repository of quality reusable classes. [Firesmith] **2.** any repository of solid reusable components, maintained by its class owners. [Lorenz]

Commentary: Classes in a reuse library are typically maintained by their owners. Reuse across applications should normally be restricted to the reuse library. The reuse library should be considered one of the organization's most important software assets. [Firesmith, Lorenz]

robustness *n.* the degree to which the software continues to function correctly under abnormal circumstances. [Firesmith]

R

role *n.* any part played by something (e.g., a person, piece of equipment, or organization). [Firesmith, Shlaer/Mellor]
Contrast with: ROLE OBJECT, DYNAMIC CLASSIFICATION.
Commentary: A role captures the purpose of something, the position it holds, or its capacity, job, or viewpoint. Roles may be implemented in the following four distinct ways. [Firesmith]
Kinds:
- MODEL ROLE
- PROTOCOL ROLE
- RELATIONSHIP ROLE
- VIEW ROLE

- **model role** *n.* any model that is an abstraction of a role. [Firesmith, Shlaer/Mellor]
Contrast with: PROTOCOL ROLE, RELATIONSHIP ROLE, VIEW ROLE.

- **protocol role** *n.* any inheritable subset of a given protocol that can be accessed as a group and used to restrict client access to only that part of the protocol that abstracts a specific role that the model may play. [Booch, Firesmith]
Contrast with: MODEL ROLE, RELATIONSHIP ROLE, VIEW ROLE.

- **relationship role** *n.* **1.** any role of something in terms of a given relationship it has with something else. [Booch, Firesmith, Jacobson] **2.** any name that qualifies a class participating in a relationship. [Coleman] **3.** one end of an association. [Rumbaugh] **4.** any specialization of the class in the connection whose objects fully participate in the relationship set in the connection. [Embley]
Contrast with: MODEL ROLE, PROTOCOL ROLE, VIEW ROLE.
See also: QUALIFIER, REFERENCE,

POINTER.
Example: The *employee* class plays the *employed-by* role in the *employment* association with the employer class. [Firesmith]
Commentary: Relationship roles are often implemented in terms of references or pointers. [Firesmith]
- **view role** *n.* any view that is used to provide access to only those resources of its model object that abstracts a specific role that the model may play. [Firesmith]
Contrast with: MODEL ROLE, PROTOCOL ROLE, RELATIONSHIP ROLE.

role class *n.* any class of role model objects or view role objects. [Firesmith]
Contrast with: ROLE, ROLE OBJECT.

role name *n.* any name that uniquely identifies a role. [Firesmith, Rumbaugh]

role object *n.* **1.** (a) any model object that is an abstraction of a role. [Firesmith] (b) any abstraction of the purpose or assignment of a person, piece of equipment, or organization. [Shlaer/Mellor] **2.** any view object that is used to provide access to only those resources of its model object that abstracts a specific role that the model may play. [Firesmith]
Contrast with: ROLE, ROLE CLASS.
See also: ROLE, DYNAMIC CLASSIFICATION.

root class *n.* **1.** any class that does not inherit from any other class. [Firesmith, Smalltalk] **2.** the master class in a system of classes that depends on (i.e., is a direct or indirect client or heir of) all of the other classes in the system. [Eiffel, Meyer]
Synonym: **1** BASE CLASS, ULTIMATE ANCESTOR. **2** MASTER CLASS.
See also: **2** SYSTEM.
Contrast with: BASE CLASS, BRANCH

CLASS, LEAF CLASS.
Rationale: This class is at the root of the inheritance tree. The term *base class* is used by C++ with a different meaning.
Commentary: Definition 1 is based on inheritance, whereas definition 2 is based on inheritance and client/server dependencies.

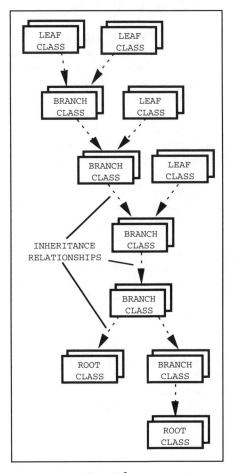

Root Classes

root object *n.* **1.** any named persistent object that can be referenced by a pro-

gram once it has opened the object database. [ODMG] **2.** the instance of the root class whose creation is the first act of system execution. [Eiffel, Firesmith, Meyer]
Contrast with: ROOT CLASS.
root type *n.* any type that does not inherit from any other type. [Firesmith]
Contrast with: BRANCH TYPE, LEAF TYPE.
Rationale: This type is at the root of the inheritance tree. The term *base type* is used by C++ with a different meaning. [Firesmith]
root type [of a derivation class] *n.* the type from which all other types in the derivation class (except associated universal types or class-wide types) are directly or indirectly derived. [Ada95]
Contrast with: ULTIMATE ANCESTOR.
See also: CLASS, DERIVATION CLASS.
round-trip gestalt design *n.* the Booch development cycle, consisting of a style of design that emphasizes the incremental and iterative development of a system, through the refinement of different yet consistent logical and physical views of the system as a whole. [Booch]
routine *n.* any computation applicable to instances of the class. A routine is either a procedure or a function. [Eiffel, Meyer]
Contrast with: FUNCTION, METHOD, OPERATION, PROCEDURE.
Kinds:
  • CURRENT ROUTINE
  • DEFERRED ROUTINE
  • EFFECTIVE ROUTINE
  • EXTERNAL ROUTINE
  • FOREIGN ROUTINE
  • INTERNAL ROUTINE
• **current routine** *n.* the routine to which the latest noncompleted rou-

R

tine call applies at some time during execution. [Eiffel, Meyer]

Contrast with: CURRENT OBJECT.

- **deferred routine** *n.* any routine that is declared as deferred, meaning that the class introducing it only gives its specification, leaving it for descendants to provide implementations. [Eiffel, Meyer]

Synonym: DEFERRED OPERATION.
Antonym: EFFECTIVE ROUTINE.

- **effective routine** *n.* any routine that is not deferred. [Eiffel, Meyer]

Antonym: DEFERRED ROUTINE.

- **external routine** *n.* any foreign routine as viewed from the text of the current language. [Eiffel, Meyer]

Antonym: INTERNAL ROUTINE.
Contrast with: EXTERNAL OPERATION.
See also: FOREIGN ROUTINE.

- **foreign routine** *n.* any routine imported from another language. [Eiffel, Meyer]

Contrast with: EXTERNAL ROUTINE.

- **internal routine** *n.* any routine written in the current language and therefore accessible to language processing tools. [Eiffel, Meyer]

Synonym: INTERNAL OPERATION.
Antonym: EXTERNAL ROUTINE.

rule *n.* **1.** any policy or condition that must be satisfied [OADSIG] **2.** any assertion or constraint. [OADSIG] **3.** any encapsulated business knowledge. [Martin]

Contrast with: ASSERTION, CONSTRAINT.
Example: For object type *Account*, account numbers must be unique. [OADSIG]

Commentary: A rule can govern either the structure or behavior of objects, classes, or types. Rules have been separated from structure and behavior be-

cause many rules address both structure and behavior. [OADSIG]

Kinds:
- BUSINESS RULE
- INTEGRITY RULE
- OPERATION POSTCONDITION RULE
- OPERATION PRECONDITION RULE

- **business rule** *n.* any rule that governs the way that the business operates. [OADSIG]

Examples: Legal requirements such as every enterprise must have a managing director and accountants, architectural principles that govern the information system, and motivational constraints such as budgets and organizational limits can all be modeled as business rules. [OADSIG]

- **integrity rule** *n.* any rule that states that something must be true. [Martin]

Synonym: ASSERTION.
Examples: A value must be within a certain range, an object relationship must have a stated cardinality, and a precondition must hold before an operation is executed are all examples of integrity rules. [Martin]

- **operation postcondition rule** *n.* any constraint that must be satisfied before an operation will perform correctly. [Martin]

Synonym: POSTCONDITION.
Antonyms: OPERATION PRECONDITION RULE, PRECONDITION.
See also: CONTRACT.

- **operation precondition rule** *n.* any constraint that guarantees the results when the operation is executed. [Martin]

Synonym: PRECONDITION.
Antonyms: OPERATION POSTCONDITION RULE, POSTCONDITION.
See also: CONTRACT.

run-time binding *n.* **1.** any binding that takes place at run-time due to compile-time ambiguities necessitated by inheritance and polymorphism. [Booch, Coad, Firesmith, Jacobson, Martin/Odell] **2.** any binding that takes place after the message is sent. [Jacobson, OMG]

Synonyms: DEFERRED, DYNAMIC BINDING, LATE BINDING, VIRTUAL BINDING.

Antonyms: COMPILE-TIME BINDING, EARLY BINDING, STATIC BINDING.

Commentary: Run-time binding allows the system to dynamically decide what method to use, based on the class of the current object. Run-time binding of methods is typically implemented via a method binding table. The term *dynamic binding* is preferred. [Firesmith]

R

S

safe method *n.* any method that has no parameters of a class type or an access type. [Atkinson]

Antonym: UNSAFE METHOD.

Commentary: All of the parameters of the method are thus of a static type. [Atkinson]

safety *n.* the degree to which the software functions without unintentional harm to life or property, regardless of how the software is used. [Firesmith]

satisfy [a type] *n.* any value satisfies a type if the predicate is true for that value. [OMG]

Contrast with: MEMBER [OF A TYPE], TYPE.

scenario *n.* **1.** (a) any single, specific, contiguous set of object interactions (e.g., instantiations, message sends, operation executions, exception raising and handling, and/or object destructions) that captures a single functional abstraction that cannot be encapsulated as an operation within a single object or class. [Firesmith] (b) any instances of a scenario class. [Firesmith] **2.** any outline of events that elicits some system behavior. [Booch] **3.** (a) any sequence of events that occurs during one particular execution of an application. [Cole-man, Henderson-Sellers, Rumbaugh] (b) any specific time-ordered sequence of object interactions used to fulfill a specific need. [Coad]

Contrast with: MECHANISM, PATH, USE CASE.

Commentary: A class of scenarios often provides a single required capability and are used for analysis, design, testing, and integration purposes. Scenarios may involve more than one thread of control. Scenarios are often, but need not be, initiated by a client terminator of the application. A typical scenario involves many objects and classes, and an object or class is typically involved in many scenarios. [Firesmith]

Kinds:
- AGGREGATE SCENARIO
- ATOMIC SCENARIO
- PRIMARY SCENARIO
- SECONDARY SCENARIO
- SUBSCENARIO
- TEST CASE
- USAGE SCENARIO

- **aggregate scenario** *n.* any scenario that contains one or more subscenarios as component parts. [Firesmith]

  Antonym: ATOMIC SCENARIO.

- **atomic scenario** *n.* any scenario that does not contain one or more subscenarios as component parts. [Firesmith]
  Antonym: AGGREGATE SCENARIO.
- **primary scenario** *n.* any scenario that represents some fundamental system function. [Booch, Firesmith]
  Antonym: SECONDARY SCENARIO.
- **secondary scenario** *n.* any scenario that represents some variation on the theme of a primary scenario. [Booch, Firesmith]
  Antonym: PRIMARY SCENARIO.
  Commentary: Secondary scenarios often reflect exceptional situations. [Firesmith]
- **subscenario** *n.* any scenario that is contained within an aggregate scenario as a component part. [Firesmith]
  See also: AGGREGATE SCENARIO.
- **test case** *n.* **1.** any sequence of one or more test messages as well as the expected responses. **2.** any single scenario that is executed to find errors as well as the expected responses. [Firesmith]
  Contrast with: TEST MESSAGE, TEST SUITE.
  Commentary: Test cases find errors by allowing testers to compare the actual behavior against the expected behavior. [Firesmith]
- **usage scenario** *n.* any scenario that captures how an application is used by its client terminators. [Firesmith]
  Synonym: ATOMIC SYSTEM FUNCTION.
  Contrast with: USE CASE.

scenario class *n.* any definition of a set of related scenarios. [Firesmith]
Contrast with: USE CASE.
Commentary: Unlike classes of objects, scenario classes are not supported by object-oriented programming languages and do not (yet) provide an automatic instantiation mechanism. [Firesmith]
Kinds:
- USE CASE
  - ABSTRACT USE CASE
  - CONCRETE USE CASE
- **use case** *n.* **1.** any scenario class of top-level usage scenarios that captures how a blackbox application is used by its client terminators. [Firesmith, Henderson-Sellers, Jacobson] **2.** (a) any behaviorally related sequence of transactions performed by a single actor in a dialogue with a system, the purpose of which is to provide some measurable value to the actor. [Jacobson] (b) any class of top-level usage scenarios that captures how a system or application is used by its client terminators (actors). c) any description of the system actions on receipt of one type of user request. [Lorenz] **3.** (formerly) any sequence of events that occur during one particular execution of an application. [Henderson-Sellers]
  Synonym: SCENARIO SCRIPT.
  Contrast with: ATOMIC SYSTEM FUNCTION, USAGE SCENARIO.
  Rationale: The term *use case* was introduced and initially popularized by Ivar Jacobson. [Firesmith]
  Commentary: Use cases are used to document user requirements in terms of user dialogs with a system that provide some measurable value to the user. [Firesmith]
  Kinds:
  - ABSTRACT USE CASE
  - CONCRETE USE CASE

  - **abstract use case** *n.* any use case that will not be instantiated on its own, but is meaningful only to describe parts shared among other

S

use cases. [Jacobson]
Antonym: CONCRETE USE CASE.
- **concrete use case** *n.* any use case that is meaningful and will be instantiated on its own. [Jacobson]
Antonym: ABSTRACT USE CASE.

scenario invariant *n.* any invariant that must evaluate to true after execution of each associated operation and exception handler if it holds prior to the start of the scenario. [Firesmith]
Contrast with: CLASS INVARIANT, EXTENT INVARIANT, INSTANCE INVARIANT, MESSAGE INVARIANT.

scenario life-cycle diagram (SLD) *n.* any diagram documenting all top-level scenarios and the transitions between them. SLDs document all valid orders of these scenarios during the life cycle of a system or cluster. [Firesmith]

scenario script *n.* any sequence of steps the user and system take to accomplish some task. [Lorenz]
Synonym: USE CASE.
Commentary: There is a script for each of the major end-user functions provided by the system.

scenario view *n.* any view presenting a specific time-ordered sequence of object interactions. [Coad]
See also: ATTRIBUTE DESCRIPTION, OBJECT MODEL, SCENARIO, SERVICE DESCRIPTION.

schema *n.* **schemata** *pl.* **1.** the set of all types whose instances may be stored in a single objectbase. [Firesmith, ODMG] **2.** any collection of object types and other schemas that constitute some form of operational system. Every schema identifies a list of object types and some schemas impose structure on this list. [OADSIG] **3.** any way of describing an operation in terms of what

must be true before it is executed (the precondition) and what is true afterward (the postcondition). [Coleman]
Example: A list of bank teller object types is a schema. [OADSIG]
Kinds:
- ACTIVITY SCHEMA
- SUBSCHEMA

- **activity schema** *n.* any diagram showing a sequence of operations [Martin/Odell]
- **subschema** *n.* any subset of the types in a objectbase schema. [Firesmith]
Contrast with: SCHEMA.

scope of definition [of an operation] *n.* the set of classes in which the operation is defined. [Firesmith]

scope of polymorphism [of an object] *n.* the set of classes or types to which the object may belong. [Firesmith]

seamless transition [between activities] *n.* any transition between development activities whereby the same concepts, terminology, and modeling techniques are used during both the activity before the transition and after the transition. [Firesmith, Henderson-Sellers]
Commentary: Object technology provides a seamless transition between development activities, unlike structured methods, which used different concepts, terms, and diagrams during requirements analysis and design. [Firesmith]

seamless transition between models *n.* any transition between models whereby it is easy to tell in a foreseeable way, how to get from concepts in the first model to concepts in the second model. [Firesmith, Jacobson]
Commentary: It is absolutely crucial for an industrial development process for the transition between development steps to be seamless because the

development process must be repeatable. [Jacobson]

secondary actor *n.* any actor that exists only so that the primary actors can use the system. [Jacobson]
Antonym: PRIMARY ACTOR.

secondary path [through a given scenario class] *n.* any of the less common or important paths through the given scenario class. [Firesmith]
Antonym: PRIMARY PATH.
See also: SCENARIO.
Commentary: The description of a scenario class is normally divided into *primary paths* and *secondary paths,* whereby the secondary paths are variants of the primary paths that often include exception handling. Secondary paths are usually developed after the primary paths. [Firesmith]

secondary scenario *n.* any scenario that represents some variation on the theme of a primary scenario. [Booch, Firesmith]
Antonym: PRIMARY SCENARIO.
Commentary: Secondary scenarios often reflect exceptional situations. [Firesmith]

secret feature *n.* any feature whose feature clause has an empty Clients list, that is to say, begins with feature [ ] and is therefore not available to any classes. [Eiffel, Meyer]
Synonym: PRIVATE FEATURE.
Contrast with: AVAILABLE FEATURE.

secured property *n.* any property, the value of which cannot be corrupted in a concurrent environment (e.g., due to the interleaving of accessor operations). [Firesmith]
Rationale: The term *secured* is used instead of the Ada95 term *protected* in order to avoid confusion with the more popular meanings of the term *protected*

in the C++ community. [Firesmith]
Commentary: Mutually exclusive access to a secured property is typically implemented efficiently via language constructs, monitors, or semaphores. [Firesmith]

security *n.* the degree to which something (e.g., the system, its software) protects itself from unauthorized access or modification. [Firesmith]
Commentary: The encapsulation of properties behind a protocol of messages and operations provides better security than structured methods which produced large amounts of common global data. [Firesmith]

security domain *n.* any identifiable subset of computational resources used to define security policy. [OMG]

seed [of a given feature] *n.* the original form of the given feature in the origin class of the feature (i.e., the most remote ancestor from which the feature *comes*). [Eiffel, Firesmith, Meyer]
See also: INHERITED FEATURE, ORIGIN.

selective inheritance *n.* any inheritance whereby the parent defines *all* of the features needed by *all* of its children and these individual children *delete* the unnecessary features of the parent rather than add new features or override inherited features. [Firesmith]
Synonym: INVERTED INHERITANCE.
Commentary: Inverted inheritance is generally rejected in the object community. It produces inheritance structures that are neither extensible nor maintainable. The parent does not capture a meaningful abstraction and is not restricted to the definition of common features. Contrary to expectations, the children are neither more abstract nor more detailed. Instead of being exten-

sions that can do more than their parents, they can only do less. Inverted inheritance is therefore a source of confusion and not recommended. [Firesmith]

selectively available feature *n.* any feature that is only available to specific classes and their descendants. [Eiffel, Meyer]
Contrast with: GENERALLY AVAILABLE.

selective visibility *n.* the ability to toggle between a fully visualized design and one in which no interface details are shown. [Henderson-Sellers]
Commentary: Selective visibility permits the complexity of diagrams to be managed visually. [Henderson-Sellers]

[message] selector *n.* the name of the type of operation a message requests of its receiver. [Smalltalk]
See also: INTERFACE, MESSAGE, OPERATION.
Commentary: The selector of a message determines which of the receiver's operations will be invoked. A class has one method for each selector in its interface. [Smalltalk]

selector [operation] *n.* **1.** any operation that accesses the state of an object but does not alter the state. [Booch] **2.** any fundamental field operation used to query the values of an object without changing its state. [Martin/Odell]
Synonym: PRESERVER [OPERATION].
Antonym: MODIFIER [OPERATION].

self *n.* the Smalltalk pseudo-variable referring to the receiver of a message (i.e., the target object of a method). [Firesmith, Rumbaugh, Smalltalk]
Synonyms: CURRENT, THIS.
Contrast with: SUPER.
Commentary: When a method contains a message whose receiver is self, the search for the method for that message begins in the instance's class, regardless

of which class contains the method containing self. Responses to messages to self are found by starting the method search in the class of the receiver, continuing up the superclass chain, and terminating at class Object. [Firesmith, Smalltalk]

self-reference *n.* the ability of any method to determine the object(s) identified in the request for the service being performed by the method. [OMG]
Contrast with: DELEGATION.
Commentary: Self-reference in Smalltalk is indicated by the keyword self. [OMG]

semantic gap *n.* the difference between an object-oriented model and what it represents. [Jacobson]
See also: IDEAL-OBJECT MODEL, REAL-OBJECT MODEL.

semantic model *n.* any object-oriented static model that documents the context of a system (or cluster) and the architecture of its component subsystems (or subclusters) in terms of the existence, abstraction, and visibility of their component objects and classes, the terminators with which these individual objects and classes directly (and indirectly) interface, and the important semantic relationships (e.g., links and associations, inheritance, classification, aggregation) between them. The semantic model consists of one or more context diagrams, general semantic nets, inheritance diagrams, aggregation diagrams, and OOSDL specifications. [Firesmith]
Synonym: OBJECT-RELATIONSHIP MODEL.
Contrast with: CONFIGURATION MODEL, INTERACTION MODEL, LANGUAGE MODEL, PRESENTATION MODEL, STATE MODEL.

semantic net (SN) *n.* any diagram using

a graph structure to represent knowledge in which the nodes represent things and the arcs represent relationships between things. [Firesmith]
Kinds:
- AGGREGATION DIAGRAM
- CONTEXT DIAGRAM
- GENERAL SEMANTIC NET
- INHERITANCE DIAGRAM
- MODEL VIEW CONTROLLER DIAGRAM

- **aggregation diagram (AGD)** *n.* any specialized semantic net that documents all or part of an aggregation hierarchy. [Firesmith]
  Contrast with: INHERITANCE DIAGRAM.

- **context diagram (CD)** *n.* any specialized semantic net used to document a system or assembly and the semantic relationships between it and its terminators. [Firesmith]

- **general semantic net (GSN)** *n.* any general semantic net that documents a collection of related objects, classes, subsystems or clusters, terminators, and the important semantic relationships (primarily links or associations) between them. [Firesmith]

- **inheritance diagram (INHD)** *n.* any specialized semantic net that documents all or part of an inheritance structure showing the relevant classes, the inheritance relationships between the derived classes and their base classes, and where useful and practical, the generic parameters of generic classes, the interfaces and implementations of classes, their instances, and the classification relationships between instances and their classes. [Firesmith]
  Contrast with: AGGREGATION DIAGRAM.

- **model-view-controller diagram (MVCD)** *n.* any semantic net documenting the dependency relationships between models, views, and controllers. [Firesmith]

send a message *v. sent, -ing* to pass a message from the sender (i.e., client) to the receiver (i.e., server). [Firesmith, Smalltalk]
Synonyms: MAKE A REQUEST, PASS A MESSAGE.

sequential *adj.* containing no separate thread(s) of control. [Firesmith]
Synonym: PASSIVE.
Antonym: CONCURRENT.

sequential class *n.* **1.** (a) any class whose instances are sequential objects. [Firesmith] (b) any class that does not contain any concurrent class feature (e.g., operation or object). [Firesmith] **2.** any class whose semantics are guaranteed only in the presence of a single thread of control. [Booch]
Antonym: CONCURRENT CLASS.

sequential message *n.* any message involving only one thread of control that is temporarily passed from the client to the server, thereby blocking the client until the server's operation(s) are completed. [Firesmith]
Contrast with: ASYNCHRONOUS MESSAGE, SYNCHRONOUS MESSAGE.

sequential object *n.* **1.** any object that does not contain any threads of control (e.g., concurrent operations or nested concurrent objects). [Firesmith] **2.** any passive object whose semantics are guaranteed only in the presence of a single thread of control. [Booch]
Synonym: **2** PASSIVE OBJECT.
Antonym: CONCURRENT OBJECT.
Commentary: All sequential objects are passive, but some concurrent objects are also passive.

sequential operation *n.* any operation

that does not contain one or more separate threads of control. [Firesmith]
Antonym: CONCURRENT OPERATION.

servant *n.* any server that is not a client. [Firesmith]
Contrast with: AGENT, MASTER.
Commentary: At either the system-level or the software-level, servants are controlled by masters or agents, but do not control others. [Firesmith]

server *n.* **1.** relative to a given unidirectional relationship, the thing on which something else (a.k.a. the *client*) depends. [Booch, Firesmith] **2.** any process implementing one or more operations on one or more objects. [OMG]

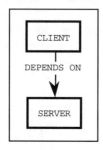

CLIENT

DEPENDS ON

SERVER

Server

Synonym: RECEIVER, SERVANT, SUPPLIER.
Antonym: CLIENT.
Contrast with: SERVANT.
Examples: Anything that provides services in response to requests is a server. [Booch, Lorenz, Wirfs-Brock] Any domain on which another domain depends via a bridge is a server. [Shlaer/Mellor]
Commentary: Clients can be many things including objects, classes, clusters, subsystems, etc. There can be many unidirectional dependency relationships from clients to servers including aggregation, association, collaboration, and inheritance.

• **servant** *n.* any server that is not a client. [Firesmith]
Contrast with: AGENT, MASTER.
Commentary: At either the system-level or the software-level, servants are controlled by masters or agents, but do not control others. [Firesmith]

server interface *n.* that part of an interface that declares all features that are required of servers. [Firesmith]
Antonym: INBOUND INTERFACE.
Contrast with: OUTBOUND PROTOCOL.
Example: The server interface of an object consists of the messages it sends to its servers, all exceptions that servers may raise to it, and any visible server properties on which it depends. [Firesmith]
Commentary: Most programming languages do not explicitly support the server part of the interface. No contract with servers will be impacted by a change to the implementation if the server interface does not change. [Firesmith]

server [object] *n.* any object providing response to a request for a service.
Antonym: CLIENT OBJECT.
Commentary: A given object may be a client for some requests and a server for other requests. [OMG]

server protocol *n.* the set of all interactions with servers, consisting of the union of the outbound message protocol and the inbound exception protocol. [Firesmith]
Antonym: CLIENT PROTOCOL.
Contrast with: SERVER INTERFACE.

service *n.* **1.** (a) any activity or behavior of a server that is individually requested by client via a message. [Firesmith, Henderson-Sellers] (b) any computation that may be performed in response to a request. [OMG] **2.** any specific behavior for which an object is responsible. [Coad] **3.** the behavior provided by a given part of a system. [Booch] **4** any capability provided by an object request broker (ORB). [OMG]

Synonyms: **2** OPERATION, RESPONSIBILITY.

Commentary: The server typically implements the service via one or more of its operations, which in turn may further subcontract (i.e., delegate) part or all of the service to the server's servers. [Firesmith]

Kinds: **2**
- BASIC SERVICE
- STATE-DEPENDENT SERVICE

Kinds: **4**
- CONCURRENCY CONTROL SERVICE
- EVENT SERVICE

- **basic service** *n.* any services that each object in an object model provides. [Coad]

  See also: SERVICE.

  Examples: The basic services are: create an object, get and set attribute values, add and remove object connections, and delete.

  Commentary: Basic services are not shown in an object model. However, they are included in a scenario view, as needed along the way.

- **concurrency control service** *n.* any service, the purpose of which is to mediate concurrent access to objects so that the consistency of the objects is not compromised when concurrently accessed. [OMG]

- **event service** *n.* any service, the purpose of which is to decouple the communication among objects. [OMG]

  Commentary: The event service defines the supplier role and the consumer role for objects. [OMG]

- **state-dependent service** *n.* any ser-

vice that is allowed only within specific states. [Coad]

Contrast with: STATE-DEPENDENT ATTRIBUTE.

service description *n.* any filled-in template of information about a service, including: inputs, outputs, description (including pseudocode or actual code, detailing the algorithm to be applied), traceability codes, and visibility. For state-dependent services, additional information may be needed, including: precondition, postcondition, trigger, terminate, exception action and performance constraints. [Coad]

See also: ATTRIBUTE DESCRIPTION, OBJECT MODEL, SCENARIO VIEW, SERVICE, TERMINATE CONDITION, TRIGGER CONDITION.

Commentary: Attribute and service descriptions express supporting detail for object models and scenario views. [Coad]

service domain *n.* the domain that provides generic mechanisms and utility functions as required to support the application domain. [Shlaer/Mellor]

Contrast with: APPLICATION DOMAIN, ARCHITECTURAL DOMAIN, IMPLEMENTATION DOMAIN.

service package *n.* the lowest-level subsystem. It is viewed as an atomic unit of change that packages services for the customer. [Jacobson]

See also: PUBLIC BLOCK, SUBSYSTEM.

Commentary: For example, service packages are atomic subsystems used in discussions with customer and product planning. [Jacobson]

service-structure model *n.* any model that documents the procedural design of a single service. [Henderson-Sellers]

set *n.* the collection of all objects to which the *object type*, or *concept*, applies. [Martin/Odell]

S

Synonym: EXTENSION.
Contrast with: CLASS.
See also: DOMAIN, RANGE.
Kinds:

- RELATIONSHIP SET
  - AGGREGATION [RELATIONSHIP SET]
  - COMPOSED-OF RELATIONSHIP
  - HIGH-LEVEL RELATIONSHIP SET
  - IS-A RELATIONSHIP SET
  - IS-MEMBER-OF RELATIONSHIP SET
  - IS-PART-OF RELATIONSHIP SET

- **relationship set** *n.* any set of relationships having a common meaning in which each relationship matches the same template and has as its name the text of the matched template. [Embley]
See also: MEMBERSHIP CONDITION, ROLE.
Commentary: The template for a relationship set has object classes designating slots for objects and phrases that express a logical connection among objects. [Embley]
Kinds:

  - AGGREGATION [RELATIONSHIP SET]
  - COMPOSED-OF RELATIONSHIP
  - HIGH-LEVEL RELATIONSHIP SET
  - IS-A RELATIONSHIP SET
  - IS-MEMBER-OF RELATIONSHIP SET
  - IS-PART-OF RELATIONSHIP SET

- **aggregation [relationship set]** *n.* any relationship set that declares an object, called a *superpart* or *aggregate*, to be composed of other objects, called *subparts* or *components*. [Embley]
Synonym: AGGREGATION, IS PART OF RELATIONSHIP SET.
Contrast with: IS-MEMBER-OF RELATIONSHIP SET.
See also: RELATIONSHIP SET, SUBPART CLASS, SUPERPART CLASS.
- **composed-of relationship** *n.* the *has part* relationship set between a

composite object and its component parts. [Martin]
- **high-level relationship set** *n.* any relationship set that groups and subsumes object classes, relationship sets, constraints, and notes. [Embley]
- **is-a relationship set** *n.* any set of relationships between specializations and generalizations. [Embley]
Synonym: GENERALIZATION–SPECIALIZATION.
See also: SPECIALIZATION.
Commentary: This definition confuses *is-a* (classification) with *a-kind-of* (specialization). [Firesmith]
- **is-member-of relationship set** *n.* any relationship set that forms a set object out of a group of members objects. [Embley]
Synonym: ASSOCIATION.
Contrast with: IS-PART-OF RELATIONSHIP SET.
See also: SET CLASS, MEMBER CLASS.
Commentary: The *is-member-of* relationship set forms a *set*, whereas the *is-part-of* relationship set forms an *aggregate*. [Embley]
- **is-part-of relationship** *n.* **1.** the inverse of the aggregation relationship from an aggregate to its component parts. [Firesmith] **2.** any relationship set that forms an aggregate object out of a group of component parts. [Embley]
Synonym: AGGREGATION.
Contrast with: IS-MEMBER-OF RELATIONSHIP SET.
See also: AGGREGATE, COMPONENT, SUBPART CLASS, SUPERPART CLASS.
Commentary: The *is-member-of* relationship set forms a *set*, whereas the *is-part-of* relationship set

forms an *aggregate*. [Embley]

set class *n.* any object class whose instances are sets. [Embley]

Synonym: ASSOCIATION.

Antonyms: MEMBER CLASS, UNIVERSE.

See also: IS-MEMBER-OF RELATIONSHIP SET.

set constraint *n.* the structural constraint that prohibits duplicate component parts in an aggregate. [Firesmith]

shadow *v. -ed, -ing* to override features that would otherwise be inherited from less specific classes. [CLOS]

Synonym: OVERRIDE.

shallow clone *v. -ed, -ing* to clone by copying properties of the source object as they appear. [Eiffel, Firesmith, Meyer]

Synonym: CLONE.

Antonym: DEEP CLONE.

Contrast with: SHALLOW COPY.

Commentary: Shallow cloning is less reliable than deep cloning because it may result in incomplete clones with dangling references. [Firesmith]

shallow copy *v. -ed, -ing* to copy properties of the source object into the existing object as they appear. [Eiffel, Firesmith, Meyer]

Antonym: DEEP COPY.

Contrast with: SHALLOW CLONE.

shallow equal objects *n.* any objects that are field-by-field identical. [Eiffel, Meyer]

Antonym: DEEP EQUAL REFERENCES.

shallow equal references *n.* any references that are either void or attached to shallow-equal objects.

Antonym: DEEP EQUAL OBJECTS.

shared feature *n.* any multiply inherited feature, only one copy of which exists because of shared repeated inheritance.

Contrast with: REPLICATED FEATURE.

See also: SHARED REPEATED INHERITANCE.

shared repeated inheritance *n.* any repeated inheritance from a common ancestor of a single feature under the same final names yielding a single feature in the current class. [Eiffel, Firesmith, Meyer]

Synonym: VIRTUAL INHERITANCE.

Contrast with: REPLICATED REPEATED INHERITANCE.

Commentary: The inherited feature is thus shared and occurs only once in the current class. [Firesmith]

shared slot *n.* any slot defined by a given class that is visible to more than one instance of that class and its subclasses and that is accessible in all instances of that class. [CLOS]

Antonym: LOCAL SLOT.

shared variable *n.* any variable that can be accessed by more than one object. [Smalltalk]

Antonym: PRIVATE VARIABLE.

Kinds:
- CLASS VARIABLE
- GLOBAL VARIABLE
- POOL VARIABLE

- **class variable** *n.* **1.** any attribute of a class-descriptor object. **2.** any CLASS ATTRIBUTE. **3.** any variable shared by all the instances of a single class. [Smalltalk]

  Synonyms: CLASS ATTRIBUTE, COMMON INSTANCE ATTRIBUTE.

  Example: In C++, a class variable is declared as a static member. [Booch]

- **global variable** *n.* any variable shared by all instances of all classes. [Smalltalk]

  Contrast with: CLASS VARIABLE, INSTANCE VARIABLE, POOL VARIABLE, TEMPORARY VARIABLE.

  Commentary: In spite of being a part of the archetypal pure object-orient-

S

ed programming language Smalltalk, global variables implement common global data and are definitely not object-oriented in that they violate the encapsulation of objects and classes.

- **pool variable** *n.* any variable shared by the instances of a subset of the classes. [Smalltalk]

  Contrast with: CLASS VARIABLE, GLOBAL VARIABLE, INSTANCE VARIABLE, TEMPORARY VARIABLE.

sheet *n.* (a) the unit of decomposition used for decomposing large diagrams into multiple pages. [Firesmith] (b) the mechanism for breaking large object models into a series of pages. [Henderson-Sellers, Rumbaugh]

short form *n.* the text of a class without its nonpublic elements. [Eiffel, Meyer]

Synonym: ABSTRACT FORM.

Commentary: The short form captures the type of the class and should be used to document its interface.

shouldNotImplement *n.* any standard exception message used to report to the user that although the superclass of the receiver specifies that the message just sent should be implemented by its subclasses, the class of the receiver could not provide an appropriate implementation. [Smalltalk]

Contrast with: SUBCLASS RESPONSIBILITY.

signal *n.* any synchronous or asynchronous stimulus that is sent between two processes. [Jacobson]

Antonym: MESSAGE.

See also: STIMULUS.

signature *n.* **1.** the complete, formal declaration of the interface of some feature. [Firesmith] **2.** the full type information associated with a feature. [Eiffel, Meyer]

Contrast with: INTERFACE, PROTOCOL.

Kinds:
- ATTRIBUTE SIGNATURE
- LINK SIGNATURE
- MESSAGE SIGNATURE
- OPERATION SIGNATURE
- RELATIONSHIP SIGNATURE

- **attribute signature** *n.* the signature of any attribute, declaring its:
  - name
  - mutability (e.g., constant or variable)
  - type
  - initial value (if any) [Firesmith, ODMG, Rumbaugh]

- **link signature** *n.* the signature of any link, declaring its:
  - name
  - mutability (e.g., constant or variable)
  - the type of the object referred to or pointed at
  - initial value (if any)
  - qualifier (if any) [Firesmith]

- **message signature** *n.* the signature of any message, declaring its:
  - name
  - destination (possibly including role, message queue, and target operation, if different)
  - parameters including their names, modes, types, and order
  - the type of the value returned by the message
  - any preconditions and postcondition
  - the names and types of any exceptions raised by the message
  - the category of the message (e.g., sequential, synchronous, asynchronous)
  - the priority of the message (if any) [Firesmith]

- **operation signature** *n.* **1.** the signa-

ture of any operation, declaring its:
- name
- parameters including their names, modes, types, and order
- the type of the value returned by the operation
- any preconditions and postconditions
- the names and types of any exceptions raised by the operation
- the category of the operation (e.g., concurrent, sequential)
- the priority of the operation (if any) [Firesmith, ODMG, OMG, Rumbaugh]

2. the complete profile of any operation's name, formal arguments, and return type. [Booch, Martin, Wirfs-Brock] 3. any description of the legitimate values of request parameters and returned results of an operation. [Jacobson]
Synonym: OPERATION PROTOCOL.

• **relationship signature** *n.* the declaration of any relationship, specifying the name of the relationship, the type of the other object or set of objects involved in the relationship, and the name of a traversal function used to refer to the related object or set of objects. [ODMG]

signature conformance *n.* any conformance of one signature to another, whereby any arguments or return type of the first signature conform to the corresponding arguments and return type of the second signature. [Eiffel, Firesmith, Meyer]
Contrast with: DIRECT CONFORMANCE, EXPRESSION CONFORMANCE, GENERAL CONFORMANCE.

simple client [of a given reference type] *n.* any class, some entity of which is of

the given type. [Eiffel, Meyer]

simple key *n.* any key that consists of a single property. [ODMG]
Antonym: COMPOUND KEY.

simple name *n.* any name with a single component. [OMG]
Antonym: COMPOUND NAME.

simple operation *n.* any operation that does not rely on knowledge of the underlying implementation of the object or class.

simple sequential message *n.* any message whose semantics are guaranteed only in the presence of a single thread of control. [Booch]
Synonym: SEQUENTIAL MESSAGE.
Contrast with: ASYNCHRONOUS MESSAGE, BALKING MESSAGE, SYNCHRONOUS MESSAGE, TIME-OUT MESSAGE.

single classification *n.* any classification whereby an instance may only have one class at a time. [Firesmith]
Antonym: MULTIPLE CLASSIFICATION.

single generalization *n.* any generalization whereby a parent has only a single child [Firesmith]
Antonym: MULTIPLE GENERALIZATION.
Contrast with: MULTIPLE INHERITANCE, SINGLE INHERITANCE.

single inheritance *n.* (a) any inheritance in which the definition of the child is constructed in terms of the definition of only a *single* parent. [Firesmith] (b) inheritance from only a single parent. [Coleman, Martin, Rumbaugh, Smalltalk, Wirfs-Brock] (c) inheritance using only a single Parent clause. [Eiffel, Meyer] (d) the construction of a definition by incremental modification of only one definition. [OMG]
Antonym: MULTIPLE INHERITANCE.
Contrast with: SINGLE GENERALIZATION, MULTIPLE GENERALIZATION.

S

Example: Single inheritance is any in-heritance whereby a single class is a child class of only a single parent class. [Firesmith]

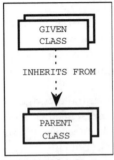

Single Inheritance

single specialization *n.* any specialization whereby a parent may only have a single child. [Firesmith]
Antonym: MULTIPLE SPECIALIZATION.
Contrast with: MULTIPLE GENERALIZA-TION, SINGLE GENERALIZATION.
singleton [object] class *n.* any class that has one and only one instance. [Embley, Firesmith]
singleton [pattern] *n.* the creational object design pattern that ensures that a class has only a single instance and also provides a global access point to the instance. [Gamma, Helm, Johnson, & Vlissides]
skeleton *n.* the object-interface-specific ORB component that assists an object adapter in passing requests to particular methods. [OMG]
slot *n.* **1.** any named part of the structure of an instance that is used to hold a value. [CLOS, Coleman] **2.** any repository for part of the state of an object. [Booch]
Synonyms: 1 ATTRIBUTE, INSTANCE VARI-ABLE, PROPERTY [ODMG].
Kinds:

- ACCESSIBLE SLOT
- BOUND SLOT
- LOCAL SLOT
- SHARED SLOT
- UNBOUND SLOT
- **accessible [slot]** *n.* any slot is *accessible* in an instance of a given class if the slot is defined by the class of the instance or is inherited from a super-class of that class. [CLOS]
Commentary: At most one slot of a given name can be accessible in an instance. [CLOS]
- **bound slot** *n.* any slot that has a value. [CLOS]
Antonym: UNBOUND SLOT.
- **local slot** *n.* any slot that is visible to exactly one instance, namely the one in which the slot is allocated. [CLOS]
Antonym: SHARED SLOT.
- **shared slot** *n.* any slot defined by a given class that is visible to more than one instance of that class and its sub-classes and that is accessible in all instances of that class. [CLOS]
Antonym: LOCAL SLOT.
- **unbound slot** *n.* any slot that does not have a value. [CLOS]
Antonym: BOUND SLOT.

Smalltalk *n.* **1.** a pure, weakly typed object-oriented programming language that only supports single inheritance. [Smalltalk] **2.** a graphical, interactive programming environment. [Smalltalk] **3.** (a) the pool that is shared by all classes and that contains all of the global variables. [Smalltalk] (b) any global variable name that refers to the dictionary of all variable names known globally in the system, in particular, the names of all classes. [Smalltalk]

Smalltalk image *n.* any integrated in-memory object repository consisting of a bound set of tightly interrelated objects. [Smalltalk]

Synonym: IMAGE.

snapshot *n.* any file in which is saved the current state of the Smalltalk image. [Smalltalk]

solicited event *n.* any external event that was generated in response to some previous operation within the current scope. [Firesmith, Shlaer/Mellor]

Antonym: UNSOLICITED EVENT.

solution domain *n.* **1.** the world of software design and implementation. **2.** the targeted implementation hardware and software platform. [Lorenz]

Synonym: SOLUTION SPACE.

Antonyms: APPLICATION DOMAIN, PROBLEM DOMAIN, PROBLEM SPACE.

Example: A solution domain could be concerned with implementing an application in Smalltalk under OS/2, running on a 386-based processor with 8 MB of memory and 60 MB of disk space. [Lorenz]

solution space *n.* **1.** the world of software design and implementation. **2.** the targeted implementation hardware and software platform. [Lorenz]

Synonym: SOLUTION DOMAIN.

Antonyms: APPLICATION DOMAIN, PROBLEM DOMAIN, PROBLEM SPACE.

Example: A solution space could be concerned with implementing an application in Smalltalk under OS/2, running on a 386-based processor with 8 MB of memory and 60 MB of disk space. [Lorenz]

special object *n.* any sequence of values, all compatible with a given type. [Eiffel, Meyer]

Contrast with: STANDARD OBJECT.

Example: A special object may be a string or an array.

specialization *n.* **1.** (a) the process of creating a specialization from one or more generalizations. [Embley, Firesmith, Martin/Odell] (b) the creation of a subclass via extension, refinement, or restriction. [Henderson-Sellers, Rumbaugh] (c) an extension of the behavior of a type of object. [Lorenz] **2.** (a) the result of using the specialization process. [Firesmith] (b) any derived class. [Embley, OMG] **3.** (a) any relationship from a generalization to one or more of its specializations. [Firesmith] (b) the relationship between a class and its par-nt(s). [Coleman] (c) the relationship between a parent and a descendant that has been modified by refinement or deletion so that the descendant is no longer behaviorally compatible with its parent. [Jacobson]

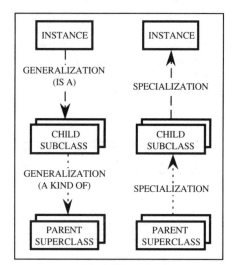

Specialization

Antonym: GENERALIZATION.

Contrast with: A-KIND-OF, CLASSIFICATION, GENERALIZATION, IS-A, SUBCLASS-

ING, SUBTYPING.

Examples: **2** A subtype of a given supertype, a child class that is an extension of its parent and an instance of its class and type are each examples of specialization. [Firesmith, Martin/Odell, OADSIG]

Commentary: The extent of the union of the specializations is a subset of the extent of the parent. Specialization can be implemented via restriction or extension. Several of the above definitions are unnecessarily restrictive. [Firesmith]

See also: IMPLEMENTATION INHERITANCE.

Kinds:
- MULTIPLE SPECIALIZATION
- SINGLE SPECIALIZATION

- **multiple specialization** *n.* any specialization whereby a parent has multiple children. [Coleman, Firesmith]

Antonym: SINGLE SPECIALIZATION.

Contrast with: MULTIPLE GENERALIZATION, SINGLE GENERALIZATION.

Commentary: The extent of the parent is a superset of the union of the extents of the children. [Firesmith]

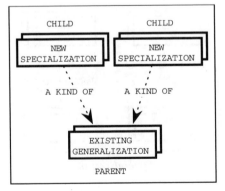

Multiple Specialization

- **single specialization** *n.* any specialization whereby a parent has only a single child. [Firesmith]

Antonyms: MULTIPLE SPECIALIZATION.

Contrast with: MULTIPLE GENERALIZATION, SINGLE GENERALIZATION.

Commentary: The extent of the parent is a superset of the extent of the child. [Firesmith]

specialization hierarchy *n.* any hierarchy consisting of classes or types and the single specialization relationships between them. [Firesmith]

Contrast with: INHERITANCE HIERARCHY.

Commentary: The use of multiple specialization may result in structures that are not true hierarchies. [Firesmith]

specialization inheritance *n.* any inheritance that implements the *a-kind-of* relationship so that the child is a specialization of its parents. [Firesmith, Henderson-Sellers]

Synonym: SUBTYPING.

Contrast with: IMPLEMENTATION INHERITANCE, INTERFACE INHERITANCE.

Example: Cars are specializations of (a kind of) vehicles.

specialize *v.* *-ed, -ing* to create a specialization from one or more generalizations. [Firesmith]

Contrast with: CLASSIFY.

Examples: To identify a subtype from a given type, to identify a more specific derived class from a given class, or to identify the instances of a given type or class is to specialize. [Firesmith]

Commentary: Specialization can be implemented via extension, refinement, or restriction. [Firesmith]

specification [of an object] *n.* the set of signatures that an object can offer. [Jacobson]

Synonym: PROTOCOL.

Antonym: IMPLEMENTATION.

See also: SIGNATURE.

specification [of a program unit] *n.* the part of a program unit that contains information that is visible to other units. [Ada95]

Antonym: BODY.

See also: PROGRAM UNIT.

specification inheritance *n.* **1.** the incremental definition of a new *specification* in terms of existing specifications. [Firesmith] **2.** any inheritance that produces consistent interfaces (i.e., inheritance in which the protocol of the derived class is a superset of the union of the protocols of its base classes). [Firesmith, Henderson-Sellers]

Synonym: INTERFACE INHERITANCE, SUBTYPING.

Antonym: IMPLEMENTATION INHERITANCE.

Contrast with: SPECIALIZATION INHERITANCE.

Commentary: Specification inheritance allows polymorphic substitution of instances of the derived class for instances of any of its base classes, even if the derived class is not a specialization of its base class(es).

specification object *n.* any object that represents rules, standards, or quality criteria (as opposed to the tangible object or role that meets these standards). [Shlaer/Mellor]

Example: A recipe represents the rules for making a certain quantity of a certain food. [Shlaer/Mellor]

Commentary: Specification objects frequently show up in inventory or manufacturing applications. They have the quality of a standard or a definition. [Shlaer/Mellor]

specific-entry operation *n.* any entry operation that depends on the incoming transition. [Firesmith]

Antonym: GENERAL-ENTRY OPERATION.

specific-exit operation *n.* any exit operation that depends on the outgoing transition. [Firesmith]

Antonym: GENERAL-EXIT OPERATION.

spontaneous transition *n.* any state transition that fires without being triggered by an incoming message. [Firesmith]

Synonym: AUTOMATIC TRANSITION.

Contrast with: NONSPONTANEOUS TRANSITION.

Examples: A spontaneous transition may result from the execution of a concurrent modifier operation, the completion of an operation associated with the source state, or result from an interrupt raised by a terminator. [Firesmith]

stair diagram *n.* any interaction diagram indicating a decentralized structure with extensive delegation of responsibilities. [Jacobson]

Antonym: FORK DIAGRAM.

See also: INTERACTION DIAGRAM.

standard-class *n.* the default metaclass, defined by *defclass*, that is appropriate for most programs. [CLOS]

See also: METACLASS, STANDARD-OBJECT.

standard object *n.* any direct instance of a class that is the direct result of a Creation instruction or clone operation executed by the system. [Eiffel, Meyer]

Contrast with: SPECIAL OBJECT.

standard-object [class] *n.* any instance of the metaclass *standard-class* and the superclass of every class that is an instance of *standard-class* except itself. [CLOS]

See also: METAOBJECT, STANDARD-CLASS.

standard system view *n.* any view that provides standard interface functions for manipulating itself, for example, for

S

moving, framing, collapsing, and closing. [Smalltalk]
Contrast with: ACTIVE VIEW, BROWSER, COLLAPSED VIEW, SUBVIEW.

start state *n.* **1.** any initial atomic state of an object or class on instantiation. [Firesmith] **2.** any first state in which an instance first comes into existence. [Shlaer/Mellor]
Synonyms: BEGIN STATE, CREATION STATE, INITIAL STATE.
Antonyms: END STATE, FINAL STATE, STOP STATE.
Commentary: Use together with the term *stop state.*

starvation *n.* the situation that occurs when a concurrent operation must wait indefinitely for execution. [Firesmith]

state *n.* **1.** (a) any status, situation, condition, mode, or life-cycle phase of an object or class during which certain rules of overall behavior (e.g., response to messages) apply. [Embley, Firesmith, Jacobson] (b) any situation or condition of the object during which certain physical laws, rules, and policies apply; a stage in the life cycle of a typical instance of the object. [Shlaer/Mellor] (c) the cumulative results of the behavior of an object or class. [Booch] (d) the information about the history of previous requests needed to determine the behavior of future requests. [OMG] **2.** the equivalence class (i.e., set of all equivalent members) of state attribute values, state links, and the states of parts that produces the same overall behavior of the associated object or class. [Firesmith, Jacobson] **3.** (a) the current value of all properties of an object or class. [Booch, Coad, Lorenz, OADSIG, Rumbaugh] (b) the time varying properties of an object that af-

fect that object's behavior. [OMG] (c) the collection of associations that an object has with other objects. [Martin/Odell] **4.** the collection of types that apply to an object. [Martin/Odell] **5.** in the ROOM method, any quiescent point where the object is waiting for an event to trigger it back into action.
Contrast with: STATE ATTRIBUTE, STATE COMPONENT, STATE LINK.
Examples: Enabled and *Disabled* are often states of device objects.
Commentary: The state of an object or class is typically implemented as the equivalence class of state attribute values, state links, and the states of parts that produce the same overall behavior. [Firesmith] States may be used to model a nondiscrete or long-running activity, or a continuous activity that must be interrupted to allow a response to events or conditions that affect an object. [Embley] Definitions **2** and **3** are quite different. Definition **2** is a way of implementing definition **1**, whereas definition **3** is inconsistent with definition **1**. Definition **4** implies dynamic typing in which the type of an object changes each time its state changes.
Kinds:
- AGGREGATE STATE
- ATOMIC STATE
- BEGIN STATE
- COMPUTATIONAL STATE
- CONCURRENT STATES
- CREATION STATE
- CURRENT STATE
- DYNAMIC STATE
- END STATE
- FINAL STATE
- HIGH-LEVEL STATE
- INITIAL STATE
- INTERNAL STATE

- PERSISTENT STATE
- PRIOR STATE
- START STATE
- STOP STATE
- SUBSEQUENT STATE
- SUBSTATE
- SUPERSTATE

- **aggregate state** *n.* any generalized superstate that is decomposed into one or more specialized substates. [Firesmith]
Synonym: COMPOSITE STATE.
Antonym: ATOMIC STATE.
Contrast with: SUPERSTATE.
Example: The aggregate state *functioning* may be decomposed into an *enabled* substate and a *disabled* substate. [Firesmith]
Commentary: The term *aggregate* state is preferred over the term *composite* state. [Firesmith]

- **atomic state** *n.* any state that does not contain any specialized substates. [Firesmith]
Antonym: AGGREGATE STATE.

- **begin state** *n.* **1.** any atomic state of an object or class on instantiation or reinitialization. [Firesmith] **2.** any first state in which an instance first comes into existence. [Shlaer/Mellor]
Synonyms: CREATION STATE, INITIAL STATE, START STATE.
Antonyms: END STATE, FINAL STATE, STOP STATE.
Commentary: Use together with the term *end state.*

- **computational state** *n.* any state that describes the current status of execution, as well as potential future execution. [Jacobson]
Antonym: INTERNAL STATE.
Commentary: In principle, object behavior should only be described in terms of computational states. [Jacobson]

- **concurrent states** *n.* any two or more states in which an object or class can be simultaneously. [Firesmith]

- **creation state** *n.* **1.** any atomic state of an object or class on instantiation or reinitialization. [Firesmith] **2.** any first state in which an instance first comes into existence. [Shlaer/Mellor]
Synonyms: BEGIN STATE, INITIAL STATE, START STATE.
Antonyms: END STATE, FINAL STATE, STOP STATE.
Rationale: Term used by Shlaer/Mellor.

- **current state** *n.* any state that an object or class currently is in. [Firesmith, Shlaer/Mellor]
Commentary: An object or class may be in multiple current states. The current state(s) of an object or class is the cumulative result of its behavior acting on its initial state(s). [Firesmith]

- **dynamic state** *n.* any state of a persistent or distributed object, which is stored in memory and is not likely to exist for the whole lifetime of the object. [OMG]
Antonym: PERSISTENT STATE.

- **end state** *n.* **1.** any terminal state from which the object or class cannot transition. [Firesmith] **2.** any state that serves as the end of the life cycle for an instance. [Shlaer/Mellor]
Synonyms: FINAL STATE, STOP STATE.
Antonyms: CREATION STATE, INITIAL STATE, START STATE.
Commentary: Use together with the term *begin state.*

- **final state** *n.* **1.** any terminal state from which the object or class cannot transition. [Firesmith] **2.** any state

S

that serves as the end of the life cycle for an instance. [Shlaer/Mellor]
Synonyms: END STATE, STOP STATE.
Antonyms: CREATION STATE, INITIAL STATE, START STATE.
Rationale: Term used by Firesmith.
Commentary: Use together with *initial state*.

- **high-level state** *n.* any state that groups and subsumes lower-level states, transitions, constraints, and notes. [Embley]
  Synonyms: AGGREGATE STATE, SUPER-STATE.

- **initial state** *n.* **1.** any atomic state of an object or class on instantiation. [Firesmith] **2.** any first state in which an instance first comes into existence. [Shlaer/Mellor]
  Synonyms: BEGIN STATE, CREATION STATE, START STATE.
  Antonyms: END STATE, FINAL STATE, STOP STATE.
  Rationale: Term used by Firesmith.
  Commentary: Use together with the term *final state*.

- **internal state** *n.* any state that is characterized by the values of all of the relevant variables. [Jacobson]
  Antonym: COMPUTATIONAL STATE.

- **persistent state** *n.* any state of a persistent or distributed object, used to reconstruct the dynamic state of the object. [OMG]
  Antonym: DYNAMIC STATE.

- **prior state** *n.* any state that an object or class is in immediately preceding a specified transition. [Embley, Firesmith]
  Antonym: SUBSEQUENT STATE.

- **start state** *n.* **1.** any atomic state of an object or class on instantiation or reinitialization. [Firesmith] **2.** any

first state in which an instance first comes into existence. [Shlaer/Mellor]
Synonyms: BEGIN STATE, CREATION STATE, INITIAL STATE.
Antonyms: END STATE, FINAL STATE, STOP STATE.
Commentary: Use together with the term *stop state*.

- **stop state** *n.* **1.** any terminal state from which the object or class cannot transition. [Firesmith] **2.** any state that serves as the end of the life cycle for an instance. [Shlaer/Mellor]
  Synonyms: END STATE, FINAL STATE.
  Antonyms: CREATION STATE, INITIAL STATE, START STATE.
  Commentary: Use together with the term *start state*.

- **subsequent state** *n.* any state that an object or class is in immediately following a specified transition. [Embley, Firesmith]
  Antonym: PRIOR STATE.

- **substate** *n.* any specialized state that is part of a more generalized superstate. [Firesmith]
  Antonym: SUPERSTATE.
  Commentary: A substate may be defined in the same class as its superstate or may be later defined in a descendant of the class that defined the superstate. [Firesmith]

- **superstate** *n.* any generalized state that is decomposed into one or more specialized substates. [Firesmith]
  Synonym: COMPONENT STATE.
  Antonym: SUBSTATE.
  Contrast with: AGGREGATE STATE.

state attribute *n.* any attribute, the value of which helps determine the state of encapsulating object or class. [Firesmith]
Contrast with: STATE COMPONENT, STATE LINK.

state component *n.* any component object the state of which helps determine the state of its aggregate object or class. [Firesmith]
Contrast with: STATE ATTRIBUTE, STATE LINK.

state consistency *n.* any consistency between the state associated with an object and the data model. [OMG]

state-controlled object *n.* any object that selects operations based on the current state as well as on the stimulus received. [Jacobson]
Antonym: STIMULUS-CONTROLLED OBJECT.

state-dependent attribute *n.* any attribute that has meaning only within specific states. [Coad, Firesmith]
Contrast with: STATE-DEPENDENT SERVICE.
Contrast with: STATE-DEPENDENT LINK.

state-dependent link *n.* any link that has meaning only during specific states. [Firesmith]
Antonym: STATE-INDEPENDENT LINK.
Contrast with: STATE-DEPENDENT ATTRIBUTE.

state-dependent object *n.* any object, the behavior of which is dependent on the state as well as on the message received. [Firesmith]
Antonym: STATE-INDEPENDENT OBJECT.

state-dependent property *n.* any property, the meaning of which is dependent on the state of its encapsulating object or class. [Firesmith]
Antonym: STATE-INDEPENDENT PROPERTY.
Contrast with: STATE-DEPENDENT OPERATION.
Kinds:
- STATE-DEPENDENT ATTRIBUTE
- STATE-DEPENDENT LINK

• **state-dependent attribute** *n.* any attribute that has meaning only within specific states. [Coad, Firesmith]
Contrast with: STATE-DEPENDENT LINK, STATE-DEPENDENT SERVICE.

• **state-dependent link** *n.* any link that has meaning only during specific states. [Firesmith]
Antonym: STATE-INDEPENDENT LINK.
Contrast with: STATE-DEPENDENT ATTRIBUTE.

state-dependent operation *n.* any operation, the method of which is dependent on the state of the object or class. [Firesmith]
Antonym: STATE-INDEPENDENT OPERATION.
Contrast with: STATE-DEPENDENT PROPERTY.
Kinds:
- ENTRY OPERATION
  - GENERAL ENTRY OPERATION
  - SPECIFIC ENTRY OPERATION
- EXIT OPERATION
  - GENERAL EXIT OPERATION
  - SPECIFIC EXIT OPERATION

• **entry operation** *n.* any state-dependent operation that executes on transition into a state. [Firesmith]
Antonym: EXIT OPERATION.
Kinds:
- GENERAL ENTRY OPERATION
- SPECIFIC ENTRY OPERATION

- **general entry operation** *n.* any entry operation that does not depend on the incoming transition. [Firesmith]
Antonym: SPECIFIC ENTRY OPERATION.

- **specific entry operation** *n.* any entry operation that depends on the incoming transition. [Firesmith]
Antonym: GENERAL ENTRY OPERATION.

S

- **exit operation** *n.* any state-dependent operation that executes on transition out of a state. [Firesmith]
  Antonym: ENTRY OPERATION.
  Kinds:
  - GENERAL EXIT OPERATION
  - SPECIFIC EXIT OPERATION
  - **general exit operation** *n.* any exit operation that does not depend on the outgoing transition. [Firesmith]
    Antonym: SPECIFIC EXIT OPERATION.
  - **specific exit operation** *n.* any exit operation that depends on the outgoing transition. [Firesmith]
    Antonym: GENERAL EXIT OPERATION.

state-dependent service *n.* any service that is allowed only within specific states. [Coad]
Contrast with: STATE-DEPENDENT ATTRIBUTE, STATE-DEPENDENT OPERATION.

state diagram *n.* any directed graph in which nodes represent states and arcs represent transitions between states. [Rumbaugh]
Synonyms: STATE NET, STATE TRANSITION DIAGRAM.

state-independent attribute *n.* any attribute that has meaning during all states. [Firesmith]
Antonym: STATE-DEPENDENT ATTRIBUTE.
Contrast with: STATE-DEPENDENT LINK.

state-independent link *n.* any link that has meaning during all states. [Firesmith]
Antonym: STATE-DEPENDENT LINK.
Contrast with: STATE-INDEPENDENT ATTRIBUTE.

state-independent object *n.* any object, the behavior of which only depends on the message received. [Firesmith]
Antonym: STATE-INDEPENDENT OBJECT.

state-independent operation *n.* any operation, the method of which is independent of the state of the object or class. [Firesmith]
Antonym: STATE-DEPENDENT OPERATION.
Contrast with: STATE-INDEPENDENT PROPERTY.

state-independent property *n.* any property, the meaning of which is independent of the state of its encapsulating object or class. [Firesmith]
Antonym: STATE-DEPENDENT PROPERTY.
Contrast with: STATE-INDEPENDENT OPERATION.
Kinds:
- STATE-INDEPENDENT ATTRIBUTE
- STATE-INDEPENDENT LINK

- **state-independent attribute** *n.* any attribute that has meaning during all states. [Firesmith]
  Contrast with: STATE-DEPENDENT ATTRIBUTE, STATE-DEPENDENT LINK.

- **state-independent link** *n.* any link that has meaning during all states. [Firesmith]
  Antonym: STATE-DEPENDENT LINK.
  Contrast with: STATE-INDEPENDENT ATTRIBUTE.

state integrity *n.* the degree to which the state of an object or class cannot be corrupted (e.g., via messages from clients). [Firesmith, OMG]
Contrast with: REFERENTIAL INTEGRITY.

state life cycle *n.* the sequence of states that an object has during its existence. [Martin]
Contrast with: BEHAVIOR, STATE SPACE.
See also: STATE.

state link *n.* any link, the existence of which helps determine the overall behavior of its client object or class. [Firesmith]
Contrast with: STATE ATTRIBUTE, STATE COMPONENT.

state matrix *n.* any matrix that indicates

all the states that can be adopted by the unit and all the stimuli that the unit is expected to receive in the various states. [Jacobson]
Contrast with: STATE TRANSITION DIAGRAM.
See also: STATE.
Commentary: In reality it is impossible to include all states in terms of all possible variable values and all variants of stimuli in terms of different parameters. [Jacobson]

state model *n.* **1.** the object-oriented dynamic model that documents the behavior of the objects and classes in terms of their states and the transitions between these states. [Firesmith] **2.** any set of states and events. [Shlaer/Mellor]
Contrast with: BEHAVIORAL MODEL, CONFIGURATION MODEL, DATA MODEL, DYNAMIC MODEL, FUNCTIONAL MODEL, INTERACTION MODEL, INTERFACE MODEL, LANGUAGE MODEL, LIFE-CYCLE MODEL, OBJECT MODEL, OPERATION MODEL, PRESENTATION MODEL, SEMANTIC MODEL, STRUCTURAL MODEL, TIMING MODEL, USE-CASE MODEL.

state-modifying request *n.* any request that by performing the service alters the results of future requests. [OMG]
Contrast with: MODIFIER OPERATION.

state net *n.* **1.** any diagram representing states and state transitions for all objects in a particular object class. **2.** any "behavior template" that specifies the expected behavior for instances of an object class. [Embley]
See also: OBJECT-BEHAVIOR MODEL.
Commentary: In OSA, state nets are used to model object behavior. When a state net is associated with an object class, every instance of the object class has the behavior described by the state net. [Embley]
Synonyms: STATE DIAGRAM, STATE TRANSITION DIAGRAM.

state of the system *n.* the values of all attributes of all instances in the system. [Shlaer/Mellor]

state operation table (SOT) *n.* any table that documents the valid prestates, poststates, and exceptions raised by each operation. [Firesmith]

state [pattern] *n.* the behavioral object design pattern that stores state as an encapsulated pointer to instances of subclasses of a state class. [Gamma, Helm, Johnson, & Vlissides]
Commentary: This pattern uses inheritance and polymorphism to eliminate the need for case statements based on state as well as the need for most state-based preconditions and postconditions.

state-process table *n.* any table that provides a compact listing of the processes in the system and the actions in which they are used. [Shlaer/Mellor]

state-process–table document *n.* any document that contains three copies of the state-process table: one sorted by process identifier, one by the state model and action in which each process is used, and one by process type. [Shlaer/Mellor]

state property *n.* any property whose value helps determine the state of its encapsulating object or class. [Firesmith]
Kinds:
- STATE ATTRIBUTE
- STATE COMPONENT
- STATE LINK

- **state attribute** *n.* any attribute whose value helps determine the state of its encapsulating object or class. [Firesmith]
Contrast with: STATE COMPONENT, STATE LINK.

S

- **state component** *n.* any component object the state of which helps determine the state of its aggregate object or class. [Firesmith]
  Contrast with: STATE ATTRIBUTE, STATE LINK.
- **state link** *n.* any link whose existence helps determine the state of its client object or class. [Firesmith]
  Contrast with: STATE ATTRIBUTE, STATE COMPONENT.

state space *n.* the set of all the possible states of an object or class, encompassing an indefinite yet finite number of possible (although not always desirable nor expected) states. [Booch, Firesmith]
Contrast with: STATE LIFE CYCLE.

state transition diagram (STD) *n.* **1.** any diagram that documents (1) the states of an object or class, (2) the triggers (e.g., operations and terminators) that cause the transitions between the states, and the corresponding operations. [Booch, Firesmith, Jacobson] **2.** a diagram that documents the sequence of states of an object. [Martin]
Synonyms: STATE DIAGRAM, STATE NET.
Rationale: This is the traditional term.
Commentary: When a class is instantiated, the instance created follows a path in this diagram throughout its lifetime. [Jacobson] Although individual objects have their own state machines, all direct instances of the same class conform to the same state transition diagram. However, if the class itself also has state properties, it typically has a different state transition diagram than its instances. [Firesmith]

state variable *n.* any part of the state of an object. [OMG]

statically tagged *adj.* describing a name or expression of tagged type whose tag is determined statically by the operand's specific type. [Ada95]
Antonym: DYNAMICALLY TAGGED.

static architecture *n.* the logical or physical partitioning of some static structure. [Firesmith]
Antonym: DYNAMIC ARCHITECTURE.
Examples: The partitioning of a system into subsystems, an assembly into clusters, or a cluster into classes. [Firesmith]

static association *n.* any association that captures a static relationship. [Jacobson]
Antonym: DYNAMIC ASSOCIATION.
Kinds:
- ACQUAINTANCE ASSOCIATION
  - CONSISTSOF ASSOCIATION
  - PARTOF ASSOCIATION
- INHERITANCE ASSOCIATION

- **acquaintance association** *n.* any static association between objects, in which one object knows of the existence of another. [Jacobson]
  See also: ATTRIBUTE, ENTITY OBJECT.
  Contrast with: STATIC ASSOCIATION.
  Commentary: An acquaintance association does not give the object the right to exchange information with the other object; for that, a dynamic association is needed. Acquaintance associations are normally implemented in the same way as attributes, namely as ordinary instance references or pointer variables to instances. [Jacobson]
  Kinds:
  - CONSISTSOF ASSOCIATION
  - PARTOF ASSOCIATION.

- **consistsOf association** *n.* any acquaintance association from an aggregate object to an object of which it consists. [Jacobson]
  Antonym: PARTOF ASSOCIATION.
  See also: ACQUAINTANCE ASSOCIATION, AGGREGATE.

Example: A food order consists of a dish and a beverage. [Jacobson]

Commentary: The associations called *consistsOf* and *partOf* are variants of the acquaintance association. They are used to express that an object is a compound of other objects. A construction of this type is called an aggregate. [Jacobson]

- **partOf association** *n.* any acquaintance association from an object to the aggregate object of which it is a part. [Jacobson]

Antonym: CONSISTSOF ASSOCIATION.

See also: ACQUAINTANCE ASSOCIATION, AGGREGATE.

Example: A dish and a beverage are parts of a food order. [Jacobson]

Commentary: The associations called *consistsOf* and *partOf* are variants of the acquaintance association. They are used to express that an object is a compound of other objects. A construction of this type is called an aggregate. [Jacobson]

• **inheritance association** *n.* any class association whereby the definition of the operations and attributes of one class is also used in the inheriting class which might do additions and redefinitions. [Jacobson]

See also: INHERITANCE.

static binding *n.* **1.** any binding that takes place statically before run-time when the associated message is sent. [Firesmith, Jacobson, Lorenz, Martin/Odell, OMG] **2.** any binding in which the name/class association is made when the name is declared (at compile time) but before the creation of the object that the name designates. [Booch]

Synonyms: COMPILE-TIME BINDING, EARLY BINDING.

Antonyms: DEFERRED, DYNAMIC BINDING, LATE BINDING, RUN-TIME BINDING, VIRTUAL BINDING.

Commentary: Static binding allows the compiler (or linker) to decide what method to use, based on the declared class of the object. The term *static binding* is preferred. [Firesmith, Lorenz]

static class *n.* **1.** any class, all instances of which are dynamic objects that are instantiated and whose memory are allocated at compile time and remains allocated until the program terminates. [Firesmith] **2.** any class with only static members [C++]

Antonym: DYNAMIC CLASS.

Commentary: A static object lasts for the duration of program execution, but not after a program ceases to execute. [Firesmith] A static class provides a facility akin to what is called a *module* in many languages: a named collection of objects and functions in their own name space. [C++]

static classification *n.* any classification whereby the class(es) of an instance may not vary over time. [Firesmith]

Antonym: DYNAMIC CLASSIFICATION.

static data member *n.* any data member of a class that has been declared static in the class declaration. There is only one copy of a static data member, shared by all objects of the class in a program. A static member is not part of objects of a class. [C++]

Commentary: The use of the word *static* to indicate that a member of a class is not associated with an individual object of a class (and not replicated in each object) parallels the use of the word static to indicate that only one copy of a local variable is to be used for all calls of a function. The purpose of *static* mem-

S

bers is to reduce the need for global variables by providing alternatives that are local to a class. [C++]

static inheritance *n.* any inheritance that does not require dynamic binding (e.g., to support polymorphism). [Firesmith]
Antonym: DYNAMIC INHERITANCE.

static invocation *n.* **1.** the construction of a request at compile time. [OMG] **2.** the calling of an operation via a stub procedure. [OMG]
Antonym: DYNAMIC INVOCATION.

static method *n.* any method is statically bound to an object at compile-time. [Firesmith]
Antonyms: DYNAMIC METHOD, DYNAMIC METHOD.

static object *n.* **1.** any object that is instantiated and whose memory is allocated at compile time and remains allocated until the program terminates. [Firesmith] **2.** any object that exists and retains the values of its properties throughout the execution of the entire program. [C++]
Contrast with: **1** DYNAMIC OBJECT, PERSISTENT OBJECT, **2** AUTOMATIC OBJECT.
Commentary: A static object lasts for the duration of program execution, but not after a program ceases to execute. [Firesmith]

static object-based application *n.* any set of related types and classes used to provide end-user functionality. [OMG]
Synonym: PROGRAM.
Antonym: DYNAMIC OBJECT-BASED APPLICATION.

static operation *n.* any operation that is statically bound to its object. [Firesmith]
Antonym: DYNAMIC OPERATION.

static type [of an entity] *n.* the type with which it is declared. [Eiffel, Meyer]
Antonym: DYNAMIC TYPE.

static type [of a given expression] *n.* the type deduced from the types of the constituents of the given expression. [Eiffel, Firesmith, Meyer]
Antonym: DYNAMIC TYPE.

static type [of a given object] *n.* the type with which the given object was declared. [Firesmith]
Antonym: DYNAMIC TYPE.

static typing *n.* any typing that occurs at compile-time. [Firesmith]
Antonym: DYNAMIC TYPING.

stereotype *n.* any characterization of a type of behavior of an object. [Lorenz, Wirfs-Brock]
Example: One stereotype would be whether the object actively drives actions in the system or passively provides information to other objects. [Lorenz]

stimulus *n.* **stimuli** *pl.* any event whereby an object communicates with another object. When received by an object, a stimulus causes an operation to be performed by the receiving object. [Jacobson]
Contrast with: OPERATION.
Commentary: The dynamics in an object-oriented model are created through the dynamic relations, by means of objects sending *stimuli* to other objects. The stimulus concept is used instead of the word *message* in order to avoid the message-semantic. [Jacobson]
Kinds:
- MESSAGE
- SIGNAL

- **message** *n.* any intraprocess stimulus. [Jacobson]
  Antonym: SIGNAL.
- **signal** *n.* any synchronous or asynchronous interprocess stimulus. [Jacobson]
  Antonym: MESSAGE.

stimulus-controlled object *n.* any object that will perform the same operation independent of the state in which a stimulus is received. [Jacobson]
Antonym: STATE-CONTROLLED OBJECT.

stop state *n.* **1.** any terminal state from which the object or class cannot transition. [Firesmith] **2.** any state that serves as the end of the life cycle for an instance. [Shlaer/Mellor]
Synonyms: END STATE, FINAL STATE.
Antonyms: CREATION STATE, INITIAL STATE, START STATE.
Commentary: Use together with the term *start state*.

storage class *n.* either any automatic or static class. [C++]
Contrast with: AUTOMATIC, STATIC.
Commentary: A named object has a storage class that determines its lifetime. [C++]
Kinds:
- AUTOMATIC CLASS
- STATIC CLASS

- **automatic class** *n.* any class of automatic objects (i.e., objects that are local to each invocation of a block). [C++]
  Antonym: STATIC CLASS.
- **static class** *n.* any class with only static members. [C++]
  Rationale: A static class provides a facility akin to what is called a *module* in many languages: a named collection of objects and functions in their own name space. [C++]

strategy [pattern] *n.* the behavioral object design pattern that defines and encapsulates a family of objectified algorithms, allowing the algorithms to vary independently of the clients that use them. [Gamma, Helm, Johnson, & Vlissides]

strict inheritance *n.* any interface inheritance whereby the new definition only adds new features to the existing definition(s), but neither deletes nor redefines inherited features from the existing definition(s). [Firesmith]
See also: INTERFACE INHERITANCE.

strong authorization *n.* any authorization on a class in an inheritance hierarchy that cannot be overridden by a descendant. [Kim]
Antonym: WEAK AUTHORIZATION.

strong typing *n.* any typing that must be declared and that is enforced, (i.e., guaranteed to be consistent). [Firesmith, Rumbaugh]
Antonym: WEAK TYPING.
Example: Ada, C++, and Eiffel implement strong typing of objects and attributes. Because Smalltalk properties are not typed, Smalltalk is not considered strongly typed. [Firesmith]

strongly typed *adj.* describing any programming language requiring the declaration of and enforcing the type consistency of each object, property, and parameter. [Booch, Firesmith]
Antonym: WEAKLY TYPED.
Examples: Ada, C++, and Eiffel are strongly typed languages. [Firesmith]

structural constraint *n.* any constraint that limits the way objects may be linked, classes may be associated, or objects may be classified into classes. [Firesmith]
Antonym: BEHAVIORAL CONSTRAINT.
Kinds:
- ANTISYMMETRIC CONSTRAINT
- ASYMMETRIC CONSTRAINT
- CARDINALITY CONSTRAINT
  - AGGREGATION-CARDINALITY CONSTRAINT
  - CLASS-CARDINALITY CONSTRAINT
  - CLUSTER-CARDINALITY CONSTRAINT

S

- OBJECT-CLASS CARDINALITY CONSTRAINT
- OBJECT-CONNECTION CONSTRAINT
- PARTICIPATION CONSTRAINT
+ CO-OCCURRENCE CONSTRAINT
- RELATIONSHIP-CARDINALITY CONSTRAINT
• INHERITANCE CONSTRAINT
- COVER CONSTRAINT
- DISJOINT CONSTRAINT
- MUTUAL-EXCLUSION CONSTRAINT
- PARTITION CONSTRAINT
- UNION CONSTRAINT
• IRREFLEXIVE CONSTRAINT
• NONTRANSITIVE CONSTRAINT
• REFLEXIVE CONSTRAINT
• SET CONSTRAINT
• SYMMETRIC CONSTRAINT
• TRANSITIVE CONSTRAINT

• **antisymmetric constraint** *n.* any structural constraint that permits a symmetric relationship between two things only if those two things are the same. [Firesmith]
Contrast with: ASYMMETRIC CONSTRAINT, SYMMETRIC CONSTRAINT.
Example: The *is-identical-to* link and association are antisymmetric. *A* is identical to *B* only if *A* and *B* are the same. [Firesmith]

• **asymmetric constraint** *n.* any structural constraint that does not permit symmetry. [Firesmith]
Contrast with: ANTISYMMETRIC CONSTRAINT, SYMMETRIC CONSTRAINT.
Example: The *is-parent-of* link and association are asymmetric. The existence of an *is-parent-of* link from *A* to *B* implies that no *is-parent-of* link can exist from *B* to *A*. [Firesmith]

• **cardinality constraint** *n.* any structural constraint that restricts the cardinality of something.

Kinds:
- AGGREGATION-CARDINALITY CONSTRAINT
- CLASS-CARDINALITY CONSTRAINT
- CLUSTER-CARDINALITY CONSTRAINT
- OBJECT-CLASS CARDINALITY CONSTRAINT
- OBJECT-CONNECTION CONSTRAINT
- PARTICIPATION CONSTRAINT
+ CO-OCCURRENCE CONSTRAINT
- RELATIONSHIP-CARDINALITY CONSTRAINT

- **aggregation-cardinality constraint** *n.* any cardinality constraint that restricts the cardinality of an aggregate. [Firesmith]

- **class-cardinality constraint** *n.* any cardinality constraint that restricts the cardinality of a class. [Firesmith]
Synonym: OBJECT-CLASS CARDINALITY CONSTRAINT.

- **cluster-cardinality constraint** *n.* any cardinality constraint that restricts the cardinality of a cluster. [Firesmith]

- **object-class cardinality constraint** *n.* any constraint used to restrict the number of objects in an object class. [Embley]
Synonym: CLASS-CARDINALITY CONSTRAINT.

- **object-connection constraint** *n.* any constraint that indicates the number of objects that an object knows. [Coad]
Synonym: PARTICIPATION CONSTRAINT, RELATIONSHIP-CARDINALITY CONSTRAINT.
See also: OBJECT CONNECTION.
Commentary: Coad's graphical placement of this constraint is just the opposite of the entity-relation-

ship convention for what the approach calls *multiplicities*. [Coad]

- **participation constraint** *n.* any constraint that defines the number of times an object in an object class can participate in a connected relationship set. Participation constraints restrict the number of relationships in which an object can appear in a relationship set. [Embley]
Synonym: OBJECT-CONNECTION CONSTRAINT, RELATIONSHIP-CARDINALITY CONSTRAINT.
Commentary: Embley et al. requires that every connection of a relationship set to an object class have a participation constraint. The basic form for a participation constraint is a par: *min:max*. [Embley]

+ **co-occurrence constraint** *n.* any constraint that specifies the minimum and maximum number of times an object or combination of objects can co-occur in the relationships of a relationship set with another object or combination of objects. [Embley]

- **relationship-cardinality constraint** *n.* any cardinality constraint that restricts the cardinality of a relationship. [Firesmith, Martin/Odell]
Synonym: OBJECT-CONNECTION CONSTRAINT, PARTICIPATION CONSTRAINT.
Examples: Common unidirectional relationship cardinality constraints are *0 or 1*, *1*, *0 or more*, and *1 or more*. Common bidirectional relationship cardinality constraints are *1 to 1*, *1 to many*, and *many to many*. More specific constraints are also possible. [Firesmith]
Commentary: Relationship-cardi-

nality constraints can be unidirectional (i.e., restricting the number on the end that is pointed to) or bidirectional (i.e., restricting the number at both ends of the relationship). [Firesmith]

• **inheritance constraint** *n.* any structural constraint that restricts the relationships among children or between the children and their parent(s). [Firesmith]
Kinds:
- COVER CONSTRAINT
- DISJOINT CONSTRAINT
- MUTUAL-EXCLUSION CONSTRAINT
- PARTITION CONSTRAINT
- UNION CONSTRAINT

- **cover constraint** *n.* the inheritance constraint which requires that the extent of the parent be a subset of the union of the extents of the children. [Firesmith]
Synonym: UNION CONSTRAINT.
Rationale: The term *cover* comes from set theory. [Firesmith]
Commentary: This constraint ensures that each instance of the parent is also an instance of at least one child. [Firesmith]

- **disjoint constraint** *n.* the inheritance constraint which requires that the extents of the children be pairwise disjoint. [Firesmith]
Synonym: MUTUAL EXCLUSION CONSTRAINT.
Rationale: The term *disjoint* comes from set theory. [Firesmith]
Commentary: This constraint ensures that no object will be an instance of two children. [Firesmith]

- **mutual-exclusion constraint** *n.* any constraint which declares that a group of specializations of gener-

S

alization are pairwise disjoint. [Embley]

Synonym: DISJOINT CONSTRAINT.

- **partition constraint** *n.* the inheritance constraint which requires that the extents of the children form a disjoint cover that partitions the parent. [Embley, Firesmith]

Commentary: The partition constraint is the conjunction of the disjoint constraint and the cover constraint. [Firesmith] A partition requires that partitioning sets be pairwise disjoint and that their union constitute the partitioned set. A partition constraint is the combination of a mutual-exclusion constraint and a union constraint. [Embley]

- **union constraint** *n.* any constraint which declares that the union of a group of specializations of a generalization constitutes the entire membership of the generalization. [Embley]

Synonym: COVER CONSTRAINT.

Commentary: A union constraint implies that every member of a generalization is also a member of at least one specialization in the group. [Embley]

- **irreflexive constraint** *n.* any structural constraint that prohibits objects or classes to be related to themselves. [Firesmith]

Antonym: REFLEXIVE CONSTRAINT.

Example: The *is-parent-of* link and association are irreflexive. No one can be its own parent. [Firesmith]

- **nontransitive constraint** *n.* the structural constraint on a given relationship *R* that requires if *A* is related by *R* to *B* and *B* is related by *R* to *C*, then

A need not be related by *R* to *C*. [Firesmith]

Antonym: TRANSITIVE CONSTRAINT.

Example: The *has-visibility-of* link and association are nontransitive. [Firesmith]

- **reflexive constraint** *n.* any structural constraint on a relationship that requires objects or classes to be related to themselves. [Firesmith]

Antonym: IRREFLEXIVE CONSTRAINT.

Example: The *is-as-old-as* link and association are reflexive. Something can be as old as other things, but must be as old as itself.

- **set constraint** *n.* any structural constraint on an extent that prohibits duplicates. [Firesmith]

- **symmetric constraint** *n.* any structural constraint on a relationship that requires the relationship to work in both directions. [Firesmith]

Contrast with: ANTISYMMETRIC CONSTRAINT, ASYMMETRIC CONSTRAINT.

Example: The *is-spouse-of* link and association are symmetric. The existence of an *is-spouse-of* link from *A* to *B* implies the existence of an *is-spouse-of* link from *B* to *A*. [Firesmith]

- **transitive constraint** *n.* any structural constraint that requires if *A* is related to *B* and *B* is related to *C*, then *A* is related to *C*. [Firesmith]

Antonym: NONTRANSITIVE CONSTRAINT.

Example: The *is-greater-than* link and association are transitive. [Firesmith]

structural model *n.* any model that describes the structure of the object types in the problem domain. [OADSIG]

Contrast with: BEHAVIORAL MODEL, CONFIGURATION MODEL, DATA MODEL, DYNAMIC MODEL, FUNCTIONAL MODEL,

INTERACTION MODEL, INTERFACE MODEL, LANGUAGE MODEL, LIFE-CYCLE MODEL, OBJECT MODEL, OPERATION MODEL, PRESENTATION MODEL, SEMANTIC MODEL, STATE MODEL, TIMING MODEL, USE CASE MODEL.

Examples: Object relationship diagrams, type hierarchies, whole-part diagrams, and subject area relationship diagrams are all structural models.

structural pattern *n.* any design pattern that is primarily concerned with how larger structures are composed out of classes and objects. [Gamma, Helm, Johnson, & Vlissides]
Kinds:
- STRUCTURAL CLASS PATTERN
  - ADAPTER
- STRUCTURAL OBJECT PATTERN
  - ADAPTER
  - BRIDGE
  - COMPOSITE
  - DECORATOR
  - FACADE
  - FLYWEIGHT
  - PROXY

- **structural class pattern** *n.* any structural design pattern that uses inheritance to compose interfaces of implementations. [Gamma, Helm, Johnson, & Vlissides]
  - **adapter [pattern]** *n.* the structural class/object design pattern that converts the interface of a class into one that clients expect, thereby allowing classes to work together that otherwise could not because of incompatible interfaces. [Gamma, Helm, Johnson, & Vlissides]
    Synonym: WRAPPER.

- **structural object pattern** *n.* any structural design pattern that documents ways to compose larger structures out of objects. [Gamma, Helm, Johnson, & Vlissides]
Kinds:
  - ADAPTER
  - BRIDGE
  - COMPOSITE
  - DECORATOR
  - FACADE
  - FLYWEIGHT
  - PROXY

- **adapter [pattern]** *n.* the structural class/object design pattern that converts the interface of a class into one that clients expect, thereby allowing classes to work together that otherwise could not because of incompatible interfaces. [Gamma, Helm, Johnson, & Vlissides]
  Synonym: WRAPPER.

- **bridge [pattern]** *n.* the structural object design pattern that decouples an interface from its implementation so that the two can vary independently. [Gamma, Helm, Johnson, & Vlissides]
  Synonym: HANDLE/BODY.

- **composite [pattern]** *n.* the structural object design pattern that composes objects into tree-like whole–part hierarchies. [Gamma, Helm, Johnson, & Vlissides]

- **decorator [pattern]** *n.* the structural object design pattern that dynamically attaches additional responsibilities to an object. [Gamma, Helm, Johnson, & Vlissides]
  Synonym: WRAPPER.

- **facade [pattern]** *n.* the structural object design pattern that provides a unified subsystem interface to a set of objects. [Gamma, Helm, Johnson, & Vlissides]

S

- flyweight [pattern] *n.* the structural object design pattern that allows a shared object (the flyweight) to be simultaneously used in multiple contexts. [Gamma, Helm, Johnson, & Vlissides]
- proxy [pattern] *n.* the structural object design pattern that provides control over an object via a surrogate or placeholder. [Gamma, Helm, Johnson, & Vlissides]
  Synonym: SURROGATE.

structure *n.* 1. (a) the physical representation of the properties of an object or class. [Booch, Firesmith] (b) the set of names of local slots in an instance. [CLOS] 2. any heterogeneous aggregate object that groups an arbitrary number of other objects, which may be instances of different types. [ODMG] 3. any expression of problem-domain complexity, pertinent to the system's responsibilities. [Coad]
Contrast with: BEHAVIOR, COLLECTION, PROPERTY.
Kinds:
- GENERALIZATION-SPECIALIZATION STRUCTURE
- WHOLE-PART STRUCTURE

- generalization–specialization (gen–spec) structure *n.* any structure produced by *is-a-kind-of* relationships between classes. [Coad]
  Contrast with: WHOLE-PART STRUCTURE.
  See also: INHERITANCE.
  Example: An example is the generalization *Vehicle* and the specialization *TruckVehicle*. A TruckVehicle is a kind of Vehicle.
  Commentary: A specialization class inherits the responsibilities of its generalization class(es).

- whole-part structure *n.* any structure produced by *has-a* relationships between wholes and their parts. [Coad].
  Contrast with: GEN-SPEC STRUCTURE.
  Example: An example is the whole *Vehicle* and the part *Engine*. A Truck has an Engine.

structure [class] *n.* any aggregate class of structure objects (i.e., aggregate objects, the component parts of which are interrelated). [Firesmith]
Antonym: COLLECTION CLASS, CONTAINER CLASS.
Commentary: A class of car engines.

structure [object] *n.* (a) any aggregate object, the component parts of which are interrelated. [Firesmith] (b) any instance of a structure class. [Firesmith]
Contrast with: COLLECTION OBJECT, CONTAINER OBJECT.
Commentary: A car engine.

structure [of a given class] *n.* the set of class properties of the given class. [Firesmith]

structure [of a given object] *n.* the set of properties of the given object. [Firesmith]

structure [of an instance] *n.* the set of names of local slots in that instance. [CLOS]
See also: INSTANCE, SLOT.

structured literal *n.* any literal that is either an immutable collection or an immutable structure. [ODMG]
Contrast with: ATOMIC LITERAL.

structurer [object] *n.* any object that maintains relationships between other objects. [Firesmith]

stub *n.* (a) any local operation that sends a message to a remote object that invokes its associated operation. [Firesmith] (b) any local procedure corresponding to a single operation which invokes that operation when called. [OMG]

subclass *n.* **1.** any class that is derived, either directly or indirectly, from the given class via inheritance. [Booch, CLOS, Firesmith, Jacobson, Smalltalk, Wirfs-Brock] **2.** (a) any specialization of a base class. [Lorenz, Rumbaugh] (b) any class that is a subtype of the given class. [Martin/Odell] **3.** any class that is a component part of the given aggregate class.

Synonym: **1** DERIVED CLASS, DESCENDANT CLASS. **3** COMPONENT CLASS.

Antonym: **1** ANCESTOR CLASS, BASE CLASS, SUPERCLASS. **3** CONTAINER CLASS.

Contrast with: SUBTYPE, SUPERCLASS.

Example: Car is a subclass of *Vehicle*. [Lorenz].

Rationale: Traditional term used by Smalltalk and CLOS.

Commentary: This term is potentially confusing and ambiguous because it could refer to either inheritance or aggregation. Similarly to substates and subsystems, the term *subclass* may be ambiguously misinterpreted to mean a component class rather than a *derived class*. On the other hand, the terms *descendent* or *derived class* are unambiguous. The term *descendant* is preferred. [Firesmith] Definition **1** is by far the most common definition. Definition **2** restricts inheritance to subtyping. Definition **3** is ambiguous, misleading, and should not be used because it confuses aggregation with inheritance. [Firesmith] *v.* **-ed, -ing** to derive a subclass from an existing class. [Firesmith]

Example: Car was subclassed from *Vehicle.*

Commentary: A subclass can add new features, modify inherited features, supply deferred features, or delete inherited features. [Smalltalk]

Kinds:
- DIRECT SUBCLASS
- INDIRECT SUBCLASS

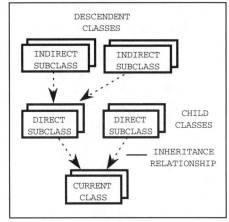

Subclasses

- **direct subclass [of a given class]** *n.* any subclass that directly inherits from the given superclass. [CLOS, Firesmith]

  Synonyms: CHILD CLASS, DIRECT-DERIVED CLASS, HEIR CLASS.

  Antonyms: DIRECT SUPERCLASS , INDIRECT SUBCLASS.

  Contrast with: ANCESTOR CLASS, INDIRECT BASE CLASS.

  Commentary: If class C_2 explicitly designates C_1 as a superclass in its definition, then C_2 is a *direct subclass* of C_1. [CLOS] A direct subclass is a descendant class that is also a child class. [Firesmith]

- **indirect subclass [of a given class]** *n.* any subclass that indirectly inherits from the given superclass via one or more intermediary superclasses. [Firesmith]

  Synonyms: DESCENDANT CLASS, INDI-

S

RECT SUBCLASS.

Contrast with: CHILD CLASS, DIRECT BASE CLASS, DIRECT SUBCLASS.

Commentary: An indirect subclass is a descendant class that is not a child class. [Firesmith]

subclassing *n.* **1.** the incremental definition of a new *class* (a.k.a. the *subclass*) in terms of one or more existing classes (a.k.a. *superclasses*), whereby the subclass inherits the features of the superclasses. [Firesmith] **2.** the incremental definition of a new *class* (a.k.a. the *subclass*) in terms of a single existing class (a.k.a. *superclass*), whereby the subclass inherits the features of the superclass. [Smalltalk]

Synonyms: 1 CLASS INHERITANCE 2 SINGLE INHERITANCE.

Commentary: Subclassing is strictly hierarchical; if any instances of a class are also instances of another class, than all instances of that class must also be instances of the other class. [Smalltalk]

subclassResponsibility *n.* any standard error message used to report to the user that a method specified in the superclass of the receiver should have been implemented in the receiver's class. [Smalltalk]

Contrast with: SHOULDNOTIMPLEMENT.

subcluster *n.* any cluster that is derived from the given cluster via cluster inheritance. [Firesmith]

subextent *n.* any subset of an extent, possibly based on a discriminator. [Firesmith]

subject *n.* any relatively arbitrary grouping of objects and classes used as a mechanism for guiding a reader (e.g., analyst, problem domain expert, manager, client) through a large, complex model. [Coad]

Contrast with: ASSEMBLY, CLUSTER, MOD-

ULE, SUBSYSTEM.

Rationale: Subjects are collections of objects and classes that form the current subject of discussion.

Commentary: Subjects are also helpful for organizing work packages on larger projects, based on initial OOA investigations. Subjects are not design entities such as clusters and subsystems. [Coad]

subject [of a given presentation] *n.* the model or view object(s) accessed by the given presentation. [Firesmith]

Contrast with: SUBJECT OF A VIEW.

subject [of a given view] *n.* the model object(s) accessed by the given view. [Firesmith]

Contrast with: SUBJECT OF A PRESENTATION.

subobject *n.* **1.** any part of an object representing the data members inherited from a base class. [C++] **2.** any complex object in an enclosing complex object. [Eiffel, Meyer]

Contrast with: **1** COMPLETE OBJECT **2** COMPOSITE OBJECT.

subpart class *n.* any object class whose instances are subparts. [Embley]

Synonym: COMPONENT CLASS.

Antonym: SUPERPART CLASS.

See also: SUBPART, IS-PART-OF RELATIONSHIP SET.

subpart [object] *n.* any object that is a component part of another (i.e., aggregate, superpart) object. [Embley]

Synonym: COMPONENT.

Antonyms: AGGREGATE, SUPERPART.

Contrast with: COMPONENT CLASS, SUBPART CLASS.

subprogram *n.* the basic program unit for expressing an algorithm. [Ada95]

Commentary: An Ada subprogram is known as an operation in other languages.

Kinds:
- ABSTRACT SUBPROGRAM
- FUNCTION
- PROCEDURE

- **abstract subprogram** *n.* any subprogram that has no body, but is intended to be overridden at some point when inherited. [Ada95]
  Synonyms: ABSTRACT METHOD, ABSTRACT OPERATION, DEFERRED OPERATION.
- **function** *n.* **1.** any sequential operation that returns a value. [Ada95, C++, Eiffel] **2.** any input/output mapping resulting from some object's behavior. [Booch]
  Antonym: PROCEDURE.
- **procedure** *n.* any operation that may perform multiple actions and modify the instance to which it is applied, but does not return a value. [Eiffel, Meyer]
  Antonym: FUNCTION.
  Contrast with: ROUTINE, SUBPROGRAM.
  Example: A procedure may read data, update variables, or produce some output. [Ada95]
  Commentary: A procedure may have parameters to provide a controlled means of passing information between the procedure and the point of call. [Ada95]

subscenario *n.* any scenario that is contained within an aggregate scenario as a component part. [Firesmith]
See also: AGGREGATE SCENARIO.

subschema *n.* any subset of the types in an objectbase schema. [Firesmith]
Contrast with: SCHEMA.

subsequent state *n.* any state that an object or class is in immediately following a specified transition. [Embley, Firesmith]

Antonyms: PRIOR STATE.

substate *n.* any specialized state that is part of a more generalized superstate. [Firesmith]
Antonym: SUPERSTATE.
Commentary: A substate may be defined in the same class as its superstate or may be later defined in a descendant of the class that defined the superstate. [Firesmith]

substitutability *n.* being able to substitute an object of some type *S* when an object of type *T* is expected, where *T* is a supertype of *S*, while guaranteeing that the substituted object will support the same operations as specified by the supertype *T.* [OMG]
Synonym: POLYMORPHIC SUBSTITUTABILITY.
Contrast with: POLYMORPHISM.

subsystem *n.* **1.** any cohesive system that is a major component part of a larger aggregate system. [Firesmith, Henderson-Sellers, Rumbaugh] **2.** (a) any encapsulation of classes and other subsystems that is not itself an object. The encapsulated classes and subsystems collaborate among themselves to fulfill a set of related responsibilities and support a set of system contracts. [Wirfs-Brock] (b) any large group of classes that work together to provide a related group of end-user functions. [Lorenz] (c) any object that encapsulates a set of related classes that fulfill a common overall purpose. [Martin] (d) any package of classes, associations, operations, events, and constraints that are interrelated and that have a reasonably well-defined and (one hopes) small interface with other subsystems. [Rumbaugh] **3.** any encapsulation of modules. [Booch] **4.** any functionally cohesive grouping

S

of objects and possibly other sub-systems that partition a system. [Jacobson] **5.** any part of a large domain in which clusters of interconnected objects remain intact. [Shlaer/Mellor]

Synonyms: ASSEMBLY, CLUSTER, ENSEMBLE, KIT.

Commentary: Subsystems should be highly cohesive and loosely coupled to other subsystems. [Firesmith, Jacobson] Definition **1** is probably preferable to definitions **2** and **3** because systems have historically contained hardware, wetware (a.k.a. personnel), and paperware (a.k.a. documentation) in addition to software. One may use the term *cluster* if either definition **2** or **3** is intended.

Kinds:
- LAYER
- PARTITION
- SERVICE PACKAGE

- **layer** *n.* **1.** any logically-related, collection of clusters or cluster instances at the same level of abstraction. [Firesmith, Henderson-Sellers] **2.** any collection of class categories or subsystems at the same level of abstraction. [Booch] **3.** any subsystem that provides multiple services, all of which are at the same level of abstraction, built on subsystems at a lower level of abstraction. [Rumbaugh]

Contrast with: PARTITION.

Examples: The user-interface layer, application-domain layer, database-independence layer, processor-communication layer, and environment-independence layer are all layers.

- **partition** *n.* **1.** the set of derived classes formed by a discriminator. [McGregor] **2.** any vertical slice of the overall architecture consisting of objects and classes that typically provide some specified functionality. **3.** one or more logically-related clusters, class categories, or subsystems that form a part of a given level of abstraction. [Booch, Firesmith, Rumbaugh]

Contrast with: DISCRIMINATOR, LAYER.

Example: **1** The derived classes of cars based on engine type is an example of a partition.

- **service package** *n.* the lowest-level subsystem. It is viewed as an atomic unit of change that packages services for the customer. [Jacobson]

See also: PUBLIC BLOCK, SUBSYSTEM.

Commentary: For example, service packages are atomic subsystems used in discussions with customer and product planning. [Jacobson]

subsystem access model (SAM) *n.* any object access model for one of the subsystems in the domain. [Shlaer/Mellor]

subsystem card *n.* any index card that is used to informally document information about a subsystem. [Wirfs-Brock]

Contrast with: CLASS CARD, CONTRACT CARD, SUBSYSTEM SPECIFICATION.

Commentary: Subsystem cards are based on the Class-Responsibility-Collaboration (CRC) cards. [Wirfs-Brock]

subsystem communication model (SCM) *n.* any object communications model for a particular subsystem. [Shlaer/Mellor]

subsystem notebook *n.* any notebook created for each subsystem or small domain that contains the work products of OOA, packaged more or less "down the column" of the project matrix. [Shlaer/Mellor]

subsystem relationship model (SRM) *n.* the entire information model for a subsystem. [Shlaer/Mellor]

subsystem responsibility specification
n. the MOSES documentation of sub-system responsibilities. [Henderson-Sellers]

subsystem specification *n.* any specification formally documenting a subsystem. [Wirfs-Brock]
Contrast with: CLASS SPECIFICATION, CONTRACT SPECIFICATION, SUBSYSTEM CARD.

subsystem testing *n.* the integration testing of a subsystem of classes.
Synonym: CLUSTER TESTING.
Contrast with: SYSTEM TESTING, UNIT TESTING.

subtype [of a given type] *n.* any more specialized type that inherits from the given type and conforms to the protocol of its supertypes (i.e., correctly responds to the same messages as the supertypes). [Firesmith, Jacobson, Martin/Odell]
Synonym: DERIVED TYPE.
Antonym: SUPERTYPE.
Contrast with: BEHAVIORALLY COMPATIBLE DESCENDANT.
Commentary: A subtype may add additional properties and operations to introduce behavior or state unique to its instances. It may also *refine* the properties and operations it inherits to specialize them to the behavior and range of state values appropriate for its instances. [Firesmith]
Kinds:
- ACTUAL SUBTYPE
- CONSTRAINED SUBTYPE
- DEFINITE SUBTYPE
- EVENT SUBTYPE
- INDEFINITE SUBTYPE
- NOMINAL SUBTYPE
- OPERATION SUBTYPE
- UNCONSTRAINED SUBTYPE

- **actual subtype [of an object]** *n.* the subtype of which the object is declared. [Ada95]
  Contrast with: NOMINAL SUBTYPE.
- **constrained subtype** *n.* any subtype whose type has neither unknown discriminants nor allows range, index, or discriminant constraints. [Ada95]
  Antonym: UNCONSTRAINED TYPE.
  Rationale: The subtype is called a *constrained* subtype because it has no unconstrained characteristics. [Ada95]
- **definite subtype** *n.* any subtype that is not indefinite. [Ada95]
  Antonym: INDEFINITE SUBTYPE.
  Commentary: All elementary subtypes are definite subtypes. [Ada95]
- **event subtype** *n.* any subtype of events that inherit trigger rules and control conditions from event supertypes. [Martin]
- **indefinite subtype** *n.* any subtype that does not by itself provide enough information to create an object without an additional constraint or explicit initial expression. [Ada95]
  Antonym: DEFINITE SUBTYPE.
  Examples: An unconstrained array subtype is an indefinite subtype, as is a subtype with unknown discriminants or unconstrained discriminants without default. [Ada95]
  Commentary: The object's *actual subtype* can be more restrictive than the nominal subtype of the view; it always is if the nominal subtype is an *indefinite subtype.* [Ada95]
- **nominal subtype** *n.* the subtype that is associated with the view when a view of an object is defined. [Ada95]
  Contrast with: ACTUAL SUBTYPE.
- **operation subtype** *n.* any specialized

S

type of operation derived from some parent type of operation. [Martin]

- **unconstrained subtype** *n.* any subtype with constrained characteristics (i.e., the subtype does not impose a constraint although its type has unknown discriminants or its type allows range, index, or discriminant constraints). [Ada95]
  Antonym: CONSTRAINED SUBTYPE.

subtype object *n.* any object representing a subtype. [Shlaer/Mellor]
Synonym: CHILD CLASS.

subtyping *n.* **1.** the incremental definition of a new *type* (a.k.a. the *subtype*) in terms of one or more existing types (a.k.a. *supertypes*), whereby the subtype conforms to all of its supertypes. [Firesmith] **2.** the relationship between types based on interface conformance. It defines the rules by which objects of one type are determined to be acceptable in contexts expecting another type. [OMG]
Synonym: TYPE INHERITANCE.
Commentary: Subtyping defines the rules by which objects of one type are determined to be acceptable in contexts expecting another type. [Firesmith]

subview *n.* any view contained as a subpart of another view. [Firesmith, Smalltalk]
Contrast with: ACTIVE VIEW, BROWSER, COLLAPSED VIEW, STANDARD-SYSTEM VIEW.

suffered operation *n.* any operation that is exported by the public interface of the current object. [Berard]
Antonym: REQUIRED OPERATION.

super *n.* the standard Smalltalk pseudo-variable that refers to the parent of the receiver of the message. When a message is sent to super, the search for the method begins in the superclass of the class containing the method instead of

beginning in the receiver's class. [Firesmith, Smalltalk]
Contrast with: SELF.
Commentary: Responses to messages to super are found by starting the method search in the superclass of the method in which super appears, continuing up the superclass chain, and terminating at class Object. The use of the term *super* allows a method to access methods defined in a superclass even if the methods have been overridden in subclasses. C++ uses the "::" scope resolution operator to accomplish approximately the same thing. [Firesmith, Smalltalk]

superclass [of a given class] *n.* **1.** any class from which the given class is derived, either directly or indirectly, via inheritance. [Booch, CLOS, Firesmith, Jacobson, Smalltalk, Wirfs-Brock] **2.** (a) any generalization from which features are inherited. [Lorenz, Rumbaugh] (b) any class that is a supertype of the given class. [Martin/Odell]
Synonyms: ANCESTOR, BASE CLASS.
Antonyms: DESCENDANT, DERIVED CLASS, SUBCLASS.
Kinds:
- DIRECT SUPERCLASS
- INDIRECT SUPERCLASS

- **direct superclass [of a given class]** *n.* any superclass from which a given derived class directly inherits. [CLOS, Firesmith]
  Synonyms: DIRECT BASE CLASS, PARENT CLASS.
  Antonym: INDIRECT SUPERCLASS.
  Contrast with: ANCESTOR, INDIRECT DERIVED CLASS.
  Commentary: If class C_2 explicitly designates C_1 as a superclass in its definition, then C_1 is a *direct super-*

class of C_2. [CLOS] A direct superclass is an ancestor class that is also a parent class. [Firesmith]

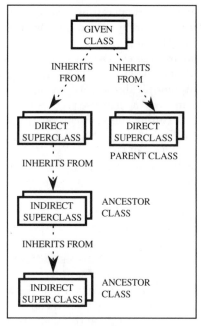

Superclass

• **indirect superclass [of a given class]** *n.* any superclass from which a given subclass indirectly inherits via intermediate superclasses. [Firesmith]
Synonyms: ANCESTOR CLASS, INDIRECT BASE CLASS.
Contrast with: DIRECT BASE CLASS, DIRECT SUPERCLASS, INDIRECT DERIVED CLASS.
Commentary: An indirect superclass is an ancestor class that is not a parent class. [Firesmith]
superpart class *n.* any object class whose instances are superparts. [Embley]
Synonym: AGGREGATE CLASS.
Antonym: SUBPART CLASS.

See also: SUPERPART, IS-PART-OF RELATIONSHIP SET.
superpart [object] *n.* any object that contains one or more other objects as component parts. [Embley]
Synonym: AGGREGATE
Antonym: COMPONENT, SUBPART.
Contrast with: SUPERPART CLASS.
superstate *n.* any generalized state that is decomposed into one or more specialized substates. [Firesmith]
Antonym: SUBSTATE.
Contrast with: AGGREGATE STATE.
supertype [of a given type] *n.* (a) any more general type from which the given type inherits and to which the given type's protocol conforms. [Firesmith] (b) any generalized type whose properties are more general than its subtypes. [Martin/Odell]
Synonym: ANCESTOR, BASE TYPE.
Antonym: SUBTYPE.
Commentary: All of the instances of the given type are also instances of the super types. [Firesmith]
• **event supertype** *n.* any supertype of events from which event subtypes can inherit trigger rules and control conditions. [Martin]
Antonym: EVENT SUBTYPE.
supertype object *n.* any object representing a supertype. [Shlaer/Mellor]
Synonym: PARENT CLASS.
supplier *n.* **1.** an object role that produces event data. [OMG] **2.** a synonym for SERVER. [Rumbaugh]
Contrast with: CLIENT, CONSUMER.
supplier class [of a given class] *n.* the class of which the given class is a client. [Eiffel, Meyer]
Contrast with: CLIENT.
supplier type [of a given type] *n.* the type of which the given type is a client.

S

[Eiffel, Meyer]
Contrast with: CLIENT.

support class *n.* (a) any class of support objects. [Firesmith] (b) any class that is not application-specific, but instead is used to support those classes that are. [Firesmith, Lorenz]
Synonyms: BASE CLASS, PERIPHERAL CLASS.
Antonym: DOMAIN CLASS.
Contrast with: APPLICATION CLASS, BUSINESS CLASS, CORE CLASS, KEY CLASS, MODEL CLASS.

support object *n.* any application domain-independent object that provides (1) a low-level utility or (2) application independence of the environment, database(s), or user-interface. [Firesmith]
Antonym: DOMAIN OBJECT.

- **utility object** *n.* any support object that provides a low-level utility such as a queue, linked-list, set, stack, transporter, relay, etc.

swizzle *v.* **-ed, -ing** to reformat an object reference when moving between address spaces. [Firesmith]
Commentary: Swizzling often occurs when an object is moved from main memory into a database. [Firesmith]

symmetric constraint *n.* the structural constraint on a given relationship *R* which requires that if *A* is related by *R* to *B*, then *B* is also related by *R* to *A*. [Firesmith]
Antonym: ASYMMETRIC CONSTRAINT.
Example: The *is-spouse-of* link and association are symmetric. The existence of an *is-spouse-of* link from *A* to *B* implies the existence of an *is-spouse-of* link from *B* to *A*. [Firesmith]

synchronization *n.* **1.** the interaction of two threads of control whereby the first thread ready to synchronize is blocked until the second thread is ready. [Firesmith] **2.** the concurrency semantics of an operation. [Booch]
Examples: **2** ASYNCHRONOUS, BALKING, SIMPLE, SYNCHRONOUS, TIMEOUT.

synchronizer operation *n.* any operation that synchronizes two threads of control. [Firesmith]

synchronous class *n.* any class whose semantics are guaranteed in the presence of multiple threads of control, but instances of the class itself are responsible for assuring mutual exclusion. [Booch]
Contrast with: GUARDED CLASS, SEQUENTIAL CLASS.

synchronous interaction *n.* any interaction used to synchronize interacting objects. [Embley]
Synonym: SYNCHRONOUS MESSAGE, SYNCHRONOUS REQUEST.
Antonym: ASYNCHRONOUS INTERACTION, ASYNCHRONOUS MESSAGE, ASYNCHRONOUS REQUEST, SIGNAL.
Commentary: Usually, the sender and receiver understand that certain conditions must be met so that communication can take place, and they see to it that these conditions are met. [Embley]

synchronous message *n.* any message that synchronizes two threads of control, thereby potentially blocking either the sender or the receiver until both are ready to communicate. [Booch, Firesmith]
Synonyms: SYNCHRONOUS INTERACTION, SYNCHRONOUS REQUEST.
Antonyms: ASYNCHRONOUS INTERACTION, ASYNCHRONOUS MESSAGE, ASYNCHRONOUS REQUEST.
Contrast with: SEQUENTIAL MESSAGE.
Kinds:
- BALKING MESSAGE
- GUARDED MESSAGE
- TIMED MESSAGE

- **balking message** *n.* any synchronous message that can be passed only if the receiver is immediately ready to accept the message. [Firesmith]
- **guarded message** *n.* any synchronous message that requires a guard condition to evaluate to true for the message to be passed. [Firesmith]
- **timed message** *n.* any synchronous message that allows a caller to pass a message, while waiting at most a limited amount of time. [Firesmith]

synchronous request *n.* any request in which the client object pauses to wait for completion of the request. [OMG]
Synonyms: SYNCHRONOUS INTERACTION, SYNCHRONOUS MESSAGE.
Antonyms: ASYNCHRONOUS INTERACTION, ASYNCHRONOUS MESSAGE, ASYNCHRONOUS REQUEST.
Contrast with: DEFERRED SYNCHRONOUS REQUEST, ONE-WAY REQUEST.

system *n.* **1.** any application consisting of software, hardware, documentation (a.k.a. paperware), and roles played by people (a.k.a. wetware). [Firesmith, Jacobson] **2.** (a) the assembly of one or more classes to produce an executable unit. [Eiffel, Meyer] (b) a group of interacting objects. [Embley]
Contrast with: 1 ASSEMBLY, SUBSYSTEM, 2 CLUSTER, UNIVERSE.

system architecture *n.* the architecture of a system in terms of its major sequential components that communicate via data flows and events. [Coleman]

system border *n.* any column in an interaction diagram that represents the interface with everything outside the blocks in the diagram, such as external actors, and consequentially it can correspond to different interfaces outside the system. [Jacobson]

See also: BLOCK, INTERACTION DIAGRAM, SYSTEM.

system browser *n.* any interactive view used to create, present, and edit the class descriptions in the system. [Smalltalk]
Contrast with: IMPLEMENTATION DESCRIPTION, PROTOCOL DESCRIPTION.

system classes *n.* any set of classes that comes with the Smalltalk system and that provides the standard functionality of a programming language and environment: arithmetic, data structures, control structures, and input/output facilities. [Smalltalk]
Examples: Classes that provide arithmetic, data structures, control structures, and input/output facilities are examples of system classes. [Smalltalk]

system diagram (SD) *n.* any configuration diagram documenting the static architecture of a system in terms of its component subsystems and the dependency relationships between them. [Firesmith]
Antonym: ASSEMBLY DIAGRAM.

system-interaction (SI) component *n.* the component which contains system interaction objects that provide an interface between problem domain objects and other systems or devices. [Coad]
Commentary: A system-interaction object encapsulates communication protocol, keeping its companion problem domain object free of such low-level, implementation-specific detail. [Coad]

system interface *n.* **1.** the interface of any system, declaring its visible objects, classes, and subsystems. [Firesmith] **2.** the set of system operations to which a system can respond and the set of events that it can output. [Coleman]
Contrast with: CLASS INTERFACE, CLUSTER INTERFACE, CONSTRUCTION INTER-

S

FACE, FUNCTIONAL INTERFACE, MESSAGE INTERFACE, OBJECT INTERFACE, OPERATION INTERFACE, ORB INTERFACE, PRINCIPAL INTERFACE, TYPE INTERFACE.

system-level validity *n.* the system-level counterpart to class-level validity, but applied to all possible dynamic types of the target. [Eiffel, Meyer]

Contrast with: CLASS-LEVEL VALIDITY.

system management facilities *n.* any horizontal CORBA facilities that provide a set of interfaces that abstract basic system administration functions (e.g., control, monitoring, security management, configuration, and policy. [OMG]

system object model *n.* the subset of the Fusion object model that determines the structure of the state of the system being built. [Coleman]

system operation *n.* any input event invoked by agents in the environment and its effect on a system. [Coleman]

system-valid call *n.* any call that satisfies the system-level validity requirement. [Eiffel, Meyer]

Contrast with: CLASS-VALID CALL.

system workspace *n.* any special workspace containing message expressions or templates for expressions that are useful for such operating system activities as opening and editing files, resetting display screen size, and accessing the references to any system changes. [Smalltalk]

Commentary: The system workspace can be used to edit and evaluate these expressions, notably expressions about accessing files, querying the system, and recovering from a crash. [Smalltalk]

T

t *n.* the CLOS superclass of every class except itself. [CLOS]
Synonyms: OBJECT [Smalltalk]

t [class] *n.* the CLOS superclass of every class except itself. [CLOS]
Synonyms: OBJECT. [Smalltalk]

tag *n.* any type descriptor ranging over the types that are members of the class. [Ada95]

tag indeterminate *adj.* describing a name or expression of tagged type whose tag is determined from context. [Ada95]
See also: TAGGED.

tagged *adj.* describing a name or expression of a tagged type when used as a controlling operand. [Ada95]
See also: DISPATCHING.
Kinds:
- DYNAMICALLY TAGGED
- STATICALLY TAGGED
- TAG INDETERMINATE

- **dynamically tagged** *adj.* describing a name or expression of tagged type, the tag of which is determined dynamically at run-time. [Ada95]
Antonym: STATICALLY TAGGED.

- **statically tagged** *adj.* describing a name or expression of tagged type whose tag is determined statically by the operand's specific type. [Ada95]
Antonym: DYNAMICALLY TAGGED.

- **tag indeterminate** *adj.* describing a name or expression of tagged type whose tag is determined from context. [Ada95]
See also: TAGGED.

tagged type *n.* any type of objects that have an associated run-time type tag, which indicates the specific tagged type with which the object was originally created. [Ada95]
Rationale: An operand of a class-wide tagged type can be used in a dispatching call; the tag indicates which subprogram body to invoke. [Ada95]
Commentary: Tagged types and type extensions support object-oriented programming, based on inheritance with extension and run-time polymorphism via *dispatching operations*. A record type or private type has the reserved word *tagged* in its declaration. [Ada95]
See also: DISPATCHING, TAG, TYPE EXTENSION.

tangible *adj.* modeling an application domain (system) object that can be touched (e.g., a hardware sensor).
Antonym: INTANGIBLE.

T

tangible object *n.* (a) any object that models something tangible in the real world. [Firesmith] (b) any abstraction of the actual existence of some thing in the physical world. [Shlaer/Mellor]
Examples: Pipes, pumps, valves, and tanks in a chemical plant are each tangible objects. [Firesmith]

task *n.* **1.** any single thread of execution. [Firesmith] **2.** any program that executes as if it were running at the same time as other programs. [Coad]
Synonym: PROCESS.
See also: TASK-MANAGEMENT COMPONENT.
Commentary: Tasks can be bigger than objects (e.g., multiple sequential objects assigned to a single process), the same size as an object (e.g., an actor object has its own single thread), or smaller than an object (e.g., a concurrent object may encapsulate multiple concurrent operations). The concurrent execution of a number of tasks is referred to as multitasking. [Firesmith]

task-management (TM) component *n.* any component containing objects responsible for handling multitasking and related issues. [Coad]

task type *n.* any composite type whose values are tasks, which are active entities that may execute concurrently with other tasks. [Ada95]
See also: TASK.
Example: The top-level task of a partition is called the environment task. [Ada95]

task [unit] *n.* any program unit for defining tasks whose sequence of actions may be executed concurrently with those of other tasks. [Ada95]
See also: TASK TYPE.
Commentary: The execution of an Ada program consists of the execution of one or more *tasks*. Each task represents a separate thread of control that proceeds independently and concurrently between the points where it interacts with other tasks. [Ada95]

template *n.* the C++ term for any parameterized metaclass or any parameterized function. [C++, Firesmith]
Synonyms: GENERIC, GENERIC CLASS, GENERIC OPERATION, PARAMETERIZED CLASS, PARAMETERIZED OPERATION.
Commentary: A class template specifies how a family of individual classes can be constructed much as a class declaration specifies how individual objects can be constructed. [C++]

template class *n.* the C++ term for a generic class. [C++]
Synonyms: GENERIC, GENERIC CLASS, PARAMETERIZED CLASS.
Commentary: A class template specifies how individual classes can be constructed much as a class declaration specifies how individual objects can be constructed. [C++]

template method *n.* any method that provides step-by-step algorithms. [Wirfs-Brock]
Commentary: The steps of the algorithm may be abstract methods that the subclass must define, base methods, other template methods, or some combination of these. [Wirfs-Brock]

temporary attribute *n.* any attribute that is local to a specific operation. [Jacobson]
Synonym: OPERATION ATTRIBUTE
Contrast with: TEMPORARY VARIABLE. [Smalltalk]

temporary variable *n.* any private variable created for a specific activity and available only for the duration of that activity. [Smalltalk]

Contrast with: TEMPORARY ATTRIBUTE.
[Jacobson]
Commentary: Temporary variables do
not include pseudovariables such as argument names and self.

terminate condition *n.* any condition that
identifies the circumstances on which a
method stops execution. [Coad, Fire-
smith]
See also: SERVICE SPECIFICATION.
Commentary: When applicable, a terminate condition is specified in a service specification. [Coad]

terminator *n.* anything external that di-
rectly or indirectly interfaces with the
current application, system, or cluster.
[Firesmith]
Contrast with: ACTOR, AUDIENCE, CLI-
ENT.

ternary association *n.* any association
among three classes. [Firesmith, Rum-
baugh]
Contrast with: BINARY ASSOCIATION.

ternary link *n.* any link among three objects. [Firesmith]
Contrast with: BINARY LINK.

ternary relationship *n.* any relationship
among three things. [Firesmith, Rum-
baugh]
Kinds:
  • TERNARY ASSOCIATION
  • TERNARY LINK

  • **ternary association** *n.* any association among three classes. [Firesmith,
  Rumbaugh]
  Contrast with: BINARY ASSOCIATION.
  • **ternary link** *n.* any link among three
  objects. [Firesmith]
  Contrast with: BINARY LINK.

test *n.* any process that tests a condition
and makes one of several conditional
control outputs. [Shlaer/Mellor]

testability *n.* the degree and ease with

which the software can be tested for
correctness, reliability, and robustness.
[Firesmith]

test case *n.* **1.** (a) any sequence of one or
more test messages as well as the expected responses. [Firesmith] (b) any series
of messages to send, along with their expected results. [Lorenz] **2.** (a) any single
scenario that is executed to find errors as
well as the expected responses. [Fire-
smith] (b) any possible instantiation of a
use case used to test the functionality of
a system. [Jacobson]
Contrast with: TEST MESSAGE, TEST SUITE.
Commentary: Test cases find errors by
allowing testers to compare the actual
behavior against the expected behavior.
[Firesmith]

test message *n.* any message including
associated parameters that is sent to
find errors. [Firesmith]
Contrast with: TEST CASE, TEST SUITE.

test suite *n.* any series of one or more
test cases. [Firesmith]
Contrast with: TEST CASE, TEST MESSAGE.

this *n.* the C++ default name of the target
object of a member function in C++.
[C++, Firesmith, Rumbaugh]
Contrast with: CURRENT, SELF.

thread of control *n.* **1.** any single process. [Booch] **2.** any logical or physical
thread (i.e., logically continuous sequence) of execution consisting primarily of operation executions linked via
messages. [Firesmith] **3.** any single path
of execution through a program, a dynamic model, or some other representation of control flow. [Rumbaugh] **4.**
the line of independent dynamic action
within an application. [OADSIG] **5.**
any sequence of actions and events that
occurs in response to the arrival of a particular unsolicited event when the system

T

is in a particular state. [Shlaer/Mellor]

Synonym: PROCESS, THREAD OF EXECU-TION.

Contrast with: CONCURRENCY, TASK.

Commentary: A given application may simultaneously support many different threads of control, which dynamically come into existence and cease to exist. [OADSIG] A thread forms a path of execution through a program. A typical thread involves multiple objects and classes, and a single object or class is typically involved in multiple threads. A given application may simultaneously support many different threads of control, which dynamically come into existence and cease to exist. [Firesmith]

thread-of-control chart *n.* any graphical representation of the succession of events and states occupied by instances that participate in a particular thread of control. [Shlaer/Mellor]

throw [an exception] *v. threw, throwing* to identify an exception, abandon local execution, and transfer execution to a local exception handler (if any) or else transfer execution to the calling operation. [Firesmith]

Synonym: RAISE AN EXCEPTION.

Contrast with: CATCH AN EXCEPTION, HANDLE AN EXCEPTION.

Rationale: The term used by C++.

Commentary: The original Ada and Eiffel term *raise an exception* is preferred. [Firesmith]

thrown away *adj.* describing classes and methods that are created and deleted during a single application development (i.e., never shipped or kept in the company's class library) [Lorenz]

timed message *n.* any synchronous message that allows a caller to pass a message, while waiting at most a limited

amount of time. [Firesmith]

Synonym: TIME-OUT MESSAGE.

Contrast with: ASYNCHRONOUS MES-SAGE, BALKING MESSAGE, SEQUENTIAL MESSAGE, SYNCHRONOUS MESSAGE.

timeline diagram *n.* any diagram documenting a scenario in terms of the temporal ordering of system operations and the events that flow to agents. [Coleman]

time-out message *n.* any synchronous message that allows a caller to pass a message, while waiting at most a limited amount of time. [Booch]

Synonym: TIMED MESSAGE.

Contrast with: ASYNCHRONOUS MES-SAGE, BALKING MESSAGE, SEQUENTIAL MESSAGE, SYNCHRONOUS MESSAGE.

timer *n.* any mechanism that can be used by an action to generate an event at some time in the future. [Shlaer/Mellor]

timing diagram (TD) *n.* any diagram documenting the temporal aspects of a scenario or thread of control in terms of the associated objects, classes, and possibly their operations and the sequencing of their behavior in terms of interactions and the execution of operations. [Booch, Firesmith]

Synonym: SCENARIO DIAGRAM.

Commentary: One should use the term *timing diagram* rather than the term *interaction diagram*, because of its emphasis on the timing involved and the fact that the term *interaction diagram* has historically been used by Colbert, Booch, and Firesmith to summarize the possible interactions prior to Jacobson's use of the term *interaction diagram* for this purpose. [Firesmith]

Kinds:

- BLACKBOX TIMING DIAGRAM
- WHITEBOX TIMING DIAGRAM

● **blackbox timing diagram (BTD)** *n.*

any timing diagram that documents the absolute or relative timing of interactions (e.g., messages, exception flows) between black-box objects and classes. [Firesmith]
Antonym: WHITEBOX TIMING DIAGRAM.

- **whitebox timing diagram (WTD)** *n.* any timing diagram that documents the duration of operation execution and the transfer of control (message or call). [Firesmith]
Antonym: BLACKBOX TIMING DIAGRAM.

timing probe *n.* the icon used on dynamic diagrams that is used to represent timing requirements and design decisions. [Firesmith]
Commentary: When connected to one or two interaction arcs, timing probes can be used to represent such information as frequency (one connection) and time differences (two connections), units of time, and deadline type (e.g., hard, soft). [Firesmith]

traceability *n.* **1.** the ability to trace requirements to object-oriented building blocks throughout analysis, design, coding, integration, and testing. [Firesmith] **2.** the ability to trace objects from analysis models to objects in design models. [Jacobson]
Commentary: Traceability is improved due to the seamless nature of model transformations in object-oriented development. [Firesmith, Jacobson] Traceability is used to ensure that all requirements are met and that unnecessary features have not been added. [Firesmith] Traceability is invaluable to the engineers who work on the maintenance and development of the system as it evolves. [Jacobson]

transaction *n.* any unit of atomicity,

consistency, and integrity into which programs that use persistent data are organized. [Firesmith, ODMG]
Commentary: A term *transaction* can be used at the method, operation, or scenario level.

transaction object *n.* any object that models a transaction (i.e., a recording or logging of any event of significance). A "transaction object" knows about a significant event, knows who the players are in that event, and calculates things pertaining to that event. [Coad]
See also: TRANSACTION PATTERN.

transaction pattern *n.* any pattern that either has a transaction player or has players that commonly play with a transaction player. [Coad]
See also: TRANSACTION OBJECT.

transformation *n.* any process whose purpose is one of computation or transformation of data: the process exists to convert its input data into a new form that is then output. [Shlaer/Mellor]

transient class *n.* any class, all instances of which are transient objects that do not exist except during the execution of the program, process, or thread in which it was created. [Firesmith]
Contrast with: PERSISTENT-CAPABLE CLASS, PERSISTENT CLASS.
Kinds:
- DYNAMIC CLASS
- STATIC CLASS

- **dynamic class** *n.* any class, all instances of which are dynamic objects that are instantiated and destroyed at run-time. [Firesmith]
Antonym: STATIC CLASS.
Commentary: A dynamic object has its memory allocated (e.g., from the heap) and deallocated during program execution. Dynamic objects are usual-

T

ly referenced via pointers. [Firesmith]

- **static class** *n.* any class, all instances of which are dynamic objects that are instantiated and whose memory are allocated at compile time and remains allocated until the program terminates. [Firesmith]

  Antonym: DYNAMIC CLASS.

  Commentary: A static object lasts for the duration of program execution, but not after a program ceases to execute. [Firesmith]

transient object *n.* any object that does not exist except during the execution of the process or thread in which it was created. [Firesmith, Martin/Odell, OMG]

Contrast with: PERSISTENT OBJECT.

Kinds:
- DYNAMIC OBJECT
- STATIC OBJECT

- **dynamic object** *n.* any object that is instantiated and destroyed at runtime. [Firesmith]

  Antonym: STATIC OBJECT.

  Commentary: A dynamic object has its memory allocated (e.g., from the heap) and deallocated during program execution. Dynamic objects are usually referenced via pointers. [Firesmith]

- **static object** *n.* any object that is instantiated and whose memory is allocated at compile time and remains allocated until the program terminates. [Firesmith]

  Antonym: DYNAMIC OBJECT.

  Commentary: A static object lasts for the duration of program execution, but not after a program ceases to execute. [Firesmith]

[state] transition *n.* **1.** any change of state. [Booch, Embley, Firesmith, Rumbaugh] **2.** any rule that specifies

what new state is achieved when an instance in a given state receives a particular event. [Shlaer/Mellor]

Synonym: 2 TRANSITION RULE.

See also: ENTRY OPERATION, EXIT OPERAITON, GUARD CONDITION.

Commentary: A transition fires (i.e., an object or class transitions to a new state) when its state attribute values, state links, or state component objects change, producing a new set of overall behaviors. [Firesmith]

Kinds:
- AUTOMATIC TRANSITION
- ENABLED TRANSITION
- FINAL TRANSITION
- GROUP TRANSITION
  - GROUP-EXTERNAL TRANSITION
  - GROUP-INTERNAL TRANSITION
- GUARDED TRANSITION
- HIGH-LEVEL TRANSITION
- INITIAL TRANSITION
- NONSPONTANEOUS TRANSITION
- SPONTANEOUS TRANSITION
- SYNCHRONIZING TRANSITION
  - REMAIN TRANSISTION
- UNGUARDED TRANSITION.

- **automatic transition** *n.* **1.** any state transition that fires without being triggered by an incoming message. [Firesmith] **2.** an unlabeled transition that automatically fires when the activity associated with the source state is completed. [Rumbaugh]

  Synonym: 1 SPONTANEOUS TRANSITION.

  Examples: An automatic transition may result from the execution of a concurrent modifier operation, the completion of an operation associated with the source state, or result from an interrupt raised by a terminator. [Firesmith]

- **enabled transition** *n.* any transition from a current state. [Embley, Firesmith]
Commentary: Triggers cannot cause transitions to fire unless the transitions are enabled. [Embley, Firesmith]
- **final transition** *n.* any transition with no subsequent states. [Embley]
Antonym: INITIAL TRANSITION.
- **group transition** *n.* any transition involving an aggregate state where substates are treated in some sense equally because they are specializations of the more general superstate. [Firesmith]
Kinds:
  - GROUP-EXTERNAL TRANSITION
  - GROUP-INTERNAL TRANSITION
- **group-external transition** *n.* any group transition from an aggregate superstate that fires regardless of the current substate. [Firesmith]
Antonym: GROUP-INTERNAL TRANSITION.
- **group-internal transition** *n.* any group transition to an aggregate superstate that is forwarded to a specific substate. [Firesmith]
Antonym: GROUP-EXTERNAL TRANSITION.
- **guarded transition** *n.* any transition that occurs only if the trigger fires while its associated guard condition evaluates to true (or to the enumeration value associated with the transition). [Firesmith, Rumbaugh]
Antonym: UNGUARDED TRANSITION.
- **high-level transition** *n.* any transition that groups and subsumes lower-level transitions, states, constraints, and notes. [Embley]
- **initial transition** *n.* any state transition that has no prior state and that is always enabled. [Embley]
Antonym: FINAL TRANSITION.
Contrast with: BEGIN STATE, INITIAL STATE, START STATE.
Commentary: Every complete state net must have an initial transition, which fires whenever its trigger is satisfied. [Embley]
- **nonspontaneous transition** *n.* any transition that requires an incoming message, and most often results from the execution of a sequential modifier operation. [Firesmith]
Antonyms: AUTOMATIC TRANSITION SPONTANEOUS TRANSITION.
- **spontaneous transition** *n.* any transition that fires without being triggered by an incoming message. [Firesmith]
Synonym: AUTOMATIC TRANSITION.
Antonym: NONSPONTANEOUS TRANSITION.
Examples: A spontaneous transition may result from the execution of a concurrent modifier operation, the completion of an operation associated with the source state, or result from an interrupt raised by a terminator. [Firesmith]
- **synchronizing transition** *n.* any transition that synchronizes two or more concurrent states. [Firesmith]
Antonym: GUARDED TRANSITION.
Examples: Two concurrent states could simultaneously transition into a single state, or conversely a single state could simultaneously transition into two concurrent states. [Firesmith]
- **remain transition** *n.* any synchronizing transition to a new state that also allows the object or class to simultaneously remaining in the original state. [Firesmith]

• **unguarded transition** *n.* any transition that does not have an associated guard condition. [Firesmith]
Antonym: GUARDED TRANSITION.

transition priority *n.* any priority assigned to transitions for a given state. [Embley, Firesmith]
See also: TRANSITION.

transition rule *n.* any rule that specifies what new state is achieved when an instance in a given state receives a particular event. [Shlaer/Mellor]
Synonym: TRANSITION.

transitive constraint *n.* the structural constraint on a given relationship R that requires if A is related by R to B and B is related by R to C, then A is also related by R to C. [Firesmith]
Antonym: NONTRANSITIVE CONSTRAINT.
Example: The *is-greater-than* link and association are transitive. [Firesmith]

transitive persistence *n.* any persistence whereby a transient object that participates in a relationship with a persistent object becomes persistent when a transaction commit occurs. [Firesmith]

trigger *n.* **1.** (a) the direct cause of one or more associated state transitions. [Firesmith] (b) any Boolean expression concerning expected events or conditions that activates a state transition on evaluating true. [Embley] **2.** the state transition that activates a service. [Coad] **3.** any operation that executes in a database when certain conditions occur.
Contrast with: FIRE, TRANSITION.
Example: An operation that changes a state property is a trigger if the new state property value represents a new state.
Kinds:
 • COMPOUND TRIGGER
 • CONDITION-BASED TRIGGER
 • EXCEPTIONAL TRIGGER

 • NORMAL TRIGGER
• **compound trigger** *n.* any conditions included in Boolean expressions with event monitors. [Embley]
• **condition-based trigger** *n.* any trigger that causes an enabled transition to fire when their logical statement is true. [Embley]
See also: CONDITION.
Commentary: The distinction between events and conditions is that an event triggers an enabled transition only at the instant the event occurs, whereas a condition triggers an enabled transition during the entire time the condition holds. [Embley]
• **exceptional trigger** *n.* any trigger that occurs during the abnormal execution of an object or class (e.g., during exception handling). [Firesmith]
Antonym: NORMAL TRIGGER.
• **normal trigger** *n.* any trigger that occurs during the normal execution of an object or class. [Firesmith]
Contrast with: EXCEPTIONAL TRIGGER.

trigger condition *n.* any condition that identifies the circumstances on which a service starts itself. [Coad]
Commentary: A trigger condition, when applicable, is specified in a service specification. [Coad]

tuple *n.* any complex object that is an immutable composition of other objects. [Martin/Odell]
See also: IMMUTABLE, OBJECT, PLACE, RELATION.
Example: If two objects are related, this is called a couple. IBM and Jane form one such Employment couple. [Martin/Odell]
Rationale: Each immutable composition is known as a tuple in relational theory. [Martin/Odell]

[object] type *n.* **1.** (a) the declaration of the interface of any set of instances (e.g., objects) that conform to this common protocol. [Firesmith] (b) any set of objects or values with similar behavior, usually expressed by the operations defined on the type, without regard for the potential implementation of the type. [Rumbaugh] (c) any set of objects defined by the manipulations that can be performed on them. [Jacobson] **2.** the definition of the domain of allowable values that an object may possess and the set of operations that may be performed on the object, without regard for the potential implementation of the type via a class. [Booch] **3.** any identifiable entity with an associated predicate (a single-argument mathematical function with a Boolean result) defined over values. [OMG] **4.** any predicate (Boolean function) defined over values that can be used in a signature to restrict a possible parameter or characterize a possible result. [OMG] **5.** any description of the form and properties of objects that can be created during the execution of a system. [Eiffel, Meyer] **6.** any definition of a set of values and primitive operations that implement the fundamental aspects of its semantics. Types are grouped into classes, whereby the types of a given class share a set of primitive operations. Classes are closed under derivation; that is, if a type is in a class, then all of its derivatives are in that class. [Ada95]

Synonym: OBJECT TYPE.

Contrast with: CLASS, DATA TYPE, INTERFACE, SUBTYPING.

Commentary: Types classify objects according to a common interface; classes classify objects according to a common implementation.

Kinds:
- ABSTRACT DATA TYPE
- ABSTRACT TYPE
  - DEFERRED TYPE
- ANCESTOR TYPE
  - DIRECT ANCESTOR
  - INDIRECT ANCESTOR
  - PARENT TYPE
  - REPEATED ANCESTOR
  - ULTIMATE ANCESTOR TYPE
- ANCHORED TYPE
- ATTRIBUTE TYPE
- BASE TYPE
- BASIC TYPE
- BUILT-IN TYPE
- CLASS-WIDE TYPE
- COMPLEX TYPE
- COMPOSITE TYPE
  - PROTECTED TYPE
- CONCRETE TYPE
- CONTROLLED TYPE
- CREATION TYPE
- DECLARED TYPE
- DERIVED TYPE
  - DIRECT DERIVED TYPE
  - INDIRECT DERIVED TYPE
- DESCENDANT TYPE
  - CHILD
    + REPEATED CHILD
  - DIRECT DESCENDANT
  - INDIRECT DESCENDANT
  - REPEATED DESCENDANT
- DYNAMIC TYPE [OF A GIVEN EXPRESSION]
- DYNAMIC TYPE [OF A GIVEN OBJECT]
- ELEMENTARY TYPE
- ENUMERATION TYPE
- EVENT TYPE
- EXPANDED TYPE
- FEATURE TYPE
- GENERATING TYPE [OF A GIVEN OBJECT]

T

- LIMITED TYPE
- NONLIMITED TYPE
- PARENT TYPE
- PRIVATE TYPE
- REFERENCE TYPE
- RELATIONSHIP TYPE
- ROOT TYPE [OF A GIVEN DERIVATION CLASS]
- ROOT TYPE [OF A GIVEN TYPE HIERARCHY]
- STATIC TYPE [OF A GIVEN EXPRESSION]
- STATIC TYPE [OF A GIVEN TYPE]
- SUBTYPE [OF A GIVEN TYPE]
  - ACTUAL SUBTYPE [OF A GIVEN OBJECT]
  - CONSTRAINED SUBTYPE
  - DEFINITE SUBTYPE
  - EVENT SUBTYPE
  - INDEFINITE SUBTYPE
  - NOMINAL SUBTYPE
  - OPERATION SUBTYPE
  - UNCONSTRAINED SUBTYPE
- SUPERTYPE
  - EVENT SUPERTYPE
- TAGGED TYPE
  - TYPE EXTENSION
    + PRIVATE EXTENSION
    + RECORD EXTENSION
- TASK TYPE
- USER-DEFINED TYPE

- **abstract data type** *n.* **1.** (a) any localization of a single data type and its associated operations, encapsulated so that the implementations of the data and operations are hidden. [Firesmith, Jacobson] (b) an encapsulated user-defined type that hides the implementations of its data and operations. [Martin/Odell] **2.** a data structure known from an official interface rather than through its representation. [Eiffel, Meyer] **3.** a user-defined type used as a description or specifi-

cation of a class without implementation details. [Henderson-Sellers] *Contrast with:* CLASS.

- **abstract type** *n.* **1.** any incomplete type that is used as a supertype to provide common features, provide a minimal protocol for polymorphic substitution, or declare missing (i.e., deferred) common features that its subtypes must supply prior to instantiation. [Firesmith] **2.** a tagged type intended for use as a parent type for type extensions, but which is not allowed to have objects of its own. [Ada95] *Antonym:* CONCRETE TYPE. *Contrast with:* ABSTRACT CLASS, DEFERRED TYPE.

  - **deferred type** *n.* any abstract type that declares the existence of one or more features (e.g., messages, exceptions) that must be provided by its subtypes. *Contrast with:* ABSTRACT TYPE, CONCRETE TYPE.

- **ancestor type [of a given type]** *n.* **1.** any type from which the given type is directly or indirectly derived via inheritance. [Firesmith] **2.** Type T1 is an ancestor of type T2 if and only if either T1 is the same as T2 or if T2 is directly or indirectly derived from T1. [Ada95] *Synonyms:* BASE TYPE, SUPERTYPE. *Antonyms:* DERIVED TYPE, DESCENDANT TYPE, SUBTYPE. *Contrast with:* PARENT TYPE, SUPERTYPE. *Rationale:* The term ancestor is preferred over the older and more popular Smalltalk term supertype because of the potential for confusion between inheritance and aggregation when the term supertype is used. The term ancestor is preferred over the C++ term base type because base class often implies direct inheritance. The term ancestor is relatively common without being language-specific. [Firesmith]

Kinds:
- DIRECT ANCESTOR
- INDIRECT ANCESTOR
- PARENT TYPE
- REPEATED ANCESTOR
- ULTIMATE ANCESTOR

- **direct ancestor [type of a given type]** *n.* any ancestor type from which the given type is directly derived via inheritance. [Firesmith]
  Synonyms: DIRECT BASE TYPE, DIRECT SUPERTYPE, PARENT TYPE.
  Antonyms: CHILD TYPE, DIRECT DESCENDANT, DIRECT DERIVED TYPE, DIRECT SUBTYPE.
  Rationale: The term parent is preferred over the term direct ancestor because of its common usage in English and in biological inheritance. [Firesmith]

- **indirect ancestor [type of a given type]** *n.* any ancestor type from which the given type is indirectly derived via inheritance. [Firesmith]
  Synonyms: INDIRECT BASE TYPE, INDIRECT SUPERTYPE.
  Antonyms: CHILD TYPE, DIRECT DESCENDANT, DIRECT DERIVED TYPE, DIRECT SUBTYPE.
  Rationale: The term indirect ancestor is preferred over the terms indirect base class and indirect superclass because of the preference of the term ancestor over the terms base class and superclass. [Firesmith]

- **parent [type of a given type]** *n.* any ancestor type from which the given type is directly derived via

inheritance. [Firesmith]
Synonyms: DIRECT ANCESTOR, DIRECT BASE TYPE, DIRECT SUPERTYPE.
Antonyms: CHILD TYPE, DIRECT DESCENDANT, DIRECT DERIVED TYPE, DIRECT SUBTYPE.
Rationale: The term parent is preferred over the term direct ancestor because of its common usage in English and in biological inheritance. The term direct ancestor is in turn preferred over the terms direct base type and direct supertype because of the preference of the term ancestor over the terms base type and supertype. [Firesmith]

- **repeated ancestor [type of a given type]** *n.* any ancestor type from which the given type is multiply derived via multiple inheritance. [Firesmith]
  Antonym: REPEATED DESCENDANT.

- **ultimate ancestor [of a given type]** *n.* (a) any ancestor type of the given type that is not a descendant of any other ancestor. [Firesmith] (b) the ancestor of the type that is not a descendant of any other type. [Ada95]
  Contrast with: ROOT TYPE.

- **anchored type** *n.* any type that carries a provision for automatic redefinition in descendants of the class where they are used. [Eiffel, Meyer]
  Commentary: An Anchored type is of the form "like anchor" where anchor, called the anchor of the type, is an entity, or Current. An anchored type avoids code duplication when you must deal with a set of entities (attributes, function results, routine arguments) that should all follow suit whenever a proper descendant redefines the type of one of them, to take

advantage of the descendant's more specific context. [Meyer]

- **attribute type** *n.* **1.** any type of objects used as attributes. [Firesmith, Jacobson] **2.** any characteristic that specifies a mapping to a nonobject type. [OADSIG] **3.** any function that links a given set of objects to another set of objects. [Martin/Odell]
Synonym: FUNCTION.
Contrast with: ATTRIBUTE CLASS, FIELD, INSTANCE VARIABLE.
See also: ASSOCIATION.
Examples: Customer Name and Customer Address would be attribute types of the Customer object type. [Firesmith]

- **base type** *n.* **1.** the C++ term for any type from which another type is derived via subtyping. [C++, Firesmith] **2.** the Eiffel term for the type of the anchor of an anchored type. [Eiffel, Firesmith, Meyer]
Synonyms: **1** PARENT TYPE, SUPERTYPE.
Antonym: **1** DERIVED TYPE.
Contrast with: **1** BASE CLASS.
See also: **2** ANCHOR.

- **basic type** *n.* any class type, defined by a nongeneric basic class of the Kernel Library. [Eiffel, Meyer]

- **built-in type** *n.* (a) any type that is defined as part of the object-oriented programming language. [Firesmith] (b) any primitive type that is defined in the language. [C++]
Antonym: USER-DEFINED TYPE.
Examples: Typical built-in types include Boolean, character, integer, float, and real. [Firesmith]

- **class-wide type** *n.* any type that is defined for (and belongs to) a derivation class rooted at a tagged type. Given a subtype S of a tagged type T, S'Class

is the subtype mark for a corresponding subtype of the tagged class-wide type T'Class. [Ada95]
See also: CLASS-WIDE PROGRAMMING, DERIVATION CLASS.
Rationale: Such types are called class-wide because when a formal parameter is defined to be of class-wide type T'Class, and actual parameter of any type in the derivation class rooted at T is acceptable. [Ada95]

- **complex type** *n.* any type whose base class is complex. [Eiffel, Meyer]

- **composite type** *n.* any type that has components. [Ada95]
Antonym: ELEMENTARY TYPE.
See also: DISCRIMINANT.
Examples: Composite types include array and record types. [Ada95]

- **protected type** *n.* any composite type whose components are protected from concurrent access by multiple tasks. [Ada95]

- **concrete type** *n.* any complete type that defines semantically meaningful instances (i.e., any type that is not abstract).
Contrast with: ABSTRACT TYPE, DEFERRED TYPE.

- **controlled type** *n.* any type that supports user-defined assignment and finalization. [Ada95]

- **creation type** *n.* either the base type of the target or the optional type appearing in the Creation instruction. [Eiffel, Meyer]

- **declared type** *n.* the type given by the associated declaration or redeclaration. [Eiffel, Firesmith, Meyer]

- **derived type** *n.* **1.** the C++ term for any subtype that is derived from a base type. [C++, Firesmith] **2.** the Ada95 term for any new, incompatible type that is derived from another type. [Ada95]

Synonyms: CHILD TYPE, SUBTYPE.
Antonyms: PARENT TYPE, SUPERTYPE.
Contrast with: BASE TYPE, DERIVED CLASS.
See also: TYPE EXTENSION.
Commentary: 2 Each class containing the parent type also contains the derived type. The derived type inherits properties such as components and primitive operations from the parent. A type together with the types derived from it (directly or indirectly) form a derivation class. [Ada95]

Kinds:
- DIRECT DERIVED TYPE
- INDIRECT DERIVED TYPE

- **direct derived type [of a given type]** *n.* the C++ term for any child type of the given type. [Firesmith]

Synonyms: CHILD TYPE, DIRECT SUBTYPE.
Antonyms: INDIRECT ANCESTOR TYPE, INDIRECT DERIVED TYPE, INDIRECT SUPERTYPE.
Commentary: A direct derived type of a given type is a descendant type that is also a child descendant type. [Firesmith]

- **indirect derived type [of a given type]** *n.* the C++ term for any derived type that is indirectly derived via intermediate base types from a given type. [Firesmith]

Synonyms: ANCESTOR TYPE, INDIRECT SUPERTYPE.
Antonyms: DIRECT DERIVED TYPE, INDIRECT BASE TYPE.
Contrast with: DESCENDANT TYPE.
Commentary: An indirect derived type of a given type is a descendant

class that is not a child type. [Firesmith]

• **descendant type [of a given type]** *n.* **1.** any type that inherits, either directly or indirectly, from the given type. [Firesmith] **2.** any class-wide type that is either the same as the given type or that is derived, either directly or indirectly, from the given type. [Ada95]

Synonyms: DERIVED TYPE, SUBTYPE.
Antonyms: ANCESTOR, BASE TYPE, SUPERTYPE.
Contrast with: CHILD TYPE, PARENT TYPE.
Kinds:
- CHILD
  + REPEATED CHILD
- DIRECT DESCENDANT
- INDIRECT DESCENDANT
- REPEATED DESCENDANT

- **child [type of a given type]** *n.* any class that is directly derived via inheritance from the given type. [Firesmith]

Synonyms: DIRECT DERIVED TYPE, DIRECT DESCENDANT, DIRECT SUBTYPE.
Antonyms: DIRECT ANCESTOR, DIRECT BASE TYPE, DIRECT SUPERTYPE, PARENT.
See also: ANCESTOR, BASE TYPE, DERIVED TYPE, DESCENDANT, SUBCLASS, SUPERCLASS.
Commentary: The given type is called the parent type of the child type. This term is preferred because it is simpler, more intuitive, and more popular than its synonyms. [Firesmith]

+ **repeated child [type of a given type]** *n.* any child type that multiply inherits from the given par-

T

ent type. [Firesmith]

Antonym: REPEATED PARENT TYPE.

- **direct descendant [type of a given type]** *n.* any descendant that inherits directly from the given type. [Firesmith]

Synonyms: CHILD TYPE, DIRECT DERIVED TYPE, DIRECT SUBTYPE.

Antonyms: INDIRECT ANCESTOR TYPE, INDIRECT DERIVED TYPE, INDIRECT SUPERTYPE.

Commentary: A direct descendant of a given type is a descendant type that is also a child class. [Firesmith]

- **indirect descendant [type of a given type]** *n.* any descendant that inherits indirectly from the given type via intermediate types. [Firesmith]

Synonyms: INDIRECT DERIVED TYPE, INDIRECT SUBTYPE.

Antonyms: DIRECT ANCESTOR TYPE, DIRECT DESCENDANT, DIRECT DERIVED TYPE, DIRECT SUPERTYPE.

Commentary: An indirect descendant of a given type is a descendant type that is not a child type. [Firesmith]

- **repeated descendant [of a given type]** *n.* any descendant that multiply inherits from the given ancestor type. [Firesmith]

Antonym: REPEATED ANCESTOR.

• **dynamic type [of a given expression]** *n.* the run-time type of the value returned by the given expression. [Eiffel, Firesmith, Meyer]

Antonym: STATIC TYPE.

See also: POLYMORPHISM.

• **dynamic type [of a given property]** *n.* the run-time type of the value of the given property. [Eiffel, Firesmith, Meyer]

Antonym: STATIC TYPE.

See also: POLYMORPHISM.

• **elementary type** *n.* any type that does not have components. [Ada95]

Antonym: COMPOSITE TYPE.

Examples: The enumeration, numeric, and access types are each elementary types in Ada95. [Ada95]

• **enumeration type** *n.* any developer-defined type whose instances are named literal objects. [Firesmith]

• **event type** *n.* any type of events that defines the common trigger rules and control conditions for a set of related events. [Martin]

• **expanded type** *n.* any type T is expanded if and only if one of the following conditions holds:

  − T is a Class_type whose base class C is an expanded class

  − T is of the form expanded CT

  − T is of the form BIT M for some nonnegative integer M. [Eiffel, Meyer]

Contrast with: EXPANDED CLASS.

• **feature type** *n.* the declared type of a feature. [Eiffel, Meyer]

Commentary: The feature type is either the declared type of an attribute or the return type of an operation (if any).

• **generating type [of a given object]** *n.* the type from which the given object is a direct instance. [Eiffel, Firesmith, Meyer]

Contrast with: GENERATING CLASS.

See also: CLASSIFICATION, IS-A RELATIONSHIP.

• **limited type** *n.* any type (or view of a type) for which the assignment operation is not allowed. [Ada95]

Antonym: NONLIMITED TYPE.

• **nonlimited type** *n.* any type (or view of a type) for which the assignment

operation is allowed. [Ada95]
Antonym: LIMITED TYPE.

- **parent type [of a given type]** *n.* (a) any direct (i.e., immediate) supertype of the given type. [Firesmith] (b) the type from which the given type was immediately derived. [Ada95]
Antonym: CHILD TYPE.
Contrast with: ANCESTOR TYPE.

- **private type** *n.* any partial view of a type whose full view is hidden from its clients. [Ada95]

- **reference type** *n.* T is a reference type if it is not a formal generic name and none of the following conditions apply:
  - T is a Class_type whose base class C is an expanded class
  - T is of the form expanded CT
  - T is of the form BIT M for some nonnegative integer M.
  [Eiffel, Meyer]
Contrast with: EXPANDED TYPE.

- **relationship type** *n.* any type that specifies a mapping from one object type to another. [OADSIG]
Examples: Borrower defined on the type Copy with a range type of Library User.
Commentary: Characteristics of a relationship type include cardinality and optionally a range type which identifies the object types that can participate in the relationship.

- **root type [of a given derivation class]** *n.* the type from which all other types in the derivation class (except associated universal types or class-wide types) are directly or indirectly derived. [Ada95]
Contrast with: ULTIMATE ANSCESTOR.
See also: CLASS, DERIVATION CLASS.

- **root type [of a given type hierarchy]** *n.* any type that does not inherit

from any other type. [Firesmith]
Contrast with: BRANCH TYPE, LEAF TYPE.
Rationale: This type is at the root of the inheritance tree. The term base type is used by C++ with a different meaning. [Firesmith]

- **static type [of a given expression]** *n.* the type deduced from the types of the given expression's constituents at compile-time. [Eiffel, Firesmith, Meyer]
Antonym: DYNAMIC TYPE.

- **static type [of a given object]** *n.* the type with which the given object was declared at compile-time. [Eiffel, Firesmith, Meyer]
Antonym: DYNAMIC TYPE.

- **subtype [of a given type]** *n.* any more specialized type that inherits from the given type and conforms to the protocol of its supertypes. [Firesmith, Jacobson, Martin/Odell]
Synonym: DERIVED TYPE.
Antonym: SUPERTYPE.
Contrast with: BEHAVIORALLY COMPATIBLE DESCENDENT.
Commentary: A subtype may add additional properties and operations to introduce behavior or state unique to its instances. It may also refine the properties and operations it inherits to specialize them to the behavior and range of state values appropriate for its instances. [Firesmith]
Kinds:
  - ACTUAL SUBTYPE
  - CONSTRAINED SUBTYPE
  - DEFINITE SUBTYPE
  - EVENT SUBTYPE
  - INDEFINITE SUBTYPE
  - NOMINAL SUBTYPE
  - OPERATION SUBTYPE
  - UNCONSTRAINED SUBTYPE

T

- **actual subtype [of a given object]** *n.* the subtype of which the given object is declared. [Ada95]
Contrast with: NOMINAL SUBTYPE.
- **constrained subtype** *n.* any subtype whose type has neither unknown discriminants nor allows range, index, or discriminant constraints. [Ada95]
Antonym: UNCONSTRAINED TYPE.
Rationale: The subtype is called a constrained subtype because it has no unconstrained characteristics. [Ada95]
- **definite subtype** *n.* any subtype that is not indefinite. [Ada95]
Antonym: INDEFINITE SUBTYPE.
Commentary: All elementary subtypes are definite subtypes. [Ada95]
- **event subtype** *n.* any subtype of events that inherit trigger rules and control conditions from event supertypes. [Martin]
- **indefinite subtype** *n.* any subtype that does not by itself provide enough information to create an object without an additional constraint or explicit initial expression. [Ada95]
Antonym: DEFINITE SUBTYPE.
Examples: An unconstrained array subtype is an indefinite subtype, as is a subtype with unknown discriminants or unconstrained discriminants without default. [Ada95]
Commentary: The object's actual subtype can be more restrictive than the nominal subtype of the view; it always is if the nominal subtype is an indefinite subtype. [Ada95]
- **nominal subtype** *n.* the subtype that is associated with the view

when a view of an object is defined. [Ada95]
Contrast with: ACTUAL SUBTYPE.
Commentary: The object's actual subtype can be more restrictive than the nominal subtype of the view; it always is if the nominal subtype is an indefinite subtype. [Ada95]
- **operation subtype** *n.* any specialized type of operation derived from some parent type of operation. [Martin]
- **unconstrained subtype** *n.* any subtype with constrained characteristics (i.e., the subtype does not impose a constraint although its type has unknown discriminants or its type allows range, index, or discriminant constraints). [Ada95]
Antonym: CONSTRAINED SUBTYPE.
- **supertype [of a given type]** *n.* (a) any more general type from which the given type inherits and to which the given type's protocol conforms. [Firesmith] (b) any generalized type whose properties are more general than its subtypes. [Martin/Odell]
Synonym: BASE TYPE.
Antonym: SUBTYPE.
Contrast with: ANCESTOR.
Commentary: All of the instances of the given type are also instances of the supertypes.
  - **event supertype** *n.* any supertype of events from which event subtypes can inherit trigger rules and control conditions. [Martin]
  Antonym: EVENT SUBTYPE.
- **tagged type** *n.* any type of objects that have an associated run-time type tag, which indicates the specific

tagged type with which the object was originally created. [Ada95]

Rationale: An operand of a class-wide tagged type can be used in a dispatching call; the tag indicates which subprogram body to invoke. [Ada95]

Commentary: Tagged types and type extensions support object-oriented programming, based on inheritance with extension and run-time polymorphism via dispatching operations. A record type or private type has the reserved word tagged in its declaration. [Ada95]

See also: DISPATCHING, TAG.

Kinds:
- TYPE EXTENSION
  + PRIVATE EXTENSION
  + RECORD EXTENSION

- **type extension [of an ancestor type]** *n.* any tagged type that has been derived from the ancestor type. [Ada95]

Synonym: EXTENSION.

See also: DERIVED TYPE, TAGGED TYPE.

Kinds:
  + PRIVATE EXTENSION
  + RECORD EXTENSION.

 + **private extension** *n.* any record type extension that extends another type by adding additional components that are hidden from its clients. [Ada95]

Antonym: RECORD EXTENSION.

 + **record extension** *n.* any type extension that extends another type by adding additional components. [Ada95]

Antonym: PRIVATE EXTENSION.

• **task type** *n.* any composite type whose values are tasks, which are active entities that may execute concurrently with other tasks. [Ada95]

See also: TASK.

Example: The top-level task of a partition is called the environment task. [Ada95]

• **user-defined type (UDT)** *n.* **1.** any type that is defined by the user rather than built into the language. [Firesmith, Martin] **2.** any class, as opposed to a built-in type. [C++]

Antonym: BUILT-IN TYPE.

type conformance *n.* any conformance of one type to another, whereby the protocol of the first type is a superset of the protocol of the second type and the semantics of the features they have in common is the same. [Firesmith]

Contrast with: SIGNATURE CONFORMANCE.

Commentary: Conformance is used as a mechanism for determining when a type is compatible with another for assignment, argument passing, or signature redefinition. If one type conforms to another, then instances of the first type can be used anywhere that instances of the second type can be used. [Firesmith]

type extension [of an ancestor type] *n.* any tagged type that has been derived from the ancestor type. [Ada95]

Synonym: EXTENSION.

See also: DERIVED TYPE, TAGGED TYPE.

Kinds:
  • PRIVATE EXTENSION
  • RECORD EXTENSION.

• **private extension** *n.* any record type extension that extends another type by adding additional components that are hidden from its clients. [Ada95]

Antonym: RECORD EXTENSION.

• **record extension** *n.* any type extension that extends another type by adding additional components. [Ada95]

T

Antonym: PRIVATE EXTENSION.

type inheritance *n.* **1.** any inheritance among types in which a new type (a.k.a. the subtype) is defined in terms of one or more existing types (a.k.a. its supertypes), whereby the subtype is a specialization of its supertypes, conforms to their protocols, and inherits their features. [Firesmith, ODMG] **2.** any inheritance among types.

Synonym: SUBTYPING.

Contrast with: CLASS INHERITANCE.

type interface *n.* **1.** the interface of a type, declaring its visible features (i.e., the set of operation signatures defined on the type). [Martin, OMG] **2.** the interface that defines the requests in which instances of this type can meaningfully participate as a parameter. [OMG]

Synonym: SUBTYPING.

Contrast with: CLASS INTERFACE, CLUSTER INTERFACE, CONSTRUCTION INTERFACE, FUNCTIONAL INTERFACE, MESSAGE INTERFACE, OBJECT INTERFACE, OPERATION INTERFACE, ORB INTERFACE, PRINCIPAL INTERFACE, SYSTEM INTERFACE.

Example: Given a document type and product type, the interface to the document type comprises edit and print and the interface to the product type comprises set price and check inventory, then the object interface of a particular document, which is also a product, comprises all four requests. [OMG]

type name *n.* any name that uniquely refers to a single type within the scope of the definition of the name. [C++]

Contrast with: CLASS NAME, OBJECT NAME.

type object *n.* any object that serves as a type. [OMG]

typing *n.* the enforcement of the type of an object or expression, which prevents objects of different types from accidentally being interchanged unless their protocols conform. [Booch, Firesmith, ODMG]

Example: The principle of polymorphic substitutability allows an instance of a subtype to be used anywhere its supertype is used because the subtype conforms to the protocol of the supertype and because a subtype is a kind of supertype (e.g., a car is a kind of vehicle). [Firesmith]

Kinds:
- DYNAMIC TYPING
- STATIC TYPING
- STRONG TYPING
- SUBTYPING
- WEAK TYPING

- **dynamic typing** *n.* any typing that occurs at run-time. [Firesmith, Wirfs-Brock]

  Antonym: STATIC TYPING.

- **static typing** *n.* any typing that occurs at compile-time. [Firesmith]

  Antonym: DYNAMIC TYPING.

- **strong typing** *n.* any typing that must be declared and that is enforced, (i.e., guaranteed to be consistent). [Firesmith, Rumbaugh]

  Antonym: WEAK TYPING.

  Example: Ada, C++, and Eiffel implement strong typing. [Firesmith]

- **subtyping** *n.* the incremental definition of a new type (a.k.a. the subtype) in terms of one or more existing types (a.k.a. supertypes), whereby the subtype conforms to all of its supertypes. [Firesmith]

  Synonym: SPECIALIZATION.

  Commentary: Subtyping defines the rules by which objects of one type are determined to be acceptable in contexts expecting another type. [Firesmith]

- **weak typing** *n.* any typing that need not be declared and that is not enforced by the compiler. [Firesmith, Rumbaugh]
Antonym: STRONG TYPING.
Example: Smalltalk is a weakly typed language. [Firesmith]

T

U

ultimate ancestor [class of a given class] *n.* any ancestor of the given class that is not a descendant of any other ancestor. [Firesmith]
Contrast with: ROOT CLASS

ultimate ancestor [type of a given type] *n.* any ancestor type of the given type that is not a descendant of any other ancestor. [Ada95, Firesmith]
Contrast with: ROOT TYPE.

unary message *n.* any message without arguments. [Smalltalk]
Contrast with: BINARY MESSAGE, KEYWORD MESSAGE.

unbounded *adj.* having dynamic and unlimited object code size.
Antonym: BOUNDED.

unbound slot *n.* any slot that does not have a value. [CLOS]
Antonym: BOUND SLOT.

unconstrained subtype *n.* any subtype with constrained characteristics (i.e., the subtype does not impose a constraint although its type has unknown discriminants or its type allows range, index, or discriminant constraints). [Ada95]
Antonym: CONSTRAINED SUBTYPE

undefined behavior *n.* any behavior that is unspecified by some standard. Implementations [of the standard] have complete freedom (e.g., they can do anything or nothing), and the behavior need not be documented by the implementor or vendor.

understandability *n.* the ease with which humans can comprehend something (e.g., the system, software). [Firesmith]

unguarded transition *n.* any transition that does not have an associated guard condition. [Firesmith]
Antonym: GUARDED TRANSITION.

unidirectional association *n.* any association directed from the client(s) to the server(s). [Firesmith]
Antonym: BIDIRECTIONAL ASSOCIATION.
Commentary: Unidirectional associations are typically implemented by one or more attributes acting as pointers or messages requesting services. [Firesmith]

unidirectional link *n.* any link directed from the client(s) to the server(s). [Firesmith]
Antonym: BIDIRECTIONAL LINK.
Commentary: Unidirectional links are typically implemented by one or more attributes acting as pointers or messages requesting services. [Firesmith]

unidirectional relationship *n.* any rela-

tionship directed from the client(s) to the server(s). [Firesmith]
Antonym: BIDIRECTIONAL RELATION-SHIP.
Kinds:
- UNIDIRECTIONAL ASSOCIATION
- UNIDIRECTIONAL LINK
- **unidirectional association** *n.* any association directed from the client(s) to the server(s). [Firesmith]
Antonym: BIDIRECTIONAL ASSOCIATION.
Commentary: Unidirectional associations are typically implemented by one or more attributes acting as pointers or messages requesting services. [Firesmith]
- **unidirectional link** *n.* any link directed from the client(s) to the server(s). [Firesmith]
Antonym: BIDIRECTIONAL LINK.
Commentary: Unidirectional links are typically implemented by one or more attributes acting as pointers or messages requesting services. [Firesmith]
uniformity *n.* the property of having the same paradigm, models, notation, and concepts consistently applied with no unnecessary differences. [Firesmith]
union *n.* any class declared with the class-key union; its members are public by default and it holds only one member at a time. [C++]
Commentary: A union is a structure capable of containing objects of different types at different times. A union is fundamentally a low-level construct for saving storage. A union may be thought of as a structure whose member objects all begin at offset zero and whose size is sufficient to contain any of its member objects. At most one of the member objects can be stored in a

union at any time. [C++].
- **anonymous union** *n.* any union that defines an unnamed object (but not a type). [C++]
Commentary: A union for which objects or pointers are declared is not an anonymous union. [C++]
union constraint *n.* any constraint which declares that the union of a group of specializations of a generalization constitutes the entire membership of the generalization. [Embley]
Commentary: When we have a union constraint, we know that every member of a generalization is a member of at least one specialization in the group. [Embley]
- **partition constraint** *n.* any constraint which declares that a group of specializations partitions a generalization. A partition requires that partitioning sets be pairwise disjoint and that their union constitute the partitioned set. [Embley]
Commentary: A partition constraint is the combination of a mutual-exclusion constraint and a union constraint. [Embley]
unit *n.* **1.** any single class. [Firesmith] **2.** any single object. [Firesmith] **3.** any single operation. **4.** any single operation, class, module, group of modules, block, or service package. [Jacobson]
Commentary: Definition **1** is based on the fact that a class is the fundamental source code module and the basic building block of design. Definition **2** is based on the premise that an object is the fundamental object-code module. Definition **3** is the object-oriented analog of the traditional definition.
unit test *n.* **1.** the test of a single unit (i.e., single class or object) in isolation. [Fire-

U

smith] **2.** the test of any single class. **3.** the test of any single object. **4.** the test of any single operation. **5.** the test of a single operation, class, module, group of modules, block, or service package. [Jacobson]

See also: UNIT.

Commentary: Definition **1** is the traditional definition interpreted in terms of what it means to be an object-oriented unit. A class is the fundamental source code module and the basic building block of design, whereas an object is the fundamental object-code module. Note that classes in most languages are not executable, and must be indirectly tested in terms of their instances. Definition **2** is based on the fact that a class is the fundamental source-code module and the basic building block of design. Definition **3** is based on the premise that an object is the fundamental object code module. Definition **4** is the object-oriented analog of the traditional definition. Operations are executable, but do not exist independently of their environment of coencapsulated features (e.g., attributes, operations, invariants, exceptions). Note that classes in most languages are not executable, and must be indirectly tested in terms of their instances. [Firesmith]

unit testing *n.* the testing of a single unit in isolation; the performance of a unit test. [Firesmith]

Contrast with: CLUSTER TESTING, SUBSYSTEM TESTING, SYSTEM TESTING.

universal identifier (UID) *n.* any system-wide unique object identifier (a.k.a. handle). [Firesmith]

Antonym: LOCAL IDENTIFIER.

Commentary: UIDs are required in distributed applications with multiple address spaces in which using the local address does not uniquely identify an object, especially if that object is to be moved around the system. [Firesmith]

universe *n.* **1.** any set of clusters, out of which developers will pick classes to build systems. [Eiffel, Meyer] **2.** any object class whose instances are members of sets. [Embley]

Synonym: **2** MEMBER CLASS.

Antonyms: **2** ASSOCIATION,.SET CLASS.

See also: **2** IS MEMBER OF RELATIONSHIP SET.

Commentary: **2** The term universe is an often-used mathematical notation that denotes the set of objects from which subsets may be formed. [Embley]

unmanaged *adj.* not managing its own garbage collection. [Booch]

Antonym: MANAGED.

unqualified association *n.* any association that is not qualified. [Firesmith]

Antonym: QUALIFIED ASSOCIATION.

unsafe method *n.* any method that contains one or more parameters of a class or access type, and may thus be used to exchange references. [Atkinson]

Antonym: SAFE METHOD.

unsolicited event *n.* any external event that was not caused to occur by some previous operation within the current scope. [Firesmith, Shlaer/Mellor]

upcast *v.* *-ed, -ing* the C++ term for changing the type of an object to that of an ancestor type. [C++, Firesmith]

Antonym: DOWNCAST.

Rationale: The ancestor type is higher in the inheritance hierarchy when the root class is drawn at the top. [Firesmith]

usage relationship *n.* any relationship in which one object type makes use of the interface provided by another object type. [OADSIG]

usage scenario *n.* any scenario that captures how an application is used by its client terminators.

Contrast with: USE CASE.

use *v.* *-ed, -ing* to reference the interface of an abstraction. [Booch, Firesmith]

use case *n.* **1.** any description of a single way of using a system or application; any class of top-level usage scenarios that captures how a blackbox application is used by its client terminators. [Firesmith, Henderson-Sellers, Jacobson] **2.** (a) any behaviorally related sequence of transactions performed by a single actor in a dialogue with a system, the purpose of which is to provide some measurable value to the actor. [Jacobson] (b) any class of top-level usage scenarios that captures how a system or application is used by its client terminators (actors). (c) any description of the system actions on receipt of one type of user request. [Lorenz] **3.** (formerly) any sequence of events that occur during one particular execution of an application. [Henderson-Sellers]

Synonym: SCENARIO SCRIPT.

Contrast with: ATOMIC SYSTEM FUNCTION, USAGE SCENARIO.

Rationale: The term use case was introduced and initially popularized by Ivar Jacobson.

Commentary: Use cases are used to document user requirements in terms of user dialogs with a system that provide some measurable value to the user. [Firesmith]

Kinds:
- ABSTRACT USE CASE
- CONCRETE USE CASE

- **abstract use case** *n.* any use case that will not be instantiated on its own, but is meaningful only to describe parts shared among other use cases. [Jacobson]

  Antonym: CONCRETE USE CASE.

- **concrete use case** *n.* any use case that is meaningful and will be instantiated on its own. [Jacobson]

  Antonym: ABSTRACT USE CASE.

use-case model *n.* any diagram that documents a system's behavior as a set of use cases, actors, and the communication arcs between them. [Jacobson]

Contrast with: BEHAVIORAL MODEL, CONFIGURATION MODEL, DATA MODEL, DYNAMIC MODEL, FUNCTIONAL MODEL, INTERACTION MODEL, INTERFACE MODEL, LANGUAGE MODEL, LIFE-CYCLE MODEL, OBJECT MODEL, OPERATION MODEL, PRESENTATION MODEL, SEMANTIC MODEL, STATE MODEL, STRUCTURAL MODEL, TIMING MODEL.

use case modelling *n.* any analysis technique for eliciting, understanding, and defining functional requirements in terms of use cases. [Jacobson]

use-case view *n.* any object model view that shows the objects and associations that participate in a specific use case. [Jacobson]

Synonym: VIEW OF PARTICIPATING OBJECTS.

Contrast with: GLOBAL OBJECT VIEW, LOCAL OBJECT VIEW.

See also: USE CASE.

Commentary: The purpose of this type of view is to illustrate how the behavior of a use case is distributed over the objects and how the objects interact to realize the course of events in a use case. The union of all views of participating objects is the global object view. [Jacobson]

user *n.* any actual person who uses the system [Jacobson]

Contrast with: ACTOR.

U

See also: USE CASE.

Commentary: The use-case model uses actors and use cases. These concepts are simply an aid to defining what exists outside the system (actors) and what should be performed by the system (use cases). [Jacobson]

user-defined class (UDC) *n.* any class that is defined by the user rather than built into the language. [Firesmith]

Antonym: BUILT-IN CLASS.

Contrast with: USER-DEFINED TYPE.

user-defined type (UDT) *n.* **1.** any type that is defined by the user rather than built into the language. [Firesmith, Martin] **2.** any class, as opposed to a built-in type. [C++]

Antonym: BUILT-IN TYPE.

user-friendliness *n.* the ease with which humans can use the software. [Firesmith]

user-interface layer *n.* the layer that provides the interface to the user. [Firesmith]

Contrast with: DATABASE-INDEPEN-DENCE LAYER, DOMAIN LAYER, ENVI-RONMENT-INDEPENDENCE LAYER, PRO-CESSOR-COMMUNICATION LAYER.

Commentary: The user-interface layer is typically built on top of the model layer and contains view and controller objects and classes. [Firesmith]

user-interface metaphor *n.* any user in-terface object type that ensures that us-ers can understand the user interface. [OADSIG]

user-interface (UI) object *n.* any object that provides an interface between the end user and the system's model ob-jects. [Lorenz]

Contrast with: MODEL OBJECT.

Example: An automatic teller machine (ATM) function menu window is a UI object for the ATM model object in a bank. [Lorenz]

Commentary: The UI object classes change relatively frequently, as new technology, screen layouts, report for-mats, and usability studies require. [Lorenz]

user-interface object type *n.* any object used to define the user interface for the application. [OADSIG]

uses association *n.* any association from an abstract use case to a concrete use case in which the description of the ab-stract use case is used in the description of the concrete use case. [Jacobson]

Contrast with: EXTEND ASSOCIATION.

See also: INHERITANCE.

utility object *sn.* any support object that provides a low-level utility, such as a queue, linked-list, set, stack, transport-er, relay, etc. [Firesmith]

V

validatability *n.* the ease with which the software can be demonstrated to be correct (i.e., that the right software was built). [Firesmith]

validity [of a call] *adj.* any call is valid if and only if it is both class valid and system valid. [Eiffel, Meyer]
See also: CLASS-VALID CALL, SYSTEM-VALID CALL.
Kinds:
- CLASS-LEVEL VALIDITY
- SYSTEM-LEVEL VALIDITY

- **class-level validity** *n.* any call to a feature of a class exhibits class-level validity (i.e., is class valid) if the class has the feature, the feature is available to the caller, and the feature has the required signature. [Eiffel, Meyer]
  Contrast with: CLASS VALID, SYSTEM-LEVEL VALIDITY.
- **system-level validity** *n.* the system-level counterpart to class-level validity, but applied to all possible dynamic types of the target. [Eiffel, Meyer]
  Contrast with: CLASS-LEVEL VALIDITY.

value *n.* **1.** (a) any data or object abstraction stored as an attribute, link, or parameter. [Firesmith] (b) any entity that can be a possible actual parameter in a request. [OMG] **2.** any objects or references to objects that are fields of a complex object. [Eiffel, Meyer]
Kinds:
- LITERAL
- NONPRIMITIVE VALUE
- OBJECT NAME
- PRIMITIVE VALUE

- **literal** *n.* any value that is not an object name. [OMG]
- **nonprimitive value** *n.* any value that is also an object. [Firesmith]
  Antonym: PRIMITIVE VALUE.
- **object name** *n.* any value that serves to identify an object. [OMG]
- **primitive value** *n.* any value that is merely a data abstraction. [Firesmith]
  Antonym: NONPRIMITIVE VALUE.
- *Examples:* Primitive values include any character, any integer, and the Boolean values true and false. [Firesmith]

value-dependent operation *n.* any operation in which the behavior of the corresponding request depends on which names are used to identify object parameters (if an object can have multiple names). [OMG]
Antonym: CONTEXT-INDEPENDENT OPERATION.

V

value of a given expression *n.* the object described by the expression. [Firesmith, Smalltalk]
Commentary: Smalltalk messages provide two-way communication. The selector and arguments transmit information to the receiver about what type of response to make. The receiver transmits information back by returning an object that becomes the value of the message expression. Even if no information needs to be communicated back to the sender, a receiver always returns a value for the message expression. Returning a value indicates that the response to the message is complete. [Smalltalk]

variable *adj.* describing anything, the values of which can change at run-time. [Firesmith]
n. anything, the value(s) of which can change. [Firesmith]
Antonym: CONSTANT.
Examples: Variables include any attributes, links, or objects the values of which can change. [Firesmith]
Kinds:
- PRIVATE VARIABLE
  - INSTANCE VARIABLE
    + INDEXED INSTANCE VARIABLE
    + NAMED INSTANCE VARIABLE
  - TEMPORARY VARIABLE
- SHARED VARIABLE
  - CLASS VARIABLE
  - GLOBAL VARIABLE
  - POOL VARIABLE

private variable *n.* any variable that is available only to a single object. [Smalltalk]
Antonym: SHARED VARIABLE.
Kinds:
- INSTANCE VARIABLE
  + INDEXED INSTANCE VARIABLE
  + NAMED INSTANCE VARIABLE

- TEMPORARY VARIABLE
- **instance variable** *n.* **1.** any attribute of an individual instance. [Firesmith, Smalltalk] **2.** any place to store and refer to an object's state data. [Booch, Lorenz] **3.** any name that allows one object (instance) to refer to another one. [Lorenz] **4.** the OOPL implementation of any attribute type [Martin/Odell]
Synonym: **1** INSTANCE ATTRIBUTE, **2** FIELD, MEMBER OBJECT, SLOT.
Rationale: In OO systems, data are made up of object instances, hence the name *instance variable.* [Lorenz] The term *instance attribute* should probably be used instead of *instance variable* because it is less language specific and because some instance attributes are constants.
Commentary: All instance variables are protected in Smalltalk, whereas C++ also allows instance variables (a.k.a. data members) to be public or protected.
Kinds:
+ INDEXED INSTANCE VARIABLE
+ NAMED INSTANCE VARIABLE.

+ **indexed instance variable** *n.* any instance variable that is not accessed by name. [Smalltalk]
Antonym: NAMED INSTANCE VARIABLE.
Example: A Smalltalk example of an indexed instance variable is names at: 1. [Smalltalk]
Commentary: An object can have indexed instance variables only if all instances of its class can have indexed instance variables. [Smalltalk]
+ **named instance variable** *n.* any instance variable that is accessed

by its instance variable name.
[Smalltalk]
Antonym: INDEXED INSTANCE VARI-
ABLE.
Commentary: All instances of a
class have the same number of
named instance variables and use
the same names to refer to them.
[Smalltalk]
- **temporary variable** *n.* any private
variable created for a specific activity and available only for the duration of that activity. [Smalltalk]
Contrast with: TEMPORARY AT-
TRIBUTE. [Jacobson]
Commentary: Temporary variables
do not include pseudovariables, such
as argument names and self.
• **shared variable** *n.* any variable that
can be accessed by more than one object. [Smalltalk]
Antonym: PRIVATE VARIABLE.
Kinds:
  - CLASS VARIABLE
  - GLOBAL VARIABLE
  - POOL VARIABLE
- **class variable** *n.* **1.** any attribute of a
class descriptor object. **2.** any class-
level attribute or variable. **3.** any
variable shared by all the instances
of a single class. [Smalltalk]
Synonyms: CLASS ATTRIBUTE, COM-
MON-INSTANCE ATTRIBUTE.
Example: In C++, a class variable is
declared as a static member.
[Booch]
- **global variable** *n.* any variable
shared by all instances of all class-
es. [Smalltalk]
Contrast with: CLASS VARIABLE, IN-
STANCE VARIABLE, POOL VARIABLE,
TEMPORARY VARIABLE.
Commentary: In spite of being a

part of the archetypal pure object-
oriented programming language
Smalltalk, global variables implement common global data and are
definitely not object-oriented in
that they violate the encapsulation
of objects and classes.
  - **pool variable** *n.* any variable shared
by the instances of a subset of the
classes. [Smalltalk]
Contrast with: CLASS VARIABLE,
GLOBAL VARIABLE, INSTANCE VARI-
ABLE, TEMPORARY VARIABLE.
variable aggregate *n.* **1.** any aggregate,
the aggregation structure and compo-
nent parts of which can change. [Fire-
smith] **2.** any aggregate with a finite
number of levels but a varying number
of parts. [Rumbaugh]
Antonym: CONSTANT AGGREGATE, FIXED
AGGREGATE.
variable attribute *n.* **1.** any attribute, the
value of which can change at run time.
[Firesmith, Jacobson] **2.** any attribute
whose value associated with a particular instance can be changed by a routine. [Eiffel, Meyer]
Antonym: CONSTANT ATTRIBUTE.
variable component *n.* any component
object, at least one property of which
can change its value. [Firesmith]
Contrast with: VARIABLE ATTRIBUTE,
VARIABLE LINK.
variable link *n.* any link, the value of
which can change at run-time. [Fire-
smith]
Antonym: CONSTANT LINK.
Commentary: A link can change by
pointing or referring to another server.
variable name *n.* any expression that describes the current value of an accessible variable. The value of a variable
name is the current value of the variable

V

with that name. [Smalltalk]

variable property *n.* any property, the value of which can change at run-time. [Firesmith]

Antonym: CONSTANT PROPERTY.

Kinds:
- VARIABLE ATTRIBUTE
- VARIABLE COMPONENT
- VARIABLE LINK

- **variable attribute** *n.* **1.** any attribute, the value of which can change at run time. [Firesmith, Jacobson] **2.** any attribute whose value associated with a particular instance can be changed by a routine. [Eiffel, Meyer]
  Antonym: CONSTANT ATTRIBUTE.

- **variable component** *n.* any component object, at least one property of which can change its value. [Firesmith]
  Contrast with: VARIABLE ATTRIBUTE, VARIABLE LINK.

- **variable link** *n.* any link, the value of which can change at run-time. [Firesmith]
  Antonym: CONSTANT LINK.
  Commentary: A link can change by pointing or referring to another server.

variant *n.* any processor-specific implementation of an object or class. [Firesmith]

Contrast with: PROXY.

variant programming *n.* any programming in which new abstractions may be constructed from existing ones whereby the programmer need only specify the differences between the new and old abstractions. [Ada95]

Contrast with: CLASS-WIDE PROGRAMMING.

Venn diagram *n.* any diagram from set theory used to show the intersection and union relationships among sets. [Wirfs-Brock]

Commentary: Venn diagrams are used to show the inheritance relationships between classes and types by showing the intersection and union relationships among their extents. Venn diagrams have sometimes been misused to show aggregation relationships. [Firesmith]

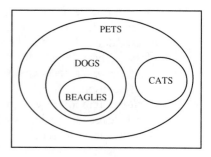

Venn Diagram

verifiability *n.* the ease with which the software products of a development activity can be demonstrated to be consistent with (1) the products of previous development activities and (2) development standards and procedures (i.e., that the software was built right). [Firesmith]

version in a descendant [of a feature] *n.* the one potential version of the feature that is inherited due to the Repeated Inheritance Consistency constraint. [Eiffel, Meyer]

Contrast with: CURRENT FEATURE.

- **potential version in a descendant [of a feature]** *n.* any feature in the descendant that is inherited from the original feature after possible redeclarations and generic derivations. [Eiffel, Meyer]
  Contrast with: CURRENT FEATURE.

vertical common facilities *n.* any COR-

BA facilities that support a vertical market such as health care, retailing, CAD, or financial systems. [OMG] *Antonym:* HORIZONTAL COMMON FACILITIES.

view *n.* **1.** (a) any domain class that exists to provide a user view of (i.e., information about and control over) one or more model classes. [Firesmith] (b) any class of view objects. [Firesmith] (c) any domain object that exists to provide a user view of (i.e., information about and control over) one or more model objects. [Firesmith] (d) any instance of a view class. [Firesmith] (e) any object displayed as a rectangular area on the display screen in which to access (view and edit) information. [Smalltalk] **2.** any higher-level abstraction used to view and manage large OSA models. [Embley] **3.** any identification of the entity (the entity of the view), plus view-specific characteristics that affect the use of the entity through that view (such as mode of access to an object, formal parameter names and defaults for a subprogram, or visibility to components of a type). [Ada95] **4.** any object diagram of a subset of an object model. [Jacobson]
Synonym: **1** WORKSPACE. **4** OBJECT-MODEL VIEW.
Commentary: The views of classes provide the fundamental mechanism to interact with the software in the system. [Smalltalk] A view class may also be a controller class of its model class(es). Most view classes are also presentation classes. A model object may have more than one view object, and a view object may also be a controller object of its model object(s). Most view objects are also presentation objects. [Firesmith]

Kinds: **1**
- ACTIVE VIEW
- BROWSER
- COLLAPSED VIEW
- EXPLODED VIEW
- IMPLODED VIEW
- PRESENTATION
- PRIVATE TYPE
- PROXY
- STANDARD SYSTEM VIEW
- SUBVIEW
- SYSTEM BROWSER

Kinds: **2**
- GLOBAL-OBJECT VIEW

Kinds: **3**
- ALIASED VIEW

Kinds: **4**
- GLOBAL-OBJECT VIEW
- LOCAL-OBJECT VIEW
- USE-CASE VIEW
- VIEW OF PARTICIPATING OBJECTS

- **active view** *n.* the view that is currently being used by the operator. [Firesmith, Smalltalk]

- **aliased view [of an object]** *n.* any view of an object that can be designated by an access value. [Ada95]
  Example: Objects allocated by allocators are aliased. Objects can also be explicitly declared as aliased with the reserved word aliased. [Ada95]
  Commentary: The Access attribute can be used to create an access value designating an aliased object. [Ada95]

- **browser** *n.* **1.** any interactive tool that allows users to view in a library the classes and their characteristics. [Eiffel, Firesmith] **2.** (a) a view that allows you to access hierarchically organized and indexable information. [Smalltalk] (b) any interactive view used to create, present, and edit the class descriptions in the system. [Smalltalk]

V

Synonym: SYSTEM BROWSER.

Commentary: The class browser is a way to present a hierarchical index of classes and messages. Browsers are set up to help one find classes either by name or by category. [Smalltalk] Browsers are typically implemented as an aggregate presentation object that allows developers to scroll through the class structure and edit the features of the classes. [Firesmith]

- **collapsed view** *n.* any [standard system] view that displays only its label part, but can be selected and expanded to show the entire view. [Firesmith, Smalltalk]

- **exploded view** *n.* any view modeled in its detailed form, making the subsumed components (relationship sets, states, and transitions) of the dominant high-level components explicit or visible. [Embley]

Antonym: IMPLODED VIEW.

- **global-object view** *n.* any object model view that shows either the entire object model or a subsystem of the object model. [Jacobson]

Antonym: LOCAL OBJECT VIEW.

Contrast with: VIEW OF PARTICIPATING OBJECTS.

- **imploded view** *n.* any view modeled in its summary form, making the subsumed components (relationship sets, states, and transitions) of the dominant high-level components implicit or invisible, while leaving the high-level component explicit or visible. [Embley]

Antonym: EXPLODED VIEW.

- **local-object view** *n.* any object model view that shows an object with all of its relations to and from other objects. [Jacobson]

Antonym: GLOBAL OBJECT VIEW.

Contrast with: VIEW OF PARTICIPATING OBJECTS.

- **presentation** *n.* **1.** (a) any specialized view class that exists to provide a formatted view of (i.e., information about and control over) one or more model or view classes. [Firesmith] (b) any class of presentation objects. [Firesmith] **2.** (a) any specialized view object that exists to provide a formatted view of (i.e., information about and control over) one or more model or view objects. (b) any instance of a presentation class.

Contrast with: 1 PRESENTATION OBJECT, PROXY CLASS **2** PRESENTATION CLASS, PROXY OBJECT.

Commentary: **1** A model or view class may have more than one presentation class, and a presentation class may also be a controller class of its model or view class(es). [Firesmith] **2** A model or view object may have more than one presentation object, and a presentation object may also be a controller object of its model or view object(s). [Firesmith]

- **private type** *n.* any partial view of a type whose full view is hidden from its clients. [Ada95]

- **proxy** *n.* **1.** (a) any local view class that represents (i.e., acts as a processor-specific variant of and communicates with) its remote model class. [Firesmith] (b) any class of a proxy objects. [Firesmith] **2.** (a) any local view object that represents (i.e., acts as a processor-specific variant of and communicates with) its remote model object. [Firesmith] (b) any instance of a proxy class. [Firesmith]

Contrast with: 1 PRESENTATION CLASS,

PROXY OBJECT. **2** PRESENTATION OBJECT, PROXY CLASS.
Commentary: **1** A proxy provides the local protocol of (and communicates with) its model on a remote processor. Proxies are used to create a single virtual address space across multiple processors. [Firesmith] **2** A proxy provides the local protocol of (and communicates with) its model on a remote processor. Proxies are used to create a single virtual address space across multiple processors. [Firesmith]

- **standard system view** *n.* any view that provides standard interface functions for manipulating itself, for example, for moving, framing, collapsing, and closing. [Smalltalk]

- **subview** *n.* any view contained as a component part of another view. [Firesmith, Smalltalk]
Contrast with: ACTIVE VIEW, BROWSER, COLLAPSED VIEW, STANDARD SYSTEM VIEW.

- **system browser** *n.* **1.** any interactive tool that allows users to explore the available classes and their features. [Eiffel] **2.** (a) any view that allows you to access hierarchically organized and indexable information. [Smalltalk] (b) any interactive view used to create, present, and edit the class descriptions in the system. [Smalltalk]
Synonym: BROWSER.
Contrast with: IMPLEMENTATION DESCRIPTION, PROTOCOL DESCRIPTION.

- **use-case view** *n.* any object-model view that shows the objects and associations that participate in a specific use case. [Jacobson]
Synonym: VIEW OF PARTICIPATING OBJECTS.
Contrast with: GLOBAL OBJECT VIEW,

LOCAL OBJECT VIEW.
See also: USE CASE.
Commentary: The purpose of this type of view is to illustrate how the behavior of a use case is distributed over the objects and how the objects interact to realize the course of events in a use case. The union of all views of participating objects is the global-object view. [Jacobson]

- **view of participating objects** *n.* any object model view that shows the objects and associations that participate in a specific use case. [Jacobson]
Synonym: USE-CASE VIEW.
Contrast with: GLOBAL-OBJECT VIEW, LOCAL-OBJECT VIEW.
See also: USE CASE.
Commentary: The purpose of this type of view is to illustrate how the behavior of a use case is distributed over the objects and how the objects interact to realize the course of events in a use case. The union of all views of participating objects is the global-object view. [Jacobson]

view [class] *n.* (a) any domain class that exists to provide a user view of (i.e., information about and control over) one or more model classes. [Firesmith] (b) any class of view objects. [Firesmith]
Contrast with: CONTROLLER CLASS, MODEL CLASS, VIEW OBJECT.
Commentary: A view class may also be a controller class of its model class(es). Most view classes are also presentation classes. [Firesmith]
Kinds:
- PRESENTATION CLASS
- PROXY CLASS

- **presentation [class]** *n.* (a) any specialized view class that exists to provide a formatted view of (i.e., infor-

V

mation about and control over) one or more model or view classes. [Firesmith] (b) any class of presentation objects. [Firesmith]

Contrast with: PRESENTATION OBJECT, PROXY CLASS.

Example: A model or view class may have more than one presentation class, and a presentation class may also be a controller class of its model or view class(es). [Firesmith]

- **proxy [class]** *n.* (a) any local-view class that represents (i.e., acts as a processor-specific variant of and communicates with) its remote model class. [Firesmith] (b) any class of proxy objects. [Firesmith]

Contrast with: PRESENTATION CLASS, PROXY OBJECT.

Commentary: A proxy provides the local protocol of (and communicates with) its model on a remote processor. Proxies are used to create a single virtual address space across multiple processors. [Firesmith]

view [object] *n.* (a) any domain object that exists to provide a user view of (i.e., information about and control over) one or more model objects. [Firesmith] (b) any instance of a view class. [Firesmith]

Synonym: PANE.

Contrast with: CONTROLLER OBJECT, MODEL OBJECT, VIEW CLASS.

Commentary: A model object may have more than one view object, and a view object may also be a controller object of its model object(s). Most view objects are also presentation objects. [Firesmith]

Kinds:

- ACTIVE VIEW
- BROWSER
- PRESENTATION OBJECT

- COLLAPSED VIEW
- PROXY OBJECT
- SUBVIEW

- **active view [object]** *n.* the view that is currently being used by the operator. [Firesmith]
- **browser [object]** *n.* any interactive tool that allows users to view in a library the classes and their characteristics. [Firesmith]

Commentary: Browsers are typically implemented as an aggregate presentation object that allows developers to scroll through the class structure and edit the features of the classes. [Firesmith]

- **presentation [object]** *n.* (a) any specialized view object that exists to provide a formatted view of (i.e., information about and control over) one or more model or view objects. [Firesmith] (b) any instance of a presentation class. [Firesmith]

Contrast with: PRESENTATION CLASS, PROXY OBJECT.

Commentary: A model or view object may have more than one presentation object, and a presentation object may also be a controller object of its model or view object(s). [Firesmith]

- **collapsed view** *n.* any view that displays only its label part, but can be selected and expanded to show the entire view. [Firesmith]
- **proxy [object]** *n.* (a) any local view object that represents (i.e., acts as a processor-specific variant of and communicates with) its remote model object. [Firesmith] (b) any instance of a proxy class. [Firesmith]

Contrast with: PRESENTATION OBJECT, PROXY CLASS.

Commentary: A proxy provides the

local protocol of (and communicates with) its model on a remote processor. Proxies are used to create a single virtual address space across multiple processors. [Firesmith]

• **subview** *n.* any view contained as a component part of another view. [Firesmith]

virtual *adj.* **1.** describing anything that has conceptual but not actual existence. [Rumbaugh] **2.** the C++ term describing any polymorphic member function that can be overridden by a descendant class. [C++, Firesmith]
See also: FLUID FEATURE.

virtual base class *n.* any base class, whose information is shared by all of its child classes that declare the base class as virtual. [C++]
Contrast with: ABSTRACT CLASS, BASE CLASS.
Example:
```
class VBC {};
class C1:virtual public VBC {};
class C2:virtual public VBC {};
class C12:public C1, public C2 {};
```
The child classes C_1 and C_2 share the information defined in the virtual base class VBC. Therefore, the ancestor derived class C_{12} does not inherit the members of VBC twice, which it would have if C_1 and C_2 had not declared VBC as virtual.
Commentary: A virtual base class provides a local point for sharing information, a statically typed interface to the information shared by its derived classes. One can cast from a derived class to a virtual base class. Casting from a virtual base class to a derived class is disallowed to avoid requiring an implementation to maintain pointers to enclosing objects. [C++]

virtual binding *n.* **1.** binding that takes place at run-time due to compile-time ambiguities caused by inheritance and polymorphism. [Booch, Coad, Firesmith, Martin/Odell, Jacobson] **2.** binding that takes place after the message is sent. [Jacobson, OMG]
Synonyms: DELAYED BINDING, DYNAMIC BINDING, LATE BINDING, RUN-TIME BINDING.
Antonyms: COMPILE-TIME BINDING, EARLY BINDING, STATIC BINDING.
See also: DYNAMICALLY TAGGED.
Commentary: Virtual binding allows the system to dynamically decide what method to use, based on the type of the current object. [Lorenz] Virtual binding of operations is typically implemented via a virtual method table. [Firesmith]

virtual function *n.* any function on an object that may be redefined by subclasses; thus, for a given object, it is implemented through a set of methods declared in various classes related via their inheritance hierarchy. [Booch]
Synonym: GENERIC FUNCTION.

virtual image *n.* all of the objects in the system. [Smalltalk]

virtual inheritance *n.* any repeated inheritance whereby the features of repeated base classes (or supertypes) are only inherited once in the derived class (or subtype). [Coleman]
Synonym: SHARED REPEATED INHERITANCE.
See also: SHARED FEATURE.

virtual machine *n.* the hardware devices and machine language (or microcode) routines that give dynamics to the objects in the virtual image. [Firesmith, Smalltalk]

virtual member function *n.* the C++ term for any member function that may be

V

dynamically bound to an object at run-time, thereby permitting redefinition by the derived class. [C++, Firesmith]
Synonym: DYNAMIC OPERATION, VIRTUAL OPERATION.
Contrast with: STATIC OPERATION.
- **pure virtual function** *n.* the C++ term for any virtual function whose implementation is deferred and must be supplied by a descendant base class before the descendant class can be instantiated. [C++, Firesmith]
  Contrast with: ABSTRACT.
  Commentary: Pure virtual functions are used to create deferred classes. [Firesmith]

virtual method *n.* any method in a base class that may be redefined in a derived class. [Coleman]

virtual node class *n.* any class that conforms to a set of rules designed to ensure that its instances do not communicate with other objects by exchanging references. [Atkinson]
Commentary: Virtual node classes are suitable for execution on the separate nodes of a loosely coupled network. [Atkinson]

virtual operation *n.* any operation that may be dynamically bound to an object at run-time. [Firesmith, Jacobson]
Synonym: DYNAMIC OPERATION, VIRTUAL MEMBER FUNCTION.
Contrast with: STATIC OPERATION.

visibility *n.* the ability of one abstraction to see another and thus reference exported features. [Booch, Firesmith]
Synonym: VISIBILITY REFERENCE.
Commentary: Visibility is determined by scoping rules and visibility control mechanisms. [Booch, Firesmith]

visibility control *n.* the mechanism by which visibility (i.e., access) to features is controlled. [Firesmith]
Synonym: ACCESS CONTROL.
Contrast with: INFORMATION HIDING, PRIVATE, PROTECTED, PUBLIC.
See also: BODY, IMPLEMENTATION, INTERFACE, PROTOCOL.

visibility graph *n.* any graph showing the visibility reference structure of classes. [Coleman]

visibility reference *n.* the connection to an object required to be able to invoke its operations. [Coleman]
Synonym: VISIBILITY.

visitor [pattern] *n.* the behavioral object design pattern that encapsulates behavior that would otherwise be distributed across classes by allowing a visitor object to traverse an object structure, visiting each node. [Gamma, Helm, Johnson, & Vlissides]

visual container *n.* any top-level view object that knows how to lay out visual components in a window and how to wrap visual components in a way that supports one or more GUI interface conventions. [Coad]
Synonym: VIEW OBJECT.
Commentary: A visual container does not know about or interact with model objects. [Coad]

void link *n.* any link to nothing. [Firesmith]
Contrast with: ATTACHED LINK, DANGLING LINK.
Kinds:
- VOID POINTER
- VOID REFERENCE

- **void pointer** *n.* any pointer that does not point to an existing object. [Firesmith]
  Synonym: NULL POINTER.
  Contrast with: ATTACHED POINTER, DANGLING POINTER.

- **void reference** *n.* any reference that does not currently refer to an object. [Eiffel, Firesmith, Meyer]
Antonym: ATTACHED REFERENCE.

volatile *adj.* a hint to the compiler to avoid aggressive optimization involving the object because the value of the object may be changed by means undetectable by a compiler. [C++]
Contrast with: CONST.
Commentary: The words const and volatile may be added to any legal type-specifier in the declaration of an object. [C++]

V

weak authorization *n.* any authorization on a class in an inheritance hierarchy that can be overridden by a descendant. [Kim]
Antonym: STRONG AUTHORIZATION.

weak typing *n.* any typing that need not be declared and that is not enforced by the compiler. [Firesmith, Rumbaugh]
Antonym: STRONG TYPING.
Example: Smalltalk is a weakly typed language.

weakly typed *adj.* describing any programming language not requiring the declaration of and enforcing the consistency of the type of each object, property, and parameter.

whitebox *n.* anything, the implementation of which is visible. [Firesmith]
Synonym: GLASSBOX.
Antonym: BLACKBOX.
Commentary: A whitebox can be viewed both from the outside and the inside. Treating something as a whitebox means that you care how it works inside. [Firesmith, Lorenz]

whitebox interaction diagram (WID) *n.* any interaction diagram in which the documented objects and classes are treated as whiteboxes, showing their interfaces and implementations. [Firesmith]
Antonym: BLACKBOX INTERACTION DIAGRAM.

whitebox timing diagram (WTD) *n.* any timing diagram that documents the duration of operation execution and the transfer of control (message or call). [Fire-smith]
Antonym: BLACKBOX TIMING DIAGRAM.

whitebox testing *n.* any testing based on the implementation of the thing being tested, which is treated as a whitebox by the test. [Firesmith]
Examples: Path coverage testing of an operation's implementation, integration testing of the interactions among a class's attributes and operations, integration testing of a cluster of classes based on message passing among the classes, and integration testing of an application based on interactions between its clusters. [Firesmith]

whole-part object connection *n.* any connection that carries the added meaning of container-content, group-member, or assembly-part. [Coad]
See also: WHOLE-PART STRUCTURE.

whole-part structure *n.* any structure

produced by *has-a* relationships be-
tween wholes and their parts. [Coad].
Synonyms: AGGREGATION HIERARCHY,
ASSEMBLY STRUCTURE.
Contrast with: GEN-SPEC STRUCTURE.
Example: An example is the whole ve-
hicle and the part engine. A truck has
an engine.

workspace *n.* any object displayed as a
rectangular area on the display screen
in which to access (view and edit) information. [Smalltalk]
Synonym: VIEW.

• **system workspace** *n.* any special
workspace containing message expressions or templates for expressions that are useful for such operat-
ing-system activities as opening and
editing files, resetting display screen
size, and accessing the references to
any system changes. [Smalltalk]
Commentary: The system workspace
can be used to edit and evaluate these
expressions, notably expressions about
accessing files, querying the system,
and recovering from a crash. [Small-
talk]

wrapper *n.* any object or set of objects
that provides an object-oriented interface to nonobject-oriented software.
[Firesmith, Rumbaugh]
Contrast with: EMBED.
Example: It is common to wrapper legacy relational databases.

write accessor *n.* any accessor operation
that updates the value of a property.
[Firesmith, Shlaer/Mellor]
Antonym: READ ACCESSOR.
Contrast with: CREATE ACCESSOR, DE-
LETE ACCESSOR.

W

References

[Atkinson]

Atkinson, Colin (1991). *Object-Oriented Reuse, Concurrency and Distribution: An Ada-based Approach.* Wokingham: England: ACM Press/Addison-Wesley Publishing Company.

[Berard]

Berard, Edward. V. (1993). *Essays on Object-Oriented Software Engineering, Volume 1.* Englewood Cliffs, NJ: Prentice Hall.

[Booch]

Booch, Grady (1987). *Software Components with Ada: Structures, Tools, and Subsystems.* Menlo Park, CA: Benjamin/Cummings.

Booch, Grady (1994) *Object-Oriented Analysis and Design with Applications,* Second Edition, Menlo Park, CA: Benjamin/Cummings.

Booch, Grady (1993). *The Booch Method: A Case Study for Rational Rose.* Santa Clara, CA: Rational.

Booch, Grady (1995). *Object Solutions.* Menlo Park, CA: Benjamin/Cummings.

[C++]

Ellis, Margaret A.; & Stroustrup, Bjarne (1990). *The Annotated C++ Reference Manual.* NJ: AT&T Bell Laboratories, Incorporated and Reading, MA: Addison Wesley.

[Coad]

Coad, Peter (1989). OOA: Object-Oriented Analysis. *American Programmer,* Summer.

Coad, Peter; & Nicola, Jill (1993). *Object-Oriented Programming,* Englewood Cliffs, NJ: Prentice Hall.

Coad, Peter; & Yourdon, Edward (1990a). *Object-Oriented Analysis,* Second Edition. Englewood Cliffs, NJ: Prentice Hall.

Coad, Peter; & Yourdon, Edward (1990b). *Object-Oriented Design.* Englewood Cliffs, NJ: Prentice Hall.

Coad, Peter; & Yourdon, Edward (1991). OOA—Object-Oriented Analysis. *IEEE Tutorial on System and Software Requirements Engineering.*

Coad, Peter; North, David; & Mayfield, Mark (1995). *Object Models: Strategies, Patterns & Applications.* Englewood Cliffs, NJ: Prentice Hall.

[Coleman]

Coleman, Derek; Arnold, Patrick; Bodoff, Stephanie; Dollin, Chris; Gilchrist, Helena; Hayes, Fiona; & Jeremaes, Paul (1994). *Object-Oriented Development: The Fusion Method.* Englewood Cliffs, NJ: Prentice Hall.

[Eiffel]

Meyer, Bertrand (1992). *Eiffel: The Language,* Englewood Cliffs, NJ: Prentice Hall.

[Embley]

Embley, David W.; Kurtz, Barry D.; & Woodfield, Scott N. (1992). *Object-Oriented Systems Analysis: A Model-Driven Approach.* Englewood Cliffs, NJ: Prentice Hall.

[Firesmith]
Firesmith, Donald G. (1993) *Object-Oriented Requirements Analysis and Logical Design: A Software Engineering Approach.* New York: Wiley.

Firesmith, Donald G. (1994). *ASTS Abbreviations and Glossary.* ASTS-G01 Version 2.0. Fort Wayne, IN: Advanced Software Technology Specialists.

[Henderson-Sellers]
Henderson-Sellers, Brian (1992). *A BOOK of Object-Oriented Knowledge.* Sydney, Australia: Prentice Hall.

Henderson-Sellers, Brian (1991). COMMA: An Architecture for Method Interoperability. *Report on Object Analysis and Design.* **1**(3) 25–28.

Henderson-Sellers, Brian; & Edwards, Julian M. (1994) *BOOKTWO of Object-Oriented Knowledge: The Working Object.* Sydney, Australia: Prentice Hall.

Henderson-Sellers, Brian; & Edwards, Julian M. (1994) Identifying Three Levels of O-O Methodologies. *Report on Object Analysis and Design.* **1**(2) 25–28.

[Jacobson]
Jacobson, Ivar; Christerson, Magnus; Jonsson, Patrik; & Övergaard, Gunnar (1992). *Object-Oriented Software Engineering: A Use Case Driven Approach.* Wokingham, England: Addison-Wesley.

Jacobson, Ivar; Christerson, Magnus; & Jacobson, Agneta (1995). *The Object Advantage: Business Process Reeingineering with Object Technology.* Wokingham, England: Addison-Wesley.

[Lorenz]
Lorenz, Mark (1993). *Object-Oriented Software Development.* Englewood Cliffs, NJ: Prentice Hall.

Lorenz, Mark (1995). *Rapid Software Development with Smalltalk.* New York: SIGS Books.

[Martin & Odell]
Martin, James; & Odell, James J. (1992). *Object-Oriented Analysis and Design.* Englewood Cliffs, NJ: Prentice Hall.

Martin, James (1993). *Principles of Object-Oriented Analysis and Design,* Englewood Cliffs, NJ: Prentice Hall.

Martin, James; & Odell, James J. (1995). *Object-Oriented Methods: A Foundation.* Englewood Cliffs, NJ: Prentice Hall.

[Meyer]
Meyer, Bertrand (1992). *Eiffel: The Language.* Englewood Cliffs, NJ: Prentice Hall.

[ODMG]
Atwood, Thomas; Duhl, Joshua; Ferran, Guy; Loomis, Mary; & Wade, Drew (1994). In R. G. G. Cattell (Ed.), *The Object Database Standard: ODMG-93.* (Release 1.1). San Francisco: Morgan Kaufmann Publishers.

[OMG]
Object Management Group. (1992). *The Common Object Request Broker; Architecture and Specification.* (Revision 1.1, OMG Document Number 91.12.1). New York: Wiley.

Object Management Group. (1993). In R. M. Soley (Ed.), *Management Architecture Guide,* (Revision 2.0, OMG Document Number 92.11.1). New York: Wiley.

Object Management Group. (1994). In J. Siegel (Ed.), *Common Object Services Specification.* (Revision 1.0, OMG Document Number 94.1.1). New York: Wiley.

Object Management Group Object Analysis and Design Special Interest Group (OAD-SIG). (1994a). In A. T. F. Hutt (Ed.), *Object Analysis and Design: Comparison of Methods.* New York: Wiley.

Object Management Group Object Analysis and Design Special Interest Group (OAD-SIG). (1994b). In A. T. F. Hutt (Ed.), *Object Analysis and Design: Description of Methods.* New York: Wiley.

[Rumbaugh]

Rumbaugh, James; Blaha, Michael; Premerlani, William; Eddy, Frederick; & Lorensen, William (1991a). *Object-Oriented Modeling and Design.* Englewood Cliffs, NJ: Prentice Hall.

Rumbaugh, James; Blaha, Michael; Premerlani, William; Eddy, Frederick; & Lorensen, William (1991b). *Object-Oriented Modeling and Design, Solutions Manual.* Englewood Cliffs, NJ: Prentice Hall.

Rumbaugh, James (1995a). OMT: The Object Model. *Journal of Object-Oriented Programming.* **7**(8) 21–27.

Rumbaugh, James (1995b). OMT: The Dynamic Model. *Journal of Object-Oriented Programming.* **7**(9) 6–12.

[Shlaer/Mellor]

Shlaer, Sally; & Mellor, Stephen J. (1988). *Object-Oriented Systems Analysis: Modeling the World in Data.* Englewood Cliffs, NJ: Yourdon Press.

Shlaer, Sally; & Mellor, Stephen J. (1990). Recursive Design. *Computer Language, 7*(3).

Shlaer, Sally; & Mellor, Stephen J. (1992). *Object-Oriented Systems Analysis: Modeling the World in States.* Englewood Cliffs, NJ: Yourdon Press.

[Smalltalk]

Goldberg, Adele (1984). *Smalltalk-80: The Interactive Programming Environment.* Reading, MA: Addison-Wesley.

Goldberg, Adele; & Robson, Dave (1989). *Smalltalk-80: The Language.* Reading, MA: Addison-Wesley.

[Steele]

Steele, Guy L. Jr. (1990). *Common LISP: The Language.* Second Edition. Newton: MA, Butterworth-Heinemann.

[Wirfs-Brock]

Wirfs-Brock, Rebecca; Wilkerson, Brian; & Wiener, Laura (1990). *Designing Object-Oriented Software.* Englewood Cliffs, NJ: Prentice Hall.

Object-Oriented Industry Groups

Appendix *A* The Object Management Group™ (OMG)

The Object Management Group (OMG) is an international trade association incorporated as nonprofit in the United States. OMG is dedicated to maximizing the portability, reusability, and interoperability of software using object technology. OMG is the leading worldwide organization dedicated to producing a framework and specifications for commercially available object-oriented environments. The OMG provides an open forum for industry discussion, education, and promotion of OMG-endorsed object technology.

The definitions appearing in this appendix are excerpted from the following sources and are reprinted with permission of The Object Management Group:

Object Management Group. (1992). *The Common Object Request Broker; Architecture and Specification.* (Revision 1.1, OMG Document Number 91.12.1). New York: Wiley.

Object Management Group. (1993). In R. M. Soley (Ed.), *Management Architecture Guide,* (Revision 2.0, OMG Document Number 92.11.1). New York: Wiley.

Object Management Group. (1994). In J. Siegel (Ed.), *Common Object Services Specification.* (Revision 1.0, OMG Document Number 94.1.1). New York: Wiley.

Object Management Group Object Analysis and Design Special Interest Group (OADSIG). (1994a). In A. T. F. Hutt (Ed.), *Object Analysis and Design: Comparison of Methods.* New York: Wiley.

Object Management Group Object Analysis and Design Special Interest Group (OADSIG). (1994b). In A. T. F. Hutt (Ed.), *Object Analysis and Design: Description of Methods.* New York: Wiley.

For more information, contact:

Dr. Jon Siegel
Director of Program Management
Object Management Group, Inc.
492 Old Connecticut Path

Framingham, Massachusetts 01701, USA
Voice: +1 (508) 820-4300, Voicemail: +1 (508) 397-1739
Fax: +1 (508) 820-4303
E-mail: info@omg.org
http://www.omg.org

abstraction *n.* "a relationship between a group of object types such that one object type represents a set of characteristics which are shared by other object types." [OADSIG 1994a, page 161]

abstract object type *n.* "an abstraction used to group common characteristics of real-world object types." [OADSIG 1994a, page 185]

activation *n.* "preparing an object to execute an operation." [OMG 1992, page 165]

Example: "Copying the persistent form of methods and stored data into an executable address space to allow execution of the methods on the stored data." [OMG 1992, page 165, OMG 1993, page 65]

Antonym: PASSIVATION.

adapter *n.* short for OBJECT ADAPTER. [OMG 1992, page 165] "an object adapter is the primary way that an object implementation accesses services provided by the ORB." [OMG 1992, page 36] "The ORB component which provides object reference, activation, and state related services to an object implementation. There may be different adapters provided for different kinds of implementations." [OMG 1992, page 168]

Synonym: OBJECT ADAPTER.

See also: BASIC OBJECT ADAPTER.

ad hoc polymorphism *n.* any polymorphism whereby "different operations on different types have the same name." [OADSIG 1994a, page 162]

Contrast with: INHERENT POLYMORPHISM.

aggregation *n.* "a relationship such as 'consists of,' 'contains,' or a similar relationship between object types; it defines the composition of an object type from other object types." [OADSIG 1994a, page 168]

Example: A 'document' contains 'text fragments,' 'diagrams,' and 'spreadsheets.'"

analysis modeling *n.* the activity that "seeks to obtain a thorough understanding of a problem domain by representing the real world as a collection of intercommunicating objects.... The purpose of analysis modeling is to obtain a thorough description of a problem domain, so that:
– The requirements in the problem domain of some application can be formalized
– The environment in which those applications are to be used is well understood." [OADSIG 1994a, page 183]

application *n.* "a dynamic object-based application is the (end-user) functionality provided by one or more programs consisting of a collection of interoperating objects. In common terminology this is usually referred to as a running application or process. A static object-based application is a set of types and classes interrelated specific to a particular (end-user) objective. In common terminology this is usually referred to as a program." [OMG 1993, page 65] "a part of an information system which is used to deliver business functionality." [OADSIG 1994a, page 187]

application facilities *n.* obsolete term for "comprise facilities that are useful within a specific application domain." [OMG 1993, page 65]

Synonym: VERTICAL COMMON FACILITIES.

Antonym: HORIZONTAL COMMON FACILITIES.

Application Object (AO) *n.* "Application Objects are specific to particular end-user applications." [OMG 1993, page 54] "Applications and their components that are managed within an object-oriented system. Example operations on such objects are open, install, move, and remove." [OMG 1993, page 66]

architecture concept *n.* any concept that is "a framework of functional components, embracing a set of standards, conventions, rules, and processes that support the integration of a wide range of information technology, enabling them to be used effectively within an enterprise." [OADSIG 1994a, page 171]

Contrast with: GROUP AND VIEW CONCEPT, OBJECT BEHAVIOR CONCEPT, OBJECT STRUCTURE CONCEPT.

assertion *n.* any rule stated as "a predicate that is part of the definition of an object type." [OADSIG 1994a, page 170]

Example: "If the due date on 'Book' is [earlier] than today's date, then the book is overdue." [OADSIG 1994a, page 170]

association *n.* "a semantic relationship with an explicit inverse relation." [OADSIG 1994a, page 165]

Examples: 'Employer' and 'Employee' relations for the object types 'Company' and 'Person.'

asynchronous request *n.* "a request where the client object does not pause to wait for results." [OMG 1993, page 66]

Synonym: ASYNCHRONOUS MESSAGE.

Antonym: SYNCHRONOUS REQUEST.

atomicity *n.* "the property that ensures that an operation either changes the state associated with all participating objects consistent with the request, or changes none at all. If a set of operations is atomic, then multiple requests for those operations are serializable." [OMG 1993, page 66]

attribute *n.* "an identifiable association between an object and a value. An at-

tribute A is made visible to clients as a pair of operations: get_A and set_A. Read-only attributes only generate a get operation." [OMG 1992, page 165]

"A conceptual notion. An attribute of an object is an identifiable association between the object and some other entity or entities. Typically, the association is revealed by an operation with a single parameter identifying the object." [OMG 1993, page 66]

Contrast with: RELATIONSHIP.

See also: PROPERTY.

attribute type *n.* "a characteristic that specifies a mapping to a nonobject type." [OADSIG 1994a, page 165]

Examples: 'Customer Name' and 'Customer Address' would be attribute types of the 'Customer' object type.

audience *n.* "the kind of consumer (caller) of the interface. An interface may be intended for use by the ultimate user of the service (functional interface), by a system management function within the system (system management interface), or by other participating services in order to construct the service from disparate objects (construction interface)." [OMG 1993, page 66]

See also: CONSTRUCTION INTERFACES, FUNCTIONAL INTERFACES, SYSTEM MANAGEMENT INTERFACES.

Basic Object Adapter (BOA) *n.* "an interface intended to be widely available and to support a wide variety of common object implementations. It includes convenient interfaces for generating object references, registering implementations that consist of one or more programs, activating implementations, and authenticating requests. It also provides a limited amount of persistent storage for objects that can be

used for connecting to a larger or more general storage facility, for storing access control information, or other purposes." [OMG 1992, page 66]
See also: OBJECT ADAPTER.

bearer *n.* "the kind of object that presents an interface. An object may be fundamentally characterized by the fact that it has a given interface (a specific object bears an interface) or an object may have an interface that is ancillary to its primary purpose in order to provide certain other capabilities (a generic object bears the interface)." [OMG 1993, page 66]

behavior *n.* "the observable effects of performing the requested operation including its results." [OMG 1992, page 165] "The behavior of a request is the observable effects of performing the requested service (including its results)." [OMG 1993, page 66]
See also: DYNAMIC INVOCATION, LANGUAGE BINDING, METHOD RESOLUTION, STATIC INVOCATION.

behavioral model *n.* any model that "describes the dynamics of the object types within the problem domain." [OADSIG 1994a, page 187]
Contrast with: FUNCTIONAL MODEL, STRUCTURAL MODEL.
Examples: Event list, state transition diagram, life cycle diagram, event diagram, event trace, scenario, use case, and object request diagram.

behavior consistency *n.* "ensures that the behavior of an object maintains its state consistency." [OMG 1993, page 66]

bind a name *v.* *-ed, -ing* "to create a name binding in a given context." [OMG 1994a, page 13]

binding *n.* "(or more specifically method binding) the selection of the method to perform a requested service and of the

data to be accessed by that method." [OMG 1993, page 66]
Synonym: METHOD BINDING.
Contrast with: METHOD RESOLUTION.
Kinds:
• DYNAMIC BINDING
• STATIC BINDING

• **dynamic binding** *n.* any "binding that is performed after the request is issued." [OMG 1993, page 68]
Antonym: STATIC BINDING.

• **static binding** *n.* any "binding that is performed prior to the actual issuing of the request." [OMG 1993, page 74]
Antonym: DYNAMIC BINDING.

business logic object type *n.* "an object type which provides the functionality of the application." [OADSIG 1994a, page 195]

class *n.* "an implementation that can be instantiated to create multiple objects with the same behavior. An object is an instance of a class. Types classify objects according to a common interface: classes classify objects according to a common implementation." [OMG 1993, page 67] "a description of a group of objects (instances) with similar properties, and common behavior, semantics, and relationships. A class represents a particular implementation of an object type. A class is composed of two parts—namely an interface and a body. [OADSIG 1994a, page 203]
Contrast with: IMPLEMENTATION, INTERFACE, TYPE.

class body *n.* "the detailed implementation of the class. It is internal structure not visible outside the class itself." [OADSIG 1994a, page 204]

class inheritance *n.* "the construction of a class by incremental modification of other classes." [OMG 1993, page 67]

class interface *n.* "defines the service which that class offers to users." [OADSIG 1994a, pages 203-204]

class object *n.* "an object that serves as a class. A class object serves as a factory." [OMG 1993, page 67]
Contrast with: FACTORY.

client *n.* "the client of a service is any entity capable of requesting the service." [OMG 1992, page 18] "The code or process that invokes an operation on an object." [OMG 1992, page 166]

client object *n.* "an object issuing a request for a service. A given object may be a client for some requests and a server for other requests." [OMG 1993, page 67]
Antonym: SERVER OBJECT.

• **managed object** *n.* "the term 'managed object' is used to refer to clients of System Management services, including the installation and activation service and the operational control service (dynamic behavior). These clients may be application objects, common facilities objects, or other object services. The term is used for compatibility with system management standards (the X/Open GDMO specification and ISO/IEC 10164 System Management Functions parts 1 to 4)." [OMG 1993, page 70]

Common Facilities (CF) *n.* "common Facilities is a collection of classes and objects that provide general purpose capabilities, useful in many applications." [OMG 1993, page 54] "Provides facilities useful in many application domains and which are made available through OMA-compliant class interfaces." [OMG 1993, page 67] "common facilities is a collection of higher-level services broadly applicable to many applications of

high-value capabilities for specific domains or vertical markets." [OMG 1995, page 9]
Synonym: CORBA FACILITIES.
Contrast with: APPLICATION OBJECTS, OBJECT SERVICES.
Kinds:
  • HORIZONTAL COMMON FACILITIES
    - SYSTEM MANAGEMENT FACILITIES
  • VERTICAL COMMON FACILITIES

• **horizontal common facilities** *n.* "The horizontal common facilities include functions shared by many or most systems, regardless of application content area." [OMG 1995, page 11]
Examples: "User interface, information management, systems management, task management." [OMG 1995, page 11]
Antonym: VERTICAL COMMON FACILITIES.

- **system management facilities** *n.* "System Management Common Facilities should provide a set of utility interfaces typically though of as system administration functions. That is, interfaces that abstract basic functions such as control, monitoring, security management, configuration, and policy that are needed to perform Systems Management operations (adding new users, setting permissions, installing software, etc.)." [OMG 1995, page 55]

• **vertical common facilities** *n.* "Vertical Market Facilities represent technology that supports various vertical markets such as health care, retailing, CAD, or financial systems." [OMG 1995, page 12]
Antonym: HORIZONTAL COMMON FACILITIES.

component *n.* "a conceptual notion. A

component is an object that is considered to be part of some containing object." [OMG 1993, page 67]
See also: PROFILE.

- **design component** *n.* "a collection of object types which create a single unit of functionality." [OADSIG 1994a, page 197]

compound name *n.* "a name with multiple components." [OMG 1994a, page 14]
Antonym: SIMPLE NAME.

compound object *n.* "a conceptual notion. A compound object is an object that is viewed as standing for a set of related objects." [OMG 1993, page 67]

concept *n.* something "used to describe an aspect of a subject area of object analysis and design." [OADSIG 1994a, page 165]

Kinds:
- ARCHITECTURE CONCEPT
- GROUP AND VIEW CONCEPT
- OBJECT BEHAVIOR CONCEPT
- OBJECT STRUCTURE CONCEPT

- **architecture concept** *n.* any concept that is "a framework of functional components, embracing a set of standards, conventions, rules, and processes that support the integration of a wide range of information technology, enabling them to be used effectively within an enterprise." [OADSIG 1994a, page 171]

- **group and view concept** *n.* any concept that "describes how a set of object types are grouped into a schema and/ or viewed in a diagram." [OADSIG 1994a, page 165]

- **object behavior concept** *n.* any concept that "describes some aspect of the dynamic behavior of the object types identified during object analysis and design. These concepts include opera-

tion, state, requests, and messages." [OADSIG 1994a, page 165]

- **object structure concept** *n.* any concept that "identifies some aspect of the object types, the attribute types, and the relationship types identified during object analysis and design." [OADSIG 1994a, page 165]

concurrency *n.* "a property which differentiates an active object from one which is not active. Active objects encompass their own thread of control." [OADSIG 1994a, page 197]

concurrency control service *n.* "The purpose of a concurrency control service is to mediate concurrent access to an object such that the consistency of the object is not compromised when accessed by concurrently executing computations." [OMG 1994b, page 7]

conformance *n.* "a relation defined over types such that type x conforms to type y if any value that satisfies type x also satisfies type y." [OMG 1993, page 67]

constraint *n.* any rule stated as "a restriction or requirement concerning instances of an object type." [OADSIG 1994a, page 170]
Examples: "The object type 'Position' has the instances of 'on' and 'off.' The attribute 'part id' on the object type 'Part' must take a value." [OADSIG 1994a, page 170]

construction interfaces *n.* "interfaces that define the operations used to communicate between the core of an Object Service and related objects that must participate in providing the service. They are typically defined by the service and inherited and implemented by participants in the service. Objects that participate in a service must support these interfaces." [OMG 1993, page 67]

Contrast with: FUNCTIONAL INTERFAC-ES, SYSTEM MANAGEMENT INTERFACES.
See also: AUDIENCE.

consumer *n.* any object role that "pro-cess[es] event data." [OMG 1994a, page 32]
Antonym: SUPPLIER.

context-independent operation *n.* "an operation where all requests that iden-tify the operation have the same behav-ior. (In contrast, the effect of a context-dependent operation might depend upon the identity or location of the cli-ent object issuing the request.)" [OMG 1993, page 67]
Antonym: CONTEXT-DEPENDENT OPER-ATION.

context object *n.* "a collection of name-value pairs that provides environmental or user-preference information." [OMG 1992, page 166]

CORBA™ **Services** *n.* CORBA Services "is a collection of services with object in-terfaces that provide basic functions for realizing and maintaining objects." [OMG 1993, page 54] "Provide basic functions for object life-cycle manage-ment and storage (e.g., creation / dele-tion, activation / passivation, identifica-tion / location)." [OMG 1993, page 71] "common facilities is a collection of higher-level services broadly applicable to many applications of high-value ca-pabilities for specific domains or verti-cal markets." [OMG 1995, page 9]
Synonym: OBJECT FACILITIES.
Contrast with: APPLICATION OBJECTS, OBJECT SERVICES.
Kinds:
- HORIZONTAL COMMON FACILITIES
  - SYSTEM MANAGEMENT FACILITIES
- VERTICAL COMMON FACILITIES

- **horizontal common facilities** *n.* "The horizontal common facilities include functions shared by many or most sys-tems, regardless of application content area." [OMG 1995, page 11]
Examples: "User interface, informa-tion management, systems manage-ment, task management." [OMG 1995, page 11]
Antonym: VERTICAL COMMON FACILI-TIES.

- **system management facilities** *n.* "System Management Common Fa-cilities should provide a set of utility interfaces typically though of as sys-tem administration functions. That is, interfaces that abstract basic func-tions such as control, monitoring, security management, configura-tion, and policy that are needed to perform Systems Management op-erations (adding new users, setting permissions, installing software, etc.)." [OMG 1995, page 55]

- **vertical common facilities** *n.* "Verti-cal Market Facilities represent tech-nology that supports various vertical markets such as health care, retailing, CAD, or financial systems." [OMG 1995, page 12]
Antonym: HORIZONTAL COMMON FA-CILITIES.

data model *n.* "a collection of entities, operators, and consistency rules." [OMG 1993, page 67]

data type *n.* "a categorization of values operation arguments, typically cover-ing both behavior and representation (i.e., the traditional non-OO program-ming language notion of type." [OMG 1992, page 166]

deactivation *n.* "the opposite of activa-tion" [OMG 1992, page 166]
Antonym: ACTIVATION.

deferred synchronous request *n.* "a request where the client does not wait for completion of the request, but does intend to accept results later." [OMG 1992, page 166]
Contrast with: ASYNCHRONOUS REQUEST, ONE-WAY REQUEST, SYNCHRONOUS MESSAGE, SYNCHRONOUS REQUEST.

delegation *n.* "the ability for a method to issue a request in such a way that self-reference in the method performing the request returns the same object(s) as self-reference in the method issuing the request." [OMG 1993, page 68]
Contrast with: SELF-REFERENCE.

design component *n.* "a collection of object types which create a single unit of functionality." [OADSIG 1994a, page 197]

design modeling *n.* the activity that "produces rigorous specifications of the interfaces provided by a set of object types.... The purpose of design modeling is to specify the external view of a set of object types." [OADSIG 1994a, page 193]

design module *n.* any design component that is "a collection of design components which are integrated together." [OADSIG 1994a, page 197]

design model object type *n.* "an object type which is used in a design model." [OADSIG 1994a, page 195]

diagram *n.* "a pictorial representation of some aspect of a set of objects. Every diagram should have a name, a notation, a graphical representation, and semantics." [OADSIG 1994a, page 171]

dialog object type *n.* a user-interface object type that "maintains the state of the interface and from the user's perception controls its overall behavior." [OADSIG 1994a, page 195]

Example: "the open file dialogue provided by a word processor." [OADSIG 1994a, page 195]

dynamic binding *n.* any "binding that is performed after the request is issued." [OMG 1993, page 68]
Antonym: STATIC BINDING.

dynamic invocation *n.* "constructing and issuing a request whose signature is possibly not known until runtime." [OMG 1992, page 166]
Antonym: STATIC INVOCATION.

dynamic state *n.* "The state of the object can be considered in two parts, the dynamic state, which is typically in memory and is not likely to exist for the whole lifetime of the object...." [OMG 1994a, page 114]
Antonym: PERSISTENT STATE.

embed *v.* *-ed, -ing* to create "an object out of a non-object entity by wrapping it in an appropriate shell." [OMG 1993, page 68]

encapsulation *n.* "the packaging of operations and data together into an object type such that the data is only accessible through its interface." [OADSIG 1994a, page 161]
Commentary: "Through encapsulation of object data (making data accessible only in a way controlled by the software that implements the object) applications are built in a truly modular fashion, preventing unintended interference." [OMG 1993, page 13]

event *n.* "an incident which requires some response, an event denotes a specific state change within an object type." [OADSIG 1994a, page 169]
Examples: 'oven overheated,' 'out of stock,' 'order arrives,' and 'phone rings.'
See also: REQUEST.
Kinds:

App
A

- EXTERNAL EVENT
- INTERNAL EVENT
- **external event** *n.* "An external event arises from outside an object type, a domain, or a module." [OADSIG 1994a, page 169]
  Antonym: INTERNAL EVENT.
- **internal event** *n.* "an event generated internally within an object type, a domain, or a module." [OADSIG 1994a, page 169]
  Antonym: EXTERNAL EVENT.

event channel *n.* "an intervening object that allows multiple suppliers to communicate with multiple consumers asynchronously." [OMG 1994a, page 32]
See also: PULL MODEL, PUSH MODEL.

event service *n.* "The event service decouples the communication between objects." [OMG 1994a, page 32]
Commentary: "The event service defines two roles for objects: the supplier role and the consumer role." [OMG 1994a, page 32]

exception *n.* "an exception is an indication that an operation request was not performed successfully. An exception may be accompanied by additional, exception-specific information." [OMG 1992, page 23] "An exception packages information indicating that some unusual event has occurred and passes that information to an exception handler." [OMG 1993, page 45] "exceptions are used exclusively for handling exceptional conditions such as error returns." [OMG 1994a, page 8]

exchange format *n.* "the form of a description used to import and export objects." [OMG 1993, page 68]

execution engine *n.* "an abstract machine (not a program) that can interpret methods of certain formats, causing the de-

scribed computations to be performed." [OMG 1992, page 25]
See also: METHOD FORMAT.

export *v.* -*ed*, -*ing* "to transmit a description of an object to an external entity." [OMG 1993, page 68]

extension of a type *n.* "the set of values that satisfy the type at any particular time." [OMG 1992, page 20]

external event *n.* "An external event arises from outside an object type, a domain, or a module." [OADSIG 1994a, page 169]
Antonym: INTERNAL EVENT.

externalized object reference *n.* "an object reference expressed as an ORB-specific string. Suitable for storage in files or other external media." [OMG 1992, page 166]

factory *n.* "A factory is an object that creates another object. Factories are not special objects." [OMG 1994a, page 68] "a conceptual notion. A factory provides a service for creating new objects." [OMG 1993, page 68]
Commentary: "As with any object, factories have well-defined IDL interfaces and implementations in some programming language.... There is no standard interface for a factory. Factories provide the client with specialized operations to create and initialized new instances in a natural way.... Factories are object implementation independent.... A factory assembles the resources necessary for the existence of an object it creates." [OMG 1993, pages 68–69]

functional interfaces *n.* any "interfaces that define the operations invoked by users of an object service. The audience for these interfaces is the service consumer, the user of the service. These interfaces present the functionality (the useful operations) of the service." [OMG 1993, page 68]

Contrast with: CONSTRUCTION INTER-FACES, SYSTEM MANAGEMENT INTERFAC-ES.

See also: AUDIENCE.

functional model *n.* any model that "describes the problem domain processing, with more emphasis on processing inputs and outputs and actions than on the events and 'things' of the domain. It may also structure the activities into a functionally based framework which may be useful when communicating the model and during design." [OADSIG 1994a, page 187]

Contrast with: BEHAVIORAL MODEL, STRUCTURAL MODEL.

Examples: Functional decomposition diagram, HIPO chart, and data flow diagram.

generalization *n.* "the inverse of the specialization relation." [OMG 1993, page 68]

Antonym: SPECIALIZATION.

generic object *n.* "an object (relative to some given Object Service) whose primary purpose for existence is unrelated to the Object Service." [OMG 1993, page 68]

generic operation *n.* "a conceptual notion. An operation is generic if it can be bound to more than one method." [OMG 1993, page 68]

group and view concept *n.* a concept that "describes how a set of object types are grouped into a schema and/or viewed in a diagram." [OADSIG 1994a, page 165]

Contrast with: ARCHITECTURE CON-CEPT, OBJECT BEHAVIOR CONCEPT, OB-JECT STRUCTURE CONCEPT.

handle *n.* "a value that unambiguously identifies an object." [OMG 1993, page 69]

Contrast with: IDENTIFIER, OBJECT NAME.

horizontal common facilities *n.* "The horizontal common facilities include functions shared by many or most systems, regardless of application content area." [OMG 1995, page 11]

Examples: "User interface, information management, systems management, task management." [OMG 1995, page 11]

Antonym: VERTICAL COMMON FACILI-TIES.

identifier *n.* "in the Core Model, each object has an identifier that provides a means to denote or refer to the object. This identifier is called an OID. OIDs label (or refer to) objects. The set of all OIDs is denoted as Obj.... OIDs in the Object Model denote the same concept as object references in CORBA." [OMG 1993, page 43]

Contrast with: HANDLE, OBJECT REFER-ENCE.

identity *n.* "each object has a unique identity that is distinct from and independent of any of its characteristics. Characteristics can vary over time whereas identity is constant." [OMG 1993, page 43]

implementation *n.* "a definition that provides the information needed to create an object, allowing the object to participate in providing an appropriate set of services. An implementation typically includes a description of the data structure used to represent the core state associated with an object, as well as definitions of the methods that access the data structure. It also typically includes information about the intended type of the object." [OMG 1993, page 69]

Synonym: OBJECT IMPLEMENTATION.

implementation definition language *n.* "a notation for describing implementations. The implementation definition language is currently beyond the scope of the ORB standard. It may contain vendor-specific and adapter-specific notations." [OMG 1992, page 166]

Antonym: INTERFACE DEFINITION LANGUAGE.

implementation inheritance *n.* "the construction of an implementation by incremental modification of other implementations. The ORB does not provide implementation inheritance. Implementation inheritance may be provided by higher level tools." [OMG 1992, page 166]

Antonym: INTERFACE INHERITANCE.

implementation object *n.* "an object that serves as an implementation definition. Implementation objects reside in an implementation repository." [OMG 1992, page 166]

implementation repository *n.* "the Implementation Repository contains information that allows the ORB to locate and activate implementations of objects." [OMG 1992, page 37] "A storage place for object implementation information." [OMG 1992, page 167]

Antonym: INTERFACE REPOSITORY.

import *n.* "creating an object based on a description of an object transmitted from an external entity." [OMG 1993, page 69]

information management object type *n.* any object type that "provides persistent storage for the application." [OADSIG 1994a, page 195]

Example: "a record definition in a logical database design." [OADSIG 1994a, page 195]

inherent polymorphism *n.* any polymorphism whereby "operations are inherited by every subtype." [OADSIG 1994a, page 162]

Contrast with: AD HOC POLYMORPHISM.

inheritance *n.* "the construction of a definition by incremental modification of other definitions." [OMG 1993, page 69] "Inheritance is a mechanism for reuse." [OMG 1993, page 47] "Inheritance is a notational mechanism for defining a type S in terms of another type T. The definition of S inherits all the operations of T and may provide other operations." [OMG 1993, page 48]

Contrast with: SPECIALIZATION, SUBTYPING.

Kinds:
- CLASS INHERITANCE
- IMPLEMENTATION INHERITANCE
- INTERFACE INHERITANCE
- MULTIPLE INHERITANCE
- SINGLE INHERITANCE

- **class inheritance** *n.* "the construction of a class by incremental modification of other classes." [OMG 1993, page 67]

- **implementation inheritance** *n.* "the construction of an implementation by incremental modification of other implementations. The ORB does not provide implementation inheritance. Implementation inheritance may be provided by higher level tools." [OMG 1992, page 166]

  Antonym: INTERFACE INHERITANCE.

- **interface inheritance** *n.* "the construction of an interface by incremental modification of other interfaces. The IDL language provides interface inheritance." [OMG 1992, page 167]

  Antonym: IMPLEMENTATION INHERITANCE.

- **multiple inheritance** *n.* "the construction of a definition by incremental modification of more than one other definition." [OMG 1992, page 167]

Antonym: SINGLE INHERITANCE.
Contrast with: SINGLE SPECIALIZATION.

- **single inheritance** *n.* "the construction of a definition by incremental modification of one definition." [OMG 1993, page 73]

  Antonym: MULTIPLE INHERITANCE.
  Contrast with: MULTIPLE SPECIALIZATION.

instance *n.* "an object is an instance of an interface if it provides the operations, signatures, and semantics specified by that interface. An object is an instance of an implementation if its behavior is provided by that implementation." [OMG 1992, page 167] "An object created by instantiating a class. An object is an instance of a class." [OMG 1993, page 69]

instantiation *n.* "object creation." [OMG 1993, page 69] "This relationship is created when an object is created as an instance of an object type." [OADSIG 1994a, page 168]

interface *n.* "a listing of the operations and attributes that an object provides. This includes the signatures of the operations, and the types of the attributes. An interface definition ideally includes the semantics as well." [OMG 1992, page 167] "A description of a set of possible uses of an object. Specifically, an interface describes a set of potential requests in which an object can meaningfully participate." [OMG 1993, page 69] "The set of operation signatures defined on a type is called the type's interface." [OMG 1993, page 44]

Commentary: "An object satisfies an interface if it can be specified as the target object in each potential request described by the interface." [OMG 1992, page 167]

Kinds:

A

- CONSTRUCTION INTERFACE
- FUNCTIONAL INTERFACE
- OBJECT INTERFACE
- ORB INTERFACE
- PRINCIPAL INTERFACE
- TYPE INTERFACE

- **construction interface** *n.* "interfaces that define the operations used to communicate between the core of an Object Service and related objects that must participate in providing the service. They are typically defined by the service and inherited and implemented by participants in the service. Objects that participate in a service must support these interfaces." [OMG 1993, page 67]

- **functional interface** *n.* "interfaces that define the operations invoked by users of an object service. The audience for these interfaces is the service consumer, the user of the service. These interfaces present the functionality (the useful operations) of the service." [OMG 1993, page 68]

- **object interface** *n.* "a description of a set of possible uses of an object. Specifically an interface describes a set of potential requests in which an object can meaningfully participate as a parameter. It is the union of the object's type interfaces." [OMG 1993, page 71]

- **ORB interface** *n.* "the ORB Interface is the interface that goes directly to the ORB which is the same for all ORBs and does not depend on the object's interface or object adapter." [OMG 1992, page 36]

- **principal interface** *n.* "the interface that describes all requests in which an object is meaningful." [OMG 1993, page 72]

- **type interface** *n.* "defines the requests

in which instances of this type can meaningfully participate as a parameter." [OMG 1993, page 74]

Example: If the interface to "document type comprises edit and print and the interface to product type comprises set price and check inventory, then the object interface of a particular document which is also a product comprises all four requests." [OMG 1993, page 74]

Interface Definition Language™ (IDL) *n.* "the language used to describe the interfaces that client objects call and object implementations provide." [OMG 1992, page 45] "The IDL Interface Definition Language defines the types of objects by specifying their interfaces." [OMG 1992, page 34] "The IDL language is used by applications to specify the various interfaces they intend to offer to other applications via the ORB layer." [OMG 1993, page 59]

Antonym: IMPLEMENTATION DEFINITION LANGUAGE.

interface inheritance *n.* "the construction of an interface by incremental modification of other interfaces. The IDL language provides interface inheritance." [OMG 1992, page 167]

Antonym: IMPLEMENTATION INHERITANCE.

interface object *n.* "an object that serves to describe an interface. Interface objects reside in an interface repository." [OMG 1992, page 167]

interface repository *n.* "the Interface Repository is a service that provides persistent objects that represent the IDL information in a form available at runtime." [OMG 1992, page 36] "A storage place for interface information." [OMG 1992, page 167]

Antonym: IMPLEMENTATION REPOSITORY.

interface type *n.* "a type that is satisfied by any object (literally, by any value that identifies an object) that satisfies a particular interface." [OMG 1993, page 69]

Contrast with: OBJECT TYPE.

internal event *n.* "an event generated internally within an object type, a domain, or a module." [OADSIG 1994a, page 169]

Antonym: EXTERNAL EVENT.

interoperability *n.* "the ability for two or more ORBs to cooperate to deliver requests to the proper object. Interoperating ORBs appear to a client as a single ORB." [OMG 1992, page 167] "The ability to exchange request using the ORB in conformance with the OMG Architecture Guide. Objects interoperate if the methods of one object requests services of another." [OMG 1993, page 69]

language binding *n.* "the means and conventions by which a programmer writing in a specific programming language accesses ORB capabilities." [OMG 1992, page 167]

Synonym: LANGUAGE MAPPING.

language mapping *n.* "the means and conventions by which a programmer writing in a specific programming language accesses ORB capabilities." [OMG 1992, page 167]

Synonym: LANGUAGE BINDING.

legacy system object type *n.* any object type that "encapsulates an existing non-object-oriented application or application component, by defining an object-oriented interface so that it can be reused." [OADSIG 1994a, pages 195-196]

Lifecycle Service *n.* "the Object Lifecycle Service provides operations for managing object creation, deletion, copy and equivalence. An Object Service Definition." [OMG 1993, page 70] "define services and conventions for creating, deleting, copying, and moving objects." [OMG 1994a, page 4]

link *n.* "a conceptual notion. A relation between two objects." [OMG 1993, page 70]

literal *n.* "a value that identifies an entity that is not an object." [OMG 1993, page 70]
Contrast with: OBJECT NAME.

managed object *n.* "the term 'managed object' is used to refer to clients of System Management services, including the installation and activation service and the operational control service (dynamic behavior). These clients may be application objects, common facilities objects, or other object services." [OMG 1993, page 70]
Commentary: "The term is used for compatibility with system management standards (the X/Open GDMO specification and ISO/IEC 10164 System Management Functions parts 1 to 4)." [OMG 1993, page 70]

meaningful request *n.* "a request where the actual parameters satisfy the signature of the named operation." [OMG 1993, page 70]

message *n.* "a communication sent or received by an object." [OADSIG 1994a, page 169]
Synonym: REQUEST.
Kinds:
- ASYNCHRONOUS MESSAGE
- SYNCHRONOUS MESSAGE

- **asynchronous message** *n.* any message "where the message is sent from originator to receiver and the originator continues processing—as would

happen between two active instances." [OADSIG 1994a, page 169]
Synonym: ASYNCHRONOUS REQUEST.
Antonym: SYNCHRONOUS MESSAGE.

- **synchronous message** *n.* any message "where the thread of control passes from the originating instance to the receiving instance—as would happen where both instances were part of the one overall process." [OADSIG 1994a, page 169]
Synonym: SYNCHRONOUS REQUEST.
Antonym: ASYNCHRONOUS MESSAGE.

metaobject *n.* "an object that represents a type, operation, class, method, or other object model entity that describes objects." [OMG 1993, page 70]

method *n.* "an implementation of an operation." [OMG 1992, page 167] "Code that may be executed to perform a requested service. Methods associated with an object may be structured into one or more programs." [OMG 1993, page 70] "that part of an object type which implements an operation." [OADSIG 1994a, page 169]

method activation *n.* "the execution of a method." [OMG 1992, page 25]

method binding *n.* "(or more specifically method binding) the selection of the method to perform a requested service and of the data to be accessed by that method." [OMG 1993, page 66]
Synonym: BINDING.
Contrast with: METHOD RESOLUTION.
Kinds:
- DYNAMIC BINDING
- STATIC BINDING

- **dynamic binding** *n.* any "binding that is performed after the request is issued." [OMG 1993, page 68]
Antonym: STATIC BINDING.

- **static binding** *n.* any "binding that is

performed prior to the actual issuing of the request." [OMG 1993, page 74]
Antonym: DYNAMIC BINDING.

method format *n.* "a method has an immutable attribute called a method format that defines the set of execution engines that can interpret the method." [OMG 1992, page 25]

method resolution *n.* "the selection of the method to perform a requested operation." [OMG 1992, page 167]
Contrast with: BINDING.
See also: RESOLVE.

multiple inheritance *n.* "the construction of a definition by incremental modification of more than one other definition." [OMG 1992, page 167]
Antonym: SINGLE INHERITANCE.
Contrast with: SINGLE SPECIALIZATION.

multiple specialization *n.* any specialization "where an object type inherits characteristics from more than one object type." [OADSIG 1994a, page 168]
Antonym: SINGLE SPECIALIZATION.
Contrast with: SINGLE INHERITANCE.

name *n.* "an ordered sequence of components." [OMG 1994a, page 14]
Kinds:
• COMPOUND NAME
• SIMPLE NAME

• **compound name** *n.* "a name with multiple components." [OMG 1994a, page 14]
Antonym: SIMPLE NAME.

• **simple name** *n.* "a name with a single components." [OMG 1994a, page 14]
Antonym: COMPOUND NAME.

name binding *n.* "a name-to-object association. A name binding is always defined relative to a *naming context.*" [OMG 1994a, page 13]

naming context *n.* "an object that contains a set of name bindings in which each name is unique." [OMG 1994a, pages 3, 13]

non-object *n.* "things that are not objects are called non-objects.... Examples of non-objects are the basic and constructed values as defined in the CORBA specification.... Each non-object can be considered to belong to a type of value, called a non-object type." [OMG 1993, page 44]

Obj *n.* "the set of all OIDs is denoted as Obj." [OMG 1993, page 43]
Contrast with: IDENTIFIER.

object *n.* "an identifiable, encapsulated entity that provides one or more services that can be requested by a client." [OMG 1992, page 19] "A combination of a state and a set of methods that explicitly embodies an abstraction characterized by the behavior of relevant requests. An object is an instance of a class. An object models a real world entity and is implemented as a computational entity that encapsulates state and operations (internally implemented as data and methods) and responds to request for services. Methods can be owned by one or more objects. Requests can be sent to (zero) one or more objects. State data can be owned by one or more objects. State data and methods can be located at one or more locations." [OMG 1993, page 70] "A basic characteristic of an object is its distinct identity, which is immutable, persists for as long as the object exists, and is independent of the object's properties or behavior." [OMG 1993, page 42] "a thing. It is created as the instance of an object type. Each object has a unique identity that is distinct from and independent of any of its characteristics. Each object offers one or more operations." [OADSIG 1994a, page 165]

Kinds:
- CLASS OBJECT
- CLIENT OBJECT
  - MANAGED OBJECT
- COMPOUND OBJECT
- GENERIC OBJECT
- INTERFACE OBJECT
- PERSISTENT OBJECT
- SERVER OBJECT
- TRANSIENT OBJECT
- TYPE OBJECT

- **class object** *n.* "an object that serves as a class. A class object serves as a factory." [OMG 1993, page 67]
Contrast with: FACTORY.

- **client object** *n.* "an object issuing a request for a service. A given object may be a client for some requests and a server for other requests." [OMG 1993, page 67]
Antonym: SERVER OBJECT.

  - **managed object** *n.* "the term 'managed object' is used to refer to clients of System Management services, including the installation and activation service and the operational control service (dynamic behavior). These clients may be application objects, common facilities objects, or other object services. The term is used for compatibility with system management standards (the X/Open GDMO specification and ISO/IEC 10164 System Management Functions parts 1 to 4)." [OMG 1993, page 70]

- **compound object** *n.* "a conceptual notion. A compound object is an object that is viewed as standing for a set of related objects." [OMG 1993, page 67]

- **generic object** *n.* "an object (relative to some given Object Service) whose primary purpose for existence is unre-

lated to the Object Service." [OMG 1993, page 68]

- **•interface object** *n.* "an object that serves to describe an interface. Interface objects reside in an interface repository." [OMG 1992, page 167]

- **persistent object** *n.* "an object that can survive the process or thread that created it. A persistent object exists until it is explicitly deleted." [OMG 1993, page 72]
Antonym: TRANSIENT OBJECT.

- **server object** *n.* "an object providing response to a request for a service. A given object may be a client for some requests and a server for other requests." [OMG 1992, page 169]
Antonym: CLIENT OBJECT.

- **transient object** *n.* "an object the existence of which is limited by the lifetime of the process or thread that created it." [OMG 1993, page 74]
Antonym: PERSISTENT OBJECT.

- **type object** *n.* "an object that serves as a type." [OMG 1993, page 74]

Object *n.* "types are arranged into a type hierarchy that forms a directed acyclic graph. The root of this type hierarchy is the type Object." [OMG 1993, page 44]

object adapter *n.* "an object adapter is the primary way that an object implementation accesses services provided by the ORB." [OMG 1992, page 36] "The ORB component which provides object reference, activation, and state related services to an object implementation. There may be different adapters provided for different kinds of implementations." [OMG 1992, page 168]
See also: BASIC OBJECT ADAPTER.

object behavior concept *n.* a concept that "describes some aspect of the dynamic

behavior of the object types identified during object analysis and design. These concepts include operation, state, requests, and messages." [OADSIG 1994a, page 165]
Contrast with: ARCHITECTURE CONCEPT, GROUP AND VIEW CONCEPT, OBJECT STRUCTURE CONCEPT.

object communication *n.* "in object-oriented systems, takes the form of one object sending requests to other objects." [OADSIG 1994a, page 162]

object creation *n.* "an event that causes an object to exist that is distinct from any other object." [OMG 1993, page 71]

object destruction *n.* "an event that causes an object to cease to exist and its associated resources to become available for reuse." [OMG 1993, page 71]

object implementation *n.* "a definition that provides the information needed to create an object, allowing the object to participate in providing an appropriate set of services. An implementation typically includes a description of the data structure used to represent the core state associated with an object, as well as definitions of the methods that access the data structure. It also typically includes information about the intended type of the object." [OMG 1993, page 69]
Synonym: IMPLEMENTATION.
Commentary: The synonym OBJECT IMPLEMENTATION is found on [OMG 1992, Page 168].

object interface *n.* "a description of a set of possible uses of an object. Specifically an interface describes a set of potential requests in which an object can meaningfully participate as a parameter. It is the union of the object's type interfaces." [OMG 1993, page 71]

object name *n.* "a value that identifies an object." [OMG 1993, page 71]
Contrast with: HANDLE, OBJECT REFERENCE.

object reference *n.* "an object name that reliably denotes a particular object. Specifically, an object reference will identify the same object each time the reference is used in a request (subject to certain pragmatic limits of space and time). An object may be denoted by multiple, distinct object references." [OMG 1992, page 19] "An object reference is the information needed to specify an object within an ORB." [OMG 1992, page 34] "A value that unambiguously identifies an object. Object references are never reused to identify another object." [OMG 1992, page 168]
Contrast with: IDENTIFIER, OBJECT NAME.

- **externalized object reference** *n.* "an object reference expressed as an ORB-specific string. Suitable for storage in files or other external media." [OMG 1992, page 166]

Object Request Broker™ (ORB) *n.* "(Object Request Broker) provides the means by which objects make and receive requests and responses." [OMG 1993, page 71]

Object Services (OS) *n.* "Object Services is a collection of services with object interfaces that provide basic functions for realizing and maintaining objects." [OMG 1993, page 54] "Provide basic functions for object life-cycle management and storage (e.g., creation / deletion, activation / passivation, identification / location)." [OMG 1993, page 71]
Synonym: CORBA SERVICES.

object structure concept *n.* a concept that "identifies some aspect of the object types, the attribute types, and the relationship types identified during object analysis and design." [OADSIG 1994a, page 165]

Contrast with: ARCHITECTURE CONCEPT, GROUP AND VIEW CONCEPT, OBJECT BEHAVIOR CONCEPT.

object type *n.* "a type the extension of which is a set of objects (literally, a set of values that identify objects). In other words, an object type is satisfied only by (values that identify) objects." [OMG 1993, page 71] "An object type represents a definition of some set of object instances with similar behavior. A type is a semantic property. Characteristics of object types are: its definition, any extension of its definition, its supertypes, and its subtypes." [OADSIG 1994a, page 167]

Contrast with: INTERFACE TYPE.

Kinds:
- ABSTRACT OBJECT TYPE
- BUSINESS LOGIC OBJECT TYPE
- DESIGN MODEL OBJECT TYPE
- DIALOG OBJECT TYPE
- INFORMATION MANAGEMENT OBJECT TYPE
- LEGACY SYSTEM OBJECT TYPE
- PRESENTATION OBJECT TYPE
- PROBLEM DOMAIN OBJECT TYPE
- REAL-WORLD OBJECT TYPE
- USER INTERFACE OBJECT TYPE
  - DIALOG OBJECT TYPE
  - PRESENTATION OBJECT TYPE
  - USER INTERFACE METAPHOR

- **abstract object type** *n.* "an abstraction used to group common characteristics of real-world object types." [OADSIG 1994a, page 185]
- **business logic object type** *n.* "an object type which provides the functionality of the application." [OADSIG 1994a, page 195]
- **design model object type** *n.* "an ob-

ject type which is used in a design model." [OADSIG 1994a, page 195]
- **dialog object type** *n.* any user interface object type that "maintains the state of the interface and from the user's perception controls its overall behavior." [OADSIG 1994a, page 195]
  Example: "the open file dialogue provided by a word processor." [OADSIG 1994a, page 195]
- **information management object type** *n.* an object type that "provides persistent storage for the application." [OADSIG 1994a, page 195]
  Example: "a record definition in a logical database design." [OADSIG 1994a, page 195]
- **legacy system object type** *n.* an object type that "encapsulates an existing non-object-oriented application or application component, by defining an object-oriented interface so that it can be reused." [OADSIG 1994a, pages 195-196]
- **presentation object type** *n.* a user interface object type that "describes the visual appearance of the user interface." [OADSIG 1994a, page 195]
  Examples: "the chart of today's stock usage, a box object, a line object, and a tree object." [OADSIG 1994a, page 195]
- **problem domain object type** *n.* "a tangible or conceptual real-world object type." [OADSIG 1994a, page 185]
- **real-world object type** *n.* "an abstraction of a tangible real-world object identified during strategic modeling." [OADSIG 1994a, page 178]
- **user interface metaphor** *n.* a user interface object type that "ensures that users can understand the user interface." [OADSIG 1994a, page 195]

- **user interface object type** *n.* "an object used to define the user interface for the application." [OADSIG 1994a, page 195]

  Kinds:
  - DIALOG OBJECT TYPE
  - PRESENTATION OBJECT TYPE
  - USER INTERFACE METAPHOR

  - **dialog object type** *n.* a user interface object type that "maintains the state of the interface and from the user's perception controls its overall behavior." [OADSIG 1994a, page 195]
  Example: "the open file dialogue provided by a word processor." [OADSIG 1994a, page 195]

  - **presentation object type** *n.* a user interface object type that "describes the visual appearance of the user interface." [OADSIG 1994a, page 195]
  Examples: "the chart of today's stock usage, a box object, a line object, and a tree object." [OADSIG 1994a, page 195]

  - **user interface metaphor** *n.* a user interface object type that "ensures that users can understand the user interface." [OADSIG 1994a, page 195]

OMA-compliant application *n.* "an application consisting of a set of inter-working classes and instances that interact via the ORB. Compliance therefore means conformance to the OMA protocol definitions and interface specifications outlined in [the OMA Guide]." [OMG 1993, page 71]

OMG object model *n.* "this model defines a common object semantics for specifying the externally visible characteristics of objects in a standard and implementation-independent way. The common semantics characterize objects that exist in an OMG-compliant system." [OMG 1993, page 33]

one-way request *n.* "a request where the client does not wait for completion of the request, nor does it intend to accept results." [OMG 1992, page 168]

operation *n.* "an identifiable entity that denotes a service that can be requested." [OMG 1992, page 22] "A service that can be requested. An operation has an associated signature, which may restrict which actual parameters are possible in a meaningful request." [OMG 1993, page 71]

Kinds:
- CONTEXT-INDEPENDENT OPERATION
- GENERIC OPERATION
- VALUE-DEPENDENT OPERATION

- **context-independent operation** *n.* "an operation where all requests that identify the operation have the same behavior. (In contrast, the effect of a context-dependent operation might depend upon the identity or location of the client object issuing the request.)" [OMG 1993, page 67]

- **generic operation** *n.* "a conceptual notion. An operation is generic if it can be bound to more than one method." [OMG 1993, page 68]

- **value-dependent operation** *n.* "an operation where the behavior of the corresponding request 'depends' upon which names are used to identify object parameters (if an object can have multiple names)." [OMG 1993, page 74]

operation dispatching *n.* "when an operation request is issued, a specific operation implementation (method) is selected for execution. This selection process is called operation dispatching." [OMG 1993, page 50]

operation name *n.* "a name used in a request to identify an operation." [OMG 1993, page 71]

ORB core *n.* "the ORB component which moves a request from a client to the appropriate adapter for the target object." [OMG 1992, page 168]

ORB interface *n.* "the ORB Interface is the interface that goes directly to the ORB which is the same for all ORBs and does not depend on the object's interface or object adapter." [OMG 1992, page 36]

OTypes *n.* "the set of all object types." [OMG 1993, page 44]

parameter passing mode *n.* "describes the direction of information flow for an operation parameter. The parameter passing modes are *IN, OUT,* and *INOUT.*" [OMG 1992, page 168]

participate *v. -ed, -ing* "an object participates in a request if one or more of the actual parameters of the request identifies the object." [OMG 1993, page 72]

passivation *n.* "the reverse of activation." [OMG 1993, page 72]
Antonym: ACTIVATION.

persistence *n.* "a property of an object by which its existence transcends time (i.e., the object continues to exist after its creator ceases to exist)." [OADSIG 1994a, page 197]

persistent object *n.* "an object that can survive the process or thread that created it. A persistent object exists until it is explicitly deleted." [OMG 1993, page 72]

persistent state *n.* "The state of the object can be considered in two parts, … and the persistent state, which the object could use to reconstruct the dynamic state." [OMG 1994a, page 114]
Antonym: DYNAMIC STATE.

polymorphism *n.* "occurs when an operation can apply to several types." [OADSIG 1994a, page 162]
Kinds:
- AD HOC POLYMORPHISM
- INHERENT POLYMORPHISM

- **ad hoc polymorphism** *n.* polymorphism whereby "different operations on different types have the same name." [OADSIG 1994a, page 162]
- **inherent polymorphism** *n.* polymorphism whereby "operations are inherited by every subtype." [OADSIG 1994a, page 162]

presentation object type *n.* a user interface object type that "describes the visual appearance of the user interface." [OADSIG 1994a, page 195]
Examples: "the chart of today's stock usage, a box object, a line object, and a tree object." [OADSIG 1994a, page 195]

principal interface *n.* "the interface that describes all requests in which an object is meaningful." [OMG 1993, page 72]

problem domain object type *n.* "a tangible or conceptual real-world object type." [OADSIG 1994a, page 185]

profile *n.* "profiles exist to group components." [OMG 1993, page 40]
See also: COMPONENT.

program *n.* "a static object-based application is a set of types and classes interrelated specific to a particular (end-user) objective. In common terminology this is usually referred to as a program." [OMG 1993, page 65]

property *n.* "a conceptual notion. An attribute the value of which can be changed." [OMG 1993, page 72]

protection *n.* "the ability to restrict the client objects for which a requested service will be performed." [OMG 1993, page 72]

App
A

pull model *n.* an approach to initiating event communication that "allows a consumer of events to request the event data from a supplier." [OMG 1994a, page 32]
Antonym: PUSH MODEL.

push model *n.* an approach to initiating event communication that "allows a supplier of events to initiate the transfer of the event data to consumers." [OMG 1994a, page 32]
Antonym: PULL MODEL.

query *n.* "an activity that involves selecting objects from implicitly or explicitly identified collections based on a specified predicate." [OMG 1993, page 72]

real-world object type *n.* "an abstraction of a tangible real-world object identified during strategic modeling." [OADSIG 1994a, page 178]

referential integrity *n.* "the property ensuring that an object reference that exists in the state associated with an object reliably identifies a single object." [OMG 1992, page 169]

relationship *n.* "a characteristic that specifies a mapping from one object to another; it is an instantiation of a relationship type." [OADSIG 1994a, page 165]
See also: USAGE.

repository *n.* either an interface repository or an implementation repository.
Kinds:
• IMPLEMENTATION REPOSITORY
• INTERFACE REPOSITORY

• **implementation repository** *n.* "the Implementation Repository contains information that allows the ORB to locate and activate implementations of objects." [OMG 1992, page 37] "A storage place for object implementation information." [OMG 1992, page 167]
Antonym: INTERFACE REPOSITORY.

• **interface repository** *n.* "the Interface Repository is a service that provides persistent objects that represent the IDL information in a form available at runtime." [OMG 1992, page 36] "A storage place for interface information." [OMG 1992, page 167]
Antonym: IMPLEMENTATION REPOSITORY.

relationship type *n.* "a characteristic that specifies a mapping from one object type to another. Characteristics of a relationship type include cardinality and optionally a range type which identifies the object types which can participate in the relationship." [OADSIG 1994a, page 167]
Examples: "Borrower" defined on the type "Copy" with a range type of "Library User."

request *n.* "an operation invocation, called a request, is an event (like a procedure invocation or function call) that indicates an operation and possibly lists some parameters on behalf of a requester (client), possibly causing results to be returned." [OMG 1993, page 45] "an event consisting of an operation and zero or more actual parameters. A client issues a request to cause a service to be performed. Also associated with a request are the results that may be returned to the client. A message can be used to implement (carry) a request and/or a result." [OMG 1993, page 72] "... 'operations being applied to objects.' This concept can be described as 'sending requests to objects.' For the purposes of the Core Object Model the two phrases mean the same thing." [OMG 1993, page 42] "an invocation of an operation on an object, comprising an operation name and a list of zero, one, or more actual parameters. A client issues a request to cause a service to be performed. Also associated with a request are the results that may be returned to the client." [OADSIG 1994a, page 169]

Synonym: MESSAGE, OPERATION INVOCATION.

Contrast with: OPERATION DISPATCHING.

See also: EVENT.

Kinds:
- ASYNCHRONOUS REQUEST
- DEFERRED SYNCHRONOUS REQUEST
- MEANINGFUL REQUEST
- ONE-WAY REQUEST
- STATE-MODIFYING REQUEST
- SYNCHRONOUS REQUEST

- **asynchronous request** *n.* "a request where the client object does not pause to wait for results." [OMG 1993, page 66]
  Synonym: ASYNCHRONOUS MESSAGE, ONE-WAY REQUEST.
  Antonym: SYNCHRONOUS REQUEST.

- **deferred synchronous request** *n.* "a request where the client does not wait for completion of the request, but does intend to accept results later." [OMG 1992, page 166]
  Contrast with: ASYNCHRONOUS REQUEST, ONE-WAY REQUEST, SYNCHRONOUS MESSAGE, SYNCHRONOUS REQUEST.

- **meaningful request** *n.* "a request where the actual parameters satisfy the signature of the named operation." [OMG 1993, page 70]

- **one-way request** *n.* "a request where the client does not wait for completion of the request, nor does it intend to accept results." [OMG 1992, page 168]
  Synonym: ASYNCHRONOUS MESSAGE, ASYNCHRONOUS REQUEST.
  Contrast with: DEFERRED SYNCHRONOUS REQUEST, SYNCHRONOUS REQUEST.

- **state-modifying request** *n.* "a request that by performing the service alters the results of future requests." [OMG 1993, page 73]

- **synchronous request** *n.* "a request where the client object pauses to wait for completion of the request." [OMG 1993, page 74]
  Synonym: SYNCHRONOUS MESSAGE.
  Antonym: ASYNCHRONOUS REQUEST.
  Contrast with: DEFERRED SYNCHRONOUS REQUEST, ONE-WAY REQUEST.

request context *n.* "a request context provides additional, operation-specific information that may affect the performance of a request." [OMG 1992, page 23]

request form *n.* "a description or pattern that can be evaluated or performed multiple times to cause the issuing of requests." [OMG 1992, page 19]

resolve [a name] *v.* *-ed, -ing* "to determine the object associated with the name in a given context." [OMG 1994a, pages 3, 13]
See also: METHOD RESOLUTION.

results *n.* "the information returned to the client, which may include values as well as status information, indicating that exceptional conditions were raised in attempting to perform the requested service." [OMG 1993, page 72]

reuse *n.* "the ability to reuse object types during the design of a system and object classes within the implementation of a system." [OADSIG 1994a, page 161]

rule *n.* "a rule can govern both the object structure and object behavior. Rules have been separated from structure and behavior because many rules address both structure and behavior. A rule can take one of two main forms—it is an assertion or a constraint." [OADSIG 1994a, page 166] "A rule is a policy or condition that must be satisfied." [OADSIG 1994a, page 170]

Contrast with: ASSERTION, CONSTRAINT.
Example: "For object type 'Account,' account numbers must be unique." [OADSIG 1994a, page 170]

- **business rule** *n.* "a rule which governs the way that the business operates." [OADSIG 1994a, page 179]

  Examples: "Legal requirements such as every enterprise must have a managing director and accountants, architectural principles which govern the information system, and motivational constraints such as budgets and organizational limits." [OADSIG 1994a, page 179]

schema *n.* "a collection of object types and other schemas which constitute some form of operational system. Every schema identifies a list of object types: some schemas impose structure on this list." [OADSIG 1994a, page 171]

Example: "a list of bank teller object types." [OADSIG 1994a, page 171]

security domain *n.* "an identifiable subset of computational resources used to define security policy." [OMG 1993, page 73]

self-reference *n.* "the ability of a method to determine the object(s) identified in the request for the service being performed by the method. (Self-reference in Smalltalk is indicated by the keyword *self.*" [OMG 1993, page 73]

Contrast with: DELEGATION.

server *n.* "a process implementing one or more operations on one or more ob-

jects." [OMG 1992, page 169]

server object *n.* "an object providing response to a request for a service. A given object may be a client for some requests and a server for other requests." [OMG 1992, page 169]

Contrast with: CLIENT OBJECT.

service *n.* "a computation that may be performed in response to a request." [OMG 1993, page 73]

Kinds:
- CONCURRENCY CONTROL SERVICE
- EVENT SERVICE

- **concurrency control service** *n.* "The purpose of a concurrency control service is to mediate concurrent access to an object such that the consistency of the object is not compromised when accessed by concurrently executing computations." [OMG 1994b, page 7]
- **event service** *n.* "The event service decouples the communication between objects." [OMG 1994a, page 32]

  Commentary: "The event service defines two roles for objects: the supplier role and the consumer role." [OMG 1994a, page 32]

signature *n.* "defines the parameters of a given operation including their number order, data types, and passing mode: the results if any: and the possible outcomes (normal vs. exceptional) that might occur." [OMG 1992, page 169] "Defines the types of the parameters for a given operation." [OMG 1993, page 73] "Each operation has a signature, which consists of a name, set of parameters, and set of results." [OMG 1993, page 44]

Contrast with: INTERFACE.

simple name *n.* "a name with a single component." [OMG 1994a, page 14]

Antonym: COMPOUND NAME.

single inheritance *n.* "the construction

of a definition by incremental modification of one definition." [OMG 1993, page 73]

Antonym: MULTIPLE INHERITANCE.
Contrast with: MULTIPLE SPECIALIZATION.

single specialization *n.* any specialization "where an object type is a specialization of one and only one object type." [OADSIG 1994a, page 168]

Antonym: MULTIPLE SPECIALIZATION.
Contrast with: MULTIPLE INHERITANCE.

skeleton *n.* "the object-interface-specific ORB component which assists an object adapter in passing requests to particular methods." [OMG 1993, page 169]

specialization *n.* "a class x is a specialization of a class y if x is defined to directly or indirectly inherit from y." [OMG 1993, page 73] "occurs when an object type inherits operations, attribute types, and relationship types from one or more supertypes (with possible restrictions)." [OADSIG 1994a, page 162] "a relationship between two object types which represents generalization or inheritance. Object types bound by this kind of relationship share attributes and operations.... Specialization in a type hierarchy is commonly called subtyping / supporting." [OADSIG 1994a, page 168]

Antonym: GENERALIZATION.
Contrast with: INHERITANCE.
Kinds:
- MULTIPLE SPECIALIZATION
- SINGLE SPECIALIZATION

- **multiple specialization** *n.* any specialization "where an object type inherits characteristics from more than one object type." [OADSIG 1994a, page 168]

  Antonym: SINGLE SPECIALIZATION.

Contrast with: SINGLE INHERITANCE.

- **single specialization** *n.* any specialization "where an object type is a specialization of one and only one object type." [OADSIG 1994a, page 168]

  Antonym: MULTIPLE SPECIALIZATION.
  Contrast with: MULTIPLE INHERITANCE.

state *n.* "the time varying properties of an object that affect that object's behavior." [OMG 1992, page 169] "The information about the history of previous requests needed to determine the behavior of future requests." [OMG 1993, page 73] "The state of an object is defined by the set of values of attributes and relationships associated with that object." [OADSIG 1994a, page 169]

Examples: "Waiting" and "Ringing."
Kinds:
- DYNAMIC STATE
- PERSISTENT STATE

- **dynamic state** *n.* "The state of the object can be considered in two parts, the dynamic state, which is typically in memory and is not likely to exist for the whole lifetime of the object...." [OMG 1994a, page 114]

  Antonym: PERSISTENT STATE.

- **persistent state** *n.* "The state of the object can be considered in two parts, ... and the persistent state, which the object could use to reconstruct the dynamic state." [OMG 1994a, page 114]

  Antonym: DYNAMIC STATE.

state consistency *n.* "ensures that the state associated with an object conforms to the data model." [OMG 1993, page 73]

state integrity *n.* "requires that the state associated with an object is not corrupted by external events." [OMG 1993, page 73]

state-modifying request *n.* "a request that by performing the service alters the results of future requests." [OMG 1993, page 73]

state variable *n.* "part of the state of an object." [OMG 1993, page 73]

static binding *n.* "binding that is performed prior to the actual issuing of the request." [OMG 1993, page 74]
Antonym: DYNAMIC BINDING.

static invocation *n.* "constructing a request at compile time. Calling an operation via a stub procedure." [OMG 1992, page 169]
Antonym: DYNAMIC INVOCATION.

structural model *n.* a model that "describes the structure of the object types in the problem domain." [OADSIG 1994a, page 187]
Contrast with: BEHAVIORAL MODEL, FUNCTIONAL MODEL.
Examples: object relationship diagram, type hierarchy, whole-part diagram, subject area relationship diagram.

stub *n.* "a local procedure corresponding to a single operation that invokes that operation when called." [OMG 1992, page 169]

substitutability *n.* "substitutability means being able to substitute an object of some type S when an object of type T is expected, where T is a supertype of S, while guaranteeing that the substituted object will support the same operation as specified by the supertype T." [OMG 1993, page 48]

subtyping *n.* "subtyping is a relationship between types based on their interfaces. It defines the rules by which objects of one type are determined to be acceptable in contexts expecting another type. [OMG 1993, page 47]

supplier *n.* an object role that "produce[s] event data" [OMG 1994a, page 32]
Antonym: CONSUMER.

synchronous request *n.* "a request where the client object pauses to wait for completion of the request." [OMG 1993, page 74]
Synonym: SYNCHRONOUS MESSAGE.
Antonym: ASYNCHRONOUS REQUEST.
Contrast with: DEFERRED SYNCHRONOUS REQUEST, ONE-WAY REQUEST.

system management interfaces *n.* "utility interfaces typically though of as system administration functions. That is, interfaces that abstract basic functions such as control, monitoring, security management, configuration, and policy that are needed to perform Systems Management operations (adding new users, setting permissions, installing software, etc.)." [OMG 1995, page 55]

thread of control *n.* "defines the line of independent dynamic action within an application. A given application may simultaneously support many different threads of control, which come into existence and cease to exist dynamically." [OADSIG 1994a, page 197]

transient object *n.* "an object the existence of which is limited by the lifetime of the process or thread that created it." [OMG 1993, page 74]
Antonym: PERSISTENT OBJECT.

transition *n.* "a change of state caused by an event." [OADSIG 1994a, page 169]
Example: the change from 'employee' to 'pensioner' when somebody retires.

type *n.* "a type is an identifiable entity with an associated predicate (a single-argument mathematical function with a Boolean result) defined over values. A value satisfies a type if the predicate is true for that value. A value that satisfies a type is called a *member of the type.*" [OMG 1992, page 20] "A predicate (Boolean function) defined over values that

can be used in a signature to restrict a possible parameter or characterize a possible result. Types classify objects according to a common interface; classes classify objects according to a common implementation." [OMG 1993, page 74]
Contrast with: DATA TYPE, INTERFACE, SUBTYPING.

type interface *n.* "defines the requests in which instances of this type can meaningfully participate as a parameter." [OMG 1993, page 74]
Example: "Given a document type and product type, the interface to the document type comprises edit and print and the interface to the product type comprises set price and check inventory, then the object interface of a particular document which is also a product comprises all four requests." [OMG 1993, page 74]

type object *n.* "an object that serves as a type." [OMG 1993, page 74]

usage *n.* "a usage relationship occurs when one object type makes use of the interface provided by another object type." [OADSIG 1994a, page 165]
See also: RELATIONSHIP.

user interface object type *n.* "an object used to define the user interface for the application." [OADSIG 1994a, page 195]
Kinds:
  • DIALOG OBJECT TYPE
  • PRESENTATION OBJECT TYPE
  • USER INTERFACE METAPHOR

  • **dialog object type** *n.* a user interface object type that "maintains the state of the interface and from the user's per-ception controls its overall behavior." [OADSIG 1994a, page 195]
Example: "the open file dialogue provided by a word processor." [OADSIG 1994a, page 195]

  • **presentation object type** *n.* a user interface object type that "describes the visual appearance of the user interface." [OADSIG 1994a, page 195]
Examples: "the chart of today's stock usage, a box object, a line object, and a tree object." [OADSIG 1994a, page 195]

  • **user interface metaphor** *n.* a user interface object type that "ensures that users can understand the user interface." [OADSIG 1994a, page 195]

value *n.* "Any entity that can be a possible actual parameter in a request. Values that serve to identify objects are called 'object names.'; values that identify other entities are called 'literals.'" [OMG 1993, page 74] "Values that serve to identify objects are called object references." [OMG 1992, page 170]

value-dependent operation *n.* "an operation where the behavior of the corresponding request depends upon which names are used to identify object parameters (if an object can have multiple names)." [OMG 1993, page 74]
Antonym: CONTEXT-INDEPENDENT OPERATION.

vertical common facilities *n.* "Vertical Market Facilities represent technology that supports various vertical markets such as health care, retailing, CAD, or financial systems." [OMG 1995, page 12]

References

[OMG 1992] Object Management Group. (1992). *The Common Object Request Broker: Architecture and Specification.* Revision 1.1, OMG Document Number 91.12.1, New York: Wiley.

[OMG 1993] Object Management Group. (1993). In R. M. Soley (ed.), *Object Management Architecture Guide.* Revision 2.0, OMG Document Number 92-11-1, New York: Wiley.

[OMG 1994a] Object Management Group. (1994). In J. Siegel (Ed.), *Common Object Services Specification*, Revision 1.0, OMG Document Number 94-1-1, New York: Wiley.

[OMG 1994b] Object Management Group. (1994). *Concurrency Control Service Proposal*, OMG Document Number 94-5-8, 1994. (Adopted as an OMG Specification in November 1994)

[OMG 1995] Object Management Group. (1995). *OMG Common Facilities Architecture Guide*, Draft, OMG Document Number 95-1-2, 1995.

[OADSIG 1994a] Object Management Group Object Analysis and Design Special Interest Group. (1994). In A. T. F. Hutt (Ed.), *Object Analysis and Design: Comparison of Methods*, New York: Wiley.

[OADSIG 1994b] Object Management Group Object Analysis and Design Special Interest Group. (1994). In A. T. F. Hutt (Ed.), *Object Analysis and Design: Description of Methods*, New York: Wiley.

Appendix **B** **The Object Database Management Group (ODMG)**

Formed in 1991, the Object Database Management Group (ODMG) is a consortium of object-oriented database management system (ODBMS) vendors and interested parties working on standards to allow portability of customer software across ODBMS products. The definitions in this appendix are excerpted from:

> Atwood, Thomas; Duhl, Joshua; Ferran, Guy; Loomis, Mary; & Wade, Drew (1994). In R. G. G. Cattell (Ed.), *The Object Database Standard: ODMG-93.* (Release 1.1). San Francisco: Morgan Kaufmann Publishers. Reprinted with permission of Morgan Kaufmann Publishers, Inc.

The ODMG-93 specification includes:

- An introductory chapter explaining the goals and discussing architectural issues and how the standards fit together.
- A chapter documenting the ODMG's object model, which is an extension of the Object Management Group (OMG) object model.
- A chapter documenting an object definition language (ODL) standard, which provides a programming-language-independent mechanism to express user object models (schema) and is an extension of the OMG IDL.
- A chapter documenting an object query language (OQL), which provides a declarative access interface for interactive and programmatic query as an extension of SQL.
- A chapter documenting a binding to C++ for all functionality, including object definition, manipulation, and query.
- A chapter documenting a similar binding for Smalltalk.
- An appendix providing a mapping of the object model to OMG's object model.
- An appendix discussing ODBMS in the OMG's object request broker (ORB) environment.
- An appendix suggesting enhancements to ANSI C++, which will allow better language integration and facilitate other, more general application needs in C++.

For more information, contact:
    The Object Database Management Group, Inc.
    13504 Clinton Place
    Burnsville, Minnesota 55337, USA
    Voice:+1 (612) 953-7250
    Fax:+1 (612) 397-7146
    E-mail:info@odmg.org
    Gopher:gopher.odmg.org, port 2073
    http://www.odmg.org

For the current release, price, and availability of *The Object Database Standard: ODMG-93*, contact:
    Morgan Kaufmann Publishers, Inc.
    340 Pine Street, 6th Floor
    San Francisco, California 94104-3205, USA
    Voice:+1 (800) 745-7323
    Fax:+1 (415) 982-2665
    E-mail:orders@mkp.com
    http://mkp.com

atom *n.* "an object that is either a type, [an] exception, or an iterator." [ODMG 1994a, page 16, 66]
Synonym: ATOMIC OBJECT.
Contrast with: LITERAL.

atomic *adj.* having no structure. [ODMG 1994a, page 16]
Antonym: STRUCTURED.

atomic literal *n.* a literal that is either an integer, a float, a Boolean, or a character. [ODMG 1994a, page 20]

atomic object *n.* "an object that is either a type, exception, or an iterator." [ODMG 1994a, page 16]
Synonym: ATOM.
Antonym: STRUCTURED OBJECT.

attribute *n.* a property that is defined between an object and a literal. "Attributes are defined on one object type and take literals as their values.... Attributes do not have OIDs.... Attributes define abstract state. They therefore appear within the interface definition of an object type rather than in the implementation." [ODMG 1994a, pages 11, 13, 21, 22]
Contrast with: PROPERTY, RELATIONSHIP.

attribute signature *n.* "defines the name of the attribute and the name and type of its legal values. Attributes take literals as values, e.g., strings, numbers, etc." [ODMG 1994a, page 13]

behavior *n.* "a set of operations" [ODMG 1994a, page 14]
Contrast with: OPERATION.

class *n.* "the combination of the type interface specification and one of the implementations defined for the type." [ODMG 1994a, page 15]
Contrast with: TYPE.
Kinds:
• PERSISTENT-CAPABLE CLASS

• TRANSIENT CLASS

• **persistent-capable class** *n.* any class "that can have both persistent and transient instances." [ODMG 1994a, page 84]
Contrast with: TRANSIENT CLASS.

• **transient class** *n.* any class "all of whose instances are transient; that is, they don't outlive the execution of the process in which they were created." [ODMG 1994a, page 84]
Contrast with: PERSISTENT-CAPABLE CLASS.

class properties *n.* "those that characterize the class itself, rather than any of its individual instances." [ODMG 1994a, page 155]

collection [object] *n.* "an object that groups other objects." [ODMG 1994a, page "Collections ... contain an arbitrary number of elements, do not have named slots, and contain elements that are all instances of the same type." [ODMG 1994a, page 27]
Contrast with: COLLECTION TYPE, STRUCTURE.

collection type *n.* "an instantiation of a collection type generator." [ODMG 1994a, page 28]
Contrast with: COLLECTION OBJECT, STRUCTURE.

compound key *n.* "a key that consists of a set of properties." [ODMG 1994a, page 12]
Antonym: SIMPLE KEY.

coterminous_with_database *adj.* "the lifetime of an object allocated out of a storage segment, page, cluster, or heap managed by the ODBMS runtime." [ODMG 1994a, page 19]
See also: PERSISTENT.
Contrast with: COTERMINOUS_WITH_PROCEDURE, COTERMINOUS_WITH_PROCESS.

App
B

coterminous_with_procedure *adj.* "the lifetime of an object that is created when the procedure is invoked and destroyed when the procedure returns." [ODMG 1994a, page 19]
See also: TRANSIENT.
Contrast with: COTERMINOUS_WITH_PROCESS, COTERMINOUS_WITH_DATABASE.

coterminous_with_process *n.* "the lifetime of an object allocated by the programming language runtime out of either static storage or the heap." [ODMG 1994a, page 19]
See also: TRANSIENT.
Contrast with: COTERMINOUS_WITH_DATABASE, COTERMINOUS_WITH_PROCEDURE

create operation *n.* an operation that "allocates storage for the representation of the object, assigns an OID, and returns that OID as the value of the operation." [ODMG 1994a, page 19]
Antonym: DELETE OPERATION.

delete operation *n.* an operation that "removes the object from the database and frees the storage used by its representation. Deleting an object removes its from any relationships in which it participated.... The OID of a deleted object is not reused." [ODMG 1994a, page 19]
Antonym: CREATE OPERATION.

Denotable_Object *n.* the root type of the hierarchy of object types. [ODMG 1994a, page 16]
See also: TYPE.

domain *n.* Synonym for scope or name space. [ODMG 1994a, page 17]

exception *n.* an object representing an error condition. "Exceptions are themselves objects." [ODMG 1994a, pages 13, 26]

extent [of a type] *n.* "the set of all instances of a given type." [ODMG 1994a, page 12]

See also: TYPE.

immutable *adj.* having constant values. [ODMG 1994a, page 16]
Antonym: MUTABLE.
Contrast with: LITERAL.

immutable object *n.* "an immutable object (value)... cannot change its intrinsic value." [ODMG 1994a, page 155]
See also: LITERAL.

implementation *n.* "the implementation ... defines data structures in terms of which instances of the type are physically represented and the methods that operate on those data structures to support the externally visible state and behavior defined in the interface." [ODMG 1994a, page 12] "An implementation of an object type consists of a *representation* and a set of *methods*. ... There may be additional methods and data structures in the implementation that have no counter-part operations in the type interface." [ODMG 1994a, page 15]
Antonym: INTERFACE.

implementation-defined [behavior] *n.* "the behavior is specified by each implementor/vendor [of the ODMG-93 standard]. The implementor/vendor is allowed to make implementation-specific decisions about the behavior. However, the behavior must be well defined and fully documented and published as part of the vendor's implementation of the standard." [ODMG 1994a, page 85]

instance property *n.* a property "for which objects of the type carry values." [ODMG 1994a, page 13]
Antonym: TYPE PROPERTY.

interface *n.* "the interface defines the external interface supported by instances of the type—that is, their properties and

the operations that can be invoked on them." [ODMG 1994a, page 12]
Antonym: IMPLEMENTATION.

inverse traversal path *n.* "The traversal path on the other side of the relationship." [ODMG 1994b]

key *n.* a property or set of properties, the value(s) of which uniquely identify individual instances of a type or class. [ODMG 1994a, pages 12, 156]
Kinds:
  • COMPOUND KEY
  • SIMPLE KEY

  • **compound key** *n.* "a key that consists of a set of properties." [ODMG 1994a, page 12]
  • **simple key** *n.* "a key that consists of a single property." [ODMG 1994a, page 12]

literal *n.* "objects whose instances are immutable." [ODMG 1994a, page 20]
Contrast with: IMMUTABLE, OBJECT.
See also: IMMUTABLE OBJECT.
Kinds:
  • ATOMIC LITERAL
  • STRUCTURED LITERAL

  • **atomic literal** *n.* a literal that is either an integer, a float, a Boolean, or a character. [ODMG 1994a, page 20]
  • **structured literal** *n.* a literal that is either an immutable collection or an immutable structure. [ODMG 1994a, page 20]

method *n.* a procedure body that implements "the behavior specified for [its] associated operation by modifying the representation of the object and/or invoking operations defined on related objects." [ODMG 1994a, page 15]

mutable *adj.* "Instances of type Object are mutable. The values of their attributes may change. The relationships in which they participate may change.

But the identity of the object remains invariant across these changes." [ODMG 1994a, page 17]
Antonym: IMMUTABLE.
See also: OBJECT.

object *n.* a thing "of which characteristics are predicated. Stated less formally, objects have state and behavior. Objects also have identity." [ODMG 1994a, page 16]
Contrast with: LITERAL.
See also: BEHAVIOR, IDENTITY, STATE.
Kinds:
  • ATOMIC OBJECT
  • IMMUTABLE OBJECT
  • ROOT OBJECT
  • STRUCTURED OBJECT

  • **atomic object** *n.* "an object that is either a type, exception, or an iterator." [ODMG 1994a, page 16]
  Antonym: STRUCTURED OBJECT.
  • **immutable object** *n.* "an immutable object (value) ... cannot change its intrinsic value." [ODMG 1994a, page 155]
  See also: LITERAL.
  • **root object** *n.* a named persistent object "that can be referenced by a program once it has opened the database." [ODMG 1994a, page 42]
  • **structured object** *n.* "an object that is either a collection or a structure." [ODMG 1994a, page 38]
  Antonym: ATOMIC OBJECT.

object database management system (ODBMS) *n.* "a [database management system] that integrates database capabilities with object-oriented programming language capabilities. An ODBMS makes database objects appear as programming language objects, in one or more existing programming languages. The ODBMS extends the language with transparent persistent data, concurrency control, data recoverability, associative queries, and other database capabilities." [ODMG 1994a, page 3]

object definition language (ODL) *n.* "a specification language used to define the interfaces to object types that conform to the ODMG Object Model." [ODMG 1994a, page 49]

object identifier (OID) *n.* that which "uniquely distinguishes the object from all other objects within the *domain* in which the object was created." [ODMG 1994a, page 17]
See also: DOMAIN.
Contrast with: OBJECT NAME.

object manipulation language (OML) *n.* "the language used for retrieving objects from the database and modifying them." [ODMG 1994a, page 83]

object name *n.* a name that refers "uniquely to a single object within the scope of the definition of the name.... A name is not explicitly defined as an attribute of an object." [ODMG 1994a, pages 17, 103]
Contrast with: OBJECT IDENTIFIER.

ODBMS profile *n.* OMG profile for object database management systems defined in the ODMG-93 standard. [ODMG 1994a, page 162]

operation *n.* a specified behavior of an instance of an object type [ODMG 1994a, page 24]
See also: BEHAVIOR, METHOD.
Kinds:
  • CREATE OPERATION
  • DELETE OPERATION

• **create operation** *n.* an operation that "allocates storage for the representation of the object, assigns an OID, and returns that id as the value of the operation." [ODMG 1994a, page 19]
Antonym: DELETE OPERATION.

• **delete operation** *n.* an operation that "removes the object from the database and frees the storage used by its representation. Deleting an object removes its from any relationships in which it participated.... The OID of a deleted object is not reused." [ODMG 1994a, page 19]
Antonym: CREATE OPERATION.

operation signature *n.* "defines the name of the operation, the name and type of any arguments, the name and type of any returned value, and the names of any exceptions (error conditions) the operation can raise." [ODMG 1994a, page 13]

overloaded operations *n.* "operations defined on different types [that] have the same name." [ODMG 1994a, page 18]

persistent *adj.* describing "data that remain after an application program execution." [ODMG 1994b]
Antonym: TRANSIENT.
See also: TRANSITIVE PERSISTENCE.

persistent-capable class *n.* any class "that can have both persistent and transient instances." [ODMG 1994a, page 84]
Contrast with: TRANSIENT CLASS.

physical pragma *n.* "a construct defined in the ODL or OML used to either (1) give a programmer some direct control over the physical storage of objects, clustering, and memory management issues associated with the stored physical representation of objects, and access structures like indices used to accelerate object retrieval or (2) enable a programmer to provide 'hints' to the storage management subsystem provided as part of the ODBMS runtime." [ODMG 1994a, page 83]

predicate *n.* "a Boolean conjunction or disjunction of operations supported by the object types that appear within the predicate." [ODMG 1994a, page 18]

property *n.* "properties may be either attributes of the object itself or relationships between the object and one or more other objects." [ODMG 1994a, page 11]

Contrast with: ATTRIBUTE, RELATIONSHIP.

Kinds:

- INSTANCE PROPERTY
- TYPE PROPERTY

- **instance property** *n.* a property "for which objects of the type carry values." [ODMG 1994a, page 13]
  Antonym: TYPE PROPERTY.

- **type property** *n.* a property of a type. [ODMG 1994a]
  Examples: EXTENT, KEY, SUPERTYPE.
  Antonym: INSTANCE PROPERTY.

raise an error *v.* either call an error routine or use "C++ exception handling once it becomes a generally available feature of most C++ environments." [ODMG 1994a, page 89]

See also: EXCEPTION.

regeneration *n.* "the automatic production of appropriate ODL declaration in order to establish communications or sharing between an existing ODBMS application and another ODMG compliant system." [ODMG 1994a, page 157]

relationship *n.* "an association between object types that may be classified as one-to-one, one-to-many, or many-to-many." [ODMG 1994a, page 13]

See also: ATTRIBUTE, PROPERTY.

relationship signature *n.* "defines the type of the other object or set of objects involved in the relationship and the name of a traversal function used to refer to the related object or set of objects. Re-

lationships are binary and are defined between two objects." [ODMG 1994a, page 13]

See also: TRAVERSAL FUNCTION.

representation *n.* "a set of data structures." [ODMG 1994a, page 15]

See also: IMPLEMENTATION, PROPERTY.

root object *n.* a named persistent object "that can be referenced by a program once it has opened the database." [ODMG 1994a, page 42]

schema *n.* "the set of all types whose instances may be stored in a single database." [ODMG 1994a, page 46]

- **subschema** *n.* "a subset of the types in a schema." [ODMG 1994a, page 46]

session *n.* "an object … used to manage a connection with a database." [ODMG 1994a, page 157]

signature *n.* a declaration of a property or behavior. [ODMG 1994a, page 13]

Kinds:

- ATTRIBUTE SIGNATURE
- OPERATION SIGNATURE
- RELATIONSHIP SIGNATURE

- **attribute signature** *n.* "defines the name of the attribute and the name and type of its legal values. Attributes take literals as values, e.g., strings, numbers, etc." [ODMG 1994a, page 13]

- **operation signature** *n.* "defines the name of the operation, the name and type of any arguments, the name and type of any returned value, and the names of any exceptions (error conditions) the operation can raise." [ODMG 1994a, page 13]

- **relationship signature** *n.* "defines the type of the other object or set of objects involved in the relationship and the name of a traversal function used to refer to the related object or set of objects. Relationships are binary and

are defined between two objects."
[ODMG 1994a, page 13]
See also: TRAVERSAL FUNCTION.

simple key *n.* "a key that consists of a single property." [ODMG 1994a, page 12]
Antonym: COMPOUND KEY.

slot *n.* a named part of a structure that contains an object or a literal. [ODMG 1994a, page 26]

state *n.* "a set of properties.... The state of an object is modified by updating its properties or by invoking operations on it." [ODMG 1994a, page 14, 102]
See also: PROPERTY.

structure *n.* "an unnamed group of elements. Each element is a (name, value) pair, where the value may be any subtype of type Denotable_Object." [ODMG 1994a, page 16]

structured literal *n.* a literal that is either an immutable collection or an immutable structure. [ODMG 1994a, page 20]
Antonym: ATOMIC LITERAL.

structured object *n.* "an object that is either a collection or a structure." [ODMG 1994a, page 38]
Antonym: ATOMIC OBJECT.

subschema *n.* "a subset of the types in a schema." [ODMG 1994a, page 46]
Contrast with: SCHEMA.

subtype *n.* "All of the attributes, relationships, and operations defined on a supertype are inherited by the subtype. The subtype may add additional properties and operations to introduce behavior or state unique to instances of the subtype. It may also 'refine' the properties and operations it inherits to specialize them to the behavior and range of state values appropriate for instances of the subtype." [ODMG 1994a, page 12]
Antonym: SUPERTYPE.

supertype *n.* a type from which another

type inherits. [ODMG 1994a, page 12]
Antonym: SUBTYPE.

transaction *n.* "programs that use persistent data are organized into transactions. Transactions are units of atomicity, consistency, and integrity." [ODMG 1994a, page 40]

transient *n.* describing "data that exist only for the duration of an application program execution." [ODMG 1994b]
Antonym: PERSISTENT.

transient class *n.* any class "all of whose instances are transient; that is, they don't outlive the execution of the process in which they were created." [ODMG 1994a, page 84]
Contrast with: PERSISTENT-CAPABLE CLASS.

transitive persistence *n.* "a transient object that participates in a relationship with a persistent object will become persistent when a transaction commit occurs." [ODMG 1994a, page 154]

traversal function *n.* a unidirectional path across a relationship. [ODMG 1994b]
Synonym: TRAVERSAL PATH.
See also: RELATIONSHIP, RELATIONSHIP SIGNATURE.

traversal path *n.* a unidirectional path across a relationship. [ODMG 1994a, page 98]
Synonym: TRAVERSAL FUNCTION.
Contrast with: RELATIONSHIP.

• **inverse traversal path** *n.* "The traversal path on the other side of the relationship." [ODMG 1994a]

type *n.* an object that categorizes other objects whereby "all objects of a given type exhibit common behavior and a common range of states.... A type defines the state and behavior of its instances." [ODMG 1994a, page 11, 12]
See also: BEHAVIOR, CLASS, INSTANCE,

STATE.
Contrast with: CLASS.
See also: DENOTABLE_OBJECT.
Kinds:
  • ABSTRACT TYPE
  • SUBTYPE
  • SUPERTYPE

• **abstract type** *n.* a type that "only de-fine[s] characteristics inherited by [its] subtypes. [It does] not define an im-plementation and therefore cannot be directly instantiated." [ODMG 1994a, page 13]

• **subtype** *n.* "All of the attributes, rela-tionships, and operations defined on a supertype are inherited by the sub-type. The subtype may add additional properties and operations to intro-duce behavior or state unique to in-stances of the subtype. It may also 're-fine' the properties and operations it inherits to specialize them to the be-havior and range of state values appro-priate for instances of the subtype." [ODMG 1994a, page 12]

Antonym: SUPERTYPE.

• **supertype** *n.* a type from which an-other type inherits. [ODMG 1994a, page 12]

Antonym: SUBTYPE.

type inheritance *n.* "If object type B is declared to be a subtype of object type A, this means that any operations de-fined on A are also available on in-stances of B, any attributes defined on A are also defined on B, and any rela-tionships defined on A are also avail-able on instances of B." [ODMG 1994a, page 18]

type property *n.* a property of a type [ODMG 1994a]

Antonym: INSTANCE PROPERTY.

Examples: EXTENT, KEY, SUPERTYPE.

undefined [behavior] *n.* "the behavior is unspecified by the ODMG-93 stan-dard. Implementations [of the standard] have complete freedom (can do any-thing or nothing), and the behavior need not be documented by the implementor or vendor." [ODMG 1994a, page 85]

References

[ODMG 1994a] Cattell, R. G. G., with Atwood, T., Duhl, J., Ferran, G., Loomis, M., & Wade, D. (1994). *The Object Database Standard: ODMG-93.* (Release 1.1) San Francisco: Morgan Kaufmann.

[ODMG 1994b] Douglas K. Barry, personal communication, 20 October 1994.

Object-Oriented Programming Languages

Appendix **C**   **Ada95** App C

The Ada95 programming language (previously referred to as Ada9X) is defined by the international standard ISO/IEC-8652:1995, and is "a general-purpose language designed to support the construction of long-lived, highly reliable software systems." [Ada94b, page ix] Ada95 incorporates significant changes to the Ada83 standard, including additional object-oriented features.

The definitions in this appendix are excerpted from the draft *Ada9X Rationale* [Ada94a] and the draft *Ada9X Reference Manual* [Ada94b]. Reprinted by permission of the U.S. Government. These documents have been finalized and the reference manual was published as international standard ANSI/ISO/IEC-8652: 1995 in January 1995 after this appendix was finalized. The reader is directed to the approved standard and its rationale for the final official definitions.

For more information, contact:
Ada Resource Association
4719 Reed Road, Suite 305
Columbus, Ohio 43220, USA
Voice: +1(614) 442-9232
Fax: +1 (614) 442-0055
E-mail: 73313.2671@compuserve.com

abstract subprogram *n.* "An *abstract subprogram* is a subprogram that has no body, but is intended to be overridden at some point when inherited." [Ada94b, page 67]

abstract type *n.* "An *abstract type* is a tagged type intended for use as a parent type for type extensions, but which is not allowed to have objects of its own." [Ada94b, page xvi]

actual *n.* "The *generic actual parameter* is either the explicit_generic_actual_parameter given in a generic_parameter_ association for each formal, or the corresponding default_expression or default_name if not generic_parameter_ association is given for the formal." [Ada94b, page 212]

Synonym: GENERIC ACTUAL PARAMETER.
Contrast with: FORMAL.

Commentary: "When the meaning is clear from context, the term 'generic actual,' or simply 'actual,' is used as a synonym for 'generic actual parameter' and also for the view denoted by one, or the value of one." [Ada94b, page 212]

actual subtype *n.* "The object's *actual subtype* can be more restrictive than the nominal subtype of the view; it always is if the nominal subtype is an *indefinite subtype.* An unconstrained array subtype is an indefinite subtype, as is a subtype with unknown discriminants or unconstrained discriminants without default." [Ada94b, page 25]

Contrast with: NOMINAL SUBTYPE.

aliased view *n.* "An aliased view of an object is one that can be designated by an access value. Objects allocated by allocators are aliased. Objects can also be explicitly declared as aliased with the reserved word *aliased.* The Access attribute can be used to create an access value designating an aliased object." [Ada94b, page 483]

ancestor [type of a type] *n.* "If a type T2 is a descendant of a type T1, then T1 is called an *ancestor* of T2." [Ada94b, page 32]

Antonym: DESCENDANT.

• **ultimate ancestor** *n.* "The *ultimate ancestor* of a type is the ancestor of the type that is not a descendant of any other type." [Ada94b, page 32]

Contrast with: ROOT TYPE.

attribute *n.* "An *attribute* is a characteristic of an entity that can be queried." [Ada94b, page 81]

body *n.* "[A body contains] the implementation details [of a program unit], which need not be visible to other units. ... The body of a program unit generally contains two parts: a declarative part, which defines the logical entities to be used in the program unit, and a sequence of statements, which defines the execution of the program unit." [Ada94b, page xv]

Antonym: SPECIFICATION.
See also: COMPLETION, PROGRAM UNIT.

class *n.* "A class is a set of types that is closed under derivation, which means that if a given type is in the class, then all types derived from that type are also in the class. The set of types of a class share common properties, such as their primitive operations." [Ada94b, page 483]

Contrast with: TYPE.
See also: ROOT TYPE, SUBTYPE.

Commentary: This assumes that derivation is via specialization, which implies that the extents of the subtypes are subsets of the extent of the class.

Kinds:
• CLASS ROOTED AT A GIVEN TYPE
• DERIVATION CLASS
• DIRECTLY DERIVED CLASS
• INDIRECTLY DERIVED CLASS

- **class rooted at a given type** *n.* "The derivation class of types for a type *T* (also called the class *rooted* at *T*) is the set consisting of *T* (the *root type* of the class) and all types derived from *T* (directly or indirectly) plus any associated universal or class-wide types." [Ada-94b, page 31]
See also: ROOT TYPE, TYPE.

- **derivation class** *n.* "In addition to the various language-defined classes of types, types can be grouped into *derivation classes*. A derived type is *derived from* its parent type *directly*; it is derived *indirectly* from any type from which its parent type is derived." [Ada94b, page 31]
See also: ROOT TYPE, TYPE.

- **directly derived class** *n.* "In addition to the various language-defined classes of types, types can be grouped into *derivation classes*. A derived type is *derived from* its parent type *directly*; it is derived *indirectly* from any type from which its parent type is derived." [Ada94b, page 31]
See also: ROOT TYPE, TYPE.

- **indirectly derived class** *n.* "In addition to the various language-defined classes of types, types can be grouped into *derivation classes*. A derived type is *derived from* its parent type *directly*; it is derived *indirectly* from any type from which its parent type is derived." [Ada94b, page 31]
See also: ROOT TYPE, TYPE.

class rooted at a given type *n.* "The derivation class of types for a type *T* (also called the class *rooted* at *T*) is the set consisting of *T* (the *root type* of the class) and all types derived from *T* (directly or indirectly) plus any associated universal or class-wide types." [Ada94b, page 31]

See also: ROOT TYPE, TYPE.

class-wide programming *n.* "Classes of related abstractions may be handled in a unified fashion, such that the programmer may systematically ignore their differences when appropriate." [Ada94a, page 4-2]
Contrast with: VARIANT PROGRAMMING.
See also: CLASS-WIDE TYPE, POLYMORPHISM.

class-wide type *n.* "Class-wide types are defined for (and belong to) each derivation class rooted at a tagged type. Given a subtype S of a tagged type *T*, S' Class is the subtype_mark for a corresponding subtype of the tagged class-wide type *T*' Class. Such types are called 'class-wide' because when a formal parameter is defined to be of class-wide type *T*' Class, an actual parameter of any type in the derivation class rooted at *T* is acceptable." [Ada94b, page 31]
See also: CLASS-WIDE PROGRAMMING, DERIVATION CLASS.

composite type *n.* "A composite type has components." [Ada94b, page 483] "[Composite types include] array and record types." [Ada94b, page xvi]
Antonym: ELEMENTARY TYPE.
See also: DISCRIMINANT.

constrained object *n.* "[If an object's] actual subtype is constrained, the object is called a *constrained object*." [Ada94b, page 26]

constrained subtype *n.* "a subtype is called an *unconstrained* subtype if its type has unknown discriminants, or if its type allows range, index, or discriminant constraints, but the subtype does not impose such a constraint; otherwise, the subtype is called a *constrained* subtype (since it has no unconstrained characteristics)." [Ada94b, page 21]
Antonym: UNCONSTRAINED TYPE.

constraint *n.* "The set of possible values for an object of a given type can be subjected to a condition that is called a *constraint* (the case of *null constraint* that specifies no restriction is also included)." [Ada94b, page 20]
See also: SUBTYPE.

controlled type *n.* "A controlled type supports user-defined assignment and finalization." [Ada94b, page 483]
Commentary: "Objects are always finalized before being destroyed." [Ada-94b, page 483]

controlling operand *n.* "A *controlling operand* in a call on a dispatching operation of a tagged type *T* is one whose corresponding formal parameter is of type *T* or is of an anonymous access type with designated type *T*." [Ada94b, page 65]
See also: DISPATCHING.

declaration *n.* "A *declaration* is a language construct that associates a name with (a view of) an entity." [Ada94b, page 483]
Contrast with: DEFINITION.
See also: COMPLETION, VIEW.
Kinds:
- EXPLICIT DECLARATION
- HOMOGRAPH
- IMPLICIT DECLARATION

- **explicit declaration** *n.* "A declaration may appear explicitly in the program text (an *explicit* declaration)." [Ada-94b, pages 19–20]
Antonym: IMPLICIT DECLARATION.
See also: OVERRIDE.

- **homograph [declaration]** *n.* "Two declarations are *homographs* if they have the same defining name, and, if both are overloadable, their profiles are type conformant." [Ada94b, page 149]
Commentary: "An inner declaration hides any outer homograph from direct visibility." [Ada94b, page 149]

- **implicit declaration** *n.* "A declaration may ... be supposed to occur at a given place in the text as a consequence of the semantics of another construct (an *implicit* declaration)." [Ada94b, page 19]
Antonym: EXPLICIT DECLARATION.
Commentary: Implicit declarations are typically those inherited in a derived type.

definite subtype *n.* "If a subtype is not indefinite, it is called a *definite* subtype. All elementary subtypes are definite subtypes." [Ada94b, page 25]
Antonym: INDEFINITE SUBTYPE.

definition *n.* "All declarations contain a *definition* for a *view* of an entity. A view consists of an identification of the entity (the entity *of* the view, plus view-specific characteristics that affect the use of the entity through that view (such as mode of access to an object, formal parameter names and defaults for a subprogram, or visibility to components of a type)." [Ada94b, page 483]
Contrast with: DECLARATION.
See also: VIEW.
Commentary: "In most cases, a declaration also contains the definition for the entity itself." [Ada94b, page 483]

derivation class *n.* "In addition to the various language-defined classes of types, types can be grouped into *derivation classes*. A derived type is *derived from* its parent type *directly*; it is derived *indirectly* from any type from which its parent type is derived. The derivation class of types for a type *T* (also called the class *rooted* at *T*) is the set consisting of *T* (the *root type* of the class) and all types derived from *T* (directly or indirectly) plus any associated universal or class-wide types." [Ada94b, page 31]
See also: ROOT TYPE, TYPE.

derived type *n.* "A derived type is a type defined in terms of another type, which is the parent type of the derived type." [Ada94b, page 483]

Antonym: PARENT TYPE.

See also: TYPE EXTENSION.

Commentary: "Each class containing the parent type also contains the derived type. The derived type inherits properties such as components and primitive operations from the parent. A type together with the types derived from it (directly or indirectly) form a derivation class." [Ada94b, page 483]

descendant [of a type] *n.* "A specific type T2 is defined to be a *descendant* of a type T1 if T2 is the same as T1, or if T2 is derived (directly or indirectly) from T1. A class-wide type T2'Class is defined to be a descendant of type T1 if T2 is a descendant of T1." [Ada94b, page 32]

Antonym: ANCESTOR.

discriminant *n.* "Discriminants can be thought of as parameters of the type." [Ada94b, page 20] "A discriminant is a parameter of a composite type. It can control, for example, the bounds of a component of the type if that type is an array type. A discriminant of a task type can be used to pass data to a task of the type upon creation." [Ada94b, page 484]

See also: COMPOSITE TYPE, GENERIC.

dispatch *v. -ed, -ing* "... using a tag to control which body to execute is called *dispatching*." [Ada94b, page 62]

See also: CONTROLLING OPERAND, TAGGED, TAGGED TYPE.

dynamically tagged *adj.* "The name or expression is *dynamically tagged* if it is of a class-wide type, or it is a call with a controlling result and at least one dynamically tagged controlling operand." [Ada94b, page 65]

Antonym: STATICALLY TAGGED.

elementary type *n.* "An elementary type does not have components." [Ada94b, page 484]

Antonym: COMPOSITE TYPE.

Examples: "enumeration, numeric, and access types." [Ada94b, page xvi]

encapsulation *n.* "[Encapsulation is] some means of defining objects and their operations and providing an abstract interface to them, while hiding their implementation details." [Ada94a, page 4-1]

exception *n.* "An *exception* represents a kind of exceptional situation." [Ada94b, page 484]

See also: EXCEPTION OCCURRENCE, HANDLE, RAISE.

exception occurrence *n.* "An occurrence of [an exception] (at run time) is called an *exception occurrence*." [Ada94b, page 484]

See also: EXCEPTION, HANDLE, RAISE.

explicit declaration *n.* "A declaration may appear explicitly in the program text (an *explicit* declaration)." [Ada94b, pages 19–20]

Antonym: IMPLICIT DECLARATION.

See also: OVERRIDE.

extension *n.* "When deriving from a tagged type ... the derived type is called an *extension* of the ancestor type, or simply a *type extension*." [Ada94b, page 62] "Every type extension is a tagged type, and is either a *record extension* or a *private extension* of some other tagged type." [Ada94b, page 64]

Synonym: TYPE EXTENSION.

See also: DERIVED TYPE, TAGGED TYPE.

Kinds:
- PRIVATE EXTENSION
- RECORD EXTENSION

- **private extension** *n.* "A private extension is like a record extension, except that the components of the extension part are hidden from its clients." [Ada94b, page 485]

Antonym: RECORD EXTENSION.

- **record extension** *n.* "A record extension is a type that extends another type by adding additional components." [Ada94b, page 485]

  Antonym: PRIVATE EXTENSION.

formal parameter *n.* "A *formal parameter* is an object directly visible within a subprogram_body that represents the actual parameter passed to the subprogram in a call." [Ada94b, page 121]

See also: FORMAL, GENERIC FORMAL.

function *n.* "A function is the means of invoking the computation of a value. It is similar to a procedure, but in addition will return a result." [Ada94b, page xv]

Antonym: PROCEDURE.

See also: SUBPROGRAM.

generic actual [parameter] *n.* "The *generic actual parameter* is either the explicit_generic_actual_parameter given in a generic_parameter_association for each formal, or the corresponding default_expression or default_name if no generic_parameter_association is given for the formal." [Ada94b, page 212]

Synonym: ACTUAL.

Contrast with: FORMAL.

Commentary: "When the meaning is clear from context, the term 'generic actual,' or simply 'actual,' is used as a synonym for 'generic actual parameter' and also for the view denoted by one, or the value of one." [Ada94b, page 212]

generic formal *adj.* "An entity is a *generic formal* entity if it is declared by using a generic_formal_parameter_declaration. 'Generic formal,' or simply 'formal,' is used as a prefix in referring to objects, subtypes (and types), func-

tions, procedures and packages, that are generic formal entities, as well as their respective declarations." [Ada94b, page 209]

Contrast with: GENERIC ACTUAL.

See also: FORMAL PARAMETER.

Examples: A generic formal procedure and a formal integer type declaration are examples of 'generic formals.'

generic [program] unit *n.* "A generic unit is a template for a (nongeneric) program unit; the template can be parameterized by objects, types, subprograms, and packages. [Ada94b, page 484] "The language provides a powerful means of parameterization of program units, called generic program units. The generic parameters can be types and subprograms (as well as objects and packages) and so allow general algorithms and data structures to be defined that are applicable to all types of a given class." [Ada94b, page xviii]

Commentary: "An instance of a generic unit is created by a generic_instantiation. The rules of the language are enforced when a generic unit is compiled, using a generic contract model; additional checks are performed upon instantiation to verify the contract is met. That is, the declaration of a generic unit represents a contract between the body of the generic and instances of the generic. Generic units can be used to perform the role that macros sometimes play in other languages." [Ada94b, page 484]

handle [an exception] *v.* "Performing some actions in response to the arising of an exception is called *handling* the exception." [Ada94b, page 484]

See also: EXCEPTION, EXCEPTION OCCURRENCE, RAISE.

homograph [declaration] *n.* "Two declarations are *homographs* if they have the same defining name, and, if both are overloadable, their profiles are type conformant. An inner declaration hides any outer homograph from direct visibility." [Ada94b, page 149]

implicit declaration *n.* "A declaration may ... be supposed to occur at a given place in the text as a consequence of the semantics of another construct (an *implicit* declaration)." [Ada94b, page 19]
Antonym: EXPLICIT DECLARATION.
Commentary: Implicit declarations are typically those inherited in a derived type.

indefinite subtype *n.* "An indefinite subtype does not by itself provide enough information to create an object; an additional constraint or explicit initial expression is necessary." [Ada94b, page 25]
Antonym: DEFINITE SUBTYPE.
Examples: "An unconstrained array subtype is an indefinite subtype, as is a subtype with unknown discriminants or unconstrained discriminants without default." [Ada94b, page 25]
Commentary: "The object's *actual subtype* can be more restrictive than the nominal subtype of the view; it always is if the nominal subtype is an *indefinite subtype*." [Ada94b, page 25]

inheritance *n.* "[Inheritance is] a means for incrementally building new abstractions from existing ones by 'inheriting' their properties—without disturbing the implementation of the original abstraction or the existing clients." [Ada94a, page 4-2]
Kinds:
- MIXIN INHERITANCE
- MULTIPLE INHERITANCE
- **mixin inheritance** *n.* "In mixin inheritance, one of the parent classes cannot have instances of its own and exists

only to provide a set of properties for classes inheriting from it. Typically, this abstract mixin class has been isolated solely for the purpose of combining with other classes." [Ada94a, page 4-34]
- **multiple inheritance** *n.* "The means of inheriting components and operations from two or more parent types." [Ada94a, page 4-3]

limited type *n.* "A limited type is (a view of) a type for which the assignment operation is not allowed." [Ada94b, page 484]

mixin inheritance *n.* "In mixin inheritance, one of the parent classes cannot have instances of its own and exists only to provide a set of properties for classes inheriting from it. Typically, this abstract mixin class has been isolated solely for the purpose of combining with other classes." [Ada94a, page 4-34]

multiple inheritance *n.* "The means of inheriting components and operations from two or more parent types." [Ada94a, page 4-3]

nominal subtype *n.* "When a view of an object is defined, a *nominal subtype* is associated with the view. The object's *actual subtype* can be more restrictive than the nominal subtype of the view; it always is if the nominal subtype is an *indefinite subtype*." [Ada94b, page 25]
Contrast with: ACTUAL SUBTYPE.

object *n.* "an *object* of a given type is a runtime entity that contains (has) a value of the type." [Ada94b, page 20]
Commentary: "Entities that have structure and state." [Ada94a, page 4-1] "An object is either a constant or a variable. An object contains a value. ... A formal parameter is (a view of) an object. A subcomponent of an object is an object." [Ada94b, page 484]

App
C

- **constrained object** *n.* "[If an object's] actual subtype is constrained, the object is called a *constrained object.*" [Ada94b, page 26]

operation *n.* "[Operations are] actions on objects that may access or manipulate that state." [Ada94a, page 4-1]

- **primitive operation** *n.* "The *primitive operations* of a type include the predefined operations of the type, plus any user-defined primitive subprograms." [Ada94b, page 24]
  See also: INHERITANCE, PRIMITIVE SUBPROGRAM.
  Commentary: "Primitive operations are the derivable (inherited) operations." [Ada94a, page 4-4]

override *v.* **overrode, -ing** "... wherever the explicit declaration is visible, it is said to *override* the implicit declaration [if an implicit declaration exists]." [Ada94b, pages 19–20]
See also: EXPLICIT DECLARATION.

package *n.* "Packages are program units that allow the specification of groups of logically related entities. Typically, a package contains the declaration of a type (often a private type or private extension) along with the declarations of primitive subprograms of the type, which can be called from outside the package, while their inner workings remain hidden from outside users." [Ada94b, pages 484–485]

parent type *n.* when a type is defined in terms of another type, that other type is called the parent type. [Ada94b, page 29]
Antonym: DERIVED TYPE.

polymorphism *n.* "a means of factoring out the differences among a collection of abstractions, such that programs may be written in terms of their common properties." [Ada94a, page 4-2]

See also: CLASS-WIDE PROGRAMMING.

private [record] extension *n.* "A private extension is like a record extension, except that the components of the extension part are hidden from its clients." [Ada94b, page 485]

private type *n.* "A private type is a partial view of a type whose full view is hidden from its clients." [Ada94b, page 485]

procedure *n.* "A procedure is the means of invoking a series of actions. For example, it may read data, update variables, or produce some output. It may have parameters, to provide a controlled means of passing information between the procedure and the point of call." [Ada94b, page xv]
Antonym: FUNCTION.

program unit *n.* "An Ada program is composed of one or more program units. Program units may be subprograms ..., packages ..., protected units ..., or generic units .... Each program unit normally consists of two parts: a specification ... and a body." [Ada94b, page xv]
See also: SPECIFICATION, BODY.
Kinds:

- GENERIC [PROGRAM] UNIT
- PACKAGE
- PROTECTED UNIT
- SUBPROGRAM
- TASK

- **generic [program] unit** *n.* "A generic unit is a template for a (nongeneric) program unit; the template can be parameterized by objects, types, subprograms, and packages. [Ada94b, page 484] "The language provides a powerful means of parameterization of program units, called generic program units. The generic parameters can be types and subprograms (as well as objects and packages) and so allow gen-

eral algorithms and data structures to be defined that are applicable to all types of a given class." [Ada94b, page xviii]
Commentary: "An instance of a generic unit is created by a generic_instantiation. The rules of the language are enforced when a generic unit is compiled, using a generic contract model; additional checks are performed upon instantiation to verify the contract is met. That is, the declaration of a generic unit represents a contract between the body of the generic and instances of the generic. Generic units can be used to perform the role that macros sometimes play in other languages." [Ada94b, page 484]

- **package** *n.* "Packages are program units that allow the specification of groups of logically related entities. Typically, a package contains the declaration of a type (often a private type or private extension) along with the declarations of primitive subprograms of the type, which can be called from outside the package, while their inner workings remain hidden from outside users." [Ada94b, pages 484–485]

- **protected unit** *n.* "A protected unit is the basic unit for defining protected operations for the coordinated use of data shared between tasks." [Ada94b, page xv]

- **subprogram** *n.* "A subprogram is the basic unit for expressing an algorithm. There are two kinds of subprograms: procedures and functions." [Ada94b, page 484]
Commentary: An Ada subprogram is known as an operation in other languages.
Kinds: ABSTRACT SUBPROGRAM, FUNCTION, PROCEDURE.

- **task [unit]** *n.* "The execution of an Ada program consists of the execution of one or more *tasks*. Each task represents a separate thread of control that proceeds independently and concurrently between the points where it interacts with other tasks." [Ada94b, page 159] "A task unit is the basic unit for defining a task whose sequence of actions may be executed concurrently with those of other tasks." [Ada94b, page xv]
See also: TASK TYPE.

protected type *n.* "A protected type is a composite type whose components are protected from concurrent access by multiple tasks." [Ada94b, page 485]

protected unit *n.* "A protected unit is the basic unit for defining protected operations for the coordinated use of data shared between tasks." [Ada94b, page xv]
See also: PROGRAM UNIT.

raise [an exception] *v.* "To *raise* an exception is to abandon normal program execution so as to draw attention to the fact that the corresponding situation has arisen." [Ada94b, page 484]
See also: EXCEPTION, EXCEPTION OCCURRENCE, HANDLE.

record extension *n.* "A record extension is a type that extends another type by adding additional components." [Ada94b, page 485]

- **private [record] extension** *n.* "A private extension is like a record extension, except that the components of the extension part are hidden from its clients." [Ada94b, page 485]
See also: RECORD EXTENSION.

root type [of a derivation class of types] *n.* The type from which all other types in the derivation class (except associated universal types or class-wide types) are directly or indirectly derived. [Ada94b, page 31]

Contrast with: ULTIMATE ANSCESTOR.

See also: CLASS, DERIVATION CLASS.

specification *n.* "[A specification contains] the information that must be visible to other units." [Ada94b, page xv]

Antonym: BODY.

See also: PROGRAM UNIT.

statically tagged *adj.* "The name or expression is *statically tagged* if it is of a specific tagged type and, if it is a call with a controlling result, it has at least one statically tagged controlling operand." [Ada94b, page 65]

Antonym: DYNAMICALLY TAGGED.

subprogram *n.* "A subprogram is the basic unit for expressing an algorithm. There are two kinds of subprograms: procedures and functions." [Ada94b, page 484]

See also: PROGRAM UNIT.

Commentary: An Ada subprogram is known as an operation in other languages.

Kinds:

- ABSTRACT SUBPROGRAM
- FUNCTION
- PROCEDURE

- **abstract subprogram** *n.* "An *abstract subprogram* is a subprogram that has no body, but is intended to be overridden at some point when inherited." [Ada94b, page 67]

- **function** *n.* "A function is the means of invoking the computation of a value. It is similar to a procedure, but in addition will return a result." [Ada94b, page xv]

  Contrast with: PROCEDURE.

  See also: SUBPROGRAM.

- **procedure** *n.* "A procedure is the means of invoking a series of actions. For example, it may read data, update variables, or produce some output. It may have parameters, to provide a controlled means of passing information between the procedure and the point of call." [Ada94b, page xv]

  Contrast with: FUNCTION.

  See also: SUBPROGRAM.

subtype *n.* "A subtype is a type together with a constraint, which constrains the values of the subtype to satisfy a certain condition. The values of a subtype are a subset of the values of its type." [Ada94b, page 485] "a *subtype* of a given type is a combination of the type, a constraint on values of the type, and certain attributes specific to the subtype. The given type is called the type *of* the subtype. Similarly, the associated constraint is called the constraint *of* the subtype. The set of values of a subtype consists of the values of its type that satisfy its constraint. Such values *belong* to the subtype." [Ada94b, pages 20–21]

See also: CLASS, CONSTRAINT, TYPE.

Commentary: "Subtypes can be used to define subranges of scalar types, arrays with a limited set of index values, and records and private types with particular discriminant values." [Ada94b, page xvii]

Kinds:

- ACTUAL SUBTYPE
- CONSTRAINED SUBTYPE
- DEFINITE SUBTYPE
- INDEFINITE SUBTYPE
- NOMINAL SUBTYPE
- UNCONSTRAINED SUBTYPE

- **actual subtype** *n.* "The object's *actual subtype* can be more restrictive than the nominal subtype of the view; it always is if the nominal subtype is an *indefinite subtype*. An unconstrained array subtype is an indefinite subtype, as is a subtype with unknown discriminants or unconstrained discriminants without default." [Ada94b, page 25]

Contrast with: NOMINAL SUBTYPE.

- **constrained subtype** *n.* "a subtype is called an *unconstrained* subtype if its type has unknown discriminants, or if its type allows range, index, or discriminant constraints, but the subtype does not impose such a constraint; otherwise, the subtype is called a *constrained* subtype (since it has no unconstrained characteristics)." [Ada94b, page 21]

Antonym: UNCONSTRAINED SUBTYPE.

- **definite subtype** *n.* "If a subtype is not indefinite, it is called a *definite* subtype. All elementary subtypes are definite subtypes." [Ada94b, page 25]

Antonym: INDEFINITE SUBTYPE.

- **indefinite subtype** *n.* "An indefinite subtype does not by itself provide enough information to create an object; an additional constraint or explicit initial expression is necessary." [Ada-94b, page 25]

Antonym: DEFINITE SUBTYPE.

- **nominal subtype** *n.* "When a view of an object is defined, a *nominal subtype* is associated with the view. The object's *actual subtype* can be more restrictive than the nominal subtype of the view; it always is if the nominal subtype is an *indefinite subtype*. An unconstrained array subtype is an indefinite subtype, as is a subtype with unknown discriminants or unconstrained discriminants without default." [Ada94b, page 25]

Contrast with: ACTUAL SUBTYPE.

- **unconstrained subtype** *n.* "a subtype is called an *unconstrained* subtype if its type has unknown discriminants, or if its type allows range, index, or discrim-

inant constraints, but the subtype does not impose such a constraint; otherwise, the subtype is called a *constrained* subtype (since it has no unconstrained characteristics)." [Ada94b, page 21]

Antonym: CONSTRAINED SUBTYPE.

tag *n.* "[A tag is] a type descriptor ranging over the types that are members of the class." [Ada94a, page 4-5]

tag indeterminate *adj.* "The name or expression is *tag indeterminate* if it is a call with a controlling result, all of whose controlling operands (if any) are tag indeterminate." [Ada94b, page 65]

See also: TAGGED.

tagged *adj.* "A name or expression of a tagged type is either *statically* tagged, *dynamically* tagged, or *tag indeterminate*, according to whether, when used as a controlling operand, the tag that controls dispatching is determined statically by the operand's (specific) type, dynamically by its tag at run time, or from context." [Ada94b, page 65]

See also: DISPATCHING.

Kinds:
- DYNAMICALLY TAGGED
- STATICALLY TAGGED
- TAG INDETERMINATE

- **dynamically tagged** *adj.* "The name or expression is *dynamically tagged* if it is of a class-wide type, or it is a call with a controlling result and at least one dynamically tagged controlling operand." [Ada94b, page 65]

Antonym: STATICALLY TAGGED.

- **statically tagged** *adj.* "The name or expression is *statically tagged* if it is of a specific tagged type and, if it is a call with a controlling result, it has at least one statically tagged controlling operand." [Ada94b, page 65]

Antonym: DYNAMICALLY TAGGED.

- **tag indeterminate** *adj.* "The name or expression is *tag indeterminate* if it is a call with a controlling result, all of whose controlling operands (if any) are tag indeterminate." [Ada94b, page 65] *See also:* TAGGED.

tagged type *n.* "The objects of a tagged type have a run-time type tag, which indicates the specific type with which the object was originally created. An operand of a class-wide tagged type can be used in a dispatching call; the tag indicates which subprogram body to invoke. Nondispatching calls, in which the subprogram body to invoke is determined at compile time, are also allowed. Tagged types may be extended with additional components." [Ada94b, page 486] *See also:* TAG, DISPATCHING, TYPE EXTENSION.

Commentary: "Tagged types and type extensions support object-oriented programming, based on inheritance with extension and run-time polymorphism via *dispatching operations.* A record type or private type that has the reserved word *tagged* in its declaration is called a *tagged* type. ... An object of a tagged type has an associated (run-time) *tag* that identifies the specific tagged type used to create the object originally." [Ada94b, page 61–62]

task type *n.* "A task type is a composite type whose values are tasks, which are active entities that may execute concurrently with other tasks." [Ada94b, page 486]

See also: TASK.

Example: "The top-level task of a partition is called the environment task." [Ada94b, page 486]

task [unit] *n.* "The execution of an Ada program consists of the execution of one or more *tasks*. Each task represents a separate thread of control that proceeds independently and concurrently between the points where it interacts with other tasks." [Ada94b, page 159] "A task unit is the basic unit for defining a task whose sequence of actions may be executed concurrently with those of other tasks." [Ada94b, page xv]

See also: PROGRAM UNIT, TASK TYPE.

type *n.* "Each object has a type. A *type* has an associated set of values, and a set of *primitive operations* which implement the fundamental aspects of its semantics. Types are grouped into *classes.* The types of a given class share a set of primitive operations. Classes are closed under derivation; that is, if a type is in a class, then all of its derivatives are in that class." [Ada94b, page 486]

See also: CLASS, DERIVATION CLASS, ROOT TYPE, SUBTYPE.

Commentary: "The main classes of types are elementary types (comprising enumeration, numeric, and access types) and composite types (including array and record types)." [Ada94b, page xvi]

Kinds:
- ABSTRACT TYPE
- CLASS-WIDE TYPE
- COMPOSITE TYPE
  - PROTECTED TYPE
- CONTROLLED TYPE
- DERIVED TYPE
- ELEMENTARY TYPE
- LIMITED TYPE
- PARENT TYPE
- PRIVATE TYPE
- ROOT TYPE
- TAGGED TYPE
- TASK TYPE

- **abstract type** *n.* "An *abstract type* is a tagged type intended for use as a parent type for type extensions, but which is not allowed to have objects of its own." [Ada94b, page xvi]

- **class-wide type** *n.* "Class-wide types are defined for (and belong to) each derivation class rooted at a tagged type. Given a subtype S of a tagged type *T*, S' Class is the subtype_mark for a corresponding subtype of the tagged class-wide type *T*' Class. Such types are called 'class-wide' because when a formal parameter is defined to be of class-wide type *T*' Class, and actual parameter of any type in the derivation class rooted at *T* is acceptable." [Ada94b, page 31]
  See also: CLASS-WIDE PROGRAMMING, DERIVATION CLASS.

- **composite type** *n.* "A composite type has components." [Ada94b, page 483] "[Composite types include] array and record types." [Ada94b, page xvi]
  Antonym: ELEMENTARY TYPE.
  See also: DISCRIMINANT.

  - **protected type** *n.* "A protected type is a composite type whose components are protected from concurrent access by multiple tasks." [Ada94b, page 485]

- **controlled type** *n.* "A controlled type supports user-defined assignment and finalization. Objects are always finalized before being destroyed." [Ada94b, page 483]

- **derived type** *n.* "A derived type is a type defined in terms of another type, which is the parent type of the derived type. Each class containing the parent type also contains the derived type. The derived type inherits properties such as components and primitive operations from the parent. A type together with the types derived from it

(directly or indirectly) form a derivation class." [Ada94b, page 483]
Antonym: PARENT TYPE.
See also: TYPE EXTENSION.

- **elementary type** *n.* "An elementary type does not have components." [Ada94b, page 484] Elementary types are comprised of "enumeration, numeric, and access types." [Ada94b, page xvi]
  Antonym: COMPOSITE TYPE.

- **limited type** *n.* "A limited type is (a view of) a type for which the assignment operation is not allowed." [Ada94b, page 484]

- **parent type** *n.* when a type is defined in terms of another type, that other type is called the parent type. [Ada94b, page 29]
  Antonym: DERIVED TYPE.

- **private type** *n.* "A private type is a partial view of a type whose full view is hidden from its clients." [Ada94b, page 485]

- **root type [of a class]** *n.* The type which is the highest ancestor type for a class. [Ada94b, page 31]
  Contrast with: ULTIMATE ANCESTOR.
  See also: CLASS, DERIVATION CLASS.

- **tagged type** *n.* "The objects of a tagged type have a run-time type tag, which indicates the specific type with which the object was originally created. An operand of a class-wide tagged type can be used in a dispatching call; the tag indicates which subprogram body to invoke. Nondispatching calls, in which the subprogram body to invoke is determined at compile time, are also allowed. Tagged types may be extended with additional components." [Ada94b, page 486] "Tagged types and type extensions support

App
C

object-oriented programming, based on inheritance with extension and run-time polymorphism via *dispatching operations*. A record type or private type that has the reserved word *tagged* in its declaration is called a *tagged* type. ... An object of a tagged type has an associated (run-time) *tag* that identifies the specific tagged type used to create the object originally." [Ada94b, page 61–62]
See also: TAG, DISPATCHING, TYPE EXTENSION.

- **task type** *n.* "A task type is a composite type whose values are tasks, which are active entities that may execute concurrently with other tasks. The top-level task of a partition is called the environment task." [Ada94b, page 486]
See also: TASK.

type extension *n.* "When deriving from a tagged type ... the derived type is called an *extension* of the ancestor type, or simply a *type extension*." [Ada94b, page 62] "Every type extension is a tagged type, and is either a *record extension* or a *private extension* of some other tagged type." [Ada94b, page 64]
Synonym: EXTENSION.
See also: DERIVED TYPE, TAGGED TYPE.
Kinds:
  - PRIVATE [RECORD] EXTENSION
  - RECORD EXTENSION

- **private [record] extension** *n.* "A private extension is like a record extension, except that the components of the extension part are hidden from its clients." [Ada94b, page 485]
Antonym: RECORD EXTENSION.

- **record extension** *n.* "A record extension is a type that extends another type by adding additional components." [Ada94b, page 485]

Antonym: PRIVATE EXTENSION.

ultimate ancestor *n.* "The *ultimate ancestor* of a type is the ancestor of the type that is not a descendant of any other type." [Ada94b, page 32]
Contrast with: ROOT TYPE.

unconstrained subtype *n.* "a subtype is called an *unconstrained* subtype if its type has unknown discriminants, or if its type allows range, index, or discriminant constraints, but the subtype does not impose such a constraint; otherwise, the subtype is called a *constrained* subtype (since it has no unconstrained characteristics)." [Ada94b, page 21]
Antonym: CONSTRAINED TYPE.

variant programming *n.* "New abstractions may be constructed from existing ones such that the programmer need only specify the differences between the new and old abstractions." [Ada94a, page 4-2]
Contrast with: CLASS-WIDE PROGRAMMING.

view *n.* "A view consists of an identification of the entity (the entity *of* the view), plus view-specific characteristics that affect the use of the entity through that view (such as mode of access to an object, formal parameter names and defaults for a subprogram, or visibility to components of a type)." [Ada94b, page 483]
See also: DEFINITION.

- **aliased view** *n.* "An aliased view of an object is one that can be designated by an access value. Objects allocated by allocators are aliased. Objects can also be explicitly declared as aliased with the reserved word *aliased*. The Access attribute can be used to create an access value designating an aliased object." [Ada94b, page 483]

References

[Ada94a] Ada 9X Mapping/Revision Team. (1994). *Ada 9X Rationale.* (Draft Version 5.0, 8 June 1994). Cambridge, MA: Intermetrics, Inc.

[Ada94b] Ada 9X Mapping/Revision Team. (1994). *Ada 9X Reference Manual.* (Draft Version 5.0, 1 June 1994). Cambridge, MA: Intermetrics, Inc.

App
C

Appendix *D*

Common Lisp Object System (CLOS)

"The Common Lisp Object System (CLOS) is an object-oriented extension to Common Lisp. It is based on generic functions, multiple inheritance, declarative method combination, and a meta-object protocol." [Steele 1990, page 770]

The definitions appearing in this appendix are excerpted from:

Steele, Guy L. Jr. (1990). *Common LISP: The Language.* Second Edition. Butterworth-Heinemann. Reprinted with permission of Butterworth-Heinemann.

For more information, contact:

Guy L. Steele, Jr.
9 Lantern Lane
Lexington, Massachusetts 02173, USA
Voice: +1 (508) 442-2620
E-mail:guy.steele@east.sun.com

Mr. Gregor Kizales
Xerox Park
3333 Coyote Hill Road
Palo Alto, California 94304, USA
Voice: +1 (415) 812-4888

accessible [slot] *n.* "A slot is said to be *accessible* in an instance of a class if the slot is defined by the class of the instance or is inherited from a superclass of that class. At most one slot of a given name can be accessible in an instance." [Steele 1990, pages 776–777]

:after method *n.* "An *:after* method specifies code that is to be run after primary methods." [Steele 1990, page 796]
Commentary: "An *:after* method has the keyword *:after* as its only qualifier." [Steele 1990, page 796]

:around method *n.* "An *:around* method specifies code that is to be run instead of other applicable methods but that is able to cause some of them to be run." [Steele 1990, page 796]
Commentary: "An *:around* method specifies code that is to be run instead of other applicable methods but that is able to cause some of them to be run." [Steele 1990, page 796]

auxiliary method *n.* ".... *auxiliary methods* modify [the main, primary action of the effective method] in one of three ways. ... An auxiliary method is a method whose method qualifier is *:before, :after,* or *:around.*" [Steele 1990, page 796]
Kinds:
- :AFTER METHOD
- :AROUND METHOD
- :BEFORE METHOD

- **:after method** *n.* "An *:after* method specifies code that is to be run after primary methods." [Steele 1990, page 796]
Commentary: "An *:after* method has the keyword *:after* as its only qualifier." [Steele 1990, page 796]

- **:around method** *n.* "An *:around* method specifies code that is to be run instead of other applicable methods but that is able to cause some of them to be run." [Steele 1990, page 796]
Commentary: "An *:around* method specifies code that is to be run instead of other applicable methods but that is able to cause some of them to be run." [Steele 1990, page 796]

- **:before method** *n.* "A *:before* method specifies code that is to be run before any primary method." [Steele 1990, page 796]
Commentary: "A *:before* method has the keyword *:before* as its only qualifier." [Steele 1990, page 796]

:before method *n.* "A *:before* method specifies code that is to be run before any primary method." [Steele 1990, page 796]
Commentary: "A *:before* method has the keyword *:before* as its only qualifier." [Steele 1990, page 796]

built-in class *n.* "[a class that is] implemented in a special, non-extensible way." [Steele 1990, page 781] "The class *built-in-class* is the class whose instances are classes that have special implementations with restricted capabilities." [Steele 1990, page 801]

call *v. -ed, -ing* "Various mechanisms in the Object System take a method object and invoke its method function, as is the case when a generic function is invoked. When this occurs it is said that the method is invoked or called." [Steele 1990, page 788]
Synonym: INVOKE.

change-class function *n.* "The function *change-class* can be used to change the class of an instance from its current class, C_{from} to a different class, C_{to}." [Steele 1990, page 812]

class *n.* "A *class* is an object that determines the structure and behavior of a set

App
D

of other objects, which are called its *instances*. A class can inherit structure and behavior from other classes." [Steele 1990, page 773] "The class of an object determines the set of operations that can be performed on the object." [Steele 1990, page 771]

See also: CLASS, INSTANCE, SUBCLASS, SUPERCLASS.

Kinds:
- BUILT-IN CLASS
- METACLASS
- STANDARD-CLASS
- STANDARD-OBJECT
- SUBCLASS
  - DIRECT SUBCLASS
- SUPERCLASS
  - DIRECT SUPERCLASS
- T CLASS

- **built-in class** *n.* "[a class that is] implemented in a special, non-extensible way." [Steele 1990, page 781] "The class *built-in-class* is the class whose instances are classes that have special implementations with restricted capabilities." [Steele 1990, page 800]

- **metaclass** *n.* "Classes are represented by objects that are themselves instances of classes. The class of the class of an object is termed the *metaclass* of that object. When no misinterpretation is possible, the term *metaclass* will be used to refer to a class that has instances that are themselves classes. The metaclass determines the form of inheritance used by the classes that are its instances and the representation of the instances of those classes." [Steele 1990, page 775]

See also: META-OBJECT, STANDARD-CLASS.

- **standard-class** *n.* "The class *standard-class* is the default class of classes defined by *defclass*." [Steele 1990, page 800] "The Common Lisp Object System provides a default metaclass, *standard-class*, that is appropriate for most programs." [Steele 1990, page 775]

See also: METACLASS, STANDARD-OBJECT.

- **standard-object [class]** *n.* "The class named *standard-object* is an instance of the [meta]class *standard-class* and is a superclass of every class that is an instance of *standard-class* except itself." [Steele 1990, page 774]

See also: META-OBJECT, STANDARD-CLASS.

- **subclass** *n.* "A class whose definition refers to other classes for the purpose of inheriting from them is said to be a *subclass* of each of those classes." [Steele 1990, page 773] "A class C_n is a *superclass* of a class C_1 if there exists a series of classes $C_2, ..., C_{n-1}$ such that C_{i+1} is a direct superclass of C_i for $1 \le i < n$. In this case, C_1 is a *subclass* of C_n." [Steele 1990, page 774]

Antonym: SUPERCLASS.

See also: CLASS.

- **direct subclass** *n.* "... if [class] C_2 explicitly designates C_1 as a superclass in its definition ... C_2 is a *direct subclass* of C_1." [Steele 1990, page 774]

Antonym: DIRECT SUPERCLASS.

- **superclass** *n.* "The classes that are designated for purposes of inheritance are said to be *superclasses* of the inheriting class." [Steele 1990, page 773] "A class C_n is a *superclass* of a class C_1 if there exists a series of classes $C_2, ..., C_{n-1}$ such that C_{i+1} is a direct superclass of C_i for $1 \le i < n$." [Steele 1990, page 774]

Antonym: SUBCLASS.

See also: CLASS.

- **direct superclass** *n.* "A class C_1 is a *direct superclass* of a class C_2 if C_2 explicitly designates C_1 as a superclass in its definition." [Steele 1990, page 774]

Antonym: DIRECT SUBCLASS.

- **t [class]** *n.* "The class named *t* has no superclasses. It is a superclass of every class except itself." [Steele 1990, page 774]

class precedence *n.* "Each class has a *class precedence list*, which is a total ordering on the set of the given class and its superclasses." [Steele 1990, page 774]

CLOS *abbr.* Common Lisp Object System *Commentary:* CLOS is pronounced "sea loss."

direct subclass *n.* "… if [class] C_2 explicitly designates C_1 as a superclass in its definition … C_2 is a *direct subclass* of C_1." [Steele 1990, page 774]
Antonym: DIRECT SUPERCLASS.

direct superclass *n.* "A class C_1 is a *direct superclass* of a class C_2 if C_2 explicitly designates C_1 as a superclass in its definition." [Steele 1990, page 774]
Antonym: DIRECT SUBCLASS.

effective method *n.* "When a generic function is called with particular arguments, it must determine the code to execute. This code is called the *effective method* for those arguments." [Steele 1990, page 793]

generic function [object] *n.* "A *generic function* is a function whose behavior depends on the classes or identities of the arguments supplied to it. A generic function object contains a set of methods, a lambda-list, a method combination type, and other information." [Steele 1990, page 771]
See also: LAMBDA-LIST.

inherit *v.* *-ed, -ing* "A class can inherit structure and behavior from other classes." [Steele 1990, page 773] "A class can inherit methods, slots, and some *defclass* options from its superclasses. … A subclass inherits methods in the sense that any method applicable to all instances of a class is also applicable to all instance of

any subclass of that class. … If a slot is defined by a superclass of C, the slot is said to be *inherited*." [Steele 1990, page 777]

initialization argument list *n.* "An *initialization argument list* is a list of alternating initialization argument names and values." [Steele 1990, page 802] "The first argument [in calling a generic function] is a class or the name of a class, and the remaining arguments form an *initialization argument* list." [Steele 1990, page 801]

instance *n.* "A *class* is an object that determines the structure and behavior of a set of other objects, which are called its *instances*." [Steele 1990, page 773]
See also: CLASS, OBJECT.

invoke *v.* *-ed, -ing* "Various mechanisms in the Object System take a method object and invoke its method function, as is the case when a generic function is invoked. When this occurs it is said that the method is invoked or called." [Steele 1990, page 788]
Synonym: CALL.

lambda-list *n.* "specifies names for the *parameters* of the functions." [Steele 1990, page 76]
See also: GENERIC FUNCTION.

local precedence order *n.* "Each class has a *local precedence order*, which is a list consisting of the class followed by its direct superclasses in the order mentioned in the defining form." [Steele 1990, page 774]
See also: CLASS PRECEDENCE.

local slot *n.* "A *local slot* is defined to be a slot that is visible to exactly one instance, namely the one in which the slot is allocated." [Steele 1990, page 776]
Antonym: SHARED SLOT.

metaclass *n.* "Classes are represented by objects that are themselves instances of classes. The class of the class of an object is termed the *metaclass* of that object. When no misinterpretation is possible, the term *metaclass* will be used to refer to a class that has instances that are themselves classes. The metaclass determines the form of inheritance used by the classes that are its instances and the representation of the instances of those classes." [Steele 1990, page 775]

See also: META-OBJECT, STANDARD-CLASS.

meta-object *n.* "The implementation of the Object System manipulates classes, methods, and generic functions. The meta-object protocol specifies a set of generic functions defined by methods on classes; the behavior of those generic functions defines the behavior of the Object System. The instances of the classes on which those methods are defined are called *meta-objects*." [Steele 1990, page 799] "The Object System supplies a standard set of meta-objects, called *standard meta-objects*. These include the class *standard-object* and instances of the classes *standard-method, standard-generic-function,* and *method-combination*." [Steele 1990, page 800]

See also: METACLASS, METHOD COMBINATION OBJECT, STANDARD-OBJECT.

method *n.* "The *methods* define the class-specific behavior and operations of the generic functions." [Steele 1990, page 786]
Kinds:
- AUXILIARY METHOD
  - :AFTER METHOD
  - :AROUND METHOD
  - :BEFORE METHOD
- EFFECTIVE METHOD
- PRIMARY METHOD

auxiliary method *n.* ".... *auxiliary methods* modify [the main, primary action of the effective method] in one of three ways.... An auxiliary method

is a method whose method qualifier is *:before, :after,* or *:around*." [Steele 1990, page 796]
Kinds:
- :AFTER METHOD
- :AROUND METHOD
- :BEFORE METHOD

- **:after method** *n.* "An *:after* method has the keyword *:after* as its only qualifier. An *:after* method specifies code that is to be run after primary methods." [Steele 1990, page 796]
- **:around method** *n.* "An *:around* method has the keyword *:around* as its only qualifier. An *:around* method specifies code that is to be run instead of other applicable methods but that is able to cause some of them to be run." [Steele 1990, page 796]
- **:before method** *n.* "A *:before* method has the keyword *:before* as its only qualifier. A *:before* method specifies code that is to be run before any primary method." [Steele 1990, page 796]
- **effective method** *n.* "When a generic function is called with particular arguments, it must determine the code to execute. This code is called the *effective method* for those arguments." [Steele 1990, page 793]
- **primary method** *n.* "*Primary methods* define the main action of the effective method.... A primary method has no method qualifiers." [Steele 1990, page 796]

method-combination facility *n.* "The method combination facility controls the selection of methods, the order in which they are run, and the values that are returned by the generic function." [Steele 1990, page 771]

method-combination object *n.* "A *meth-*

od combination object is an object that encapsulates the method combination type and options specified by the *:method-combination* option to forms that specify generic function options." [Steele 1990, page 795]
See also: META-OBJECT, METHOD-COMBINATION FACILITY, METHOD OBJECT.

method [object] *n.* "A method object contains a method function, a sequence of *parameter specializers* that specify when the given method is applicable, a lambda-list, and a sequence of *qualifiers* that are used by the method combination facility to distinguish among methods. A method object is not a function and cannot be invoked as a function." [Steele 1990, page 788]
See also: METHOD COMBINATION OBJECT, PARAMETER SPECIALIZER.

nil *n.* specifies the empty set. [Steele 1990, page 807]
See also: SLOT.

object *n.* "Every Common Lisp object is an *instance* of a class." [Steele 1990, page 771]
See also: CLASS, INSTANCE.
Kinds:
- META-OBJECT
- METHOD-COMBINATION OBJECT
- METHOD OBJECT

- **meta-object** *n.* "The implementation of the Object System manipulates classes, methods, and generic functions. The meta-object protocol specifies a set of generic functions defined by methods on classes; the behavior of those generic functions defines the behavior of the Object System. The instances of the classes on which those methods are defined are called *meta-objects.*" [Steele 1990, page 799] "The Object System supplies a standard set of meta-objects, called *standard meta-*

objects. These include the class *standard-object* and instances of the classes *standard-method, standard-generic-function,* and *method-combination.*" [Steele 1990, page 800]
See also: METACLASS, METHOD-COMBINATION OBJECT, STANDARD-OBJECT.

- **method-combination object** *n.* "A *method combination object* is an object that encapsulates the method combination type and options specified by the *:method-combination* option to forms that specify generic function options." [Steele 1990, page 795]
See also: META-OBJECT, METHOD-COMBINATION FACILITY, METHOD OBJECT.

- **method [object]** *n.* "A method object contains a method function, a sequence of *parameter specializers* that specify when the given method is applicable, a lambda-list, and a sequence of *qualifiers* that are used by the method combination facility to distinguish among methods. A method object is not a function and cannot be invoked as a function." [Steele 1990, page 788]
See also: METHOD-COMBINATION OBJECT, PARAMETER SPECIALIZER.

override *v.* "… more specific classes can *shadow*, or override, features that would otherwise be inherited from less specific classes." [Steele 1990, page 774]
Synonym: SHADOW.

parameter specializer *n.* "… specify when the given method is applicable…" [Steele 1990, page 788] "Each required formal parameter of each method has an associated parameter specializer, and the method will invoked only on arguments that satisfy its parameter specializers." [Steele 1990, page 771]
See also: METHOD.

primary method *n.* "*Primary methods*

define the main action of the effective method. ... A primary method has no method qualifiers." [Steele 1990, page 796]

redefine *v. -ed, -ing* "Redefining a class modifies the existing class object to reflect the new class definition; it does not create a new class object for the class.... When the class *C* is redefined, changes are propagated to its instances and to instances of any of its subclasses. Updating such an instance occurs at an implementation-dependent time, but no later than the next time a slot of that instance is read or written. Updating an instance does not change its identity as defined by the *eq* function. The updating process may change the slots of that particular instance, but it does not create a new instance." [Steele 1990, page 810]

shadow *v. -ed, -ing* "... more specific classes can *shadow*, or override, features that would otherwise be inherited from less specific classes." [Steele 1990, page 774]
Synonym: OVERRIDE.

shared slot *n.* "A *shared slot* is defined to be a slot that is visible to more than one instance of a given class and its subclasses. A shared slot defined by a class is accessible in all instances of that class." [Steele 1990, page 776]
Antonym: LOCAL SLOT.

slot *n.* "An object that has *standard-class* as its metaclass has zero or more named slots. The slots of an object are determined by the class of the object. Each slot can hold one value. The name of a slot is a symbol that is syntactically valid for use as a variable name." [Steele 1990, page 776]
See also: NIL, UNBOUND.
Kinds:
- ACCESSIBLE SLOT
- LOCAL SLOT

- SHARED SLOT
- UNBOUND SLOT

- **accessible [slot]** *n.* "A slot is said to be *accessible* in an instance of a class if the slot is defined by the class of the instance or is inherited from a superclass of that class. At most one slot of a given name can be accessible in an instance." [Steele 1990, pages 776–777]

- **local slot** *n.* "A *local slot* is defined to be a slot that is visible to exactly one instance, namely the one in which the slot is allocated." [Steele 1990, page 776]
Antonym: SHARED SLOT.

- **shared slot** *n.* "A *shared slot* is defined to be a slot that is visible to more than one instance of a given class and its subclasses. A shared slot defined by a class is accessible in all instances of that class." [Steele 1990, page 776]
Antonym: LOCAL SLOT.

- **unbound slot** *n.* "When a slot does not have a value, the slot is said to be *unbound*." [Steele 1990, page 776]

standard-class *n.* "The class *standard-class* is the default class of classes defined by *defclass*." [Steele 1990, page 800] "The Common Lisp Object System provides a default metaclass, *standard-class*, that is appropriate for most programs." [Steele 1990, page 775]
See also: METACLASS, STANDARD-OBJECT.

standard-object [class] *n.* "The class named *standard-object* is an instance of the [meta-]class *standard-class* and is a superclass of every class that is an instance of *standard-class* except itself." [Steele 1990, page 774]
See also: META-OBJECT, STANDARD-CLASS.

structure [of an instance] *n.* "The structure of an instance is the set of names of local slots in that instance." [Steele 1990, page 778]

See also: INSTANCE, SLOT.

subclass *n.* "A class whose definition refers to other classes for the purpose of inheriting from them is said to be a *subclass* of each of those classes." [Steele 1990, page 773] "A class C_n is a *superclass* of a class C_1 if there exists a series of classes C_2, ..., C_{n-1} such that C_{i+1} is a direct superclass of C_i for $1 \leq i < n$. In this case, C_1 is a *subclass* of C_n." [Steele 1990, page 774]
Antonym: SUPERCLASS.
See also: CLASS.

- **direct subclass** *n.* "... if [class] C_2 explicitly designates C_1 as a superclass in its definition ... C_2 is a *direct subclass* of C_1." [Steele 1990, page 774]
Antonym: DIRECT SUPERCLASS.

superclass *n.* "The classes that are designated for purposes of inheritance are said to be *superclasses* of the inheriting class." [Steele 1990, page 773] "A class C_n is a *superclass* of a class C_1 if there exists a series of classes C_2, ..., C_{n-1} such that C_{i+1} is a direct superclass of C_i for $1 \leq i < n$." [Steele 1990, page 774]
Antonym: SUBCLASS.
See also: CLASS.

- **direct superclass** *n.* "A class C_1 is a *direct superclass* of a class C_2 if C_2 explicitly designates C_1 as a superclass in its definition." [Steele 1990, page 774]
Antonym: DIRECT SUBCLASS.

t class *n.* "The class named *t* has no superclasses. It is a superclass of every class except itself." [Steele 1990, page 774]

unbound slot *n.* "When a slot does not have a value, the slot is said to be *unbound*." [Steele 1990, page 776]

App
D

Reference

[Steele] Steele, Guy L. Jr. (1990). *Common LISP: The Language,* second edition, Butterworth-Heinemann.

Appendix *E*

"C++ is a general purpose programming language based on the C programming language. In addition to the facilities provided by C, C++ provides classes, inline functions, operator overloading, constant types, references, free store management operators, and function argument checking and type conversions." [Ellis & Stroustrup 1990, page 1].

The definitions appearing in this appendix are excerpted from:

Ellis, Margaret A.; & Stroustrup, Bjarne (1990). *The Annotated C++ Reference Manual.* NJ: AT&T Bell Laboratories, Incorporated and Reading, MA: Addison Wesley. Reprinted with permission of Addison-Wesley Publishing Company, Inc.

For more information, contact:

Bjarne Stroustrup
AT&T Bell Labs
Murray Hill, New Jersey 07974, USA
Fax:+1 (908) 482-7393
E-mail:bs@research.att.com

The book may be ordered as follows:

Margaret Ellis & Bjarne Stroustrup, *The Annotated C++ Reference Manual,* ISBN 0-201-51459-1, $45.95
Attn.: Order Services Department
Addison-Wesley Publishing Company, Inc.
One Jacob Way
Reading, Massachusetts 01867, USA
Telephone: (800) 822-6339
Fax: +1 (617) 942-1117
http://www.aw.com

abstract class *n.* "Classes can be declared *abstract* to ensure that they are used only as base classes." [Ellis & Stroustrup 1990, page 195]. "An *abstract class* is a class that can be used only as a base class of some other class; no objects of an abstract class may be created except as objects representing a base class of a class derived from it. A class is abstract if it has at least one *pure virtual function*." [Ellis & Stroustrup 1990, page 214]
Contrast with: PURE VIRTUAL, VIRTUAL.

access control *n.* "... it is access to members that is controlled, not their visibility" [Ellis & Stroustrup 1990, page 241] "A few basic principles pervade the system: [1] Protection is provided by compile-time mechanisms, against accident, not against fraud or explicit violation. [2] Access is granted by a class, not unilaterally taken. [3] Access control is done for names and does not depend on the type of what is named. [4] The unit of protection is the class, not the individual object. [5] Access is controlled, not visibility." [Ellis & Stroustrup 1990, pages 256–257] "Access control is based on the use of the keywords *public*, *private*, and *protected* to control access to individual members of a class and on the use of *private* and *public* specifiers to control whether a derived class is considered a subtype of a base class or not. The *friend* mechanism provides a way of granting individual functions and class access to members of a class." [Ellis & Stroustrup 1990, page 239]
See also: ACCESS DECLARATION, FRIEND, NAME, PRIVATE, PROTECTED, PUBLIC, VISIBLE.
Commentary: "The reason access control rather than visibility control was chosen was to ensure that changes in access status would not quietly change the meaning of a program." [Ellis & Stroustrup 1990, page 241] "The C++ access control mechanisms provide protection against accident, not against fraud. Any programming language that supports access to raw memory will leave data open to deliberate tampering in ways that violate the explicit type rules specified for a given data item." [Ellis & Stroustrup 1990, page 239]

access declaration *n.* "The access to a member of a direct or indirect base class in a derived class can be adjusted by mentioning its *qualified-name* in the public or protected part of a derived class declaration. Such mention is called an *access declaration*." [Ellis & Stroustrup 1990, page 244]
Contrast with: ACCESS CONTROL, DECLARATION.
Commentary: "An access declaration may not be used to restrict access to a member that is accessible in the base class, nor may it be used to enable access to a member that is not accessible in the base class." [Ellis & Stroustrup 1990, page 245]

aggregate *n.* "An *aggregate* is an array or an object of a class with no constructors, no private or protected members, no base classes, and no virtual functions." [Ellis & Stroustrup 1990, page 151]

ambiguous *adj.* "Access to a base class member is ambiguous if the expression used refers to more than one function, object, type, or enumerator." [Ellis & Stroustrup 1990, page 202] "When virtual base classes are used, more than one function, object, or enumerator may be reached through paths through the directed acyclic graph of base classes. This is an ambiguity unless one of the names found *dominates* the others. [Ellis & Stroustrup 1990, page 204]

See also: BASE CLASS, DOMINANCE.

Commentary: "When virtual base classes are used, a single function, object, type or enumerator may be reached through more than one path through the directed acyclic graph of base classes. This is not an ambiguity." [Ellis & Stroustrup 1990, page 204]

anonymous union *n.* "... an anonymous union ... defines an unnamed object (and not a type)" [Ellis & Stroustrup 1990, pages 182–183]

Commentary: "A union for which objects or pointers are declared is not an anonymous union." [Ellis & Stroustrup 1990, pages 182–183]

argument *n.* "A function call is a postfix expression followed by parentheses containing a possibly empty, comma-separated list of expressions which constitute the actual arguments to the function." [Ellis & Stroustrup 1990, page 49]

assignment *n.* "The assignment operator [=] is the only operator function that is not inherited. Assignment has a useful and necessary generalization across all classes (memberwise copy)." [Ellis & Stroustrup 1990, page 335]

automatic object *n.* "Automatic objects are local to each invocation of a block." [Ellis & Stroustrup 1990, page 21]

Contrast with: STATIC OBJECT.

base class *n.* "A class can be *derived* from another class, which is then called a *base* class of the derived class." [Ellis & Stroustrup 1990, page 195] "A class is called a *direct base* if it is mentioned in the *base-list* and an *indirect base* if it is not a direct base but is a base class of one of the classes mentioned in the *base-list*." [Ellis & Stroustrup 1990, page 197]

Contrast with: DERIVED CLASS, VIRTUAL CLASS.

Commentary: "The terms *base class* and *derived class* were chosen in preference to the alternatives *superclass* and *subclass* because of confusion experienced by Simula users about which was which." [Ellis & Stroustrup 1990, page 197]

Kinds:

- DIRECT BASE CLASS
- INDIRECT BASE CLASS
- VIRTUAL BASE CLASS

● **direct base class** *n.* "A class is called a *direct base* if it is mentioned in the *base-list....*" [Ellis & Stroustrup 1990, page 197]

Antonym: INDIRECT BASE CLASS.

● **indirect base class** *n.* "A class is called ... an *indirect base* if it is not a direct base but is a base class of one of the classes mentioned in the *base-list*." [Ellis & Stroustrup 1990, page 197]

Antonym: DIRECT BASE CLASS.

● **virtual base class** *n.* "The keyword *virtual* may be added to a base class specifier. A single subobject of the virtual base class is shared by every base class that specified the base class to be virtual." [Ellis & Stroustrup 1990, page 200]

Contrast with: ABSTRACT CLASS.

Commentary: "A virtual base class provides a local point for sharing information, thus improving locality of reference and data hiding beyond what can be achieved without such classes. A virtual base class provides a statically typed interface to the information shared by its derived classes." [Ellis & Stroustrup 1990, page 201] "One can cast from a derived class to a virtual base class.... Casting from a virtual base class to a derived class is disallowed to avoid requiring an implementation to maintain pointers to enclosing objects." [Ellis & Stroustrup 1990, page 227]

built-in type *n.* "We refer to classes (including structures and unions) as *user-defined* types and other types as *built-in* types." [Ellis & Stroustrup 1990, page 25] *Contrast with:* USER-DEFINED TYPE.

call *n.* "A function call is a postfix expression followed by parentheses containing a possibly empty, comma-separated list of expressions which constitute the actual arguments to the function." [Ellis & Stroustrup 1990, page 49]

cast *n.* "An explicit type conversion can be expressed using either functional notation or the cast notation." [Ellis & Stroustrup 1990, page 67]
Contrast with: CONVERSION FUNCTION.
Commentary: "A pointer to a derived class may be implicitly converted to a pointer to a base class, but a pointer to a base class may not be implicitly converted to point to a derived class." [Ellis & Stroustrup 1990, page 223]

catch *v.* **caught, -ing** "Exceptions of arbitrary types can be *thrown* and *caught* and the set of exceptions a function may throw can be specified." [Ellis & Stroustrup 1990, page 353]
See also: EXCEPTION HANDLING.
Commentary: "… the word *catch* was chosen in preference to *handle* because handle is a common identifier in C programs for PC and Mac computers." [Ellis & Stroustrup 1990, page 355]

class *n.* "'Class' is the key concept of C++. A class is a user-defined type. The class is the unit of data hiding and encapsulation. The class is the mechanism supporting data abstraction by allowing representation details to be hidden and accessed exclusively through a set of op-erations defined as part of the class. Polymorphism is supported through classes with virtual functions. The class provides a unit of modularity." [Ellis & Stroustrup 1990, page 165] "… *classes* [contain] a sequence of objects of various types, a set of functions for manipulating these objects, and a set of restrictions on the access to these objects and functions." [Ellis & Stroustrup 1990, page 24] "A *class* is a user-defined type…. Its name becomes a *class-name*, that is, a reserved word within its scope." [Ellis & Stroustrup 1990, page 163]
Contrast with: TYPE.
Commentary: "We refer to classes (including structures and unions) as *user-defined* types and other types as *built-in* types." [Ellis & Stroustrup 1990, page 25]
Kinds:

- ABSTRACT CLASS
- BASE CLASS
  - DIRECT BASE CLASS
  - INDIRECT BASE CLASS
  - VIRTUAL BASE CLASS
- DERIVED CLASS
  - MOST DERIVED CLASS
- LOCAL CLASS
- NESTED CLASS
- STATIC CLASS
- STORAGE CLASS

- **abstract class** *n.* "Classes can be declared *abstract* to ensure that they are used only as base classes." [Ellis & Stroustrup 1990, page 195]. "An *abstract class* is a class that can be used only as a base class of some other class; no objects of an abstract class may be created except as objects representing a base class of a class derived from it. A class is abstract if it has at least one *pure virtual function.*" [Ellis & Stroustrup 1990, page 214]

See also: PURE VIRTUAL, VIRTUAL

- **base class** *n.* "A class can be *derived* from another class, which is then called a *base* class of the derived class." [Ellis & Stroustrup 1990, page 195] "A class is called a *direct base* if it is mentioned in the *base-list* and an *indirect base* if it is not a direct base but is a base class of one of the classes mentioned in the *base-list*." [Ellis & Stroustrup 1990, page 197]

  Contrast with: DERIVED CLASS, VIRTUAL CLASS.

  Commentary: "The terms *base class* and *derived class* were chosen in preference to the alternatives *superclass* and *subclass* because of confusion experienced by Simula users about which was which." [Ellis & Stroustrup 1990, page 197]

  Kinds:
  - DIRECT BASE CLASS
  - INDIRECT BASE CLASS
  - VIRTUAL BASE CLASS

- **direct base class** *n.* "A class is called a *direct base* if it is mentioned in the *base-list*...." [Ellis & Stroustrup 1990, page 197]

  Antonym: INDIRECT BASE CLASS.

- **indirect base class** *n.* "A class is called ... an *indirect base* if it is not a direct base but is a base class of one of the classes mentioned in the *base-list*." [Ellis & Stroustrup 1990, page 197]

  Antonym: DIRECT BASE CLASS.

- **virtual base class** *n.* "The keyword *virtual* may be added to a base class specifier. A single subobject of the virtual base class is shared by every base class that specified the base class to be virtual." [Ellis & Stroustrup 1990, page 200]

  Contrast with: ABSTRACT CLASS.

  Commentary: "A virtual base class provides a local point for sharing information, thus improving locality of reference and data hiding beyond what can be achieved without such classes. A virtual base class provides a statically typed interface to the information shared by its derived classes." [Ellis & Stroustrup 1990, page 201] "One can cast from a derived class to a virtual base class.... Casting from a virtual base class to a derived class is disallowed to avoid requiring an implementation to maintain pointers to enclosing objects." [Ellis & Stroustrup 1990, page 227]

- **derived class** *n.* "A class can be derived from another class, which is then called a base class of the derived class" [Ellis & Stroustrup 1990, page 195]

  Contrast with: BASE CLASS, COMPLETE OBJECT, DERIVED TYPE.

  See also: INHERITANCE.

  Commentary: "the derived class can override virtual functions of its bases and declare additional data members, functions and so on." [Ellis & Stroustrup 1990, page 195] "A pointer to a derived class may be implicitly converted to a pointer to a base class, but a pointer to a base class may not be implicitly converted to point to a derived class." [Ellis & Stroustrup 1990, page 223] "The terms *base class* and *derived class* were chosen in preference to the alternatives *superclass* and *subclass* because of confusion experienced by Simula users about which was which." [Ellis & Stroustrup 1990, page 197]

- **most derived class** *n.* "A *complete object* is an object that is not a subobject representing a base class. Its class is said to be the *most derived* *class* for the object." [Ellis & Stroustrup 1990, page 293]

- **local class** *n.* "A class can be declared within a function definition; such a class is called a *local class*. ... The local class is in the scope of the enclosing scope." [Ellis & Stroustrup 1990, page 188]
  See also: SCOPE.

- **nested class** *n.* "A class may be declared within another class. A class declared within another is called a *nested* class" [Ellis & Stroustrup 1990, page 185]
  Commentary: "Note that simply declaring a class nested in another does not mean that the enclosing class contains an object of the enclosed class. Nesting expresses scoping, not containment of sub-objects." [Ellis & Stroustrup 1990, page 187]

- **static class** *n.* "... a class with only static members provides a facility akin to what is called a 'module' in many languages: a named collection of objects and functions in their own name space." [Ellis & Stroustrup 1990, page 165]

- **storage class** *n.* either any automatic or static class. [C++]
  Contrast with: AUTOMATIC, STATIC.
  Commentary: A named object has a storage class that determines its lifetime. [C++]

- **class declaration** *n.* "A class declaration is the complete specification of the interfaces provided by a class." [Ellis & Stroustrup 1990, page 175] "A class declaration introduces a new type.... A class declaration introduces the class name into the scope where it is declared and hides any class, object, function, or other declaration of that name in an enclosing scope." [Ellis & Stroustrup 1990, page 165]

Synonym: CLASS SPECIFICATION.
Commentary: "C++ provides a single declaration for a class that acts as the interface to both users and implementors of the member functions. There is no direct support for the notions of 'interface definition' and 'implementation module.'" [Ellis & Stroustrup 1990, page 191]

class-specifier *n.* "A *class-specifier* is commonly referred to as a class declaration." [Ellis & Stroustrup 1990, page 164]
Synonym: CLASS DECLARATION.

complete object *n.* "A *complete object* is an object that is not a sub-object representing a base class. Its class is said to be the *most derived class* for the object." [Ellis & Stroustrup 1990, page 293]

const *adj.* "Adding *const* to a declaration ensures that an object to which the *const* is applied cannot have its value changed through an expression involving the name being declared unless an explicit type conversion is used to remove the 'constness.'" [Ellis & Stroustrup 1990, page 109]
Contrast with: VOLATILE.
Commentary: "... *const* does not simply mean 'store in read-only memory' nor does it mean 'compile-time constant.' Fundamentally, saying *const* obliges and enables the compiler to prevent accidental updates of the value of an object using a specific name." [Ellis & Stroustrup 1990, page 109] "The words *const* and *volatile* may be added to any legal *type-specifier* in the declaration of an object." [Ellis & Stroustrup 1990, page 108]

constructor *n.* "A member function with the same name as its class is called a constructor; it is used to construct values of its class type. If a class has a constructor, each object of that class will be initialized before any use is made of the object." [Ellis & Stroustrup 1990, page 262] "... the job of the constructor is to create the basic structure of the object.... a constructor turns raw memory into an object for which the rules of the type system hold." [Ellis & Stroustrup 1990, page 262]

Antonym: DESTRUCTOR.

Contrast with: CONVERSION FUNCTION.

Kinds:
- COPY CONSTRUCTOR
- DEFAULT CONSTRUCTOR

- **copy constructor** *n.* "A *copy constructor* for a class X is a constructor that can be called to copy an object of class X; that is, one that can be called with a single argument of type X." [Ellis & Stroustrup 1990, page 264]

- **default constructor** *n.* a constructor that can be called without arguments. A default constructor may have default arguments. [Ellis & Stroustrup 1990, page 264]

  Examples:
  ```
  X::X();
  X::X(int=0);
  ```

conversion *n.* "Type conversions of class objects can be specified by constructors and by conversion functions." [Ellis & Stroustrup 1990, page 270]

conversion function *n.* "A conversion function specifies a conversion between a class object and another type." [Ellis & Stroustrup 1990, page 261]

Contrast with: CAST, CONSTRUCTOR.

Commentary: "Conversion functions can do two things that cannot be specified by constructors: 1. Define a conversion from a class to a basic type, 2. Define a conversion from one class to another without modifying the declaration for the other class." [Ellis & Stroustrup 1990, page 273]

copy constructor *n.* "A *copy constructor* for a class X is a constructor that can be called to copy an object of class X; that is, one that can be called with a single argument of type X." [Ellis & Stroustrup 1990, page 264]

Contrast with: DEFAULT CONSTRUCTOR.

declaration *n.* "A declaration introduces one or more names into a program and specifies how those names are to be interpreted." [Ellis & Stroustrup 1990, page 95] "... the name of a type must be specified. This is done with a *type-name*, which is syntactically a declaration for an object or function of that type that omits the name of the object or function." [Ellis & Stroustrup 1990, page 130] "A name is introduced into a program by a declaration.... A name has a type, which determines its use.... A declaration is a definition unless it declares a function without specifying the body." [Ellis & Stroustrup 1990, page 13] "Declarations specify the interpretation given to each identifier; they do not necessarily reserve storage associated with the identifier." [Ellis & Stroustrup 1990, page 95]

Contrast with: CLASS, DEFINITION, NAME, TYPE.

- **class declaration** *n.* "A class declaration is the complete specification of the interfaces provided by a class." [Ellis & Stroustrup 1990, page 175] "A class declaration introduces a new type ... A class declaration introduces the class name into the scope where it is declared and hides any class, object, function, or other declaration of that name in an enclosing scope." [Ellis & Stroustrup 1990, page 165]

  Synonym: CLASS SPECIFICATION.

  Commentary: "C++ provides a single

declaration for a class that acts as the interface to both users and implementors of the member functions. There is no direct support for the notions of 'interface definition' and 'implementation module.'" [Ellis & Stroustrup 1990, page 191]

declarator *n.* "A declarator declares a single object, function, or type, within a declaration." [Ellis & Stroustrup 1990, page 129]
Contrast with: DECLARATION.

default constructor *n.* a constructor that can be called without arguments. A default constructor may have default arguments. [Ellis & Stroustrup 1990, page 264]
Contrast with: COPY CONSTRUCTOR.
Examples:
```
X::X();
X::X(int=0);
```

definition *n.* "A declaration is a definition unless it declares a function without specifying the body." [Ellis & Stroustrup 1990, page 13] "... declarations can be repeated whereas definitions cannot." [Ellis & Stroustrup 1990, page 14] "There must be exactly one definition of each object, function, class, and enumerator used in a program." [Ellis & Stroustrup 1990, page 14]
Contrast with: DECLARATION.

• **inline definition** *n.* "A member function may be defined in the class declaration, in which case it is *inline*." [Ellis & Stroustrup 1990, page 178]

delete *n.* "The delete operator destroys an object created by the new operator." [Ellis & Stroustrup 1990, page 62]
Contrast with: DESTRUCTOR.

derived class *n.* "A class can be derived from another class, which is then called a base class of the derived class" [Ellis & Stroustrup 1990, page 195]
Contrast with: BASE CLASS, COMPLETE OBJECT, DERIVED TYPE.
See also: INHERITANCE.
Commentary: "the derived class can override virtual functions of its bases and declare additional data members, functions and so on." [Ellis & Stroustrup 1990, page 195] "A pointer to a derived class may be implicitly converted to a pointer to a base class, but a pointer to a base class may not be implicitly converted to point to a derived class." [Ellis & Stroustrup 1990, page 223] "The terms *base class* and *derived class* were chosen in preference to the alternatives *superclass* and *subclass* because of confusion experienced by Simula users about which was which." [Ellis & Stroustrup 1990, page 197]

derived type *n.* "There is a conceptually infinite number of derived types constructed from the fundamental types in the ways: *arrays ... functions ... pointers ... references ... constants ... classes ... structures ... unions ... pointers to class members.*" [Ellis & Stroustrup 1990, page 24]
Contrast with: DERIVED CLASS.

descriptor object *n.* "... a [potentially] standard class for containing 'useful information about a class' ... the 'descriptor object' for the class." [Ellis & Stroustrup 1990, page 213]

destructor *n.* "A member function of class *c1* named ~*c1* is called a destructor; it is used to destroy values of type *c1* immediately before the object containing them is destroyed.... Explicit calls of destructors are rarely needed." [Ellis & Stroustrup 1990, pages 276–277] Destructors are invoked when class objects are destroyed; they are useful for cleaning up." [Ellis & Stroustrup 1990, page 261]

Contrast with: CONSTRUCTOR, DELETE.

direct base class *n.* "A class is called a *direct base* if it is mentioned in the *base-list.* ..." [Ellis & Stroustrup 1990, page 197]

Contrast with: INDIRECT BASE CLASS.

dominance *n.* "A name *B::f dominates* a name *A::f* if its base class *B* has *A* as a base. If a name dominates another no ambiguity exists between the two; the dominant name is used when there is a choice.... Note that dominance applies to names and not just to functions." [Ellis & Stroustrup 1990, page 205]

Contrast with: AMBIGUOUS.

exception *n.* "Exception handling provides a way of transferring control and information to an unspecified caller that has expressed willingness to handle exceptions of a given type. Exceptions of arbitrary types can be *thrown* and *caught* and the set of exceptions a function may throw can be specified." [Ellis & Stroustrup 1990, page 353]

exception handling *n.* "Exception handling provides a way of transferring control and information to an unspecified caller that has expressed willingness to handle exceptions of a given type. Exceptions of arbitrary types can be *thrown* and *caught* and the set of exceptions a function may throw can be specified." [Ellis & Stroustrup 1990, page 353] "A handler will be invoked only by a throw-expression invoked in code executed in the handler's *try-block* or in functions called from the handler's *try-block.* ... A *try-block* is a *statement.* A *throw-expression* is a *unary-expression* of type *void.* A *throw-expression* is sometimes referred to as a '*throw-point.*' Code that executes a *throw-expression* is

said to 'throw an exception'; code that subsequently gets control is called a '*handler.*' [Ellis & Stroustrup 1990, page 354]

Commentary: "The word *throw* was chosen in preference to the more commonly used *signal* and *raise* because both *signal* and *raise* are functions in the ANSI C standard library. Similarly, the word *catch* was chosen in preference to *handle* because handle is a common identifier in C programs for PC and Mac computers." [Ellis & Stroustrup 1990, page 355]

friend *n.* "The *friend* specifier is used to specify access to class members." [Ellis & Stroustrup 1990, page 108] "A friend of a class is a function that is not a member of the class but is permitted to use the private and protected member names from the class.... Friendship, like all other access, is granted by the class - *not* unilaterally grabbed by the friend." [Ellis & Stroustrup 1990, page 248] "If a function is explicitly declared *friend*, it is not a member of the class in which the *friend* declaration occurs, though it may be a member of some other class." [Ellis & Stroustrup 1990, page 175]

See also: ACCESS CONTROL.

Commentary: "The *friend* mechanism provides a way of granting individual functions and classes access to members of a class." [Ellis & Stroustrup 1990, page 239]

function call *n.* "A function call is a postfix expression followed by parentheses containing a possibly empty, comma-separated list of expressions which constitute the actual arguments to the function." [Ellis & Stroustrup 1990, page 49]

function overloading *n.* "A single name may be used for several different functions in a single scope; this is *function overloading*." [Ellis & Stroustrup 1990, pages 138]

handler *n.* "A handler will be invoked only by a throw-expression invoked in code executed in the handler's *try-block* or in functions called from the handler's *try-block....* A *try-block* is a *statement*. A *throw-expression* is a *unary-expression* of type *void*. A *throw-expression* is sometimes referred to as a '*throw-point*.' Code that executes a *throw-expression* is said to 'throw an exception'; code that subsequently gets control is called a '*handler*.' [Ellis & Stroustrup 1990, page 354]

identifier *n.* "An *identifier* is a *name* provided it has been suitably declared." [Ellis & Stroustrup 1990, page 48] "An identifier is an arbitrarily long sequence of letters and digits." [Ellis & Stroustrup 1990, page 6]
Contrast with: DECLARATION.

indirect base class *n.* "A class is called ... an *indirect base* if it is not a direct base but is a base class of one of the classes mentioned in the *base-list*." [Ellis & Stroustrup 1990, page 197]
Antonym: DIRECT BASE CLASS.

inheritance *n.* "The derived class inherits the properties of its base classes, including its data members and member functions." [Ellis & Stroustrup 1990, page 195]
See also: DERIVED CLASS, BASE CLASS.

- **multiple inheritance** *n.* "The use of more than one direct base class is often called multiple inheritance." [Ellis & Stroustrup 1990, page 198]
Commentary: "One important aspect of multiple inheritance as compared to single inheritance is that classes within a class lattice can share information without pushing that information to-

wards the single root of an inheritance tree." [Ellis & Stroustrup 1990, page 200]

inline *adj.* "A member function may be defined in the class declaration, in which case it is *inline*." [Ellis & Stroustrup 1990, page 178]

layout *n.* How something, e.g. an object, is represented and sequenced in memory. "An object of a class is typically represented by a contiguous region of memory." [Ellis & Stroustrup 1990, page 217]

local class *n.* "A class can be declared within a function definition; such a class is called a *local class....* The local class is in the scope of the enclosing scope." [Ellis & Stroustrup 1990, page 188]
See also: DECLARATION, SCOPE.

local type name *n.* "... names defined within a class declaration cannot be used outside their class without qualification." [Ellis & Stroustrup 1990, page 189]

lvalue *n.* "an *lvalue* is an expression referring to an object or function. An obvious example of an lvalue expression is the name of an object." [Ellis & Stroustrup 1990, page 25]

member *n.* "A *member-list* may declare data, functions, classes, enumerations, bit-fields, friends, and type names.... The *member-list* defines the full set of members of the class." [Ellis & Stroustrup 1990, pages 169–170]

member function *n.* "A function declared as a member (without the *friend* specifier) is called a member function." [Ellis & Stroustrup 1990, page 173]
Commentary: "Member functions are sometimes referred to as 'methods.' The analogy is not exact." [Ellis & Stroustrup 1990, page 174]

most derived class *n.* "A *complete object* is

App
E

an object that is not a subobject representing a base class. Its class is said to be the *most derived class* for the object." [Ellis & Stroustrup 1990, page 293]

multiple inheritance *n.* "The use of more than one direct base class is often called multiple inheritance." [Ellis & Stroustrup 1990, page 198]
Commentary: "One important aspect of multiple inheritance as compared to single inheritance is that classes within a class lattice can share information without pushing that information towards the single root of an inheritance tree." [Ellis & Stroustrup 1990, page 200]

name *n.* "A name denotes an object, a function, a set of functions, an enumerator, a type, a class member, a template, a value, or a label. A name is introduced into a program by a declaration.... A name has a type, which determines its use." [Ellis & Stroustrup 1990, page 13] "A name *S* can be declared as a type (struct, class, union, enum, typedef) and as a nontype (function, object, value, and so on) in a single scope." [Ellis & Stroustrup 1990, page 27] "Declarations containing the *decl-specifier typedef* declared identifiers that can be used later for naming fundamental or derived types.... A *typedef-name* is thus a synonym for another type." [Ellis & Stroustrup 1990, pages 105–106] "Fundamental and derived types can be given names by the *typedef* mechanism, and families of types and functions can be specified and named by the *template* mechanism." [Ellis & Stroustrup 1990, page 25]
Contrast with: DECLARATION, IDENTIFIER, LVALUE, OVERLOAD, TYPE.

nested class *n.* "A class may be declared within another class. A class declared within another is called a *nested* class" [Ellis & Stroustrup 1990, page 185]
Commentary: "Note that simply declaring a class nested in another does not mean that the enclosing class contains an object of the enclosed class. Nesting expresses scoping, not containment of sub-objects." [Ellis & Stroustrup 1990, page 187]

new *n.* "The *new* operator attempts to create an object of the *type-name* to which it is applied." [Ellis & Stroustrup 1990, page 58]
See also: CONSTRUCTOR.

object *n.* "An object is a region of storage. A named object has a storage class that determines its lifetime." [Ellis & Stroustrup 1990, page 13]
Kinds:
- AUTOMATIC OBJECT
- CLASS OBJECT
- COMPLETE OBJECT
- DESCRIPTOR OBJECT
- STATIC OBJECT

- **automatic object** *n.* "Automatic objects are local to each invocation of a block." [Ellis & Stroustrup 1990, page 21]
Contrast with: STATIC OBJECT.

- **class object** *n.* "... class objects must be objects of previously declared classes." [Ellis & Stroustrup 1990, page 171] " ... 'class objects' can be structures and unions." [Ellis & Stroustrup 1990, page 53]

- **complete object** *n.* "A *complete object* is an object that is not a sub-object representing a base class. Its class is said to be the *most derived class* for the object." [Ellis & Stroustrup 1990, page 293]

- **descriptor object** *n.* "A [potentially] standard class for containing 'useful information about a class.' ... The 'descriptor object' for the class." [Ellis & Stroustrup 1990, page 213]

• **static object** *n.* "Static objects exist and retain their values throughout the execution of the entire program." [Ellis & Stroustrup 1990, page 21] *Contrast with:* AUTOMATIC OBJECT.

object-oriented programming *n.* "The use of derived classes and virtual functions is often called *object-oriented programming.* [Ellis & Stroustrup 1990, page 209]

overloading *n.* "Overloading allows multiple functions with the same name to be defined provided their argument lists differ sufficiently for calls to be resolved. [Ellis & Stroustrup 1990, page 307] *Contrast with:* NAME, RESOLVED.

override *v.* **overrode, -ing** "If a class *base* contains a *virtual* function *vf*, and a class *derived* derived from it also contains a function *vf* of the same type, then a call of *vf* for an object of class derived invokes *derived::vf* (even if the access is through a pointer or reference to *base*). The derived class function is said to *override* the base class function." [Ellis & Stroustrup 1990, page 208]

polymorphism *n.* "The ability to call a variety of functions using exactly the same interface—as is provided by virtual functions—is sometimes called *polymorphism.*" [Ellis & Stroustrup 1990, page 209] *Contrast with:* VIRTUAL. *Commentary:* "Polymorphism is supported through classes with virtual functions." [Ellis & Stroustrup 1990, page 165]

private *adj.* "Access control is based on the use of the keywords *public, private,* and *protected* to control access to individual members of a class and on the use of *private* and *public* specifiers to control whether a derived class is considered a subtype of a base class or not.... A member of a class can be *private*; that is, its name can be used only by member functions, member initializers, and friends of the class in which it is declared." [Ellis & Stroustrup 1990, page 239] "Private members of a base class remain inaccessible even to derived classes unless friend declarations within the base class declaration are used to grant access explicitly." [Ellis & Stroustrup 1990, page 242] *Contrast with:* PROTECTED, PUBLIC. *See also:* ACCESS CONTROL.

protected *adj.* "Access control is based on the use of the keywords *public, private,* and *protected* to control access to individual members of a class.... A member of a class can be ... *protected*; that is, its name can be used only by member functions, member initializers, and friends of the class in which it is declared and by member functions and friends of classes derived from this class." [Ellis & Stroustrup 1990, page 239] "One way of understanding *protected* is as a mechanism for the writer of a class to give other programmers the right to grant themselves access to a specific subset of the representation and operations." [Ellis & Stroustrup 1990, page 254] "A friend or member function of a derived class can access a protected static member of a base class. A friend or a member function of a derived class can access a protected nonstatic member of one of its base classes only through a pointer to, reference to, or object of the derived class." [Ellis & Stroustrup 1990, page 253] *Contrast with:* PRIVATE, PUBLIC.

App
E

See also: ACCESS CONTROL.

public *adj.* "Access control is based on the use of the keywords *public*, *private*, and *protected* to control access to individual members of a class and on the use of *private* and *public* specifiers to control whether a derived class is considered a subtype of a base class or not.... A member of a class can be ... *public*; that is its name can be used by any function or initializer." [Ellis & Stroustrup 1990, page 239]

Contrast with: PRIVATE, PROTECTED.

See also: ACCESS CONTROL.

pure virtual function *n.* "A class is abstract if it has at lease one *pure virtual function*. A virtual function is specified *pure* by using a *pure-specifier* in the function declaration in the class declaration." [Ellis & Stroustrup 1990, page 214]

Contrast with: ABSTRACT.

Commentary: "Pure virtual functions are inherited as pure virtual functions." [Ellis & Stroustrup 1990, page 214]

qualify *v. -ied, -ing* "Names of nested types can be qualified by the names of their enclosing class." [Ellis & Stroustrup 1990, page 112] "Explicit qualification with the scope operator suppresses the virtual call mechanism." [Ellis & Stroustrup 1990, page 209] "As a rule of thumb, explicit qualification should be used only to access base class members from a member of a derived class." [Ellis & Stroustrup 1990, page 210]

See also: SCOPE RESOLUTION OPERATOR.

reference *n.* "A variable declared to be a *T&*, that is 'reference to type *T*', must be initialized by an object of type *T* or by an object that can be converted into a *T*." [Ellis & Stroustrup 1990, page 153]

Commentary: "A reference cannot be changed to refer to another object after

initialization. This means that references are not first class citizens in C++. In a very real sense a reference is not an object." [Ellis & Stroustrup 1990, page 153].

scope *n.* "There are four kinds of scope: local, function, file, and class." [Ellis & Stroustrup 1990, page 15]

Contrast with: STORAGE CLASS.

static *adj.* "*Static* objects exist and retain their values throughout the execution of the entire program." [Ellis & Stroustrup 1990, page 21] "All global objects have storage class *static*. Local objects and class members can be given static storage class by explicit use of the *static* storage class specifier." [Ellis & Stroustrup 1990, page 22] "A data or function member of a class may be declared static in the class declaration. There is only one copy of a static data member, shared by all objects of the class in a program. A static member is not part of objects of a class." [Ellis & Stroustrup 1990, page 179]

Commentary: "The use of the word *static* to indicate that a member of a class is not associated with an individual object of a class (and not replicated in each object) parallels the use of the word static to indicate that only one copy of a local variable is to be used for all calls of a function.... The purpose of *static* members is to reduce the need for global variables by providing alternatives that are local to a class." [Ellis & Stroustrup 1990, pages 180–181]

static class *n.* "... a class with only static members provides a facility akin to what is called a 'module' in many languages: a named collection of objects and functions in their own name space." [Ellis & Stroustrup 1990, page 165]

static object *n.* "Static objects exist and

retain their values throughout the execution of the entire program." [Ellis & Stroustrup 1990, page 21]
See also: AUTOMATIC OBJECT.

storage class *n.* "There are two declarable storage classes: automatic and static." [Ellis & Stroustrup 1990, page 21]
Contrast with: AUTOMATIC, STATIC.
Commentary: "A named object has a storage class that determines its lifetime." [Ellis & Stroustrup 1990, page 13]

template *n.* "A *template* declaration is used to specify families of types or functions." [Ellis & Stroustrup 1990, page 108] "A class template defines the layout and operations for an unbounded set of related types.... A function template defines an unbounded set of related functions." [Ellis & Stroustrup 1990, page 341] "A class template specifies how individual classes can be constructed much as a class declaration specifies how individual objects can be constructed.... In other words ... a parameterized type." [Ellis & Stroustrup 1990, pages 342–343]
Synonym: PARAMETERIZED TYPE.
Contrast with: CLASS.

this *n.* "The keyword *this* names a pointer to the object for which the function was invoked." [Ellis & Stroustrup 1990, page 47] "In a nonstatic member function, the keyword *this* is a pointer to the object for which the function in called." [Ellis & Stroustrup 1990, page 176]
Commentary: "In many languages, notably Smalltalk, the equivalent construct for identifying the object for which a function is invoked is called *self*." [Ellis & Stroustrup 1990, page 176]

throw *v.* *threw, -ing* "Exception handling provides a way of transferring control and information to an unspecified caller that has expressed willingness

to handle exceptions of a given type. Exceptions of arbitrary types can be *thrown* and *caught* and the set of exceptions a function may throw can be specified." [Ellis & Stroustrup 1990, page 353] "Code that executes a *throw-expression* is said to 'throw an exception'; code that subsequently gets control is called a '*handler*.' [Ellis & Stroustrup 1990, page 354]
Commentary: "The word *throw* was chosen in preference to the more commonly used *signal* and *raise* because both *signal* and *raise* are functions in the ANSI C standard library. Similarly, the word *catch* was chosen in preference to *handle* because handle is a common identifier in C programs for PC and Mac computers." [Ellis & Stroustrup 1990, page 355]

type *n.* "A name is introduced into a program by a declaration.... A name has a type, which determines its use." [Ellis & Stroustrup 1990, page 13] "A name *S* can be declared as a type (struct, class, union, enum, typedef) *and* as a nontype (function, object, value, and so on) in a single scope. [Ellis & Stroustrup 1990, page 27] "There are two kinds of types: fundamental types and derived types." [Ellis & Stroustrup 1990, page 22]
Contrast with: CLASS.
See also: DECLARATION, DEFINITION, NAME.
Kinds:
- BUILT-IN TYPE
- DERIVED TYPE
- USER-DEFINED TYPE

- **built-in type** *n.* "We refer to classes (including structures and unions) as *user-defined* types and other types as *built-in* types. [Ellis & Stroustrup 1990, page 25]

App
E

Antonym: USER-DEFINED TYPE.

- **derived type** *n.* "There is a conceptually infinite number of derived types constructed from the fundamental types in the ways: *arrays … functions … pointers … references … constants … classes … structures … unions … pointers to class members.*" [Ellis & Stroustrup 1990, page 24]
  Contrast with: DERIVED CLASS.

- **user-defined type** *n.* "We refer to classes (including structures and unions) as *user-defined* types. [Ellis & Stroustrup 1990, page 25]
  Antonym: BUILT-IN TYPE.

union *n.* "A union is a class declared with the *class-key* union; its members are public by default and it holds only one member at a time." [Ellis & Stroustrup 1990, page 165] "… *unions* … are structures capable of containing objects of different types at different times." [Ellis & Stroustrup 1990, page 24] "… a union is fundamentally a low-level construct for saving storage." [Ellis & Stroustrup 1990, page 181] "A union may be thought of as a structure whose member objects all begin at offset zero and whose size is sufficient to contain any of its member objects. At most one of the member objects can be stored in a union at any time." [Ellis & Stroustrup 1990, page 181]

- **anonymous union** *n.* "… an anonymous union … defines an unnamed object (and not a type)" [Ellis & Stroustrup 1990, pages 182–183]
  See also: UNION.
  Commentary: "A union for which objects or pointers are declared is not an anonymous union." [Ellis & Stroustrup 1990, pages 182–183]

user-defined type *n.* "We refer to classes (including structures and unions) as *user-defined* types and other types as *built-in types.* [Ellis & Stroustrup 1990, page 25]

virtual *adj.* "The keyword *virtual* may be added to a base class specifier. A single sub-object of the virtual base class is shared by every base class that specified the base class to be virtual." [Ellis & Stroustrup 1990, page 200] "The *virtual* specifier implies membership, so a *virtual* function cannot be a global (non-member) function. Nor can a virtual function be a *static* member, since a virtual function call relies on a specific object for determining which function to invoke." [Ellis & Stroustrup 1990, page 209] "The *virtual* specifier may be used only in declarations of nonstatic class member functions within a class declaration." [Ellis & Stroustrup 1990, page 105] "The access rules for a virtual function are determined by its declaration and are not affected by the rules for a function that later overrides it." [Ellis & Stroustrup 1990, page 255] "A virtual function can be declared a *friend* in another class." [Ellis & Stroustrup 1990, page 209]
Contrast with: BASE CLASS, CALL, FRIEND, QUALIFY.

- **pure virtual** *adj.* "A class is abstract if it has at lease one *pure virtual function.* A virtual function is specified *pure* by using a *pure-specifier* in the function declaration in the class declaration." [Ellis & Stroustrup 1990, page 214]
  Contrast with: ABSTRACT.
  Commentary: "Pure virtual functions are inherited as pure virtual functions." [Ellis & Stroustrup 1990, page 214]

virtual base class *n.* "The keyword *virtual* may be added to a base class specifier. A single subobject of the virtual base class is shared by every base class

that specified the base class to be virtual." [Ellis & Stroustrup 1990, page 200]
Contrast with: ABSTRACT CLASS, BASE CLASS.
Commentary: "A virtual base class provides a local point for sharing information, thus improving locality of reference and data hiding beyond what can be achieved without such classes. A virtual base class provides a statically typed interface to the information shared by its derived classes." [Ellis & Stroustrup 1990, page 201] "One can cast from a derived class to a virtual base class.... Casting from a virtual base class to a derived

class is disallowed to avoid requiring an implementation to maintain pointers to enclosing objects." [Ellis & Stroustrup 1990, page 227]

volatile *adj.* "... *volatile* is a hint to the compiler to avoid aggressive optimization involving the object because the value of the object may be changed by means undetectable by a compiler." [Ellis & Stroustrup 1990, page 110]
Contrast with: CONST.
Commentary: "The words *const* and *volatile* may be added to any legal *type-specifier* in the declaration of an object." [Ellis & Stroustrup 1990, page 108]

Reference

[Ellis & Stroustrup 1990] Ellis, Margaret A., & Stroustrup, Bjarne (1990), *The Annotated C++ Reference Manual*, Reading, MA: Addison-Wesley.

Appendix **F**

Eiffel (and Bertrand Meyer)

Eiffel is a strongly typed, pure object-oriented specification, design, and coding language. Eiffel emphasizes the software engineering of quality components. It is best known for its use of assertions and compatibility with Bertrand Meyer's Design by Contract method.

The definitions appearing in this appendix are excerpted from:

Meyer, Bertrand (1992). *Eiffel: The Language,* Englewood Cliffs, NJ: Prentice Hall.

© 1992 by Bertrand Meyer. Reprinted by permission of Bertrand Meyer.

For more information, contact:

Mr. Bertrand Meyer
Interactive Software Engineering, Inc.
270 Storke Road, Suite 7
Goleta, California 93117, USA
Voice: +1 (805) 685-1006
Fax: +1 (805) 685-6869
E-mail:bertrand@eiffel.com
http://www.eiffel.com

abstract data type *n.* "… data structures known from an official interface rather than through their representation." [Meyer 1992, page 4]
Contrast with: TYPE.

abstract form *n.* **1.** a synonym for SHORT FORM. [Meyer 1992, page 103] **2.** "a text which has the same structure as the class but does not include non-public elements. The short form is the one that should be used as interface documentation for the class." [Meyer 1992, page 103]

ancestor [class] *n.* "Class A is an ancestor of class B if and only if A is B itself or, recursively, an ancestor of one of B's parents." [Meyer 1992, page 77]
Contrast with: DESCENDANT.

• **proper ancestor** *n.* "The proper ancestors of a class C are its ancestors other than C itself." [Meyer 1992, page 78]
Contrast with: PROPER DESCENDANT.

anchored type *n.* "a type that carries a provision for automatic redefinition in descendants of the class where they are used." [Meyer 1992, page 211]
Commentary: "An Anchored type is of the form 'like *anchor*' where *anchor*, called the anchor of the type, is an entity, or Current." [Meyer 1992, page 211] "An anchored type avoids code duplication when you must deal with a set of entities (attributes, function results, routine arguments) which should all follow suit whenever a proper descendant redefines the type of one of them, to take advantage of the descendant's more specific context. [Meyer 1992, page 215]

ANY (Kernel Library Class) *n.* "A general-purpose class, ANY, serves as parent to any class without an Inheritance clause, and hence as universal ancestor." [Meyer 1992, page 85]

assertion *n.* "Eiffel software texts—class-

es and their routines—may be equipped with elements of formal specification, called assertions, expressing correctness conditions." [Meyer 1992, page 117]

attached reference *n.* "If [a reference is] attached, it gives access to an object; it is said to be attached to that object. The object will also be said to be attached to the reference." [Meyer 1992, page 270]
Antonym: VOID REFERENCE.

attachment *n.* "… one of the effects of a Creation instruction … is to attach the instruction's target [to] an object." [Meyer 1992, page 310] "The attachment status of an entity is not eternal. It may be changed one or more times during system execution by … reattachment operations." [Meyer 1992, page 310]

attribute *n.* "Attributes represent data items associated with [class] instances" [Meyer 1992, page 6] "… attributes, represent fields of the class's direct instances." [Meyer 1992, page 44] "Attributes are one of the two kinds of feature.… The other kind is routines." [Meyer 1992, page 261] "There are two kinds of attribute: variable and constant." [Meyer 1992, page 261]
Contrast with: FIELD.
Kinds:

• CONSTANT ATTRIBUTE
• VARIABLE ATTRIBUTE

• **constant attribute** *n.* "… the value is the same for every instance, and it cannot be changed at run time." [Meyer 1992, page 261]
Contrast with: VARIABLE ATTRIBUTE.

• **variable attribute** *n.* "… it is possible to write routines that will change the attribute values associated with particular instances." [Meyer 1992, page 261]
Contrast with: CONSTANT ATTRIBUTE.

available [feature] *adj.* "A feature of a

App
F

class S is said to be available to a class C if and only if it is either selectively available to S or generally available." [Meyer 1992, page 100]

Contrast with: SECRET.

Kinds:
- GENERALLY AVAILABLE
- SELECTIVELY AVAILABLE

- **generally available [feature]** *adj.* "… available to all classes." [Meyer 1992, page 100]

  Synonym: EXPORTED.

- **selectively available [feature]** *adj.* "The feature may be available to specific classes only. In that case it is also available to the descendants of all these classes. Such a feature is said to be selectively available to the given classes and their descendants" [Meyer 1992, page 100]

base class *n.* "A type T of any category is derived, directly or indirectly, from a class, called the base class of the type." [Meyer 1992, page 198]

Contrast with: BASE TYPE.

Commentary: "The base class of a type is always the same as the base class of its base type." [Meyer 1992, page 198]

base type *n.* "… if [type] T is anchored, the type of its anchor is the base type of T, and the base class of T's base type also serves as the base class of T.… The base class of a type is always the same as the base class of its base type.…" [Meyer 1992, page 198]

basic type *n.* "The basic types are class types, defined by non-generic classes of the Kernel Library called basic classes." [Meyer 1992, page 209]

belong to *adj.* "The objects belonging to an environment *env* are defined as follows.

1. Any persistent object of *env* belongs to *env*.

2. Any object created while *env* is open belongs to *env*.

3. Any dependent of an object belonging to *env* belongs to *env*.

4. No object belongs to *env* other than through the application of rules 1, 2 and 3." [Meyer 1992, page 463]

browser *n.* "An interactive browser allows users to explore the available classes and their features." [Meyer 1992, page 22]

call *n.* "A call is the application of a certain feature to a certain object, possibly with arguments. As a consequence, it has three components:

– the target of the call, an expression whose value is attached to the object;

– the feature of the call, which must be a feature of the base class of the object's type;

– an actual argument list." [Meyer 1992, page 340]

See also: VALIDITY.

C-Eiffel Call-In Library *n.* "… a library of C functions." [Meyer 1992, page 406]

Commentary: Cecil is used by developers who wish to write C routines "which create Eiffel objects and apply features to these objects, without relying on features explicitly passed by the Eiffel side." [Meyer 1992, page 406]

check-correct *adj.* "… the conditions of Check instructions are satisfied." [Meyer 1992, page 258] "An effective routine r is check-correct if, for every Check instruction c in r, any execution of c (as part of an execution of r) satisfies all its assertions." [Meyer 1992, page 129]

See also: EFFECTIVE ROUTINE.

Contrast with: EXCEPTION-CORRECT, LOOP CORRECT.

class *n.* "The constituents of Eiffel software are called classes.… A class is a modular unit." [Meyer 1992, page 34]

Viewed as a type, a class describes the properties of a set of possible data structures, or objects. [Meyer 1992, page 43]
Kinds:
- • ANCESTOR CLASS
  - - PROPER ANCESTOR
- • BASE CLASS
- • CLIENT
  - - EXPANDED CLIENT
  - - GENERIC CLIENT
  - - SIMPLE CLIENT
- • COMPLEX CLASS
- • DEFERRED CLASS
  - - FULLY DEFERRED CLASS
- • DESCENDANT CLASS
  - - PROPER DESCENDANT
- • EXPANDED CLASS
- • GENERATING CLASS
- • GENERIC CLASS
- • ROOT CLASS

• **ancestor [class]** *n.* "Class A is an ancestor of class B if and only if A is B itself or, recursively, an ancestor of one of B's parents." [Meyer 1992, page 77]
Contrast with: DESCENDANT.

  - **proper ancestor** *n.* "The proper ancestors of a class C are its ancestors other than C itself." [Meyer 1992, page 78]
  Contrast with: PROPER DESCENDANT.

• **base class** *n.* "A type T of any category is derived, directly or indirectly, from a class, called the base class of the type. …The base class of a type is always the same as the base class of its base type." [Meyer 1992, page 198]
See: BASE TYPE.

• **client [class]** *n.* "A class C is a client of S if some ancestor of C is a simple client, an expanded client or a generic client of S." [Meyer 1992, page 90]
Contrast with: SUPPLIER.

Kinds:
  - EXPANDED CLIENT
  - GENERIC CLIENT
  - SIMPLE CLIENT

- **expanded client** *n.* "A class C is an expanded client of a type S if S is an expanded type and some entity of C is of type S." [Meyer 1992, page 94]
- **generic client** *n.* "A class C is a generic client of a type S if for some generically derived type T of the form B [..., S, ...] one of the following holds:
  1. C is a client of T.
  2. One of the Parent clauses of C, or of a proper ancestor of C, lists T as a parent." [Meyer 1992, page 94]
- **simple client** *n.* "A class C is a simple client of a type S if S is a reference type, and some entity f of C is of type S." [Meyer 1992, page 92]

• **complex class** *n.* "Every class other than BOOLEAN, CHARACTER, INTEGER, REAL and DOUBLE is said to be a complex class. Any type whose base class is complex is itself called a complex type, and its instances are complex objects." [Meyer 1992, page 273]

• **deferred class** *n.* "Deferred classes describe a group of implementations of an abstract data type rather than just a single implementation. A deferred class may not be instantiated." [Meyer 1992, page 20] "A deferred class describes an incompletely implemented abstraction, which other classes (its proper descendants) will use as a basis for further refinement." [Meyer 1992, page 47] "You will declare a class as deferred if you plan to include one or more features which are specified but not implemented, with the expecta-

App
F

tion that proper descendants of the class will provide the implementations." [Meyer 1992, page 50] "A class which is declared as deferred but has no deferred features is invalid." [Meyer 1992, page 51]

- **fully deferred class** *n.* "a class whose features are all deferred." [Meyer 1992, page 146]

• **descendant [class]** *n.* "Class B is a descendant of class A if and only if A is an ancestor of B, in other words if B is A or (recursively) a descendant of one of its heirs." [Meyer 1992, page 77]
Contrast with: ANCESTOR.

- **proper descendant** *n.* "The proper descendants of class B are its descendants other than B itself." [Meyer 1992, page 78]
Contrast with: PROPER ANCESTOR.

• **expanded class** *n.* "Declaring a class as expanded indicates that entities declared of the corresponding type will have objects as their run-time values." [Meyer 1992, page 47]

• **generating class [of an object]** *n.* "The base class of the generating type is called the object's generating class, or generator for short." [Meyer 1992, page 270]
Synonym: GENERATOR.

• **generic class** *n.* "A generic class is a class declared with formal generic parameters; this mechanism supports type parameterization.... Generic classes describe flexible structures having variants parameterized by types." [Meyer 1992, page 200]

• **root class** *n.* "A system is a set of classes, one of which has been designated as the root of the system, such that all the classes on which the root depends belong to the system." [Meyer 1992, page 35]

Contrast with: ROOT OBJECT.

class abstracter *n.* "A class abstracter produces an interface version of a class, providing client programmers with a specification of the exported features." [Meyer 1992, page 22]

class flattener *n.* "A class flattener produces an inheritance-free version of a class, with all inherited features brought into the class itself, taking care of redefinition, renaming and invariant accumulation." [Meyer 1992, page 22]

class-level validity *n.* a call to a feature of a class exhibits class-level validity (i.e., is class-valid) if the class has the feature, the feature is available to the caller, and the feature has the required signature. [Meyer 1992, pages 356–358]
Contrast with: SYSTEM-LEVEL VALIDITY.

class name *n.* "The Class_name part [of the Class_header] gives the name of the class." [Meyer 1992, page 50]
See also: REDECLARATION.

class-valid call *n.* "Calls which satisfy this [class-level validity] condition." [Meyer 1992, page 357] "A class-valid call is not necessarily system-valid." [Meyer 1992, page 358]
Contrast with: SYSTEM-VALID CALL.

client [class] *n.* "A class C is a client of S if some ancestor of C is a simple client, an expanded client or a generic client of S." [Meyer 1992, page 90]
Contrast with: SUPPLIER.
Kinds:
  • EXPANDED CLIENT
  • GENERIC CLIENT
  • SIMPLE CLIENT

• **expanded client** *n.* "A class C is an expanded client of a type S if S is an expanded type and some entity of C is of type S." [Meyer 1992, page 94]

• **generic client** *n.* "A class C is a generic

client of a type S if for some generically derived type T of the form B [..., S, ...] one of the following holds:
1. C is a client of T.
2. One of the Parent clauses of C, or of a proper ancestor of C, lists T as a parent." [Meyer 1992, page 94]
- **simple client** *n.* "A class C is a simple client of a type S if S is a reference type, and some entity f of C is of type S." [Meyer 1992, page 92]

clone *v. -ed, -ing* "A variant of copy is clone, which produces a fresh object by duplicating an existing one." [Meyer 1992, page 295]
Contrast with: COPY.
Kinds:
- DEEP CLONE
- SHALLOW CLONE
- **deep clone** *v. -ed, -ing* "... will replicate an entire data structure, starting at the source and creating new objects as needed." [Meyer 1992, page 302]
Contrast with: DEEP COPY, SHALLOW CLONE.
- **shallow clone** *v. -ed, -ing* "... just copy fields of the source object as they appear." [Meyer 1992, page 302]
Contrast with: DEEP CLONE, SHALLOW COPY.

cloning *n.* "A ... mechanism ... for duplicating objects." [Meyer 1992, page 277]

cluster *n.* "A cluster is a set of related classes." [Meyer 1992, page 33] "As the number of classes in your system grows, you will need to arrange these classes into groups, called clusters. The figure [] illustrates a typical system structure as a set of layers, each representing a cluster." [Meyer 1992, page 37]

complex class *n.* "Every class other than BOOLEAN, CHARACTER, INTEGER, REAL and DOUBLE is said to be a complex class." [Meyer 1992, page 273]

complex object *n.* "Any type whose base class is complex is itself called a complex type, and its instances are complex objects." [Meyer 1992, page 273]

complex type *n.* "Any type whose base class is complex is itself called a complex type...." [Meyer 1992, page 273]

composite object *n.* "objects with sub-objects" [Meyer 1992, page 204]
Contrast with: SUB-OBJECT.

conformance [of a type] *n.* "Conformance determines when a type is compatible with another for assignment, argument passing or signature redefinition." [Meyer 1992, page 195]
Kinds:
- DIRECT CONFORMANCE
- EXPRESSION CONFORMANCE
- GENERAL CONFORMANCE
- SIGNATURE CONFORMANCE
- **direct conformance** *n.* "the case of a class conforming to a different one through no intermediary." [Meyer 1992, page 219]
- **expression conformance** *n.* "An expression v of type VT conforms to an expression t of type TT if and only if they satisfy any one of the following four conditions.
1. VT conforms to TT.
2. VT is like t (t in this case must be an entity).
3. VT and TT are both of the form like x for the same x.
4. TT is like x where x is a formal argument to a routine r, v is an actual argument in a call to r, and VT conforms to the type of the actual argument corresponding to x in the call." [Meyer 1992, page 226]
- **general conformance** *n.* "Let T and V be two types other than Bit_type. V

App
F

conforms to T if and only if one of the following holds:

1. V and T are identical.
2. V is NONE and T is a reference type.
3. V is $B[Y_1,...Y_n]$ for some generic class B, T is $B[X_1,...X_n]$, and every one of the Y_i conforms (recursively) to the corresponding X_i.
4. T is a reference type and, for some type U, V conforms directly to U and U conforms (recursively) to T." [Meyer 1992, page 219]

- **signature conformance** *n.* "A signature t conforms to a signature s if and only if every element of t (the type of an argument or result) conforms to the corresponding element of s." [Meyer 1992, page 218] "The type of every argument (for a routine) must conform to the corresponding argument type in the ... original; and the result type, if any, must conform to the result type of the original." [Meyer 1992, page 219]

consistent *adj.* "A class is ... consistent [if] every Routine_body, started in a state satisfying the precondition and the invariant, terminates in a state satisfying the postcondition and the invariant." [Meyer 1992, page 258]

constant attribute *n.* "... the value is the same for every instance, and it cannot be changed at run time." [Meyer 1992, page 261]
Contrast with: VARIABLE ATTRIBUTE.

contract *n.* "... the goal that [a routine or other software component] is meant to achieve—what in Eiffel theory is called the contract. The component provides just one way to achieve the contract; often, other implementations are possible." [Meyer 1992, page 249]

copy *v.* "... to copy the contents of an existing object onto those of another. This is the copy operation...." [Meyer 1992, page 295]
Contrast with: CLONE.
Kinds:
- DEEP COPY
- SHALLOW COPY

- **deep copy** *v.* "... will replicate an entire data structure, starting at the source and creating new objects as needed." [Meyer 1992, page 302]
Contrast with: DEEP CLONE, SHALLOW COPY.

- **shallow copy** *v.* "... just copy fields of the source object as they appear." [Meyer 1992, page 302]
Contrast with: DEEP COPY, SHALLOW CLONE.

correct *adj.* "A class is correct if and only if it is consistent and every routine of the class is check-correct, loop-correct and exception-correct." [Meyer 1992, page 132]
Kinds:
- CHECK-CORRECT
- EXCEPTION-CORRECT
- LOOP-CORRECT

- **check-correct** *adj.* "... the conditions of Check instructions are satisfied." [Meyer 1992, page 258] "An effective routine r is check-correct if, for every Check instruction c in r, any execution of c (as part of an execution of r) satisfies all its assertions." [Meyer 1992, page 129]
See also: EFFECTIVE ROUTINE.

- **exception-correct** *adj.* "... the rescue block must be such that any branch terminating with a Retry ... ensures the precondition and the invariant, and that any other branch ... ensure the invariant.... A routine satisfying these conditions ... is said to be exception-correct." [Meyer 1992, page 132]

- **loop-correct** *adj.* "loops maintain their invariant and every iteration decreases the variant" [Meyer 1992, page 258]

correctness *n.* "ability [for a valid component] to operate properly at run-time." [Meyer 1992, page 29]

Creation instruction *n.* "the principal mechanism used to produce new objects." [Meyer 1992, page 285]
Contrast with: CLONING.

creation type *n.* "The creation type is the optional Type appearing in the [Creation] instruction ... if present; otherwise it is the base type of the target." [Meyer 1992, page 285]

Current *n.* "The predefined entity used to represent a reference to the current object." [Meyer 1992, page 275]

current object *n.* "At any time during execution, the current object ... is the object to which the latest non-completed routine call applies, and the current routine ... is the feature of that call." [Meyer 1992, page 349]
Contrast with: CURRENT ROUTINE.

current routine *n.* "At any time during execution, the current object ... is the object to which the latest non-completed routine call applies, and the current routine ... is the feature of that call." [Meyer 1992, page 349]
Contrast with: CURRENT OBJECT.

declared type *n.* "the type given by the declaration or redeclaration." [Meyer 1992, page 146]

deep clone *v.* "... will replicate an entire data structure, starting at the source and creating new objects as needed." [Meyer 1992, page 302]
Contrast with: DEEP COPY, SHALLOW CLONE.

deep copy *v.* "... will replicate an entire data structure, starting at the source and cre-

ating new objects as needed." [Meyer 1992, page 302]
Contrast with: DEEP CLONE, SHALLOW COPY.

deep equality *n.* "Two references x and y are deep-equal if and only if they are either both void or attached to deep-equal objects. Two objects OX and OY are deep-equal and only if they satisfy the following three conditions:

1. The objects obtained by setting all the reference fields of OX and OY (if any) to void references are equal.
2. For every void reference field of OX, the corresponding field of OY is void.
3. For every non-void reference field of OX, attached to an object PX, the corresponding field of OY is attached to an object PY, and it is possible (recursively) to show, under the assumption that OX is deep-equal to OY, that PX is deep-equal to PY" [Meyer 1992, page 305]
Contrast with: SHALLOW EQUALITY.

deferred *adj.* "The parent's version, deprived of any implementation (but with a signature and specification) is said to be deferred." [Meyer 1992, page 135]
See also: EFFECTING.

- **fully deferred** *adj.* "... features are all deferred." [Meyer 1992, page 146]

deferred class *n.* "Deferred classes describe a group of implementations of an abstract data type rather than just a single implementation. A deferred class may not be instantiated." [Meyer 1992, page 20] "A deferred class describes an incompletely implemented abstraction, which other classes (its proper descendants) will use as a basis for further refinement." [Meyer 1992, page 47] "You will declare a class as deferred if you plan to include one or more features which

App
F

are specified but not implemented, with the expectation that proper descendants of the class will provide the implementations." [Meyer 1992, page 50] "A class which is declared as deferred but has no deferred features is invalid." [Meyer 1992, page 51]

deferred routine *n.* "A routine may further be declared as deferred, meaning that the class introducing it only gives its specification, leaving it for descendants to provide implementations." [Meyer 1992, page 107]

Contrast with: EFFECTIVE ROUTINE.

depend *v. -ed, -ing* "Here a class C is said to depend on a class A if one of the following holds:
– C is an heir of A.
– C is a client of A.
– Recursively, there is a class B such that C depends on B and B depends on A." [Meyer 1992, page 35]

dependent *n.* "The dependents of an object are the object itself and (recursively) the dependents of its direct dependents." [Meyer 1992, page 456]

● **direct dependent** *n.* "The direct dependents of an object O, at some time during the execution of a system, are the objects attached to the reference field of O." [Meyer 1992, page 456]

descendant [class] *n.* "Class B is a descendant of class A if and only if A is an ancestor of B, in other words if B is A or (recursively) a descendant of one of its heirs." [Meyer 1992, page 77]

Contrast with: ANCESTOR.

● **proper descendant** *n.* "The proper descendants of class B are its descendants other than B itself." [Meyer 1992, page 78]

Contrast with: PROPER ANCESTOR.

Design by Contract *n.* "The underlying

theory of Design by Contract views software construction as based on contracts between clients (callers) and suppliers (routines), relying on mutual obligations and advantages made explicit by the assertions." [Meyer 1992, page 11]

direct conformance *n.* "the case of a class conforming to a different one through no intermediary." [Meyer 1992, page 219]

See also: ANCHORED TYPE.

direct instance *n.* "a class is the description of similar run-time data elements, or objects, called the direct instances of the class." [Meyer 1992, page 34]

direct repeated inheritance *n.* "corresponds to the following scheme (where D is a 'repeated heir' of A):

```
class D inherit
    A
    rename … redefine … end;
    A
    rename … redefine … end;
```

[Meyer 1992, page 168]

dynamic class set *n.* "The dynamic class set of an entity is the set of base classes of all types that the entity may take on at run-time, as a result of polymorphic reattachments and creation instructions." [Meyer 1992, page 364]

Contrast with: DYNAMIC TYPE SET.

dynamic type *n.* "The dynamic type of an entity or expression x, at some instant of execution when x is not void, is the type of the object to which x is attached." [Meyer 1992, page 323]

See also: POLYMORPHISM.

Contrast with: STATIC TYPE.

dynamic type set *n.* "The set of possible dynamic types for an entity for expression x is called the dynamic type set of x. The set of base classes of these types is called the dynamic class set of x." [Meyer 1992, page 323]

Contrast with: DYNAMIC CLASS SET.

effecting *n.* "[a mechanism] which provides an implementation (or 'effective' version) for a feature which did not have one in the parent." [Meyer 1992, page 135]
See also: DEFERRED, REDECLARATION.

effective routine *n.* "A routine which is not deferred is said to be effective." [Meyer 1992, page 107]
Contrast with: DEFERRED ROUTINE.

Eiffel shelf *n.* "A distribution mechanism known as the Eiffel shelf is available to make reusable classes from various sources … accessible to Eiffel users worldwide." [Meyer 1992, page 430]

ensure *n.* "Routine postconditions, introduced by the keyword *ensure*, express conditions that the routine (the supplier) guarantees on return, if the precondition was satisfied on entry." [Meyer 1992, page 9] "The keyword *ensure* introduces an Assertion, called the Postcondition of the routine. This expresses the conditions that a routine call will ensure on return if called in a state satisfying the precondition." [Meyer 1992, page 112]
Contrast with: REQUIRE.

entity *n.* "An entity is a name used by a class text to refer to values which may at runtime become associated in some way to the instances of the class. In a class context, four kinds of entity may appear:
1. Attributes of the class.
2. Local entities of routines, including the redefined entity Result for functions.
3. Formal routine arguments.
4. Current, the predefined entity used to represent a reference to the current object (the target of the latest not yet completed routine call)." [Meyer 1992, page 275]

environment *n.* "An environment—an instance of class ENVIRONMENT—simply represents a set of objects. It is always complete under dependency: in other words, if an object belongs to an environment, all of its dependents, direct or indirect, also belong to the environment." [Meyer 1992, page 461]

equality expression *n.* "An Equality expression serves to test equality (with the = symbol) or inequality (with the /= symbol) of values…. the expression e=f has two possible meanings:
1. If both e and f are of reference types, the expression denotes reference equality….
2. If either e or f is of an expanded type, the expression denotes object equality." [Meyer 1992, pages 374–375]
Kinds:
• DEEP EQUALITY
• SHALLOW EQUALITY

• **deep equality** *n.* "Two references x and y are deep-equal if and only if they are either both void or attached to deep-equal objects. Two objects OX and OY are deep-equal and only if they satisfy the following three conditions:
1. The objects obtained by setting all the reference fields of OX and OY (if any) to void references are equal.
2. For every void reference field of OX, the corresponding field of OY is void.
3. For every non-void reference field of OX, attached to an object PX, the corresponding field of OY is attached to an object PY, and it is possible (recursively) to show, under the assumption that OX is deep-equal to OY, that PX is deep-equal to PY" [Meyer 1992, page 305]
Contrast with: SHALLOW EQUALITY.

• **shallow equality** *n.* "To determine if the objects attached to x and y are field-by-field identical, you may use the Call equal(x,y)." [Meyer 1992, page 303]

Contrast with: DEEP EQUALITY.

exception *n.* "Exceptions—contract violations—may arise from several causes. One is assertion violations, if assertions are monitored. Another is the occurrence of a signal triggered by the hardware or operations system to indicate an abnormal condition such as arithmetic overflow or lack of memory to allocate a new object.... Failure of a routine is a third cause of exception: a routine that fails triggers an exception in its caller." [Meyer 1992, page 12] "If a routine executes a component and that component fails, this will prevent the routine's execution from proceeding as planned; such an event is called an exception.... an exception is the consequence of a failure." [Meyer 1992, page 248]

See also: RAISE, RECIPIENT, RESCUE BLOCK, SUCCESS.

exception-correct *adj.* "... the rescue block must be such that any branch terminating with a Retry ... ensures the precondition and the invariant, and that any other branch ... ensure the invariant.... A routine satisfying these conditions ... is said to be exception-correct." [Meyer 1992, page 132]

Contrast with: CHECK-CORRECT, LOOP CORRECT.

expanded class *n.* "Declaring a class as expanded indicates that entities declared of the corresponding type will have objects as their run-time values." [Meyer 1992, page 47]

Contrast with: EXPANDED TYPE.

expanded type *n.* "A type T is expanded if and only if one of the following conditions holds:

1. T is a Class_type whose base class C is an expanded class.
2. T is of the form expanded CT.
3. T is of the form BIT M for some non-negative integer M." [Meyer 1992, page 208]

Contrast with: EXPANDED CLASS.

exported [feature] *adj.* ".... available to all classes." [Meyer 1992, page 100]

Synonym: GENERALLY AVAILABLE.

external routine *n.* "The name 'external' refers to the routine as viewed from the Eiffel text." [Meyer 1992, page 399]

See also: FOREIGN ROUTINE.

Contrast with: INTERNAL ROUTINE.

feature *n.* "A class ... describes a set of run-time objects, characterized by features (operations) applicable to them, and by the formal properties to these features.. .. Features are of two kinds: Routines [and] Attributes." [Meyer 1992, pages 5–6]. "Viewed as a module, a class introduces, through its class text, a set of features. Some features, called attributes, represent fields of the class's direct instances; others, called routines represent computations applicable to those instances." [Meyer 1992, page 44] "A feature is either an attribute, describing information stored with each instance, or a routine, describing an algorithm." [Meyer 1992, page 55] "The features of a class C include its inherited features and its immediate features." [Meyer 1992, page 56]

See also: CALL, NAME [OF A FEATURE], SEED [OF A FEATURE].

Kinds:

• AVAILABLE FEATURE
  - GENERALLY AVAILABLE
  - SELECTIVELY AVAILABLE

- FROZEN FEATURE
- IMMEDIATE FEATURE
- INHERITED FEATURE
- POTENTIALLY AMBIGUOUS FEATURE
- SECRET FEATURE

- **available [feature]** *adj.* "A feature of a class S is said to be available to a class C if and only if it is either selectively available to S or generally available." [Meyer 1992, page 100]
  Contrast with: SECRET.
  Kinds:
    - GENERALLY AVAILABLE
    - SELECTIVELY AVAILABLE

  - **generally available [feature]** *adj.* ".... available to all classes." [Meyer 1992, page 100]
    Synonym: EXPORTED.

  - **selectively available [feature]** *adj.* "The feature may be available to specific classes only. In that case it is also available to the descendants of all these classes. Such a feature is said to be selectively available to the given classes and their descendants" [Meyer 1992, page 100]

- **frozen feature** *n.* "... the keyword frozen, appearing before the feature name to express that the declaration is final (not subject to redefinition in descendants)." [Meyer 1992, page 63]
  See also: REDEFINITION.

- **immediate feature** *n.* "a new feature, said to be immediate." [Meyer 1992, page 56]
  Contrast with: INHERITED FEATURE.

- **inherited feature** *n.* "The features obtained by [class] C from its parents, if any." [Meyer 1992, page 56]
  See also: PRECURSOR [OF A FEATURE], SEED [OF A FEATURE].
  Contrast with: IMMEDIATE FEATURE.

- **potentially ambiguous feature** *n.* "A

feature is potentially ambiguous in a repeated descendant if it presents more than one choice for dynamic binding." [Meyer 1992, page 190]

- **secret [feature]** *n.* "The feature may be available to no classes." [Meyer 1992, page 100] "... if the Feature_clause has an empty Clients list, that is to say, begins with feature [ ], then the features it introduces are secret." [Meyer 1992, page 102]
  Contrast with: AVAILABLE [FEATURE].

feature redefinition *n.* "[a mechanism] which may change an inherited feature's original implementation, signature or specification" [Meyer 1992, page 133] "The redeclaration is a redefinition if and only if it is not an effecting. This is the case if [a Feature_declaration] and the inherited form of the redeclared feature are both deferred or both effective." [Meyer 1992, page 163]
  See also: EFFECTING, PRECURSOR, REDECLARATION.

feature type *n.* "The 'type' of a feature or entity, without further qualification always means its declared type (rather than its base type." [Meyer 1992, page 164]

field *n.* "A direct instance of a complex type is a sequence of zero or more values, called fields. There is one field for every attribute of the type's base class. ... The field is itself an object, called a sub-object of the enclosing object." [Meyer 1992, pages 273–274]
  Contrast with: ATTRIBUTE, INSTANCE.

final name [of a feature] *n.* "Every feature f of a class C has a final name in C, defined as follows:

1. If f is immediate in C, its final name is its original name.

2. If f is inherited, f is obtained from a feature of parent B of C. Let parent_

App
F

name be (recursively) the final name of that feature in B.

Then: If the Parent clause for B in C contains a Rename_pair of the form rename parent_name as new_name, then the final name of f in C is new_name. Otherwise, the final name is parent_name." [Meyer 1992, page 82]

Contrast with: ORIGINAL NAME.

See also: FINAL NAME SET.

final name set *n.* "The final names of all the features of a class constitute the final name set of a class." [Meyer 1992, page 82]

Contrast with: ORIGINAL NAME.

foreign routine *n.* "… the form of the routine as it appears in its original language." [Meyer 1992, page 399]

Contrast with: EXTERNAL ROUTINE.

formal arguments *n.* "Within the routine, the arguments are represented by entities called formal arguments." [Meyer 1992, page 108]

frozen [feature] *adj.* "… the keyword frozen, appearing before the feature name to express that the declaration is final (not subject to redefinition in descendants)." [Meyer 1992, page 63]

See also: REDEFINITION.

fully deferred class *n.* "a class whose features are all deferred." [Meyer 1992, page 146]

function *n.* "A function returns a result and may also perform operations." [Meyer 1992, page 61]

Contrast with: PROCEDURE, ROUTINE.

garbage collector *n.* "… reclaims the storage associated with unused objects, relieving programmers from this tedious and error-prone task." [Meyer 1992, page 21] "… a garbage collection mechanism which will take care of detecting unreachable objects." [Meyer 1992, page 335]

general conformance *n.* "Let T and V be two type other than Bit_type. V conforms to T if and only if one of the following holds:

1. V and T are identical.
2. V is NONE and T is a reference type.
3. V is $B[Y_1,...Y_n]$ for some generic class B, T is $B[X_1,...X_n]$, and every one of the Y_i conforms (recursively) to the corresponding X_i.
4. T is a reference type and, for some type U, V conforms directly to U and U conforms (recursively) to T." [Meyer 1992, page 219]

generally available *adj.* "…. available to all classes. Such a feature is said to be exported, or generally available." [Meyer 1992, page 100]

Synonym: EXPORTED.

generating class [of an object] *n.* "The base class of the generating type is called the object's generating class, or generator for short." [Meyer 1992, page 270]

Synonym: GENERATOR.

generating type [of an object] *n.* "Every standard object is a direct instance of some type of the system, called the generating type for the object, or just 'the type of the object' if there is no ambiguity." [Meyer 1992, page 270]

generator *n. short for* GENERATING CLASS.

generic *adj.* "… with formal generic parameters." [Meyer 1992, page 200]

generic class *n.* "A generic class is a class declared with formal generic parameters; this mechanism supports type parameterization…. Generic classes describe flexible structures having variants parameterized by types." [Meyer 1992, page 200]

generic client *n.* "A class C is a generic client of a type S if for some generically derived type T of the form B [..., S, ...] one of the following holds:

1. C is a client of T.
2. One of the Parent clauses of C, or of a proper ancestor of C, lists T as a parent." [Meyer 1992, page 94]

genericity *n.* "To make a class generic is to give it formal generic parameters representing arbitrary types." [Meyer 1992, page 13] "The mechanism which permits generic classes and the corresponding types is called genericity." [Meyer 1992, page 51]

heir *n.* "If class C has a Parent clause for B., then C is said to inherit from B; B is said to be a parent of C, and C is said to be an heir of B." [Meyer 1992, page 77] *Contrast with:* PARENT.

identifier *n.* "An important category of variable tokens is identifiers, describing symbolic names which Eiffel texts use to denote various components such as classes, features or entities." [Meyer 1992, page 417]

indirect repeated inheritance *n.* "arises when one parent of D is a proper descendant of A, and one or more other parents are descendants of A. (Some of the paths may be direct.)" [Meyer 1992, page 168]

information hiding *n.* "By keeping ... features private, the designer of the supplier class protects clients against the effects of later reversals of these choices. This policy is known as information hiding." [Meyer 1992, page 95]

inherit *v.* "If class C has a Parent clause for B., then C is said to inherit from B; B is said to be a parent of C, and C is said to be an heir of B." [Meyer 1992, page 77]

inheritance *n.* "Inheritance, [a] fundamental generalization mechanism, makes it possible to define a new class by combination and specialization of existing classes rather than from scratch." [Meyer 1992, page 14] "As a module extension mechanism, inheritance makes it possible to define new classes from existing ones by adding or adapting features. As a type refinement mechanism, inheritance supports the definition of new types as specializations of existing ones, and plays a key role in defining the type system." [Meyer 1992, page 75]
Kinds:
- MULTIPLE INHERITANCE
- REPEATED INHERITANCE
  - DIRECT REPEATED INHERITANCE
  - INDIRECT REPEATED INHERITANCE
  - REPLICATED REPEATED INHERITANCE
  - SHARED REPEATED INHERITANCE
- SINGLE INHERITANCE

App
F

- **multiple inheritance** *n.* "When ... there are two or more Parent clauses, inheritance is said to be multiple." [Meyer 1992, page 76]
  Contrast with: SINGLE INHERITANCE.

- **repeated inheritance** *n.* "[in multiple inheritance] if more than one Parent clause ... all refer to the same parent class." [Meyer 1992, page 76] "Prohibiting cycles does not mean prohibiting a class D from being a descendant of another class A in more than one way. This case, [is] known as repeated inheritance." [Meyer 1992, page 79] "Repeated inheritance occurs whenever (as a result of multiple inheritance) two or more of the ancestors of a class D have a common parent A." [Meyer 1992, page 168]

  - **direct repeated inheritance** *n.* "corresponds to the following scheme (where D is a 'repeated heir' of A):
    ```
    class D inherit
        A
        rename ... redefine ... end;
    ```

A

rename ... redefine ... end"
[Meyer 1992, page 168]

- **indirect repeated inheritance** *n.* "arises when one parent of D is a proper descendant of A, and one or more other parents are descendants of A. (Some of the paths may be direct.)" [Meyer 1992, page 168]

- **replicated repeated inheritance** *n.* "[where] any two of these features inherited under a different name yield two features of [class] D." [Meyer 1992, page 170]
  Contrast with: SHARED REPEATED INHERITANCE.

- **shared repeated inheritance** *n.* "[where] any subset of these features inherited by [class] D under the same final name yields a single feature of D." [Meyer 1992, page 170]
  Contrast with: REPLICATED REPEATED INHERITANCE.

- **single inheritance** *n.* "With only one Parent clause, we would have "single" inheritance. [Meyer 1992, page 76]
  Contrast with: MULTIPLE INHERITANCE.

inherited *adj.* "... obtained from ... a parent." [Meyer 1992, page 82]

inherited feature *n.* "The features obtained by [class] C from its parents, if any." [Meyer 1992, page 56]
See also: PRECURSOR [OF A FEATURE], SEED [OF A FEATURE].

inherited name *n.* "The inherited name of a feature obtained from a feature f of a parent B is the final name of f in B." [Meyer 1992, page 82]
Contrast with: ORIGINAL NAME.

instance [of a class] *n.* "... objects are called the instances of the class." [Meyer 1992, page 44] "An instance of a class C is an instance of any type T based on C,

and similarly for direct instances." [Meyer 1992, page 271] "... objects, called the direct instances of the class." [Meyer 1992, page 34]

instance [of a type] *n.* "Every object is an instance of one or more types. More precisely: ... The instances of a type TX are the direct instances of any type conforming to TX. In other words, the instances of TX are the direct instances of TX and, recursively, the instances of any other type conforming to TX." [Meyer 1992, page 272]
Contrast with: ATTRIBUTE, FIELD.

internal routine *n.* "... any Eiffel routine accessible to language processing tools." [Meyer 1992, page 399]
Contrast with: EXTERNAL ROUTINE.

invariant *n.* "A class invariant must be satisfied by every instance of the class whenever the instance is externally accessible: after creation, and after any call to an exported routine of a class." [Meyer 1992, page 9] "The invariant specifies properties which any instance of the class must satisfy at every instant at which the instance is observable by clients." [Meyer 1992, page 126] "The invariant of a class C is an assertion obtained as follows:

– Determine (recursively) the invariants of all parents.

– Concatenate the resulting assertions in order of the corresponding Parent clauses, followed by the Assertion in C's Invariant clause, if any." [Meyer 1992, page 127]

Lace *n.* "Language for Assembling Classes in Eiffel.... You may use Lace to write an Assembly of Classes in Eiffel, or Ace." [Meyer 1992, page 40]

loop-correct *adj.* "loops maintain their invariant and every iteration decreases

the variant" [Meyer 1992, page 258]
See: EFFECTIVE ROUTINE.
Contrast with: CHECK-CORRECT, EXCEPTION CORRECT.

multiple inheritance *n.* "When ... there are two or more Parent clauses, inheritance is said to be multiple." [Meyer 1992, page 76]
Contrast with: SINGLE INHERITANCE.

name [of a feature] *n.*
Kinds:
- FINAL NAME
- INHERITED NAME
- ORIGINAL NAME

- **final name [of a feature]** *n.* "Every feature f of a class C has a final name in C, defined as follows:
  1. If f is immediate in C, its final name is its original name.
  2. If f is inherited, f is obtained from a feature of parent B of C. Let parent_ name be (recursively) the final name of that feature in B.

  Then: If the Parent clause for B in C contains a Rename_pair of the form rename parent_name as new_name, then the final name of f in C is new_ name. Otherwise, the final name is parent_name." [Meyer 1992, page 82]
  Contrast with: ORIGINAL NAME.
  See also: FINAL NAME SET.

- **inherited name** *n.* "The inherited name of a feature obtained from a feature f of a parent B is the final name of f in B." [Meyer 1992, page 82]
  Contrast with: ORIGINAL NAME.

- **original name [of a feature]** *n.* "The original name of a feature is the name under which it is declared in its class of origin." [Meyer 1992, page 82]
  Contrast with: FINAL NAME, FINAL NAME SET.

NONE (Kernel Library Class) *n.* "This class is considered to inherit from all classes—assuming appropriate renaming to remove any resulting name clashes. It does not actually exist as a class text in the library..., but serves as a convenient fiction to make the class structure and the type system complete." [Meyer 1992, page 88]

object *n.* "Objects are described as instances of abstract data types—that is to say, data structures known from an official interface rather than through their representation." [Meyer 1992, page 4] "... objects, called the direct instances of the class." [Meyer 1992, page 34] "... objects ... may exist during the execution of a system that includes the class; these objects are called the instances of the class. An object may represent a real-world thing such as a signal in a process control software, a document in a text processing software or an electron in physics software. Objects may also be pure artifacts of computer programming, such as an abstract syntax tree in compilation software. [Meyer 1992, page 43]
Kinds:
- COMPLEX OBJECT
- COMPOSITE OBJECT
- CURRENT OBJECT
- PERSISTENT OBJECT
- ROOT OBJECT
- SPECIAL OBJECT
- STANDARD OBJECT
- SUB-OBJECT

- **complex object** *n.* "Any type whose base class is complex is itself called a complex type, and its instances are complex objects." [Meyer 1992, page 273]

- **composite object** *n.* "objects with sub-objects" [Meyer 1992, page 204]
  Contrast with: SUB-OBJECT.

- **current object** *n.* "At any time during

App
F

execution, the current object ... is the object to which the latest non-completed routine call applies, and the current routine ... is the feature of that call." [Meyer 1992, page 349]

Contrast with: CURRENT ROUTINE.

- **persistent object** *n.* "The persistent objects of an environment are all the objects recorded under some key in the environment, and their dependents." [Meyer 1992, page 463]

See also: ENVIRONMENT.

- **root object** *n.* "... the instance of the root class whose creation is the first act of system execution." [Meyer 1992, page 349]

Contrast with: ROOT CLASS.

- **special object** *n.* "There are two kinds of object, standard and special: ... A special object is a sequence of values, all compatible with a given type. It may be a string or an array." [Meyer 1992, page 270]

Contrast with: STANDARD OBJECT.

- **standard object** *n.* "There are two kinds of object, standard and special: A standard object is the direct result of a Creation instruction or clone operation executed by the system." [Meyer 1992, page 270] "A standard object is a direct instance of a class." [Meyer 1992, page 395]

Contrast with: SPECIAL OBJECT.

- **sub-object** *n.* "In other words, the field is itself an object, called a sub-object of the enclosing object." [Meyer 1992, page 274]

Contrast with: COMPOSITE OBJECT.

object-oriented design *n.* "the construction of software systems as structured collections of classes, or abstract data type implementations." [Meyer 1992, page 4]

original name [of a feature] *n.* "The original name of a feature is the name under which it is declared in its class of origin." [Meyer 1992, page 82]

Contrast with: FINAL NAME, FINAL NAME SET.

origin [of a feature] *n.* "Every feature of a class C has ... an origin, which is a class.. .. Any immediate feature of C ... has C as its origin.... The origin of a feature is the most remote ancestor from which the feature 'comes.'" [Meyer 1992, page 162]

parent [class] *n.* "If class C has a Parent clause for B., then C is said to inherit from B; B is said to be a parent of C, and C is said to be an heir of B." [Meyer 1992, page 77]

persistent object *n.* "The persistent objects of an environment are all the objects recorded under some key in the environment, and their dependents." [Meyer 1992, page 463]

See also: ENVIRONMENT.

polymorphism *n.* "... ability to have more than one dynamic type is called polymorphism; an entity or expression which has two or more possible dynamic types (that is to say, which may become attached at run time to objects of two or more types) is itself a polymorphic entity. Only entities or expressions of reference types may be polymorphic." [Meyer 1992, page 323]

See also: FEATURE REDEFINITION.

postcondition *n.* "Routine postconditions, introduced by the keyword ensure, express conditions that the routine (the supplier) guarantees on return, if the precondition was satisfied on entry." [Meyer 1992, page 9]

potentially ambiguous feature *n.* "A feature is potentially ambiguous in a repeated descendant if it presents more

than one choice for dynamic binding."
[Meyer 1992, page 190]

precondition *n.* "Routine preconditions express the requirements that clients must satisfy whenever they call a routine." [Meyer 1992, page 9]

precursor [of an inherited feature] *n.* "A precursor of an inherited feature is a version of the feature in the parent from which it is inherited." [Meyer 1992, page 165]
See also: REDEFINITION.

procedure *n.* "A procedure does not return a result; it may perform a number of operations, some of which may modify the instance to which the procedure is applied." [Meyer 1992, page 61]
Contrast with: FUNCTION, ROUTINE.

proper ancestor *n.* "The proper ancestors of a class C are its ancestors other than C itself. The proper descendants of class B are its descendants other than B itself." [Meyer 1992, page 78]
Contrast with: PROPER DESCENDANT.

proper descendant *n.* "The proper ancestors of a class C are its ancestors other than C itself. The proper descendants of class B are its descendants other than B itself." [Meyer 1992, page 78]
Contrast with: PROPER ANCESTOR.

raise *n.* "Class EXCEPTION also provides a way to raise an exception on purpose. This is called a developer exception and is triggered by the procedure call raise(exception_name)." [Meyer 1992, page 259]
See also: EXCEPTION.

recipient [of an exception] *n.* "When the component's execution fails, this will trigger an exception in the current routine, which becomes the recipient of the exception.... Any exception has a recipient, which is a routine." [Meyer 1992, page 250]

redeclaration *n.* "A class that contains a redefinition or effecting of an inherited feature will be said to redeclare that feature.... Redeclaration never introduces a new feature, but simply overrides the original declaration of an inherited feature, deferred or not." [Meyer 1992, pages 136–137]
Contrast with: EFFECTING, REDEFINITION.

redefinition *n.* "[a mechanism] which may change an inherited feature's original implementation, signature or specification" [Meyer 1992, page 133] "The redeclaration is a redefinition if and only if it is not an effecting. This is the case if [a Feature_declaration] and the inherited form of the redeclared feature are both deferred or both effective." [Meyer 1992, page 163]
See also: EFFECTING, PRECURSOR, REDECLARATION.

reference [to an object] *n.* "A reference is a value which is either void or attached. If a reference is void, no further information is available on it. If it is attached, it gives access to an object; it is said to be attached to that object. The object will also said to be attached to the reference." [Meyer 1992, page 270]
Contrast with: VALUE.
Kinds:
- ATTACHED REFERENCE
- VOID REFERENCE

- **attached reference** *n.* "If [a reference is] attached, it gives access to an object; it is said to be attached to that object. The object will also be said to be attached to the reference." [Meyer 1992, page 270]
Contrast with: VOID REFERENCE.

- **void reference** *n.* "If a reference is void, no further information is available on it." [Meyer 1992, page 270]

**App
F**

Contrast with: ATTACHED REFERENCE.

reference type *n.* Any type T where

"1. T is a Class_type whose base class C is an expanded class.

2. T is of the form expanded CT.

3. T is of the form BIT M for some non-negative integer M.

T is a reference type if it is not a Formal_generic_name and none of the above condition applies." [Meyer 1992, page 208]

Contrast with: EXPANDED TYPE.

renaming *n.* "… a renaming mechanism, enabling a class to be known to others, within a system, under a name different from its actual class name." [Meyer 1992, page 39]

repeated inheritance *n.* "[in multiple inheritance] if more than one Parent clause … all refer to the same parent class." [Meyer 1992, page 76] "Prohibiting cycles does not mean prohibiting a class D from being a descendant of another class A in more than one way. This case, [is] known as repeated inheritance." [Meyer 1992, page 79] "Repeated inheritance occurs whenever (as a result of multiple inheritance) two or more of the ancestors of a class D have a common parent A." [Meyer 1992, page 168]

Kinds:

- DIRECT REPEATED INHERITANCE
- INDIRECT REPEATED INHERITANCE
- REPLICATED REPEATED INHERITANCE
- SHARED REPEATED INHERITANCE

- **direct repeated inheritance** *n.* "corresponds to the following scheme (where D is a 'repeated heir' of A):

```
class D inherit
  A
  rename … redefine … end;
  A
  rename … redefine … end"
```

[Meyer 1992, page 168]

- **indirect repeated inheritance** *n.* "arises when one parent of D is a proper descendant of A, and one or more other parents are descendants of A. (Some of the paths may be direct.)" [Meyer 1992, page 168]

- **replicated repeated inheritance** *n.* "[where] any two of these features inherited under a different name yield two features of [class] D." [Meyer 1992, page 170]

Contrast with: SHARED REPEATED INHERITANCE.

- **shared repeated inheritance** *n.* "[where] any subset of these features inherited by [class] D under the same final name yields a single feature of D." [Meyer 1992, page 170]

Contrast with: REPLICATED REPEATED INHERITANCE.

replicated repeated inheritance *n.* "[where] any two of these features inherited under a different name yield two features of [class] D." [Meyer 1992, page 170]

Contrast with: SHARED REPEATED INHERITANCE.

require *n.* "The keyword *require* introduces an Assertion, called the Precondition of the routine. This expresses the condition under which a call to the routine is correct." [Meyer 1992, page 111]

Contrast with: ENSURE.

rescue block [of a routine] *n.* "To define the semantics of exception handling, it is convenient to consider that every routine has an implicit or explicit 'rescue block'" [Meyer 1992, page 257]

Result *n.* "… the predefined entity Result for functions." [Meyer 1992, page 275]

root class *n.* "A system is a set of classes, one of which has been designated as the root of the system, such that all the classes on which the root depends belong to the

system." [Meyer 1992, page 35]
Contrast with: ROOT OBJECT.

root object *n.* "... the instance of the root class whose creation is the first act of system execution." [Meyer 1992, page 349]
Contrast with: ROOT CLASS.

routine *n.* "Routines ... represent computations applicable to instances of the class." [Meyer 1992, page 6] "... routines represent computations applicable to [a class's direct] instances." [Meyer 1992, page 44] "A routine is either a procedure or a function." [Meyer 1992, page 61] "Routines describe computations.... A routine is either a procedure, which does not return a result, or a function, which does." [Meyer 1992, page 107]
Kinds:
- CURRENT ROUTINE
- DEFERRED ROUTINE
- EFFECTIVE ROUTINE
- EXTERNAL ROUTINE
- FOREIGN ROUTINE
- INTERNAL ROUTINE

- **current routine** *n.* "At any time during execution, the current object ... is the object to which the latest non-completed routine call applies, and the current routine ... is the feature of that call." [Meyer 1992, page 349]
Contrast with: CURRENT OBJECT.

- **deferred routine** *n.* "A routine may further be declared as deferred, meaning that the class introducing it only gives its specification, leaving it for descendants to provide implementations." [Meyer 1992, page 107]
Contrast with: EFFECTIVE ROUTINE.

- **effective routine** *n.* "A routine which is not deferred is said to be effective." [Meyer 1992, page 107]
Contrast with: DEFERRED ROUTINE.

- **external routine** *n.* "The name 'exter-

nal' refers to the routine as viewed from the Eiffel text." [Meyer 1992, page 399]
See also: FOREIGN ROUTINE.
Contrast with: INTERNAL ROUTINE.

- **foreign routine** *n.* "... the form of the routine as it appears in its original language." [Meyer 1992, page 399]
Contrast with: EXTERNAL ROUTINE.

- **internal routine** *n.* "... any Eiffel routine accessible to language processing tools." [Meyer 1992, page 399]
Contrast with: EXTERNAL ROUTINE.

secret [feature] *n.* "The feature may be available to no classes." [Meyer 1992, page 100] "... if the Feature_clause has an empty Clients list, that is to say, begins with feature [ ], then the features it introduces are secret." [Meyer 1992, page 102]
Contrast with: AVAILABLE [FEATURE].

seed [of a feature] *n.* "The origin of a feature is the most remote ancestor from which the feature 'comes,' and its seed is its original form in that ancestor." [Meyer 1992, page 162]
See also: INHERITED FEATURE.
Contrast with: ORIGIN.

selectively available feature *n.* "The feature may be available to specific classes only. In that case it is also available to the descendants of all these classes. Such a feature is said to be selectively available to the given classes and their descendants" [Meyer 1992, page 100]

shallow *adj.* "copying only one object" [Meyer 1992, page 295]
Contrast with: DEEP.

shallow clone *v.* "... just copy fields of the source object as they appear." [Meyer 1992, page 302]
Contrast with: DEEP CLONE, SHALLOW COPY.

shallow copy *v.* "... just copy fields of the

source object as they appear." [Meyer 1992, page 302]

Contrast with: DEEP COPY, SHALLOW CLONE.

shallow equality *n.* "To determine if the objects attached to x and y are field-by-field identical, you may use the Call equal(x,y)." [Meyer 1992, page 303]

Contrast with: DEEP EQUALITY.

shared repeated inheritance *n.* "[where] any subset of these features inherited by [class] D under the same final name yields a single feature of D." [Meyer 1992, page 170]

Contrast with: REPLICATED REPEATED INHERITANCE.

short form *n.* "a text which has the same structure as the class but does not include non-public elements. The short form is the one that should be used as interface documentation for the class." [Meyer 1992, page 103]

Synonym: ABSTRACT FORM.

signature *n.* "A signature gives the full type information associated with a feature: the type" [Meyer 1992, page 218]

signature conformance *n.* "A signature t conforms to a signature s if and only if every element of t (the type of an argument or result) conforms to the corresponding element of s." [Meyer 1992, page 218] "The type of every argument (for a routine) must conform to the corresponding argument type in the … original; and the result type, if any, must conform to the result type of the original." [Meyer 1992, page 219]

simple client *n.* "A class C is a simple client of a type S if S is a reference type, and some entity f of C is of type S." [Meyer 1992, page 92]

single inheritance *n.* "With only one Parent clause, we would have 'single' inheritance. [Meyer 1992, page 76]

Contrast with: MULTIPLE INHERITANCE.

special object *n.* "There are two kinds of object, standard and special: … A special object is a sequence of values, all compatible with a given type. It may be a string or an array." [Meyer 1992, page 270]

Contrast with: STANDARD OBJECT.

standard object *n.* "There are two kinds of object, standard and special: A standard object is the direct result of a Creation instruction or clone operation executed by the system." [Meyer 1992, page 270] "A standard object is a direct instance of a class." [Meyer 1992, page 395]

Contrast with: SPECIAL OBJECT.

static type *n.* "… the 'type' of x (called it static type if there is any ambiguity), which an entity is the type with which it is declared, and for an expression is the type deduced from the types of its constituents." [Meyer 1992, page 323]

Contrast with: DYNAMIC TYPE.

sub-object *n.* "In other words, the field is itself an object, called a sub-object of the enclosing object." [Meyer 1992, page 274]

Contrast with: COMPOSITE OBJECT.

supplier [type or class] *n.* "[type] S is a supplier of [class] C if and only if C is a client of S; similarly, S may be a simple supplier of C, a direct or indirect generic supplier and so on." [Meyer 1992, page 91]

Contrast with: CLIENT.

system *n.* "A system results from the assembly of one or more classes to produce an executable unit." [Meyer 1992, page 33]

See: ROOT.

system-level validity *n.* "System-level validity is the same property as its class-level counterpart, but applied to all possible dynamic types of the target x." [Meyer 1992, page 288]

Contrast with: CLASS_LEVEL VALIDITY.

system-valid call *n.* "Calls which satisfy [the system-level validity requirement] will be said to be system-valid." [Meyer 1992, page 358]

Contrast with: CLASS-VALID CALL.

type *n.* "Types describe the form and properties of objects that can be created during the execution of a system." [Meyer 1992, page 193] "The 'type' of a feature or entity, without further qualification, always means its declared type (rather than its base type)." [Meyer 1992, page 164] "For non-generic classes the difference between [class C] and [any type T based on C] is irrelevant, but for a generic class you must remember that by itself the class does not fully determine the shape of its direct instances: you need a type, which requires providing a set of actual generic parameters." [Meyer 1992, page 271]

See also: ABSTRACT DATA TYPE, VERSION.

Kinds:
- ABSTRACT DATA TYPE
- ANCHORED TYPE
- BASE TYPE
- BASIC TYPE
- COMPLEX TYPE
- CREATION TYPE
- DECLARED TYPE
- DYNAMIC TYPE
- EXPANDED TYPE
- FEATURE TYPE
- GENERATING TYPE
- REFERENCE TYPE
- STATIC TYPE

- **abstract data type** *n.* "... data structures known from an official interface rather than through their representation." [Meyer 1992, page 4]

  Contrast with: TYPE.

- **anchored type** *n.* "The originality of anchored types ... is that they carry a provision for automatic redefinition in descendants of the class where they are used. An Anchored type is of the form 'like anchor' where anchor, called the anchor of the type, is an entity, or Current." [Meyer 1992, page 211] "An anchored type conforms directly to no type other than implied by these rules. No type conforms directly to an anchored type." [Meyer 1992, page 225]

- **base type** *n.* "... if [type] T is anchored, the type of its anchor is the base type of T, and the base class of T's base type also serves as the base class of T.... The base class of a type is always the same as the base class of its base type...." [Meyer 1992, page 198]

- **basic type** *n.* "The basic types are class types, defined by non-generic classes of the Kernel Library called basic classes." [Meyer 1992, page 209]

- **complex type** *n.* "Any type whose base class is complex is itself called a complex type...." [Meyer 1992, page 273]

- **creation type** *n.* "The creation type is the optional Type appearing in the [Creation] instruction ... if present; otherwise it is the base type of the target." [Meyer 1992, page 285]

- **declared type** *n.* "the type given by the declaration or redeclaration" [Meyer 1992, page 146]

- **dynamic type** *n.* "The dynamic type of an entity or expression x, at some instant of execution when x is not void, is the type of the object to which x is attached." [Meyer 1992, page 323]

  Contrast with: STATIC TYPE.

  See: POLYMORPHISM

- **expanded type** *n.* "A type T is ex-

App
F

panded if and only if one of the following conditions holds:

1. T is a Class_type whose base class C is an expanded class.
2. T is of the form expanded CT.
3. T is of the form BIT M for some non-negative integer M." [Meyer 1992, page 208]

Contrast with: REFERENCE TYPE.

- **feature type** *n.* "The 'type' of a feature or entity, without further qualification always means its declared type (rather than its base type)." [Meyer 1992, page 164]

- **generating type [of an object]** *n.* "Every standard object is a direct instance of some type of the system, called the generating type for the object, or just 'the type of the object' if there is no ambiguity." [Meyer 1992, page 270]

- **reference type** *n.* "Any type T where
  1. T is a Class_type whose base class C is an expanded class.
  2. T is of the form expanded CT.
  3. T is of the form BIT M for some non-negative integer M.

  T is a reference type if it is not a Formal_generic_name and none of the above condition applies." [Meyer 1992, page 208]

  Contrast with: EXPANDED TYPE.

- **static type** *n.* "... the 'type' of x (called it static type if there is any ambiguity), which an entity is the type with which it is declared, and for an expression is the type deduced from the types of its constituents." [Meyer 1992, page 323]

  Contrast with: DYNAMIC TYPE.

universe *n.* "A universe is a set of clusters, out of which developers will pick classes to build systems." [Meyer 1992, pages 33, 38]

See also: CLUSTER.

validity [of a call] *adj.* "A call is valid if and only if it is both class-valid and system-valid." [Meyer 1992, page 367]

See also: CLASS-VALID CALL, SYSTEM-VALID CALL.

Kinds:
- CLASS-LEVEL VALIDITY
- SYSTEM-LEVEL VALIDITY

- **class-level validity** *n.* "... the actual type constraint ... still applies to a class D the conditions defined ... for class-level validity:
  1. D must have a feature corresponding to fname, available to C.
  2. That feature must have the required signature." [Meyer 1992, page 358]

  Contrast with: SYSTEM-LEVEL VALIDITY.

- **system-level validity** *n.* "System-level validity is the same property as its class-level counterpart, but applied to all possible dynamic types of the target x." [Meyer 1992, page 288]

  Contrast with: CLASS_LEVEL VALIDITY.

value *n.* "... the fields of a complex object are values.... all values are objects or references to objects." [Meyer 1992, pages 270–271]

Contrast with: REFERENCE.

variable attribute *n.* "... it is possible to write routines that will change the attribute values associated with particular instances." [Meyer 1992, page 261]

Contrast with: CONSTANT ATTRIBUTE.

version [of a feature] *n.* "The definition of inherited features yields a precise definition for yet another important notion...: the version of a feature in a descendant. It is convenient to define first the potential versions. If a feature has two or more potential versions in a class, one of them will be the version. Informally, a potential version of a feature f is any feature which, in a descendant of f's class, comes from f after possible redeclarations and generic derivations." [Meyer 1992, page 189] "Let f be a feature of a class A and D a descendant of A. The version of f in D is the feature df defined as follows:

V1. If D has only one potential version of f, then df is that feature.

V2. If D has two or more potential ver-

sions of f, the Repeated Inheritance Consistency constraint ... states that exactly one of them must appear, under its final D name, as part of a Select clause in D; then df is that feature." [Meyer 1992, page 190]

Contrast with: CURRENT FEATURE.

void reference *n.* "If a reference is void, no further information is available on it." [Meyer 1992, page 270]

Contrast with: ATTACHED REFERENCE.

Reference

[Meyer 1992] Meyer, Bertrand (1992). *Eiffel: The Language,* Englewood Cliffs, NJ: Prentice Hall.

Appendix G

Smalltalk

Smalltalk is a weakly typed, pure object-oriented programming language and integrated environment. Smalltalk is generally considered to be the archetypal object-oriented language, against which other OOPLs are compared.

The definitions appearing in this appendix are excerpted from:

Goldberg, Adele (1984). *Smalltalk-80: The Interactive Programming Environment.* Reading, MA: Addison-Wesley. © 1984 by ParcPlace Systems. Reprinted by permission of Addison-Wesley Publishing Company, Inc.

Goldberg, Adele; & Robson, Dave (1989). *Smalltalk-80: The Language.* Reading, MA: Addison-Wesley. © 1984 by the Xerox Corporation. Reprinted by permission of Addison-Wesley Publishing Company, Inc.

For more information, contact:

Ms. Adele Goldberg
ParcPlace Systems Inc.
999 E. Arques Avenue
Sunnyvale, California 94086, USA
Voice: +1 (408) 481-9090
Fax: +1 (408) 481-9095
E-mail: adele@parcplace.com
http://www.parcplace.com

The books may be ordered as follows:

Adele Goldberg and David Robson, *Smalltalk-80: The Language,*
ISBN 0-201-13688-0, $30.95
Adele Goldberg, *Smalltalk-80: The Interactive Programming Environment,*
ISBN 0-201-11372-4, $39.95
Attn.: Order Services Department
Addison-Wesley Publishing Company, Inc.
One Jacob Way

Reading, Massachusetts 01867, USA
Voice: +1 (800) 822-6339
Fax: +1 (617) 942-1117
http://www.aw.com

App
G

↑ *symbol* "When used in a method, indicates that the value of the next expression is to be the value of the method." [Goldberg & Robson 1989, page 53]

abstract class *n.* "A class that specifies protocol, but is not able to fully implement it; by convention, instances are not created of this kind of class." [Goldberg & Robson 1989, page 73]

Contrast with: SUPERCLASS.

Commentary: "Abstract superclasses are created when two classes share a part of their descriptions and yet neither one is properly a subclass of the other. A mutual superclass is created for the two classes which contains their shared aspects." [Goldberg & Robson 1989, page 66]

active process *n.* "The process whose actions are currently being carried out is called active." [Goldberg & Robson 1989, page 254]

active view *n.* "The view in which you are currently working." [Goldberg 1984, page 28]

Contrast with: BROWSER, COLLAPSED VIEW, STANDARD SYSTEM VIEW, SUBVIEW.

argument name *n.* "Name of a pseudo-variable available to a method only for the duration of that method's execution; the value of the argument names are the arguments of the message that invoked the method." [Goldberg 1984, page 102; 1989, page 53]

binary message *n.* "A message with one argument whose selector is made up of one or two special characters." [Goldberg & Robson 1989, page 37]

Contrast with: KEYWORD MESSAGE, UNARY MESSAGE.

block *n.* "Blocks are objects used in many of the control structures in the Smalltalk … system. A block represents a deferred sequence of actions." [Goldberg &

Robson 1989, page 31]

Commentary: "Blocks are used to implement control structures." [Goldberg & Robson 1989, page 18]

block expression *n.* "Block expressions describe objects representing deferred activities…. A block expression consists of a sequence of expressions separated by periods and delimited by square brackets." [Goldberg & Robson 1989, pages 18, 31]

Contrast with: LITERAL, MESSAGE EXPRESSION, VARIABLE NAME.

browser *n.* "A view that allows you to access hierarchically organized and indexable information." [Goldberg 1984, page 28]

Contrast with: ACTIVE VIEW, COLLAPSED VIEW, STANDARD SYSTEM VIEW, SUBVIEW.

Commentary: The class browser "is a way to present a hierarchical index to classes and to messages. Browsers are set up to help you find classes either by name or by category." [Goldberg 1984, page 99]

cascaded message expression *n.* "A cascaded message expression consists of one description of the receiver followed by several messages separated by semi-colons." [Goldberg & Robson 1989, page 30]

cascading messages *n.* "A description of several messages to one object in a single expression." [Goldberg 1984, page 103; Goldberg & Robson 1989, page 37] "Cascading specifies multiple messages to the same object" [Goldberg 1984, page 103]

class *n.* "A class describes the implementation of a set of objects that all represent the same kind of system component." [Goldberg & Robson 1989, page 8] "A description of a group of similar objects…. An object that describes the

implementation of a set of similar objects." [Goldberg 1984, page 102; Goldberg & Robson 1989, pages 16, 53]
Commentary: "All instances of a class respond to the same set of messages and use the same set of methods to do so. All instances of a class have the same number of named instance variables and use the same names to refer to them. An object can have indexed instance variables only if all instances of its class can have indexed instance variables.... Every object is an instance of a class." [Goldberg & Robson 1989, pages 56, 269]
Kinds:
- ABSTRACT CLASS
- METACLASS
- ROOT CLASS
- SUBCLASS
- SUPERCLASS

- **abstract class** *n.* "A class that specifies protocol, but is not able to fully implement it; by convention, instances are not created of this kind of class." [Goldberg & Robson 1989, page 73]
  Contrast with: SUPERCLASS.

- **metaclass** *n.* "A class whose instances are themselves classes." [Goldberg 1984, page 94]

- **root class** *n.* "Object is the single root class; it is the only class without a superclass.... The class that is the root of the tree-structured lass hierarchy." [Goldberg & Robson 1989, pages 58, 73]

- **subclass** *n.* "A class that inherits variables and methods from an existing class." [Goldberg & Robson 1989, page 73] [Goldberg 1984, page 103] "A subclass can add new functionality or private memory, and modify or prohibit existing functionality." [Goldberg 1984, page 78]

Antonym: SUPERCLASS.
- **superclass** *n.* "The class from which variables and methods are inherited." [Goldberg 1984, page 103; 1989, page 73]
  Antonym: SUBCLASS.

Class *n.* "The abstract superclass of all classes other than metaclasses." [Goldberg & Robson 1989, page 89]

class name *n.* "Each class has a name that describes the type of component its instances represent." [Goldberg & Robson 1989, page 40]
Commentary: "A class name serves two fundamental purposes; it is a simple way for instances to identify themselves, and it provides a way to refer to the class in expressions." [Goldberg & Robson 1989, page 40]

class variable *n.* "A variable shared by all the instances of a single class." [Goldberg 1984, page 102; Goldberg & Robson 1989, page 53]
Contrast with: GLOBAL VARIABLE, INSTANCE VARIABLE, POOL VARIABLE, TEMPORARY VARIABLE.

collapsed view *n.* "A standard system view that displays only its label part, but can be selected and expanded to show the entire view." [Goldberg 1984, page 28]
Contrast with: ACTIVE VIEW, BROWSER, STANDARD SYSTEM VIEW, SUBVIEW.

context *n.* "Objects representing organizational structures for classes and methods help the programmer keep track of the system, and objects representing histories of software modification help interface with the efforts of other programmers. These objects are classed contexts and are analogous to stack frames or activation records in other systems." [Goldberg & Robson 1989, page 15]

App
G

Example: "Even the execution state of a method is represented by an object." [Goldberg & Robson 1989, page 15]

control manager *n.* "A system object that maintains a list of screen views; it lets you point to a view and interact with either the view itself or with information inside the view." [Goldberg 1984, page 27]

dependents *n.* "Access objects that have been declared as dependents of one another." [Goldberg 1984, page 506]
Example: A particular view is dependent on the object it views." [Goldberg 1984, page 506]

doesNotUnderstand *n.* A standard message used to "report to the user that the receiver does not understand the argument ... as a message." [Goldberg & Robson 1989, page 102]

expression *n.* "A sequence of characters that describes an object; the object is called the *value of the expression*." [Goldberg 1984, page 103; Goldberg & Robson 1989, page 18]
Commentary: The four types of expressions in Smalltalk are block expressions, literals, message expressions, and variable names.
Kinds:
- BLOCK EXPRESSION
- LITERAL
- MESSAGE EXPRESSION
  - CASCADED MESSAGE EXPRESSION
- VARIABLE NAME

- **block expression** *n.* "Block expressions describe objects representing deferred activities.... A block expression consists of a sequence of expressions separated by periods and delimited by square brackets." [Goldberg & Robson 1989, pages 18, 31]
- **literal [constant]** *n.* "An expression describing a constant [object]." [Goldberg & Robson 1989, page 37]
Examples: "a number or a string." [Goldberg & Robson 1989, page 15]

- **message expression** *n.* "Message expressions describe messages to receivers. The value of a message expression is determined by the method the message invokes. That method is found in the class of the receiver.... A message expression describes a receiver, selector, and possibly some arguments." [Goldberg & Robson 1989, pages 18, 25]
  - **cascaded message expression** *n.* "A cascaded message expression consists of one description of the receiver followed by several messages separated by semicolons." [Goldberg & Robson 1989, page 30]

- **variable name** *n.* "Variable names describe the accessible variables. The value of a variable name is the current value of the variable with that name.... An expression describing the current value of a variable." [Goldberg & Robson 1989, pages 18, 37]

global *n.* "Names in Smalltalk other than classes and pools." [Goldberg 1984, page 506]

global variable *n.* "A variable shared by all the instances of all classes." [Goldberg 1984, page 102; Goldberg & Robson 1989, page 53]
Contrast with: CLASS VARIABLE, INSTANCE VARIABLE, POOL VARIABLE, TEMPORARY VARIABLE.

implementation description *n.* "An implementation description shows how the functionality described in the protocol description is implemented. An implementation description gives the form of the instances' private memory and the set

of methods that describe how instances perform their operations.... A description of a class in terms of its instances' private memory and the set of methods that describe how instances perform their operations." [Goldberg & Robson 1989, pages 41, 53]
Contrast with: PROTOCOL DESCRIPTION.

indexed instance variable *n.* "Instances of some classes can have instance variables that are not accessed by names. These are called indexed instance variables." [Goldberg & Robson 1989, page 46]
Antonym: NAMED INSTANCE VARIABLE.
Example: "names at: 1" [Goldberg & Robson 1989, page 46]
Commentary: "An object can have indexed instance variables only if all instances of its class can have indexed instance variables." [Goldberg & Robson 1989, page 56]

instance *n.* "One of the objects described by a class; it has memory and responds to messages" [Goldberg 1984, page 102; Goldberg & Robson 1989, page 53]

instance variable *n.* "An object's private properties are a set of instance variables that make up its private memory.... A part of an object's private memory.... A variable available to a single object for the entire lifetime of the object; instance variables can be named or indexed." [Goldberg 1984, page 102; Goldberg & Robson 1989, pages 8, 16, 53]
Contrast with: CLASS VARIABLE, GLOBAL VARIABLE, POOL VARIABLE, TEMPORARY VARIABLE.
Commentary: Instance variables "represent the current state of an object." [Goldberg 1984, page 94]
Kinds:
- INDEXED INSTANCE VARIABLE
- NAMED INSTANCE VARIABLE

- **indexed instance variable** *n.* "Instances of some classes can have instance variables that are not accessed by names. These are called indexed instance variables." [Goldberg & Robson 1989, page 46]
Antonym: NAMED INSTANCE VARIABLE.
Example: "names at: 1" [Goldberg & Robson 1989, page 46]
Commentary: "An object can have indexed instance variables only if all instances of its class can have indexed instance variables." [Goldberg & Robson 1989, page 56]

- **named instance variable** *n.* "An implementation description includes a set of names for the instance variables that make up the individual instances. Each instance has one variable corresponding to each instance variable name." [Goldberg & Robson 1989, page 45]
Antonym: INDEXED INSTANCE VARIABLE.
Commentary: "All instances of a class have the same number of named instance variables and use the same names to refer to them." [Goldberg & Robson 1989, page 56]

interface *n.* "The messages to which an object can respond." [Goldberg 1984, page 102; Goldberg & Robson 1989, page 16]
Synonym: PROTOCOL.
Commentary: "The only way to interact with an object is through its interface." [Goldberg & Robson 1989, page 6] "The instances of a class all have the same message interface; the class describes how to carry out each of the operations available through the interface." [Goldberg & Robson 1989, page 40]

App
G

keyword message *n.* "A message with one or more arguments whose selector is made up of one or more keywords." [Goldberg & Robson 1989, page 37]
Contrast with: BINARY MESSAGE, UNARY MESSAGE.
Commentary: A keyword is "an identifier with a trailing colon." [Goldberg & Robson 1989, page 37]

literal [constant] *n.* "An expression describing a constant...." [Goldberg & Robson 1989, page 37]
Examples: "a number, symbol constant, string, or array constant." [Goldberg 1984, page 103]
Contrast with: BLOCK EXPRESSION, MESSAGE EXPRESSION, VARIABLE NAME.
Commentary: "A literal constant will always refer to the same object...." [Goldberg & Robson 1989, page 22]

message *n.* "A request for an object to carry out one of its operations." [Goldberg 1984, pages 27, 102; Goldberg & Robson 1989, page 16]
Commentary: "A message specifies which operation is desired, but not how that operation should be carried out.... A crucial property of messages is that they are the only way to invoke an object's operations.... Messages insure the modularity of the system because they specify the type of operation desired, but not how the operation should be accomplished." [Goldberg & Robson 1989, pages 6–7] "Messages represent the interactions between the components of the Smalltalk ... system." [Goldberg & Robson 1989, page 24] "Messages make an object's functionality available to other objects, while keeping the object's implementation hidden." [Goldberg & Robson 1989, page 40]
Kinds:

- BINARY MESSAGE
- KEYWORD MESSAGE
- UNARY MESSAGE

- **binary message** *n.* "A message with one argument whose selector is made up of one or two special characters." [Goldberg & Robson 1989, page 37]
- **keyword message** *n.* "A message with one or more arguments whose selector is made up of one or more keywords." [Goldberg & Robson 1989, page 37]
Commentary: A keyword is "an identifier with a trailing colon." [Goldberg & Robson 1989, page 37]
- **unary message** *n.* "A message without arguments." [Goldberg 1984, page 104; Goldberg & Robson 1989, page 37]

message argument *n.* "An object that specifies additional information for an operation." [Goldberg 1984, page 103; Goldberg & Robson 1989, page 37]

message category *n.* "Messages that invoke similar operations are grouped together in categories. The categories have names that indicate the common functionality of messages in the group.... A group of methods in a class description." [Goldberg & Robson 1989, pages 42, 53]

message category name *n.* "The [message] categories have names that indicate the common functionality of messages in the group." [Goldberg & Robson 1989, page 42]

message expression *n.* "Message expressions describe messages to receivers. The value of a message expression is determined by the method the message invokes. That method is found in the class of the receiver.... A message expression describes a receiver, selector, and possibly some arguments." [Goldberg & Robson 1989, pages 18, 25]

Contrast with: BLOCK EXPRESSION, LITERAL, VARIABLE NAME.

- **cascaded message expression** *n.* "A cascaded message expression consists of one description of the receiver followed by several messages separated by semicolons." [Goldberg & Robson 1989, page 30]

message pattern *n.* "Messages in a protocol description are described in the form of message patterns. A message pattern contains a ... message selector and a set of argument names, one for each argument that a message with this selector must have." [Goldberg 1984, page 102; 1989, pages 41, 53]

Commentary: "A message pattern matches any messages that have the same selector. A class will have only one method with a given selector in its message pattern." [Goldberg & Robson 1989, page 49]

message selector *n.* "The name of the type of operation a message requests of its receiver." [Goldberg 1984, page 103; Goldberg & Robson 1989, page 26] "The selector of a message determines which of the receiver's operations will be invoked." [Goldberg & Robson 1989, page 37]

See also: INTERFACE, MESSAGE, OPERATION.

Commentary: "The selector of a message determines what type of operation the receiver should perform, so a class has one method for each selector in its interface." [Goldberg & Robson 1989, page 40]

message send *n.* "A message sent to an object." [Goldberg 1984, page 116]

Commentary: "In a view of an interrupted process, the term message-send usually refers to a message from which a response has not yet been received." [Goldberg 1984, page 104]

metaclass *n.* "A class whose instances are themselves classes." [Goldberg 1984, page 94] "The class of a class." [Goldberg & Robson 1989, page 89]

Example: Metaclass.

Commentary: "Every class is an instance of a metaclass." [Goldberg & Robson 1989, page 269]

Metaclass *n.* "A class whose instances are classes of classes." [Goldberg & Robson 1989, page 89]

method *n.* "A procedure describing how to perform one of an object's operations." [Goldberg 1984, page 27] "A description of one of an object's operations; it is made up of a message pattern, temporary variable declaration, and a sequence of expressions [separated by periods]. A method is executed when a message matching its message pattern is sent to an instance of the class in which the method is found." [Goldberg 1984, page 102; Goldberg & Robson 1989, pages 48, 53]

Commentary: "A method is executed when a message matching its message pattern is sent to an instance of the class in which the method is found." [Goldberg & Robson 1989, page 53]

- **primitive method** *n.* "A small subset of the methods in the Smalltalk... system are not expressed in the Smalltalk... programming language." [Goldberg & Robson 1989, page 9] "An operation performed directly by the Smalltalk... virtual machine." [Goldberg 1984, page 103; Goldberg & Robson 1989, page 16] "It is not described as a sequence of Smalltalk... expressions." [Goldberg & Robson 1989, page 53]

named instance variable *n.* "An implementation description includes a set of names for the instance variables that make up the individual instances. Each instance has one variable corresponding to each instance variable name." [Goldberg & Robson 1989, page 45]
Contrast with: INDEXED INSTANCE VARIABLE.
Commentary: "All instances of a class have the same number of named instance variables and use the same names to refer to them." [Goldberg & Robson 1989, page 56]

nil *n.* A pseudo-variable name that "refers to an object used as the value of a variable when no other object is appropriate. Variables that have not been otherwise initialized refer to nil." [Goldberg & Robson 1989, page 23]
Commentary: "The only instance of class UndefinedObject; it is typically the value of variables that have not been assigned as yet." [Goldberg 1984, page 116]

object *n.* "An object is a representation of information consisting of private memory, and a set of operations to manipulate information stored in the private memory or to carry out some actions relative to that information." [Goldberg 1984, page 1] "A component of the Smalltalk... system represented by some private memory and a set of operations." [Goldberg 1984, pages 27, 103; Goldberg & Robson 1989, page 6] "An object is a uniform representation of information that is an abstraction of the capabilities of a computer ... to store information and ... to manipulate information." [Goldberg 1984, page 76] "An object represents a component of the Smalltalk ... software system.... An ob-

ject consists of some private memory and a set of operations." [Goldberg & Robson 1989, pages 16]
Examples: "Numbers, character strings, queues, dictionaries, rectangles, file directories, text editors, programs, compilers, computational processes, financial histories, views of information." [Goldberg & Robson 1989, page 6]
Commentary: "Every object is an instance of a class." [Goldberg & Robson 1989, page 269]

Object *n.* "A system class named Object describes the similarities of all objects in the system, so every class will at least be a subclass of Object.... Object is the single root class; it is the only class without a superclass.... The class that is the root of the tree-structured class hierarchy." [Goldberg & Robson 1989, pages 58, 73]
Commentary: "Every class is ultimately a subclass of class Object, except for Object itself, which has no superclass." [Goldberg & Robson 1989, page 269]

object pointer *n.* "Each object is associated with a unique identifier called its object pointer. The object memory and interpreter communicate about objects with object pointers. The size of object pointers determines the maximum number of objects a Smalltalk... system can contain." [Goldberg & Robson 1989, page 440]

override [a method] *v. overrode, -ing* To "[specify] a method in a subclass for the same message as a method in a superclass." [Goldberg & Robson 1989, page 73]
Commentary: "If a subclass adds a method whose message pattern has the same selector as a method in the superclass, its instances will respond to messages with that selector by executing the

new method. This is called overriding a method." [Goldberg & Robson 1989, page 59]

pool *n.* "Variables that are shared by more than one object come in groups called pools. Each class has two or more pools whose variables can be accessed by its instances. One pool is shared by all classes and contains the global variables; this pool is named Smalltalk. Each class also has a pool which is only available to its instances and contains the class variables." [Goldberg & Robson 1989, pages 47–48]
See also: CLASS VARIABLE, POOL VARIABLE, SMALLTALK.

pool variable *n.* "A variable shared by the instances of a subset of the classes." [Goldberg 1984, page 103; Goldberg & Robson 1989, page 53]
Contrast with: CLASS VARIABLE, GLOBAL VARIABLE, INSTANCE VARIABLE, TEMPORARY VARIABLE.

primitive method *n.* "A small subset of the methods in the Smalltalk... system are not expressed in the Smalltalk... programming language." [Goldberg & Robson 1989, page 9] "An operation performed directly by the Smalltalk... virtual machine." [Goldberg 1984, page 103; Goldberg & Robson 1989, page 16] "It is not described as a sequence of Smalltalk... expressions." [Goldberg & Robson 1989, page 53]

private property *n.* "An object's private properties are a set of instance variables that make up its private memory and a set of methods that describe how to carry out its operations." [Goldberg & Robson 1989, page 8]

private variable *n.* A variable that is "available only to a single object." [Goldberg & Robson 1989, page 44]

Kinds:
• INSTANCE VARIABLE
  - INDEXED INSTANCE VAIRABLE
  - NAMED INSTANCE VARIABLE
• TEMPORARY VARIABLE

• **instance variable** *n.* "An object's private properties are a set of instance variables that make up its private memory.... A part of an object's private memory.... A variable available to a single object for the entire lifetime of the object; instance variables can be named or indexed." [Goldberg & Robson 1989, pages 8, 16, 53]
Kinds:
  - INDEXED INSTANCE VARIABLE
  - NAMED INSTANCE VAIRABLE

  - **indexed instance variable** *n.* "Instances of some classes can have instance variables that are not accessed by names. These are called indexed instance variables." [Goldberg & Robson 1989, page 46]
  Example: "names at: 1" [Goldberg & Robson 1989, page 46]

  - **named instance variable** *n.* "An implementation description includes a set of names for the instance variables that make up the individual instances. Each instance has one variable corresponding to each instance variable name." [Goldberg & Robson 1989, page 45]

• **temporary variable** *n.* "A variable created for a specific activity and available only for the duration of that activity." [Goldberg & Robson 1989, page 53]
Commentary: Temporary variables do not include pseudo-variables such as argument names and self.

process *n.* "A process is a sequence of actions described by expressions and performed by the Smalltalk... virtual machine." [Goldberg & Robson 1989, page 251]

• **active process** *n.* "The process whose actions are currently being carried out is called active." [Goldberg & Robson 1989, page 254]

project *n.* "A collection of views of information that takes up an entire display screen for the presentation of its views." [Goldberg 1984, page 28]

protocol *n.* "The messages to which an object can respond." [Goldberg 1984, pages 102, 103]

Contrast with: INTERFACE.

protocol description *n.* "A protocol description lists the messages in the instances' message interface. Each message is accompanied by a comment describing the operation an instance will perform when it receives that type of message.... A protocol description lists the messages understood by instances of a particular class.... A description of a class in terms of its instances' public message protocol." [Goldberg & Robson 1989, pages 41, 53]

Contrast with: IMPLEMENTATION DE-SCRIPTION.

See also: SYSTEM BROWSER.

pseudo-variable name *n.* "An expression similar to a variable name. However, unlike a variable name, the value of a pseudo-variable name cannot be changed by an assignment." [Goldberg & Robson 1989, page 37]

receiver *n.* "The object to which a message is sent." [Goldberg 1984, page 103; Goldberg & Robson 1989, page 16]

Commentary: "The receiver ... determines how to carry out the requested operation." [Goldberg & Robson 1989, page 6]

root class *n.* "Object is the single root class; it is the only class without a superclass.... The class that is the root of the tree-structured class hierarchy." [Goldberg & Robson 1989, pages 58, 73]

selector *n.* Short for message selector: "The name of the type of operation a message requests of its receiver.... The selector of a message determines which of the receiver's operations will be invoked." [Goldberg & Robson 1989, pages 26. 37]

self *n.* "A pseudo-variable referring to the receiver of a message." [Goldberg 1984, page 104; Goldberg & Robson 1989, page 53]

Contrast with: SUPER.

Commentary: "Responses to messages to self are found by starting the method search in the class of the receiver, continuing up the superclass chain, and terminating at class Object." [Goldberg 1984, page 104] "When a method contains a message whose receiver is self, the search for the method for that message begins in the instance's class, regardless of which class contains the method containing self." [Goldberg & Robson 1989, page 62]

send a message *v.* "... the Smalltalk way to invoke a procedure." [Goldberg 1984, page 103]

shared variable *n.* A variable that "can be accessed by more than one object." [Goldberg & Robson 1989, page 44]

Kinds:
- CLASS VARIABLE
- GLOBAL VARIABLE
- POOL VARIABLE

• **class variable** *n.* "A variable shared by all the instances of a single class." [Goldberg & Robson 1989, page 53]

• **global variable** *n.* "A variable shared by all the instances of all classes."

[Goldberg & Robson 1989, page 53]
• **pool variable** *n.* "A variable shared by all the instances of a subset of the classes in a system." [Goldberg & Robson 1989, page 53]

shouldNotImplement *n.* "A message to report the error that this is a message inherited from a superclass, but explicitly not available to instances of the superclass." [Goldberg & Robson 1989, page 73]
Contrast with: SUBCLASSRESPONSIBILITY.
Commentary: "Report to the user that, although the superclass of the receiver specifies that a message should be implemented by subclasses, the class of the receiver cannot provide an appropriate implementation." [Goldberg & Robson 1989, page 103]

Smalltalk *n.* **1.** "Smalltalk is a graphical, interactive programming environment." [Goldberg & Robson 1989, page viii] **2.** "A pool shared by all classes that contains the global variables." [Goldberg & Robson 1989, page 53] "A global variable name that refers to the dictionary of all variable names known globally in the system, in particular, the names of all classes." [Goldberg 1984, page 117]

snapshot *n.* "A file in which you save the current state of your Smalltalk... system image." [Goldberg 1984, page 27]

standard system view *n.* "A view that provides standard interface functions for manipulating itself, for example, for moving, framing, collapsing, and closing." [Goldberg 1984, page 28]
Contrast with: ACTIVE VIEW, BROWSER, COLLAPSED VIEW, SUBVIEW.

subclass *n.* "A class that inherits variables and methods from an existing class."

[Goldberg 1984, page 103; Goldberg & Robson 1989, page 73]
Contrast with: SUPERCLASS.
Commentary: "A subclass can add new functionality or private memory, and modify or prohibit existing functionality." [Goldberg 1984, page 78]

subclassing *n.* "A less general relaxation of the nonintersection limitation on classes is to allow a class to include all instances of another class, but not to allow more general sharing ... We call this approach subclassing.... Subclassing is strictly hierarchical; if any instances of a class are also instances of another class, than all instances of that class must also be instances of the other class." [Goldberg & Robson 1989, pages 57–58]

subclassResponsibility *n.* "A message to report the error that a subclass should have implemented one of the superclass's messages." [Goldberg & Robson 1989, page 73]
Contrast with: SHOULDNOTIMPLEMENT.
Commentary: "Report to the user that a method specified in the superclass of the receiver should have been implemented in the receiver's class." [Goldberg & Robson 1989, page 103]

subview *n.* "A view contained as a subpart of another view." [Goldberg 1984, page 27]
Contrast with: ACTIVE VIEW, BROWSER, COLLAPSED VIEW, STANDARD SYSTEM VIEW.

super *n.* "The pseudo-variable super refers to the receiver of the message, just as self does. However, when a message is sent to super, the search for the method does not begin in the receiver's class. Instead, the search begins in the superclass of the class containing the method." [Goldberg & Robson 1989, page 62] "A pseudo-variable that refers to the receiver of a message; differs from self in where to start the search for methods." [Goldberg 1984, page 104; Goldberg & Robson 1989, page 73]

Contrast with: SELF.

Commentary: "Responses to messages to super are found by starting the method search in the superclass of the method in which super appears, continuing up the superclass chain, and terminating at class Object." [Goldberg 1984, page 104] "The use of super allows a method to access methods defined in a superclass even if the methods have been overridden in subclasses." [Goldberg & Robson 1989, pages 63–64]

superclass *n.* "A class from which variables and methods are inherited." [Goldberg & Robson 1989, page 73]

Contrast with: SUBCLASS.

system browser *n.* "A third way to present classes is an interactive view called a system browser.... The view [that] allows the class descriptions in the system to be viewed and edited.... A browser is a view of the classes in the Smalltalk... system. Existing classes are examined and changed using a browser. New classes are added to the system using a browser." [Goldberg & Robson 1989, pages 41, 297]

Contrast with: IMPLEMENTATION DESCRIPTION, PROTOCOL DESCRIPTION.

system classes *n.* "The Smalltalk... system includes a set of classes that provides the standard functionality of a programming language and environment: arithmetic, data structures, control structures, and input/output facilities." [Goldberg & Robson 1989, page 13] "The set of classes that come with the Smalltalk ... system." [Goldberg 1984, page 103;

Goldberg & Robson 1989, page 16]

system workspace *n.* "A workspace that contains many useful message expressions that you can edit and evaluate, notably expressions about accessing files, querying the system, and recovering from a crash." [Goldberg 1984, page 28] "A special workspace containing expressions or templates for expressions that are useful for such operating system activities as opening and editing files, resetting display screen size, and accessing the references to any system changes." [Goldberg 1984, page 117]

temporary variable *n.* "A variable created for a specific activity and available only for the duration of that activity." [Goldberg 1984, page 103; Goldberg & Robson 1989, page 53]

Contrast with: CLASS VARIABLE, GLOBAL VARIABLE, INSTANCE VARIABLE, POOL VARIABLE.

Commentary: "Temporary variables "represent the transitory state necessary to execute a method." [Goldberg 1984, page 94] Temporary variables do not include pseudo-variables such as argument names and self. [Goldberg & Robson 1989, page 51]

unary message *n.* "A message without arguments." [Goldberg 1984, page 104; Goldberg & Robson 1989, page 37]

Contrast with: BINARY MESSAGE, KEYWORD MESSAGE.

value of an expression *n.* An expression is "a sequence of characters that describes an object called the value of the expression." [Goldberg & Robson 1989, page 18]

Commentary: "Smalltalk... messages provide two-way communication. The selector and arguments transmit information to the receiver about what type of response to make. The receiver transmits information back by returning an object that becomes the value of the message expression.... Even if no information needs to be communicated back to the sender, a receiver always returns a value for the message expression. Returning a value indicates that the response to the message is complete." [Goldberg & Robson 1989, page 27]

variable *n.* "[part of] the memory available to an object" [Goldberg 1984, page 85] "The memory available to an object is made up of variables. Most of these variables have names. Each variable remembers a single object, and the variable's name can be used as an expression referring to that object." [Goldberg & Robson 1989, pages 21–22]
Kinds:
- • PRIVATE VARIABLE
  - - INSTANCE VARIABLE
    - + INDEXED INSTANCE VARIABLE
    - + NAMED INSTANCE VARIABLE
  - - TEMPORARY VARIABLE
- • SHARED VARIABLE
  - - CLASS VARIABLE
  - - GLOBAL VARIABLE
  - - POOL VARIABLE

• **private variable** *n.* A variable that is "available only to a single object." [Goldberg & Robson 1989, page 44]
Kinds:
- - INSTANCE VARIABLE
  - + INDEXED INSTANCE VARIABLE
  - + NAMED INSTANCE VARIABLE
- - TEMPORARY VARIABLE.

- **instance variable** *n.* "An object's private properties are a set of instance variables that make up its private memory." [Goldberg & Robson 1989, page 8] "A part of an object's private memory.... A variable

available to a single object for the entire lifetime of the object; instance variables can be named or indexed." [Goldberg 1984, page 102; 1989, pages 16, 53]
Commentary: Instance variables "represent the current state of an object." [Goldberg 1984, page 94]
Kinds:
- + INDEXED INSTANCE VARIABLE
- + NAMED INSTANCE VARIABLE

+ **indexed instance variable** *n.* "Instances of some classes can have instance variables that are not accessed by names. These are called indexed instance variables." [Goldberg & Robson 1989, page 46]
Example: "`names at: 1`" [Goldberg & Robson 1989, page 46]

+ **named instance variable** *n.* "An implementation description includes a set of names for the instance variables that make up the individual instances. Each instance has one variable corresponding to each instance variable name." [Goldberg & Robson 1989, page 45]

- **temporary variable** *n.* "A variable created for a specific activity and available only for the duration of that activity." [Goldberg 1984, page 103; Goldberg & Robson 1989, page 53]
Commentary: Temporary variables "represent the transitory state necessary to execute a method." [Goldberg 1984, page 94]

• **shared variable** *n.* A variable that "can be accessed by more than one object." [Goldberg & Robson 1989, page 44]
Kinds:
- - CLASS VARIABLE
- - GLOBAL VARIABLE
- - POOL VARIABLE

App
G

- **class variable** *n.* "A variable shared by all the instances of a single class." [Goldberg 1984, page 102; Goldberg & Robson 1989, page 53]
- **global variable** *n.* "A variable shared by all the instances of all classes (that is, by all objects)." [Goldberg 1984, page 102; Goldberg & Robson 1989, page 44]
- **pool variable** *n.* "A variable shared by all the instances of a subset of the classes in a system." [Goldberg 1984, page 103; Goldberg & Robson 1989, page 44]

variable name *n.* "Variable names describe the accessible variables. The value of a variable name is the current value of the variable with that name." [Goldberg & Robson 1989, page 18] "An expression describing the current value of a variable" [Goldberg 1984, page 104; Goldberg & Robson 1989, pages 37]

Contrast with: BLOCK EXPRESSION, LITERAL, MESSAGE EXPRESSION.

Commentary: "Each variable remembers a single object, and the variable's name can be used as an expression referring to the object.... A literal constant will always refer to the same object, but a variable name may refer to different objects at different times." [Goldberg & Robson 1989, pages 15, 22]

view *n.* "A rectangular area on the display screen in which to access information." [Goldberg 1984, page 27] "The Smalltalk... system includes classes of objects that can be used to view and edit information." [Goldberg & Robson 1989, page 15]

Commentary: "The views of classes provide the fundamental mechanism to interact with the software in the system." [Goldberg & Robson 1989, page 15]

Kinds:

- ACTIVE VIEW
- BROWSER
- COLLAPSED VIEW
- STANDARD SYSTEM VIEW
- SUBVIEW

- **active view** *n.* "The view in which you are currently working." [Goldberg 1984, page 28]
- **browser** *n.* "A view that allows you to access hierarchically organized and indexable information." [Goldberg 1984, page 49]
- **collapsed view** *n.* "A standard system view that displays only its label part, but can be selected and expanded to show the entire view." [Goldberg 1984, page 28]
- **standard system view** *n.* "A view that provides standard interface functions for manipulating itself, for example, for moving, framing, collapsing, and closing." [Goldberg 1984, page 28]
- **subview** *n.* "A view contained as a subpart of another view." [Goldberg 1984, page 27]

virtual image *n.* "The virtual image consists of all of the objects in the system." [Goldberg & Robson 1989, page 418]

virtual machine *n.* "The virtual machine consists of the hardware devices and machine language (or microcode) routines that give dynamics to the objects in the virtual image." [Goldberg & Robson 1989, page 292]

workspace *n.* "The view [that] contains text that can be edited or evaluated." [Goldberg & Robson 1989, page 292]

- **system workspace** *n.* "A workspace that contains many useful message expressions that you can edit and evaluate, notably expressions about accessing files, querying the system, and recovering from a crash." [Goldberg 1984, page 28]

References

[Goldberg 1984] Goldberg, Adele (1984), *Smalltalk-80: The Interactive Programming Environment*, Reading, MA: Addison-Wesley.
[Goldberg & Robson 1989]
Goldberg, Adele, and Robson, David (1989), *Smalltalk-80: The Language*, Reading, MA: Addison-Wesley.

App
G

Add these essential books to your object technology reading list!

Explore the leading methodologies

OBJECT DEVELOPMENT METHODS

(Part of the ADVANCES IN OBJECT TECHNOLOGY series)

edited by Andy Carmichael

Object Development Methods addresses how object technology can be applied to systems analysis and design. It includes:

- a comprehensive survey and comparison of the leading methodologies including Booch, Texel, Rumbaugh, Shlaer/Mellor, Jacobson, and Coad/Yourdon among others

- an exploration of the common concepts and underlying structure of each methodology.

A must-read for anyone interested in distinguishing and learning how to evaluate, the leading object-oriented methods.

ISBN: 0-9627477-9-3   347 pages $39

A book whose time has come...

Objectifying Real-Time Systems

(Part of the ADVANCES IN OBJECT TECHNOLOGY series)

by John R. Ellis

This essential book presents a methodology for creating a real-time information processing system Requirements Model. The methodology presented is an evolution of popular Real-Time Structured Analysis (RTSA) techniques into object-based Real-Time Object-Oriented Structured Analysis (RTOOSA).

By reading this book, you'll get:

- leading-edge information including more than 100 helpful figures and examples;

- a guided tour through the steps of applying object-oriented techniques to daily projects;

- an accompanying diskette which contains the source programs used throughout the book, to enable the reader to experiment and verify executions without having to key in code.

ISBN: 0-9627477-8-5   525 pages (including diskette) $44

SIGS BOOKS ORDER COUPON

YES! Please rush me the following books:

❑ ___copy(ies) of **Inside the Object Model** (ISBN: 1-884842-05-4)
at the low price of $39 per copy.

❑ ___copy(ies) of **Object Lessons** (ISBN: 0-9627477-3-4)
at the low price of $29 per copy.

❑ ___copy(ies) of **Directory of Object Technology** (ISBN: 1-884842-08-9)
at ❑ $69 (Individual Rate) per copy.
    ❑ $169 (Corporate Library Rate) per copy.

❑ ___copy(ies) of **The Dictionary of Object Technology** (ISBN: 1-884842-09-7)
at the low price of $55 per copy.

❑ ___copy(ies) of **Object Development Methods** (ISBN: 0-9627477-9-3)
at the low price of $39 per copy.

❑ ___copy(ies) of **Objectifying Real-Time Systems** (ISBN: 0-9627477-8-5)
at the low price of $44 per copy (including diskette).

RISK-FREE OFFER! *If you are not completely satisfied with your purchase, simply return the book within 14 days and receive a full refund.*

Total Purchase

Inside the Object Model	$_____
Object Lessons	$_____
Directory of Object Technology	$_____
The Dictionary of Object Technology	$_____
Object Development Methods	$_____
Objectifying Real-Time Systems	$_____
Postage	$_____
NY Resident Sales Tax	$_____
TOTAL	$_____

METHOD OF PAYMENT
❑ Check enclosed (Payable to SIGS Books)
❑ Charge my: ❑ Visa ❑ MasterCard ❑ AmEx

Card#:_____ Exp. date:_____

Signature: _____

SEND TO:

Name _____

Company _____

Address _____

City/State _____

Country _____ Postal Code_____

Phone _____

Fax _____

Postage and handling per Item: U.S. orders add $5.00; Canada and Mexico add $10.00; Outside North America add $15.00. Note: New York State residents must add applicable sales tax. Please allow 4-6 weeks from publication date for delivery.
Note: Non-U.S. orders must be prepaid. Checks must be in U.S. dollars and drawn on a U.S. bank.
PBA1

Distributed by Prentice Hall. Available at selected book stores.

RETURN ORDER TO: SIGS Books, P.O. Box 99425, Collingswood, NJ, 08108-9970, USA.
Fax: 609-488-6188 Phone: 609.488.9602